The Global Internet Economy

The Global Internet Economy

Edited by Bruce Kogut

The MIT Press
Cambridge, Massachusetts
London, England

This book was set in Baskerville on 3B2 by Asco Typesetters, Hong Kong, and was printed and bound in the United States of America.

Library of Congress Cataloging-in-Publication Data

The global internet economy / Bruce Kogut, editor.
  p.   cm.
Includes bibliographical references and index.
ISBN 0-262-11272-8 (hc. : alk. paper)
  1. Internet—Economic aspects—Cross-cultural studies. 2. Internet—Social aspects—Cross-cultural studies. 3. Information technology—Cross-cultural studies. 4. Electronic commerce—Cross-cultural studies. I. Kogut, Bruce Mitchel.
HC79.I55 G5783   2003
338.4'7004678—dc21   2002075120

To Edward Bowman, the first director of the Reginald H. Jones Center and a friend to my colleagues at Wharton and myself, who believed that the world of ideas can reflect and yet guide the action we observe.

Contents

Acknowledgments   ix

List of Contributors   xiii

1 Introduction: The Internet Has Borders   1
Bruce Kogut

I Country Chapters   41

**2 From Pockets of Experimentation to Institutional
Change**   43
Bruce Kogut

**3 The Growth and Development of the Internet in
the United States**   69
Martin Kenney

**4 Sweden's Wireless Wonders: The Diverse Roots
and Selective Adaptations of the Swedish Internet
Economy**   109
Henrik Glimstedt and Udo Zander

**5 Technological National Learning in France: From
Minitel to Internet**   153
Pierre-Jean Benghozi and Christian Licoppe

**6 Creativity under Constraint: Technological
Imprinting and the Migration of Indian Business to
the New Economy**   191
Srilata Zaheer and Radhika Rajan

**7 The German Internet Economy and the "Silicon
Valley Model": Convergence, Divergence, or
Something Else?**   223
Steven Casper

8 The Internet Economy of Korea   263
Sea-Jin Chang

**9 Between Bit Valley and Silicon Valley: Hybrid
Forms of Business Governance in the Japanese
Internet Economy**   291
Mari Sako

II Cross-cutting Themes   327

**10 Is There Global Convergence in Regulation and
Electronic Markets?**   329
Bruce Kogut

11 Suppliers and Intermediaries   331
Susan Helper and John Paul MacDuffie

12 Regulation in Europe   381
Alain Jeunemaître and Hervé Dumez

**13 Non-Market Strategies and Regulation in the
United States**   407
Dennis Yao

14 Conclusions   437
Bruce Kogut

References   473

Index   509

Acknowledgments

This book was conceived by curiosity, a plague that wiser minds avoid. It began by observing a global euphoria over the potential of a new body of technologies lumped under the label of the Internet. Many colleagues and friends were fascinated by the Internet's effects on productivity, and surely almost all were infected by the lure of astronomical valuations placed on companies run (dare one say managed?) by talented and enthusiastic entrepreneurs, often with very little experience.

I had the fortune to be on sabbatical in Paris at the Centre de Recherche en Gestion, attached to the Ecole Polytechnique and constituted as a national scientific research center, for the years 1999–2001. The Internet economy was in full swing in France in the fall of 1999. There was already an active research program, coordinated loosely among several French centers. Having long been affiliated with the Institute of International Business at the Stockholm School of Economics and periodically with the Science Center in Berlin, I learned that these institutes were also engaged in research on the Internet. In all of these countries, the reports indicated the emergence of hundreds of new firms, venture capitalists, and graduates defecting from the traditional employment markets to enter new firms that promised options and equity sharing.

How odd this reality seemed compared to the many stylized models of national systems that had been studied for the past decade! Clearly, a global cultural movement was in gear, the leading indicator being the replacement of the business suit by the black T-shirt worn by the new entrepreneurs in Palo Alto, New York, Paris, and Tokyo. Could a cultural shift be powerful enough to overturn the institutions that guided the educational systems, the funnelling of engineers and managers to large industry, and the traditional bank finance?

These observations drive a theoretical stake into the undeveloped side of the national systems approach, for economic history has always shown the fundamental role played by the diffusion of ideas, methods, and technologies across borders. Indeed, the Reginald H. Jones Center had financed a volume a decade ago, entitled *Country Competition*, that examined this historical tension among national context, technological capability, and the global diffusion of organizing principles. The Internet economy reflected these familiar patterns of international diffusion, only played at a faster tempo. But more poignantly, this new economy was also marked by the transport of an economic model, often called the Silicon Valley model, to countries that had long been shown by researchers to be inhospitable to these institutions. How important is the concept of the nation if cultural ideas can coerce national systems to converge toward new global understandings of how technology should be developed and people rewarded?

These are intriguing questions that could not be ignored. A project was born after discussion with colleagues who came to join the endeavor. Most of them responded first with the reply, "It is still too early to study these questions, and I don't know enough in any event." And then came the second response, "But still, I would like to know the answer ..." The dangers and wonders of curious minds. I would like to thank above all these participants who had to give so much of their time to learn about the Internet, to gather the facts, and then to write their interpretations of what they observed.

We thank as well the participation of many people who helped us along the way. These include above all Patrick Fridenson and his students at the École Hautes des Etudes en Sciences Sociales and Dan Raff of the Wharton School, who contributed a sense of historical sobriety to our deliberations. Olivier Bomsel at the École des Mines, Susan Lucas-Cornwall of VEO, Michel Fleuret of CCF in Paris, and Frédérique Sachwald of the Institut Francais des Relations Internationals provided comments on several of the draft chapters presented in March 2001 at an event sponsored by the Centre de Recherche en Gestion, the Reginald H. Jones Center, and the Wharton Alumni Club of France. We would also like to thank the Institute of International Business, and especially Malin Ekberg, for organizing the first of our meetings, held on an island near Stockholm, to discuss early drafts in June 2000.

This project was financed by the Reginald H. Jones Center of the Wharton School at the University of Pennsylvania. The center receives funding from the private sector and government agencies to conduct research on the concerns of the chief executive officer. We would like to thank DuPont, General Electric, General Motors, the IBM Institute for Knowledge-Based Organizations, and Pitney Bowes, and their managers who give us their time and support. These include Paul Costello, James Parke, Reginald Jones, Julie Beamer and Mark Hogan, Doug Sweeny, and Johnna Torsone. I would like to express my thanks especially to Larry Prusak and to John Seely Brown, with whom we organized a series of conferences on "The Internet and Virtual Communities." Our cooperation with Larry's Institute for Knowledge-Based Organizations has been intellectually vital to this research program. We would also like to mention the help of Mukul Pandya and Robbie Shell, who disseminated the results of our work and conferences through *Knowledge@Wharton*, a great example of the educational power of the Internet.

John Covell, Deborah Cantor-Adams, and the MIT Press provided us with excellent support and productive criticism. My co-directors at the Reginald H. Jones Center, John Paul MacDuffie and Sid Winter, gave enthusiasm and, in the case of John Paul, their time to this project. Sue McMullen, a valued colleague and associate at the center, watched with care the financial management.

And above all, my thanks to Rachel Barrett, who more patiently than we deserve, managed the various parts to a completed manuscript.

Contributors

Pierre-Jean Benghozi is presently the research director at the National Center for Scientific Research (CNRS) and teaches regularly at University of Paris (Panthéon-Sorbonne, Dauphine, Nanterre). He created and leads a research group on Information Technology, Telecomunications, Media, and Culture at the Centre de Recherche en Gestion (CRG) at the École Polytechnique. His current projects draw attention to adoption and uses of ITC in large organizations, structuring of e-commerce, and ITC-supported markets and supply chains. Pierre-Jean Benghozi publishes on these topics in French and English.

Steven Casper is a university lecturer at the Judge Institute of Management Studies and a senior research fellow at the Center for Business Research, both at the University of Cambridge. His research focuses on cross-national comparisons of the organization of science-based industry and the relationship between law and technical change. He is currently writing a book examining the diffusion of institutions to support entepreneurial technology firms across Europe.

Sea-Jin Chang is currently Professor of Business Administration at Korea University. Previously, he was a faculty member at the Stern School of Business of New York University and a visiting professor at Stanford and INSEAD. Professor Chang is primarily interested in the management of diversified multinational enterprises. His research interests include diversification, corporate restructuring, organizational learning, corporate growth through joint ventures and acquisitions, and comparative management studies of Japan and Korea.

Hervé Dumez is Director of Research at the CNRS (Centre de Recherche en Gestion de l'École Polytechnique). He has been a visiting professor at MIT. His main stream of research focuses on regulatory policy, the globalization of markets, and EU integration.

Henrik Glimstedt is an associate professor at the Institute of International Business, Stockholm School of Economics. He has been a visitor to the Wharton School of the University of Pennsylvania; the Wissenschaftszentrum in Berlin, Germany; the Norwegian School of Management; and University of Wisconsin–Madison. He has mainly published on globalization and national and international industry governance in historical and comparative perspective. His recent writing includes articles on global standardization and governance of technological development in the information and communications industry.

Susan Helper is Professor of Economics at the Weatherhead School of Management of Case Western Reserve University in Cleveland. Her research focuses on how innovation is affected by the structure incentive systems and channels of information flow within supply chains. Current research projects include investigating the impact of industry clusters on productivity and innovation in Midwest and Mexican component manufacturing, the determinants of worker satisfaction in low-wage manufacturing, and the impact of e-business on small automotive suppliers. She is a research associate of the National Bureau of Economic Research, the MIT International Motor Vehicle Program, and Gerpisa (European automotive research group).

Alain Jeunemaître, Director of Research at CNRS–Maison Française d'Oxford, is affiliated with Nuffield College and the Regulatory Policy Institute (Hertford College) at the University of Oxford. His main stream of research focuses on regulatory policy, the globalization of markets, and the EU integration.

Martin Kenney is a professor in the Department of Human and Community Development at the University of California at Davis, as well as a senior project director at the Berkeley Roundtable on the International Economy. He has been a visitor at the Copenhagen Business School, Hitotsubashi University, the University of Tokyo, and Kobe University. He works on regional innovation complexes, venture capital, and industry globalization issues.

Bruce Kogut is the Dr. Felix Zandman Professor of International Management at the Wharton School of the University of Pennsylvania, and co-director of the Reginald H. Jones Center. He has been a visitor at the Stockholm School of Economics, the Wissenschaftszentrum in Berlin, the Centre de Recherche en Gestion at the École Polytechnique, and INSEAD. He works on the diffusion of ideas across borders and the economic potential of information technologies for developing countries.

Christian Licoppe has been trained in the history and sociology of science and technology. He has published a book on the history of experimental practices and is currently working on the analysis of mediated interaction practices in the field of electronic exchanges and e-commerce. He is director of the social and cognitive science laboratory at the France Telecom R&D research facility in Paris.

John Paul MacDuffie is an associate professor in the Management Department at the Wharton School, University of Pennsylvania and co-director of the Reginald H. Jones Center. His research focuses on the rise of lean production as an alternative to mass production; the consequences for economic performance and the organization of work; the diffusion of this approach across company and country boundaries; and patterns of collaborative problem-solving and knowledge transfer within and across firms. For many years, he has been a core researcher for MIT's International Motor Vehicle Program (IMVP), and he was recently named as IMVP's co-director.

Radhika Rajan works with the TCG Group, an investment house in New York City focused on technology investments. She has first-hand knowledge of the issues discussed in this book, from her experience as executive vice president of a global IT company, headquartered in the United States with substantial Indian operations and customers on every continent. She has worked in the financial markets at JP-Morgan Chase, Union Bank of Switzerland, Bank of America, and other prime financial institutions. She is a graduate of the Indian Institute of Technology in Bombay, and the Indian Institute of Management in Ahmedabad. She combines a career in investments with strong academic interests in international business strategies, especially cross-border issues in Asia.

Mari Sako is P&O Professor of Management Studies at the Said Business School and a professorial fellow of Templeton College, University of Oxford. She had previously taught at London School of Economics, and has been a visitor at Kyoto University's Economics Department and the Institute of Social Science at Tokyo University. Her research is on comparative business systems with a specific focus on inter-firm relations, human resources, and the automobile sector.

Dennis A. Yao is Professor of Business and Public Policy and associate professor of Management at the Wharton School, University of Pennsylvania. From 1991–1994 he served as commissioner of the U.S. Federal Trade Commission, where he and his colleagues had responsibility for antitrust and consumer protection matters. Professor Yao has published a number of papers concerned with economics and policy in the areas of antitrust, consumer protection, regulation, procurement contracting, and innovation and intellectual property.

Srilata Zaheer (Ph.D., MIT) is the Carlson School Term Professor of International Management at the University of Minnesota's Carlson School of Management, and chair of the International Management Division of the Academy of Management (2001–2002). Her research interests revolve around international strategy and organization, and focus on the legitimacy of multinational enterprises, the value of international location in a digital economy, knowledge creation, and diffusion across borders and time-based strategies.

List of Contributors

Udo Zander is Professor of International Business at the Stockholm School of Economics, where he is the acting director of the Institute of International Business. Dr. Zander has been a visitor at the Wharton School, University of Pennsylvania, and Stanford University. He is the author of several articles that cover the internationalization of R&D, the theory of the firm as a social community, and a comparative study of the Zeiss firms in East and West Germany. His most recent area of research is the impact and power of ideas on international firms and society, addressing the myth of unidirectional and smooth globalization.

1

Introduction: The Internet Has Borders

Bruce Kogut

Technologies diffuse rapidly in the modern global economy. Certainly, the diffusion of the technologies that make up the Internet occurred with great rapidity over the past two decades. This is hardly surprising given the global web of ties among people, firms, and institutions. Many of the Internet's key components were created in universities and public research institutions that viewed their research mission as public dissemination. Multinational companies recognized the global demand for the infrastructure of the Internet: fiber optics, routers, data terminals, computers, software. Any country with sufficient financial and economic resources could have rendered its communication and data transmission infrastructure capable of supporting Internet connections. Though countries varied in the speed and the extent by which these investments were made, all but a handful of countries were connected to the global Internet by 2002.

This story of the global Internet gold rush hides another and a fascinating tale. Here we have an intrinsically global technology—for once a country is connected, it becomes virtually co-located with all other countries—but its development occurs within the physical and institutional geography of nations. The Internet relies, after all, on two technological components: a network among distributed computers, and the digitalization of content (e.g., music, text, data). In Nicholas Negroponte's (1995) powerful phrasing, the movement of atoms that had been the core of world trade since the dawn of human history gave way to the transmission of electrons, or bits, that do not comply with the economic geography we learn in school and through travel. By this view, this is not the end of history, but the end of distance.

There are elements of truth to this vision. The Internet arrived at a particularly critical junction in economic history, for its exploitation is closely intertwined with the powerful force of the globalization of finance, corporate governance, and trade. This coincidence of the Internet and globalization poses deep challenges to the historical institutional models that govern the development and exploitation of technologies and innovations within nations. Historically, countries have been defined by more than just political borders, but also by more or less coherent institutions and conventions that shape the skill formation of a work force and the entrepreneurial modes by which technologies are commercially developed and marketed. The Internet technologies crashed on the shores of most countries about the same time, challenging existing institutions and powerful interests, as their diffusion was coupled with global ideas about venture capital financing, start-ups, and radical business models. The Internet technology was global, but its economic and business development was molded in the context of prevailing national institutions.

The ambition of this book is not to give an assessment of the "average" impact of the Internet. By comparing seven different country experiences, we analyze how the Internet was developed and what has been the impact on changing national institutions. Three additional chapters analyze specific Internet sectors and regulation across countries. By this comparative analysis, we assess the extent that the Internet presented a revolutionary opening for economic and cultural change and served as an impetus for institutional readjustments to a global economy.

The Two Explosions of the Internet

The Internet technologies evolved far more steadily and incrementally than their economic and commercial exploitation. One date by which to mark the explosion of the Internet onto the business and cultural scene is 1994, the year an easy-to-use Internet browser with secured transactions called Netscape was launched. From this date to 2000, the number of web hosts grew from 2.2 million to over 94 million. The number of "internauts" worldwide grew by some estimates to over 400 million, 40

percent of these in North America and half divided almost evenly between Europe and Asia/Pacific.[1] Thousands of new firms were created.
Stock markets boomed. Venerable firms trembled before the astronomic
rise in valuations of firms no more than a few years old. Suddenly, there
was an old and "new economy." The literary gazette of the new American economy, *Wired* magazine, predicted in September 1999 that the
Dow Jones Index for Wall Street would hit 50,000 in the year 2010.

The euphoria ended in the implosion of April 2000, during which the
stock market values of new economy companies fell dramatically. Suddenly, there was wide recognition that the stock market looked like a
classic speculative bubble. Fundamentals mattered after all, and rules of
discounted cash flow returned to remind investors that even the most remarkable growth opportunities could not explain the valuations of the
new economy companies. Sobriety returned.

History is not reversible. This simple learning means that the cycle by
which expectations started and ended close to their long-term steady state
did not leave companies, consumers, and national systems the same. In
the course of these six years, a wave of innovation carried on its crest
new firm creation and the transformation of existing companies that
permanently influenced the trajectories of national economies around the
world.

The Internet as a Cultural Event
The Internet offered the possibility for the delivery of new services. Some
of these services were the provision of information. Some promised to
rationalize the supply chains of entire industries. Others offered opportunities for people to communicate and to help each other through online
communities.

Workers abandoned traditional companies to work for start-ups.
Graduates of engineering schools turned down offers from prestigious
companies to take up offers to work for companies that had no revenues.
Clad in jeans, open shirts, and casual shoes, these workers labored long
hours to realize the dream that their stock options they would receive
from an Initial Public Offering (IPO) would be worth more than what
their parents had earned in the course of their entire working lives. They
attended gatherings where investors and twenty-something entrepreneurs

would meet in the midst of a cultural happening. Organizations such as *First Tuesday* opened operations in a dozen European cities to offer business happenings over cocktails, lavish food, and cultural fanfare. The business icons of this new culture were Jeff Bezos, founder of Amazon, David Filo and Chih-Yuan "Jerry" Yang of Yahoo!, and Marc Andreesen of Netscape. There were dozens more, many of them young, fresh from meetings with venture capitalists and Wall Street investment bankers. These founders and their companies were worth billions of dollars and had yet to earn a profit. In Silicon Valley, it was reported that 250,000 people were millionaires (Kaplan 1999). Stories abounded of secretaries gifted company shares, and who could now buy homes in the hills of Los Altos.

The cultural significance of the Internet went far beyond business culture. The Internet brought new *worlds* to internauts. People entered chat rooms, tried out new identities, and encountered dialogues outside their local lives. The quip that on the Internet no one knows you are a dog summarized the potential for anonymous exploration of new selves.[2]

The Internet economy promised a new economy. It represented radical changes in labor markets, a change in cultural expectations and exploration, and the introduction of new products and services. The entry of new firms into these new economic spaces shook the strategies and fates of industrial and financial giants. In this regard, the Internet poses a *cognitive* reframing of work and entrepreneurship that vies with traditional job definitions and aspirations of labor market participants.

The Internet economy is also the digital economy. The content of cultural and material life increasingly became encoded in bits. A generation of children "growing up digital" understood the broad possibilities of converting the familiar image, text, and sound to data encoded digitally, as 0s and 1s.[3] Their digital CDs could now be transmitted as a steady stream of binary numbers, transporting the sounds of favorite artists through a digital compressed format called MP3. Businesses such as Napster, which began as a teenager's hobby, supported these exchanges between individuals. The Internet culture had its own rhythm, took little heed of conventional ideas of property rights, and expanded by the participation of millions of people who pursued their interests in new worlds that William Gibson called in his novel *Neuromancer* "cyberspace."

National Systems and Institutional Recoupling

If the Internet was a cultural and economic wave, it broke upon very different national shores. The rapid expansion of Internet-related businesses challenged national systems consisting of firms, governments, consumers, and workers. The Internet appeared deeply engrained in the American model of entrepreneurship and new firms, and threatened the ideological foundations of these national systems, already unbalanced by global investors and the end of the Cold War. The economy of Germany is organized by corporatist principles: business and labor are represented by their associations, banks and firms are highly intertwined by cross-holdings, and the government actively supports programs to maintain the contract of a social economy. The Japanese and Korean economies—though quite different in their economic logics—consist of competing business groups; labor unions are often fragmented, and tax rates are low, pushing many social programs onto individuals and companies. Dominated by business groups in a historical context of socialist economic and social policies, India is a classic dual economy, with a backward and advanced agriculture (depending on the region) and with a backward retail sector coupled with relatively advanced industries, with pockets of global activity in software design.

The United States often appears as the exception in national system comparisons. Highly decentralized, it has weak business and labor associations. Its government pursues active policies in antitrust, but relatively weak policies in providing guarantees for health insurance or equal access to basic education. Labor markets are relatively flexible, which also means workers have less job security than in many other countries. Ties between universities and companies are unusually strong, and patent and intellectual property law encourages universities to invest in commercially relevant research. Yet the United States provides an inegalitarian primary and secondary education, and its deficit of skilled technicians and engineers is compensated for by an immigration policy, partly implemented by university admission criteria. Venture capital is predominantly an American institution in its origins. Small firm creation is an unusually powerful engine for innovation.

Because of the particular role played by Silicon Valley in driving the American Internet economy, the American national system is often called the "Silicon Valley model."[4] This model, for us, consists of a few distinctive elements that might be summarized as an embrace of the institutions that promote new firm innovations. These institutions include:

1. Early venture capital financing

2. Equity markets for Initial Public Offers (IPOs) of recently founded firms

3. Fluid regional labor market for global talent

4. Fiscal policies that lower the costs of starting and operating a business

5. Proximity of university and research institutes within a region.

There is, of course, debate over this description. Indeed, our larger point is that the ambiguity around this definition, and the causal claims, permits countries to use such a model as a *prototype* to influence the national discourse and struggles. The list is also in some respects too short, especially in underestimating the pervasive influence of government military and industrial policies. In Leslie Stuart's (2000) phrasing, the US government was the "biggest Angel of all," where an angel refers to the initial investors backing an entrepreneur. Surely, an immigration policy that uses the educational system to screen for world talent and grants visas to these graduates and other skilled workers, is an essential ingredient. More importantly, a list of institutions distracts attention from the arenas of discourse and coordination that are embedded in the social and professional communities.[5] Whether we call this a network, or social capital, a community of practice, or simply "connections," the business transaction is a strand within a greater social fabric.

These regional and national systems exist in a global economy. The world economy is vastly different today than a hundred years ago, when the revolutionary technologies of the automobile, electricity, and communications were developed in western countries. The Internet economy confronted a world that was already networked by communications, by television transmission, and by cross-cultural exposure. People shared common learning in their experiences interacting with computers, computer games, and software. International trade was not only large, but the network of trade was far more expansive in the number of countries than before. Multinational corporations span across borders, and their arteries transport the spread of new technologies and managerial practices. International institutions, such as the World Trade Organization and the International Communications Union, are transnational actors. The global economy is a networked society, as Manuel Castells (2000) claims, though as I explain in this chapter, these networks still reveal the importance of place and personal relationships.

Here lie the initial questions of our study. Does the rapidity by which the Internet economy exploded, once and then again, in many countries mean that borders are inconsequential? Is the evidence that new firms rose in Germany, France, Sweden, and many other countries contrary to the traditional logic of their economic systems? Is the Internet an intrinsically global technology, riding upon the already existing backbone of the global communication network?

The simple answer to these questions is that the Internet has borders. The Internet economy developed differently in each country, reflecting different national systems of law and regulation, business networks, competition, and technological legacies. Each country ultimately faced the entrepreneurial challenge of developing the competence needed to compete in this new space. Each country "bootstrapped" from their traditional ways by which competence is created through educational institutions and organized and further developed by firms.

In some sense, however, the above observation is equivalent to what in statistics is called "testing the null." After all, should not the expectation be that national characteristics persist over fairly short durations of time? A more revealing point of departure for our inquiry is that the global Internet did pierce borders, but with effects depending upon the national specificities. The Internet of the 1990s did not represent a major new technological trajectory, for the basic technologies were already known. The Internet instead represented a revolutionary and cultural challenge to the traditional models by which the relevant competence should be organized to explore the new economic space. Many national models were in crisis; many European countries failed to provide growth and jobs during a time of American resurgence in the first two-thirds of the 1990s; Korea and Japan were in economic crisis; India had begun to liberalize certain sectors. The Silicon Valley model provided proof that this space could be filled by new firm creation. The slowness of incumbent actors to exploit the Internet gave an opportunity for entrepreneurs to bootstrap as well from the American experience. The global reach of venture capital and investment banks invested in these entrepreneurs. Suddenly, traditional national systems were seeded by foreign institutions.

We propose that these national systems are best understood not as rigid templates but as capable of a political and economic process permitting a *recoupling* of institutions that allow for entrepreneurial exploration of a global technology. Surely, Silicon Valley produced specific institutional patterns in which innovation was promoted and sustained. As we will see, the Internet evolved in other countries by very different means and by different paths of innovative exploration, and yet in deference to other national experiences and the role played by transnational actors. In some countries, the availability of capital to finance entrepreneurial firms in specific pockets of the economy created enough momentum to tip the institutional balance. These local pockets of experiments constructed bridges by which older systems could migrate toward new institutional arrangements of a perceptibly different logic. In most countries, the effects have been transient, with no major changes in the institutional landscape yet to be seen.

The Internet

But this is getting ahead of our story. Before understanding the national experiences, it is important to pose first the question of what is the Internet. There are many ways to answer this question, and we will try several.

A Modular Technological System

The technological answer is that the Internet is a complex technological system consisting of a body of protocol agreements that permit individuals to use resident software (or middleware) to send and retrieve text, information, and images in a distributed physical network by digital signals. Let's parse this sentence into its components. The Internet is a complex technological system because it relies upon several essential subsystems: the physical infrastructure, terminals and servers, software, and technical agreements. The distributed network consists of the communication backbone, the local access points, and local network and packet switches and terminals (including an isolated computer). For individuals behind their computers or equipped with other devices that are Internet capable (such

Introduction

as advanced mobile telephones), they must have middleware such as a browser to send information in a form that can be recognized by a recipient. This recipient will very often be using different equipment and resident software. The last elements then are the protocol agreements that allow people using different machines to communicate and that govern the transmission of a signal over a distributed network. We say distributed because the transmission does not follow a determined path, but is broken up into packets and sent along multiple paths to be reassembled at the destination.

From this engineering perspective, the Internet consists of several layers, illustrated in figure 1.1. These technological layers have experienced dramatic increases in functionality, with technological progress in one layer driving the complementary engine of change in other layers. These technologies provide the enabling capabilities that constitute the Internet.

Layer	Examples
Business webs	Portals, communities, supply chains
Applications	Word processing, productivity applications
Middleware	Browsers, database management systems
Software Interface: Information standards and protocols Addressing and routing Data Protocols	 HTML, XML, WAP Domains, HTTP TCP/IP
Operating Systems	Unix, Linux, Windows NT
Hardware: Backbone Servers	 "Leased lines" Sun stations

Figure 1.1
The Internet as a technological system
Source: Based on Feldman 1999.

Political Economy of the Infrastructure
The Internet, however, is not simply the product of technological solutions. There are many competing and complementary technologies, the creation and success of which are indelibly tied to the actions and decisions made by firms, consumers, and governments. For example, the distributed network could consist of fiber optic lines owned by a telephone company and leased to Internet Service Providers (ISP). These ISPs might be the telephone company, owners of the backbone, or companies that specialize in these services. An example of a private ISP is America Online (AOL). An individual must rely upon an ISP, or a web server, in order to access the Internet. Who provides the ISP service is not a technological question.

It is common that conflict exists between the specialized ISP companies and the ISP services provided by a regulated or state-owned telephone monopoly. Because the telephone companies often control local access to the home (often called the "last mile"), historically they have had monopoly powers in providing connection. In addition, telephone companies owned the vast proportion of the infrastructure and ISPs, so other telephone operators were forced to rely on leased lines for transmission. Governments and courts have been active in regulating the fees that telephone monopolies can charge. In some countries, such as the United States, consumers pay these fees as part of the fixed charges for telephone access; no fees are usually imposed on local calls. In other countries, such as many European countries, there is also a fee for the time connected, even for local calls. In fact, one of the major problems in pricing for Internet services is that there is no standardized measure of usage (e.g., how much information is sent and received) other than access time. In the United States, even access time is not charged, as long as the dial-up access call is local. Thus, an American consumer does not pay for basic telephone charges for time connected to the Internet, whereas a European pays for the time connected to the Internet by telephone lines. Internet usage was clearly promoted in countries that have unmetered pricing, as in Australia, Canada, New Zealand, and the United States (OECD 2000, 30).

Given the initial difficulty of accessing the home (and the current challenge of providing high-speed connections), three new ways of link-

ing people to the Internet have emerged that avoid the telephone company leased lines. The first is cable that had often already been installed
in people's homes to provide television programming. By installing a
digital coder and decoder that is connected to a computer at the premises, the cable company can also offer Internet services. Cable can be expensive because it requires investment to connect physically the home or
office premises to the cable company. Satellite transmission also works
on the same principle insofar that signals are sent by radio waves and
then decoded. However, because individuals do not have the equipment
to send signals with adequate power to reach space, they still rely upon
terrestrial stations connected to a local exchange. Thus the telephone
company again is able to charge for access.

The last way to avoid the telephone access charges is wireless transmission. Wireless transmission avoids the costly investment in installing
lines and equipment at the local premises. The wireless device (such as a
mobile telephone) is itself a coder and decoder that has sufficient energy
to send and receive signals between itself and a local station. This station
might then be connected to the backbone owned by the telephone
company (or companies) or by a third-party vendor or by the company
providing the mobile transmission service. Newer technologies bypass
the wireline network entirely for short-distance transmission. Not surprisingly, for many countries, new competition has arisen quickly in mobile
transmission services.

For the consumer, the choice among these competing services often
appears complex and is influenced by a combination of price and quality
elements. An important element in quality is the speed of the transmission. "Broadband" refers to the transmission of signals at high speeds,
measured in the number of bits transmitted per second. Conventional
phone lines using a modem can send data up to 56,000 bits per second (kbps). Broadband transmits at speeds 10–100 times as fast. This
speed enables video or television programs, for example, to be sent at a
speed that can be seen at a high quality at home. Telephone companies,
or operators leasing telephone lines, provide high-speed connections
by installing expensive digital subscriber lines (DSL) exchanges. Cable
operators are already sending television programs at fast speeds, and
are expanding into data transmission. Recent developments in mobile

telephony enable wireless transmission at fast speeds. The introduction of broadband access has permitted companies to break from the tariff rates of the phone system to charge for value-added services.

Competition among these different ways of transmitting signals is influenced strongly by the regulatory and legal environment. In some countries, the state or regulated telephone monopoly is permitted to control or compete in mobile and, less frequently, cable transmission. Even if the traditional monopoly company is not permitted to compete, governments usually control licenses to companies that can compete in cable or wireless. The methods by which licenses are granted vary dramatically across market and geography. Increasingly, market-based mechanisms such as auctions have been used to allocate licenses. Still, an important issue is how many licenses a government will permit to provide service to a geographical area, and whether the monopoly company will be permitted to compete in these new services.

In addition, the state or regulated monopoly is often permitted to operate ISP services in competition with private companies. A new ISP company faces the problem of how to be paid. Some companies, such as AOL or Earthlink in the United States, charge a fixed rate. Others do not charge a fee, but try to earn revenues by selling advertising. For the telephone company, this problem is often solved by offering free ISP services that can be subsidized by charging access and connection fees. It also earns money from fees when users connect to other ISPs. Clearly, the traditional telephone monopoly operator has an advantage that can deter new competitors. As a result, in the European Union, the United States, and other countries, there have been intense conflicts between the traditional monopoly and new competitors.

Standards, Protocols, and the Internet
The Internet is not simply the physical infrastructure. It also consists of a body of protocol agreements that permits the exchange of data between computers and other devices in a distributed environment. The physical infrastructure provides interconnection so that people with the appropriate equipment can be connected to a common network. The physical infrastructure does not, however, guarantee interoperability, or the ability of people with different types of equipment to communicate. To enable interoperability, protocols are needed.

Protocols establish a set of rules, which when obeyed, allow communications to be sent, received, and understood. Protocols are ubiquitous. A protocol is used to start even simple appliances and may look something like this: press the button of the dishwasher. There may be a second protocol that says: if the dishwasher does not start, press again. If the dishwasher itself is "intelligent," it might also be programmed to light up a red button to indicate that the door is not closed. Perhaps the easiest example of a protocol is: shake hands when you meet someone. Or is it bow to someone? Or is it kneel down? This plurality of ways to greet someone is emblematic of the problem of choosing a protocol.

Protocols then are rules that govern the interface among people and devices. Some of the rules are simple as illustrated above. Some are complex, involving rules about how to represent data. When one technology relies upon an interface with other technologies, technological change frequently requires changes in protocols or new protocols. Even in the absence of conflict and competition, establishing protocols requires coalitions. Sometimes these coalitions are built through private initiatives, frequently ratified *subsequently* by governments or their delegates. Sometimes they are created directly by official standard bodies created by treaty or by law by governments. In all cases, standard setting faces the problem of who has jurisdictional control and how broad this jurisdiction is.

Two sets of protocol are especially important for the Internet. The first is TCP/IP. The second is HTML and HTTP. These protocols have many competitors, and many people created them. However, particular people succeeded in implementing these protocols because they were able to have them accepted as standards, often under the control of particular standard-setting bodies.

The TCP/IP is a compilation of rules that guarantee interoperability. The Internet Architecture Board (IAB) standardizes these protocols, and changes to them. The Transmission Control Protocol establishes the rules for the packaging of data, their transmission, and assurance of their reception. The TCP software verifies ahead of transmission to arrange for reception and to guarantee that the packet will arrive. The sending and receiving computers "handshake" and establish a control number for the incoming packets and a clock to control the permitted transmission time.

Bruce Kogut

The Internet Protocol manages the addressing system by recognizing individual network nodes and providing information to route packages in the network. Thus, the Internet Protocol operates closely with an addressing system called Domain Names. These names describe a tree-like structure to locate the final address. Top-level names include .edu (educational institution) and .org (non-profit organization), which form the suffix to addresses. There are also more than two hundred country suffixes, such as .fr (France) or .kr (Korea). These addresses are stored on servers located throughout the Internet.

The Internet Protocol is the background to important issues regarding privacy and secure transmission of data. A computer, or any Internet device, need not be assigned a permanent IP address. When it is turned "on" and "connected" to the Internet, it is assigned a temporary IP address that is returned to the system when the device is no longer logged on. Because it slows the system to send data that will be reused every time a computer logs on and is assigned an address, a server often sends a "cookie" to be installed in the memory of the user's computer. These cookies provide log-on information or identification mechanisms to permit secure transactions, and they often expire after a period of time. However, because companies want to know the preferences of potential customers, they also send cookies that monitor the Internet activity of the users. Some of the information is just to tell the company that a previous user is back online; the IP address cannot do this, as a new one is assigned every time. Some cookies serve as a common key that identifies the users across sites, allowing for a consumer research company to profile a customer. There have been proposals to provide permanent IP addresses that are encoded in the microprocessor. Permanent addresses would increase efficiency and permit more security in doing online purchases, but they also make it easier to track users.

The second set of protocols is the rules for addressing documents and formatting data. Browsers and other middleware software operate on top of the operating system of a computer and manage the TCP and IP interface with the net. When a user issues a request for information from an address, the browser sends a request encoded in the Hypertext Transfer Protocol (HTTP) to a web server. The web server sends a script of Hypertext Markup Language (HTML), along with embedded graphics and other scripts. The browser reads and executes the script, recreating the page on the computer screen. For this system to work, both computer and servers must be able to recognize and transmit the scripts.

National and Global Webs of People

In retrospect, protocols and standards needed to operate the web seem so obvious that it is a wonder that they were not invented all at once from the very beginning. This point brings us to an alternative way of understanding the Internet as a complex system that evolved in response to the efforts of particular people who pieced the various parts together. As explained in chapter 3 by Martin Kenney, the Internet evolved out of many actions that often sought only to resolve a local problem. The implications for a large system that provided interconnection and interoperability among distributed computers emerged only over time. In Paul David's phrasing, the Internet was the consequence of the "accidental evolving information super-highway" (2001).

It is useful to review aspects of this history—treated also briefly by Kenney in his chapter—to highlight the importance of national and global communities to the evolution of Internet technology. (For a more complete history, see ⟨http://www.isoc.org/Internet-history⟩ and Abbate 1999.) The story of the creation of the Internet is unmistakably about the role of the U.S. government and a few remarkable people. But it is also about the creation of a computer science, and sometimes hacker, community, and the expansion of this community across national borders. Indeed, the history suggests that the technological capabilities, and some of the innovations, were not exclusive to the United States. The United States got there first because of massive physical investments to support an already existing community of researchers that had the technical expertise and hence the political power to shape the technology.

Designed and Emergent Innovation   The Internet as a concept did not arise out of the commercial sector. It is somewhat stunning to realize that even as late as 1990, there were very few who understood the potential to create interoperability among computers. The Internet stemmed from the efforts of the U.S. military under the Advanced Research Projects Agency (ARPA) program to connect its research installations and university partners and to build a communication system that would be robust to the destruction of part of the system. For this latter purpose, the transmission of data by packets that could be routed through a network had clear advantages over a network optimized to send data through a centralized and hierarchical communication structure. It was this purpose that TCP/IP addressed.

The concept of distributed nodes and routing by "packet" switching is often attributed to Paul Baran, a researcher at RAND, an American think-tank that consulted heavily for the military. The conventional approach to switching was to set up a direct communication between two parties. Starting about 1959, Baran realized that with the advent of distributed computing, communication could be digitized and broken up into discrete packages that were addressed to the final destination; then the switching nodes would allocate a route. At the destination, the packets were reassembled, with appropriate testing to verify that all packets were received. This idea was proposed a little later by Donald Davies of the National Physical Laboratory (NPL) outside of London, who was unaware of Baran's work. Davies understood from the start that this distributed system could support interactive computing in a distributed network.

The United Kingdom did not have the resources to implement the idea, but the United States did under ARPA. The NPL via the University College of London became an ARPANET node by 1972—three years after the first one was established at the University of California at Los Angeles—but almost lost the honor due to the lack of funding and duty relief to import the necessary equipment. The French government established in 1969 the Cyclades program that was to create a network among public administrations. Under the direction of Louis Pouzin, the Cyclades program pioneered a more software-based approach to networking, relying for example on dynamic addressing rather than on physical addresses. Pouzin also insisted on a more hierarchical system that was contrary to the ARPANET design (Abbate 1999). In the 1970s, joint European efforts also succeeded in building a packet switching data network among the U.K., Swiss, French, and Italian sites, called EIN.[6]

In other words, European countries had the technological capability but lacked the public commitment of resources and orchestrating vision that yet did not stifle local experimentation. They also made an important strategic error in trying to coordinate development around an "open standard," the X.25, that rivaled the IP/TCP and was promoted by the national telecommunication operators. The Cyclades project was not sponsored by the French government, because the telecom monopoly favored a digital network called Transpac that later became the back-bone to the first commercialization of digital services in the world, the Minitel. Davies's efforts at the NPL, which had been a leader in Internet development, were similarly neglected. The British pushed instead the X.25 to be implemented by the Post Office. The U.K. academic commu-nity developed a network called JANET that for the first five years was registered to the Queen because the royal family did not need a license to operate a private network (Gillies and Cailliau 2000). In both the United Kingdom and France, the institutional logic was to develop a network that would permit payments through metering of use, similar to the model of circuit switching. The X.25 protocol was adopted throughout Europe.

The American net did not simply follow a technological blueprint; as in the European case, it emerged within a specific institutional and decentralized context. The European experience recapitulated in many ways Thomas Hughes's (1983) description of the creation of large tech-nological systems, such as the electrical grid. For reasons linked to the relationship of a strong and independent university system and military industrial policy, the ARPANET did not evolve out of a hierarchical but rather a modular design that focused on common interfaces.[7] Advanced Research Projects Agency wanted to reduce its large outlays for com-puters and hence proposed the ARPANET as a way to connect research centers and to exploit better the computer resources in a distributed en-vironment. The visionary head of the information-processing unit at ARPA, Joseph Licklider, appointed Lawrence Roberts from Lincoln Lab to coordinate the efforts to build the ARPANET. Roberts understood that the ARPANET would require the cooperation of headstrong com-puter scientists managing the various research sites (Abbate 1999). Partly in response to this political reality, Roberts recognized the importance of allocating the major responsibility to the local centers. In practice, this meant keeping the network itself simple and letting the intelligence reside in locally controlled computers. Roberts thus decided not to impose ho-mogeneous choices of computers and software on all the centers. Instead, he focused on creating a system that would integrate the diverse centers by relying upon common protocols.

Intermediate to the computers and the network were switching nodes that represented the additional layer created by the ARPANET. Indeed, the notion of "layers" (as seen in our fig. 1.1) derived from the ARPA experience as an engineering design principle to assign responsibilities to the local hosts and to the switches. Thus, the system was modular: components (the centers) could be treated as black boxes as long as they worked with a common interface dictated by the protocols. This system was first demonstrated in 1972.

The growing complexity and the diversity of demands on ARPA lead in the 1980s to a number of changes. Advanced Research Projects Agency spun off the military net (milnet) into its own domain and the year after, in 1984, handed the management over the system to the National Science Foundation, which re-named it the NSFNET. In 1990, the NSF announced it intended to privatize the net, and it withdrew entirely from its management by 1995. During this time, the ARPANET grew to include NATO partners linked by satellite transmission to the NSFNET, which linked an international research community, including the NPL and the University College of London, Cyclades in France (which contributed several important design ideas), and CERN in Geneva. Because the infrastructure was built by and around institutional actors (such as Bolt, Beranek & Newman (BBN), which received a dominant share of the early contracts to develop and build the network), many of them became major players in providing the backbone services to the Internet. The role of U.S. government funding cannot be underestimated; Langlois and Mowery (1996) calculate that NSF and DARPA funding between 1956 and 1995 amounted to over a billion constant dollars.

This short technical history of the ARPANET misses, however, two important aspects relating to the role of community. Roberts, in charge of creating the ARPANET, understood that the job of creating the net would lead to cooperation across the difference centers and disciplines. The researchers involved in these efforts, many of them doctoral students, would later come to populate the regulatory associations that governed the assignment of domain names, decisions on new protocols, and broad policy issues. These people included Robert Metcalfe, who invented the Ethernet while at Xerox PARC; Paul Mockapetris of the University of Southern California (USC), who proposed the Domain Name System; Vinton Cerf and Robert Kahn at Stanford, who designed the TCP/IP interface as well as the idea of "gateway" switches that bridged different national and commercial networks; and such legendary figures in Internet history as Jon Postel, a graduate student at USC. The strength of this community is pervasive in the history of the Internet. Thus the company Cisco, which leads the market in the provision of routers to support packet switching, came out of Stanford University; the Berkeley version of UNIX early on incorporated the TCP/IP functionality, allowing for individual efforts to experiment with local networks.

The other important aspect of the ARPANET experience was the primary role played by the user in a distributed environment.[8] Once users were able to use the net for communication, they began to send messages. It was e-mail that quickly dominated use on the early net and it has never since then relinquished its place. E-mail is "asynchronous"; a party can send a message that can be retrieved later at the will of the recipient. These messages provided an exchange of partly tacit knowledge that would otherwise remain local, or be exchanged at conferences. They also intimated the explosive implications of the net for the social engagement of users. E-mail predates the early ARPANET, but the date of 1971 when Ray Tomlinson of Bolt, Beranek & Newman sent the first e-mail message on ARPANET represents a critical juncture.

The USENET is another example of a spontaneous innovation. It arose at Duke University and the University of North Carolina when three computer scientists met to establish a news server in 1978. The year after, the first MUD (multi-user dungeon) was invented at the University of Essex. For the designers of the ARPANET, the *network intermediated between computers*. The emergent reality imposed a different conception: *the network intermediated between people*.

The ARPANET vision dominated alternatives because of these emergent properties. Distributed computing and public financing were not unique to the United States, though the size of the ARPANET budget dwarfed European efforts in this particular domain. (We should recall, though, the massive European and national government support for the computer and electronic industries.) The American Internet expanded because its protocols emerged everywhere: in routers, software languages, operating systems, local area networks (such as Ethernet), and user groups. This distributed model of innovation and diffusion overwhelmed the coordinated efforts of computer companies and telecommunication operators in Europe and the United States to build a network by design. The irony is that this model of distributed innovation is evident in historical hindsight; it was not planned but driven by a growing community of users.

The Web It is not surprising, in this perspective, that the Internet moved from research community to popular use once technologies were developed that facilitated broad access. The demand for social communication trumped the technocratic vision of file transfer and remote computing. The ARPANET had developed the principles of distributed and modular design and built an infrastructure to permit digital packet switching. The Internet was subsequently launched out of two important contributions that addressed the popular user: the software that permits documents to be addressed and found, and the browser software that permits an easy interface between the local computer and the retrieved contents from the Internet.

The first contribution consisted of the creation of HTML and HTPP as a standard used in the scientific community. A British computer scientist, Tim Berners-Lee, largely deserves the credit for this contribution, though many of the components were assembled from pre-existing solutions. After his education in the United Kingdom, Berners-Lee was employed at the physics research laboratory CERN, located in Geneva, Switzerland. CERN, as a research institute, was connected to the NSFNET. (It is important to note that the ARPANET branched overseas in 1973 when it connected to the University College of London in the United Kingdom, and the Royal Radar Establishment in Norway; at that time, the number of US nodes consisted only of a dozen or more sites). Berners-Lee took on the task of improving the ability of researchers to send hypertext documents to each other. Hypertext is a defining feature of the Internet, in which a user can begin one document and easily find related documents, if a word or concept is linked.[9] He called his software the "World Wide Web." A key element to Berners-Lee software was the creation of a Universal Resource Identifier that can be used to find anything on the web using an HTTP address. (The standard term now used is the Universal Resource Locator, or URL.) In 1991, Berners-Lee released the first version of his software, which could be installed at no charge on any server that was connected to other servers, either by dedicated lines or by telephone using a modem. The code was *open source*, meaning anyone could use and alter the code. It use as *copyleft* was protected by a license.

(See chapter 14 for a discussion of open source.) Any document that had a URL and was located on a machine connected to the Internet thus became part of the World Wide Web (or www).

Thus, the World Wide Web represents that part of the Internet that is accessible through this addressing system. The original domains were the scientific laboratories that chose voluntarily to install the software and to make their documents accessible. Berners-Lee and his colleagues diffused the software through presentations at scientific conferences and voluntary international standard bodies, such as the Internet Engineering Task Force. At an IETF meeting, he met researchers from Xerox Parc and MIT's Media Lab, and he spent several months at each in 1992. By 1993, the World Wide Web software had diffused sufficiently that MIT and CERN agreed to host a consortium to develop standards and monitor quality. The World Wide Web consortium, labeled W3C, was announced by Martin Bangemann, part of a European Commission that was responsible for developing the EC's plan for a Global Information Society. In 1995, INRIA, a French national laboratory for information technology, became the European host, and in 1996, Keio University became the Asian host of the consortium.

The second contribution that permitted the growth of the Internet was the creation of browsers to provide users with an interface to access easily information from distributed locations. Browsers developed independently of the World Wide Web software, though Berners-Lee immediately understood the importance of a browser (plus an editor, he thought) for developing the Internet. He approached several research communities to see if they would adapt their hypertext editors to be used as a browser. Many of these editors were developed at European institutes. For example, in 1991, just after the first release of the World Wide Web software, Berners-Lee tried to persuade a company called Grif to adapt its software to the net. Grif sold an editor that was invented at France's national laboratory INRIA, from which the company was spun off. Berners-Lee writes:

I tried to persuade the people at GRIF to add the software needed for sending and receiving files over the Internet, so their editor could become a Web browser, too. I told them I would give them the software outright; they would just have to hook it in. But they said the only way they would do that was if we could get the European Commission to fund the development. They didn't want to risk taking the time. I was extremely frustrated. There was a growing group of people who were excited about the possibilities of the World Wide Web, and here we had the technology for a true hypertext browser/editor mostly developed, and we couldn't bridge the gap. Getting Commission funding would have put eighteen months into the loop immediately. This mindset, I thought, was disappointingly different from the more American entrepreneurial attitude of developing something in the garage for fun and worrying about funding it when it worked! (Berners-Lee 1999, 45).

Even at a commercial company, Berners-Lee was unable to find a European partner for further development of his idea.

Instead, American efforts were largely responsible for the diffusion of browser software. However, the revolutionary development was the creation of a browser with a graphical interface, called Mosaic, by a researcher Marc Andreesen, a student at the government-financed National Center for Supercomputing Applications (NCSA) at the University of Illinois at Urbana-Champaign. Testing out his ideas with user groups on the web, Andreesen worked out a way to transmit graphical images embedded in Mosaic text.

In February 1993, the NCSA released the Mosaic browser, which offered point-and-click access to the web and could be easily downloaded and installed. By the end of that year, Andreesen had founded a company along with Jim Clark, a former Stanford University professor who had founded a start-up company called Silicon Graphics. They hired a large number of employees at the NCSA Illinois site, plus others from the Internet community. In April 1994, they renamed themselves Netscape— as part of a settlement with the University of Illinois that had lodged a suit against the use of Mosaic in the company name—and made their program available for downloading from the Internet. It included an important feature of permitting security transactions, thus facilitating commercial payments. The same month, Bill Gates, chief executive officer at Microsoft, decided that the next version of the Windows operating system should include access to the Internet.

These two contributions of the addressing system and text editor developed by Berners-Lee and the browser—of which the most important commercial breakthrough was made by Andreesen and Netscape— made the Internet available to a large public. These technologies did not arrive from nowhere, but were developed, in Berners-Lee's (1999) expression, in "webs of people." The initial versions were free; the source code could be downloaded, used, and changed without violation of a license protection.[10] People knew each other, interacted in electronic communities, and built consortia. Many of the early contributions came from European research institutes. This point cannot be emphasized enough: the technology and technological capabilities existed in many parts of the world. European, Japanese, Israeli, New Zealand, and Australian research institutes were part of an international infrastructure by 1989 that supported interconnections among distributed sites. Yet it was in the United States that commercial development occurred at the fastest speed.

The Search for Profit

Who are users in the United States? A Stanford University study found 55 percent of the U.S. population in 2000 was connected to the Internet, 17 percent of these solely by access at the place of work (Nie and Erbring 2000). By far, the primary use was e-mail and chat rooms, underscoring that the Internet amplifies existing relationships. The time allocated to television declined. Though little use was found of telecommuting, the study found that Internet use correlated with more time at work, both regarding time in the office and time at home. Internet access was strongly affected by educational differences; college education increased access by 40 percent. Aside from an age effect, the study found no digital gap in usage among those connected.[11]

These cultural and demographic factors are not unique to the United States and they also influenced the diffusion of the Internet internationally. In other words, those online share similar demographic profiles throughout the world, with access and usage particularly high among the wealthier and educated. The OECD (2001) study on the digital divide indicated that Internet penetration has been highly concentrated in richer countries, with household income as an important predictor of access and use. With 90 percent of world secured sites in English, the access to the Internet for many did not translate into commercial access to its diverse content.

The statistics published by the International Telecommunications Union (2001a) on global use show the same inequality in the Internet penetration, but also a rapid acceleration in users. In 1991, it was estimated that Internet users numbered 4.4 million; by 1997, 96 million, and by 2000, 361 million. These figures are open to considerable problems of interpretation given that Internet access is often available through the workplace, libraries, and cybercafes. NUA provides more recent data, using a different methodology than the ITU. It estimates the world total to be 513 million in August 2001, with 181 million users in the United States and Canada, 155 million in Europe, 143 million in Asia, 25 million in Latin America, and 4.5 million in the Middle East. African users are estimated at 4 million, about equivalent to the number of Swedes connected.[12]

These data indicate the massive extent of the digital divide, but they also underestimate the limitations. Even if poor countries should be connected, they still face poverty. It may be easier to locate medical information, but medical services will still be priced by the wage rates where the physicians, nurses, and technicians live. Even the costs of connection pose a barrier. Most studies show a perceptible relationship between online pricing and use; not surprisingly, countries that deregulated tend to have lower prices and higher penetration rates (Mowery and Simcoe 2001). However, with penetration rates reaching 30 to 50 percent in most OECD countries, the Internet is available to many strata of society in *developed* countries, though how they use the Internet will still reflect the overall divide in education and opportunity.

An interesting observation from these statistics is that the growth of the Internet is not the same phenomenon as the development of Internet businesses. The Internet opened up several sectors that appeared ripe for entrants that bypassed traditional channels: portals serving consumer to consumer, business sales to consumers, or brokering sales between businesses (respectively called "C2C," "B2C" and "B2B"). Figure 1.2 provides a schema by which these markets are related. The strategies of portals, ISPs, e-commerce, and brokers are oriented toward engaging consumers in repeat business. Business-to-Business (B2B) consists of online auctions, but the bulk of this exchange is the substitution for previous electronic supply stems.

The Internet has been by far most successful in the B2B sectors and in the back office. The B2B sector represents 85 percent of the reported value of transactions globally; most of the country chapters to this book report similar findings. Back office efficiencies include the conversion of

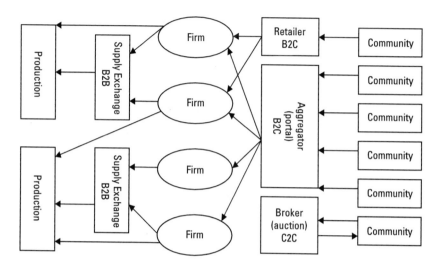

Figure 1.2
Source: Gensollen 2000.

paper documentation to electronic media. This conversion has the radical implication that documentation can be handled remotely, by customers from their home filling out mortgage applications or by agents in call centers located in India providing customer service. Companies such as General Electric estimate these savings to be valued at billions of dollars (see Litan and Rivlin 2001).

There is, though, an overall paradox in the figures on Internet connection by the wealthier countries and households and the relatively modest estimates of Internet retail purchasing. To paraphrase the famous quip by the Nobel economist Robert Solow, we see the Internet everywhere but in the figures for commercial sales. One body of explanation for this gap points to the problem of providing information services. Another line of explanation, to which I hold, is that this gap between overall use and commercial sales reflects an ongoing tension between the Internet as an extension of, or the creation of, communities and the delicate intrusion of business to commercialize these activities.

In large part, the origins of the Internet from the public sector created a natural tension between the culture of the early users and the subsequent commercial development.[13] However, the tension was not only due to these historical origins, but also was inherent in the social attraction of the Internet for the creation of new, or the expansion of existing, communities. It is this notion of community that first struck researchers of the Internet who studied such phenomena as the Well, with its origins in the Whole Earth movement of northern California (Rheingold 1993). The Internet was quickly recognized as offering some of the dangers of wandering from safe to dangerous parts of a city, with some sites specializing in violence, sex, or ideological movements. The Internet thus posed the question of how to develop trust and membership in distributed networks (Kollock 1999; Wellman 1999).

Most studies make an observation that is central to understanding the net: the Internet is not separate from traditional social networks. Or as one pair of researcher summarized, surfers don't ride alone (Wellman and Gulia 1999). The data on Internet penetration show rather remarkable rates of penetration within a decade. As a social phenomenon, the Internet has been revolutionary in its rate of adoption. As a business phenomenon, the Internet has had considerable difficulty. Indeed, the total amount of B2C business by Internet is a fraction of national economic income even for the countries with the highest usage.

The business and economic literature has focused on the market failure of markets for information, almost oblivious to the wider cultural conflict in the logics of community and market that percolates in the background. The economics of information consist of a series of what appears at first to be a fundamental paradox: information is costly to create, but easy to replicate.[14] Tolstoy may have labored hard at *War and Peace*, and the copies that his wife made by hand to send to publishers is itself a labor not to be replicated. But today, the digital encoding of *War and Peace* means it is easy to post the text on the web and let consumers pay the marginal costs of reading or printing it. In other words, creation of content is a standard economic good, but once digitally encoded as information, content is a public good: it is re-created at close to zero marginal costs and its consumption does not reduce its availability for others to consume.

Business by the Internet, at first glance, appears to be a bonus for the customer and a terror for the seller. Because the Internet permits browsing and easy verification of prices, the customer is potentially far more informed when browsing in the virtual space than in strolling in the shopping mall. The importance of information encouraged early on the appearance of what John Hagel and Mark Singer (1999) named the "infomediary," that is a company that unbundled the value chain and directed customers to the sites where a product or service could be purchased at the lowest price. Yet, the problem for the infomediary was the same for the other businesses, that it "unbundled." How can an infomediary earn money if other companies can offer the same service? Why would customers return to any vendor rather than simply search the Internet every time they wanted to purchase a product or service? In other words, what would be the source of differentiation to support repeat business in an environment that gives customers the power to compare prices while sitting at home?

The analysis of business models quickly pointed to two elements that differentiate products and services. The first element is that the Internet transmits information. The market for information is notoriously pitted with low barriers to entry and market failures. The failure arises because buyers and sellers cannot easily verify the information. The buyer does not know if the information is true or, in the case of a purchase of an item, whether the product would be shipped and in what state it will arrive. The seller does not know if the buyer can pay or if the buyer will not resell the information. An obvious way to solve such a failure is to post a bond that is lost in the case of default. An easy bond to establish is a credit rating for customers, so that customers that do not pay incur damaged credit. (See chapter 13 for a discussion of these and other solutions.) The seller can post a bond by establishing a costly *reputation* that would be damaged if bad information or goods were sold. Thus, brand label recognition and reputation are especially important for an e-business.

The second element is the exploitation of positive network externalities: the value of the network increases with the number of connected users. The benefits of membership derived from network externalities are more powerful in the presence of the attributes of interconnection and interoperability in a distributed environment. In an odd way of art preceding reality, the concept of a *network externality* predates the commercial exploitation of the largest of all social networks, the Internet. The Internet evaporates the constraints of physical space and local networks. Bob

Metcalfe encapsulated this idea when he proposed that the value of a network is the number of connections, $N(N-1)$, or N^2 when the number of nodes is large; this observation is called Metcalfe's Law.

In many respects, network externalities imply the possibility of a "cascade" in which users are attracted to only one or a few sites, products, or technology. The promise of network externalities is that a large enough share might "tip" a market toward your site. Hence, many companies offer free services to grab dominant market share, or to prevent someone else from doing so. The latter motive clearly might have been operating in Microsoft's acquisition and support of the free e-mail service Hotmail, and its free distribution of an Internet browser. More recently, it has freely offered a messenger service. These free services countered inroads by new competitors (AOL and Netscape, later acquired by AOL). Many ISP and e-mail service providers attracted large numbers of non-paying customers by offering free service with the hope of recovering costs by advertising fees or by more sophisticated provisions. For example, search engine providers such as Google earn fees from sales on sites to which they direct customers.

Some sites sought to charge for the software (such as Netscape did originally) or for access. An example of such a strategy is AOL. It offered, eventually for a flat fee, the possibility for users to engage in chat room discussions with other members. It also offered multiple accounts that permitted not only individuals to take on multiple identities, but more importantly families to assign individual names to family members. These services were supported in a software interface that provided a number of services: access to the Internet, e-mail and instant messaging, and the availability of special promotions. It is interesting to note that by 2002, AOL listed 20 million paying customers, along with 50 million users of its instant messaging service.

The AOL strategy exploits a particular kind of network externality, namely a *virtual community*, where the externality is the value of communicating and participating with "like-minded members." This strategy is particularly interesting, for in such commercial communities, the two logics of the social and the market are jointly at play. In the social network literature, these kinds of networks are called homophilous, that is, they consist of people sharing similar tastes and values. They are in many ways the engines behind the expansion of the Internet. Such online mes-

saging communities as ICQ (I seek you), developed by an Israeli company, bootstraps on the communication among pre-existing relationships
to widen the social net to users who meet, often on a sustained basis.[15]

A strategy of benefiting from virtual communities highlights the efforts
to escape from the economics of information. Economic information is a
public good. Its marginal cost of replication is negligible because the information content is easily codified electronically. Yet the substance of a
social relationship is contextual and situated; communication and transaction are lodged in a sense of shared affect and value that traditionally is
enjoyed by sharing physical proximity: the café, bookstore, or religious
assembly. This sticky knowledge, to use a common phrasing, is the by-
product of social affiliation and, in the eyes of new online businesses, the
elixir to render the customer loyal to its site.[16]

The commercial value of a community highlights the tender balance
between the social and commercial dimensions of the Internet. Because
creating communities is costly and hard, a logical strategy is to form alliances with existing or "natural" ones. After all, the Internet rides super-
ficially upon anonymity, whereas in fact it reveals the emergence of
groups built on existing relationships or preferences. The Internet quickly
provided opportunities for social groups to communicate, especially useful for social pariahs by the norms of one country to find similar people in
other countries. Sites for homosexuals, women, ethnicities, religions,
hobbies, and intellectual, cultural, and political interests bloomed.

A few of these sites recognized the potential commercial value of these
communities, as did for-profit firms. Thus, companies such as e-GM
struck alliances with these communities to provide selective advertisements to their members in return for payment. These alliances, even
if founded on transparent agreements, nevertheless touched upon the
perennial clash between the norms of social communities (sometimes
nonprofits) and commercial interests.

The efforts to create or ally with a community reflected the ambition of
companies to make customers loyal to their sites. The early measurements of success rested on "eyeball" counts. This measure was particularly relevant if the primary source of revenue was advertising. But
"eyeballs" did not result in sales on the site, and hence the idea of "sticky
eyeballs" became increasingly important: how long a customer visited the
site. Sites wanted to replicate the feel of a "locale," much as bookstores

offer chairs and coffee. Ultimately, measurements migrated to ratios of how many visitors actually made a purchase. To encourage returns, companies such as Amazon pioneered loyalty programs that offered incentives for subsequent purchases. This program creates a tie between the customer and the company and hence does not rely upon a community. But companies such as Amazon also developed rating mechanisms by which customers provided comments on books and products, and other customers rated the value of these comments, thus creating anonymous profiles of the customers' average value to the community.

The purest example of a strategy to gain from a community is an online auction house, such as eBay, which has no inventory and no products to sell, but earns a profit as a percentage of the transacted price. What is its advantage relative to other online auction houses? Surely its reputation helps bond eBay to providing service. But eBay also leverages its existing customer base by having customers rate their experience with each other, while maintaining their anonymity.

There is, in other words, an uneasy tension between the service provider and customers. Information can be analyzed to suggest how much a customer might pay. Evans and Wurster (2000) call this use of information to personalize offers and prices the creation of "segments of one." But the merits of this strategy illustrate the hazards posed by electronic transactions, already surfaced by the use of scanner data. In usual transactions, the customer understands that if a payment is made on credit, the company has recourse to his or her credit history; in addition, the company itself might sell information to a mail listing company. Both parties gain in this system, and thus customers volunteer to provide personal information. There are, of course, rules and laws regarding the dissemination of this information by the company. The digital records of customers, however, make it far easier to aggregate information to provide an extraordinarily detailed profile. At the same time, some companies earned reputations as guardians of virtual communities, serving as the cyber equivalent of "gated communities" that populate the US real estate market (Lessig 1999b). Thus, eBay established a department to monitor the sale of illegal goods, and other sites provide users means to filter out undesired sites. Again, we see the tension between the classic concept of community and the commercial interests of the service provider.

There is now a greater understanding of the causes and effects of successful Internet strategies in general. If one of the points of attraction of the Internet is the convenience of shopping or accessing services remotely, it is also true that variations in convenience influence the choice of sites. Consumers are surprisingly sensitive to the number of clicks needed to access a page, especially at slow bandwidth access. Studies of pricing on the Internet often show the same variation in price as found in physical retail stores (Smith, Bailey, and Brynjolfsson 2000). Johnson and his colleagues (2002) found the degree of search sometimes declines with user experience. The use of meta-search engines that conduct comparison shopping over sites is easily frustrated by "bait and switch" strategies that attract consumers to the site by advertising low price and low quality goods but then tries to persuade them to buy higher priced goods.[17] Latcovich and Smith (2001) find that some sectors, such as retail book selling, are more concentrated on the Internet than traditional markets. The strategies of advertising for reputation and for attracting customers lead to higher fixed costs, hence greater concentration.

It is not surprising, as a consequence, to observe a power law distribution among sites, whereby a few sites receive the bulk of traffic and sales. (See the discussion in chapter 14 of this book.) In other words, among consumer sites, Internet strategies quickly lead to maturation of product markets in which a few players dominate. A logical consequence is a shake-out of marginal firms. This pattern is hardly unique to the Internet and shares striking similarities to previous waves of revolutionary technologies and entrepreneurial activities, such as those associated with the automobile or electrical industry at the close of the nineteenth century. (See Klepper and Grady 1990, for a stylized description of this evolution common to the history of many industries.) Given that these firms were frequently new entrants, their exit from the market often was marked by their bankruptcy.

These strategies stumble, as intimated above, upon the barriers of addressing foreign markets, for few communities are global. The expectation of many is that the Internet, being built upon a global technology, provides a business instantaneous access to customers wherever they be. A few companies quickly internationalized. Boo.com, a Swedish clothing retailer with large French and international investments, opened up sites to address several countries. It failed within a short time, partly because of the gap between its managerial capability and the demands of serving diverse national markets. Retailers such as Amazon also discovered that duty tax, shipping charges, and logistics created losses large even by early Internet standards. In addition, laws regarding payments, privacy, and content (see the discussion of the Yahoo! case in France by Yao in this volume, chapter 13) rendered global strategies far more difficult than addressing national markets. Not surprisingly, these factors often suggested that foreign entry proceed by partnering with local players, a pattern that is discussed by the country chapters below.

Far from being global, then, the companies that ventured across borders employed "multidomestic" strategies that took into account national differences. Even domestically, relatively few businesses could avoid transporting atoms, engaging in what became called "brick and mortar" strategies. Warehouses and even store fronts were necessary investments for many online companies. In fact, for many consumers, online services were primarily informational, regarding flight times, reservations, and product search, with purchase and sale still being handled at retail premises.

There are, however, differences among countries regarding demand for services and products, as discussed in the country chapters. One area that has developed considerable online business (other than sex and gambling, which are increasingly becoming regulated by national laws) is finance and stock trading, especially in the Scandinavian countries; the United Kingdom has also witnessed one of the few successful cases of an entirely online bank. But even here, such activities are associated with traditional and local names in banking and finance. In most countries, B2B has been an expansive area for the Internet, but primarily because of the existing electronic networks among suppliers and buyers. In other words, previous relationships predated the Internet commerce.

If the effects of the Internet on competition has not been the predicted one of atomistic markets—to the contrary!—this still leaves open the issue of the impact on the traditional dominant players and the broader institutions. One of the most important questions addressed by studies of the Internet is whether the Internet served to disrupt the position of incumbent firms in the countries under study. There are two related but more ambitious questions of interest: did the Internet economy provide the window of opportunity for new firms and new entrants to create fundamental institutional change in national economies, and has this change caused a convergence among nations toward a more global model? The analysis of both of these questions is related to the role of transnational actors in transporting the new business models across borders.

Global Actors and Regulation

The Internet economy is global not only because communication networks span the globe. Surely, this feature provides a *necessary* and powerful dynamic for its diffusion, if by global, we accept that users are confronted with a cultural content largely dominated by American Web servers. But the Internet did not simply diffuse because communication networks ignited these factors; they were enabling but not sufficient conditions. The Internet economy is global because transnational actors diffused an entrepreneurial model of development. Under closer scrutiny, many of these transnational actors are deeply embedded in the American system, posing deep challenges of how to regulate globally the Internet. Global actors increasingly confront an environment that is regulated by international organizations or by cooperation among national regulators.

Global Actors

A critical agent in the diffusion of the Internet is the multinational corporation. One of the intriguing findings of the Stanford study cited earlier is the important role, for better or worse, played by work in the diffusion of Internet access. Because multinational corporations operate existing networks of subsidiaries, they serve to diffuse the Internet by two powerful mechanisms. First, they enter into new opportunities on a global basis, both to enter new markets and to support their sourcing needs. Second, they diffuse information technologies as part of their communication networks, as foreign customers and suppliers must adopt Internet technologies in order to coordinate on a world wide basis. Indeed, the multinational corporation is a "wired network," intensive in information technologies (Hagstrom 1991).

As noted earlier, the new dot.com enterprises, such as AOL (founded in the 1980s), Amazon, and Yahoo!, aggressively sought international opportunities. Because of regulatory hurdles and their desire to enter countries rapidly, these companies often formed alliances with established players in foreign markets. For companies such as Amazon that sold atoms called books, their entries were troubled by problems of logistics and import duties. For companies that provided pure information services, alliances with local telecommunication companies provided the immediate access to infrastructure and companies. In a few cases, international alliances were made between two Internet start-ups.

Perhaps the most fascinating part of the diffusion of the Internet, and of the American model, has been the role played by investment banks, consulting companies, and venture capital. These American companies were eager to replicate internationally their success in the United States, partly to explore the still uninhabited economic space of the Internet, partly to sell their "learning" from the United States to foreign countries. To a large extent, they followed the path beaten by American investment and consulting companies over the past century that transported Taylorism, divisionalization, and information systems to Europe and elsewhere (Kipping 1999; McKenna 1999; Djelic 1998). Yet the rapidity by which consultants and bankers of the cyberage brought the new learning is only explicable by an important difference compared to the past: these actors were already global in their reach. The investment bank of Goldman Sachs, the consulting firm McKinsey, and American law firms had existing affiliates in foreign markets.

If there were a new category of actors, these were American venture capitalists and American-style stock markets. American venture capitalists themselves expanded into foreign markets, and they also inspired local venture capitalists and new imitators. An example is APAX in France, a venture fund started by a Harvard Business School graduate. APAX historically focused on management buyouts, and then grew aggressively in financing the sudden emergence of new companies. These imitators sought to recreate new financial networks, just like the "webs of people" that seeded Berners-Lee's ideas of the World Wide Web. The organization of *First Tuesday* arose in London, and then spread to other European capitals. Entrepreneurs wore yellow nametags, investors wore red, and they mingled among cocktails to meet each other; venture capitalists usually faced a line of eager and young faces. These meetings attracted crowds over a thousand every Tuesday of the month. First Tuesday itself was a loose confederation of national organizations, sold collectively to an American company, before being bought out by the national organizations that were not originally consulted on the sale. Its own experience reflects the inexperience and uncertainties of entrepreneurs during this time. It is not possible to know how many deals this type of association consummated, but they indicate a groping for investment means outside of the traditional capital and banking institutions.

Venture capitalists are interested in recovering their money by bringing a company public (Black and Gilson 1998). Hence, an important element to this expansion was the co-evolution of small firm stock markets to support the initial public offers of the new start-ups. Stock markets were organized in many of the countries in our study in response to the growing demand by entrepreneurs to find capital outside the banking-based systems of most countries; it is hard to gauge how much of this demand also stemmed from venture capitalists who depended upon these markets to reap their returns. Governments too were convinced that such markets were critical to new firm development and innovation. Thus, with public subsidies, new stock exchanges for small companies grew up in Germany, France, and many other countries. As reviewed in chapter 14, venture capital may be the most important legacy of the first Internet explosion.

Global Regulation

An area of tremendous importance, as we have explained above, is international regulation. Again, the early lead of the United States has deeply influenced the Internet regulation of foreign countries. The U.S. power derives from its large share of web servers and the overall Internet infrastructure. Partly because of the much higher price of leased lines in Europe, it is often less expensive to route Internet traffic from one point to another by the way of the United States. The United States also has had the vast majority of Internet web hosts.

However, the growth of the Internet outside of the United States has clearly changed the power dynamics as well. These changes can be seen in the wireless sector, as briefly discussed by Glimstedt and Zander in this volume (chapter 4), because many of the dominant players are non-American. A stunning example of the transformation in U.S. influence on world regulation that serves as a useful illustration is the registry of names. For the browser to receive information from a site, it must know the address of a web server, its domain name. Though the actual routing of packet relies upon 32-bit numerical addresses, sites are given alphabetical names in order to facilitate user convenience. (Due to the large demand, 128-bit addresses have been created.) There must, therefore, be a way for names and numbers to be matched in order for packets to reach their destination.

The Internet relies upon a centralized hierarchy to locate these servers. For example, the address ⟨http://www.wharton.upenn.edu⟩ is the domain name of an Internet server. Wharton owns this domain name, for which it received permission from the University of Pennsylvania. The University of Pennsylvania registered its name with the owner of .edu. The Internet Assigned Numbers Authority, IANA, administered this structure. In 1992, the United States government privatized the registry authority to Network Solutions, Inc. For a minimal fee, parties could then register their names and receive a .com, .net, or .org address. Firms and individuals could also register with non-American government agencies and receive a country code domain, such as .fr for France. In 2000, 10 of the 13 root name servers were located in the United States, with three others located in Stockholm, London, and Tokyo.

The United States deregulated their service in 1998 by permitting competition among registrars.[18] Private companies compete as registrars, relying on a common database to ensure that the requested name is available. Names are registered on a "first come" basis. The United States transferred the coordinating function of the Internet to a private and non-public organization, the Internet Corporation for Assigned Names and Numbers (ICANN) that started real operations in 2000. ICANN is responsible for managing the Domain Name System, the allocation of Internet Protocol addresses, the coordination of new IP parameters, and the root name server system. Despite very different regulatory traditions, the European Union has nevertheless accepted the United States' lead in domain name registration because it has no choice.

ICANN's board consists of 19 directors, nine from the three supporting organizations, nine directors at-large, and the president. (This structure is outlined in fig. 1.3.) These latter directors are elected by the membership at large, and members can also be individuals. To ensure international representation, no more than 50 percent of the at-large directors can come from a single country. This has had a curious effect. The EU has explicitly encouraged individuals and public service organizations to join. To ensure that governments exercise some influence, public authorities created a Government Advisory Committee, which in

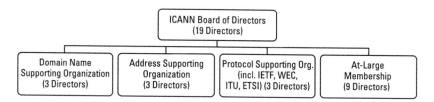

Figure 1.3
Structure of ICANN Board of Directors

2000 consisted of 35 members, including international organizations of the International Telecommunication Union (ITU), World Intellectual Projects Organization (WIPO) (responsible for intellectual property), and the OECD. There were no governments from Africa represented, and few in general from developing countries.

Domain names can, obviously, conflict with intellectual property in the form of trademarks. Because IANA and Network Solutions did not interfere with the issue of trademarks, there quickly developed a business called "cybersquatting" that took advantage of the "first come" principle of registration. Trademarked names or names of famous people were registered in bad faith by entrepreneurs who then sought to sell their "property" to the interested parties. The more liberal definition of intellectual property law in the United States conflicts with European law that favors the creator. American law eventually evolved to sort a good deal of this mess, but it remains still an area of conflict.

As for Network Solutions, Inc., competition policy did not eradicate its first mover advantage. It has merged with VeriSign, in a deal estimated at $21 billion. Verisign has a dominant market position in digital certification. The combination of dominant positions in domain name registration and digital certifications provides potential economies, but it also raises issues of privacy and data protection laws that differ among countries.

Plan of the Book

The Internet economy results from a global technology and a transnational infrastructure, but has developed commercially in the context of historical and institutional factors that vary within and across national borders. It is important to understand what is the quantity of change that interests the chapters of these books. One quantity is simply "how much?" For our purposes, this might mean how much has the Internet economy contributed to a country's growth? How much does a country dominate the world Internet? A second quantity of change is the assessment of "how different." What have been the evolutionary histories and institutional consequences among countries in their response to the emergence of the Internet economy?

It is this second quantity that interests us in this book. The "how much" question poses complex problems of measurement, as seen in the many efforts to resolve the so-called Solow paradox of trying to find the productivity effects of information technologies in productivity numbers. However, this is not our question, because we are after another elusive prey.[19] We would like to understand the meaning of a global Internet economy as a cultural and economic force that influenced the organization and institutions of seven countries and a world system.

The term "global Internet economy" is not a statement that presumes such an economy exists. This is not true, any more than we can that there are national Internet economies. The claim is that the Internet appeared in the 1990s as a radical technology that upset not only business practices, but also economic institutions. It is global in the extent that it organized latent tendencies, even frustrations, under a cultural rubric that was associated with a technology but also a conception of lifestyles and market participation.

The book is organized in two parts. The first consists of seven country chapters: United States (chapter 3), Sweden (chapter 4), France (chapter 5), India (chapter 6), Germany (chapter 7), Korea (chapter 8), and Japan (chapter 9). A preface to these chapters explains the framework, common themes, and their relative positions according to the penetration and development of the Internet. The country chapters meet three objectives: describe how the Internet developed, evaluate to what extent the Silicon Valley model diffused or was adopted, and analyze the features that explain why certain sectors and technologies developed faster than others.

The second part of the book consists of four chapters. Chapter 11 focuses on B2B, as this sector is evaluated by far to be the most extensive globally and in each of our countries; it also permits a chance to see how country environments influence the development of this sector. The next two chapters discuss regulatory influences. Chapter 12 considers the interesting question of whether the European Union mattered to the national histories; chapter 13 offers a prospective evaluation of how different regulatory traditions will handle some of the most pressing challenges, such as privacy. Chapter 14 evaluates the results.

This book provides an analysis of the historical and institutional roots to a cross-section in time. It reveals the massive tensions in national systems in adapting to the pressure of a global Internet economy. The choices made by countries reflect wide differences in cultural, institutional, and political values. But the intriguing element of the Internet is that it connects individuals, who though still embedded in their local webs of friends and family, are able to participate in and influence wider transnational communities. This possibility did not exist before, and its consequences, so this book shows, are perceptible in the evolution of national systems and their place in a global economy.

Acknowledgments

I would like to thank Henrik Glimstedt, Martin Kenney, Eleanor Westney, and Udo Zander for comments on the written text, the anonymous reviewers, and the participants in the project for their help.

Notes

1. These estimates are given by Internet Software Consortium (⟨http://www.isc.org/⟩) for the hosts, and by Nua Internet Surveys (⟨http://www.nua.ie⟩) for the online estimates. Estimates vary by source, and these should be taken as indicative.

2. The study *Life on the Screen* by Sherry Turkle (1995) is one of the earliest and most penetrating investigations into this multiple role-playing.

3. See Tapscott 1998.

4. See Kenney in this volume, and also Kenney 2000 and Lee et al. 2000.

5. For other arguments regarding the relevance of government, see Rowen 2000; Castilla et al. (2000) analyze the social network that supports Silicon Valley; immigration policies are discussed in Kogut 2000 and Saxenian 1999, and labor mobility in Almeida and Kogut 1999.

6. An excellent account of European efforts is in Gillies and Cailliau 2000.

7. I hesitate to call this the contemporary American model, but surely it bears strong similarities to the development of the personal computer as described by Langlois (1992); see also von Burg's (2001) study of the Ethernet as one "module" in the Internet.

8. More broadly, the Internet permits users to contribute rapidly to product innovation, reinforcing von Hippel's (1988) findings that users drive innovative advances in some industries and sectors.

9. Ted Nelson coined the term "hypertext" in the mid 1960s, though the idea is often attributed to Vannevar Bush in the late 1940s and the technological innovation to Xerox's Palo Alto Research Center's scientist, Doug Engelbart, who also invented the mouse to service hypertext searches.

10. It was an odd feature of Internet history that Netscape did copyright their intellectual property. But due to competitive pressures, it later endorsed open source software and released its source code of later products into the public domain.

11. This study looks at whether the Internet complements or substitutes for other social relationships, finding a substitution effect. Castells (2001) criticizes these results and summarizes positive findings from other studies. It is clear though that a "selection" bias is at play, with Internet use screening for other attributes. It is too early to evaluate these claims.

12. ⟨http://www.nua.ie/surveys/how_many_online/⟩.

13. Interesting histories of these communities are given in Levy 1994 and Hafner and Lyon 1996.

14. Shapiro and Varian (1999) offer an accessible and in-depth discussion of the economics of information, network externalities, and Internet strategies to profit in information markets.

15. Beaudouin and Velkovska (1999) provide an excellent observational analysis of ICQ communities.

16. These observations are reflected in the revolt against the belief that information technology destroys the meaning of spatial proximity at work. See Brown and Duguid 2000 and Cohen and Prusak 2001 for two articulate criticisms.

17. Shapiro and Varian 1999 suggest several strategies, one of the more interesting ones being "versioning," by which a company attracts a customer to its site by a low offer with the hope of selling the more expensive and upscale version.

18. This section is based on Commission of the European Communities 2000a.

19. For an excellent analysis of productivity studies, see Litan and Rivlin 2001.

I

Country Chapters

2
From Pockets of Experimentation to Institutional Change

Bruce Kogut

The growth of the Internet represented a challenge to national systems that structure the relationships among firms, businesses, workers, and government. As a confusing blend of complement and substitute technologies for traditional communication systems, the Internet posed the question, who should be allowed to offer Internet services. The potential of the Internet to substitute for telecom services appeared as manna from heaven for policymakers and new entrants who were frustrated in their attempts to deregulate telecom. Thus, the Internet rode upon the wave of liberalization that had already started to shake the institutional agreements between the state, the public sector, and business.

However, the Internet posed more than a challenge to the existing infrastructure; it also opened up virgin competitive arenas. Suddenly, a new economic space, unpopulated by existing firms, appeared in the midst of these economies. The emergence of this space permitted the creation of a variety of new business models that often were exploited by new firms. Once this space was "seeded," this new ecology resulted in competitive patterns that looked at odds with the historical institutions and practices in some countries.

The perceived success of the American institutional model surely also influenced these national challenges. Many of the new start-up firms were American subsidiaries or joint ventures with American partners, themselves often less than a decade old. American finance, often in the form of venture capital, extended across borders. Governments encouraged new stock markets, entertaining or changing laws to support stock options as compensation, and subsidized new firm development. The American model was seen as the Silicon Valley and as the causal explanation for why in the 1990s the United States grew faster overall and in the new economy in particular.

The Silicon Valley model, defined in the introductory chapter, poses concretely the problem of identifying complex causality and competing explanations. At the core of these issues is the question of why better institutions or technologies do not simply diffuse across national borders. What is causally responsible for differences in national performances? Is it venture capital, flexible labor markets, new firm development, or are all of these elements joined together as factors individually necessary and jointly sufficient for growth?

Yet, the discussion of the causality of institutions obscures a more fundamental level of analysis. After all, the efficacy of these institutions depends, as I claim below, on the beliefs and social networks inscribed within geography. The commercial promise of the Internet was coupled with a cultural wave that potentially appeared to shift the expectations of entrepreneurs and the career decisions of workers to switch into these new pockets of experimentation. More radically, the demands of the new technologies and market opportunities promised a "rewiring" of the traditional social connections within and across countries. People could dare to try new careers because the rise of the Internet rode on the back of new institutional players and organizational forms. The question confronted in these chapters on national histories is whether the cultural and institutional change ultimately made a difference to the traditional national systems.

National Systems

Let's consider first the preliminary equation of what constitutes national systems and how institutions, technologies, and practices interact in the production of goods and services. Accepting that causality is complex, a body of literature called "national systems" developed in the 1990s that sought to understand the comparative advantage of countries in terms of institutional advantages. The early works often noted that countries differ systematically in their institutions and politics, and these factors influence the capabilities of firms, as well as the broad technological and organizational trajectories in a country. Certainly firms compete, but the claim is, they compete on the basis of resources and expectations formed and shaped by the national institutional environments. This literature migrated from explaining why one country is richer to why many countries are rich and yet are institutionally different. This is an important distinction. The former emphasis implies that there is a best configuration of institutions and practices. The second approach attempts to explain the variety of institutional configurations that support particular innovatory and productive capabilities.

Some of the work on national systems attempts to describe and analyze the institutional differences. Along the lines of sorting out the implications of institutions on countries' comparative advantage, Richard Nelson (1993) conducted a project to detail cross-country differences in how science and technology are organized as an explanation for national patterns in innovation. Whitley (1992) opened a broader inquiry into business systems that seeks to outline the distant and proximate factors in explaining economic behavior. In a less obvious way, the magisterial history by Alfred Chandler (1990) of the relative success of American, British, and German firms relied upon notions of stylized country differences that influenced the capabilities of national firms. As discussed below, I propose that nations are marked by trajectories of organizing principles that diffuse more rapidly across the boundaries of firms than those of countries, thus providing waves of national innovation and eventual diffusion (Kogut 1991; Dosi and Kogut 1993). Berger and Dore (1996) captured the spirit of these exercises by proposing that the international division of labor reflects the *institutional* advantage of countries. In these approaches, nations demarcate institutions that provide the resources available to resident firms.

Another line of work amends these descriptive approaches to argue that nations are not simply the geography of institutions, but consist of institutional systems that are coupled by a political and economic logic. A national system is then a bundle of *complementary* institutions and practices. For example, Aoki (1990) argues that the competitive advantages of Japanese firms stem from three complementary elements: the financial system that monitors performance, the vertical hierarchy that monitors managerial behavior, and horizontal governance that encourages workers to monitor each other. Soskice (1990), Boyer and Orléan (1991), and Hall and Soskice (2001) argue similarly that successful national systems transform the inherent conflict among corporatist actors such as labor and capital into a coordination game. This game is facilitated by institutional complements that permit the monitoring of workers, managers, and investors. These models depart from the tradition in political economy of corporatist versus liberal systems, in which the former is characterized by bargaining among macro-institutional players, such federal unions, business associations, and the government, and the latter is a very large residual category consisting of systems that are not coordinated.

Configurations and Causality

The national systems approach implies that there are multiple viable combinations of institutions. A useful representation of the problem is the comparative methodology of Charles Ragin (1987) that utilizes the following Boolean rule. A cause A can be present (denoted as A) or absent (denoted as "a"). In one case, AB are two factors that are both present and are associated with a truth condition of high performance. In a second case, factor A is still present but factor B is not, and yet the outcome is still high performance. By Boolean algebra, the truth condition is the same, $AB + Ab = A$. In other words, only cause A is causally related to the outcome of high performance. Indeed, for this comparison, A is sufficient to cause high performance. In the absence of other causes, A also appears as a necessary factor. There may be other factors that also explain high performance that cannot be reduced to factor A. For example, it is possible that $Ab + Ca$ represent two configurations that produce high performance; the two configurations do not reduce to a simpler expression. Thus, Ragin's methodology permits multiple national systems to be viable, while identifying some combinations that deteriorate economic performance; it also eliminates configurations that are not jointly causal in their effects.

The advantage of Ragin's approach is that it teases out spurious causality and identifies *functional equivalents* that are not uniquely causal. Ragin's method has the advantage of asking why don't we observe these combinations, or asking what if we did? In part, these chapters address these issues. They describe the traditional elements of a national economy and analyze the emergence of Internet-driven innovation. In this way, they observe the consequences of what did happen when new configurations of institutions and organizational forms began to take hold in a new sector of the national economy.

Convergence and Divergence in Global Systems

The national system approach poses another set of issues in addition to that of causality. Given different national systems, is diffusion between systems possible? Can practices diffuse without institutional diffusion? The heuristic rule would be to discover the causal elements to the Silicon Valley model and transfer these to foreign sites. However, the implicit notion behind national systems as institutional complements is that to remove any one element is to cause the system to decay. This claim is difficult to reconcile with the evidence that national systems are communicating members of a global system. The diffusion of practices and institutions marks world history, to cite the example of religions as one of the most obvious examples. In many ways, globalization is primarily a cultural diffusion, though sometimes carried on the backs of agents of social integration (Meyer et al. 1997).

Though sympathetic to national systems approach, the alternative framing that I have proposed for the development of national trajectories begins with the observation that nations are lodged in a wider global and evolving system in which ideas, technologies, and organizing methods diffuse (Kogut 1991; Dosi and Kogut 1993). Long-term data show that certain nations appear to lead at certain historical times. In recent modern history, this leadership is often associated with distinctive principles by which technologies are developed and work is organized, such as the British division of labor, American mass production and divisionalization, German applied research institutes and industrial laboratories, or Japanese production methods. This observation implies that it is major organizing innovations that account for persistence of national leadership. Because organizational innovations diffuse much more slowly across national borders than firm borders, they create persisting competitive advantages for firms that are geographically co-located.

There is considerable evidence that technologies themselves are relatively quickly imitated, either by a process of diffusion or by indigenous capabilities. After all, technologies often rely upon codified knowledge: the underlying science is shared in an international community, teaching manuals are used in schools and by companies, and patents provide detailed information. The geographic dispersion of Nobel Prize winners before World War II, for example, shows a fairly broad European participation and an absence of American scientists, and yet the United States was leading in productivity and per capita income by 1920. The surge in American Nobel Prize winners after 1945 reflected the increased military expenditures, but also the migration of scientific minds to the United States. This latter aspect suggests the importance of knowledge that is held by individuals, as well as a general feature of the US system: its designed bias to encourage inward flows of human capital.

Organizing principles are often less codified and also less institutionally neutral. The great rise of American multinationals was predicated on their transfer of American principles of organization abroad, a point that I analyze qualitatively and statistically elsewhere (Kogut 1992). As an organizational medium, the multinational corporation exists, by this argument, as a conduit of the diffusion of embedded and tacit organizing knowledge. The international growth of American consulting firms amplifies this contention, for such firms as Arthur D. Little and McKinsey expanded on the basis of their promise to teach the American secret of productivity, the former in the way of scientific management and the latter in the way of the multidivisional corporation.[1]

The international diffusion of methods is hardly uniform across countries for at least three reasons. The first is that, as in any diffusion model, some countries are "exposed" more than others. A great difference today versus a hundred years ago is that multinational corporations, global consultants, and investment firms exist to bridge borders to varying degrees among nations; not all countries are as tightly integrated in this world system. Second, countries differ in their sectoral composition. The Japanese production model evolved in the context of the automobile and electronic industries (Nishiguchi 1994), and it diffused more rapidly overseas in these sectors. Diffusion patterns differ by sector, and countries differ in their sectoral activities; thus, global diffusion shows a country pattern.

The more interesting explanation for the geographic and country heterogeneity in diffusion of organizing principles is that recipient nations differ in their characteristics. They have to reject or rework methods to fit their own needs. The classic study of this reworking is Eleanor Westney's

(1987) history of how Meiji Japan gradually emulated, rather than imitated, foreign institutions. Of course, history is filled with cases where methods are rejected as culturally anathema or are politically blocked. Not only do notions of authority differ among countries (see the massive literature on cross-cultural management problems), but political groups may block new methods, such as the opposition of German unions to the introduction of teams as threatening the power and role of work councils.

Often, these oppositions are characterized as upsetting the historical agreements among players, but there is another and, in my view, more penetrating observation. The adoption of new work methods also upsets the work categories, and hence the associated notions of prestige and professional identities, categories that define the division of labor and the trajectories by which workers learn and specialize, and generate the social understandings the support coordination among specializations and hierarchic ranks.[2] In short, the obstacles to adoption are *political* and *cognitive*, with the latter referring to the social anticipations that are taken for granted as part of everyday life. In fact, the notion of complementarities is far more elastic than realized, because the beliefs held in common about "what practices go with what" are often cultural and hence open to cultural re-interpretation!

This process of heterogeneous diffusion points to the possibility of "hybridization," that is, the ways by which industry, labor, and other actors recombine old and new skills. (Boyer 1996 and 1998 provide several studies along these lines.) In other words, new methods often consist of elements that differ along a critical characteristic: the extent to which they are complementary, neutral, or hostile not only with existing work practices, but more critically with existing institutions. Some characteristics will be seen as incompatible at the firm level, such as mass production and piece rate pay. Others will be seen as incompatible at the institutional level, such as increasing worker mobility when wages are centrally bargained. We thus have two interacting levels of analysis, practices within and between firms and broader social and political institutions.

These two levels of analysis, firm-level work practices and national institutions, are theoretically often blurred, but powerfully distinct. Paying options as part of salary might be a necessary complement to attracting skilled labor to take on the risk of a start-up, but might be institutionally incompatible with notions of solidarity, law, or the bargain between labor and capital. More interestingly, and I would like to stress this observation, the difficulty of sorting out the causal effects on economic performance means that interested parties will seize upon cultural movements or new ideas of management to change the institutional bargain in their favor. Indeed, the problem of sorting out causality also opens the door to the creative minds of academic scholars in creating numerous explanations for the performance effects of particular national systems or business strategies, a problem not foreign to analyses of the Internet. The problems of causal inference are not then simply the plague of comparative research, they are the stuff of daily life that permits individual and collective groping toward new definitions of work practices and institutions.

The Silicon Valley Model

These methodological concerns have a particular relevance for understanding the subject of this book, namely the American system and, more narrowly, Silicon Valley. The American model poses for theorists of national systems the antithesis of the German description. As the ideal case of the liberal market economy, it consists of equity-based corporate governance systems, relatively fluid labor markets, atomized large businesses, and hierarchical management. Richard Nelson would surely add the factor of strong university/industry research cooperation. The outcome of this model is relatively high performance in producing radical innovations.

One might ask if this causal list, given in chapter one and in the chapter by Kenney (chapter 3), is complete. Surely what comes to mind is the inequitable distribution of wealth, health benefits, and educational opportunity. Few people have sought to argue that these facets are positive causal elements in the American national system. Their consideration raises the mundane question of why such social factors do not act as causal impediments to the national innovative performance. After all, the data on education shows a scarcity of engineers, technicians, mathematicians, and many kinds of scientists. How could the United States produce radical innovations if it doesn't invest to broadly educate its citizens, not to mention provide them with adequate health care? Surely, part of the answer is the design of the U.S. immigration system.[3] This line of inquiry leads to the hypothesis of the benefits of global free-riding in human capital investment as an explanation for the U.S. success, with the compensating externality that American innovations diffuse globally.

This discussion brings to the fore a well-brewed debate: Do we discuss region or nation? Saxenian's (1994) celebrated study on the sources of innovation in Silicon Valley used the Route 128 area outside of Boston as the counter example of the wrong institutions. Many of the chapters in this book use the term of the Silicon Valley model, and seek to define it, as we did in the introduction to this volume, by key attributes: venture capital, equity markets for IPOs, new firms, university relationships, and mobile labor markets.

These factors seem to be plausible, and theoretically, they make sense. Still, such a description poses the question of how did this model develop within the broader institutional perimeters of the U.S. national system. Can we see other regions in the world that meet the stylized description of the Silicon Valley model? Or to rephrase this question, are there regions that share the same institutional properties that can generate and sustain a Silicon Valley? The history of Silicon Valley suggests a property of *emergence* whereby institutions became coupled through a fluid labor market for skilled talent *prior* to the creation of large hierarchical firms.[4] This is the central historical observation: the education of researchers and engineers by local educational institutions preceded the creation of large firms that already dominated in the East Coast.

For example, studies by Baron, Burton, and Hannan (1996) show that new firms in Silicon Valley share an imprinting of their environment; they tend to be built around project-based management and similar human resource practices. This outcome is surely influenced by prototypical understandings of labor and managerial practices; and it reflects the decisions of early entrepreneurs, such as Robert Noyce at Fairchild, to avoid the hierarchy of the large East Coast firms (Castilla et al. 2000). But the proliferation of these practices is the emergent outcome of the institutional ecology of Silicon Valley. Under conditions of mobile labor markets, management by project in flat organizations makes sense rather than requiring employees to walk up the hierarchy to gain responsibility and salary. To maintain talent, newer firms need to bond employees with options. To attract venture capital, equity markets permit early investors to capitalize on success.

These factors imply a chain of complex causality that operates at the regional level of the United States. The disparity in regional practices that mark other countries is a critical feature of the American federal system. (See Locke 1995 and Putnam 1993, for an analysis of regional experimentation in Italy.) Perhaps then the way to understand the American model is the tolerance of regional and organizational variety within the perimeter of national systems. The Route 128 model was suited to a regime of military/industrial contracting, not for the disbundled and distributed economy of the Internet. But the languishing region of the Silicon Valley consisted of an institutional logic that generated a different experimental trajectory in organizational forms and technological paths. It was this local island of experimentation that fitted the early development of the Internet.

As the chapters below show, these pockets of experimentation are not unique to United States Internet history. However, variety might be an evolutionary outcome especially suited to American economic institutions. Franklin Allen and Douglas Gale (1999) argue that the advantage of an equity versus banking system is that the former is more efficient in the collection of diverse information by which to evaluate radical and uncertain technologies. As is always the case, others argue that German banks resolve this problem better. Consider first that Myers and Majluf (1984) argue that new innovations prevent firms from full disclosure in equity due to the threat of competitive imitation. Venture capital and private equity agreements resolve some of the problems of information asymmetry in equity-based systems.

I raise the caution that this functional resolution is a by-product of social relations that characterize venture capital funding, or more broadly, exchange in social regions.[5] That venture capital has historically funded companies that are in close proximity indicates that such asymmetries, as well as the provision of managerial advice, are mitigated within local social and business networks. It is not surprising that the geographical clustering of Internet domains appears to be correlated with the institution of venture capital that favors particular locations, such as Silicon Valley and New York (Zook 2002). Money and ideas do not flow without friction across geographic space, even in the Internet industry. It is the generation of variety in regional institutional experiments that appears to mark the United States.

Experimentation and Discourse in Social Networks

I have emphasized above that the term "systems" itself is best seen as varying sets of complements among countries. National systems differ, cross-sectionally and historically, in the degree of the tight coupling of their institutions and their tolerance of islands of experimentation. National systems consist of institutional logics expressed by the prevalent cultures, historical political bargains, and, we would like to add here, economic and social networks. These logics are expressed and replicated in the behavioral patterns that they validate, that is, actors take them for granted as part of their background knowledge of everyday life.[6]

Whereas such logics can be viewed as economic systems, this would be short-changing how political and economic actors exploit autonomous cultural influences to re-negotiate agreements of social consensus. In this regard, national debates are not over a model, but rather conflicting models of change. There is not one Silicon Valley but many, with knowledgeable actors posing competing *prototypical* configurations as ways to influence the direction and saliency of change.

This formulation allows for more leniency in permitting autonomous influences, such as cultural forces and the play of ideas, to allow institutions to decouple and recouple. More importantly, it displaces the analytical attention on the prisoner's dilemma type of reasoning toward a more historically amenable characterization of social action as acting on learned rules. As noted above, an approach to understanding problems of shared cognition is to treat cooperation as a coordination dilemma. In the classic formulation of Schelling (1960), this dilemma poses the problem of how two people lost in a city might find each other, with the insight that they would tend to use rules that say go to the most famous site in the city. Such rules are derived from the specific dilemma but must be borrowed from cultural icons that are shared among people.

The advantage of this approach is that it opens a path toward a more sociologically grounded view of institutions and economic change. Indeed, it might well be that this approach so successfully opens the door that one might as well close it once entering the room. For at the heart of this approach are the concerns of what is the *common knowledge* held by people. Formally, this issue has been treated by what two parties know, recursively, about each others' beliefs: does she know that I know that she knows? Such knowledge may be gained by observation over repeated interactions, or normative understandings that guide people to ignore such recursive calculations in favor of "rule of thumb" beliefs on what to expect. Governments play a role in alleviating some of the cognitive burden of recursive calculations by announcing standards and regulations that serve as common knowledge. But common knowledge rephrases the conundrum of how "knowing" what to do is shared among people. In other words, the core of cooperation is the procedural knowledge by which people coordinate (Kogut 1997).

These ideas are the traditional concerns of economic sociology. Such tacit beliefs are the "taken for granted" postulate that forms the cornerstone in the new economic sociology.[7] Life would indeed be difficult, as Garfinkel (1967) likes to remind us, if we had to establish anew in every social setting what our primitive and prior beliefs are! For those who cross from one nation to another or from one coast to the other, the (apocryphal?) quip of Churchill on England and the United States as two nations divided by a common language becomes salient. What is the expectation of a career in the Silicon Valley? Is it the same as in Germany? Expectations, which are impacted by broad cultural forces, influence the calibration of people whether to become an engineer or poet, or once an engineer, to work for a large firm or a new one. This claim seems almost too innocuous to propose, but it has an interesting theoretical flag to it. Such choices are made unconsciously on a daily basis insofar that any time in liberal societies workers can quit and leave their jobs, or while at breakfast, to become entrepreneurs. But these choices are *not* made, because such recursive formulations would exhaust our cognitive and emotional capacities.

Institutional Change

These considerations lie at the heart of the phenomena that interest this book: how can we expect developed market economies to change? Common to economics and sociology is the question if institutions are defined as stable expectations shared as common knowledge, then how can institutions evolve? The studies in this book on the global Internet economy identify three interrelated and yet autonomous influences: technological paths, politics, and culture.

Technological Paths

The Internet represents a body of protocol agreements that permit interconnection and interoperability in a distributed network. As a technological system, it confronted existing systems. Benghozi and Licoppe (chapter 5), for example, argue that Internet penetration in France proceeded relatively slowly because of prior investments by France Telecom in the Minitel, a hierarchical communication system. Glimstedt and Zander (chapter 4) explain that Sweden had already developed an expertise in wireless technologies that served as a major trajectory to innovate for Internet applications and infrastructure equipment. It is important to underline that this knowledge was shared within local regional and national communities. Prior learning and trajectories varied among countries, influencing their points of entry into the stream of innovations that constitute the Internet: wireless for Sweden, software for Germany, the ARPANET experience for the United States.

The technological system of the Internet differs dramatically from the point to point circuitry of the traditional communication system and hence represented a radical challenge to the national competence gained in specific technologies. The economics of these innovations arguably appear in the shift of relative prices that favored packet over circuit switching. In this regard, the technological change of the Internet is a recapitulation of the thesis that sufficient movements in relative prices can cause institutional change, much like the rising price of labor created markets in the Middle Ages (North and Thomas 1973). But though the Internet represented a new technological architecture, its interpretation was formed within the technical communities of existing practice and on the basis of existing infrastructural investments.

Politics

A discussion of technological paths quickly reveals the presence of actors who differ in their preferences and power. Feasible paths of technological and commercial exploration are embedded in the industrial politics of a country. The Internet grew fastest, initially, in countries that deregulated their telecommunication sector. Monopoly telecom operators saw the Internet as a substitute for their investments in circuit switching, backed by a pricing policy challenged by packet switching. In the United States, the Internet pioneers were not the traditional phone companies; AT&T even declined control over the Internet as late as the 1990s (see the discussion in Kenney, chapter 3). These state monopolies evolved during a period of Keynsian policies and also labor and social policies to support the "welfare state" or, to use a German expression, as a "social market economy." The Internet is, in this regard, a prototype of the technologies of the second industrial divide that forced a re-ordering of macro-economic social policies (Piore and Sabel 1984).

There were two interrelated factors that allowed these political strongholds to waiver in the 1980s and later. The first is the disbundling of an integrated system that permitted pockets of competition to develop and expand. Did deregulation lead to the "unbundling" of this system, or did the inherent modularity of packet switching break up the national monopolies? Such recursive questioning begs a more fundamental question: are there complementarities between the regulatory order and the technological evolution of the Internet? In these country studies, with the exception of India for reasons that might be argued to be a special case, the Internet is associated with deregulation. There are too many points of entry into the system, and too many subsystems that can be assembled, to leave it under the purvey of a single national company. These services include the ISPs, the retail sites, the B2B exchanges, the infrastructural investments, the computers, terminals, and handsets, and of course the pervasive presence of software. The days when a national monopoly would write millions of lines of software code to operate and govern a network are not long ago, but they seem oddly ancient in light of the distributed and unbundled technologies that fall under the rubric of the Internet.

The second is the penetration of national markets by foreign participants: expanding telecommunication operators (such as MCI), new Internet firms, consulting companies, and venture capital and investment companies. These participants often targeted specific sectors, such as financing new firms or telephony. Once a system is disbundled, it allows for "seeding" of sectors that, in isolation from a central regulatory order, might succeed in expanding, a point to which we return below.

Market creation is, as Fligstein (2001) argues, a political process. The Internet was not simply a complement to existing products and services. It was, and is, a substitute threat to many firms and political interests, such as unions in the public sector. In some countries, particularly India and Korea, the disruptive effects of the Internet occurred during a time of broader political and institutional change, as discussed in the following chapters. Yet the presence of politics is also perceptible in every country account.

Cultural Prototyping

A striking feature of the Internet economy is the hype. However, beneath this hype is Plato's marketplace for ideas: people selling ideas, people searching for them, and a tatonnement consisting of trial and error, imitation, and experimentation. Prototypes, as we discussed earlier, are important aspects of this discourse. What is a successful career? What does a successful Internet company need to do? What are the features that make the Silicon Valley successful? These prototypes are ideal types, but they are also notional beliefs, cultural images, that guide the groping toward better practices or desired personal outcomes.

Discourse does not occur in the abstract but in the context of existing institutions and societies. Capitalism emerged among vastly different cultural spaces, forcing every country to develop its own managerial ideology to support the new contract between owner and worker (Bendix 1956). The Internet, as we discuss in the final chapter, is oddly marked by a reworking of a 1960s hacker culture and a 1980s financial "ethic," a blending found in many spheres of modern economic life (Boltanski and Chiappello 1999).

We have described above how social networks influenced the technological direction of the Internet and its diffusion. The distinctions in the social fabric of regions and countries point to why transporting institutions is not the simple fix. A young German engineer who watches online the bubble of Internet start-ups in the United States lives still in a local community with German banks, customers, and families. She or he needs to engage the money of investors and friends and to attract the labor of associates. Indeed, few countries outside the United States have an equivalent of American bankruptcy law that leniently relieves by limited liability the owners of a company from personal risk in the case of failure (Gompers and Lerner 2001). Yet the power of the cultural imagery of the Internet and the Silicon Valley model lead many regulators and lawmakers in diverse countries to discursively engage in a collective rethinking of these institutions. The chapters on regulation in this book reflect the articulated debates within professional communities of economists, lawyers, and public servants. In a number of cases, discourse leads to decisive action, such as the creation of new equity markets, changes in bankruptcy and fiscal law, or the seeding by governments of high technology and high-risk enterprises to encourage the new cultural prototype: the entrepreneur dressed in a black shirt.

This cultural imagery is easy to discount but it reflects two important dynamics. The first is the changes in the values of workers and entrepreneurs regarding their choices. These changes can have vast implications. Gittelman (2000), for example, found that the science of biotechnology was as well developed in France as in the United States and that new French biotechnology firms did as well as their American counterparts in producing patented discoveries. There simply were a lot fewer French start-ups, partly because French scientists did not engage in the same entrepreneurial activities as the American scientists. The second dynamic is that the cultural imagery has, unintendedly so at least in its origins, the benefits of signalling to others that change is occurring; here we have a replay of the theme of network externalities. Behind the cultural hype is the tweaking of the emergent properties of social change: the probability of one individual to move into a "new economy" is influenced by the expectation that others have done or will do so as well. Behind this cascading effect is also the creation of new social links; as people switch to the new economy, social networks are rewired and people encourage friends and friends of friends to switch to these new pockets. After all, an established finding of how people get jobs is through local searches among friends and acquaintances, or so-called "weak ties" (Granovetter, 1973). The experimentation of the Internet, and through new institutional linkages, provided people the opportunity to find new contacts, e.g., sources of funding and jobs in the "new economy" that did not exist before or were not recognized.

The economics of the Internet appeared to favor this emergence, for the entry costs of setting up a business site were relatively low. More radically, the Internet appeared to promise an escape from local social networks. Entrepreneurs could find each other in the Net, or barring this, new links were to be forged in entrepreneurial meetings (such as "First Tuesday" discussed in the previous chapter). Here is the interesting road test played out across national economies: did the cultural impetus and the enlarged social networks that drove business entry echo in a demand for their services? In the absence of business success, can these pockets of experiments be expected to succeed in sustaining an institutional alternative to national models? Or is change less discrete and more of a gradual evolution than models of national systems suggest?

Evolutionary Change

These three autonomous factors of technology, politics, and cultural prototyping have the attractive property of explaining how institutional change might proceed on the basis of local experiments. The national system approach stumbles on the enormity of the theoretical implications of its argument. How can a society jump from one institutional equilibrium to another? In fact, this language of jumping between complementary bundles of institutions is misleading. It implies a static dimensional space (i.e., the claim that there are four institutions that describe societies) that no theory has been shown to cover the variety across countries. Instead, we find cases where countries succeeded in decoupling and recoupling institutions and practices, and cases where they failed; the chapters in this book show as well a variety of national experiments.

To recall Ragin's Boolean reduction, a dimensional space may in fact collapse to a smaller consideration of factors. Distant institutional bundles can suddenly seem closer by reducing a dimension.[8] Cultural shifts can serve to render practices acceptable that were before anathema— that is, they can reconfigure configurations. The creation of cultural communities renders these reconfigurations more feasible. Local experiments often show that simple ridges, or bridges, built on recoupling existing and new practices can evolve from distinct bundles of national practices and institutions that appear notionally distant. Being local, they have a higher chance of being observed and imitated in social networks, thus cascading into sustained social change.[9]

A concrete example is the main banking system that has been described by some as fundamental to Japanese success, but only in the presence of other Japanese factors (Aoki 1990). But in fact, Japanese practices diffused widely to American and European firms without adopting the banking system (a rather fortunate circumstance). As Florida and Kenney (1991) note, these practices were often adopted through the massive investments by Japanese firms in specific regions. Of course, these practices were adapted in the process, as shown by numerous studies on the international diffusion of organizing principles (Westney 1987; Zeitlin and Herrigel 2000). Though absolute cultural explanations—"practices don't diffuse because they are embedded in national cultures"—are disproven by this diffusion, cultural change provides the symbolic forum by which foreign practices are re-contextualized and accommodated in a world system (Brannen, Liker, and Fruin 1999; Meyer et al. 1997).

Charles Tilly (1984) has noted that comparative national studies fail to account effectively for diffusion in world systems. The study of the global expansion of the Internet economy cannot treat each national case in isolation from each other. Much as David Stark (1996) noted that Eastern Europe rebuilt itself by recombining its institutional debris with imported capitalist institutions, the countries under our study also struggled to define their prototypical understandings of what constituted the "new economy," what had to be changed, what could be preserved. It is this discursive search, coupled with a sudden burst of broad experimentation in organizational forms, that was instigated by the technological and commercial innovations called the Internet. And it informs the central question of this book: to what extent did these innovations transform the institutional bargains and cognitive frameworks in diverse national systems?

Country Chapters

A solid lesson of research design is that you can't discover more than what the design itself allows. The theoretical and methodological challenge of the national system approach is to sort out the combinations of institutional features that explain a given economic outcome, such as high growth or innovations. Our design is to compare the process by which a cultural and economic "disturbance" called the Internet seeded the business ecologies of various nations with a new institutional configuration, while encouraging each chapter to offer its own interpretation on the observed national experience. This configuration, referred to as the Silicon Valley model in this text, consists of new firm start-ups, rapid innovation and market exploration, and equity-linked compensation and finance. To analyze this process, this book reports on the experiences of seven countries: the United States, Sweden, France, India, Germany, Korea, and Japan. These countries were chosen because they provide a reasonable geographic and institutional diversity and because of an *a priori* understanding of what would be useful comparisons.

One of the important elements of a good design is to understand how inferences are made from the "absence" of a condition. We consciously did not choose countries that had no or little Internet activity. To understand why the Internet developed in some but not all countries, we would have to sample countries, particularly in developing regions, where the Internet has not been important. Partly this choice was made because of our belief that this comparison would be either too obvious or still too complicated, at least initially—too simple, because the level of development would be an important criteria; too complicated, because explaining development itself opens up a large number of candidate explanations that involve a different ambition than ours. However, the inclusion of India is designed to play the role of a country vastly poorer than the other six country cases.

We want to understand ultimately not only how different national systems explored the new economic space of the Internet, but also how these national experiences fit into a world economy with transnational actors and infrastructure. We recognize, as suggested above, the word "global" is to be taken with caution. Wealthy countries, especially the United States, dominate the global infrastructure. Transnational actors reflect as well the relative power and importance of nations and corporations. Still, against these national contours, the Internet represents a cultural and technological revolution on a global scale.

The next seven chapters are in-depth country studies. As can be seen in figure 2.1, these countries witnessed a fairly rapid diffusion of Internet connections; India's per capita penetration is, not surprisingly, much lower. The prominence of Sweden is also clear in these data. The similarities across these countries extend also to the expectations built into financial evaluations. Figure 2.2 graphs the performance of the large

Bruce Kogut

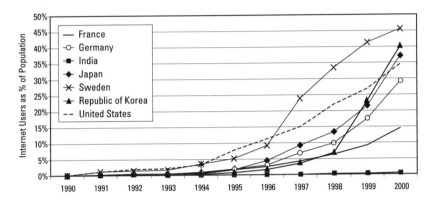

Figure 2.1
Penetration of Internet connections 1990–2000
Source: International Telecommunication Union 2001b.

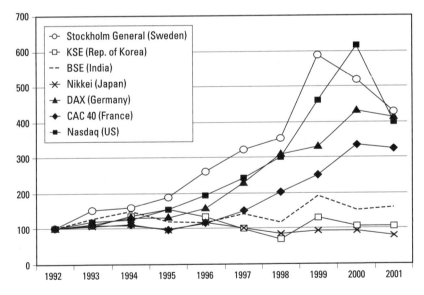

Figure 2.2
Changes in the major stock market indices 1992–2001
Note: The indices were standardized by dividing by the 1992 index.
Source: ⟨http://finance.yahoo.com⟩.

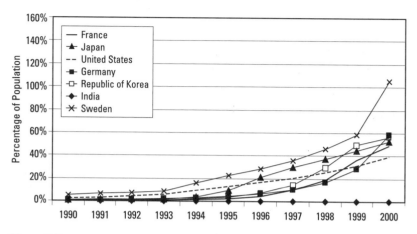

Figure 2.3
Penetration of portable phones 1990–2000
Source: International Telecommunication Union 2001b.

national stock markets in these countries. For the United States, two explosions are evidenced in the burst of valuations toward the end of the 1990s, and the sudden drop in April 2000. Other national markets show a more gradual increase. For Japan and Korea, this reflects their economic crisis that dominates the Internet effect. Still, for Sweden, Germany, France, and India, the deflation in Internet values had a perceptible effect, even if more mild than that in the United States.

There are, however, important national differences. Figure 2.3 shows, as explained above, that mobile telephony represented an important technological path for the development of the Internet outside the United States, primarily due to the control of the national telephony monopoly over the fixed network communication. Figure 2.4 graphs the dominance of the United States in the number of servers registered in the United States. This graph represents, at a minimum, the early lead in the United States to develop the Internet and the system to register web addresses, even though the World Wide Web started in Europe. It reflects also that the United States still dominates the world in the location of web servers and commercial activity.

The chapter by Martin Kenney presents a core argument in the book that the United States lead resulted from the innovative dynamic located

64

Bruce Kogut

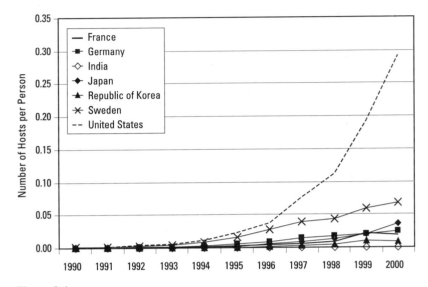

Figure 2.4
Number of web host servers
Source: International Telecommunication Union 2001b.

in Silicon Valley and was driven by the institutions of venture capital and new firm formation. Kenney's thesis of how venture capital drove the Silicon Valley model presents an explanation of the genesis of the Internet that may not be the same as the explanation for its subsequent development.

Indeed, the country cases point to the advantages of incumbent firms located in countries that lagged the United States and the persisting influence of national histories. Sweden, for example, shows a harmonious relationship among old and new companies, especially as exemplified by Ericsson's role in seeding scores of new companies in the Stockholm area and in establishing international standards. Henrik Glimstedt and Udo Zander (chapter 4) argue that a combination of historical accident—a loophole in the regulatory code—and technological capabilities integrated by Ericsson around wireless technologies made Sweden a major center of Internet activity. Thus, the national telecommunications monopoly is broken, favoring the emergence of new Internet businesses, but the underlying technology is developed in a classic industrial region setting with a dominant and coordinating company. France, on the other hand, reveals less. Pierre-Jean Benghozi and Christian Licoppe (chapter 5) show that France Telecom adjusted over time to play a major role in the development of the economy, partly because of the reprieve it enjoyed due to its control over access to, and pricing of, leased lines and local access. They argue that an earlier technology, the Minitel, retarded the French adoption of the Internet, but this experience also served as a springboard for rapid learning. Their chapter provides a very grounded demonstration of the legacy of accumulated knowledge in France and how in specific knowledge domains, such as linguistics, this learning influenced the development of the Internet by major technological actors.

India and Germany present an unusual pairing in many regards, and yet share the strong commonality that they both entered the Internet economy on the back of their software capabilities. For India, Radhika Rajan and Srilata Zaheer (chapter 6) explain how the Internet drove the rapid expansion of companies in a few regions in order to meet the huge demand for software. Software, because it is digital and transported as bits and not atoms, is unusually favored by the Internet. They argue most forcefully that the software industry developed as a major institutional departure. Older companies were not the major players, labor markets behaved differently, venture capital was pivotal for funding the new companies. Indeed, for India, the Internet has succeeded in opening a major path of institutional exploration. Steven Casper (chapter 7) argues that the German experience failed to produce institutional change. This case represents a more troubled evolution, in which its incumbent firms do not rapidly migrate to the Internet economy, nor play a role in fostering regional centers of small firm development. The traditional German strength of incremental innovation was not suited for the radical disruption posed by the Internet. Casper predicts Germany will play its traditional role as an effective contributor to incremental innovation.

Korea and Japan reveal an extraordinary tension between the traditional business groups and the appearance of hundreds of new Internet companies. The Internet economy developed at a moment when both of these countries were in economic crisis and their national systems challenged by competing models imported from abroad. Sea-Jin Chang (chapter 8) concludes that the Korean Internet economy launched a wave of new businesses and initiated new financial markets that are only partly dominated by the traditional business groups. Ultimately, however, the largest business groups, or chaebols, reasserted dominance over the Internet, even if they were forced to evolve in response to the more broad economic crisis. His chapter poses the question of whether the cognitive models by which workers and graduates value employment in large corporations changed sufficiently to support alternative institutions.

Mari Sako (chapter 9) finds that Japan saw the rise of new major players that still converged to national models of corporate organization. The one major new entrant in the Japanese system, Softbank, remade itself along a modern version of the traditonal keiretsu. By the end of the period of observation for this book, Softbank withdrew from many of its ventures, posing the wider possibility that its maverick institutional status endured as long as an inflated stock valuation could support it. Sako and Chang do not find major institutional departures.

These chapters provide recent histories of the national experiences of commercializing the Internet. Each provides an individual perspective on the meaning and implication of the Internet for the country under study. Whether we can infer a larger pattern is discussed in the final chapter of this book.

Notes

1. Empirical tests of the relationship between the degree of tacitness and the speed of transfer are given in Zander and Kogut 1995. On consulting firms, see McKenna 1999; Kipping 1999; and Djelic 1998.

2. Boltanski (1982) gives a crisp analysis of these cognitive obstacles in his study of the emergence of the *manager* as a classification; Swidler (2001) provides a sympathetic analysis along these lines but in a rather different domain. See Kogut 1997 for a discussion of the distinction between power and cognition. That chapter was written while visiting David Soskice's group at the Science Center as the Karl Deutsch Professor, held jointly with Peter Hall at the time, which provided the occasion for me to benefit from many useful discussions.

3. I discuss these policies, along with immigration data, in Kogut and Almeida 1999.

4. The importance of labor mobility is discussed by Angel (1989) for all kinds of workers; Almeida and Kogut (1999) demonstrate empirically that for the Silicon Valley, innovations move through regional labor markets.

5. See Uzzi 1996 for a discussion of social networks in the garment industry, Baker 1984 for stock trading, and Sorenson and Stuart 2001. These studies belong to a long tradition of studies on economic regions and cooperative behavor; see Piore and Sabel 1984.

6. I draw the idea of an institutional logic from Hamilton and Biggart's (1988) identification of three developmental logics seen in east Asian development. Fligstein's (1990) notion of "conceptions of control" is related, though it carries a Weberian baggage ("control") that strikes me as too restrictive for our purpose here.

7. See DiMaggio and Powell 1991; the concept derives from Alfred Schutz, among others.

8. We can only abbreviate this discussion. The implication is that the the "hamming" distance between these Boolean configurations can be misleading. By logical reduction, two configurations of {1 0 0} and {1 1 1}, with a hamming distance of two out of a maximum of three may reduce to {1 0} and {1 1}, a difference of one step. We should treat very skeptically these a priori arguments that do not confront the empirical evidence!

9. There are many models that display this property, with one of the earlier and most interesting ones found in Boorman and Levitt 1980.

3

The Growth and Development of the Internet in the United States

Martin Kenney

Rarely does a new technology emerge that galvanizes a dramatic rethinking of the nature of commerce. The Internet is such a technology. At this early stage, it is difficult to appreciate fully the importance of the Internet, but some speculate it might be as momentous as the arrival of the telegraph (Cohen, Delurg, and Sysmar 2000; Standage 1999). Radically new communication technologies such as the Internet have multiple applications and often become ubiquitous. As such, the adoption, diffusion, and development of this new technology provide an especially penetrating view of how different national innovation systems have responded to and shaped the commercial possibilities inherent in the Internet. Of course, such an assessment for an economy as large as that of the United States is difficult. It is further complicated by the peculiar way in which communications technologies permeate and facilitate connections and relationships. Often the action of such technologies is imperceptible to most of the actors involved and even to aggregate statistics; for example, better information transfer between customers and suppliers is not manifested in the finished good, though it is embodied in the good in terms of lower cost and/or higher quality. Given the diffuse nature and the speed of the Internet's evolution, any analysis can only be tentative.

Government and universities played vital roles in the gestation of the Internet in the pre-commercial and early commercialization phases. The apparent ease of entry encouraged many start-ups. Many established firms were laggards in the early commercialization process, though ultimately they were counted among the greatest beneficiaries. In this respect, the commercialization of the Internet parallels the commercialization of university-based biology research in the late 1970s and early 1980s that led to the formation of a biotechnology industry (Kenney 1986). In the biotechnology case, venture capital was the midwife for the creation of the biotechnology industry, but the large pharmaceutical firms were able to later integrate the techniques of biotechnology into their technological toolkit.

National exceptionalism is a difficult argument to advance and validate. Nevertheless, in the case of the commercialization of the Internet, certain characteristics of the U.S. political economy contributed to the head start that U.S. firms enjoyed, their ability to grow rapidly, and, after the 2000 NASDAQ decline, a large number of firm failures. With respect to commercialization, the U.S. institution of venture capital played a central role in the rapid formation of new dedicated Internet firms that were established to define and occupy the new economic space. With respect to the Internet, there were three advantageous features of the U.S. national system of innovation: a unique telecommunications infrastructure, an active government in funding university research, and a capable set of private sector institutions dedicated to funding new high-technology enterprises.

The enormity of the U.S. market and the variety of impacts and uses of the Internet dictate that this discussion must necessarily be a limited examination of the role of the National System of Innovation (NSI) and the development of the Internet. For example, the significant impacts of intranets upon firm organization, internal information flow, and human resources practices, and so on are simply ignored, though they will surely be profound. The chapter by Helper and MacDuffie (chapter 11) examines the business-to-business (B2B) area in more detail; I will focus on those issues with respect to the role of the NSI in funding B2B startups. One of the most intriguing impacts or initiatives that has emerged from the Internet is not examined, namely the effort in a wide variety of industries to standardize descriptors of all parts of the value chain, so that commerce can be transacted entirely electronically.[1] Despite these and numerous other omissions, the pervasive nature of the Internet as a communications medium, and the wide variety of experiments underway that are aimed at exploiting the Internet, mean that the scope of this chapter remains immense.

Setting the Stage

The commercialization of the Internet and the speed with which it became a medium for commerce depended upon the already extensive diffusion of the Internet's infrastructure and its noncommercial use. This section describes some of the organizational features that provided the preconditions for the U.S. commercialization process. Despite the formation of the European Union, the United States was (and remains) the largest single market united by common laws, a common language, a common currency, and various features of a modern nation-state.[2] A more prosaic, but nonetheless important, feature for the diffusion of the Internet was a well-developed telephone system with uniform rates and usage rules. Widespread credit card usage and the large number of U.S. consumers who were comfortable using their credit cards for telephone and catalog sales also helped ensure the rapid growth of Internet commerce.

In an entirely different vein, the United States had an enormous research university system with a number of global-class engineering and science departments that were among the largest and most lavishly funded in the world. This was complemented by a large number of global-class corporate research laboratories, led by AT&T/Lucent's Bell Laboratories, IBM's Yorktown Heights and San Jose Laboratories, and Xerox's Palo Alto Research Center, to name the most prominent. No other nation or, perhaps even group of nations possessed institutions that could rival these as sources of technology and well-trained personnel. In terms of computers, computer firms, and resources dedicated to computing, the United States was the acknowledged global leader. The United States not only trained many engineers, but also had a liberal immigration policy that permitted qualified immigrants to enter, particularly for postgraduate education. These institutions and policies created an enormous pool of engineers and scientists.

The United States was the leader in developing and using computers in government, university, and industry. The importance of military spending in this process is well known (Flamm 1988), though often exaggerated. In the adoption of computers for commercial or general use, the United States was the world's leader.[3] The rapid adoption and large installed base created positive feedback loops, reinforcing the U.S.

advantage. Though IBM was a global colossus, U.S. antitrust enforcement ensured a semblance of competition and fettered IBM's ability to throttle new entrants: witness Microsoft, DEC, or Sun Microsystems. In most other nations, one national champion for computing and another for telecommunications equipment were chosen and subsidized by the national government; other entrants were discouraged. The evolution of the computer sector in the United States was characterized by repeated waves of new computing and data communications industry entrants, whose innovations were more capable and/or less expensive than those of the dominant vendors. Thus, there was continuing turbulence—a feature not as prevalent in Europe or Japan.

In technical terms, the Internet is the result of an evolutionary path that has been affected by two fundamental reconceptualizations of the architecture of computing: distributed networked personal computers, and the connection of a wide variety of data processing devices. At each step of this evolution, U.S.-based start-ups were the delivery mechanism for and the beneficiaries of leaps in functionality caused by a set of technological trajectories (Dosi 1984).[4] The dominant tendency has been an evolution from centralized computing to distributed, networked computing. The distributed portion of this computing system consists of the millions of computers in workplaces and homes across the United States and the world. The networked portion refers to the various media, including radio waves, electrical pulses, and photons, which permit these computers to intercommunicate.

The adoption of the Internet and the WWW was predicated upon the earlier diffusion of personal computers at home and work in the form of local area networks (LANs) in institutional settings (von Burg 2001a) and modems on home PCs (Jimeniz and Greenstein 1998). When the WWW software was first released in 1992, the majority of adopters were in institutions, especially universities, where they utilized a desktop computer connected to a LAN. These groups were already using their computers to access files through Gopher and communicating by e-mail through systems such as Telnet. They were the early adopters that downloaded browsers to access the WWW.

Though not the initial adopters of the WWW, U.S. home users rapidly embraced the Web (see table 3.1). The earlier diffusion of online services such as AOL (which was venture capital-funded), Compuserve, Prodigy,

Table 3.1
U.S. World Wide Web Users in Millions, 1996–2000

Year	Home	Work	Total
1996	13	15	28
1997	20	20	40
1998	27	30	57
1999	35	45	80
2000*	42	60	102

Note: *Estimated
Source: Computerworld, ⟨http://www.computerworld.com/home/emmerce.NSF/All/pop⟩

and the Well had created a large, relatively sophisticated population of home users that were comfortable online (Jimeniz and Greenstein 1998). For the online services, the emergence of the WWW and the privatization of the Internet initially appeared to be a challenge because their revenue was generated by per-minute access fees and further fees to use proprietary services. The no-cost Internet appeared threatening, but their response was to continue their proprietary online services that were inaccessible to nonmembers, while implementing flat monthly fees and converting themselves into Internet service providers (ISPs) that provided their home customers with e-mail addresses and Internet access points globally (e.g., AOL).

The United States had a far greater installed base of computers than any other country; moreover, many were already connected to a network. This can be seen in table 3.2, which indicates that there were more domain names registered in the United States than in the rest of the world. This massive installed base and the large number of users experienced with computer networks meant that the adoption of the Internet could advance at breakneck speed. The next section discusses the ways in which the unique U.S. regulatory regime encouraged the development of the data communications market.

Regulatory Preconditions in the Telecommunications Sector

The low-cost and open U.S. telecommunications system was the outcome of a gradual evolution of the U.S. regulatory regime.[5] As important as the contemporary regulatory environment, which is discussed in the chapter

Table 3.2
Growth of Domains in the United States and the World

	.com, .org, .net and .edu		% in U.S.	Country code domains	Total	Percent of total in U.S.
	U.S.	World				
Jul. 98	1,610,689	543,945	74.8%	1,127,483	3,282,117	49.07%
Jan. 99	3,003,950	1,033,925	74.4%	1,466,276	5,504,151	54.58%
Jul. 99	4,886,550	2,165,800	69.3%	2,045,716	9,098,066	53.71%
Jan. 00	6,673,650	3,334,825	66.7%	3,393,973	13,402,448	49.79%
Jul. 00	10,120,208	7,294,171	58.1%	6,450,232	23,864,611	42.41%

Source: Adapted from Zook 2000, ⟨http://socrates.berkeley.edu/~zook/domain_names/Domain⟩

by Dennis Yao (chapter 13), were a series of telecommunications policies that took effect before the birth of the Internet. These policies opened the telephone system to new entrants and accelerated the pace of innovation, encouraging the private sector to increase bandwidth and lower costs. United States government policy toward AT&T differed markedly from those of European and Asian governments toward their dominant telephone company. The result was that the United States had a more dynamic and open telecommunications system earlier than did most other countries.

In nearly every other OECD nation, the telephone system was a government-operated monopoly, whereas in the United States, AT&T was a private corporation regulated by federal and various independent state regulatory commissions. The roots of the U.S. telecommunications environment can be traced to a marketplace struggle during the first two decades of the twentieth century that ended with the triumph of AT&T and the imposition of regulation. Beginning in 1893, when the central Bell patents expired, and ending about 1920, AT&T engaged in vicious competition with a large number of local (city-based) phone firms. AT&T's strategy was to offer low rates for local calls (i.e., where there was competition), while garnering its profits from the long-distance system that it alone controlled. The result was a brutal price competition, leading to a dramatic decrease in local rates, an increase in telephone penetration and usage,[6] overbuilding of the telephone infrastructure, and rapid adoption of new cost-saving technologies such as the Strowger mechanical switch. AT&T used its long-distance income, the ability to block access to its long-distance lines, and selective purchases of local telephone companies to defeat the locals and unify the entire system under monopoly control (Lipartito 1997). In the process of this competition, a flat-rate price for local calls and "universal service" became an accepted norm and was enshrined in the U.S. regulatory structure.[7] This arrangement was stable for the next fifty years, despite the fact that telecommunications technology continually improved. The flat rate for local calls would become an important factor in the adoption of online services and Internet penetration into the home.

With AT&T's triumph, the U.S. system now outwardly resembled the government-owned European situation, with one entity controlling nearly the entire U.S. telephone system.[8] In most European countries, the government post office and telegraph monopolies quickly asserted control of the telephone system, and the cutthroat competition phase never occurred, so market penetration was retarded and there was no consideration of flat-rate local call pricing. Technology adoption also lagged, and service was the best an entrenched bureaucracy decided to deliver.[9] Moreover, the telephone service became a government revenue source and employer, so any deregulatory moves had budgetary and employment implications. Thus a different user profile, regulatory regime, and market structure distinguished the United States from other countries.

In the mid-1950s, AT&T owned and operated the entire phone system, from the consumer handsets to the network—it was a classic case of vertical integration. The U.S. government had no vested interest in the system, however, and it was committed to encouraging competition. The opening of the AT&T monopoly to competition can be understood as a disintegration of telecommunications into the following independent market layers (Moore 1996):

1. Terminal equipment (e.g., phone-sets, extension cables, and switches)

2. Long-distance services (e.g., MCI and Sprint)

3. The local loop

4. Encoding mechanisms (e.g., modems/multiplexing/protocols)

5. Value-added services (e.g., Tymnet, Telnet, and the Internet).

Each layer was gradually opened to competition. In parallel to this, though not directly related, was an inexorable increase in the volume of data versus voice transmission through telecommunications pipelines. Roberts (2001) estimated in August 2000 that the data transmitted by the Internet protocol surpassed all other telecommunications combined. AT&T's near monopoly in the voice area forced new entrants to focus on the data transmission market—a fortuitous decision, as data transmission grew exponentially, whereas voice transmission grew incrementally.

The first move toward opening the telephone network was the 1956 Hush-a-Phone decision by the U.S. Court of Appeals, which permitted mechanical devices such as receivers to be connected to the network. The 1968 Federal Communications Commission (FCC) Carterphone ruling allowed the Carter Electronic Corporation to connect its mobile radio system to the AT&T telephone network. Thus the first liberalization occurred at the edge of the network, and created a market for telephones and subsequently for telephone answering devices, fax machines, and computer modems.

The next step in deregulation occurred in the area of transmission. In 1969, MCI received FCC permission to establish microwave service between St. Louis and Chicago. This permission was soon extended to other markets, which enabled large long-distance users to bypass the AT&T network and extended competition closer to the center of the network. MCI and other specialized carriers soon undercut AT&T on the most lucrative routes, while AT&T's long-distance service was hobbled by its commitment and the regulatory requirement to serve less lucrative routes and provide highly regulated local service.[10] Moreover, the new entrants installed the newest and most up-to-date (and non-AT&T) equipment, thus providing a market for other equipment suppliers. Most important, though not recognized at the time, were FCC decisions separating data from voice communications, thereby permitting new entrants to specialize in data communications.[11]

The 1974 challenge from MCI to AT&T's right to maintain a monopoly over long-distance service set in motion antitrust proceedings against AT&T. These were settled in 1982, with the consent decree stipulating the conditions for the dismemberment of AT&T: long distance was separated from local phone service, and six regional operating companies were created. Retaining the long-distance profit center appeared a brilliant decision; little did AT&T suspect that long distance would become a commodity, and that "ownership" of the consumer would become a critical control nexus.

This gradual deregulation of the AT&T monopoly was driven by a desire to accelerate competition and innovation. It would be tempting to attribute the process entirely to far-sighted government regulators and legislators, but it was entrepreneurs who pressed for deregulation, which, to their credit, government regulators and the courts did not strongly resist. The relationship of the U.S. government to the dominant telephone vendor made deregulation much easier and more gradual. This progressive deregulation allowed new firms to emerge in every aspect of telecommunications. Repeatedly, the new entrants ignited cutthroat competition, rapidly decreasing costs and/or increasing functionality. The outcome of this gradual deregulation was a low-cost, comparatively open market for telecommunications services.

The relatively open U.S. telecommunications market and the rapidly changing technologies created many new market opportunities. However, the conversion of opportunities into new firms—as opposed to having them actualized in existing firms—required entrepreneurs, an encouraging environment, and a capital market willing to support these new ventures. In the decades since World War II, a set of institutions evolved in the United States that were centered on venture capital, which profits from converting such opportunities into successful firms.

Venture Capital—A Critical Component of the U.S. Innovation System

Venture capital, as an institution intimately related to clusters of high-technology start-ups, was largely confined to the United States until the mid 1980s, when Israel developed a venture capital industry. The U.S. commercialization of the Internet cannot be understood without reference to venture capital and the complex of institutions for supporting entrepreneurship that have evolved with it. As we shall see, the largest concentration of firms commercializing the Internet is in the San Francisco Bay area, which is also the center of the world's venture capital industry (Kenney and Florida 2000). Simply put, the willingness of venture capitalists to fund Internet start-ups was responsible for the U.S. pattern whereby start-ups rapidly commercialized the Internet.

The first venture capital firms were established after World War II with the express purpose of assisting in and profiting from the foundation and growth of entrepreneurial firms. During the following decades, venture capital gradually became a more formal institution, as the venture capitalists profited from and concentrated on investing in high technology, where they funded many of the defining firms of the late twentieth century. The rapidity of the increase is amazing—total venture capital investments increased from $45 million in 1969 to $6 billion in 1995 and the unheard of sum of $103 billion in 2000 (NVCA 2000b). However, for the first two quarters of 2001, venture capital investments were roughly half that of the comparable quarter in 2000. Moreover, there was reason to believe that the pace would continue to slow for the remainder of 2001.

As the venture capital industry evolved in regions such as Silicon Valley and Route 128, there was also a co-evolution of a plethora of other organizations, including law firms, accountants, employment agencies, executive search firms, and investment banks; all of these services specialized in accelerating the growth of small firms (Kenney and von Burg 1999; Bahrami and Evans 2000). This ecosystem of organizations operates to lower entry barriers and accelerate a new firm's growth, thereby decreasing what Stinchcombe (1965) termed the "liability of newness." Curiously, for the constituents of the ecosystem, newness is not entirely a liability—it is also a desired attribute. Under normal conditions, usually the greatest single entry barrier for any fledgling firm is the lack of capital. Venture capital is the primary accelerant because it eliminates the need for new firms to grow slowly out of retained earnings and frees the founding team from a continual, time-consuming search for capital. The law firms are able to advise their small-firm clients on how best to structure their business, bargain with the venture capitalists, handle intellectual property issues, and assist with myriad other details necessary to establish a firm (Suchman 2000). Furthermore, there are a wide variety of consultants and firms capable of undertaking many corporate functions, allowing the small firm to postpone expenditures it otherwise would have to make immediately upon constitution, thereby freeing it to concentrate on product development and market introduction.

Another critical institution for this innovation system was the NASDAQ stock exchange, which gradually evolved to specialize in raising capital for fast-growing young firms as well as providing an exit strategy for the investors and entrepreneurs. It would be on the NASDAQ that the Internet stock bubble would be most pronounced and, after March 2000, where the decline in Internet stocks was the greatest.

In Silicon Valley, but also in other high-technology regions, entrepreneurs began establishing firms even before the Internet was officially privatized. Figure 3.1 is an indication that as of January 1999, Silicon Valley had many more significant e-commerce and software tools-based Internet start-ups than any other U.S. region.[12] This is not surprising because the individuals making up Silicon Valley's institutions are constantly searching for new opportunities, and they were already active in data communications. The potential of the Internet quickly attracted their interest, and the funding extended by venture capitalists provided the financial wherewithal for these start-ups to grow very rapidly.

The importance of Silicon Valley-like institutions is the rapidity with which they responded to the opportunities that the Internet and WWW presented. Figure 3.1, perhaps, in some measure, over-represents the percentage of firms because of the dominance of Silicon Valley venture capitalists among the top 20 venture capitalists and the aggressiveness of firms funded by venture capitalists in undertaking public offerings. Having said that, all evidence suggests that Silicon Valley was the center of the explosion of Internet start-ups and, more recently, as a recent report by Webmergers (2001) of Internet firm closures indicates, California is massively over-represented, having experienced 32 percent of all closures they catalogued. Notice that in California the number of Internet-focused start-ups is evenly divided between e-commerce sites and software tools for the Internet. This differs from the two other major start-up concentrations. It is interesting to note that Boston's start-ups are concentrated in the software tools area, whereas New York is more e-commerce oriented. These results fit very well with the high-technology character of the Boston area and the more creative and commercial New York area. These three clusters account for over 50 percent of total

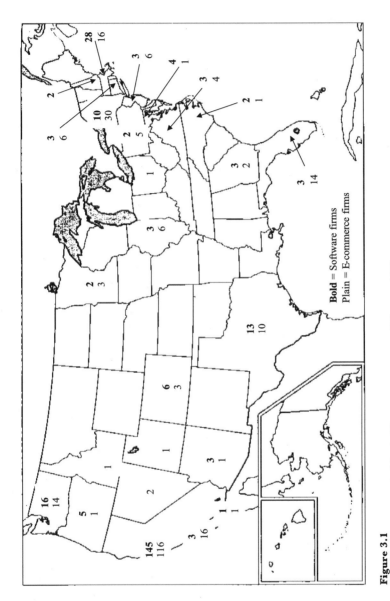

Figure 3.1
Significant venture capital-funded Internet start-ups as of January 1999
Note: Compiled from initial public offerings and investments by first-tier venture capitalists. This likely overestimates Silicon Valley firms. However, it is indicative of where the main firm concentrations are and the regions with greater technology or e-commerce emphasis. Most important, Silicon Valley indicates high concentrations of both.
Source: Author's own compilation.

Bold = Software firms
Plain = E-commerce firms

venture capital disbursements in the United States, and, not surprisingly, the highest visibility Internet start-ups were formed in these three regions.

The University—An Important Initial Repository of Capabilities

At the dawn of commercialization of the Internet, the single largest concentration of users (i.e., expertise) was to be found among university faculty, particularly computer science faculty, and their students. In the initial commercialization phase, students were as important or more important than faculty. Given this expertise, it is not surprising that universities were the source of several early start-ups. Firms tracing their origins to university computer science departments include the three major portals, Yahoo!, Excite, and Lycos, and the first important commercial browser firm, Netscape. Two of the most-used search engine firms, Inktomi and Google, had university roots (UC Berkeley and Stanford, respectively). An MIT faculty member established the Web-caching firm Akamai. The university was not only a source of knowledge and expertise; it was also a source of entrepreneurs.

Computer science students and faculty formed the vanguard, but soon students in other departments, particularly business school students, began launching e-commerce start-ups. The ensuing "dot.com" fever would make entrepreneurship an important career goal for students and faculty, and many ventures were first conceived and then launched from campus. During 1997–1999, the enthusiasm was infectious. Career goals for MBA students changed from joining an investment bank or consulting firm to establishing or joining a start-up. Whether the changed goals are merely a short-term response to the increase of dot.com stock prices, or will persist for the longer term, is not clear.

From the Internet to E-commerce

The Internet began as a U.S. Department of Defense project for interlinking defense researchers at various universities and military research establishments (Abbate 1999). The first Internet server was installed at UCLA in September 1969. The next server computer went to the Stanford Research Institute, soon to be followed by servers at UC Santa

Barbara and the University of Utah. After this initial burst, further nodes proliferated slowly because only research sites funded by the Department of Defense were allowed to connect to the ARPANET, so, by 1979, there were only 61 servers. On the network, e-mail quickly became the compelling application, and soon other academic research groups clamored for e-mail access. In the mid 1970s, the U.S. Department of Energy (DOE) inaugurated MFENET for its magnetic fusion energy researchers, and then DOE'S high-energy physicists built HEPNET. NASA's space physicists established their own network. In 1981, non-DARPA-funded computer scientists launched CSNET with funding from the National Science Foundation (NSF), and this spread quickly to more than seventy sites (Haffner and Lyon 1996, 244). Contemporaneously, AT&T's dissemination of the UNIX computer operating system spawned USENET, and then in 1981, BITNET was introduced to link academic mainframe computers; it also offered a simple e-mail program (Rogers 1998).[13] In 1985, DARPA transferred the ARPANET to the NSF. In an effort to increase usage, the NSFNET was open to all universities with the requirement that they must make a connection "available to all qualified users on campus" (quoted in Leiner et al. 2000). The NSFNET diffused e-mail and file-sharing to the rest of academe, thereby enlarging the installed base and providing students with experience in using the Internet. In 1985, NSF also decreed that all NSF-related sites should use the TCP/IP protocol, and it became the dominant data transmission protocol. In the late 1980s, a lack of interest among AT&T and the other established firms in operating the NSF Internet backbones created market opportunities for startup Internet Service Providers such as UUNET and PSINET, both of which were funded by venture capitalists.

In March 1991, certain restrictions on commercial use of the NSFNET were loosened, providing an early indication that eventually the Internet would be privatized and opened fully to commercial use. In September 1994, NSF announced its intention to end subsidies for the Internet backbone by May 1995 (Ferguson 1999; Howe 2000). Even as NSF was moving in this direction, a national commercial online service began offering Internet access to its subscribers by opening an e-mail service in July 1992, followed by full Internet service in November 1992.

In 1992, the dominant program for using the Internet was Gopher, which had been written and released by University of Minnesota professors, but graphical browsers based on the WWW specifications would soon displace it. The technological breakthrough that dramatically increased the functionality of the Internet was the development and the 1991 release by Timothy Berners-Lee at the CERN high-energy physics laboratory in Switzerland of the software and specifications that would form the basis of the WWW. In May 1991, the first Web server was introduced at the Stanford Linear Accelerator. By the beginning of 1992, there were 26 servers, and the number began increasing exponentially. Berners-Lee released a UNIX browser, but use of the WWW was still confined to a small number of academic and corporate researchers.

In February 1993, Marc Andreessen and Eric Bina, working at the University of Illinois National Center for Supercomputer Applications, wrote the Mosaic Web browser for the Microsoft Windows platform. Their user-friendly graphical browser simplified use of the WWW. Moreover, they made it freely available by posting it on the WWW, and as a result millions of copies were downloaded in a few months. This browser began the process of bringing the commercial potential of the Internet and WWW into focus. Moving to capitalize on the software, the University of Illinois licensed the Mosaic browser technology to the venture capital-funded firm Spyglass, and then later Microsoft. The creation of Mosaic, the connection of commercially operated networks to the old NSF Internet, and the withdrawal of NSF, signaled the end of the pre-commercialization phase.

The rapidity with which the terms "Internet" and "WWW" merged in the public mind is remarkable. For example, the 1994 book *The Internet Unleashed* contained 62 chapters devoted to various issues surrounding the Internet, but only one chapter was devoted to the WWW and another to Mosaic. The other chapters largely ignored the WWW. In the index, there were 42 headings for Gopher, 25 for Telnet, and only 21 for the WWW (Sams Publishing 1994).

The commercialization of the WWW bears a certain resemblance to the Oklahoma Land Rush memorialized in the 1934 movie *Cimmaron* (Kenney and Curry 1999).[14] The Web created a new, rich interactive experience and a spatial-like feeling for cyberspace. A new universe of fast and inexpensive "virtual" applications promised to allow commercial transactions that would be far less costly and/or more convenient than those in the physical world. Because this new economic space is simply software constructions, there would be enormous opportunities to exper-iment and create novel applications. Many processes conducted in physi-cal space could be modeled in software and manipulated in cyberspace. The WWW transmits information not only through sound or words, but also through graphics, thereby creating enormous flexibility and bandwidth. The old adage "a picture is worth a thousand words" applies well. Like a phone conversation, the WWW is interactive: it allows a form of dialogue to occur between the user and the Web site. Because the in-teraction is digitized, it can be informated (Zuboff 1988). The removal of humans from the interaction means that if the demand for a product or service increases, then the site can be rapidly scaled up or turned off. The intense pace of WWW developments is the result of an interaction between the telephone-like speed, the ease of reproduction and trans-mission, and omniaccessibility (Curry and Kenney 1999). All of this is facilitated by the Internet's ease of use. In combination, this made the Internet an attractive medium for commerce.

By early 1993, the technology was ready, and a few existing firms and several start-ups were experimenting with harnessing the technology to commercial purposes. However, for the most part, industry and entre-preneurs were more interested in the implications of interactive television delivered through the cable system. In most respects, the Internet was still a university-driven technology, and for the users it was free. From the perspective of hardheaded businesspersons, the Internet was attractive, but it was difficult to decide whether there was a valid business model for its commercialization. The first significant report to the general public about the commercial implications of the Internet was the December 8, 1993 *New York Times* article by John Markoff entitled "A Free and Simple Computer Link." Markoff described how firms were putting documenta-tion online, preparing online magazines, and thinking about advertising applications. Online sales were not mentioned.

E-commerce

The U.S.'s advantages for an early start commercializing the Internet were substantial and multidimensional. Both U.S. start-ups and established firms moved quickly to establish an Internet presence. The strength of the U.S. firms is best illustrated in table 3.3, which indicates that Micro-

Table 3.3
Media Metrix Global Top 20 Web and Digital Media Properties for November 2001

Rank	Top Web and digital media properties	Unique visitors (000)
	All Digital Media	189,357
1	MSN-Microsoft Sites*	127,379
2	AOL Time Warner Network*	113,119
3	Yahoo!*	100,990
4	X10.COM	44,528
5	Vivendi-Universal Sites*	39,518
6	About/Primedia*	39,076
7	Google Sites*	36,541
8	Terra Lycos*	35,225
9	Amazon*	35,133
10	eBay*	33,418
11	LYCOS SITES	31,956
12	Excite Network*	27,031
13	CNET Networks*	27,005
14	Walt Disney Internet Group*	26,019
15	Infospace Network*	23,012
16	American Greetings*	20,410
17	Real.com Network*	20,237
18	Ask Jeeves*	20,216
19	eUniverse Network*	18,555
20	FortuneCity Network*	17,437

Note: *Aggregated from a variety of sites
Source: Media Metrix, ⟨http://www.mediametrix.com⟩

soft, AOL, and Yahoo! were the world's leading Internet sites on the basis of unique visitors as of November 2001. The strongest European site is Lycos, which was purchased by the Spanish telecommunications firm Telefonica. Research on the Internet in Mexico found that many of the most popular "Mexican" e-commerce sites were actually hosted on computers in the United States (Curry, Contreras, and Kenney 2001). Thus, to some degree the statistics might understate the centrality of U.S. industry to the Internet. In the following sections we briefly detail the responses of established firms to the Internet. This is followed by four short subsections discussing the actions of the start-ups and the responses of the established firms in four areas: portals and other miscellaneous sites, business-to-consumer (B2C) e-commerce, B2B e-commerce, and software tools. One salient feature of these sections is the sheer volume of entrants and rivals in each area and the proliferation of niches within those areas.

Existing Firms and the Internet

The responses by existing firms varied widely in type and rapidity. At the initial stage of commercialization, full comprehension of the impact of the Internet was not easy. For example, it was only on May 16, 1995, with the release of Bill Gates's memo entitled "The Internet Tidal Wave," that Microsoft demonstrated it grasped the implications of the Internet (Ferguson 1999). Given Microsoft's comparative tardiness, it is no surprise that in the period from 1995 to 1997 most non-technology firms had little appreciation of the possible impacts of the Internet on their businesses.

Among the first established firms to understand the Internet's potential were Silicon Valley firms such as Cisco, Sun Microsystems, and Oracle, all of which had been financed by venture capitalists in the 1980s. Cisco was particularly advantaged: it produced the routers and switches that directed much of the Internet traffic, so it became aware of the Internet's implications almost immediately. Sun, with its roots in the engineering and networking community, also saw the potential, and its servers would become the standard for large Web sites. Sun also introduced the Java programming language. Oracle's database software became the platform upon which most Web sites operated. These firms became critical Internet infrastructure firms.

Technology firms such as IBM and Hewlett Packard also responded, though they both lagged behind Sun and Oracle. Other firms such as DEC were less successful. In the case of DEC, this is particularly surprising because it was the owner of Altavista, which was one of the most successful early search engines. DEC might have been able to create a successful portal and become a rival to start-ups such as Yahoo! A comparison of the rival PC makers Dell and Compaq also illustrates that the Internet did not necessarily lead to commercial advantage. Dell rapidly transferred its build-to-order model to the Internet and was rewarded with lowered costs and increased sales. In contrast, Compaq, dependent as it was upon its retail channels, found it difficult to convert its operations to the Internet. For Dell the Internet was a competitive weapon, whereas for Compaq the Internet proved to be a difficult media to use effectively (Kenney and Curry 2001). Although the Internet was beneficial for most technology firms, it also created difficulties for firms whose business model could not easily integrate the Internet.

For existing firms, the WWW enabled the provision of new services to their customers. For example, Federal Express first provided a one-way information service that enabled customers to track the location and arrival times of shipments (Lappin 1996; Grant 1997). The positive customer response to this experiment spurred Federal Express to develop yet other Internet services. Based on its experience with the tracking service, an application was developed to permit customers to use the Internet for all their shipping functions. The features now available include scheduling pick-ups and obtaining detailed maps for all their drop-off locations, rate charts, and other information such as international customs regulations. FedEx also provided free downloadable software capable of automating shipment by allowing the user to create an address book, maintain a shipping history log, and create and print labels (FedEx 2001). In other words, FedEx and other package shippers quickly integrated the WWW into their business.

For every FedEx and Dell, there were many established firms that initially were oblivious to the possible impact of the WWW. Of course, many firms, including General Motors, Ford, and Wal-Mart, operated sophisticated EDI (electronic data interchange) systems, not only internally, but also with a core group of suppliers or customers; however, they were not the first to switch to the Internet. Whereas FedEx and Dell began integrating the Internet into their operations in 1995, most firms only recognized the possibilities and dangers posed by the Internet in late 1996 and 1997. The store-based retail industry was especially slow in responding, and established Web sites after 1998. Catalog-based firms such as REI, Eddie Bauer, and Land's End moved more rapidly. The response of manufacturers was more variable. For example, Cisco and Intel began online customer service in 1995 and 1996, respectively. From these beginnings, the early adopters gradually deepened the functionality of their site. In 2000, Cisco had online sales of over $12 billion and resolved over 70 percent of its support requests over the Internet (Cisco Systems, Inc. 2000).

The safest generalizations about the established firms is that the more technologically sophisticated they were, the closer they were to computer networking, and the more entrepreneurial they were, the more likely they were to begin experimenting with the Internet and the WWW. However, many established firms were largely oblivious to the Internet's possibilities until start-ups actually entered their market with the threat of disintermediating them (if they were retail operations) or reorganizing the value chain (if they were manufacturers). Either way, the strategic threats from the start-ups soon forced every established firm to consider the implications of the Internet for business.

The Start-ups
The role of start-ups in the commercialization of the Internet did not begin with the WWW. As mentioned earlier, the Internet data communications firms PSINET and UUNET were funded by venture capitalists in the late 1980s.[15] It is accurate to say that outside of these firms, there were only a few start-ups and fewer investments until 1994. This was a function of the time it took for entrepreneurs to comprehend the opportunities that the WWW represented, and the slightly greater time for venture capitalists to be convinced that the Internet presented a valuable investment opportunity; however, the lag was not long, particularly in Silicon Valley. By early 1994, venture capitalists began receiving business plans from entrepreneurs with ideas about how to exploit the WWW. Given the greater venture capital resources and large numbers of entrepreneurs, Silicon Valley quickly became the center for Internet start-ups.

With the release of Mosaic, a few existing small firms and some start-ups began developing browsers. A few of these were funded by venture capitalists, but most were self-financed. The first major start-up to attract venture capital and become a firm dedicated to exploiting the WWW was Netscape. It was established in April 1994, by Jim Clark, an ex-Stanford professor and founder of Silicon Graphics Inc., and Marc Andreessen, a former student at the University of Illinois and leader of the team that created Mosaic. After hiring the others on the Mosaic team, they rewrote Mosaic and rapidly captured the browser market (Cusumano and Yoffie 1998). Netscape went public in August 1995 at a price that gave it a valuation of nearly $1 billion. This alerted every venture capitalist to the capital gains one might reap in the Internet field. By March 9, 2000, more than 370 self-identified Internet firms had gone public; their total valuation was $1.5 trillion, though they had only $40 billion in sales (Perkins 2000).

As the number of users grew rapidly and new business ideas proliferated, the Internet became an economic space that continually expanded, providing yet further commercial opportunities. The greater the number of users, the more reason there was to create Web pages, which meant there was more content. The result was a virtuous circle of increasing returns. This provided opportunities for still other start-ups to develop new software and Web-based services. There was an explosion of software tools firms, Web-hosting services, and so on. For example, businesses could be built on searching and cataloging the other sites. The earliest examples of these catalogues and search engines were created in universities, but they were soon transformed into for-profit firms, such as Yahoo!, Excite, and Lycos. Each success attracted still more entrepreneurs experimenting with other business models.

The chaotic but rapidly growing user base, reinforced by the high valuations that Internet-related start-ups commanded in the stock market, unleashed a frenzy of venture investing. Naturally, this willingness to fund experiments encouraged ever greater experimentation. Moreover, during the stock market boom, all of these experiments could be listed on the stock market for massive capital gains. One example of a failure was "push" technology, which enabled WWW content providers to automatically send information to users. In 1997, pundits hailed push as a killer application, but by 1999, it became clear that it was only a niche market, at best. Venture capitalists had funded many firms to exploit push technology, but with only a limited market, the firms either limped along, were acquired, or ceased operations.

Despite the scattered failures, overall the Internet sector burgeoned and more firms entered the space. The investments in the pioneers returned excellent results as firms went public. From 1995 through March 2000, the willingness of public markets to purchase the shares of newly formed Internet firms fluctuated, but in general the market was very positive and small firms were able to raise large amounts of capital. For example, eBay went public at a split-adjusted price of $7.64 per share in September 1999 and rose as high as $121 per share before falling to

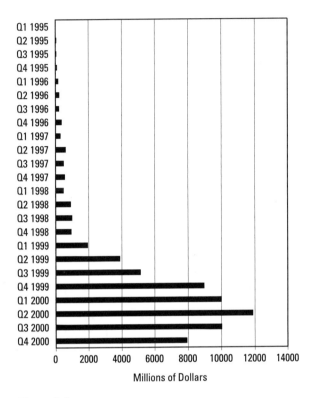

Figure 3.2
Internet-related investments by venture capitalists by quarter, 1995—Q4, 2000

about $45 per share in February 2001. This illustrates how by mid-1999
there was what might be termed a full-scale investment frenzy as public
investors drove the price of new issues skyward. As a result, some venture
capital funds reported annualized returns of one hundred percent or
greater. In 1999, the *average* return for early stage funds was 91.2 percent, the highest in history (NVCA 2000a).[16] As figure 3.2 indicates, the
amount of venture capital invested in Internet-related firms grew from
a nearly negligible $12 million in the first quarter of 1995 to nearly
$12 billion in the second quarter of 2000 (NVCA 2000b). In percentage
terms, the increase was equally dramatic, growing from a negligible percentage in 1995 to nearly 40 percent of total investment in 1999.

The money going to first-round financing clearly can be seen in the estimated figures (NVCA, 2001). In 1994, only 15 firms in the Internet-related sector received such funding (including spin-offs from existing firms); by 1999 and 2000, these figures rose to 1,044 and 1,546, respectively. Similarly, IPOs increased from four in 1994 to 134 and 56 by 1999 and 2000; these figures exclude the communication equipment market and a small number of buyouts.

In this bubble, massive sums were committed to multiple firms intent on entering the same business segment, even when it was likely that only one firm could survive. However, if these investments are thought of as being experiments, it means that the United States launched an enormous number of experiments. This large number, even if accompanied by foolishness and even stupidity, increased the probability of having made a correct investment; indeed, some of the start-ups have become global leaders. As important, this feverish investment alerted established firms to the potential of the WWW and forced them to react. In effect, these investments both created new firms and changed the environmental conditions for established firms. Finally, the concentration of these firms in Silicon Valley meant that they were able to benefit from the knowledge gained from previous start-up attempts and from access to advanced users providing insight into other opportunities to create new firms (von Hippel 1988).

An intense emphasis on speed is a central attribute of the U.S. venture capital-driven commercialization process. Speed is vital because usually there are other start-ups seeking to occupy the same space, and because it is necessary to reach critical mass before larger, established firms enter the market. The fuel for this growth is sufficient capital and the ability to offer new employees equity that might quickly appreciate in value. Combined with the head start, this emphasis on rapid execution meant that the United States would repeatedly have the earliest and then the largest firms in nearly every Internet segment. Moreover, because a number of these sectors exhibit winner-take-all characteristics, the earliest entrants to grow to substantial size often acquire an insurmountable first-mover advantage.

The genesis of the Internet in the United States, the large number of U.S. and English-language users, and the preponderance of English-language content were all advantages for U.S. firms establishing Internet firms. United States firms quickly established dominance in English-language Web sites, and foreign Web sites had to cede their own national English-language market. Moreover, they were soon faced with established U.S. firms trying to capture their local language market.

The success of U.S. firms in other countries was not assured, however, for a variety of reasons. Customization for a local market was not so simple. Different cultures might appreciate different layouts, designs, and logics. Beyond this are the individual national idiosyncrasies and legal regimes. Thus the English-language Yahoo! auction site was sued in French courts for allowing Nazi paraphernalia to be offered to the French. (See Yao's discussion of this case in chapter 13.) The technology opens the world to the user, but national governments continue to enforce their local laws. Examples such as the Yahoo! case indicate that the emergence of dominant global players is not a foregone conclusion.

The transformation of cyberspace into an economic space was characterized by a construction process in which commercial entities were formed at various levels.[17] The uppermost level is the location of actual sites, such as Amazon, Yahoo!, Chemdex, and eBay, which the user visits. At this level, the diversity of sites is almost infinite. The level below encompasses the various software toolmakers and services. At this level, there are established firms, such as IBM, Oracle, and SAP, and also a large number of start-ups, such as Viant, Scient, Ariba, CommerceOne, and Microstrategy, to name only a few. The firms at the next level provide services much closer to the network, including Web-hosting firms such as Exodus and those providing network software such as Inktomi and Akamai. At the infrastructural level are the firms actually owning the data pipelines of all types. Then there are the firms providing the infrastructure equipment, including routers, fiber optics-related components, DSL equipment, cable modems, and so on. In the infrastructure sector both established firms and start-ups competed, and in most of these areas the competition was between established U.S. firms such as Cisco, Lucent, and 3Com; established non-U.S. firms such as Ericsson (Sweden), Nortel (Canada), Alcatel (France), Siemens (Germany), and NEC (Japan); and many start-ups.

Deciding the boundaries for a discussion of the Internet is complicated indeed. In fact, when Hunt and Aldrich (1998) described the organizational ecology of the Internet, they included firms ranging from AT&T to the newest start-up. For the purposes of this chapter, such a definition would be too inclusive. Therefore, my discussion concentrates upon only two levels: the Web sites and the software and services directly related to creating and delivering those sites. To accomplish this, the sites are parsed into general commercial Web sites and software and services. Among the general Web sites, two genres, the B2C and B2B sites, are described in separate subsections. This division is somewhat artificial, but given the number of sites and the proliferation of activities on the Web, it provides a certain order and structure.

Portals, Communities, Auctions, and More
The sheer diversity of WWW-based commercial activities is remarkable. Many of these businesses simply would not exist if it were not for the WWW. For example, portals and search engines such as Yahoo! and Google are only possible because of the WWW. It is impossible to even categorize all the experiments in creating new businesses that the Internet has sparked. One way to think about this is that cyberspace is being "settled" and people are building economic activities in the space. Some of these activities are directly analogous to those in physical space, such as B2C and B2B commerce (discussed below), but others are unique to cyberspace.

Portals are important because they have established themselves as central destinations for Web users. The dominant portals were established during the earliest days of commercialization. Due to the U.S. head start, nearly all of the dominant global portals such as Yahoo!, Excite, Altavista, and Infoseek were U.S.-based.[18] These U.S. portals have successfully penetrated foreign markets. In November 2000, Yahoo! operated 23 overseas properties (Yahoo's term). In the most important markets, such as France, Germany, the United Kingdom, and Japan, Yahoo! is either the first or second most-visited site. In France and Germany, it is second only to the sites established by the dominant telecom providers, Deutsche Telecom and France Telecom. The strength of the U.S.-based portals is predicated on a number of advantages. The precocity of the U.S. market and its large size meant that the vast preponderance of sites continue to be in English. Not surprisingly, this is an advantage to the U.S. portals, not only in terms of content, but also in terms of an ability to increase content and services that could be distributed over more users. They also had an advantage because they had more technological and marketing experience. Their early growth allowed them to establish global brand names, before other sites could compete in the English-language market. In other countries, indigenous portals were forced to defend their language market from the U.S. portals, which had already captured their English-language traffic. However, the U.S. portals also translated their sites into foreign languages, while leveraging their underlying architecture, software, server farms, and technical talent.

Another group of sites are those involved in consumer-to-consumer (C2C) e-commerce. This category refers to Web sites that connect consumers. Because C2C sites are not based on direct sales, their profits come from other revenue sources such as advertising, commissions, referral fees, and so on. The premier example is the auction site eBay, which was established in September 1995 and grew rapidly to be the largest C2C auction site on the Internet, with revenues of $431 million in 2000, with a profit of $48 million. In 1998, it expanded overseas by establishing a subsidiary in the United Kingdom. In June 1999, it purchased Alando.de, the largest C2C German auction site. In February 2000, it launched a joint venture with NEC for the Japanese market. EBay claims that it is the leading C2C auction site in Australia, Canada, Germany, and the United Kingdom (figure 3.3). It expects to operate in 10 countries by the end of 2001 and plans to expand to 25 countries by 2006 (eBay 2001). Whether eBay can successively translate its model for each of these national markets is difficult to predict; however, it now has critical mass, brand awareness, significant technical advantages, and a strong financial base.

There are many other examples of C2C sites. For example, a number of sites allow users to engage each other in games. There are community sites such as Geocities, which was purchased by Yahoo! for more than $4 billion. Firms such as Napster provide software downloads that allow registered users to trade various digital content such as MP3 files. There are online services that provide notification, registration, and verification through the Internet for meetings. These are only examples of the enormous variety of services created to exploit the Internet.

For students of technology, the development of C2C business is fascinating because it did not simply translate existing commerce online;

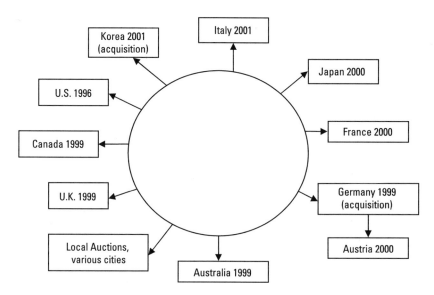

Figure 3.3
EBay's global auctions

rather, it was a field for experimentation with extremely wide parameters of possibility. Of course, such experimentation was under way in other countries, but there can be little doubt that the United States undertook a far greater number of experiments than any other single country.[19]

Business-to-Consumer E-commerce
From late 1995 through late 1998, great attention was focused on the proliferation of start-ups in the B2C sector. These start-ups meant to replace physical stores (bricks and mortar) with online sales. Put differently, the online operations would disintermediate the traditional retailers, because virtual storefronts on the Internet would substitute for physical storefronts. One idea was to create e-malls, retail sites that, like physical-world shopping malls, would be where retailers would "locate" their various shops. The proposition was that these B2C sites would attract consumers because of the convenience of having a centralized "shopping center" online. This was a flawed vision and these malls failed, though interestingly the portals and other heavily visited sites then set up shop-

ping sites that resembled the mall idea. They have played, however, a role in the development of the Internet in Korea, as analyzed by the chapter by Chang.

The theory underlying B2C e-commerce was that the elimination of the costs of stores and sales employees and the use of a more efficient supply chain due to taking customers' orders directly should allow online retailers to sell at a discount. The proponents of online retailing were predicting nothing short of revolution—there would be a massive shift of purchasing to the Internet. There is precedent for such shifts in retailing. For example, the "category killers" such Wal-Mart, Home Depot, Borders, Barnes & Noble, Office Depot, Rite Aid, and so on transformed retailing and thereby devastated both small independent stores and the department stores. The Internet appeared to be an opportunity to galvanize a shift in consumer purchasing habits that could have transformative consequences for retailing.

With any new technology there are two ideal-typical possibilities. New entrants displace the existing firms, or the incumbents fend off the threat either by adopting the entrant's model or by reinforcing their own advantages, thereby undercutting the entrant's advantages. In B2C e-commerce, the incumbents were caught unaware by the start-ups, which mushroomed seemingly overnight. Moreover, many, but certainly not all, of the early efforts by the incumbents to develop Web-based businesses failed. For example, both Wal-Mart and Levi's created Web sites that proved to be disasters, though later their efforts would improve. Retailers that had substantial mail order businesses were generally far more successful in switching to Web-based operations.[20]

In July 1994, only a few months after the establishment of Netscape and Yahoo!, Amazon was established; its online bookstore opened in July 1995. Amazon's founder, Jeff Bezos, was not particularly attracted to books; rather, he was searching for a retail sector that would be easy to penetrate. Books were chosen because they are an easy-to-ship, undifferentiated product. Moreover, there was an existing set of distributors that could be used for fulfillment. But, most critical, from its inception Amazon aimed to expand from books to other items, with the eventual goal of becoming a multiproduct retailer—in other words, Wal-Mart was the real target. As indicated in figure 3.4a, by 2001, parts of Amazon's empire had gone bankrupt. Even though Amazon consistently lost money,

The Growth and Development of the Internet in the United States

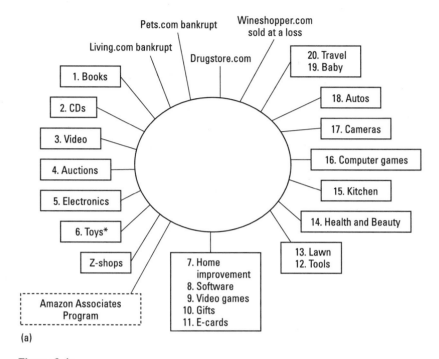

(a)

Figure 3.4a
Amazon's growing empire
Source: Author's compilation from various sources
* In 2000, became joint venture with Toys "R" Us.

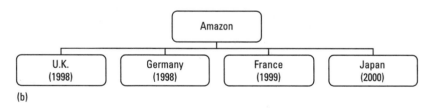

(b)

Figure 3.4b
Amazon's international operations

and it did not have the advantage of being the first online bookstore, it was able to grow rapidly because of the venture capital backing it received in June 1996. As of fall 2001, Amazon was not yet profitable, but management promised pro forma profitability in the near future.

The early investments in the B2C space by venture capitalists and the successful listing of Amazon on the NASDAQ ignited a frenzy of investment in online retail start-ups. Very soon there were specialized sites selling groceries, pet supplies, air travel, vitamins, pharmaceutical prescriptions, stocks, CDs, electronics, PCs, home improvement supplies, and nearly every other commonly consumed item. In this investment frenzy, often four or five online firms were established in each product category. At times these firms would have different business models, but for the most part they were simply clones. For example, in January 2000, *Upside* magazine listed six dedicated online cosmetic start-ups: Eve.com, Gloss.com, Sephora.com, Beauty.com, Beautyscene.com, and Beautyjungle.com (Garner 2000). Similarly, there was a plethora of online toy stores launched by start-ups and traditional players. However, by the end of 2000, all of them had failed or were consolidated (table 3.4). Many of those that had gone public were by early 2001 in the process of being delisted by the NASDAQ. Even more odd was the proliferation of high-visibility online pet stores that rapidly disappeared, taking millions of investor dollars with them. When the IPO boom ended

Table 3.4
Status of Most Important Online Toy Stores in 2000

Firm	Status	Investors
Toysmart.com	Closed 2000	Disney
Toytime	Closed 2000	Unavailable
RedRocket.com	Closed 2000	Viacom
KB Kids.com	For sale	Consolidated Stores
EToys	Since going public, down 95%	Idealab (public investors)
SmarterKids.com	Since going public, down 90%	Venture capitalists (public investors)
Toys "R" Us	Merged Web site with Amazon	Toys "R" Us
Amazon.com	Merged Web site with Toys "R" Us	Venture capitalists (public investors)

Sources: Wall Street Journal 2000; author's research

in early 2000, many of these e-retailers still had not gone public and were not profitable. With no exit opportunity, their backers rejected entreaties for more funds, sparking a wave of distress mergers and bankruptcies.

After establishing a Web site, these e-tailers discovered that simply posting an image of an item online and booking an order did not remove the need to deliver the purchases to the customer. Managing the delivery logistics would be as important as booking a sale. In Christmas 1999, many e-tailers were simply not prepared for the volume of Internet purchases, and their systems were overwhelmed. As a result, many purchases were not delivered in time for Christmas. Finally, the online retailers discovered what offline retailers had always known: predicting demand is one of the most difficult skills in retailing. For example, Amazon discovered that it had purchased the wrong toys and after Christmas had to write-off $35 million in unsold inventory. In response to these problems, in August 2000, Amazon.com came to an arrangement with Toys "R" Us.com in which Toys "R" Us would be responsible for buying and managing the inventory, while Amazon would operate the Web site development, order fulfillment, and customer service for a new joint site. The inventory for both companies would be housed in Amazon's warehouses (Farmer and Junnarkar 2000). In effect, Amazon conceded that it did not have the expertise to predict toy demand effectively, while Toys "R" Us conceded that it was not so successful in interfacing with Internet buyers and handling fulfillment.

Traditional retailers such as Macy's and J. C. Penney found it difficult to establish online operations. The world's largest retailer, Wal-Mart, launched its first Web site in late 1996, but it generated minimal sales. Simultaneously, Amazon extended its product offerings beyond books and CDs, presaging a possible competitive threat. In 1999, Amazon hired 15 of Wal-Mart's logistics and retailing executives to strengthen its logistics operations, making the threat more palpable. In January 2000, believing that its own site operating from corporate headquarters in Bentonville, Arkansas, was not successful, Wal-Mart established a joint-venture agreement with a venture capital firm to re-establish Wal-Mart.com, with headquarters in Palo Alto. Effectively, Wal-Mart decided that it had to develop an organization entirely separate from its Arkansas headquarters (Waxer 2000). This is not surprising, as selling in the online world is very different from selling from stores.

Without venture capital, there could not have been such a proliferation of B2C startups. Although creating possible competitors, it also alerted U.S. retailers to the threats and opportunities this new method of interacting with customers posed. The start-ups discovered the difficulties of fulfillment, inventory control, and handling of returns. In general, the firms most successful in launching online operations were those that had strong order fulfillment operations already in place. These firms already fulfilled remote orders, so for them it was a matter of switching their incoming order stream from voice and catalog to the Internet.

It is too early to judge the ultimate result of the willingness to risk hundreds of millions of dollars in e-tailing. What is certain, even if most of these investments are lost, is that the U.S. retail system will have been forced to become more efficient than ever. Further, there is the possibility that a number of the start-ups such as Amazon will survive and create an entirely new channel that has a global reach. Given the estimate that as much as one-quarter of Amazon's sales originate from outside the United States, Amazon has already become a global brand. As of 2001, there were mixed signals about the ability of U.S. firms to compete globally: firms such as eToys closed their overseas subsidiaries prior to closing themselves, whereas eBay and others continued to compete globally.

Business-to-Business E-commerce
Only six months to one year after the establishment of the first B2C firms, venture capitalists began funding entrepreneurs to establish Web sites aimed at becoming online marketplaces where businesses could buy and sell, business-to business (B2B) sites. The B2B market quickly outstripped B2C in sales, though it is interesting to note that the first B2B operations that were successful were those of firms such as Dell, Cisco, and Intel that sold through their dedicated sites to other businesses. These were neither sites developed by newly established firms nor the consortia sites established by oligopolistic groups of firms. Helper and MacDuffie examine the B2B sector, especially in regards to the auto industry in greater detail (chpater 11). This section limits its focus to the aspects of B2B e-commerce that directly relate to the responses of the U.S. economy to the opportunities for harnessing the Internet and especially the role of venture capitalists in funding the establishment of firms

to exploit what were perceived to be new business opportunities that resulted from the commercialization of the Internet.

By mid 1998, independent marketplaces had been established for nearly every business imaginable. A 1999 report by a Robertson Coleman analyst listed 253 separate B2B sites (Upin 1999). VerticalNet was one of the first independent B2B sites. In October 1995, it established the first vertical trading community, and by November 2000, VerticalNet operated over sixty separate industry sites (VerticalNet 2001). The Plastics Network, which was launched in September 1995 and relaunched in 1999 with funding from Internet Capital Group (ICG), was another early site. In fact, ICG was a publicly listed firm established in 1996 with the express purpose of investing in fledgling B2B startups. ICG's investments were an indicator of the growth in interest in B2B e-commerce. In 1996, ICG committed only $14 million, but by 1999, this had increased to $572 million. Moreover, it expected to commit in excess of $1 billion in 2000, though this has been dramatically reduced due to the collapse of ICG's stock price. ICG was not alone. Beginning in 1997, there was a rising tide of investment in B2B startups (Internet Capital Group 2001). For example, Chemdex Corporation was funded by several venture capital funds in September 1997. The receptivity of the public market to B2B stock offerings in 1998 and 1999 led to a plethora of new firms funded by both traditional venture capital and the new publicly held venture capital firms such as ICG and CMGI.

The establishment of B2B sites was initially uncontested by existing firms and industries. In this respect, the B2B marketplace resembled that of the B2C sector, because the first movers were start-ups funded by venture capital. These start-ups aimed to attract established firms to their sites. This was easiest when there was no dominant firm or set of firms in the value chain. However, as Helper and Macduffie so ably indicate, if the value chain contained oligopolists, be they suppliers or purchasers, often they exerted significant power over adjacent segments at the least and perhaps even over the entire chain. In such markets, success in moving the chain onto the start-up's platform was predicated upon attracting these oligopolists. For the oligopolists there was no compelling reason to join any specific platform. Though the potential efficiencies were substantial and could not be ignored indefinitely, joining a marketplace controlled by another firm would create vulnerability and permit the other firm to reap the benefits.

Hesitant to join marketplaces owned by others, larger firms soon decided to create their own Web sites. The problem was that each oligopolist created his or her own unique site. This reintroduced an inefficiency because it divided the market, forcing suppliers to adapt to different sites, and thereby limited any efficiency gains. Thus, if the oligopolists all created their own sites, then the threat of a market organized by an independent firm remained. The independent could divide and conquer the market, because the independent could offer incentives, such as a preferential position, equity, or lower trading costs, to a few oligopolists that were willing to break ranks and join the independent site. Then the late movers would be the losers, because after the site gained momentum they would be compelled to join the site under unfavorable bargaining conditions. The oligopolists responded to this threat by creating consortia to own the platforms they joined.

In terms of commercialization, the B2B space also exhibited characteristics similar to those in the B2C area. Entrepreneurs quickly entered the field, and there was a proliferation of sites in each category as venture capitalists funded many "me-too" firms. After a significant lag, the established firms reacted by creating their own Web sites. As Helper and MacDuffie indicate, by the end of 2001, many of the venture capital-funded B2B sites had been closed and others were in great difficulty, whereas some of the consortia sites did appear to be gaining traction. At the close of 2001, what seemed most certain is that key firms such as Intel, Cisco, and Dell have had significant success with their B2B operations.

Software Tools and Internet Services

The early and rapid development of e-commerce, the large number of leading-edge users, and an already strong position in software provided significant advantages to US firms intent upon developing software tools for Internet users. As von Hippel (1999) pointed out, the needs of cutting-edge users can alert toolmakers to marketable improvements, or what could be termed "learning from lead customers." Further, the needs of customers such as Yahoo!, Amazon, and/or eBay meant that software and services would be severely tested, thereby exposing limitations and problems. The intense competition among the users as they sought technological advantages meant that software innovators had a ready market. A symbiosis between software designers and leading-edge users developed. This created a virtuous circle in which improved tools accelerated the development of the Web sites and vice versa.

For established software firms such as Microsoft, Oracle, and Seibel Systems, the start-ups were both competitors and potential acquisition targets. United States firms quickly grasped the importance of the WWW and rewrote their software to operate on the Internet. The German firm SAP did not grasp the movement to the WWW as quickly, and by the time it became conscious of its significance it had lost ground to aggressive U.S. competitors. In contrast, Oracle rapidly reengineered its database software to be WWW compatible and captured market share from its competitors.

Rationalizing and transferring business processes and B2B e-commerce to the Web-based protocols created significant new demand for software, and many start-ups were funded by venture capitalists to meet this new demand. Venture capital-funded startups such as CommerceOne, Ariba, E.phiphany, and Kana Communications, to name only a few, became global competitors, and very often the U.S. firms (and, most often, these had roots in Silicon Valley) were competing globally against each other. In the Internet services arena, U.S. start-ups such as Exodus Communications became global leaders in corporate web-hosting. Other firms offered to manage corporate Web sites, e-mail, and a wide variety of other Internet-related functions. Software firms such as Inktomi and Akamai developed software used for Internet infrastructure.

United States firms have occupied nearly every important Internet-related software niche. These firms have rapidly expanded their businesses into other countries, either by establishing offices or using their stock to purchase the much smaller national competitors. Whether American or foreign, most Web sites operate on U.S. software and hardware. Regardless of the outcome of international competition concerning portals or e-commerce, or the different privacy issues and government policies, it will be U.S. software toolmakers and service providers that will become the dominant vendors. Judging from the current situation, there will be fewer significant European and Asian firms. The exception will be if mobile phones become a dominant Internet access device—an unclear proposition.

Regardless of what happens to the e-commerce start-ups, in the arena of WWW software tools, the U.S. firms have important first-mover advantages. Whether the bulk of the sector will be captured by existing firms such as Oracle or Seibel or by the start-ups such as Ariba and Kana is not as important as the fact that most of the tools will be provided by U.S. firms. The one significant exception is the German enterprise resource planning software firm SAP, whose software is used by firms around the world (see Casper, chapter 7 in this book). SAP seems to have made the transition to the Internet world. With a few other exceptions, such as the German firm Intershop, the Internet software tools industry, which is centered in Silicon Valley, makes it likely that U.S. firms will be able to benefit from the further evolution of the Internet infrastructure. The one possible exception to this scenario would be if wireless applications were to become dominant, requiring a set of competencies that U.S. firms lack, but as Sako and Glimstedt and Zander show are more prevalent in Japan and Scandinavia.

Conclusion

In summary, the speed with which the U.S. NSI reacted to the commercial possibilities inherent in the Internet was remarkable and, perhaps, unprecedented. In nearly every facet of the Internet, from the infrastructure and equipment to e-commerce, U.S. firms became global leaders, with the possible exception of two fields: wireless Internet and optical switching. It would be simplistic to attribute the achievement of such dominance to any single variable; rather, it was the result of a confluence of factors.

The first bundle of factors that favored U.S. industry was the unique political economy of the telecommunications system. Early and gradual (though thoroughgoing) deregulation made the United States the leading economy for innovation. In sharp contrast, in most of Europe and Asia the dominant government-owned monopolist (even in 2000) exerted undue influence. The flat-rate tariff structure for local phone calls was remarkably important for the diffusion of online services and the uptake of the Internet in the home market. The macro-level deregulation created a powerful competition that drove bandwidth costs down, encouraging ever-greater use of the telecommunications system and the Internet.

A second bundle of factors involved the willingness of Americans to order remotely. United States consumers already had ample experience using credit cards to purchase through catalogs or over the phone. Thus they were comfortable purchasing from a Web site. Similarly, U.S. firms were already using Electronic Data Interchange (EDI) systems, so they were a receptive audience for Internet-based trading systems, particularly because they believed such systems would be less expensive and easier to use. Moreover, U.S. firms were under intense price competition from foreign and domestic producers, so the idea of a potentially more convenient, easier to operate, and cost-effective system was attractive. Many leading firms such as Intel, Cisco, and Dell quickly moved to implement Web-based systems because of these advantages.

The third and probably the most unusual bundle of factors centered upon a unique feature of the U.S. economy, the infrastructure centered upon venture capital meant to support high-technology entrepreneurship. Earlier this infrastructure had supported the establishment of critical e-commerce and Internet infrastructure firms such as Sun Microsystems, Oracle, and Cisco Systems. With the successful public offerings of Netscape, Yahoo!, and Amazon, venture capitalists were eager to fund Internet-related investments of all types. From one perspective, the massive outpouring of capital was spectacularly wasteful, but from another perspective, it created a large number of experiments to be winnowed out by a Darwinian selection process. This infrastructure not only funded these experiments, it also attracted many of the society's best managers and technologists.

When the preparation of this chapter began, Internet firms were still the toast of Wall Street, and there was a perception that the venture capital-funded Internet boom was contributing to a fundamental transformation of the economy. By the end of 2001, the situation appeared very different. A powerful shakeout struck public and private start-ups as firms were delisted and venture capitalists refused to provide further support for many of these firms. Undoubtedly, billions of dollars have disappeared, and firms are rapidly writing down their investments. Many firms, such as Lucent in January 2002, are selling their venture funds to outside brokers at substantial reductions of their value a year ago.

Nevertheless, the Internet has become an almost taken-for-granted utility. Entrepreneurs and established firms alike are deploying the Internet to reorganize the way commerce is conducted. In retail commerce, it is an important new sales and information channel. There are innumerable small enterprises that never received venture capital that now use the WWW as their sales channel. Similarly, as MacDuffie and Helper (chapter 11) will show for B2B commerce, the use of the Internet is becoming an accepted medium for handling mundane interfirm transactions and various co-design processes. An observation made on other technological changes will likely be proven true again: in the short run, the impact was overhyped, but in the long run, the changes set in motion were much greater than anyone imagined.

The heights of the Internet gold rush not only affected the United States, but as the other papers in this book show, spread around the globe. Nations that previously had had low levels of technology-related entrepreneurship and minimal or nonexistent venture capital resources experienced an explosion of venture capital investing, much of it targeted at Internet start-ups. To encourage this efflorescence, many of these nations created new markets with looser listing requirements, thereby encouraging even greater investment and start-up activity. However, the bursting of the U.S. NASDAQ bubble in early 2000 led to a stock price collapse and closing of public markets as an exit strategy for technology and especially Internet firms globally. The outcome of this reversal of fortunes is as yet uncertain; however, in a number of nations it may result in a vicious cycle of decline that destroys these fledgling institutions that had just been introduced to encourage new firm formation.

The Internet investment craze of the second half of the 1990s was wasteful in the extreme. Wild ideas of all sorts received funding. And yet, even after the evisceration of large amounts of this speculative capital, U.S. firms remain dominant in nearly every area related to the Internet, except in mobile telephony, where European and North Asian firms have been most successful. From a systemic perspective, it is likely that in a decade hence we will reflect upon the Internet investment bubble and conclude that the willingness of investors to experiment resulted in U.S. firms capturing a leadership role, and that the survivors gained the resources, experience, and market share that only a few firms in other nations were able to achieve.

Acknowledgments

The author would like to thank Suzy Iacono of the National Science Foundation and the Alfred Sloan Foundation for providing funding for the research reported in this paper.

Notes

1. For developments in the personal computer industry value chain, see Kenney and Curry 2001.

2. It is worth noting that in the United States, many different entities including state, county, and city governments can affect e-commerce. These jurisdictions have different taxation schemes and laws pertaining to retail sales, particularly with respect to tobacco, firearms, alcohol, and pornography. Despite these differences, it is accurate to call the United States a unified market.

3. The U.S. lead was not always at the invention stage. Frequently, there was simultaneous invention in several nations, but nearly always the United States triumphed in the commercialization of the idea.

4. Four "technological trajectories" contributed to the rapid growth of these industries (Dosi 1984). The first is Moore's Law (named after one of the founders of Intel). It states that the cost of a transistor on a semiconductor will be halved every 18 months. The second is Metcalfe's Law (named by George Gilder after Robert Metcalfe, co-inventor of Ethernet and founder of 3Com), which postulates that the functionality of a network will increase exponentially with the addition of each user. The third law is Shugart's Law (coined by me for Al Shugart, founder of the hard disk drive firm Seagate Technology), and is based upon the observation that the price per bit of magnetic storage halves every 18 months. The importance of this law is ignored, but Web sites such as Yahoo!, Amazon, etc. require enormous amounts of data storage. The final law, which Gilder (2000) terms the Law of the Telecosm, observes that the price of transmitting a bit of data over the communications network is halved every 12 months.

5. See, for example, Davies 1994.

6. In 1900, there was one telephone per 60 Americans, one for every 115 Swedes, and one for every 1,216 Frenchmen (de Sola Pool 1977, 30).

7. The term "universal service," when first coined by Theodore Vail, did not refer to every American having access to a telephone. It referred to the ability for anyone having an AT&T-provided phone being able to contact any other phone in the system (Dordick 1990, 230).

8. In rural areas and some towns, independents survived and had interconnection agreements with AT&T.

9. Few would argue that AT&T service was the best possible, but most would agree that in the 1950s and 1960s it was superior to service in other countries.

10. The value of the local loop would only come in the late 1990s, when the Regional Bell Operating Companies would benefit from their control of the customer.

11. For AT&T, losing data communications did not appear serious in the 1970s, as it was such a small market. In fact, AT&T was uninterested in packet-switched data communications when it was first proposed. The result was that AT&T did not have the dominant role in the Internet data transmission business, and its equipment subsidiary, Western Electric, which became Lucent, fell behind in the data transmission equipment business (Hafner and Lyon 1996, 63–66).

12. The definition of a "significant" start-up was a firm that either had gone public or received funding from the top 20 venture capital firms. Thus the map is not exhaustive or necessarily complete; it is only illustrative. Not included in this map are network equipment start-ups, Internet Service Providers, and other physical network-related firms.

13. Contemporaneously, several firms introduced various networking technologies, such as DECNet and IBM's SNA, but these were all proprietary.

14. A salient expression of this was the individuals who rushed to occupy various URLs with no intention of using them. They then offered to sell the URLs. To translate this into the land rush metaphor, they "staked a claim" to an address in cyberspace. One response to this was legislation forbidding "cybersquatting," a reference to the registration by entrepreneurs of addresses that were trademarks and/or established firms' names.

15. Venture capitalists had funded AOL in the 1980s as an online service; at the time its operations were unrelated to the Internet.

16. The three-year compounded average annual return was a more modest 47.9 percent!

17. The richness of this economic space is based on a small number of universally agreed-upon open protocols. The most important are HTML, HTTP, TCP/IP, etc. A metaphor for this is the richness of life being based on the DNA molecule, which operates on the basis of quite simple protocols.

18. Microsoft and AOL are also leading destinations. AOL is successful because it has its captive audience of AOL subscribers. Microsoft attracts visitors for many reasons; for instance, it is the default option on the Internet Explorer browser, and users need software assistance, etc.

19. Entrepreneurs and venture capitalists in other countries often simply observed the experiments in the United States and then reproduced them in their own countries. This was the case for the German auction site Alando.de and numerous Asian sites. The Japanese firm Softbank adopted this as its strategy for creating Japanese sites.

20. For Dell, see Curry and Kenney 1999.

4

Sweden's Wireless Wonders: The Diverse Roots and Selective Adaptations of the Swedish Internet Economy

Henrik Glimstedt and Udo Zander

Sweden—Why and How?

Fascination for the Internet and the Web grew quickly in Sweden in the early 1990s. Like so many times before in the twentieth century, the Swedes rapidly took a promising new technology to their hearts. The story of early and fast adoption of the telephone, radio, TV, color TV, personal computer, and cellular phone repeated itself with the Internet. Unlike PCs, which at introduction were surrounded by a certain skepticism and hesitation as to their effects on childrens' learning and family life, the Internet was from day one perceived as a gift from heaven. The often shy and interaction-hungry people in the sparsely populated north of Europe saw the beauty of the net and embraced it.

Our contribution to this volume develops the argument that the development of the Swedish Internet economy came about through the *disbundling of network elements* and *the existence of entrepreneurial pockets of competition*. The Swedish telecommunications network was modularized and it became possibly, under the deregulated telecommunications market regime, for private actors to add innovations that improved network elements without changing the system as a whole. This opened business opportunities not only for large and established actors, but also for small and more focused firms specializing in more narrow technologies or Internet services. Once the system was disbundled, new actors in the financial arena—venture capital—targeted the emerging technological specialists and creators of Internet services, leveraging the emerging new specialist firms. But this raises the issue of how technological coordination between large multinational telecom operators and the small firms took place. Our investigation draws attention to the importance of modularity and interoperability interfaces in disbundled systems. We thus emphasize the role of standardization of bodies and the relaxed antitrust regimes that permit large corporations to abandon the slow formal standard setting organizations and create new private ones. It is in this intersection between the entrepreneurs' ideas as to how to appropriate rents in modular systems and his or her ideas for re-arrangements of factor markets, it seems to us, that crucial processes are defined and shaped.

Indeed, much suggests that Sweden's Internet economy took off early in a particularly forceful way (IDC 2001). It was not just that the number of users and Web sites grew more quickly than elsewhere in Europe. The quality of the IP infrastructure also improved rapidly, as did the quality of the services. Throughout the 1990s, the Swedish information and communication technology sector became increasingly populated by new firms that made heavy contributions to Swedish economic growth (Näringsdepartementet 2000).

Given these developments that were underpinned by the disbundling of the network elements, what can be said about the nature of change? Sweden did not stand out as a likely candidate for rapid transformations. The Swedish economy has been shaped by a coherent set of institutions and policies: centralized bargaining, active labor market policy, and solidarity wage policy. A tight coalition between the two core units of the social democratic movement—the party and the labor union—was central to the realization of these policies. Although there are significant differences, Sweden furthermore shared many features with, for example, the German economy[1]: a centralized labor market, conservative banks with a long-term view on investments, strong employer associations, and home-market-centered large multinational firms (Glete 1994; Henrekson and Jakobsson 2000; Jagrén 1993; Lindbeck 1997; Lindholm Dahlstrand 1997; Pontusson 1992) In the embedded capitalism view, Sweden would be a laggard in launching start-up firms in the Internet economy due to relative centralization of capital, absence of venture capital, and obstructive taxation of entrepreneurial labor (Isaksson 1999; King and Fullerton 1984; Södersten 1984).

But contrary to Germany—a tightly integrated national model held to be based on a relatively stable institutional configuration—Sweden experienced a "punctuated equilibrium" as the institutional configuration provided the economic and political actors with insufficient conditions to react to external economic shocks (Pontusson and Swensson 1996; Thelen 2000; Wallerstien 2000). One type of explanation for the breakthrough of the Swedish Internet economy would, hence, focus on the radical effects of globalization. It would make the principal point that once the national protective cousins have been removed by deregulation, in combination with free trade and the internationalization of finance, something will happen. In this view, there are no alternatives but adaptation to competitive pressures and best practice solutions. That view would emphasize the effects of the breakdown of centralized bargaining and the continued dismantling of peak-level unions, leading to the rise of entrepreneurship and more flexible organizations. Growth of the Internet economy would thus be associated with the spread of institutional reform and new organizational principles at the level of firms. In the case of the Swedish Internet economy, this implies a transfer of Silicon Valley's recipe for institutional solutions to achieve ends such as strengthened SME-entrepreneurship, more flexible organizational forms, and collective sharing of information and risks (Henrekson and Rosenberg 2000b). This notion is predicated on a belief in the convergence toward a single form of global capitalism.

An alternative view, one that comes closer to our own views and the introduction to this volume, is that the Internet economy is associated with a variety of different sorts of organizational solutions. Under this assumption, elements of economic strategies are much more modular and less tightly coupled to each other. Actors thus experience some degrees of freedom to create a mix of elements from both the new and the old systems. If that were the case, we would find evidence not of a full adoption of the Silicon Valley model, involving the scrapping of the old established organizations and institutions representing the old telecom system, but rather *evidence of selective adaptation, building on new re-combinations of new and old technologies and organizational principles.* This is a perspective that often is associated with the concept of hybridization and selective adaptation (Kogut and Zander 1992; Tolliday et al. 1998; Zeitlin and Herrigel 2000). This pattern supports the idea that the parts that make up the national systems are sometimes loosely coupled, which would allow continued diversity both within and across countries.

A closely related idea is that change occurs through re-combinations as economic actors explore diverse solutions. Previous case studies of Swedish industrial development by Glimstedt (2000) develop the argument that the Swedish model supported more than one type of industrial equilibrium. Rather than pushing firms onto a singular industrial trajectory, firm-level studies show that the centralized institutional framework supported selective adaptation and extensive borrowing of elements from different growth strategies. Moreover, studies of innovation in large Swedish firms suggest that strategies often have been fragmented, leaving room for independent skunk works and peripheral innovations (Regnér 1999). Spin-offs of large-firm-based entrepreneurial activities and subsequent acquisitions of entrepreneurial firms were also vital to innovative capacity of Swedish corporations before the much-discussed rise of Swedish venture capital (Granstrand and Alänge 1995).

What gets shattered here is not so much the idea of the large firm's weak innovative capacity, as the idea of Sweden's industrial structure as a homogenous reflection of certain more or less fixed institutional conditions. In this view, diversity within systems facilitates change. The important question is, then, how re-combinations occur as loosely coupled social systems develop as a historical process. Selective adaptation is here the operative word. By that term we flag the centrality of reflexive actors, their experiments, and their capacity to re-conceptualize the ways that organizations may work but also the logic of institutional structures and factor markets. In our view, they do this by "discursive" learning as they explore different ways and mechanisms to coordinate innovation, create markets, tweek production systems through recombining elements from different models, and adapt labor market systems. We place special emphasis on how "pockets of competition" served to bootstrap the larger process of change.

This chapter is structured as follows. The first section outlines when and how the ground for the Internet economy was prepared in Sweden. This section is of a historical nature. It bears the burden of explaining why disbundling network elements is so fundamental, also linking historical actors to institutional transformation of the Swedish communication business. The second section focuses on the take-off and the shape of the Swedish Internet economy, in order to investigate the extent of selective adaptation to Silicon Valley models of business. This section hence explores the interaction between the new economy and the old economy, with specific reference to how old parts of the communication economy interact with IP-based communication business. Part of this section is also an investigation of the way that enabling institutions supports decentralized innovation in disbundled networks.

From Bundled Telecom to Disbundled Infocom Networks
With few exceptions, telecommunications developed as vertically integrated national monopolies. The logic behind this particular structure was the conventional wisdom that telecoms were an example of a natural monopoly, because due to the increasing returns to scale, services could only be provided efficiently by a monopoly provider. The monopoly was considered to be "natural" because a new entrant would have to build parallel infrastructures, which in turn would drive down returns.

Integration of service providing (by operators) and manufacturing of telecom equipment (by vendors) went furthest in the United States, where complete vertical integration took place when the American Bell Company purchased the telecom equipment-manufacturing arm of Western Electric. We remember this vertically integrated system as the AT&T monopoly, which was fully established in 1934 (Vietor 1994).

The combination of monopoly and national suppliers resulted in stand-alone black-box telecommunications systems. Under this regime, telecommunication network architectures consisted of a set of tightly bundled subtechnologies consisting of three layers (see figure 4.1). Until the 1980s, the topology of telecommunications was such that all switches in the network and the transmission link connecting them constituted the *trunk network*. Access was mainly over copper, and early mobile markets such as radio were only developed slowly, although the technology existed. In particular, the fixed backbone, the trunk system, was only accessed from traditional phones that lacked independent intelligence, such as processor capacity memory and so on. All vital forms of *intelligence* resided in the switches in Layer 2, the network layer. Interconnections

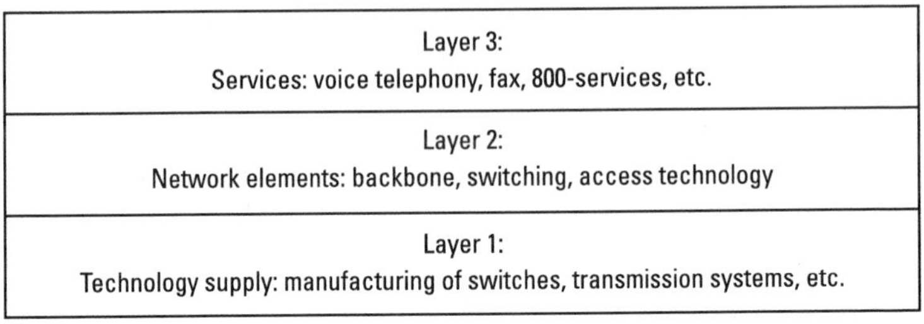

| Layer 3:
Services: voice telephony, fax, 800-services, etc. |
| Layer 2:
Network elements: backbone, switching, access technology |
| Layer 1:
Technology supply: manufacturing of switches, transmission systems, etc. |

Figure 4.1
Layers of the old telecom system

between national systems were made possible through international interface standardization under the auspices of ITU, the International Telecommunications Union.

Historically, there have been important variations of the national configurations with cooperation emerging as a dominant form of economic organization between monopoly network operators and the specialist technology suppliers (Fransman, 2002; Helgesson 1999; Lipartito 2000; Vogel 1996). Sweden represents another variation of this theme of long-standing integration between services and manufacturing. But a few unique features of the Swedish system merit our attention. On the one hand, the Swedish Postal, Telegraph, and Telephone (PTT) was active in system design and manufacturing of both telephones and electromagnetic switches designed for small towns and the less densely populated Swedish countryside. From 1970 on, innovative efforts in designing digital switches were more closely coordinated with those of Ericsson, the large Swedish private manufacturer of telephone systems. In 1970, Ericsson and Telia (formerly Swedish Telecom) formed a joint venture, Ellemtel, that successfully developed the Swedish digital switching system, AXE (Fridlund 1998b; Meurling, Jeans, and Ericsson 1995).

Creating Diversity from Within
Sweden's path to deregulation and technological renewal is rooted in the dual structure of the telecom market. Although Sweden in many ways looked precisely like many other monopoly markets, the resemblance was only superficial. There are two main sources of the unique structure that typified Sweden's post-1945 telecom market. First, the public operator,

Swedish Telecom, grew as a de facto monopoly through aggressive acquisitions in the inter-war era. Even in the postwar years, which constituted fertile grounds for nationalization across Europe, the Swedish
monopoly was not coded in Swedish law. According to the 1980 investigation of the status of the Swedish monopoly in telecommunications,
Sweden was lacking a formal monopoly in telecommunication and there
were no binding legal obstacles against private networks (Karlsson 1998).

From a legal point of view, the Swedish de facto monopoly was only
regulated through the PTT's legally defined right to deny interconnection between the public telecom network and any private network. In
fixed telephony, the economics of natural monopoly remained stable until
the late 1970s to the extent that Swedish Telecom had faced no serious
competition from private operators since the early 1920s. In mobile telecommunications and data communication, however, infrastructure competition had already emerged by the mid 1960s.

Within the framework of de facto monopoly, the Swedish PTT both
operated the public network and regulated the industry because it also
governed the degree of public-private networks interconnectedness. It
also issued frequency licenses for mobile operators that used the regulated spectrum. In addition, the regulations stipulated that PTT could
deny the potential private network operators the right to interconnect to
the public network, greatly limiting the growth potential of private networks. But the law nevertheless opened space for private networks in
areas such as cellular mobile telecommunication services and data communications. We will argue that the existence of two *pockets of competition*
(mobile telephony and data communications) shaped the introduction
of new information technology and information services from the mid
1960s on.

Pocket of Competition #1: Mobile Telephony Early movers in
mobile telephony came from diverse backgrounds. Test systems grew out
of military radio communication applications that were transformed to
civilian systems. In the late 1950s, the military radio arm of Svenska Radio Aktiebolaget (SRA), the Ericsson/Marconi joint venture, took initiatives to pull together engineers from the private industry and Swedish
Telecom to define signaling and switching interfaces, resulting in the
first Swedish mobile telecom standards. The MTA standard thus laid

the foundation for subsequent upgrades through the 1960s. Although Swedish plans for national mobile telecommunications were developed in the 1950s, these technological efforts were stimulated by the growth of private operators in the mid 1960s. End-users of the systems were banks, transport companies, top executives, public institutions (such as the police and custom authorities) and a limited number of small entrepreneurs (such as locksmiths, photographers, and freelance reporters). By the late 1960s, a total of 13 operators offered mobile telecom services. As of the early 1970s, these mobile operators were integrated into two main groups (Mölleryd 1999).

A significant boost to mobile telephony came in the late 1970s with the entry of Mr. Jan Stenbeck, a Swedish entrepreneur based in the United States. As the main owner of Kinnevik, Stenbeck was already involved in the mobile business through his company Millicom and through a joint venture with Racal, which later developed into Vodafone. On Swedish soil, Stenbeck's first move was to buy a small private operator, Företagstelefon, in order to turn it into a leading private operator. What attracted Stenbeck's interest was the fact that Företagstelefon, which operated a small regional network with transport companies as its main customers, had received a legally binding right to switch their calls into the fixed telecom network. With this right to public interconnection as its stepping stone, Stenbeck took steps to rapidly erect a nationwide mobile telecom network under the brand Comviq. To set up the initial mobile system, Stenbeck employed approximately twenty talented engineers (interviews with Håkan Ledin; Daniel Johannisson; Tony Hagström; Karlsson 1998).

Under the new competitive conditions, private entrepreneurs were moving to supply the emerging mobile telecom networks with key technologies. In all areas, system suppliers emerged. Of particular significance were companies such as Magnetics in radio base stations, and AGA-Sonab, Technophone, and Spectronic in portable mobile telephones (terminals). Both the private and the publicly owned operators profited from the technological radicalism that emerged in the unregulated subsector of Swedish telecommunications.

In response to this development within the private sector, Swedish Telecom's radio laboratory initiated development work under Östen Mäkitalo's legendary leadership. Sweden Telecom successfully initiated a joint Nordic effort to specify and set a standard for mobile telecommunications at the 450 MHz band. As the NMT 450 system was co-developed and recognized by the PTTs across the Nordic region, it constituted an important step toward global standards in mobile telephony (McKelvey, Texier, and Alm 1998; Mölleryd 1999).

Ericsson was surprisingly late entering into this game (Regnér 1999). It is true that its radio subsidiary, SRA, was among the early movers in many related radio technologies (police radio, military radio communications, and radio links) in the 1960s and early 1970s, but lack of technological sophistication in key areas such as radio base stations hampered SRA's market plans. Radio technology received only limited support from Ericsson's central management teams, which were concerned more with day-to-day operations and the core business of fixed systems than with new markets. As the first opportunities to sell mobile telecom systems in the international market emerged by the late 1970s, SRA successfully tapped into its parent company's main technology, digital switching. Although satisfactory to some of the initial customers, this combination was not judged as being advanced enough to meet the needs of more sophisticated buyers. The insight that Ericsson's subsidiary could not deliver entire systems that would meet market demands was the starting point for Ericsson's effort to gain control of the Swedish mobile telecom sector. Toward the end of the 1970s and the early 1980s, SRA took steps to vertically integrate the more advanced competitors, beginning with Sonab and Magnetics (Meurling and Jens 1994; Mölleryd 1999). A significant trend since the mid 1960s was the emergence of suppliers in mobile telecommunications. In fixed telecommunications, the quest for advanced services produced the same result. Swedish Telecom's strategy to meet international pressures to open the Swedish telecom sector to foreign competition involved a number of steps toward more advanced so-called value-added services. On the whole, these tendencies created opportunities for new suppliers to emerge.

In sum, Stenbeck's initial investments in Comviq's mobile network fed into the already established technology trend, further stimulating the growth of the still independent manufacturers such as Radiosystems.

Pocket of Competition #2: Data Communications Data communication is the other area where the lack of legal status of the Swedish monopoly created and allowed the emergence of private communication networks. By the late 1960s, the cost of data processing was still prohibitive for many firms, as well as many state agencies (Karlsson 1998). The private computer industry reacted by creating so-called data processing centers, to which firms could turn for outsourcing of the computer processing needs. Swedish Telecom identified the possibility of creating a public computer utility that could be networked over the telecommunication system.

For a few years in the late 1960s and early 1970s, this was clearly a priority within the public agency. But several obstacles were also identified. The main architects of the public utility proposal realized that the agency lacked skills and would have to rely on the private computer industry. In this situation, Swedish Telecom lacked the protection from a de jure monopoly, which possibly would result in fierce competition from other private firms. Therefore, key strategists in the public telecom authorities developed a plan aimed at forming a partnership with the computer industry and data processing centers. An increasing number of private networked data processing centers, relying on the telecom network for data communication, were established in the early 1970s. Actors such as Bull, IBM, and Honeywell offered data communication via modems. Others such as WM-Data built private communication networks between the user's facilities in and around Stockholm and the data processing centers. All in all, about 1,250 modems were installed by 1971, of which only a fraction operated at 2,400 baud. More common were baud rates around two hundred, but the speed of modems increased during the 1980s.

One should not overestimate the amount of data that actually was distributed via the telecom network to data processing centers. Neither should one focus too much on the offshoots of these activities in terms of domestic hardware and software production, because they were far more limited than in the case of mobile telecommunications. However, these findings reinforce the argument that the nature of Swedish regulation created pockets in which private entrepreneurs could establish and operate private communication networks.

The Take-off
The deregulation of Swedish telecommunications in the 1980s and the early 1990s stands out as a highly ambivalent affair. As we have already

noted above, the de facto monopoly allowed for pockets of competition. In particular, the absence of a legally based de jure monopoly made it possible for strong actors to emerge within the telecom sector. As may be predicted, it was precisely this kind of already established private actors that made the first major assaults. Together with organized business interests within the Swedish Employers Confederation, which already in the 1970s had formed a forum for communication policy, entrepreneurs with interests in operating companies started to exercise increased pressure on the Swedish government to remove the de facto monopoly in fixed telecommunication networks. Taking the lead in this battle, Stenbeck formulated the basic vision for a re-regulation of the Swedish telecom sector. In his assault on the Swedish de facto monopoly, he used his own operating company. Stenbeck aimed to restructure the telecommunications regulatory system in such a way that an independent network operator with no end customers could operate the public network. The idea was that all operating companies selling telecom and data communication services would have equal status as customers of the public network operator. Hence, in this vision, the Swedish PTT would not enjoy the benefit of controlling the last mile that connects homes and offices to the network. But the more narrow goal and immediate concern was to make Comviq's interconnect agreement, which was disputed by Sweden Telecom, permanent (interviews with Daniel Johannisson and Tony Hagström).

In response, the director general of Sweden Telecom, Mr. Tony Hagström, created an alliance drawing together a number of political and commercial interests with long-term and short-term interests in the de facto monopoly. Significantly, industry actors such as Ericsson and the Association of Mobile Telephone Equipment appeared in the media in support of de facto monopoly, arguing that the construction of a national mobile telecommunication network was only feasible under a natural monopoly situation (interview with Tony Hagström).

But this was mainly a way of buying time, preparing for the inevitable. Against the background of the antitrust case against AT&T, Sweden Telecom ordered an investigation of future value-added services enabled by technological advances in information technology (interview with Bertil Thorngren). In conjunction with the experience of rapidly advancing communication services that Sweden had experienced since the 1960s, this report reinforced the claim that it would be extremely hard for any

PTT to single-handedly create and operate such a wide range of services. When faced with the pressures for a radical break-up of the Swedish de facto monopoly, the director general initiated a series of moves preparing the public operator for increased competition, including the creation of separate companies for value-added services such as a telecom-linked alarm system, TeleLarm (interview with Tony Hagström).

Despite frequent measures aiming at undermining Stenbeck's position, the transformation of the Swedish telecom market was relatively smooth. In the mid 1980s, the Social Democrats, who were back in power began a search process that lead to a more open stance in these issues. Public investigations into the matter brought forward the view that competition was already a reality and that it was time to reconsider the defense of the de facto monopoly. It was against this background that the responsible government officials, such as the minister of transport and communication, as well as the director general of Sweden Telecom, Tony Hagström, voiced a new approach to infrastructure competition. In particular, Swedish Telecom launched a three-year program that proposed full competition in value-added service based on leased lines and the introduction of third-party traffic (Karlsson 1998).

The new telecom laws that finally codified privatization and deregulation were passed in the early 1990s. They soon resulted in what by international comparison stands out as one of the most competitive and advanced markets. Following the introduction of a new telecom regime, competition increased rapidly as new players gained access to the Swedish telecom market. In international calls, BT, AT&T, and Tele2 soon gained large market shares. In fixed national telephony, Stenbeck's Tele2 and Telenordia (BT and Telenor) were established as competitors to Swedish Telecom. Mobile telephony was dominated by Comviq, Europolitan (Vodafone), and Telia Mobile (Swedish Telecom).

In addition, a host of international firms emerged in advanced value-added services and data communication. Private networks, including BT, Tele2 (40 percent cable and wireless), GEIS, Tymnet, and IBM, were established in Sweden, reflecting the increased demand for international corporate communications (Hagström 1997). As the demand for corporate services soared under the new regulatory regime, large public actors such as Telia, Swedish Railways, and the Swedish Power Board initiated a rapid expansion of the national fiber optic grid. Also, in response to the development of national grid, local authorities started to build municipal networks that connected to the local access network owned by Telia (PTS 2000). Although the principal operator, Telia, does not publish detailed data on investments in fiber optic networks, informed observers estimate that the growth rate has been at least a hundred percent on a yearly basis throughout the 1990s (OECD 2001). Although the public actors are making investments in the nationwide data communication network, private operators in the Swedish telecom market, Tele2, NETnet, and WorldCom, have made only very limited investments. For the services offered by the private operators, they instead rely on the surplus capacity in public investments (PTS 2000).

Package Switching—From Leased Lines and X.25 to TCP/IP
The concept of Wide Area Networks (WANs) raised questions concerning robust data communication protocols that would allow cheap broadband connections and, more generally, the issue of the coordination of development of national and international data communication. European initiatives to standardize data communication involved formalized ex-ante standards set by government agencies and international standard defining organizations, such as CCITT (Comité Consultatif International Télégraphique et Téléphonique) or ITU (International Telecommunications Union). Established in 1983 by the International Organization for Standardization (CCITT), the Open System Integration (OSI) model divided network protocols (standardized procedures for exchanging information) into seven functional "layers." The layering provides a modularization of the protocols and hence of their implementations. Each layer is defined by the functions it relies upon from the next lower level and by the services it provides to the layer above. Open System Integration can be perceived as an umbrella under which the CCITT technical committees gradually developed new services, such as the X.25 protocol for package switching and X.400 for e-mail.

In early packet switching networks, such as X.25 protocol networks, data was "piggy-backed" on existing circuit switched networks, which limited throughput to 64,000 bps. These early networks performed extensive error checking at each switching node, which ensured very low error rates, but also precluded higher transmission rates. Despite the advances in package switching, many leased lines were built on circuit switching. In Sweden, for example, the DATEX network, a circuit switched network operated by the Swedish PTT, was long seen by the operator as the preferred solution. Compared to the Swedish X.25 network, DATEX had more customers and transferred more data communication across the network until the breakthrough of IP in the early 1990s (Närings- och Teknikutvecklingsverket 1993).

The Trickle-down of the TCP/IP Begins Compared to point-to-point protocols, TCP/IP has significantly stronger functions, particularly addressing/routing, which generates far more "talk" between nodes of the network. (For the development of the TCP/IP protocol, see chapters 1 and 3 in this volume.) Therefore, TCP/IP was seen as a powerful but costly solution. Although package switching is more efficient than closed circuits in general, the TCP/IP standards used in the Internet only gained popularity over other package switched protocols, such as X.25, as the bandwidth prices dropped significantly due to the development of fiber optics as a carrier of information.[2]

But more than sheer network economics slowed down the spread of TCP/IP networks. In particular, the European telecommunication scene was clearly dominated by a strong political effort to undermine the U.S. dominance in data communication technology. European governments and their telecom agencies sponsored alternative network protocols developed under the umbrella of the International Telecommunication Union. Open System Integration led to a number of data communication services, such as the unsuccessful X-400 protocol for e-mail. Because European policymakers strongly backed the X.25 related datacom services, there were political barriers against adoption of the IP-based services (Schmidt and Werle 1998). Although Sweden remained outside the European Union until 1995, the blocking effect of OSI was felt also in Sweden through Telia's longstanding collaboration with public telecom operators within European standardization bodies.

However, the tide was turning against these European efforts, as network operators were looking toward IP. As in many other countries, early Swedish IP-based networks were initiated and run by universities. The Royal Institute of Technology (KTH) was the pioneering force through its effort to implement IP network technology in the Swedish university system, SUNET. (The IP protocol also received pioneering support by Swedish Radio, the public broadcasting company.) Links were then built to bridge islands of university IP networks across the Nordic countries, NORDUNET. The Nordic network was later linked to the growing European university IP network through Ebone, a European IP backbone also involving private IP network operators outside academia (Närings- och Teknikutvecklingsverket 1993).

The successful development of an IP network required financial resources. Also, managers of KTH's network operating unit felt that there was an increasing demand for IP services outside the strictly academic world. But commercialization of the IP network required that the network be spun-off to an outside operator that could tap into private sector demand. Björn Ericsson of KTH turned to Telia and proposed that SUNET should be operated by Telia. But the public operator was by then deeply involved in the development X.25 and OSI. At best, Telia's strategists thought, IP could be seen as a step toward full implementation of OSI. Hence, the offer was rejected. Having been unable to convince Telia that IP was not just a short-lived transitional stage, Björn Eriksson initiated contacts with Jan Stenbeck, the owner of Telia's main challenger, Tele2. Stenbeck did not need much time. By accepting KTH's business proposal, Stenbeck jump-started the Swedish proliferation of Internet services outside the university sector. Stenbeck saw what Telia failed to realize: the university's infrastructure was an excellent stepping stone for any operator that wanted to offer IP solutions to the corporate sector and even to private households. Rather than Telia, it was Stenbeck who saw the potential of TCP/IP as an alternative to traditional leased lines and to the X.25 protocol stack (Lindström 2001; Söderlund 2001).

We should, however, note that there was no direct convergence. Rather, a mix of protocols came to typify Swedish data communications. In the end, as concluded by Hagström, "What constitutes a typical corporate communications network are elements drawn from all ... categories. Private leased lines, dial-up modems, common public package- and circuit-switched links, and value-added communication services more often than not coexist in a corporate data communication network" (Hagström 1991, 219).

Summary

The absence of formal regulations created space for new technologies, as well as entrepreneurs with big ambitions and some experience of the nascent value-added services. In this context, the new regulations meant that the Swedish telecom market exploded with new initiatives and investments. According to OECD, Sweden emerged as the most open and most contested telecom market both in terms of deregulated subsectors and number of competitors (Boyland and Nicoletti 2000; OECD 1996). The transition was so rapid because the ground was already well prepared. A case in point is, of course, the fact that Stenbeck's operating company was already in place when the opportunity to operate the Swedish IP network emerged.

The new conditions created a new type of network structure. Compared to the closed network structure typifying the traditional telecom monopoly, deregulation resulted in a disbundled network structure. Many of the benefits of such an infrastructure can only be realized if the means to transfer information and interconnect its parts is effective and reliable. To establish meaningful communication the system has to take connectivity to a higher order of *interoperability*. Because computers need to communicate, the computer industry has had to tackle network-to-network communications issues in a more complex way.

To describe the technological architecture of the Internet, the world of communication engineering relies on the so-called "layered functional model." This model enables engineers and companies to handle increasingly complex technology as a modular design. A modular system is composed of units (modules) that may be designed independently but still function as an integrated whole. The principal means of achieving network externalities and developing a common infrastructure is the adoption of "technical compatibility standards" that provide rules for interconnecting parts of the communication system.

This type of network structure is also referred to as an open or disbundled network. Our next point is that the disbundling of the Swedish telecom network opened the scene for entrepreneurial efforts on a far larger scale.

The Swedish Internet Economy in the 1990s

It is hard to imagine better preconditions for being an early adapter of the Internet than the ones existing in Sweden. The rational, modernist, pro-technology mentality of many Swedes led to early high penetration of computer systems and personal computers.[3] This in combination with the country being a long-time world leader in the number of telephone

Layer	Service	Typical Firm Types
4	*Application Layer:* E-mail, FTP, Web design, including online information for business or private use, software platforms for B2B and B2C e-commerce, etc.	Entrepreneurial software firms
3	*Navigation and Middleware Layer:* WWW browsers, electronic payment systems, WAP related applications, search engines	Entrepreneurial software firms
2	*Connectivity Layer:* Internet access, Web server parks	Primarily large firms due to sunk costs of network provision
1	*Network Layer:* trunk networks, fixed local access networks, radio networks, Ethernet LANs	Large, integrated network equipment manufacturers

Figure 4.2
The layered functional model of the Internet

lines per capita made the Internet immediately accessible to interested Swedes. Early deregulation in 1992, leading-edge competing telecom equipment companies such as Ericsson and Nokia, and sophisticated international telecom operators such as Telia, Tele2, and Europolitan have not hurt adoption rates.

The general picture, including widespread use and high-quality infrastructure, was built on accelerating IT investments. From lagging behind the average EU members and the United States in 1980, Sweden picked up steam in the early 1990s. Today, Sweden invests more in IT and telecom in relation to its GDP than any other nation—almost 8 percent (OECD 1999a). Larger parts of its GDP are invested in education, software, and R&D than in any other country, according to OECD. As a result, Sweden has become one of the world's most wired nations. The national digital mobile network is a particularly important part of Sweden's telecommunications infrastructure, and three Global System for Mobile Communication networks cover all of Scandinavia. More than 40 telecom operators, both Swedish and foreign, are active in the market.

Internet Penetration and Usage
The rates of Internet penetration, cellular penetration, and home-PC penetration are among the highest in the world. Mirroring the U.S. figures, almost 70 percent of the Swedish population has a PC with Internet

access at home, and over 60 percent own a cellular phone. The percentage of Swedish firms using Internet (93 percent), e-mail (94 percent), home pages (58 percent), and firms where more than three-quarters of the employees have a computer (47 percent) is consistently higher than for firms in the European Union. In the last five years, the share of the working population owning cellular phones has increased from 25 to 80 percent. Among young people (age 16–29), 90 percent own a cellular phone (International Data Corporation 2001; Statens Institut för Kommunikationsanalys 2001; TELDOK 2000).

The high levels of Internet penetration in the household sector is partly explained by the local entrepreneur Stenbeck's aggressive entry into this area. But the high levels were underpinned by public policies. As for increased diffusion of on-ramps to the Internet, the Swedish government's decision to heavily subsidize private personal computer ownership was a decisive factor. In particular, a chain of tax benefits, starting with firms and ending with employees, reduced the purchasing cost of PCs by some 50 percent. By 1998, about 20 percent of privately owned PCs were subsidized through the agreement (Statens Institut för Kommunikationsanalys 2001).

But the state was not the only one that developed schemes to increase the use of home PCs and the Internet penetration rate. To get more traffic through the network, Internet Service Providers initiated experimenting with the same tactics as previously used with great success in mobile ˙telephony: private sector hardware subsidies. By bundling the PC with an Internet subscription, ISPs such as Tele2 contributed to an even higher penetration of Internet-connected PCs in ordinary Swedes' homes.

Seven out of 10 Swedes have used the Internet, according to figures from the Swedish Bureau of Statistics. There are clear patterns as to the demography and work situation. Not surprisingly, the use of Internet decreases with age. Although over 90 percent of teenagers use the net, fewer than 50 percent of those 55–64 are surfing. As for work groups, over 90 percent of salaried employees in higher positions use the net, in comparison to 50 percent of the workers. The most frequent Internet users are men aged 30–49, moderately educated (high school plus), who live in a major city. Interestingly, Sweden's northern region and the capital Stockholm are in the fast lane, displaying technological optimism, high use of PCs, online surfing, and shopping (Forrester Group 1999). In the north, communication is important due to the large, sparsely populated landmass. The Internet is, for example, used for ordering and paying for goods from former mail-order companies. Auto parts, hand tools, and clothes are some examples of northern shopping needs catered for via the net.

In world rankings of the quality of the Swedish IT infrastructure, Sweden regularly occupies first or second place together with the United States, which implies that the Swedish citizens are enjoying the benefits of a particularly useful infrastructure (Sveriges Tekniska Attachéer 1999). So what do they do on the Internet? Looking at the total population, the Internet is used mainly for information gathering (62 percent of the total population), e-mail (60 percent), Internet banking (29 percent), purchasing of goods or services (29 percent), communication with the public sector, such as tax authorities (27 percent), and discussion or chat groups (15 percent) (TELDOK 2000). Let us briefly comment on the three categories less obvious than information gathering and e-mail.

In international comparison, the relatively early and rapid penetration of Internet banking in Swedish society is especially interesting (Berg 1999; Finansinspektionen 2000). In 2000, there were two million bank accounts using the Internet. Over 30 percent of all Swedish customers of the five largest private banks used the Internet for accessing their accounts. A public Swedish analyst unit in a recent survey found that the percentage of households paying their bills via Internet banking has jumped from 9 percent in 1998 to 29 percent in 2001. In the age group 25–45 years, the use of the Internet for financial services reached 40 percent in December 2000 (Finansinspektionen 2000; Statens Institut för Kommunikationsanalys 2001; TELDOK 2000). Bank offices are increasingly populated with elderly clients, which makes the service slower and turns away younger clients pressed for time. The latest possibility is to use your cellular phone for banking (including transfer to other banks' accounts), paying bills, trading securities, and analyses. In SEB, a leading Swedish bank, 50 percent of all private account transactions are made via the Internet. In the financial markets, more and more Swedes are conducting trade from home. By the end of 2000, almost half a million private customers used the Internet for trading stock and other financial instruments (Finansinspektionen 2000).

Using the Internet, banks try to solve retail-banking dilemmas such as dealing with unprofitable transaction-intensive clients. New product penetration and customer understanding is up, commission-based income is added, and profits are leveraged on a large customer base. A study by IBM and Interbrand concludes that three of the five best Internet banks (as determined by the range quality of services offered) in the world are Swedish.

Purchasing of Non-financial Goods and Services (B2C plus B2B) In the retailing sector, 5 percent of Sweden's shops sell via Internet, as do 13 percent of the department stores and 93 percent of the mail-order companies. The Swedish purchase pattern follows what is going on in other countries: the main products for purchase are music, books, computer software and hardware, clothes, and movies. Once again, Sweden's northern region and the capital Stockholm are in the fast lane, displaying technological optimism and Internet shopping.

As indicated in figure 4.3, the financial sector in the Swedish context stands out as a stronghold of B2C transactions. But it should also be noted that outside of this sector, the impact of e-commerce is still very limited. E-commerce revenues as a percentage of all revenues on a yearly basis in retailing is insignificant, but has gone from 0.7 percent to 1.8 percent over the period 1999–2001 (Svensk Handel 2001). For 2000, the turnover relating to e-commerce trade is less than US $25 per capita for B2C. In B2B, the turnover relating to e-commerce is less than US $15 per capita. Secondly, there is strong evidence that only a handful of retailers are depending on the Internet for their distribution. A recent investigation of the e-commerce sector shows that less than 0.5 percent of all firms that have Web sites with functions that support e-commerce depend on the Internet for more than 50 percent of revenues (Statens Institut för Kommunikationsanalys 2001).

First Deep Technology, Then Web Applications

Not since the early twentieth century have so many new companies been established in one Swedish industry in a limited time as in the Internet-related boom in the late 1990s. Currently some 950 Internet companies operate in Stockholm, more than in any other city outside the United States. In addition to the hot spot for new companies in Stockholm, cities

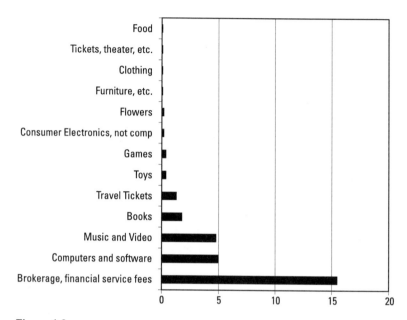

Figure 4.3
Internet sales in percent of total sales
Source: Statens Institut för Kommunikationsanalys 2001.

such as Gothenburg (home to the Chalmers Institute of Technology), Malmö/Lund, and Karlskrona/Ronneby host new Internet firms. However, if there is little evidence of a real breakthrough in e-commerce applications, there is more to be said about the predominance of deep technology as a defining aspect of the Swedish Internet economy. First, the IT sector's contribution to the Swedish economy has been relatively stable during the 1990s. The IT industry added value as share of GNP, for example, remained at levels around 3.0–3.5 percent between 1980 and 1996 (Söderström 2001).

At this point one might wonder to what *kind* of IT industry do these numbers refer? Is it hardware or software? Web consultants or complex data network technology? Is it relatively standardized and simple tasks or is it innovative and highly demanding tasks that require experienced system integrators and complex software modeling tasks? First, it should be pointed out Swedish IT, as compared to other European countries, has been characterized by a high degree of R&D intensity. Investments in

R&D have been significant. Together with a group of countries including Finland, Ireland, Greece, Italy, and Norway, Sweden scores high in terms of private R&D investments in IT as compared to all other R&D expenditures. Since the mid 1990s, Sweden has scored somewhat lower in relative terms (Söderström 2001).

A quick glance at the listings of the most important Swedish IT firms explains this pattern. Recent rankings of the firms constituting the Swedish IT sector (including software, hardware, IT consultants, multimedia, telecom and datacom equipment, telecom operators/ISP) show a complex layered structure with some large players at the bottom and hundreds of small firms in the higher layers.

In the basic layers we find Ericsson, Sweden's giant in infrastructure equipment manufacturing and Sweden's most important company in terms of employment, turnover, and exports. (For the distrubution of firms by subsector, see fig. 4.4.) In addition, there are a number of technology intensive suppliers of basic system integration solutions for this segment. In the next layer, we also find large telecom operators that are more and more dependent on Internet service providing and on data communications than the traditional core business, voice services. Just as

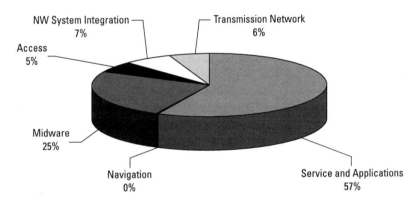

Figure 4.4
Distribution of Swedish Internet firms by sub-sector
Note: The distribution is based on a sample of firms with more than 10 employees, in total 407 joint stock companies. All in all, about 950 firms declare that they are active in Internet related technology or services.
Source: MarketManager; the analysis of the precise orientation of firms is based on the firm's mix of end-products as stated on the individual firms' Web sites (visited in June/July 2001).

important, but significantly smaller in terms of sales, turnover, employment, and revenues, are middleware firms that sell their services to Ericsson and the large operators/ISPs. The main function of the technology consultants is to implement sophisticated technologies relating to infrastructure, middleware, and corporate IT projects for large firms such as ABB. The large technology consultants, such as WM-Data, Tietoenator, and AU-Systems, are deeply rooted in the first wave of deregulations leading to demand for new communication technologies. Much smaller ones, such as Bluetail and E-Hand, are equally technologically capable but with a far more narrow focus in terms of products and services.

In the upper layers we find the Web integrators or Web consultants that provide basic technology for home pages and dot.com companies. In general, even the large Web consultancies, such as Icon MediaLab, have far more limited capacity than, say, middleware specialists. Their specialty is in creation of Web sites and they tend to migrate toward management consulting rather than the deep technologies. Hence, they often find themselves to be in an area typified by fierce competition because the technologies are fully standardized. Therefore, a large number of firms are marketing general e-commerce platforms that can be adapted to fit specific needs at relatively low cost. Costs, and to some extent brands, more than technology account for success in this business. Only a handful of Web integrators are successfully moving from the relatively simple tasks of constructing stand-alone Web sites to more demanding tasks. Infovention, for example, has successfully specialized in solutions for Internet banking, which involves the construction of complex middleware systems that integrate Web interfaces with the banks' computerized transaction systems.

Only above this level do we find the large Internet and Web consultants that are focused on creating Web applications and platforms for e-commerce solutions.

By the way of summary, there is something remarkably "complete" about the Swedish Internet economy. Although the large R&D intensive firms still remain stable players in the high-tech race, there has been a phenomenal growth in the higher strata of the layered functional model of the Internet. In the European setting, Sweden is a special case because it has players of relative importance not just in areas where it is relatively easy to enter, such as Web applications, but also where the U.S.-

Number of Start-ups

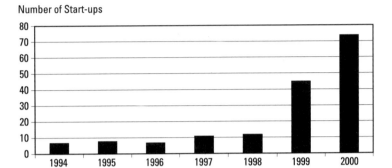

Figure 4.5
Number of start-up firms in the wireless sector
Source: Gustafsson 2000.

dominance is most well established by players such as Cisco, Microsoft,
IBM, and Compaq, in networks, sophisticated middleware, and on-ramp
technology.

... And Now a Focus on Wireless

As is often asserted by observers of the communications industry, the establishment of Ericsson as principal hub in the development of mobile
Internet technologies has attracted wider investments, resulting in a large
number of entrepreneurial start-up firms. But also already large, established firms have located "centers of excellence" of wireless solutions in
Stockholm. As indicated in figure 4.5, a remarkable number of firms have
been established since 1999.

A large chunk of these firms are trying to take the concept of portals
and e-commerce into the world of mobility and wireless Internet. Many
of these companies, at least judging from the financial performance as of
fall 2001, seem to have an uncertain future. Even the more successful
producers of wireless portals, WAP and SMS Solutions, have announced
major layoffs, as owners and financiers have become more careful. But
more interesting, and perhaps promising in a commercial sense, are the
technologically more sophisticated firms that develop middleware technologies. Middleware firms focusing on enterprise databases, such as E-
Hand, are using the WAP protocol to provide links between enterprise
databases and smart wireless phones. In other words, they work as

bridges between the enterprise software industry and the makers of advanced wireless terminals (Nokia Communicator, Palm VII, etc.). Even more sophisticated Internet solutions providers, such as Infovention and Entra, have targeted the financial sector with relatively standardized platforms for the development of Internet banking services. WirelessCar, a Volvo/Ford joint venture with Ericsson and Telia, has inaugurated a lab focused on wireless safety systems. This lab is closely linked to the research and development at Ford's two centers of excellence located in Sweden for safety technology and computerized electrical systems. General Motors is currently forming an alliance with Ericsson and Delphi, the world's dominating supplier of automobile components, to develop mobile Internet solutions.

Ericsson's strength in international standardization games is well documented (Funk 2002; Glimstedt 2001). The company was early in emancipating itself from the idea that standard wars should be fought according to national industrial policy agendas. By promoting global standards and marketing equipment based on non-Ericsson technology, such as AMPS and TACS, the company built a large customer base outside the "natural" Nordic camp. Moving away from national technological priorities helped Ericsson secure a central position in the GSM standardization process as the European Union tried to free it from parochial interests. In the marketplace, Ericsson's bet on global analog standards before GSM paid off in terms of securing a wide customer base of mobile operators using other analog standards than the Nordic NMT standard. It was precisely those operators that turned to their supplier of analog systems—Ericsson—as they were upgrading to the digital GSM standard.

The fact that Ericsson has become a key player in the development of mobile Internet solutions has certainly reinforced this aspect of the Swedish Internet economy. Leading foreign firms have established Swedish subsidiaries on their own or in cooperation. What is notable about these investments is that the large IT multinationals are not just setting up small outlets to monitor the development in Sweden—listening posts—but they are establishing themselves in a much more extensive way. IBM, Sun, Oracle, Intel, Compaq, Motorola, Nortel, and Microsoft hired 4,825 engineers to work in their respective Stockholm subsidiaries, focusing on wireless solutions. Oracle emerged on the Swedish scene as a partner to Telia and Ericsson as they co-developed added value services for GSM. Microsoft acquired a successful Swedish start-up company with strong technology for e-mail that promised rapid transfer into the wireless services. In 1998, Microsoft invested in a joint venture with Ericsson to co-develop applications that would link the wireless applications to Windows and the Office suite. Intel, IBM, and Sun have chosen a different path by establishing centers of excellence for the development of wireless technologies (Leijonhufvud 2001).

Judging from the size and number of firms operating in the Swedish Internet economy, disbundling of network elements has led to a new type of organizational solutions: small firms can enter into this industry because they can focus on narrow tasks. Even if they develop new network functions or even if they are just an improvement of a single aspect of the network, this improvement tends to leverage the functionality of the network as a whole. This, it seems to us, is undisputable. But it only raises another question: if the number of independent actor increases, how then is innovation coordinated across firms?

Enabling Institutions in Transformation

Sweden has historically experienced many cases of public technology procurement that have served the purpose of influencing technical development and contributing to the competitiveness of national firms (Edquist 2000). Well-known cases involved the creation of a public/private interface through so called "development pairs" based on joint R&D efforts by public agencies and large, export-oriented private firms. Examples of industries in which this happened are telecommunications, power generation, and communications. In successful cases, the creation of development pairs led to organized pools of competencies across organizational boundaries (Fridlund 1998a; Glete 1983).

The development pair as a mechanism for knowledge transfers between public institutions and the private corporate sector was closely associated with monopoly markets. Under deregulated market conditions, the telecom operators are assuming a much smaller share of the R&D costs. Given the transformation associated with the deregulation of the Swedish communication market, private industry and the university sector generally assume a larger share of the R&D costs, as a recent study by Martin Fransman (2002) reports. Although the Swedish governments—be they social democratic or liberal right wing—have long taken the view that basic research is key to economic gains derived from applied R&D, the most recent tendency indicates that this is even more so under deregulated market regimes. Since the mid 1980s, Sweden has had the highest R&D/GDP ratio of all OECD countries (Henrekson and Rosenberg 2000a).

The large volume of R&D raises, nevertheless, the issue of changing connections between public R&D and the private corporate sector. New mechanisms and organizational solutions are thus emerging to bridge public and private R&D efforts.

As in most other European countries, a number of additional mechanisms aimed at bridging university research and entrepreneurship in the private sector have been created. At least twenty science parks have been established to host small start-ups and R&D departments of large companies. Together these parks employ more than ten thousand engineers. The Swedish National Board for Industrial and Technical Development, NUTEK, has set up "broker institutions" that aim at helping university researchers commercialize their patents. The government has also been instrumental in developing legal and financial infrastructures aimed at facilitating exploitation of university R&D efforts, including granting university personnel full patent rights for their innovations.

A recent investigation of the effects of the most celebrated industrial park, Telecom City located in Karlskrona, in the southeast of Sweden, shows how government's top-down processes are connected to localized SME-programs. The government's re-location subsidies explain, at a first glance, why large-scale telecom and IT-related activities were transferred to Karlskrona. Additional decisions to create an IT-focused university college as part of the decentralization of the Swedish university systems were also part of the top-down process. Having received these resources, the local actors started programs to facilitate the creation and recruitment of new IT start-ups to the Telecom City project. After these resources had been moved to the region, start-ups focusing on mobile and Internet technology began to crop up (Engstrand 2002).

The success of these bridging institutions can be questioned. Little is known about the effect on technology transfer between firms and universities within regional parks. Our view is rather that the standardization process is a more deep and profound factor in technology coordination than sheer co-location of firms and institutions. This takes us into the area of standards and how larger firms direct smaller firms' R&D through stacks of interoperability protocols.

Open Interoperability Standards

The Internet is a "system product." Several products need to work together simultaneously to produce the desired output. The components of the system must be compatible with one another or, differently put, must be held together by a set of interoperability standards and system architectures. For firms, the strategic value of standards is increasing with the number of actors in an industry. "Network externalities" is thus an economic term that reflects the fact that the value of networks increases as the number of connected users increases. As more users adapt to the standard, that standard becomes increasingly attractive to others—and so on, in a way that can be described as a positive feedback loop. In cases where the network effects are not exhausted at a small scale relative to the market size, Paul David demonstrated in his landmark article on QWERTY typewriting that the market "tips" when a standard has gathered a critical mass of adherents (David 1985).

It should thus not come as a surprise that efforts to tip the market in favor of standards sponsored by leading Swedish actors, such as Ericsson in alliance with Nokia of Finland and Motorola of the United States, have been a prominent feature of the Internet economy. Some of these standards have been intensely contested. A case in point is the battle over interface standards for mobile Internet services, or the so-called "third generation" of mobile telephony, known as Universal Mobile Telecom Services in the European context[4] (Glimstedt 2001). UMTS covers only a single aspect of mobile Internet, namely the air interface that connects the handheld phone to the radio base station in the spectrum. On closer inspection, the mobile Internet initiative consists of a set of open standards that have been far less contested. Table 4.1 shows the key areas of standardization in wireless Internet services in which Ericsson, together with mainly Nokia and Motorola, figures as a main sponsor or co-sponsor of particular mobile Internet related standards.

Two different but interrelated sets of ideas underpin the development of open standards. First, traditional ways of creating and agreeing upon

Table 4.1
Service by Standardization Body and Type

Service	Standard	Comment
Radio Interface for wireless broadband services	W-CDMA	This is Ericsson's version of CDMA technology, which was adopted by ETSI in 1999 for UMTS. Europe's UMTS strategy is coordinated with other GSM-related standards within the global Third Generation Partner Program (3GPP).
Package switched and faster GSM, also kown as GSM 2.5.	GPRS + EDGE	Voluntary standards set by ETSI
MultiLayerSwitchingProtocol for integration of ATM and IP in mobile swirches	MLSP/ATM	Voluntary standards set by ATM Forum, MPLS Forum and adopted by IEFT. Co-sponsored by Cisco, Nortel, and Ericsson, among others, which have participated in joint interoperability tests.
Wireless LAN and WLAN	IEEE 802.11	Widely used voluntary industry standard sponsored by IEEE, adopted by Ericsson.
Short distance wireless connections	Bluetooth	Voluntary industry standard with Ericsson and Nokia as major sponsors and developers
Enhanced SMS, adds graphics and sound to the popular SMS standard	MMS	Sponsored by Ericsson and Nokia through 3GPP and WAP Forum
Wireless internet access via WAP browsers	WAP Forum	Voluntary industry standard sponsored and co-developed by Ericsson and Nokia with support of a large group of firms
OS for handheld communicators	Symbian	Open-but-owned OS standard developed by joint venture between Motorola, Psion, Ericsson, Nokia, and Panasonic.

telecommunication standards have proved too slow and cumbersome to be effective in a world in which technology changes at a fast rate. Second, it is a well-established fact that Europe's bodies that develop ex-ante standards (i.e., standards that are set before products are put to the market) suffer from being too late and being out of touch with end-user demand. The fate of OSI, which was unsuccessful compared to the TCP/IP protocol, is a particularly illuminating example of this. It shows, in particular, the dangers of creating standards in splendid isolation from end-users' preferences (Schmidt and Werle 1998).

As indicated in table 4.1, which lists the main technological standards involved in the convergence between Internet and mobile communications, there is movement toward small and focused standardization groups sponsored by several firms. These so-called standardization consortia's set publicly available specifications that are used as interoperability standards. A major implication of communication standards is that they make the thorny task of system integration relatively simple because the standards provide the developer with a clear interface and protocols for how functions should be implemented.

Take the recent version of the ATM technology (asynchronous transfer mode), also known as Multi Protocol Layer Switching (MPLS). This technology has become significant because it underpins a series of applications, ranging from fixed multi-service networks to next-generation radio base stations and mobile switches. Standardization consortia are heavily used to develop quickly new standards and get firms onboard the project.[5] In the case of ATM/MPLS, the private consortia (ATM Forum and MPLS Forum) developed standards that were coordinated with end-customer demands in the corporate LAN sector in order to ensure compatibility between end customers' preferences and the development of core network technology. Large-scale voluntary standardization bodies, such as the Internet Engineering Task Force, IETF, can later adopt these standards.

Network externalities are also generated through the creation of a growing community of producers of a particular technology. From a firm's perspective, the common adoption of a particular communication technology or a stack of communication protocols by a large number of firms tends to create a pool of skilled developers of that technology. In other words, open standards have become attractive because they allow many actors to improve technology at the level of the modules in parallel lines to the extent that the innovations improve the parts of the system and not the way that the parts are hooked up to each other.

To continue our ATM example here, the involved firms have arranged joint interoperability tests to demonstrate to the end customers that ATM-based products by Nortel, Ericsson, and Cisco are fully compatible with each other and that the components live up to the promises of differentiated quality-of-service across the whole network. So one aim behind the combined standardization and interoperability tests is to build markets for products that can be derived from the generic protocols. Another effect is that the standardization consortia enable the large firms to connect to the smaller but technologically sophisticated ones. In case of the ATM-related standardization processes, connections were built up between Ericsson, Cisco, and smaller firms such as General Data Communications, Mariposa, and ACC through the work within the standardization organizations. Later, these firms were acquired by Ericsson or gained position as first tier system suppliers of advanced routers and switches.

Seen from this perspective, the Internet economy is typified by both intense *inter*system competition and *intra*system competition. Open standards are critical to both forms because they (1) allow sponsors of new architectural designs to rapidly define new standards, and (2) facilitate the modular innovations that increase the number of innovative actors and the number of entry points for innovation.

These two forms of competition and collaboration are, in practice, indistinguishable. Take Symbian, the joint venture by the three major wireless phone manufacturers (Motorola, Nokia, and Ericsson, later joined by Panasonic and Sony) to leverage an operating system known as Epoch for use in future smart phones. This was popularly regarded as an "anti-Microsoft" strategy, as it was widely reported that Microsoft had been courting the manufacturers to use PocketPC (earlier Windows CE). Because the Epoch operating system was technologically superior to PocketPC (consuming less memory and having better real-time determinism), it provided the manufacturers with an alternative that made them stay independent of Microsoft, and let them keep control of the "smart phone" market.[6] Symbian opens new entry points for innovation. The main sponsors share the burden of improving the basic core of the operating system within Symbian's basic operations while the modular design facilitates adapting the OS it to firm-specific user interfaces. Thus Ericsson has to develop one user interface while Nokia is collaborating with Palm Computing to implement its popular interface on top of Epoch. Also, Symbian has become an attractive partner for a wider range of actors seeking to explore wireless technologies.

Similarly, an effort to create industry standards for mobile games has been linked to Symbian's operating system and related standards such as Wireless Application Protocol (WAP) and Multimedia Messaging Service (MMS) (interview with Bo Nordblom). Ericsson, Motorola, Nokia, and Siemens have launched the Mobile Games Interoperability Forum, paving the way for gaming on multiple servers and wireless networks. By fall 2001, about ten producers and publishers of digital games had joined this consortium. The MGI Forum aims to write global standards so that users can play games across different servers, on wireless networks, and on different mobile devices in the same way that Counterstrike is played across the Internet. This strategy calls for implementation at many levels of the mobile network: in dedicated game servers inside the networks, in network functions in Epoch, and in WAP browsers or in MMS. The main sponsors thus aim at providing other industry leaders and innovators, game developers, mobile operators, game service providers, and systems integrators with a platform that makes designing and launching mobile games simpler because the platform contains standardized routines for complex software design and programming tasks. The four companies define application programming interfaces (APIs) and a Software Development Kit (SDK), developing certification procedures to ensure wide acceptance of the standard and providing recommendations to ensure an open environment for developing mobile games.

Standardization of Software Tools within Local Developer Environments As we have seen above, network externalities are generated through the creation of a growing community of users for a particular technology. From an employer's perspective, the common adoption of a particular communication technology or a stack of communication protocol by a large number of firms tends to create a pool of skilled software designers and programmers in the use of that technology. In other words, common technological standards are a way of solving the problem of technological coordination across firms.

From the perspective of software development, major actors such as Ericsson have adopted the use of standardized tool kits that are well established in the local environments that embed the development units. Instead of their old in-house proprietary software languages, such as PLEX and Erlang, Ericsson is aiming to use open industry standards such as Unified Modeling Language (UML) in combination with object oriented languages such as Java and C++ in the new platforms (interview with Hans Brolin).

The decision by Swedish firms to use UML has a lot to do with the reported productivity increases that users of formal UML modeling have experienced, but there is also the recruitment question. One might ask rhetorically what developer in his or her right mind would develop software expertise in languages that are not used outside Ericsson. The decision to stop using PLEX had a clear bearing on making Ericsson an attractive employer for ambitious programmers (interview with Hans Broström).

There are equally strong incentives for relatively small firms to use the same kind of high-level software language. Even E-Hand, a 25-programmer software house specializing in middleware for wireless connections between SAP databases and handheld devices, is implementing UML in order to prepare for rapid scaling up and increased complexity in software tasks (interviews with Eric Boman and Viktor Kotnik).

UML has become a standard for large-scale software projects in the Swedish telecom and data communication sector, serving as a widely understood language spoken by most programmers. This common language makes it possible for programmers to help each other independently. In light of this, it should be noted that software development tools vendors (such as Telelogic and Rational) with more than 60 percent of the Swedish market for software tools in the telecom sector have experienced a soaring demand for UML-based modeling methods (Svensson 2000).

Privatization of the Standardization Process and the Relaxed Competition Law

Collaboration within private standardization bodies facilitates collaboration in the market. But are standard consortia really different from cartels? Fundamental to the technological exchange between the private firms is, for example, an emerging private regime for exchange and distribution of revenues from intellectual property rights or patents. In the case of mobile Internet services, the world's leading wireless companies have completed the definition of what is known as the *3G Patent Platform* (UMTS Intellectual Property Association 2001). This arrangement provides a system for evaluating, certifying, and licensing "essential" 3G patents. The platform specifies the maximum amount of royalties per product category to be paid by any licensee. Patent fees are to be collected and distributed through a system in which the last manufacturer in the value chain constitutes the collection point so that all formerly involved activities that result in the product are covered.

One would think that this type of combined arrangement would raise the eyebrows of, say, Ms. Ann-Christin Nykvist, the vigorous director general the Swedish Competition Authority, or her European counterparts. All this organized technological collaboration between groups of firms, including the IPR platform described above, has only been possible under the relaxed antitrust legislation in Europe and in the United States (Jorde and Teece 1992). On a strict legal interpretation of antitrust regulations in both the United States and in Europe, sharing technical information between firms is similar to sharing pricing and other types of essential market information. Recent case law permits sharing technical information in connection with standardization processes without interference from antitrust enforcement since the late 1980s. In the United States, the passing of the National Cooperative Research and Production Act in 1993 made it safer for firms to relocate standardization from formal standardization bodies to private consortia (Tate 2001).

The core of the more recent thinking in European and U.S. antitrust law is that it, in modular technologies, construes the firm's and the standardization consortia's problems as being related to long-term innovation rather than to short-term profits. To work properly, complex modular technologies require collaboration between suppliers and users of the various components. In Europe, the commission has allowed the possibility of exemption under Article 81(3), which regulates information sharing. In both cases, information sharing is seen as crucial in network markets, which may ultimately benefit consumers (Seabright and Halliday 2001; Toth 1996).

Open standards allow intrasystem competition, which is consistent with variety through recombinations of modules rather than through competition between different systems. In other words, the existence of private standardization consortia is tolerated by recent competition policy because the modular systems provide more entry points for innovation. A variety of design and organizational alternatives become available to end customers on this assumption. What needs to be watched most carefully by antitrust authorities, in this perspective, is how patents with a broad scope (e.g., covering more than one module) can create barriers to this experimentalism.

Venture Capital

Of course, standards and disbundling alone are not sufficient for the creation of start-ups; finance is also needed. To a considerable extent, Sweden has followed the U.S. model in developing a venture capital market to invest in entrepreneurs.

At a limited scale, venture capital has been available in Sweden since the early 1980s. Limitations applied not only to volume but also to direction of funds—the emerging Swedish VC industry first and foremost aimed at already existing business firms. Few financial resources were supplied to the establishment of new firms or in the first critical phase of expansion in firms' development (Isaksson 1999). The public sector has, within the framework of regional policy, tried to offset the lack of private venture capital by introducing numerous support schemes. In 1998, there were more than 140 such schemes. There is no coordination of the different schemes, and the net effect is far from clear. Bold regional projects, however, proved unsuccessful and the failure of the so-called Uddevalla Package effectively cooled off both the state's and regional authority's interest in regional development programs (Landell 1998; Landström 1993).

The tide has, however, turned in terms of availability of finance. As in the United States, the emergence of small Internet companies is closely related to a particular transformation of the financial sector, the emergence of independent venture capital firms. Swedish venture capital investment between 1995 and 1999 showed an approximately 200 percent annual average growth (Isaksson 1999; Karaömerlioglu and Jacobsson 2000).

In February 2000, there were some two hundred venture capital firms in Sweden, of which 40 were foreign-owned. These firms together man-

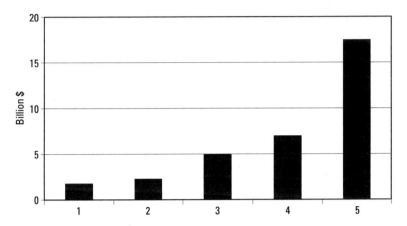

Figure 4.6
Available venture capital
Source: Swedish Venture Capital Association 2000.

age funds of $18 billion, to be invested over the next three to seven years. By January 2001, the amount had jumped to $25 billion (see fig. 4.6).

A very large number of the firms that focus on IT, Internet, and wireless were founded within a few years in the late 1990s. In 2000, they provided almost $2.5 billion to some five hundred Swedish IT projects. In 1999, around $1 billion were invested in 335 projects.

As indicated in figure 4.7, our estimations show that the high-tech subsectors—middleware and networking technologies—received 42 percent of the investments, whereas application oriented firms that dominate in terms of the number of firms received 58 percent of the invested venture capital.

Specialized VCs, such as BrainHeart Ventures, which raised $200 million, and Ericsson Ventures with $290 million, have focused all investments on the wireless Internet business, building on the expertise in third generation mobile telephony. BrainHeart's CEO, Ulf Jonströmmer, left his position as CEO of the leading telecom and networking technology consultancy (AU Systems) to invest in and help develop wireless Internet start-ups.

Although VC firms function as focused investors in IT, they rely principally on three types of sources for the available VC funds: institutional

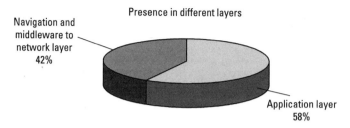

Figure 4.7
Distribution of invested funds
Source: Swedish Venture Capital Association 2000.

investors (49 percent of the invested capital), private placement (41 percent), mother companies (5 percent), and others (5 percent). Initially, however, the existing Swedish venture capitalists were very cautious and did not take high risks. Their security portfolios included blue-chip companies and the expected returns were 15–25 percent over 10 years. Around 65 percent of the capital was traditionally invested when the business concept and management team already functioned. In 1992, only 10 of these old-style cautious private venture capital firms worked with technology endeavors.

Among the new American-style actors were business angels, senior entrepreneurs (often former CEOs of large companies), new venture capitalists, and foreign capital interests. There are thus today two types of Swedish venture capital companies. One consists of newly formed firms focusing on IT and the Internet from the very start. A small team with entrepreneurial background manages the typical venture capital company of this type. The average company is capitalized by the owners' private funds combined with institutional investors' funds. During the last year, mutual funds, funds managers, and insurance companies have also supplied around $10 billion. The other is a group of older, established investment companies and venture capital companies with a recent interest in the Internet and biotechnology. The old industrialist spheres, including the traditional financial families, are represented in this group.

Venture Capital and the Point of Exit   Generally, venture capital investments are based on exit points, the moment when the VC firm sells off its equity in a particular firm to reap profits from the investment. This ties the venture capital closely to the stock market, which provides the venture capital firms an institutionalized solution to the problem of exits. For Sweden as elsewhere, we thus note that the number of initial public offerings (IPOs) has been fueled by stock market expectations. For example, the Swedish AFGX index for IT and telecommunication stocks reveals the nature of the boom. Information Technology and Internet stocks soared from the level of roughly 300 points to the 800 level in 1999 alone. Telecommunication stock displayed an even more spectacular boom, going from the 350 level to 1,500 points between February 1999 and February 2000.

Between 1996 and 2000, the number of IT and telecom stocks on the OM Stockholm Stock Exchange increased tenfold. In 2000 alone, there were about 35 initial public offerings by IT and telecom-related companies, a new record high. Of the total of 311 companies listed on the OM Stockholm Stock Exchange at the end of 2000, 95 were IT and telecom companies, some 30 percent of the market's total value. This made OM Stockholm Stock Exchange one of Europe's leading markets for technology stocks, and a viable alternative to listing on NASDAQ or other exchanges.

Venture Capital and Competency Orchestration One of the most vital functions of the VC industry in the United States has been the combination of financial services and strategic advice, although the sheer number of ventures supported in recent years clearly limits the venture capital firms' ability to monitor each venture (Kenney and Florida 2001). Investigations of the Swedish VC industry reveal a skill shortage. Compared to their US counterparts, for example, the Swedish VC firms have less management and technology expertise. Isaksson (1999) shows that only about 20 percent of the firms that have received VC investment have also received significant inputs in terms of strategic advice, networks, and recruitment of key personnel.

At the level of boards, we note that interlocking directorates is of increasing importance. A recent study shows that at least 30 percent of Swedish Internet firms are linked through interlocking directorates. Although the bulk of these firms are parts of small networks with only two or three nodes, there are examples of larger networks involving 10–20 firms (White and Coronado 2000).

In particular, the institutionalized family ownership in Swedish business has resulted in strong ties between financial actors, leading IT firms, and main users of IT solutions. Investor, the Wallenberg family's main holding company, has strong ties to Ericsson, WM Data, and to a host of smaller IT firms through Investor's interlocks with venture capital firms (Adams-Ray and Sandberg 2001). In this regard, we note that the historical financial institutions have remained actors in investing in Internet-related businesses.

On the content side, Sweden's dominant private publishing group, Bonnier, is interlocked directly to Internet consultants, software producers, and to other Internet media actors. Another hub, Icon MediaLab, also has a large set of direct interlocking directorates that ensure direct information flows from firm to firm. Other actors, such as RamsinCoMedia, are less impressive in numbers of direct links but hold positions as mediators between larger networks (White and Coronado 2000).

Conclusion: Convergence or Cross-fertilization?

Many analysts suggest that entrepreneurial activity ushers in venture capital-backed high-tech industries; newly financed companies compete with and then overturn the established firms. It is also widely believed that the Internet economy is closely associated with a particular organizational model, involving (1) decentralized innovation in networked production networks, (2) high-risk oriented venture capital firms, and (3) high-powered personal incentive structures. In particular, the Silicon Valley model is a societal machinery that rapidly produces start-up companies, aiming at commercialization of new technologies quickly in a highly flexible labor market (see Kenney in this volume, chapter 3). Proponents of this view are suggesting that because venture capital has overcome the liquidity and incentive dilemmas that traditionally have limited the small firm's level of innovative activity, the rise of venture capital will be associated with systematic pro-competitive consequences. Ultimately, small-firm financing is accelerating the "gale of creative destruction" (Christensen 1997; Forster 1986). Many analysts seem to agree, at least until recently, that the Swedish Internet economy needs to adapt to this pattern.

The interesting question is to what extent the coming of the Internet economy in Sweden has been associated with international pressures to converge with Silicon Valley, and to what extent it has evolved historically as a series of selective adaptations from within? In assessing this issue, we have looked at two main themes: stability and change (actors and institutional transformation), and hybridization (patterns of cross-fertilization between old and new elements).

Stability and Change

A core argument has been that the historical roots of the disbundling of the Swedish telecom network were not a result of convergence pressures; change did not assume the character of a punctuated equilibrium. Rather, "change through diversity within" seems to be a more accurate thematic description. Swedish regulatory style allowed pockets of competition in which new services, new technologies, and new challengers grew into serious conflicts between regulators and private actors. Sweden's telecommunications system was already a hybrid at the outset.

As we compare the realities of the more bundled network of the 1960s and 1970s with the disbundled network of present days, we are hence struck by the degree of cumulative developments. An essential feature of the developments within Sweden's information and communication technology sector is the continued co-existence of new and old elements. Although balance between old and new elements may shift over time, it is still true that the old organizations, such as Ericsson and Telia that formed the core of the old network, still remain key players. What is new, however, is the intensified exchange between small and large firms under disbundled network structures. Rather than introducing new organizational forms, the Swedish Internet economy stands out because it makes far more intensive use of the organizational opportunities available to firms.

Hybridization

The sheer intensity in the exchange between small and large established firms needs to be understood in terms of a set of underlying problems. These arise in connection with established forms for preservation of firm-specific skills in large organizations and the need for destruction of these skills as new disruptive technologies come into the large organizations from the small firms. The introduction of new technologies in disbundled systems has been conceived as closely related to horizontal specialization that is facilitated by standardization; firms are specializing in a subset of technologies without actually having to tackle the more complex task of mastering all technologies that make up the network structure. Disbundled networks are often associated with emergence of small- or medium-sized business organizations that make efforts to commercialize new IT innovations.

We have certainly mentioned venture capital supporting start-ups and different approaches to coordinating innovation, such as virtual communities and standardization of software tools, facilitating cooperation between horizontal specialists. These are elements that we associate with Silicon Valley. But unlike the Silicon Valley start-up machinery, Sweden's Internet economy is associated with *reinforcement* of incumbent market power. Although the emergence of TCP/IP was heralded as a force of creative destruction, market leadership has remained constant.

We can explain this pattern by two factors. First, innovative start-ups are often closely coordinated with the large incumbent, Ericsson, through collaborative standardization consortia. This collaboration allows for a high rate of innovativeness by start-ups alongside stability in the product market. A second explanation for this pattern is that the Internet, or the TCP/IP protocol to be more precise, is less dominant than often assumed. It should be remembered that the network structure still contains some elements that are relatively stable over time. Older and newer protocols are moreover often mutually dependent, as demonstrated by the discussion of MPLS ("IP over ATM"). Under these circumstances, it is not surprising that incumbents such as Ericsson, with their expertise in network architecture and large-scale system integration, remain significant market forces.

In other words, the unusual strength of the Swedish Internet economy has been its ability to operate at several points in the overall system: from infrastructure, to modular innovations, to software, and to commercial business models. This wide diversity, for a country with about a fifth of the population of California, is a remarkable achievement. It suggests that large national systems can migrate to new institutional settings when the critical players, namely the government and the established firms, carve a future for themselves in this new economic order. They were not passive observers, or victims, but active participants in their roles of providing the resources and the regulatory frameworks to exploit the innovative potential in a disbundled network. But the ultimate source of this diversity was the entrepreneurial pockets of competition that gave the impetus to a radical institutional change, based upon an evolving technological progress. It is these two elements, disbundled networks and entrepreneurial pockets of competition, that explain the Swedish transformation from a corporatist to an innovative economy.

Acknowledgments

In writing this essay, we are indebted to a number of friends and colleagues. Much was initially gained from the close interactions within the so-called Kråkmarö Group at the Institute of International Business. We have also profited from discussions with the participants of the Global Internet Economy Project. We especially thank Mr. Håkan Ledin for financial support and access to his vast personal network in the world of communications. But that was not Håkan's main contribution to this project. Above all, we have gained immensely from his inspired visions of the effects of technological dynamism within the communication business.

Notes

1. Economic institutions within Germany, Japan, and some Scandinavian countries have more regulative and "organized" characteristics that, although conducive to many successful innovation strategies within established industries, seem to hinder the creation of technology start-ups (see Casper et al. 1999). Deep patterns of vocational training within firms, consensual decisionmaking norms, long-term employment, and patient finance are all linked to the systematic exploitation of established technologies to a wide variety of niche markets, a strategy Streeck (1992), focusing on Germany, labels "diversified quality production." By contrast, the more regulative nature economic institutions combined with pervasive non-market patterns of coordination within the economy create constraints against the organization of industries that best perform within shorter-term, market based patterns of industrial organization (Soskice 1997).

2. We thank Axel Fromell pointing this out to us.

3. The majority of surveyed Swedes believe that IT creates new jobs and that most people (young and old) want to adapt it. Only 10 percent were scared by the development, although 20 percent felt that the development is too fast to follow.

4. In sum, Europe's bold strategy for 3G services—UMTS—was perceived in negative terms by leading American firms, such as Qualcomm, as well as trade strategists in the US Congress. It was Ericsson's and Nokia's move to punch through its version of so-called spread spectrum air interface standards (W-CDMA) that irked the Americans, who insisted that the ITU should adopt a approach that allowed a family of interoperable standards. At this point, the original champion of CDMA technology, Qualcomm, threatened to block the international standardization process through aggressive protection of its vast intellectual property rights in CDMA. The United States positioned weakened as Motorola, the holder of the majority of the essential GSM patents, and the US GSM operators joined forces with the European 3G effort. United States GSM operators also cut a deal with US TDMA operators, agreeing to make TDMA and GSM compatible. Qualcomm was thus isolated. The Europeans, on the other hand, became troubled by Qualcomm's success in the Asian markets. China's sudden interventions as the Chinese authorities hinted they would consider Qualcomm's technology if the United States were to adopt a positive stance toward China in the upcoming WTO-negotiations. These developments constituted the backdrop to the deal between Ericsson and Qualcomm in March 1999, which resulted in (1) extensive cross-licensing of patents, (2) Ericsson's acquisition of Qualcomm's network manufacturing operations in United States, and (3) an agreement on how CDMA and W-CDMA should constitute the core of a family of interoperable 3G standards backed by the ITU. According to congressional sources, Trans-Atlantic Business Dialogue, a private industry forum for coordination of European and US business interests, provided the venue for the final rounds of negotiations between the parties.

5. The following draws on Glimstedt 2001.

6. Although the independence of Microsoft is routinely questioned by analysts (Shosteck 1999), the selection of an independent browser (Opera) for Symbian's reference products indicates the parties' ambition to remain outside Microsoft's control.

5

Technological National Learning: From Minitel to Internet

Pierre-Jean Benghozi and Christian Licoppe

In France, the development of the Internet has been influenced by the evolution of the inherited information technology. France had the institutional elements needed for the Internet to flourish: excellent engineering schools, participation of scientists and academic researchers in data networks, financial markets with venture capital companies, a supportive government, and high incomes. Thus, France had many of the components that constitute the American, or even the Silicon Valley, model. And yet, the Internet economy did not begin until some years after it did in the United States, Sweden, and the United Kingdom. Many have argued that the monopoly of France Telecom slowed the Internet's development in France. In this chapter, we shall show that it was instead France's early lead in electronic commerce that hindered this development.

The Internet is the most recent phase of a movement to rationalize and computerize communication. This movement began in the 1960s and has entailed increasingly sophisticated iterations of information and communication technologies (ICT). This incremental revolution makes it hard to characterize Internet usage today, as the technological base underlying the Internet is not limited only to the latest generations of technology. The various waves of ICT did not simply follow each other; rather, their effect was cumulative and many different layers of technology still coexist. These successive layers have influenced current forms of organization and communication. Over time, these choices have defined a technological base and determined organizational structures and specific areas of competence.

Information technologies cannot therefore be considered independently and separately from one another. Technologies function in clusters as parts of diverse technical applications. They require systems that combine defined infrastructure capabilities and autonomous technical applications. They are also embedded in configurations and operational procedures that imply specific organizational forms. Consumer and business demand for ICT rests on declared needs that are poorly defined in terms of the technologies required, their possible uses, and their functional characteristics. Users are confronted with complex needs that can be met only by combinations of services and technologies. There is a trade-off level between the various technologies and the types of services they support. Functionalities overlap each other, and a single technology can be used to fulfill a variety of functions.

Prior experience with computerization often makes it possible to better prepare, facilitate, and structure the integration of past and recent technological generations. The Minitel, which was launched in the 1980s, encouraged the emergence of a computerized communications sector. More than 17 million people regularly use 25,000 Minitel services, which range from secure access to bank accounts, electronic commerce, and online payment systems (including reservation of train or cinema tickets) to communications forums and information searches.

We hypothesize that although the French Minitel slowed the emergence of the Internet, it gave space to what we call a national learning. This learning can be seen at the level of economic actors, public groups, and users, which together compose a national system of innovation. Such a national learning explains why the Internet emerged later in France than it did in other countries, yet emerged at a comparatively higher growth rate. We will develop this thesis using evidence primarily from e-commerce rather than from the global Internet economy because few data are available about the latter. The first part of the chapter presents the status of the Internet in France and some details about its development. The second part analyzes what lessons we can draw from the Minitel experience.

National Differences Exist

The French Delay
France developed early and noticeable initiatives regarding the Internet. They were for the most part supported by administrative bodies and

aimed at technical development or academic and research support. One can mention, in particular, the *Cyclades* computer network launched in 1972, inspired by the ARPA project and run by the P&T administration for general purpose. Another case of such early initiatives is the national Internet network for academics and research, Renater, developed on researchers' initiative and putting an immediate, powerful, and up-to-date Internet infrastructure at the disposal of French academics. Nevertheless, academic literature, public reports, and comments from economic players frequently evoke the "French delay" in developing the Internet. Relative to other European countries and Canada, the penetration rate for PCs and Internet connections in France has long been low. As pointed out by Rallet (2001), in 1998, there were only five hundred French retail Web sites open to the public that had on-line sales capabilities, which is 2 percent of the worldwide total and less than 8 percent of the European total. These outlets' combined sales were only €0.2 billion ($180 million) in 1998, which was only one-seventh the amount that the Minitel took in during the same period. In 2000, two years later, e-commerce sales were estimated at €6.098 billion ($5.49 million) for B2B[1] and, according to sources, within a range from €380–€900 million ($342–$810 million) in B2C.[2]

The low B2C figure is partly the outcome of competition with Minitel, as discussed below. It is interesting to note that the estimates vary by source; our estimates reflect the assessment of the French government. The €380 million corresponds approximately to 0.14 percent of total retail trade in France. As a comparison, the total amount of mail order trade is €8 billion ($7.2 billion), including electronic and telephone selling. Total B2C online sales in France may be estimated at around €1.660 billion ($1.49 billion): Internet e-commerce (€670 million [$603 million] —the average of the above estimates), the e-commerce sales through Minitel (€550 million [$495 million]), and €440 million ($396 million) corresponding to "Minitel kiosque" payback made by France Telecom and indirectly remunerating information and services providers.

In recent years, however, there has been a noticeable sense of urgency relating to Internet use and computerization in France. Since 1999, France has begun to catch up with its European partners: that year, the Internet in France grew 60 percent, compared with an average growth of 41 percent in other European Union nations. According to figures published by Jupiter MMXI Europe, France had nearly 8 million home

Internet users as of February 2001. This penetration represents a growth rate of 16 percent from the end of 2000. During this same period, growth in home-based Internet usage was 5 percent in Germany and 6 percent in Great Britain. Despite the stagnant growth level, growth of households online was 14.1 percent in France (vs. 9.3 percent in Great Britain and 5.6 percent in Germany) from January to June 2001, according to Net-Value. This sustained growth rate has made France one of the largest European markets for the Internet, though still lagging. In 2000, 14 percent of French citizens used the Internet. For Germany and Sweden, the degree of penetration was 29 percent and 46 percent in 2000 (see table 14.1). It is important to keep this lower penetration of the Internet in perspective of the overall behavior of the French consumer. Less than 10 percent of French citizens regularly purchase national daily newspapers and only a few percent see films regularly.[3] The French exception sometimes rests on the exceptional behavior of a minority of its citizens.

This same pattern of an initial delay followed by increased growth also occurred in the business world. Although only 28 percent of industrial concerns were connected to the Internet in 1997, the number rose to 69 percent in 1999. Table 5.1 shows that among these firms large corporations, for obvious reasons (readily available means and expertise, information systems needs, and business-to-business relations), were the forerunners, with three-quarters of them already connected to the Internet in 1997 and 97 percent currently connected. It is probably even more interesting, however, to observe the situation within smaller companies. Eighty-eight percent of companies with 100–249 employees are now connected, which is twice the rate of 1999. For small companies (20–49 employees), the rate has tripled, reaching nearly 60 percent. This phenomenon can be seen in all industrial sectors, especially the "traditional"

Table 5.1
Internet Connection in Relation to Company Size (in percentage of companies)

	Overall	20–49 employees	50–99 employees	100–249 employees	250–499 employees	500 or more employees
1997	28.2	19.2	28.7	41.4	61.5	75.4
1999	68.7	58.5	76.7	88.3	93.3	97.3

Sources: SESSI 1997; SESSI 1999.

sectors, which were not widely computerized until recently. In fact, as tables 5.2 and 5.3 show, the number of companies in the machine, textile, metalworking, wood/paper, and clothing/leather sectors has grown quickly.

French Industry and Services in ICT

In the French ICT sector, industry and services are of comparable economic significance, despite the fact that services comprise 53 percent of total sales and 57 percent of jobs in this sector (see table 5.4).[4] In 1998, ICT industrial businesses realized overall total sales of €56 billion ($50.4 billion), whereas ICT services had €61 billion ($54.9 billion) in sales. The industrial sector employs approximately 270,000 people (as many as the automobile sector does); the service sector employs approximately 400,000. Jobs in the latter sector require a much higher skill level than do

Table 5.2
The Spread of the Internet 1997–1999

	Internet connection (in percentage of company size)	
	1997	1999
Apparel and leather industries	13.6	49.6
Mineral product industries	21.5	53.2
Wood and paper industries	18.2	59.6
Metals processing and metalworking	18.8	60.5
Textile industries	21.9	64.3
Shipbuilding, aircraft, and railroad equipment	40.8	67.4
Automobile manufacturing	31.3	69.4
Mechanical engineering products	23.7	69.9
Home appliances, furniture, and other durables	28.9	72.8
Chemicals, rubber, and plastics	34.5	74.5
Printing, publishing, and reproduction	38.9	78.1
Pharmaceuticals, fragrances, and cleaning products	53.9	80.0
Electrical and electronic components	45.2	89.7
Electrical and electronic equipment	61.3	91.2
All industrial sectors	28.2	68.7

Sources: SESSI 1997; SESSI 1999.

Table 5.3
Industrial Companies and the Internet

In % of companies	Internet connection	Website	Online ordering capability	Intranet network	Extranet network
Large companies	97.7	70.5	13.6	79.1	37.2
Small- and medium-sized industries	67.6	38.1	8.9	19.3	8.6
High technology	85.6	51.5	9.2	36.5	16.8
Low technology	64.3	36.2	8.9	17.4	7.8
Export ratio >25 percent	83	52.4	10.2	33.4	16.7
Export ratio <25 percent	64	35	8.6	17.3	7.3
Subsidiaries of groups	82.1	47.9	9.5	38.4	15.8
Incl. foreign groups	*85.7*	*46.3*	*9.8*	*6.5*	*20*
Independents	59.2	33.3	8.6	9.5	5.3
Innovative companies	80.5	49.6	11.1	28.6	13.2
Incl. Product innovation	*81.6*	*51.1*	*11.3*	*29.5*	*13.5*
Non-innovative companies	58.7	30.5	7.3	15.2	6.6

Source: SESSI 1999.

jobs in the industry as a whole. Executives have 32 percent of these jobs, workers have 31 percent, and intermediary professions (i.e., technicians and first-line supervisors) have 2 percent.

The ICT sector in France covers four areas. Two of these areas are information technology and telecommunications, including both industry and services. The third field, electronics, is specifically industrial, and the last, the audiovisual sector, is essentially service-oriented. Table 5.4 shows that among ICT services, telecommunication services predominate in terms of sales revenue (47 percent) and jobs (48 percent). The sector of information technology services has 34 percent of total revenue and 41 percent of the jobs; the audiovisual sector has 19 percent of total revenue and 11 percent of the jobs. In the telecommunications sector, services are particularly predominant, with total sales of €29 billion ($26.1 billion) (as compared with €20 billion [$18 billion] in industry) and 190,000 people employed, or more than twice as many as in industry. In the information technology sector, services (e.g., software, data processing, and maintenance) also predominate, with total revenue of €21 billion ($18.9 billion) in 1998, as compared with €14 billion ($12.6 billion) for industry.

Along with this spectacular development in the service sector, ICT is providing other sectors of the French economy with new growth opportunities. Indeed, the development of this sector consists of the massive production of items that are used by most sectors of the French economy. It is not surprising that the information and communication technology sector contributes to the overall productivity of the economy, as outlined in the first chapter of this book.

France is the eighth largest exporter of ICT products in the world, an average performance. Yet the results are particularly noteworthy in the telecommunications industry, which is one of the strongest areas of French manufacturing and French international trade. This sector has been very successful in the last few years (table 5.5), and its contribution to the trade balance of France with other countries is considerable: more than €5 billion ($4.5 billion), even as trade, particularly with the United States and Japan, has increased significantly, despite the worldwide downturn in the Internet economy. The French telecommunications industry is relatively concentrated: 18 large companies (those with more than 500 employees) represent 9 percent of the total number of companies in the sector, but employ 81 percent of workers, realize 90 percent of total sales and 95 percent of exports, and account for 91 percent of investments in equipment. The export propensity (exports/total sales) is 55.8 percent in these companies, whereas it remains lower than 20 percent for small- and medium-sized enterprises (SMEs, having fewer than 500 employees). Conversely, small companies with fewer than 20 employees only produce 4 percent of the total sales for the ICT sector, as compared with 8 percent for the manufacturing sector as a whole.

Until the year 2000, growth in the world market for telecommunications equipment was supported by growth in equipment and services for mobile networks. It was also stimulated by data transmission and networking. The European market, for its part, was rapidly expanding because of fewer constraints on competition, which resulted in a proliferation of infrastructures and the democratization of the mobile phone. Because of its late start, the average annual growth rate of the French market is, at 42 percent, higher than that of most other European and worldwide markets.

In France, the mobile terminals segment is now the largest, but French industry is also well positioned in the communications equipment seg-

Table 5.4
TIC: Industry or Services

Industry = more than 20 employees Services = more than 30 employees or 4.5 M	Computers		Telecommunications	
	Industry	Services	Industry	Services
Companies	59	1379	258	120
Employees	41,877	161,920	92,560	189,729
Turnover excl. taxes	12,426 M	20,464 M	18,410 M	28,474 M
Exportation rate	44%	8%	46%	5%
Value-added rate	28%	56%	29%	60%
Investment rate	8%	15%	10%	29%
Profitability	−2%	5%	35%	54%
Profit margin	26%	27%	17%	51%

Source: SESSI 2000.

ment because the growth of the market for mobiles required infrastructure equipment. This market includes interface equipment (modems, repeaters, multiplexers, and amplifiers) and is profiting from the development of the Internet and from the proliferation of transmission media (fiber optics in particular). The telecommunications techniques that were once reserved for academics and defense are spreading rapidly. This expansion explains why French companies are increasing their sales, particularly their exports. Production outlets are located primarily, but not exclusively, among the European partners (table 5.6). The deregulation of telecommunications services in the European Union, which went into effect on January 1, 1998, and the proliferation of television channels and radio stations, have fuelled the business equipment market. Moreover, emerging countries, such as South Africa, Mexico, and Central and Eastern European nations, are becoming choice market outlets as they modernize their infrastructures and develop their telecommunications networks. As a result, the telecommunications field has the largest share of the French trade surplus.

The telecommunications sector in France is dominated by four large groups: Alcatel (one of the world leaders in consumer telephony, along with the Scandinavian companies Nokia and Ericsson), Thomson, Matra

	Electronics Industry	Media Services	Total ITC Industry	Services
Companies	874	352	1191	1841
Employees	138,106	40,541	272,543	392,190
Turnover excl. taxes	23,900 M	11,779 M	54,736 M	60,717 M
Exportation rate	47%	7%	46%	6%
Value-added rate	29%	47%	29%	56%
Investment rate	13%	11%	11%	21%
Profitability	−5%	1%	9%	29%
Profit margin	18%	54%	20%	43%

Table 5.5
Exports in the Telecommunications Industry

	Companies	Employees	Turnover (excl. taxes)	Export rate
1990	200	69,903	7.24 B	16.5%
1991	196	62,578	7.77 B	19.5%
1992	205	58,113	7.46 B	23.7%
1993	174	53,111	7.62 B	26.2%
1994	189	54,840	8.77 B	30.8%
1995	221	62,881	10.28 B	30.1%
1996	208	69,222	11.31 B	32.4%
1997	208	69,689	12.31 B	40.2%
1998	203	75,357	15.62 B	47.2%

Source: SESSI 2000.

Table 5.6
Exporting French Telecommunications: Europe First

Most important export destinations	Sales (1999)
U.K.	13%
Germany	11%
Netherlands	7%
Spain	6%
Italy	5%
Total worldwide exports	€6.6 M

Source: SESSI 2000.

(oriented more toward business communications and defense), and Sagem. In order to fund the high level of investment required for development in this sector (these firms allot €1.4 billion [$1.26 billion] per year to R&D), companies must achieve critical mass. Substantial levels of corporate integration are occurring at both the national and worldwide levels. Firms are forging alliances in order to exploit a technology and quickly achieve low costs or to penetrate a promising market segment. Alcatel thus made up for its late start in the consumer mobile telephony segment by negotiating license exchange agreements with Motorola; it also bought Newbridge, a Canadian company, to strengthen its position in high-bandwidth transmission in North America. To ensure progress in R&D, telecommunications firms are now among the largest French employers of management-level staff: because the capacity for innovation is key to corporate development, these companies are hiring increasing numbers of engineers, researchers, and other highly qualified workers.

Companies are also streamlining their production by not performing certain activities or by increasing their use of subcontracting. Alcatel, for example, which is a non-specialized company, is liquidating certain activities such as cables and components, standardizing its production, and subcontracting its lower value-added activities (e.g., the manufacture of its mobile terminals, which have become consumer electronics products), thereby reducing the number of its factories. This subcontracting trend favors small- and medium-sized enterprises specializing in equipment assembly or installation. Relative to their larger counterparts, SMEs have less-skilled personnel, do less research, and are less profitable.

Table 5.7
Concentration in Computer Industries

	0–19 employees	Portion of computer industry
Companies	295	82.9%
Employees	1,484	4.2%
Turnover (excl. taxes)	197 M	1.7%
Investments	3 M	1.1%
Export rate	5.5%	0.2%

Source: SESSI 2000.

The situation in the information technology sector is slightly different: it includes activities in which both manufacturing and services co-exist. French production is oriented toward complex products, such as large IT systems intended for large corporations, even though French firms also manufacture a significant number of personal computers. This sector is very concentrated (table 5.7). Although companies with fewer than 20 employees account for 82.9 percent of the businesses in this sector, they employ only 4.2 percent of the total number of employees and mainly assemble and install personal computers and perform wiring and maintenance functions. Because of corporate restructuring,[5] concentration is high and few firms dominate this sector: subsidiaries of two American firms (IBM and Hewlett-Packard) and the French company, Bull. Faced with competition from abroad for standard products, especially from Asia, firms in this sector are refocusing their activities on three key sectors: software production, technology services, and sales. They have also formed partnerships. After six software manufacturing companies were acquired in 1998, IBM entered into joint ventures with Dell, Bull joined forces with Microsoft, and Siemens teamed up with the Japanese company, Fujitsu.

Firms in this sector invest 15.7 percent of added value in R&D, a rate that is double of the average of other French industries. For the same reason, the employment structure in this sector is distinct from most other French industries: most personnel are executive staff or researchers. Workers represent barely 10 percent of personnel, as compared with almost 50 percent in other industries.

The French components sector is also expanding rapidly. This growth can be explained in part by the vitality of the telephone market and by the development of embedded electronics in the automobile sector. French manufacturers, which are the leading players in the field of smart (microprocessor) cards, have also profited greatly from the development of this market and are eager to broaden the field of applications into electronic commerce, management, and secure access. This passive component sector is made up, for the most part, of SMEs, which are responsible for nearly 50 percent of total sales, although they account for only 20 percent of sales in the active component sector. This industry is labor-intensive (20.7 percent of unskilled workers), which is characteristic of sectors in which there is a significant amount of subcontracting. Conversely, industrial groups predominate in the active component sector, in which employees are highly skilled and large investments are required to fit out semiconductor plants.

A Recurrent Development Model
When it comes to new technologies, the pattern of development we have described is part of a long French tradition. France perceives itself as a world leader in terms of technology, however, and the perception of a delay, whether accurate or not, has always stirred public opinion and motivated those in positions of power to promote new technologies and develop catch-up strategies by organizing projects, visits, and business trips for industrialists and decisionmakers to the United States. The same trends occurred during the 1960s when continuous production techniques and enterprise information techniques were developed, during the 1970s and 1980s, when automated manufacturing was developed and the success of the Japanese industrial model was touted, and during the 1990s, when information technologies were developed.

Within this fairly general framework, the new economy has some special characteristics. In fact, there are several possible reasons why the French experience is unique.

The Evolution of the Entrepreneurial Spirit in France
Until the 1980s, "the company," especially the small- or medium-sized company, was not viewed as important in France. There were several origins of this perspective: inertia in the higher levels of the civil service,

the mercantilist tradition (handed down from Louis XIV's minister Colbert in the seventeenth century), and the high regard for public activity, especially as part of the post–World War II efforts led by the state to make France into an industrial and technological leader. Conversely, the end of the 1990s saw increased emphasis of the entrepreneurial spirit, particularly regarding the new economy. This shift induced changes in how the French government intervened in the economy and fostered the emergence of financing structures (such as venture capital and innovation aid) that had previously encountered a great deal of opposition.

The entrepreneurial tradition in France is weak, despite public officials' regular attempts to shore it up by supporting small- and medium-sized industries, innovation, business start-ups, and so on. Several factors have exacerbated this paradox in its current form:

• sector idiosyncrasies and growth that occurs too rapidly for public bodies to react

• a greater emphasis on deregulation, which requires new tools for public action

• growing liberalization of the telecommunication sector.

These new conditions focus intervention on modernizing administrative procedures and support activities (promotion, training, and information) rather than on traditionally "French" forms of industrial policy (Cohen 1992).

The emergence of the Internet has fostered the proliferation of new initiatives. About 250 start-ups were financed in 1999, and more than eight thousand new companies have been formed annually in the ICT and telecom sectors (table 5.8). Most of these firms sell telecommunication services and data processing. The average annual growth rate of telecommunication services since 1996 has been 85 percent, and this sector has been stimulated by deregulation. In computer service activities, the average annual growth rate has been only 6 percent. Nonetheless, new firms have capitalized on opportunities associated with data processing, information systems, the transition to the Euro, and Y2K compliance. The financial and economic evolution these firms brought about (e.g., new capital investment, IPOs, and innovation in capital investment and venture capital) has resulted in structural changes to entrepreneurship in more traditional industries.

Table 5.8
Newly Created Firms

	1996	1997	1998	1999
Technology suppliers (computers, infrastructure ...)	339	345	299	286
Services and technology users (retail, telecommunications services, software ...)	5,386	5,652	6,312	6,681
Multimedia services (radio, TV, media ...)	1,082	1,068	1,007	1,160
Total ITC firms	6,807	7,065	7,618	8,127
Total of newly created firms in France	171,628	166,850	166,191	169,674

Source: SESSI 2000.

The Availability and Importance of Means of Financing and Capitalization These developments have also led to increasingly sophisticated forms of financing and capitalization for new firms. There is more segmentation and hierarchy among forms of financing: new financial intermediaries, friends and family, venture capital, and investment funds. Firms such as the Bernard Arnault Group, Dassault, Andersen Consulting, and Accenture have funds designed to secure a foothold on the Internet or guard their traditional markets. Audiovisual and telecom companies (Vivendi, France Telecom, and Sagem) are anxious to sell their services to new, innovative enterprises. Banking organizations, insurance companies, and the new financial service providers (Morgan, Rothschild Finance, Lazard-Axa, Galileo, and ABN Amro), along with "opportunistic" investors, small investors, and mutual funds are eager to take advantage of strong growth opportunities. As a result, available funds (€ billion, ±15 percent, in 1999) for investment capital increased sharply. In 1999, venture capital funds (42) invested nearly €6.2 million ($5.58 million), on average, for an overall total of €427 million ($389.3 million) (up 64 percent from 1998) in Internet firms. Venture capital firms that previously focused on innovation (Sofinnova, Innovacom, CDC Innovation, and Axa Innovation) were among the most active investors. There were, however, comparatively few IPOs: only about thirty initial public offerings occurred in 1999, and the number of listed companies was only 113 at the end of 1999. The recent stock market crisis has further reduced the number of IPOs. Clearly, French firms have preferred other forms of financing to IPOs.

In contrast, large and medium-sized existing companies that were expanding onto the Internet (platforms, websites, intranets, web portals, etc.) generally used equity capital to finance these activities. The private nature of these investments and the lack of available data about them make it difficult to assess the extent to which self-financing was used. This phenomenon is probably related to the relatively important role played very early on by business-to-business exchanges in Europe, compared to the United States, according to a study published by ActivMedia in 2000. Although nearly half the websites in North America and the Asia-Pacific region cater to consumers, only one in four European sites and one in three sites in other countries do. Half of European websites are B2B, as are just over a third of North American sites, one in four Asia-Pacific sites, and nearly one in three sites in other parts of the world.

The Role of National Characteristics in the Development of the Internet The global convergence of communications and networking protocols has not prevented national differences in how consumers use the Internet. This divergence is influenced by national cultural traditions. Not all types of content are directly transferable from one means of communication to another, and the culture of each country affects how this content is adapted, assimilated, and adopted. Accordingly, IT penetration rates and usage patterns (i.e., professional/private use, preferred services, and how recently users were connected) differ from country to country (see table 5.9).

In France, language has also probably hindered the entry of the larger American sites. In most other countries, including even other European nations, large international sites generate the most Internet traffic (Nielsen Netratings 2001). In France, however, most sites with the highest rates of traffic are national sites. This trend holds both for general interest sites, such as search engines or access portals, as well as for more specialized sites such as travel services and online auction sites, for which national enterprises were able to establish niches early because they were among the first on the scene. In several instances, foreign participants (e.g., American, English, and German firms) established a presence in France only by acquiring these successful national forerunners.

Table 5.9
Examples of Internet Usage Distribution Data

	France	Great Britain	Germany	United States
Web	97.3%	97.2%	96.2%	97.9%
Mail	64.9%	58.1%	51.1%	37.5%
Audio-Video	12.6%	12.1%	11.3%	4.0%
Forums (news)	8.0%	8.7%	5.9%	1.3%
Online discussion (chat)	10.2%	5.4%	4.6%	1.2%
Household connection times				
Less than 6 months	30.1%	27.1%	27.4%	16%
6 months to 1 year	17.2%	18.3%	13.8%	10%
Greater than 1 year	52.7%	54.8%	58.8%	74%

Source: NetValue 1999.

France Telecom Had Been Able to Adapt Itself

Despite privatizing fairly late as compared with other operators (e.g., in England, Scandinavia, or Germany), France Telecom established a strong presence on the Internet. Wanadoo, its service provider subsidiary, is the most frequently visited French domain, with a 55 percent penetration rate and 4.5 million single visitors (a million more than its closest runner-up). There are a number of possible explanations for its success: its ability to establish a strategic position and anticipate the transition to a competitive market (in terms of pricing, full-scale development campaigns, spin-offs or division into subsidiaries of certain activities, and negotiations with labor organizations), a considerable degree of integration of networks and services, a good public image, unique expertise in research and development, and financial capacity.

France Telecom was the prime example of the strong past presence of the state, and was characteristic of an engineering and professional culture coupled with a technical and research-based sense of legitimacy. The company underwent its first break-up in the 1980s, marking its evolution toward a private firm and the revision of its corporate raison d'être to a focus on customer service. By favoring new entrants under the guise of the deregulation of telecoms and mobile phone providers, the French regulatory association indirectly caused France Telecom to become more sales-oriented as it anticipated changes in its competitive environment,

Table 5.10
Number of European Users in 1998 (millions)

	Number of users (millions)	Percentage of population
Germany	4.3	5.1
U.K.	4.1	6.6
Sweden	1.4	15.6
France	1.2	2.1
Norway	0.9	20.5
Netherlands	0.8	5.1
Finland	0.7	13.7
Spain	0.6	1.5

Source: eStats 1999.

notably with regard to the Internet. This cultural transformation, carried out via a series of reforms, was brutal in many ways. Moreover, as we will see in the second section, the technical skills that were built and the experience that was gained through developing the Minitel created an expertise and knowledge of networks that could be quickly mobilized for later Internet developments.

Monopoly and Barriers to Entry   We see in several chapters of this book that access to the telecommunication infrastructure is a critical factor influencing the expansion of the Internet. The Swedish study points to the importance of "pockets of competition" that were able to play the role of a Trojan horse, allowing for competitive access to the infrastructure. Deregulation was fundamental to the United States, United Kingdom, and eventually Japanese and Korean cases. What has been the case in France?

The standard thesis emphasizes that France Telecom's former monopoly status slowed the development of Internet networks and services in France (Bomsel and Leblanc 2000). Our qualitative studies show that entrepreneurs that were to launch Internet businesses became aware of these opportunities as recently as 1996–1998. In France at the time, the number of Internet users as a percentage of total population was lagging behind most European countries (table 5.10), and the number of Internet hosts per 100 inhabitants was lagging even more (table 5.11). Before

Pierre-Jean Benghozi and Christian Licoppe

Table 5.11
PCs per 100 Inhabitants (1993–1997)

	1993	1994	1995	1996	1997
France	10	12	13	18	20
Germany	13	14	17	24	26
Great Britain	13	15	19	25	27
U.S.	27	30	33	48	49

Source: Konert 1999.

Table 5.12
Internet Hosts per 100 Inhabitants in Western Europe and the United States, January 1998

Country	Hosts per 100 inhabitants
Denmark	3.1
Finland	8.8
France	0.6
Germany	1.2
Greece	0.3
Italy	0.4
Netherlands	2.4
Norway	6.6
Spain	0.4
Sweden	3.6
U.K.	1.7
U.S.	7.8

Source: Konert 1999.

arguing for a French delay based on the Telco monopoly, it must be noted that France was also lagging (though less) in PC penetration rates in homes, which rose from 10 percent in 1993 to 20 percent in 1997, compared to the case of Germany, for which it rose from 13 percent to 26 percent. The latter figure provides a constraint to the development of the Internet audience in France, which is largely independent of monopolistic tendencies in telecommunication policies (table 5.12). The issue is better discussed if one looks at R&D and firm policies at the same time.

Several plausible arguments support the thesis of the retarding effects of a monopolistic and state-owned telecommunications carrier. On the technical side, France Telecom's R&D labs were still promoting ATM protocols over Internet protocols for data packet transmission well into the 1990s. On the managerial side, most of French Telecom's managers were engineers who belonged to the elite administrative corps that composed the top ranks of French administration. Also, the multiplicity of career bridges through the top levels of the French public service ensured strong couplings and influence networks for France Telecom within the French state, and provided it with the political clout to affect decisions relevant to its interests.

France Telecom also wished to preserve the profits it derived from both the Minitel and its telecommunication services. As a monopoly, it was able to charge high prices for landline phone calls. These prices have probably slowed the penetration of the Internet in France. Studies of lead domestic Internet users experimenting with ADSL access in 1998 showed that most of them were very cost-sensitive, and that they wished to have flat rate billing.[6]

Commuted access is likely to remain the dominant form of connection for the next few years, as high-speed networks (cable, ADSL) are diffusing slowly. Today, there are two different economic and technical models for commuted access. For a direct interconnection, the user is invoiced by France Telecom. For an indirect interconnection, the user is invoiced by a telecom supplier, by an access provider, or by France Telecom. The service provider charges either a flat rate fee or a fee that is based on the time the user is connected. As competition has increased during the last two years, suppliers have developed sophisticated pricing offers. Some in France have explained that it is difficult to implement and provide unlimited commuted access to the Internet so long as Internet penetration and connection level remain low in France. Although a few suppliers tried to offer unlimited commuted access, they had to suspend these offers after a few months because their own connection costs, which still depended on the number of user connections and the time that users stayed online, increased. Moreover, these providers had technical problems because their equipment could not handle the new subscribers' high demand. Several operators and access suppliers pressured the national authority regulator to require France Telecom to supply a global interconnection for a flat rate so that they could provide unlimited access and still make money. (See the discussion in chapter 12 on the legal challenges by MCI in the United Kingdom.)

We believe, however, that France Telecom's monopoly status provides only a partial explanation for the delays we have described. In the mid 1990s, French civil servants and entrepreneurs were blind to the possibilities prevented by the Internet. The three main public reports of the time scarcely mention the Internet (the Thery report on information superhighways, the Breton report on teleservices, and the AFTEL report on the future of telematics). It is possible that the interests of the Minitel service providers were aligned with those of France Telecom because of the peculiarities of the Minitel billing system (the *kiosque multimedia*): consumers paid for using the Minitel services through their phone bills, and France Telecom gave back part of that money to the service providers. Yet according to consulting and engineering firms trying to sell Web sites to French firms in 1995, officials from the public sector were utterly unaware of the existence of the Internet and of the potential of Web services.[7] That situation began to change from 1996 to 1998 due to several initiatives, which included state reports and private sector efforts that targeted France's need to catch up with the United States in developing web-based services. Examples include the Yolin report, which stressed that small French firms were lagging in developing advanced Internet services, and the Lorentz report on e-commerce, appearing in 1997 and 1998, respectively. Among private sector efforts, one needs to mention the "Atelier de la Compagnie Bancaire," under the aegis of Jean Michel Billaut, self-proclaimed French guru of the Web, who enlightened prospective French electronic entrepreneurs about the latest trends in Web experiences. We believe that this ignorance of the Internet in France was largely a by-product of the tight bonds that linked influential individuals from the public and private sector into a collective network.

Moreover, arguments that highlight monopolistic effects conceal the deep transition that occurred in the 1990s in France Telecom. The same men who had been civil servants within the French telecommunication administration quickly became the staunchest defendants of the private sector over a few months in the mid 1990s. Various kinds of hybrid organizational forms supported that move. First, although France Telecom did not have private sector contracts, it was largely separate from the civil service (this separation was legal so long as the state remained the absolute majority shareholder in France Telecom). France Telecom thus spanned the public and the private sector. Beginning in the late 1990s, France Telecom also began developing subsidiaries (the latest of which is the Orange group) in France and abroad that had private sector contracts. In some of these subsidiaries, such as the Internet access oriented Wanadoo, a distinct ethos emerged among the founders that combined elements pertaining both to the spirit of start-ups and the practices of the larger structure. Such evolution led to the development of new hybrid career paths for key actors.

Second, the coexistence of public and private interests relied on some interfering practices, such as the accounting procedures for this growing halo of firms around France Telecom. Also, R&D outputs have been gradually defined, with much fanfare, to emphasize marketing and services development that is helping to unite the large R&D force and the marketing organization. The rhetoric of services became pervasive in the late 1990s, in part replacing, in part supplementing a more traditional focus on networks and infrastructures.

To put it provocatively, it is essential not to reduce the French trajectory to the negative effects of the state and the interplay of public sector and monopolistic practices. It is instead important to understand how the complex networks that supported a mostly public organization until the mid 1990s could evolve into a mostly private one in the early 2000s, and how the former public and monopolistic system that today's market advocates are so keen to criticize could also be construed positively as a resource for negotiating a complex transformation within a very risky international context.

Organizational Learning Takes Place for the Various Actors
In short, we argue that a detailed analysis favors an explanation focusing on the systemic elements of the so-called French delay than one based on a thesis of administrative or monopolistic inertia. It is important to take into account, on the one hand, the Internet's late takeoff and its ensuing rapid growth rate, and, on the other hand, low penetration statistics that still reflect the initial time-lag and usage figures that show the diversity of situations and modes of appropriation, which are sometimes very intense for certain activities. The development of the Internet sheds light on a specific developmental mode for technology and related economic forms,

one that operates continually, even as exchanges are being displaced and transformed, without being leveled-out by technology. This specific form of development and adaptation is central to the interpretations that are suggested by the learning experiences and successive waves of technological change outlined here. We will illustrate this point by describing the importance of the Minitel to the French experience. In France, the Minitel is still very relevant for operators and firms, particularly actors already present in distant retail, new entrants, operators, technology suppliers and services suppliers, and final users.

From the Minitel to the Internet

Establishing a Chronology
As we pointed out in the introduction, the attempt to characterize Internet usage today and to place such usage in historical perspective is difficult because it is impossible to define precisely the systems and technologies in question. This usage depends on a modular technical base that combines various infrastructure components, autonomous applications, implicit organizational forms embedded in the technical configurations, and diverse procedures for use. Establishing even a simplified chronology of the transition from more basic forms of telecommunications (telematics) to the Internet perfectly illustrates the overlapping phenomenon of the various technological layers. It is thus particularly difficult to distinguish which developments stem from the creation of networks (beginning with packet switching), servers, protocols (from Videotex to HTML), and terminals (from the dedicated Minitel to the individual computer and the net box) from both the services provided and the related management and billing methods (e.g., the invention of kiosk-type billing services and subscriptions). Terms such as "Minitel" are inherently ambiguous because they lump together all these elements. We will attempt to be precise in our discussion below, focusing on services and usage.

Without trying to isolate one single event, the origin of Minitel data communications (telematics) can be dated to the 1970s. As with the Internet in France, this origin involved a late start that had to be overcome. At the time, observers believed this delay was related to both the level of installed telephone equipment and the relatively undeveloped state of the French computer industry. The Minitel project was undertaken to address both issues: it let the industrialists and the telecommunications authorities further their efforts to update the French telephone system, and allowed these efforts to be oriented toward computer technologies.[8]

There were several important technical trends and milestones in the Minitel's development. The core service was designed around a national electronic directory, provided at the expense of the operator; the planned method of consultation was based on a moderately priced dedicated terminal, which was supplied free of charge to all users in order to encourage its use. The service was also open to other applications. After an initial period of hostility from traditional media outlets that were wary of possible competition from this new information medium, the DGT (the Telecommunications Branch) was able to unite and to enter into numerous partnerships with private operators (the press, media, service, and information base providers). The Minitel was deployed gradually and relied heavily on local experimentation; electronic messaging and forums constituted (along with the electronic directory) "killer applications" that strongly stimulated connections and the supply of new services.

Initially, the Minitel was economically viable because of its technical and service product offering. Its development rapidly leveled off, however, and was subsequently revived only by initiatives that focused on the organization of payments and on the remuneration of the various service providers. It was, in fact, the kiosk billing mode—invented by the DGT—that was responsible for the take off in the use of services by the general public. The kiosk offered a unique form of fee-for-service billing directly debited from the telephone account, with France Telecom being responsible for subsequently reimbursing their tolling revenues to the service providers. This system replaced the traditional telephone billing system based on call distance, which was not well suited to online services; it was also quite different from the subscription arrangements offered by some service providers, which met with little success because they required users to accumulate several subscriptions in order to access all the services they wished to use. The kiosk's success was astounding. As a means for accessing an increasingly diversified base of services and

customers caused the billing system to evolve from a single billing system
in the beginning to a differentiated "step variable" system instituted in
1986.

Although the plan was initially limited to the Minitel, it was soon
extended to certain telephone numbers (Audiotel). In this way, the DGT
inaugurated a new era of telecommunication services by stimulating
the provision of content, thanks to a new partnership model between
the telecommunications administration and a diversified base of content
providers that differed radically from the strictly monopolistic models. It
offered content providers a profitable and simple economic model, which
continues to be nostalgically evoked today, even by Internet participants.
We should add that because network development and the supply of
terminals was largely, if not exclusively, a state-subsidized venture, the
Minitel reached its break-even point only in the mid 1990s. As a state-
subsidized venture, the Minitel reached its break-even point only in the
mid 1990s.

Although the 1980s were the key years for the Minitel venture, the
"information superhighway" rhetoric did not flourish until the 1990s,
when the telecommunications sector was opened up to competition in
France. The key word was digital convergence, and the belief was that
wideband networks would make it possible, with the digitizing and interoperability of services, to support an almost infinite range of applications. During this period, France Telecom, the successor to the DGT
within the framework of deregulation, deployed long-term R&D initiatives to expand on the Minitel's success and to develop new value-added
telecommunications media. At this time, the integrated services digital
network (ISDN) was set up and the first electronic messaging services
(using the X.400 standard), electronic-mail services (Teletex) and an
enriched facsimile system were launched. The Internet will eventually
displace all of these services with platforms that integrate all forms of
mediation around networks.

The success of the Minitel and the resultant attempts to expand its
reach probably explain why the Internet was not viewed as important. It
was alluded to only very belatedly, and only once in a public report (the
Théry report in 1994), and then only to harshly criticize its lack of a
simple billing system and its overly open and cooperative nature, which
was thought unlikely to encourage the development of commercial ser-

vices. Far from the perspective of open interconnection and distributed innovation that characterized the Internet and the web as they were developed in the United States, the Breton report (1994) continued to advocate that the service offering should be adjusted to usage via large-scale experimentation, based on the Minitel model.

Most actors assumed future telecommunications would continue along the lines of the Minitel experience. In this shared vision of the world, the perspectives and strategic challenges of the various economic operators seemed to converge. It is not surprising that France Telecom would be wary of embracing the Internet. It wished to preserve present and expected gains from Minitel that had finally reached its break-even point after paying off the heavy investments required to develop it. It should be noted, however, that the service providers had just as many reservations: they worried about rushing headlong into a new system and preferred to preserve the hard-won gains they had obtained by constructing this large public market. France Telecom expressed these concerns through the intermediary of Aftel, their professional association.

As a consequence, both the number of Minitel terminals and yearly consultation times have decreased much more slowly than was projected since the Internet appeared (see table 5.13). It is thus likely that the Minitel will continue to be used heavily for the next several years, because it is available to a wide audience, an important fraction of which has not yet gained access to the Internet or developed the skills to use it effectively. For these segments of the population, using the Minitel for banking or retailing services remains an attractive option. Indeed, the Minitel is offered as a for-fee service bundled with French versions of Microsoft's operating system pre-installed on some computers.

As we saw in the first part of this chapter, the transition toward the Internet began in France only at the end of the 1990s. Two public reports sum up this change in mentality particularly well: the first was the Yolin report, which appeared in 1997 and focused on the experiences of small- and medium-sized companies; the second was the Lorentz report, which appeared a year later. Both took up, the theme of French delay, but emphasized the inadequate use of the Internet by French companies and society. The omnipresence of the Internet in this new wave of official reports is just as striking as the corresponding absence of the Minitel, which received only cursory treatment in the Lorentz report. This report

Pierre-Jean Benghozi and Christian Licoppe

Table 5.13
Comparing Uses of Minitel and Internet

Use of Minitel	1993	1994	1995	1996	1997	1998	1999	2000
Minitel terminals (millions)[1]	6.71	6.91	7.16	7.77	8.00	8.06	8	—
Cumulated Minitel consultation time[1] (millions of hours per year)	112	115	106	104	101	n.s.	n.s.	—
Cumulated Minitel consultation time excluding electronic directory[2] (millions of hours per year)	89.7	87	84	85	83	80.5	74.7	—
Cumulated Internet consultation time (millions of hours per year)	—	—	—	0.6	3	8	17.02	—
Use of Internet	1993	1994	1995	1996	1997	1998	1999	2000
Cumulated Internet consultation time (millions of hours per year)[3]	n.s.	n.s.	n.s.	0.6	3	8	17.02	54.6
French Internet hosts (millions)[4]	0.05	0.07	0.14	0.22	0.35	0.49	1.21	1.12

Notes: (1) Sagatel 2001; (2) OECD 1998; (3) Internet Access Provider French Association 2001; (4) AFNIC (French Network Information Center) 2001.

also accorded prime importance to e-commerce, whereas the Breton report gave only passing mention to television shopping as but one of many types of telecommunications services. The re-emergence of the rhetoric of the French delay revealed that the Internet is widely perceived as exogenous to the French situation. At an elementary level, this rhetoric reflected the fact that, once again, those responsible for French public policy had to turn to the United States as a source of new technology.

At another level, this language indicated that the Minitel and the Internet were not being developed in France as an integrated technical system, as was, for example, electricity (Hughes 1993). In fact, Internet protocols and services were not perceived as a possible response to problems and were not understood as such within the framework of the implementation and development of a telecommunications system. They seemed to come from somewhere else (Flichy 1999) and were supported by other networks or subnetworks, other protocols and standards (Edwards 1998), other service providers, other terminals and other operators, and had a different ideology (i.e., whether or not to bill for certain services, or the association of open systems and the interoperability of architectures with a libertarian bias).

The Dominant Interpretation of the French Experience, From Telematics to the Internet

The characterization of the Internet as an exogenous entity in a series of several significant official reports between 1985 and 2000 raises several questions.

The first question that widely captured the attention of French and foreign analysts is why telematics was so much more successful in France than it was in other countries, such as Great Britain and Germany (Cats and Jelassi 1994). Castells addresses this question by proposing three reasons. First, the Minitel's success resulted from intervention by the state, which subsidized the network and terminals and thereby directly created the conditions for a large public market. This intervention was then strengthened by the public authorities' ability to develop the partnerships and billing structures that facilitated the deployment of a private system of content providers, which combined the efforts of traditional companies, software and IT services companies (SITS), and new "telematic" companies (Charon 1987). Finally, this success was made possible by the fact that the construction of the Minitel system was gradual, took advantage of the experience and ergonomics of prior projects (e.g., an aborted project to develop a facsimile system for the general public), and relied on a large number of experiments. By relying on public feedback regarding potential uses, the developers increased the probability that the general public would accept the Minitel. This acceptance was later reinforced by the kiosk fee-for-service billing system, which enhanced the Minitel's flexibility and ease of access. Ultimately, usage was anchored by offering services such as the "rose-colored" lonely hearts messaging system, which resonated deeply with many French people and created conditions favorable for a collective learning experience. It should be noted, moreover, that, beginning in the 1990s, these initial services (games and rose-colored services) began to decline in popularity while more "serious" services (various types of information, TV shopping, remote order-taking, etc.) became more widely used. It is interesting to note that Castells feels obliged to justify the later success of the Internet by highlighting how the Internet would resolve the problems inherent in Minitel telematics: exceedingly hierarchical network architectures that do not favor horizontal gateways, and the low intelligence levels of the terminals. Like many other writers, he starts by assuming that the Internet and its related services take similar forms in all European countries, and feels he must simultaneously explain the phenomenal success of the Minitel in France and its apparent disappearance in a wave of cultural leveling at the European level.

A statement that contends a country-wide learning effect existed provides another interpretation because differences in both substance and form exist between the Minitel and the Internet (e.g., billing methods, ways of acquiring the terminal, and public policy development and the status of operators, with France Telecom moving from a monopoly position to a competitive relationship with its former suppliers). This perspective entails a post hoc interpretation of these effects. By contrast, reports dating from the middle of the 1990s identify limitations in the use of the Minitel and the Videotex for home shopping (such as the difficulty of producing a description of the products). There is, however, no immediate resolution proposed in these reports. The tentative solutions that are advanced rely on TV shopping and interactive television, and do not refer at all to HTML interfaces (Breton 1994). Further, the Internet did not develop in France as a response to the Minitel's problems, nor—as we noted above—has it caused this medium to disappear. Even though the Minitel has declined in popularity, it still realizes five to ten times more sales (depending on the sector) than the Internet does for e-commerce services intended for the general public. Certain Internet-oriented companies continue to open Minitel servers, even though their consultants advise them not to advertise the fact. The coexistence of these two media has, however, led almost all of the multimedia participants to contrast the Minitel, which they categorize as essentially an ordering system, to the web, which they regard as a true sales and marketing tool.[9]

This framework is the basis for interpretations that are similar to Castells's. By framing the Internet as the successor to the Minitel, actors view the former as a response or solution to the limitations of the latter. Thus, for instance, the ease with which HTML interfaces can manage detailed product descriptions and promotional and marketing materials can thus appear to be a response to the limited resources of the Minitel screens. HTML interfaces are then considered to be the prototype of the functional interface par excellence. Incidentally, present-day critics who decry the lack of user-friendliness of WAP screens on mobile phone terminals repeatedly compare these screens to Minitel screens.

This framework of technical evolution is quite deterministic. To resist it, we must abandon the idea that a higher performance technology has replaced a precursor system that is limited in scope and, based on experiential knowledge, to assume that the French telematic experience produced specific effects. At any rate, we believe the most interesting question is quite different: how does one identify, within the telematic experience, the effects of formatting, continuity, and learning that influenced how the various operators in France, whether they were directly or indirectly involved in the telematic world, appropriated Internet technologies and services?

Clearly Identifiable Transfer Ranges and Learning Effects
In order to identify the characteristics that the Minitel and the Internet share, we consider two levels of analysis, and two particular examples, that focus on the operators that provide e-commerce services to the general public on the Internet.

Pierre-Jean Benghozi and Christian Licoppe

Research and Development by France Telecom Mastery and control of technological resources are crucial, but often are overlooked when sites are developed. Labor markets for engineers, technicians' capacity to master technology, interoperability, databases, hosting, maintenance, and new application development are all strategic considerations. Given the importance of these resources, it is important to assess the extent to which the development of the Internet relied on both the technical expertise developed and the research conducted for the Minitel. Regarding the latter,[10] the historic operator's research center was directly involved.[11] Telematic research was split up into several different units and allocated to three different locations: the Lannion center in Brittany dealt mainly with network questions; the Rennes center concentrated on interfaces and telematic services (e.g., the development of the electronic directory); and the Caen center specialized in the services related to the postal interface and value-added networks (electronic mail, facsimile, finance, and security).

As reflected in the major reports of this period, researchers at the CNET found the telematic framework confining to their attempts to take into account the deployment of Internet protocols in America. At Lannion, the attitude of neglect regarding Internet-related issues centered on a discussion of protocols and standards for future networks. For the most part, the center defended solutions based on the ATM standards (*La Recherche* 2000). At Rennes, the center was aware of the limitations of the Minitel interfaces, but it focused on the deployment of more elaborate interfaces, with its sights on the PC operating systems of the period. According to the first-hand accounts of participants at the time, these efforts ran up against the lethargy of the terminal manufacturers, which were not inclined to develop more advanced terminals, because the current arrangement with the operator was already very profitable for them. One visible sign of the research centers' lack of sensitivity to new services and of their Minitel bias is evidenced by the following development: when the CNET decided to launch Internet plans in the second half of the 1990s, its management decided, in principle, to concentrate efforts in the center located at Caen, which until then had been the least involved with the Minitel.

At first view, these developments confirm the argument that the deployment of the Internet was checked by a lack of vision and blocked by actors who had interests in telematics, and that the slate needed to be wiped clean of past telematic experiences. Nevertheless, the experience of the Rennes center and its later evolution suggest other interpretations. In fact, this center had developed a high level of competence in Internet services in just a few years and was radically repositioning itself at the beginning of 2000. By developing more specifically targeted efforts to interface Minitel screens with PC screens in a manner that accounted for digital convergence, the Rennes center gradually oriented its research toward hypermedia languages. It focused especially on developing dynamic editors, which enable the automatic updating of data and methods-oriented interfaces on any platform ("edit once, publish many times"). Today, these concerns are viewed as one of the most important problems of multimedia design. The competence of the research center in the areas of language translation and the portability of information, services, and interfaces to all types of platforms clearly benefited from the prior learning experiences provided by telematics. By taking advantage of these learning experiences, the Rennes center was able to preserve some space for Internet research with the historic operator.

It is important to point out that this use of technical skills that were initially developed for the Minitel in developing the Internet occurred not only in R&D departments but also in the operational units of France Telecom. In fact, in the second half of the 1990s, a single unit, the multimedia division of the branch devoted to the general public, was responsible both for Minitel telematics and Internet services. One could reasonably conclude that this division put the experience developed by the DGT with the Minitel to good use in terms of the dialog it created and the partnerships it built with private content providers. This experience made it possible to put together a framework and skills base that could be used to design and implement the operator's Internet activities. It explains, to a large extent, the rapid transition described earlier.

Analogous learning experiences also occurred at other operational levels. For example, more than half of France Telecom's sales by its Internet subsidiaries (Wanadoo S. A., founded in 2000) comes from the Yellow Pages, which is an area of expertise falling under directory services. This expertise had been transposed to the Minitel very early on in the form of the electronic directory, the development of which in fact was viewed as a valuable resource that would help make the Minitel profitable. Beginning in the 1980s, the development of this directory led France Telecom to construct, develop, and mobilize its competence in the area of languages and databases, including the capability of deploying them and transporting them to different platforms (Minitel, local networks, and various IT standards). Transporting this electronic directory to the Internet was thus only a problem of setting up a new platform and did not require France Telecom to design the service from scratch. France Telecom was thus able to set the directory up very quickly, and it very rapidly increased Internet usage. It would appear that the same learning effect influenced the management of the marketing side of these directory solutions, which could, for the most part, be re-used for the Internet (partnerships with advertisers, fee structure, customer follow-up, and so on).

Consumer E-commerce Market   A second example of the relationship of the Minitel to the Internet is in the consumer space. As noted earlier, information systems can be characterized as much by their technical components as by the implicit organizational models that they represent. It is particularly interesting to note that the learning curve provided by the Minitel also operated at this second level. It is therefore possible to identify transfers of experience and solutions from the Minitel to the Internet that prefigure the widespread use of certain models that are now found everywhere on the Internet. Such transfers are especially noteworthy for how they are used to diversify and cross-fertilize markets, for their capacity to manage multichannel processing (the Minitel, fax, telephone, and telex) and for their application in business models that take into account the constraints related to multiplicity and the appropriate allocation of transactions and billings (i.e., the kiosk model). This learning curve affects not only the historic operator but also all of the economic participants that participated in the Minitel venture (technology providers, service companies, content creators, and the like). To illustrate this point, we will analyze the effects of this learning experience for the strategies and operating modes of market participants, especially participants in e-business to consumers (B2C). This section is based on fieldwork systematically conducted over 18 months with retail operators on the Internet, which were questioned about the links between their experience and the various aspects of telematics. We will distinguish between two types of participants: the true new entrants on the Internet scene (the "pure players") and the service providers that have already acquired sales experience on the Minitel and telematic servers.

Generally speaking, vis-à-vis e-business, strategies typically developed by French firms are very cautious. "Brick and mortar" firms in France are very skeptical about the ability of e-business to rapidly capture significant market share with the general public; such firms believe their experience of selling via the Minitel distinguishes them from the Internet neophytes. The evidence for this contrast is particularly clear-cut in the ergonomics of the services offered on the Internet. Toward the end of the 1990s, American web designers developed a rhetoric of the commercial website as a genre by contrasting it with two "foil" models. The first model concerns sites that contain essentially written text (thereby too closely resembling print formats); in the second model, the designers allow themselves to be carried away with technical feats, constructing highly animated sites that "flicker and flash all over the place" but are very difficult to load, even with the state-of-the-art equipment that is now available to the general public. From the perspective of several Minitel service providers that recounted their approach to the websites they had set up, the American sites exhibited the latter shortcoming, with an excess of multimedia. French companies with Minitel experience feel, on the contrary, that they must try to profit from their mass-market experience by offering sites or design elements that retain the functional and graphic simplicity of the Minitel. These firms believe such simplicity is essential to capturing significant market share.

As an example of this attitude, a large online travel agency, which was the offshoot of a telematic holding company at the outset, put its principles into practice by setting up its site on the basis of two different ergonomic styles. The first offers an extremely simplified area, based on the lessons drawn from the Minitel experience. By its side is a more difficult-to-use version, which uses search engines, for example, to call up requests, and which is more "Internet-oriented," according to the site managers. It has two distinct usage formats that are layered one on top of another: inside what appears to be a typical web screen, the site offers a quasi-specific reference to the Minitel—but it has been re-appropriated and re-invested with web-type formats to such an extent that the reference becomes almost imperceptible.

Second, numerous operators with past telematic experience in online commerce insist on trivializing the web. According to them, it offers nothing really new; it is just another sales channel that offers a concrete example of expertise in remote sales that they feel they already possess because of their Minitel experience. The correlate of this perspective of e-business is that these operators insist on creating a shared base of specific knowledge and skills, which they use to develop diversified sales platforms. Moreover, in the background of the customer relationship, they strive to construct a back office and, to the extent possible, a middleware common to all of the various distribution channels. Many pursue this goal even when doing so creates a surprising degree of heterogeneity; for example, the Internet site of a specialized distributor was only just being connected, in 1999, to an AS400 networked system shared by the telephone and Minitel ordering channels. Indeed, databases, products, and customers are the focus of this resource-sharing process, rather than the communication technologies themselves. These databases are thereby organized in terms of descriptive traits, categories, reference numbers, and structure, in order to be able to feed each channel. This preoccupation is ubiquitous with former telematic participants, but some new entrants share it as well, especially if they arrived early on the Internet scene prior to 1998. This tendency also appears to be reinforced by the opportunities created by the new mobile telephony services (WAP and UMTS), which are opening up opportunities for a multiplicity of future distribution channels. Another specialized distributor had its Web site constructed by a Web agency that initially specialized in telematics: this site was set up so that a single database could simultaneously feed an Internet site and a "phantom" Minitel site, one of the functions of which was to test the overall coherence of this system. For another client, the database produced for the Minitel was simply expanded with new fields, enabling it to adjust to accommodate the capacity to include images of the product, something that is possible on Internet sites.

One can see how this successive expansion of a database exemplifies the comparison between the Minitel as an ordering channel and the Internet as a sales channel, for which product description can be enriched with descriptive multimedia formats. The database, as a device, incorporates a method for comparing and evaluating these two forms of service that varies according to how categories are defined therein. Certain traits are either included or excluded in the construction and use of the database: invisible and embedded in information systems, databases incorporate a network and services policy (Bowker and Star 1999).

Returning to the initial question, the experience of the former participants in telematic ventures tends to push them to pursue increased interoperability, portability, and fluidity of the information systems working in the background of the customer interfaces. This concern with interoperability is widely found in their discourse, if not in their actions. These concerns, which are the offshoots of their experience, are for the most part not evident to the user.

There is a second issue that is central to the development of e-commerce. It involves the capacity for redistributing the transaction itself over several platforms and media. The experience of the call centers of a large shipper illustrates the significance of this issue. This firm's managers have stated that they learned from the Minitel experience that it is important to have dedicated phone lines so that information or advice regarding the transaction can be provided via this channel. This example of an early learning experience concerning the processing and consideration of a request resulted from the company's past experience with Minitel callers. This learning experience not only contributed to creating an awareness in the shipping company of the need to provide a similar link between the online sales site on the Internet and the call center; it also made the managers aware of the difficulties generated on the Minitel by their past hesitancy to equip the call center operators with a terminal and telematic access. When they made the transition to e-commerce via the Internet, these managers were thus more easily inclined to quickly equip their operators with Internet access stations. This point is important, and it has been confirmed by a number of firms that engage in online sales. For the telephone operators dealing with Internet users, the capacity to consult the electronic platform (if possible, during the call from the Internet user) is indispensable for establishing and confirming a common reference point with the customer. This shared framework is an absolute prerequisite for enabling the parties to establish a basis for agreement concerning the transaction. Here again, the Minitel learning experience is hidden from view, but it has enabled French Internet companies to speed up the introduction of electronic Internet access in call centers.

Conclusion

By searching for common elements between the telematic experience and the implementation of Internet and commercial online services, we have identified a body of effects related to both the interoperability of formats and the simultaneous management and distribution of interactions over several platforms. The telematic experience thus provided us with a number of concrete examples of the capacity to combine and use several different formats for interaction. We can speak of capacity inasmuch as the nature of this learning experience makes conceivable, and directly structures, a body of knowledge that can then be exploited to increase the number of technical broadcast channels and to combine and manage the numerous and diversified platforms and exchange formats. This orientation of the cognitive economy of the participants—and the configuration of software technologies on which it is based—is at the heart of the philosophy of networks to such an extent that it is difficult to objectify and measure. Indeed, how do we account for what is only a tendency to integrate a more distributed and spread-out commercial relationship? Can it be reduced to a concern and a set of skills that can be mobilized in other contexts of networked technologies in order to share databases and make formats and languages interoperable? Do these properties underlie the ability to simultaneously integrate a more distributed commercial relationship?

These findings prevent us from rejecting the thesis proposed by Castells that the limits of the telematic experience explain, once and for all, its replacement by services based on Internet protocols. The model underlying the description that we have given of the telematic "late start" in fact operates by two stages. We first observed the neglect of the Internet's potential for exploiting the profitability of a new and difficult mass market. We then noticed that the rapid appropriation of the Internet was based on expertise acquired within the telematic framework, and allowed a variety of informational formats and the corresponding distribution of interactions to be co-managed over different platforms. The limits of telematic services that some have pointed out, and the idea that the Internet could provide a solution for them, essentially stemmed from a post hoc perspective that has been constructed during a time when both types of service were operative.

The task of simultaneously reinterpreting the past and contrasting its different types of technologies is never-ending. The challenge of providing economically viable online services for a mass market is, from this perspective, plagued with the same tensions and unresolved arguments. For example, it is not clear if a service should be provided free of charge or, if there should be a fee, which billing method should be used. The rise of successful services based on fee-for-service billing methods (i.e., based on the quantity of data exchanged) thus leads French observers, analysts, and professionals to recall fondly the telematic experience and to advocate the implementation of business models tested on the Minitel. The kiosk-type billing model is thus suddenly regarded as a panacea for an entire class of unresolved economic problems. This appropriation of the Minitel business model by Internet service providers is an ironic but telling reminder that technologies in themselves are never truly radical, but evolutionary.[12]

Acknowledgments

We thank John Lafkas for his help in editing the chapter.

Notes

1. From IDC ⟨http://www.idc.fr⟩.

2. The source is the Ministère d'Economie, des Finances, et de l'Industrie, ⟨http://www.minefi.gouv.fr/minefi/chiffres/comelec/tbce/indi/indi.htm⟩.

3. See Mediangles 1999.

4. Most of the data in the following section are taken from SESSI 2000.

5. Restructuring reduced staffing by 20 percent between 1990 and 1998!

6. Cf. Beaudoin 1999.

7. This finding appears in the current series of interviews performed independently by both authors.

8. The DGT (Direction Générale des Télécommunications) was a public administrative body that became a state-owned company under the name of France Telecom and was later privatized under the same name.

9. Interviews were conducted in an on-the-job setting.

Pierre-Jean Benghozi and Christian Licoppe

10. This section is based on a series of preliminary interviews, at a historical research center, with the participants in the telematic experience at the CNET, conducted by one of the authors (C.L.).

11. In the middle of the 1990s, at the time when deregulation of the sector transformed the former DGT into the historic operator now called France Telecom, it was still known as the National Centre for Telecommunications Studies (CNET).

12. cf. *Newbizz* no. 135094, Jan. 25, 2001, special issue "Au secours, le Minitel revient!," edited by Pierre Agède, ⟨http://www.01net.com/rdn?oid=135094&rub=1569&page=0-135094⟩.

6

Creativity under Constraint: Technological Imprinting and the Migration of Indian Business to the New Economy

Srilata Zaheer and Radhika Rajan

India will have a globally-focused outward-looking IT services sector and a domestically-focused manufacturing sector—just the reverse of Japan
—*Indian dot.com CEO, 2000*

India presents a paradox as far as IT (information technology) services and e-business are concerned. With an installed base of 5 million PCs, 2 million Internet subscribers (as compared to over 22 million in China), and 5.5 million Internet users as of December 2001, and a population of over 1 billion, India ranks among the lowest in the world in terms of per capita PC and Internet penetration (Mehta 2001a, 2001b; NFO-MBL 2000). Yet some facts stand out. With over 410,000 employees, India's information-technology services industry is estimated to be the second largest in the world in terms of employment, second only to the United States. India is one of the fastest growing personal computer markets in the world today, with the *installed base* of PCs growing by 85 percent between 2000 and 2001. There are close to 20 million cable TV subscribers and 38 million households with cable TV access in India, who could potentially become Internet users. The number of mobile phones in India grew 76 percent in 2001 alone. Indian firms exported $6.24 billion worth of software in 2000–2001, of which $1.2 billion was directly e-business related. Further, although India has just a 2 percent world market share in software exports, it has a 19.5 percent world market share in the export of customized software services—and despite the global economic slowdown, the industry grew 50 percent in 2000–2001 (Mehta 2001b;

ITU 2000, 79; NASSCOM-Mckinsey Study 2000). In the public mind and in the private sector, IT and web-enabled services are clearly seen as some of the most promising areas for growth. As one of the managers we interviewed put it, in India, "IT and e-business are in your face, *every* day, in *every* newspaper."

Despite the number of PCs per capita and the level of Internet penetration not being particularly encouraging, many of the major Indian business groups have set up e-business arms, and dot.com advertisements fill the billboards of every major city. Both domestic and international venture capitalists are establishing footholds in India, with the amount of cumulative venture capital commitments through 2000 estimated at around $1 billion (Wright, Lockett, and Pruthi 2001). Silicon Valley–style entrepreneurship also appears to be gaining legitimacy, especially in pockets such as Bangalore, with several well-publicized moves of executives from established firms to start-ups, some of which are seamlessly connected to the valley itself. At the governmental level, IT services and in particular, the Internet, are seen as having the potential to deliver on multiple fronts—on employment, on development, and even on improving the efficiency and transparency of the governance process.

We explore this paradox as we address the question of to what extent the promise of IT services, and of e-business in particular, are being realized in India. We focus in this chapter on the private sector, and in particular on the challenges faced by established Indian IT firms as they attempt to migrate their technological capabilities and skills toward higher value-added software and e-business activities. The question is how a country without a sophisticated domestic customer base or intense domestic rivalry, and without strong related and supporting industries can create and sustain competitive advantage in industries such as software or e-business (Porter 1990; Ramamurti and Kapur 2001). In essence, although there have been some efforts at developing the Internet economy in terms of e-commerce and e-business in India, the drivers of e-business and higher value-added software development in India have been predominantly global rather than local.

This study is essentially an inductive, exploratory study, where we attempt to both describe the evolution and the current state of the Internet economy in India as of 2000–2001, and to develop some preliminary ideas on the factors that influence the migration of Indian businesses to the new economy, focusing particularly on the Indian software industry. We base our analyses on a combination of data from archival sources and from over sixty interviews with managers, entrepreneurs, venture capitalists, and government officials, conducted in 2000 and 2001 in India and in the United States. In developing this chapter, we interviewed senior managers (including several CEOs) from all the major software firms in India, and of several U.S. multinational companies' Offshore Development Centers (ODCs) there. We talked to senior government officials in three of the most dynamic states in India as far as IT is concerned—Karnataka, Andhra Pradesh, and Maharashtra—as well as to several Indian and foreign venture capitalists, entrepreneurs engaged in e-commerce and e-business start-ups, and members of the Bombay and National Stock Exchanges (BSE and NSE). Although our access was far from random, we believe our interviewees represent a wide cross-section of stakeholders interested in the phenomenon of the Internet.

We start this chapter with a description of the state of local-for-local and local-for-global software and e-business activities in India (Bartlett and Ghoshal 1989). Although the paper will touch on the state of B2C and B2B within India, India perhaps provides one of the best examples of how the Internet economy is more than just commerce on the Web, but spans the gamut of value-added activities in ways that transform work. This section will provide a brief report on the types and volumes of different IT and Internet-enabled activities in India, and draw some theoretical lessons on how digitization of content and electronic networking might change the structures of value-added globally.

The paper then moves to a discussion of how the institutional environment, in particular, deregulation, the institutions of higher education, and the types of firms involved in new economy businesses have influenced the development of e-business in India. This section starts with a brief discussion of the role of government, especially the telecom sector, and the dismantling of the Videsh Sanchar Nigam Limited (VSNL) monopoly that controlled bandwidth out of India, and of the educational and training institutions that sprang up in software (some of which—NIIT, Aptech—are now multinationals in their own right), in influencing the infrastructure and manpower base for the Internet economy. We then discuss the historical evolution and the symbiotic relationships among three types of firms that dominate the e-business landscape in

India: the software export houses such as TCS, Wipro, Infosys, and Satyam (the top four as of 1999–2000); the Silicon-Valley style entrepreneurs such as Fabmart.com, Ittiam, MindTree, and Silicon Automation Systems; and the old-economy bricks-and-mortar firms, in particular multinational corporations (MNCs) such as GE, all of which have driven the growth of e-business in India. We discuss examples of each of these types of firms. Each draws on different capabilities and contributes differently to the growth of the Internet economy in India and to the other firms.

Finally, the paper examines how the 30-year history of the development of technological capability in software exports affected the ability of Indian firms to migrate up the value chain to e-business/e-commerce activities. The paper examines the role of technological trajectories in influencing the path of e-business growth in India. Specifically, the traditional software houses are both hampered and helped by their history of involvement in IT software exports as they attempt to migrate their technological capabilities to the needs of e-commerce and e-business. Their ability to migrate appears to be influenced by their being technologically imprinted with the routines and processes that were most suited to conditions that prevailed when they were founded. We conclude this chapter with a discussion of some of these challenges.

The State of IT and Internet-enabled Services in India

Local-for-local B2B and B2C

Estimates as to the current and potential size of the indigenous business-to-business (B2B) and business-to-consumer (B2C) markets in India vary widely, and our interviews over the past two years have led us to believe that even the more conservative projections tend to err on the high side. For example, estimates from respected market research agencies and consulting firms in 2000 suggesting that the B2B market in India would be between $5 billion and $10 billion in 2001 and that B2C would gross $1 billion to $3.6 billion, have proven to be excessively optimistic. Revised estimates suggest that in 2000–2001, the volume of B2C retail transactions in India (excluding stock trading) is expected to reach $12 million. It is estimated that another $240 million worth of stocks were traded online during this period. As for B2B transactions, in 1999–2000, they stood at $90 million, and revised estimates for 2000–2001 suggest they might reach a volume of $240 million. It is estimated that less than one-sixth of the total investment in these sectors comes from venture capitalists, with the bulk of the investment coming from Indian corporate houses. Estimates on VC investments tend to converge on a cumulative commitment figure of $1 billion till 2000, though several sources suggest that this figure may have more than doubled in 2001 (Manzar, Rao, and Ahmad 2001; NASSCOM 2001; NASSCOM-McKinsey Study 2000; GIIC 1999; Charles 1999). All these figures are provided with the caveat that even historical data in areas such as venture capital funding in India tend to be inconsistent across different sources, with the figures rarely explained. In this context, we have had to exercise judgment by looking for convergence across sources and by asking industry experts to assess the validity of the data.

Our interviews also indicate that true industry-wide B2B exchanges are at a fairly nascent stage in India, and even the B2B networks that are being implemented are mostly firm-centered extranets, often with an MNC subsidiary at the hub, which is linked electronically to its current suppliers (Sawhney and Kaplan 1999). Hindustan-Lever (a Unilever subsidiary) is one of the firms moving forward in this direction. However, a few industry-wide B2B exchanges have been set up. For example, Satyam is involved with the plastics Industry Association in setting up a plastics exchange, Wipro has been involved in setting up a B2B computer exchange, and Mindtree has been involved in setting up a tire industry exchange on an ARIBA platform.

As for B2C, even some of the biggest and best-known retail Indian Web sites, such as Rediff.com and Fabmart.com, processed fewer than ten thousand transactions a month in 2000. This is not surprising in a country where, despite the proliferation of cybercafés, 58 percent of regular Internet users access the Web from their place of work, where presumably consumer transactions are less likely to occur than at home. Only 29 percent of Internet users access it from their homes, and another 9 percent access it from a cybercafé (NFO-MBL 2000). It should be noted, however, that these results are based on a survey of users in the top eight urban centers of India—the proportion of users accessing the Web from cybercafes is likely to be higher in smaller urban centers and in rural areas.

Further, 76 percent of Internet users in India use the web primarily for e-mail messaging, and only 3 percent have ever used it to make a purchase. Again, this is not unexpected in a country with only 3.8 million credit card holders as of 2000, even though the major B2C retailers have come up with several creative ways through which to receive payments. Fabmart.com, for instance, allows direct debits from a customer's bank account through relationships with Citibank and other banks, and also uses the traditional cash-on-delivery system that has been a long-established feature of the Indian postal service. It has also created "Fabmoney"—coupons with tamper-proof account numbers that can be purchased for fixed amounts at selected cybercafé's (designated as "Fabpoints")—which can be used to buy products from Fabmart on the Web. Fabmart claims that, as a result of these innovations, fewer than 50 percent of its transactions are now credit card based.

Local-for-global IT Services

Taking a broader view of IT and web-enabled services to include the software that goes into e-commerce and e-business applications, and other remote services that are facilitated by improved telecommunications and the Internet, the picture that emerges of the impact of the new economy in India looks considerably brighter. The Indian software industry has emerged as one of the major e-commerce facilitators to industry worldwide. As the CEO of Infosys, put it, "It has become critical for those companies [US e-business infrastructure firms and dot.coms, and Fortune 1000 firms] to have this India connection ... as their applications, their tools, their websites have all been built out of here." As another manager interviewed commented, "E-commerce stands on the shoulders of traditional software." Indian software houses have been active in the software industry since 1974, when Tata Consultancy Services (TCS), a privately held firm of the Tata industrial group, first began software exports. The primary focus of the major Indian software houses has been on overseas customers, especially in the United States. The largest Indian software house, TCS, had total revenues of $450 million (Rs. 2,115 crores) in 1999–2000, of which the domestic component was only $49 million (Rs. 230 crores). The other major software houses are even less domestically focused, with Infosys, for instance, reporting just $3.8 million (Rs. 18 crores) of domestic revenue out of a total revenue of

$195 million (Rs. 918 crores). With so much exposure to global business, the software industry in India is vulnerable to global economic downturns. Later in this chapter, we will explore the migration of these software firms to e-business and to other higher value activities, and the impact of the worldwide economic downturn on their fortunes.

IT-enabled Services In addition to software, a range of IT and Internet-enabled services such as engineering design, remote customer access, data search and analysis, and transcription and localization services, facilitated by digitization, by the Internet, and by improvements in telecommunications, have begun to grow rapidly in India. Although the total revenues from such services were only of the order of $250 million and these services employed about twenty-five thousand workers in 1998–1999, they are estimated to grow to over 1 million workers and revenues of $17 billion by 2008 (Mehta 1999). The higher projected growth rates in IT-enabled services compared to indigenous e-commerce is based on the fact that these services are "local-for-global" activities that are less dependent on household and business Internet penetration in India.

In 2000, there were 141 firms providing remote services from India who were members of NASSCOM (the Indian software industry association). Fourteen of these firms were associated with multinationals such as GE Capital, British Telecom, and Ernst & Young. Some of the MNC affiliates service the parent and affiliate firms' offshore needs. For example, the American Express affiliate operates as a captive offshore software development center for all of American Express worldwide. However, the majority of Indian IT-enabled service providers and several of the MNC-affiliated providers such as CSIL (Citicorp Securities and Investments Limited) provide remote services to a range of overseas customers. These remote services include activities all across the value chain, from downstream customer interaction through call centers and Web-based technical support, to upstream engineering and design services and supply-chain management and support services such as finance, accounting, and data-processing.

GE Capital, for instance, has the stated objective of moving a significant part of its IT-enabled global services to India and it alone has established two major call centers in India (handling both outgoing and incoming calls), apart from several offshore software development centers, employing over three thousand people. Swissair does its accounting in India, CISCO and Oracle have advanced software development centers, Bechtel does engineering design there, and hundreds of small entrepreneurs offer remote services as varied as market research, medical transcription, animation, security services, and text entry. In providing these services, the India-based firms and software centers compete with firms in Ireland, Israel, China, and the Philippines. The outsourcing of such services to India and other emerging economies could potentially contribute to a global shift in such value-added activities, supporting the product-cycle hypothesis of Ray Vernon, who suggested that as a product "matured," the location where it was manufactured would move from the innovating home country to other developed countries and finally to developing countries. It is interesting to find this pattern in technologically based service activities, though the length of the cycle is relatively short compared to product life cycles in manufacturing, and perhaps more to the point, it is not clear that only more "mature" activities move in the software case.

With projected net cost savings of 50–60 percent for firms in developed countries from "outlocating" processes in India and the expected technological advances in bandwidth and connectivity, in theory, a significant proportion of process value-added could be remotely accessed from India (estimated at around 50 percent of total process costs). The accelerating trend toward more and more offshore services (i.e., software development in India rather than near the client), which have grown from 10 percent of India's software exports in 1993–1994 to 42 percent in 1999–2000, bears this out. Such services could represent a major growth opportunity for firms in India and in other emerging markets (Mehta 2001b; Apte and Mason 1995). However, the value added from IT-enabled services that have moved to India so far is a negligible fraction of the total volume of such services worldwide, and it remains to be seen how many MNCs will follow the GE example.

Indian firms have certain natural advantages in terms of labor costs and time-zone benefits in providing IT-enabled services, and over the years some of the software firms have also acquired the capabilities required to develop software for e-business and other higher value-added services. At the "medium technology" level represented by large-scale

Management Information Systems (MIS) projects, several Indian software firms have developed a reputation for software development process capabilities. As of 2000, 195 Indian software firms have obtained an ISO9000, SEI, or other quality certification. Twenty of the best software houses had attained the highest "Level 5" software development quality certification defined by the "Capability Maturity Model" (CMM) of Carnegie Mellon University (Mehta 2001b; Arora and Asundi 1999). In fact, Indian firms had obtained the highest numbers of CMM Level 5 certifications—only 37 firms worldwide had acquired this level of certification as of January 2001. Arora and Asundi (1999) find that these certifications do correlate to improvements in software development processes. Some of these software firms have been able to begin competing not just on cost but on value delivered on a few of their projects, though the bulk of their software exports still focus on large-scale MIS projects that depend on low-cost labor (Arora et al. 2001). Indian firms have a limited presence in the higher technology end of the software industry represented by embedded chips or 3D video game software. Firms located in India also enjoy a time-zone advantage in providing some of these services, from their ability to have work completed when it is night in the United States (Zaheer 2000). In the long run, improvements in telecommunication, digitization, data compression, and bandwidth could potentially alter the economics and motivations for foreign direct investment in a particular location, for instance, by prompting a cost-driven relocation of the customer-relationship aspects of market-seeking investments (Balasubramanian, Krishnan, and Sawhney 1999; Zaheer and Manrakhan 2001). This would mean that MNCs might relocate their after-sales service hotlines or their technical help desks to India and to other emerging markets from their current locations in the developed world.

Remote IT-enabled services also contribute to the employment of individuals other than software engineers in significant numbers, and thus touch the lives of a broader population than just a quarter of a million educated software professionals. Projections of revenue/employee, average offshore salary, projected revenues for Indian firms, and growth rates in the various sectors of IT-enabled services, drawn from the NASSCOM-McKinsey study (2000) and from a Barings Private Equity report (2000), are provided in table 6.1.

Table 6.1
IT-enabled Services in India (remote access services)

Service	Annual Revenue/ employee ($)	Average offshore salary in India ($)	Projected revenues for Indian firms 2004 ($ billion)	Projected employment 2008	Projected compound annual growth rate
HR services	31,000	12,000	2.5	143,000	71%
Remote customer interaction	18,000	3,000	1.6	212,000	18%
Data services	26,000	4,000	2.2	160,000	NA
Finance and accounting services	31,000	15,000	0.2	24,000	26%
Remote education	18,000	10,000	0.5	42,000	NA
Network management	35,000	14,000	0.1	7,000	NA
Engineering and design services	20,000	8,000	1.0	87,000	29%
Web site services	26,000	7,000	0.05	12,000	NA
Transcription and localization	11,000	3,000	0.5	32,000	21%
Animation	15,000	7,000	0.2	30,000	4%
Market research	12,000	5,000	0.1	19,000	NA
Average or total	21,000	7,000	9.0	~800,000	30%

Sources: NASSCOM-McKinsey Study 2000; Baring Private Equity Report 2000.

The Institutional Environment for the Internet and for IT Services

Although the earliest efforts to promote Indian networking came from the education and research network (ERNET), funded by the United Nations Development Program (UNDP), they were isolated from performance and market demands, and their service was often unreliable (Press, Foster, and Goodman 2000). Below we examine the institutions of government, venture capital, and education in influencing the growth of the Internet in India and the migration of the Indian software industry toward e-business.

The Role of Government

It is practically axiomatic that government matters in India. It has traditionally been seen more as barrier than as a facilitator to industry. At the time of Indian independence from British rule in 1947, partly in reaction to their colonial history, Indians internalized the values of democracy and self-reliance, which led to a series of actions by the Indian government that had far-reaching consequences. For one, there was a strong push to become self-sufficient in technology, which led in the 1950s to investment in a fairly large network of elite engineering schools (the Indian Institutes of Technology and the Regional Engineering Colleges), without doubt at the expense of primary education and universal literacy. The focus on self-sufficiency also led to controls on foreign direct investment and on telecommunications, especially on communications with the rest of the world, which remained a government-controlled monopoly until 2000. Self-reliance also fostered a misguided fascination with Soviet-style planning that kept investment in heavy industry in the hands of state-owned enterprises, fostered protectionism, and kept the Indian economy growing at rates below 5 percent for most of the 45 years that followed.

However, there were some bright spots in this picture. For one, the value of democracy was also strongly entrenched in Indian society. India never succumbed to military rule or to civilian dictators, as happened in so many post-colonial emerging markets (except for a brief hiccup in the early 1970s when the prime minister, Indira Gandhi, tried to assume "emergency" powers). Further, there was always free movement of people and ideas into and within India. Books and magazines could be imported duty free. There were few, if any, restrictions on individual liberty. Further, and this is fairly critical to the development of the software industry, the government's focus on heavy industry and large-scale enterprises meant that many service industries (with the exception of banks and insurance companies), such as advertising and media, film production, and to a large extent software, thrived under a regime of benign neglect from the Indian government, even before the much-vaunted reforms of 1991–1992 that accelerated the process of deregulation. As the CEO of NASDAQ-listed *Rediff.com*, one of India's largest portals and an offshoot of an advertising agency that he had founded in the mid 1970s, remarked, "The only time we had to go to Delhi [in the history of the firm] was to get approval for the International IPO" (Ajit Balakrishnan, personal interview, August 2000).

As for governmental involvement in shaping the evolution of software and e-business in India, the central government has had a fairly "hands-off" attitude toward information technology services and e-business except for, until recently, controlling communications and connectivity into and out of India (Heeks 1996). The government has mainly had an influence on IT and e-business through its shaping of the institutions of capital, labor, and the telecom infrastructure, which we discuss later in this chapter. A timeline of major governmental actions affecting software and e-business is provided in table 6.2.

Some of the more critical developments on this timeline include the creation of the Department of Electronics (DOE) in 1970, with an explicit computer policy targeting software exports (India was the first developing country to this). The 1980s saw continued liberalization and encouragement for software exports and development. For example, the DOE broke 26 separate rules to accommodate Texas Instruments' hundred percent Indian subsidiary in 1986. The Software Technology Parks (STP) scheme was introduced in 1988 to encourage offshore development centers to set up business in India. These parks were structured like export-processing zones, in which state governments would invest substantially in infrastructure and high-bandwidth telecommunications, and software and IT service firms could rent space and start up relatively easily. Many states now have STPs and have been able to attract multinational investment into these parks. Hyderabad's "Hi-Tech City," for instance, has attracted firms such as Oracle and GE, and is being substantially expanded.

Telecom Policy   Until 1984, the telecom sector in India was wholly government owned and was "characterized by underinvestment, outdated equipment, and growth well below the potential of the market" (Jain 2001, 189). One of the first steps taken by the government was the separation of the Department of Telecommunications (DOT) from the department of Posts and Telegraphs in 1985. Recognizing the national importance of telecom and its underperformance in India, the government embarked on a further series of reforms involving deregulation and privatization—in early 2001, even embarking on corporatizing the Department of Telecommmunications.

Since independence, the share of the telecom sector in the national budget has increased from 2.4 percent in the early 1950s to 7.4 percent in 1990–1992 and surging to over 19 percent in 1999–2000. Telephone

Table 6.2
Time Line of Key Government Initiatives Affecting Software and E-business in India

1947+	India attains independence, commits to goal of self-reliance. Domestic industries (including computer hardware & software) protected by tariffs, licensing procedures & restrictions on imports, controls on foreign direct investment. Educational institutions such as IITs set up.
1970+	Department of Electronics (DOE) created, explicitly targets & promotes generation of software for export. Growth of software hampered by contradictory policies of difficulty in importing computer hardware.
1972	Emphasis on computer & software education & training. Lower import duties on hardware imports by training institutes.
1985	The Department of Telecommunications (DoT) spun off from the Department of Post and Telegraphs.
1986	Two state-owned enterprises created under DoT to handle telecommunications inside the country (MTNL—Mahanagar Telephone Nigam Limited) and internationally (VSNL—Videsh Sanchar Nigam Limited)
1986	New Software Policy announced, allowing liberal imports that are expected to lead to exports.
1988	Software Technology Park (STP) scheme introduced. STPs are export processing zones where the government provides infrastructure, buildings, power & high-speed satellite links.
1990–91	Major liberalization & reforms initiated, precipitated by severe financial crisis. Restriction on imports abolished for capital goods. Telecom equipment manufacturing opened to private sector. Multinationals (Alcatel, AT&T, Ericsson, and others) enter market.
1993	Private telecom networks allowed in industrial areas.
1994–95	Licensing of cellular mobile service in four major cities and nineteen other circles to private firms begins.
1998	VSNL monopoly on Internet Service Provision removed. Private ISPs allowed.
1999	National Telecom Policy announced liberalizing licensing and connectivity. Allows private firms to lay cable and set up networks within India, and to set up gateways for international connections. Several state governments allow private firms free rights to lay cable along highways. Bandwidth available increases rapidly.
2000	Information Technology Act passed, provides the legal infrastructure for e-commerce by allowing digital signatures and giving legal sanction to e-mail as evidence.

Sources: Based on Mehta 2001b; Jain 2001; Lateef 1997; interviews and archival data.

lines trebled, from 5 million in 1990 to 17.8 million in 1997–1998. However, 80 percent of these lines were in urban areas, serving just 26 percent of the population, and fully 30 percent of the lines were concentrated in the four largest cities. As of 2001, about 50 percent of the villages in India still had no phone line at all. Teledensity, the number of telephones (both fixed and mobile) per 100 people, has been growing rapidly in India, but is still very low as compared to China or other East Asian countries. For example, in 1998, teledensity in India was at 2.2 telephones per 100 people, lower even than Indonesia's 2.7, and far lower than Malaysia's 19.76 and the United States' 66.13 telephones per 100 people. However, in India, the more relevant criterion may be "tele-access," defined as the percentage of the population having access to telecom services within a specified distance. The proliferation of calling booths through urban, semi-rural, and rural areas improves the tele-access statistic (Jain 2001).

Two areas of relevance to software and e-business that the central government did continue to regulate until 1998 and 1999, respectively, were Internet access and international bandwidth. The state-owned enterprise Videsh Sanchar Nigam Limited (VSNL) used to have a monopoly on Internet service provision in India until November 1998, and until the new IT policy was adopted in 2000, a monopoly on bandwidth to and from India as well. However, the government has been gradually diluting its stake in VSNL by issuing Global Depository Receipts (GDRs), and as of March 2000, its stake was down to 53 percent.

When the ISP market was liberalized overnight in 1998, more than a hundred firms registered to become Internet Service Providers, though since then the number of active providers appears to have stabilized at around a dozen. The VSNL monopoly had severely limited total connectivity out of India, and international bandwidth stood at around 800 megabits per second (MBPS) as of December 2000, compared to China's 55,000 MBPS, with bandwidths within India also at levels significantly below that of China (Press, Foster, and Goodman 2000). However, with the new IT policy completely opening up investment in IT infrastructure to private companies and to foreign investment, firms such as Reliance Industries have been moving fairly quickly to lay fiber optic cable across the country. Private investments in international bandwidth have also begun to appear—the first privately owned submarine cable was landed in Chennai in the summer of 2000. International telecom has seen faster deregulation in India than domestic telecom, resulting in declining costs and quicker introduction of new technologies.

Since deregulation in 1999, bandwidth available has expanded rapidly to approximately 10–30 gigabits per second (GBPS) internationally, and 2.5 GBPS between major Indian cities as of March 2001. What came up repeatedly in our interviews was that although past restrictions on bandwidth may have slowed the growth of domestic B2C, and perhaps a few high-bandwidth global IT services such as video, to date, it has not been a major constraint in the local-for-global business, particularly in software exports, as firms could lease satellite uplinks through VSNL, and set up private networks.

Progess on bandwidth, especially within India, has not been without setbacks. In fact, with connectivity within India growing more slowly than connectivity out of India (see figure 6.1), many e-mail messages within the same city travel not just through that city or even just within India, but travel all the way to the United States and back to be delivered. The Sankhyavahini project was meant to fix this with the creation of a national fiber optic data backbone connecting ten cities and over a hundred universities and research centers, with investment from the DOT and from professors at Carnegie Mellon University (CMU). The project ran into opposition after CMU had signed a memorandum of understanding with DOT in 1999, ostensibly because participation by a foreign institution (CMU) in a domestic network was a breach of national security that

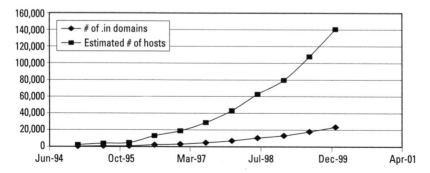

Figure 6.1
Growth in hosts in India (dot-in and all hosts)

would violate the Indian Telegraph Act of 1885, the Indian Wireless Act of 1933, the National Telecom Policy of 1994, and the New Telecom Policy of 1999. The old distrust of foreigners and focus on self-reliance had raised its head again. This was despite assurances that a fiber optic network was far more secure than satellite or cellular networks. Carnegie Mellon University had to pull out of the project in 2001.

As for the pricing of Internet services, VSNL plans to cut end-user rates to between 67 and 44 cents an hour for dial-up IP connections in 2002 (down 20–47 percent from the current 84 cents; service started in 1995 at $1.70 an hour), and phase out its dial-up login shell accounts (priced at 27 cents an hour) altogether. As it still has more than a 50 percent market share in Internet service provision, VSNL's pricing drives the marketplace. For the moment however, the DOT, which provides the service in smaller cities where VSNL itself has no presence, has not agreed to VSNL's proposed price reductions. It should be noted that India has no history of flat rate pricing in any telecom services; VSNL, despite declining prices, has stuck to usage-based pricing. How much this hurts consumers is an open question. If VSNL reduces prices, an Indian subscriber could pay under $20 per month for 90 minutes a day of dial-up IP, comparable to effective real use at an American flat-rate ISP. Although this may seem high compared to average Indian salaries, the 2 million Internet subscribers in India are overwhelmingly from the upper end of the income distribution.

India has also had an indigenous government-owned satellite program since 1969, which has been fairly successful, with many multipurpose satellite systems in place since 1979. Satellite technology has strengthened existing telegraphy, telephony, wireless telegraphy, and radio communication. There have also been a number of private initiatives in the satellite field, by groups such as Reliance and ZeeTV. These initiatives have seen a slowdown in 2001 with the downturn in the telecom industry worldwide. The emergence of firms such as Reliance, primarilly a successful chemicals company, as major players in the telecom infrastructure sphere is interesting as it supports what other authors in this volume find in Korea (Chang) and in Japan (Sako): the repetition of traditional corporate forms (in this case, the successful family business) in the new areas of the economy.

State Governments What has been interesting about the nature of governmental involvement in the development of software and e-business is that the state governments have been at the forefront in pushing the center on liberalization. For example, the Karnataka government played a major role in persuading the center to break the rules to allow a Texas Instruments subsidiary to be established in Bangalore. More recently, the chief minister of Andhra Pradesh (AP) has been particularly vocal in persuading the center to allow free access to cable companies to lay cable along the national highways. In fact, the story of government's role in IT in India in recent years has been of a few dynamic state chief ministers pulling a somewhat indifferent and sluggish central government down the IT path.

Some of the particularly forward-looking state governments, such as those of AP and Karnataka, have been far ahead of the central government in acting as catalysts for private investments in IT. They have been active promoters of software technology parks, offering tax and investment incentives to private investors. The government of Andhra Pradesh has also been at the forefront in using IT to increase the efficiency and transparency of the governance process. The AP government has invested heavily in programs to train bureaucrats and officials in different state agencies in how to use the Internet and in how to develop web-based projects for their departments to facilitate information dissemination to the public. Andhra Pradesh has for instance, been putting daily power-generation statistics of the state-owned power companies on its website, to create an incentive for the firms to do better on capacity utilization, with an informed public. Karnataka is making a major effort to "take IT to the common man" by setting up IT training centers with the assistance of private sector training institutions such as NIIT and Aptech in smaller towns, and in a thousand government-run high schools throughout the state, and by setting up Internet access points in rural areas.

These much publicized efforts of the state governments have, in fact, forced the central government to take a more positive and proactive stance toward the IT industry, and in 1999–2000, there were a series of initiatives that essentially deregulated much of what had been under government control.

Venture Capital

Venture capital is a relatively new phenomenon in India (Verma 1997). Traditionally, entrepreneurs relied on family and friends and their ethnic networks for start-up financing; once they were established, they could get some financing from banks against assets or inventories. In the past few years, venture capital financing has been available through the venture arms of national financial institutions such as the Industrial Credit and Investment Corporation of India (ICICI) and the Industrial Development Bank of India (IDBI), and state financial institutions such as Gujarat Venture Finance Corporation (GVFC), Andhra Pradesh Industrial Development Corporation (APIDC), and Kitven in Karnataka. It used to be that firms needed to have an established a track record of profitability for an initial public offering on the Bombay Stock Exchange (BSE) or the National Stock Exchange (NSE). The rules have been loosened to allow firms that have not yet become profitable to list on the exchanges, provided they are 10 percent owned by one of the public financial institutions.

Since the early 1990s, there have been a few private Indian venture capital firms, such as Global Technology Ventures (GTV), a division of Sivan Securities, one of the largest private retail brokers in South India, which as of August 2000 had financed 24 start-ups, including seven U.S.-headquartered start-ups, with a 1999 valuation of about $100 million. Several traditional business houses, such as the Tatas, the Birlas, and Reliance, have also set up venture capital arms. A point to note is that many of the Indian VCs—both public and private—are themselves funded by foreign institutions and individuals. Several foreign players, some of them headquartered in Mauritius to take advantage of the tax treaty between India and Mauritius, also entered the fray in the late 1990s, such as HSBC and Barings Private Equity from the United Kingdom and Draper International, Walden-Nikko, Citibank, and Alliance Capital from the United States. Since March 2001, there appears to have been a fairly steep drop in the amount of VC funding in India, with only $73 million going to about twenty start-ups in the first nine months of 2001, and firms such as Draper International claiming to be fully invested. In addition, there have been small investments from individual Indian-American angel investors from Silicon Valley. It is sobering to examine comparable figures from Israel, a country with 6 million people to India's 1 billion, and which had $4 billion in committed VC funding for high-tech start-ups in 1998 (Arora et al. 2001; IVCA 1998; Mishra 1996).

What is interesting about venture capital in India is that some of the start-ups (several financed by GTV, for instance) begin their existence in Bangalore, where the "burn rate" for new ventures is estimated at between one-third and one-half that in Silicon Valley. Private estimates suggest that an early stage venture in India usually requires less than $700,000 in financing, whereas an equivalent stage comparable venture started in the United States might require at least $2 million. Once a prototype has been developed in India, some of these entrepreneurs move a significant part of their operations to the United States in order to be closer to the market, and to attract U.S. venture capital. We noticed this "seamless integration" between Bangalore and the United States (Silicon Valley in particular) in several of the most recent start-ups, a feature of the latest generation of entrants, who appear to have more of a global mindset than the old-line software houses (see table 6.3).

An issue for the development of venture capital in India is the absence of a NASDAQ-type stock exchange that can facilitate exit (Sagari and Guidotti 1992). The listing requirements on India's main exchanges are fairly stringent, with substantial capital and profitability requirements that have made private placements the main exit avenue for Indian VCs. As mentioned earlier, the Indian government has made a start at capital market reform by easing some of these requirements.

As for the influence of U.S. venture capital firms in India, the direct impact as of 2000 has been fairly insignificant. Indian VCs, however, clearly model themselves on U.S. venture capital. As one of them put it, "Our role model is Kleiner Perkins." Indian VCs engage in significant relationship-based funding, acting as "venture catalysts" rather than as just venture capitalists. Global Technology Ventures (GTV) for instance, is involved in creating technology campuses, which are industrial parks fully wired with fiber optic cable and high-speed links, so that entrepreneurs (especially those arriving in Bangalore from the United States) can immediately set up their businesses without having to worry about basic infrastructure issues. Global Technology Ventures itself receives funding

Table 6.3
Evolution of Indian Software Houses toward New Economy Businesses

	Pioneering firms	Technology focus	Marketing/Delivery channel	Vertical or industry focus	Domestic/International focus
1970s	TCS, IBM	Mainframes, Maintenance, Coding, Testing	Offshore development, Onsite-development (body-shopping)	Banking, Manufacturing, Engineering	*"Export"* mindset
1980s	TI, HP (100 percentsubs), WIPRO, CITIL, COSL, Motorola, NIIT	Client-server systems, PC applications, Breakthroughs in UNIX-based computing	Offshore development, Body-shopping Key Foreign partnerships, some direct marketing	Applications in varied vertical markets such as Finance & Telecom, Operating systems	Offshore & onsite development, *"Cost reduction"* mindset
1990–1995	Infosys, NIIT	Y2K, Legacy systems, Distributed computing	Direct marketing, Partnerships	Financial institutions, Retail, Healthcare	Overseas offices Domestic/international strategies
1996–2000	Infosys, CITIL, WIPRO, Satyam	Consulting & Architecture design, Legacy migration/Integration to the web	Branding, (NASDAQ listings), Direct customer relationships	Many verticals	*"Multinational"* mindset
2000 and beyond	Mindtree, Silicon Automation	Internet technologies, E- and M-commerce, Legacy migration, Pervasive computing, Wireless ASP, Embedded software		Opportunistic; High value/margin, 3G Telecom, Backbone/ Infrastructure providers	*"Global"* mindset, Silicon Valley-India seamlessness, mergers/ acquisition of foreign companies

Note: TCS (Tata Consultancy Services) was founded in 1974 (marking the birth of the Indian software industry). Through the 1970s, 1980s, and 1990s, TCS has continued to remain the market leader in terms of both revenues and manpower. TCS is not a public company.

from several overseas venture capitalists and individual investors. Bank of America Securities and Nomura Securities, for instance, have invested in GTV.

Labor—The Role of Technological Education
After independence from Britain in 1947, the Indian government under then prime minister Jawaharlal Nehru embarked on an ambitious plan to develop technological talent in the country by creating five Indian Institutes of Technology and a supporting network of Regional Engineering Colleges. This investment in a higher technical education system has often been criticized as an elite system invested in at the expense of primary education and universal literacy. However, one result of this investment is that India now produces one of the largest pools of trained English-speaking software engineers every year. Indian universities graduated about 122,000 engineers in all disciplines in 1999 (compared to about 63,000 in the United States), and about 68,000 software professionals are trained in over eighteen hundred higher education institutions every year in India. As an indication of just how important a role the Indian IT-services industry plays in the economy, over 67 percent of all the engineering graduates who registered for placement at the Indian Institute of Technology, Mumbai, between 1995 and 2000, were placed in IT-services firms (IIT Mumbai Placement Office).

There have also been some success stories of private IT training institutions, which provide software education, most often to non-engineers, typically at a lower level than that provided by the computer-science departments of engineering colleges or by the in-house software training institutions of the software firms. The National Institutes of Information Technology and Aptech International have both grown into successful multinational enterprises.

The favorable institutional environment for higher education in general, and for training in software development in particular, combined with a vast pool of young people hungry for work, has created an abundant supply of labor to feed the IT-services industry worldwide. Indian software talent has been migrating to where the demand has been highest, the United States, in large numbers. Forty-three percent of H-1B ("specialty occupation workers") visa petitions approved by the United States between October 1999 and February 2000 were from India

(19,209 new workers from India were admitted in this period, far out-numbering the next highest number of new workers admitted—5,394—from China). Most of the Indian H-1B workers were in computer-related occupations. This "brain drain" does not appear to have as yet seriously affected the ability of the best Indian software houses to attract talent, as several of these firms interviewed claimed to hire just 0.5–1 percent of the applicants for their positions. Still, competition from U.S. demand for labor has been raising software salaries in India and forcing several firms such as TCS and WIPRO to look beyond the Indian Institutes of Technology for their entering pool of engineers. They have also been trying to find ways to retain talented engineers, often by preempting an overseas offer by sending their best talent overseas on short-term assignments. Although average software wages in India are reported to have grown by 25 percent in 2000, the wages of experienced, senior software professionals grew in one year by more than 60 percent. Even so, the major software houses are estimated to lose between 17 percent and 25 percent of their trained engineers every year.

The quality of this seemingly unlimited software labor supply does, however, span the entire gamut. At the lowest end are the poorly trained graduates of the many hundreds of non-accredited computer institutes that have sprung up all over the country, many of whom may not even have had much of an opportunity to use a computer. At the high end are the Masters graduates in computer science and computer engineering from some of the most respected institutions such as the IITs, the Tata Institute of Fundamental Research, and the Indian Institute of Science.

The Migration of Indian Firms to the Internet Economy

The Internet economy in India is primarily being driven by three types of players (see figure 6.2).

The first and perhaps most important drivers are the traditional software and IT service houses, such as Tata Consultancy Services (TCS), Wipro, Infosys, and Satyam, who are trying, with varying degrees of success, to move up the value chain into becoming global providers of software and services to e-commerce and e-business worldwide. The second group consists of the bricks and mortar firms, in particular the financial services of MNCs such as Citicorp and GE Capital, who are

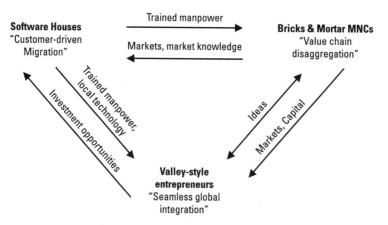

Figure 6.2
Major e-business players in India

seeking the benefits of remote services and value-chain disaggregation. Finally, there is a small but growing new generation of Valley-style entrepreneurs, such as Fabmart.com, India's largest exclusively retail-oriented site, and MindTree.com, a global B2B architecture provider, funded by both domestic and foreign venture capitalists, some of whom have strong ties to entrepreneurs in the United States. Each of these players brings a different set of resources and capabilities to the table, and they all have a symbiotic relationship with the other groups.

The software houses are one of the main nurturers of technical talent, as they take raw engineering graduates and provide them with extensive training to tackle the most challenging demands of e-business. Tata Consultancy Services, for instance, spends 5 percent of its revenues on training. Every entering consultant in TCS goes through a 72-day training program, some of it at their Trivandrum training center that can accommodate over five hundred consultants. TCS also targets another 20 days of training per year per consultant, much of it self-paced computer-based training.

The software houses have often been the launching pad for the entrepreneurs and the CEOs of MNCs and start-ups alike, and have also often provided higher-end software workers to the entire industry. In 1979, when IBM opted to leave India rather than dilute its ownership, it released twelve hundred software engineers into the marketplace. Many of them became entrepreneurs and set up software development shops. Unable to grow in the domestic market due to the low level of computerization, these firms targeted exports. In turn, some of the software houses such as Infosys developed their own investment arms, typically investing in later-stage ventures. The new entrepreneurial firms thus provide investment and growth opportunities to the traditional software houses.

The bricks-and-mortar MNCs are a little less homogeneous. Some of them generate lower-end employment, whereas others such as Oracle and Texas Instruments' subsidiaries in India operate as design and development centers at the high end, but they all share one characteristic, demonstrating to the world what can be done in terms of remote services from India. They play a vital role in *providing the link to global markets* for both the software houses and the entrepreneurial community. General Electric is perhaps unique in generating employment across the spectrum, from low-end call-center type work to high-end testing and design work at some of its offshore development centers housed in the offices of Satyam and TCS. Historically, the role of the MNCs in stimulating the growth of the Indian software industry is even more significant, as the very birth of the Indian software industry can be traced to demand from MNCs for low-cost software development work from India.

The third group—the new entrepreneurs—represent the creative edge in this system. As a group, they seem to have more global aspirations than do the software houses (they appear to move more quickly on overseas partnerships and acquisitions, for instance), and they also appear to be more willing and able to take on high-risk and high-value-added projects in areas such as embedded software and e-business tools. Pioneers in this group include Ittiam, MindTree, and Silicon Automation Systems.

Silicon Automation Systems, for example, is a chip design operation; it is somewhat older than the other firms in this group, having been started in 1989 by an ex-Intel engineer. The firm was originally based in California but moved to Bangalore in 1994. It designs and markets embedded software, focusing on products for mobile telephone and Internet applications for the telecommunications industry. Another example of the new-generation entrepreneurship is MindTree, which sees itself as a "next generation" software firm focused on e-business solutions. Mind-

Tree is a "born global" firm. Of its 10 founder-directors, five are from Wipro in India, three from Cambridge Technology Partners, and two from Lucent; four of the 10 currently work in the United States.

In order to truly understand the nature and depth of the "seamless integration" that exists between Silicon Valley and some of the new firms in the Bangalore-Hyderabad axis of the "Silicon Plateau," it is instructive to examine the case of Gray Cell/Unimobile, once a member of this new breed of globally minded firms. Unimobile used to be a California company providing wireless data solutions to major multinational corporations worldwide. In May 2002, it was bought out by the U.S. printing technology firm Electronics for Imaging (EFI), a move designed to ensure its continued existence in the face of difficult financing conditions. Unimobile was based in Santa Clara, California, with a network operating center and development facility in Bangalore, India, and a sales office in Barcelona, Spain; at its peak, it had just 90 employees worldwide. The firm offered a platform for developing and delivering secure, real-time wireless data on any mobile device across multiple network protocols, a capability that was attractive to EFI, which hopes to use Unimobile's technology to get mobile phones to direct documents to nearby printers on EFI's PrintME network technology.

Unimobile was not always a Silicon Valley firm. It was founded in 1996 as Gray Cell Applied Technologies Private Limited in Bangalore, India. Gray Cell pioneered Internet-to-mobile communications and developed the world's first wireless-internet gateway in 1996. The name Gray Cell was taken from the British epithet for intellect and reflected the ambitious vision of its founder to set up a world-class, cutting-edge IT company in India. The founder of Gray Cell was a homegrown entrepreneur who had not spent any significant time outside India until then. After about three years of trying to grow the company in Bangalore, he realized that Gray Cell needed a jump-start and decided to approach VCs in Silicon Valley. The timing was right, and a leading VC in Silicon Valley was receptive to his pitch—with the caveat that to achieve its objectives, Gray Cell, and in particular its marketing and business development arms, needed to be based in Silicon Valley. In June 1999, Gray Cell received its Series A venture capital funding, a total of $2 million from Draper International, Walden International Investment Group, and two Silicon Valley entrepreneurs of Indian origin who had founded Exodus

Communications. After the Series A funding, Gray Cell moved to Silicon Valley and acquired a CEO who was born and educated in India. At that point, the company was renamed Unimobile, Inc.

Technological Imprinting and Mindsets
To some extent, the technological trajectories followed by these different types of firms, and the challenges they face as they seek to migrate toward e-business and other higher value-added solutions, appears to be loosely coupled to when they came into existence and what areas they were pioneers in (Kogut 1993). This "technological imprinting" appears to stay with them and shape their mindsets as they go forward and seek to upgrade to higher value-added activities (see table 6.3).

For example, many of the early software houses (such as HCL and Wipro) began as hardware firms diversifying into the software area (Arora et al. 2001). These firms have tended to remain most wedded to work on legacy systems and large-scale MIS projects in areas such as banking and financial services that were typical of the body-shopping era. Even some of the later entrants who did not bring a hardware legacy with them, such as Infosys and Satyam, were not able to completely move away from these fairly low-technology projects. All of these firms have developed certain key capabilities such as deep knowledge of legacy systems software and the systematic documentation and software development process capabilities that are involved in coordinating large numbers of programmers. These skills and discipline have earned many of these software houses the coveted CMM Level 4 and 5 classifications, based on the sophistication of their software development process capabilities.

The earliest entrants, such as TCS, Datamatics, Wipro, BFL, and Birla Software, and to some extent the ones that followed them, such as Infosys and Satyam, tended to get pieces of outsourced work on systems that had typically been architected by someone else. As a result, they did not need to develop much of a marketing orientation, or the capabilities required to proactively pull customers up the technological trajectory by "telling them what to do" rather than being in the position of "being told what to do," even though they often had the knowledge in-house to be able to provide such a service. Their migration up the value chain has thus been largely "reactive migration," being pulled by customer demands rather than being one step ahead of their customers. As one of the later-generation entrepreneurs interviewed put it, the traditional software houses' "customers were the MIS departments of multinationals, or other consultants—our customers are marketing departments and we deal directly with our customers' customers."

This generational technological imprinting also affects the mindsets of the firms in terms of their aspirations and operational structures. The earliest firms continue to have a largely ethnocentric "exporter" mindset, with mostly India-based operations; some of the slightly later firms appear to have developed a slightly more "polycentric" or "multinational" orientation, with FDI in several countries, and a few of the latest generation of entrepreneurs appear to have coordinated global operations with employees and owners of different nationalities, although there are perhaps fewer than a handful of such truly "geocentrically" minded firms in India as yet (Perlmutter 1969). In general, the pioneers in each era have found it harder than new entrants to develop the appropriate mindset that might enable them to make the required transformations to migrate up the value chain.

In the short- to medium-term, being the low-cost provider of low-end services can be a profitable niche for these firms (especially if they can locate most of their labor offshore, in India, rather than on-site where their clients are, in order to capture higher margins). However, in the long run, this is likely to be an unsustainable competitive position, as their margins come under pressure. A cause for concern is that the revenue per employee in the software industry in India in 1998 stood at around $15,000 p.a., whereas the comparable figure for Israel and Ireland was $100,000 p.a. (Arora et al. 2000). More recent figures put the revenue per employee of non-CMM certified software firms in India at $23,710 and of CMM-certified firms at $35,120 (Arora et al. 2001), still far below the Irish or Israeli average. Indian software houses thus still compete primarily on the basis of cheap labor, judging from these figures, whatever their rhetoric. There is, however, some variance in the revenues per employee across the Indian software firms. Excluding firms such as IBM in India, whose revenues per employee tend to be inflated by the fact that their projects often also involve hardware installation, and focusing on the pure software firms, Tata Consultancy Services, the oldest and largest of these firms and the top software exporter in the country, is also at the top of the "big four" (TCS, Wipro, Infosys, Satyam), with revenues per employee of over $45,000 in 2000–2001. Satyam, the worst performer on revenues per employee in this group, received a little over $22,000 per employee in 1999–2000. Infosys and Wipro both had revenues of around $32,000 per employee in 1999–2000. Even the best of these firms thus fares much worse on revenues per employee than the Israeli or Irish companies. There are many software firms in India that continue to supply software labor for as little as $12–$15 an hour.

The role of technological imprinting and the associated mindsets becomes particularly important in dealing with the realities of e-business software development, which differs on many dimensions from traditional software development (see table 6.4).

Although comfort with legacy systems and with constantly changing platforms and their strong tradition of continuous training in new software applications has been helpful to the traditional software firms as they migrate toward yet another set of platforms and software skills, certain features of the new technology—in particular speed and the customer-driven, design-as-you-go character of development in e-business—tend to conflict with some of the software development process capabilities that these firms have built. The methodical approach to documentation and the discipline involved in the staged testing and sequential development processes of traditional software development translates imperfectly into the e-business world. The constant need to interact with the ultimate customers and end users during the development process calls for marketing skills, non-Indian employees, and a global mindset. These are characteristics that many Indian software firms that have honed their human resource and operational routines doing "body-shop" work may find difficult to develop.

Further, the traditional software houses pride themselves on their ability to cobble together solutions that integrate existing legacy systems and pieces of new off-the-shelf software into seamless applications at a reasonable price—an ability that stems from a tradition of creativity under conditions of resource constraint. As one entrepreneur put it, "Culturally, the idea of IT as a consumable is not pervasive in Indian industry." These skills are not to be scoffed at. There are not many firms capable of working with and around old, often badly written and documented code. However, the learning from each such integration project tends to be idiosyncratic and largely tacit, carried by the individuals who

Table 6.4
Differences between Traditional Software and E-business Software Realities for Indian Software Suppliers

	Traditional software development	E-business software development
Development cycle times	6–24 months	1–3 months
Problem-solving approach	"Throw *people* at the problem"	Use sophisticated *tools* (often requires alliances)
Growth model	*Slow, organic growth*	*Rapid growth* through alliances and acquisitions
Design architecture	Design for *stability*, few major changes expected over life of software	Design for *modification*, frequent changes expected
Design sequence	*Sequential*, "Waterfall"	*Simultaneous*, build entire core and modify
Design specifications	*Clear* specifications	*Ambiguous* specifications
Competencies	*Scale* Legacy systems knowledge *Process Skills* Staged testing Extensive documentation	*Speed* Marketing *Customer relationships*
Frequency of end-user or customer involvement in design and development	Up front, *one-time* or infrequent	*Continuous* end-user/ customer involvement
Pricing model	*Cost based* pricing	*Value based* pricing
Locus of development	*Offshore* (i.e., in India) High margins	At least partly *on-site* (at customer location) Lower margins on on-site component
Typical client within the MNC	*MIS* departments	*Marketing departments*
Firm's relationship with customer	*Customer leads*—software firm follows	*Customer needs to be led*

work on it. This makes it difficult to reuse the code, replicate the system, or to package and "productize" this knowledge. Only 24 percent of Indian software revenues come from the sale of scaleable "products" as opposed to the sale of services (NASSCOM-McKinsey Study 2000).

There may be some silver linings to this technological trajectory, however. In a global economic slowdown, the ability to pull together low-cost system integration solutions that work within the constraints of existing legacy systems might actually be a highly desirable capability in a software supplier, and a source of competitive advantage. Certainly the undisputed lead position held by the first and today Asia's largest software export house—TCS—for over 25 years, building on exactly this type of systems integration knowledge, leads one to believe that there is value in these capabilities. Furthermore, the cost-cutting drive in IT departments in U.S. companies observed in 2001 has resulted in more outsourcing of large IT projects in India; TCS, for instance, continues to show growth rates over 40 percent even in the face of the sharp economic downturn worldwide. Although other emerging countries such as the Philippines and China are emerging as competitors, India still retains the advantage of "branding," being perceived as a superior production site for software. Indian software firms are keenly aware of how other countries, notably China, are playing catch-up: Infosys recently announced plans to open an office in China, in keeping with its strategy to be a truly global company.

The tacitness of the knowledge created in the provision of customized services and its non-scalability, however, do pose some special challenges to Indian software firms as they attempt to institutionalize their knowledge and move into higher-margin areas. Specifically, in a global market for talent, the retention of senior systems people who are the carriers of the tacit technological knowledge becomes critically important, as does the development of strong globally oriented marketing people who can talk to customers and end users worldwide. As the market for labor in this area becomes increasingly global, to maintain growth and profitability, the traditional software houses may need to break free from their generational technological imprinting and become more truly global players themselves. In the process, they may have to abandon routines developed in the body-shop era of cost-based pricing, which will not be easy without a focused organizational change effort.

As an example of the specific technological competencies Indian firms may draw on as they try to move up the value chain, specific competencies in digital signal processing software (DSP) are enabling some Indian firms to break into higher technology areas. India has the highest concentration of DSP-literate programmers in the world, a consequence of companies such as TI, Motorola, and Analog Devices lobbying India's technical institutes to add DSP courses to their curricula. A recent entrant into this area is Ittiam ("I think therefore I am"), one of the new generation firms set up by exiles from Texas Instruments (India) and funded by Global Technology Ventures. This firm is positioning itself as a product firm, providing DSP systems for embedded applications, reference boards, and customized solutions to customers worldwide. Even with the downturn in global telecom, this firm appears to be attracting both investment and paying customers.

In conclusion, did the Internet radically alter Indian institutions? At the level of government and governance, it has certainly begun to transform transparency and access to the public of several state governments, most notably Andhra Pradesh and Karnataka. It has also demonstrated that one individual, in this instance, the chief minister of Andhra Pradesh, Chandrababu Naidu, could use technology to bring about significant transformation in the governance of a state. That Chief Minister Naidu could get re-elected to a second term despite resistance from vested interests that stood to lose from the greater transparency of e-governance, is a testament to the widespread acceptance (no urban-rural divide here!) of the transforming powers of technology.

At the industry level, software and e-business are entrenched in the Indian psyche as an area where Indian firms can compete and win in global competition. Attempting to replicate the success of the Indian IT story, many small and large Indian firms have now turned their sights on biotech, which is viewed as an area of growth over the next two decades. As a cultural phenomenon, the software industry in general, and more specifically, the new entrepreneurial start-ups of 1999–2001, have shown a generation of Indians accustomed to seeking out sinecures in government jobs and particularly in the bureaucracy of the Indian Administrative Services that careers in the private sector in general, and entrepreneurship in particular, are viable and indeed lucrative and satisfying career options. This trend toward seeing entrepreneurs as heroes, entrepreneurship as a desirable career choice, and computer literacy as key to personal advancement, represents a major cultural shift at the end of the twentieth century in India. Although this transformation began in the late 1980s in the software industry, with entrepreneurs such as Mr. Narayanamurthi of Infosys attaining near-iconic status, this cultural shift was undoubtedly accelerated by the advent of the Internet, and with it, the new Indian-American entrepreneur-heroes of Silicon Valley, who are widely recognized across all classes of Indian society. These contributions to the cognitive institutions of Indian society and the cultural transformation this has wrought may be the most far-reaching impact of the Internet economy on India.

Acknowledgments

We thank the Reginald H. Jones Center of the Wharton School for financial support for this project. We would also like to thank the many managers, entrepreneurs, and venture capitalists who willingly gave their time to us in India and in the United States, and the chief minister of Karnataka, the commissioner of Bangalore, and the IT secretaries of Andhra Pradesh and Karnataka for sharing their insights. Needless to say, all opinions expressed in this chapter are our own, and we apologize for any factual or interpretive errors we may have made.

7

The German Internet Economy and the "Silicon Valley Model": Convergence, Divergence, or Something Else?

Steven Casper

Introduction

Over the postwar period, the German economy has excelled, but not in high technology. Although the Internet economy has had a profound effect over many areas of German economic and social life, this article focuses on one core issue: has the Internet economy driven a fundamental change in the German economy, such that it can support high-technology entrepreneurial activity? In particular, can "Silicon Valley" forms of technological start-ups prosper in Germany?

Evidence based on the financing and growth of new economy firms suggests they can. There is no doubt that over the last few years the new economy has taken hold in Germany. Information technology has, over the course of the 1980s, become the fastest growing segment of the German economy (at over 10 percent growth per year) and the largest new employment generator. Whereas few entrepreneurial start-ups existed in the 1980s and early 1990s, hundreds of technology start-ups have been founded over the last few years, most with venture capital, and well over 250 technology firms have successfully taken initial public offerings on a new NASDAQ-inspired stock market. The goal of this chapter is to examine the combination of institutional incentives and technological drivers supporting this boom.

A reversal of fortunes surrounding the fate of new technology companies has occurred in Germany, with the growth of the Internet playing a key role. However, this turnaround is of a particular sort. This chapter provides an overview of the development of competitive competencies within German Internet technology firms, emphasizing important human resource characteristics in addition to high-risk financing. This overview suggests that important continuities remain within the German business system, particularly with regard to the ability of firms to quickly hire and fire personnel—a key requirement of firms hoping to compete in technologically intensive markets where "competency destruction" is high.

Although institutions are important, technology drivers can also promote innovation. To examine these effects in Germany, I examine the role of large German firms in encouraging new economy start-ups through technological leadership. This survey shows the weaknesses of German large firms in core networking technologies driving the growth of the Internet. However, it also identifies important demonstration effects in non-infrastructure areas of software: first by SAP in showing German firms how to compete in enterprise software markets, and more recently by Intershop, a key German player in international e-commerce software markets.

In order to present a detailed analysis of the activities of German entrepreneurial Internet firms, the chapter focuses on patterns of subsector specialization within German Internet software firms. What is the level of technological intensity among these firms? How are their business models organized? Do these firms appear sustainable? The analysis is based on visits to over a dozen of these companies, supplemented by performance and structural statistics on all Internet software-related companies listed on Germany's technology oriented stock market as of January 2001.

The chapter is organized in three parts, followed by a conclusion. To set the stage, the first section examines the broad shape of the emerging German Internet economy, focusing in particular on a range of regulatory and demand driven factors that have shaped a large market for Internet technologies, but with some important differences compared to the United States. The second section focuses more narrowly on a range of institutional and technology driven factors that are influencing the development of technologies in Germany. The section focuses in particular on the management of key competencies within entrepreneurial firms, demonstrating how a number of institutional and technological drivers have hampered the sustained orchestration of entrepreneurial technology firms in Germany. The third section then examines the emerging Internet economy in Germany, first through a broad lens focusing on macro-institutional changes spurring the entry of new economy firms, then in more detail through an analysis of business models and related organizational structures of key groups of German Internet software firms.

The conclusion to this analysis, briefly stated, is that though important changes are taking place, the German economy cannot easily support "Silicon Valley" types of organization. This carries with it the implication that German Internet firms will have a difficult time competing in markets with a high level of technological intensity. However, the analysis also demonstrates that certain types of entrepreneurial competencies can be developed in Germany and that, interestingly, Germany's nascent new economy financial institutions, intertwined with old economy labor market institutions, may promote patterns of competitive advantage not easily sustained in massively deregulated labor markets, such as those in the United States.

The German Internet Economy: An Overview

At about $250 billion in 2001, Germany's information technology sector, driven in recent years by the Internet, is the third largest in the world, behind the United States and Japan (6 percent of the world market) and the largest in Europe (21 percent). This market has grown by over 10 percent a year during the late 1990s, slowing down to around 5 percent in 2001 and 2002 (BITCOM 2001). Employment in the IT sector is over 820,000 as of early 2001, of which 47 percent work in software related market segments. Employment growth, an issue of high political importance in post unification Germany, has been substantial in the IT area—averaging around 5 percent per year in the late 1990s and peaking at over 10 percent in 2000 (BITCOM 2001).

Germany's IT infrastructure, though well behind the United States, is impressive. Figure 7.1 presents some summary statistics. The United States is far ahead of Germany in important areas, such as the density of PCs, the percentage of the population who are Internet users, and the number of Internet hosts as a percentage of the population. The United States is also far ahead of Germany in most areas of broadband imple-

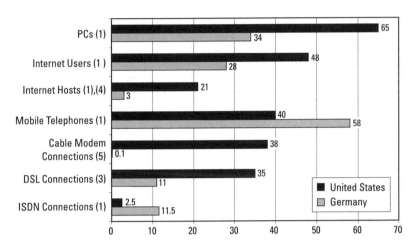

Figure 7.1
Information technology infrastructure in the United States and Germany, 2000
Notes: (1) per 100 inhabitants, (2) per 100 households, (3) per 1000 households, (4) as of
September 2000, (5) NetValue estimates found at ⟨www.cyberatlas.com⟩.
Source: BITCOM, found at ⟨www.bitcom.de⟩.

mentation (i.e., cable modems and DSL), though, for reasons explained
shortly, Germany has a much higher percentage of middleband ISDN
connections than the United States. As with most European economies,
Germany's wireless communications networks are well developed, fostering hopes that the implementation of third generation, higher bandwidth
wireless networks will drive innovation for German firms in this area.
Overall, although generally lower than the United States, Germany's
Internet infrastructure is strong by global standards.

Germany has well-developed markets for most e-commerce Internet
activities. German business-to-business activities have grown strongly. A
recent survey of data from a number of market research organizations
estimates the size of German B2B markets to be between $10 and $40
billion in 1999, $40 to $80 billion in 2000, $80 to $160 billion in 2001,
and to grow to $160 to $300 billion in 2002 (ECIN 2001). In a related
statistic, German business appears to be leading the major European
economies in e-procurement. A survey of small- and medium-sized businesses conducted by the U.K. Department of Trade and Industry revealed that 54 percent of German firms have moved at least part of their

procurement process online, a percentage equal to that in the United States and only slightly behind the United Kingdom (Moran 2000).

Turning to business-to-consumer e-commerce, markets in this area are also maturing. According to a recent survey, German consumers spent $3.87 billion online for the year beginning July 2000 and ending June 2001 (GfK, 2001a, 2001b). Germany has fostered a number of successful home-grown sites, particularly in books and travel markets, even while most of the large American e-commerce firms, such as Amazon.com or eBay have moved aggressively into the German market. Within Europe, anecdotal reports indicate that the United Kingdom is leading in overall business to consumer shopping. For example, one recent study reports that German consumers spend 15.3 minutes per month shopping online, compared to 19.7 minutes in the United Kingdom (Pastore 2001). The structure of "indigenous" German e-commerce marketplaces is relatively strong, however. As of April 2000, seven of the top 10 German e-commerce sites were of German origin (Pastore 2000). The country's dot.com segment is weaker than that in the United States, with only a handful of firms that have successfully taken initial public offerings on the German stock market for growth companies. However, a number of private firms are doing well, particularly in the online travel and book-selling businesses (see PriceWaterhouseCoopers 2001).

Within most European countries, the development of large-scale data communications networks has been crucially dependent on telecom deregulation processes (see Glimstedt 2001). Following most European countries, German policymakers began a long discussion over the liberalization of its telecommunications sector during the 1980s, leading to a partial liberalization of the sector in 1990, and, in 1993, a decision to fully privatize Deutsche Telekom, the long-established monopoly service provider (see Vogel 1996). Although competition has gradually developed in long-distance provision and many high value-added corporate services, the ownership structure created by the privatization process has strongly shaped the structure of Internet service provision in Germany. Though allowing new entry, the German deregulation process has given Deutsche Telekom large if not dominating stakes in each of the three core connectivity technologies over which broadband networks have developed. Together with local municipalities, Deutsche Telekom owns a controlling interest in Germany's cable infrastructure (impacting cable modem access), is the dominant player in traditional land-based local and long-distance networks (impacting DSL-type technologies), and is one of three dominant network providers in the wireless market. This industry structure has limited competition across competing connectivity technologies, and through doing so generally slowed the introduction of broadband Internet technologies in Germany (see Wittke and Hanekop 1999).

Deutsche Telekom has focused its efforts on maximizing the value of existing copper-based networks. Its most substantial broadband investments are in DSL technologies, leading to relatively high early penetration by German households of this technology (about 1 percent in early 2001). As seen in figure 7.1, virtually no substantial investments in cable modem technologies have occurred in Germany, due in large part to the ownership structure of Germany's extensive cable television network (Wittke and Hanekop 1999). Third generation wireless technologies, as of late 2001, are far from emerging in Germany, but could spur competition with Deutsche Telekom from successful independent wireless carriers such as Mannesmann Vodafone.

From a comparative perspective, the very high concentration of German households using ISDN technology (11 percent) is interesting and relates directly to early, somewhat ill-fated investments in digital technologies by Deutsche Telekom's public predecessor, the Deutsche Bundespost. Throughout the 1970s and 1980s, the Deutsche Bundespost channeled large research and development grants to Siemens, then the national champion network equipment provider, to create switching technologies integrating voice and data (Cawson et al. 1990). Siemens hoped to become an international leader in integrated digital switching technology. During the 1970s, it focused on a proprietary system but, when this effort failed, turned to international standards surrounding ISDN during the 1980s. As discussed in more detail below, Siemens largely failed in this ambition, and has struggled to gain a strong foothold in Internet networking technologies partially as a result.

Because of its relatively low bandwidth by today's standards (66 kilobits per channel), ISDN has been dwarfed by a variety of newer technologies such as ATM. Nevertheless, large investments by the Deutsche Bundespost before the Internet boom have given it a large capacity to serve domestic telephone customers with ISDN service at relatively low prices, relatively simple connection processes, and reliable service that does not block voice telephone lines. Due to its advantages over dial-up modems, access to middleband Internet might serve as a valuable tool to introduce German households to the Internet, driving demand for both Internet services, and, eventually, higher value-added broadband connections.

In general, this survey of the German Internet economy highlights two broad points. First, in line with the general argument of this book, it suggests that important cross-national variation exists in the structure of the German Internet economy, highlighting the importance of country-specific policy traditions, particularly surrounding telecommunications deregulation, in explaining technological development. Second, it establishes that, though far behind the United States, Germany ranks high by most international comparisons in developing a dense information technology infrastructure supporting the Internet.

The demand for Internet technologies is high in Germany, as it is in most of Germany's core trading partners. How have German firms performed in supplying this technology? The remainder of the chapter investigates this theme, focusing first on institutional and technological factors related to the creation of entrepreneurial technology firms in Germany.

Building New Technology Firms within the German Economy: Institutions and Technology

Institutional Drivers

One way to analyze the types of entrepreneurism found in technological hot beds such as Silicon Valley is through examining types of competency development found consistently within these firms (for overviews of Silicon Valley, see Saxenian 1994; Kenney 2000; and the chapters by Kogut and Kenney in this volume). The entrepreneurial business models organized within small innovative firms are associated with the development of three key competencies: the management of high-risk finance, the development of human resources within a "competency destroying" environment, and the creation of sufficiently high-powered motivational incentives for personnel.

Managing High-risk Finance Successful Internet start-ups often create enormous financial returns. However, high technological volatility, reliance on often unproven business models, and appropriability risks created by low entry barriers can produce substantial financial risks. Internet firms generally have high "burn rates," generated by large R&D and marketing costs coupled with low profitability in start-up and expansion phases. To obtain investment funds, most entrepreneurial technology firms use equity leveraged financing schemes—trading equity within the firm for finance at different periods in the firm's development. At early stages, equity deals are made with venture capitalists, and then later through the investment banking community and third-party investors through stock offerings.

From a competency development perspective, managers of Internet firms must manage complex relationships with venture capitalists, investment bankers, and other financiers to enable funding of high-risk ventures. Within the firm, this usually necessitates the creation of business strategies that can accommodate the creation of milestones negotiated with VCs to justify further funding. However, the viability of equity leveraged financial plans is also strongly dependent on viable exit options for financiers within financial markets (both to quickly close out unsuccessful investments, but more importantly to exit successful ones through IPOs or, in some cases, mergers or acquisitions). Knowing that the investors can (and will) exit if projects under-perform puts continual pressure on managers of Internet firms to demonstrate at key milestones that their projects have met growth or earnings targets that justify on-going capital investments.

Developing Human Resources within a "Competency Destroying" Environment Attracting and retaining staff and managers to work in the risky and dynamic environments of technology start-ups is a second challenge facing most Internet firms. Staff mobility within entrepreneurial start-up firms is generally much higher than at firms within established industries. Extensive hiring and firing is routine at many Internet start-ups. This is particularly true in firms engaged in the development of new Internet technologies, such as middleware firms involved in the creation of software interfaces to exploit new standards or protocols. A large number of projects fail on technological grounds, are cut for commercial reasons (due to the failure of surrounding business models), or change focus over time.

Where competency destruction is high, asset recycling becomes an important organizational problem (Bahrami and Evans 2000). To achieve flexibility, managers of technology firms must have the ability to develop quickly new research and development competencies while cutting others. To do this, they must have access to a pool of software developers, technicians, and other specialists with known reputations in particular areas that can quickly be recruited to work on projects. If "asset recycling" is difficult or if there is a cultural stigma attached to failing or changing jobs regularly, then engineers and managers may choose not to commit to firms with high-risk research projects, for fear that if the project fails the value of his or her engineering and/or management experiences could significantly decline.

Organizing High-powered Motivational Incentives for Personnel Many Internet software firms must create organizational structures facilitating innovation in complex technological fields. Managers must motivate staff to commit to what are often demanding, competitive, and time-intensive work environments. Technology start-ups often employ performance-based incentive schemes to induce employees to commit to intense work environments and reduce hold-up risks. The prospect of large financial rewards acts to align the private incentives of engineers and software developers with those of commercial managers (see Miller 1992). In addition to salary increases and performance pay, over the last decade, companies have primarily used share-options packages, made attractive by the expectation that share value will multiply many times if the company goes public or is sold at a high valuation to another firm. A third competency challenge faced by most managers of Internet firms is credibly maintaining such high-powered performance incentives.

The successful orchestration of each of these three competencies is strongly influenced by institutional environments within which firms are embedded. Firms situated in economies with abundant high-risk venture capital and follow-on capital market institutions, robust labor markets for highly trained personnel, and a company law and industrial relations

environment conducive to the orchestration of high-powered performance incentives should prosper relative to firms in impoverished institutional environments.

A brief survey of the U.S. case supports this argument. In the financial
area, U.S.-based Internet firms have been able to organize financial
resources through turning to a huge market for high-risk venture capital embedded within supportive, facilitative financial institutions. Most
importantly, through the NASDAQ exchange, massive capital markets
exist in which thousands of technology firms have successfully taken
listings. This exit option allows early stage investors to adopt a portfolio
strategy by diversifying risks across several investments. It also creates
a viable refinancing mechanism for venture capitalists (Gompers and
Lerner 2001). Turning to the issue of competency destruction, generally
deregulated labor markets in the United States are conducive to the
development of extremely active markets for engineers and managers
within clusters of high-technology firms that have adopted complementary human resource policies (see Saxenian 1994; Hyde 1998). Through
lowering the career risk faced by talented personnel that sign on with
technologically speculative firms, clusters of technologically intense firms
can easily develop. Finally, the prospect of large financial rewards
through realistic IPO scenarios for successful firms coupled with a series
of stock-option friendly finance and industrial relations laws help U.S.
technology start-ups easily craft high-powered performance instruments
—a prime reason why U.S. high-tech firms have become associated with
extremely long work-weeks and general dedication to projects.

Until recently, none of these institutional characteristics existed in
Germany. Its economy has long been categorized as "organized" or
"coordinated" (Hall and Soskice 2001). German institutions facilitate the
creation of organizational competencies necessary for firms active in sectors characterized by incremental innovation processes within established
industries, such as many segments within the metal-working, engineering,
and chemicals sectors (Streeck 1992). Deep patterns of vocational training within firms, consensual decisionmaking, long-term employment, and
patient finance are all linked to the systematic exploitation of established
technologies to a wide variety of niche markets, a strategy Streeck (1992)
labels "diversified quality production." On the other hand, the regulatory
nature of German economic institutions combined with pervasive non-

market patterns of coordination within the economy create constraints against the organization of industries that best perform within shorter term, market-based patterns of coordination (Soskice 1997).

A brief survey demonstrates this weak institutional support for competency development within German entrepreneurial technology firms.

High-risk Finance   Germany's traditionally credit-based financial system excels at providing "patient finance" to firms in traditional sectors with relatively low long-term risk, but provides obstacles toward the financing of more risky entrepreneurial projects (Edwards and Fischer 1994). As late as 1996, market capitalization as a percentage of GDP in Germany was only 26 percent, compared to 121 percent in the United States and 151 percent in the United Kingdom (Deutsche Bundesbank 1997). Venture capital is hard to sustain in countries without large capital markets willing to support high-risk initial public offerings. In addition to often discussed financing "gaps" in high-risk capital within bank-centered financial systems, the lack of experienced venture capitalists with in-depth industry knowledge and contacts creates additional difficulties. Investors rely on experts to monitor investments, whereas young firms often rely on venture capitalists for strategic advice and access to personal networks that often prove crucial in arranging key business alliances and recruiting key managers or scientists (see Tylecote and Conesa 1999).

Human Resource Development   In Germany, stake-holder based company laws combine with high financial burdens on employee dismissals to promote long-term employment within firms. Labor law cedes a formal right for staff at all firms with over five employees to form a works council, which holds important bargaining rights over personnel policy, training, and overtime. Within German manufacturing firms, works councils usually demand long-term employment guarantees in return for flexibility in work organization and overtime negotiations (see Streeck 1984). This helps the management of German firms to convince their workers to invest in skills or knowledge that are often tacit or firm-specific and thus difficult to sell on the open labor market. Although "competency enhancement" within organizations is strong in Germany, it systematically inhibits the creation of active labor markets needed to create incentives for firms and their employees to embark on high-risk projects with a strong possibility of failure. Similarly, limits on hiring and firing make it difficult for firms to compete in rapidly developing fields in which necessary research competencies change quickly.

Employee Financial Motivation Germany's bank-centered financial system tends to dampen ownership related incentives through muting the effectiveness of share dispersal schemes. Without a realistic possibility of making an initial public offering, the performance incentive provided by stock options or outright share dispersals is weakened (though merger activity or management buy-outs provide weaker exit options). Prior to 1998, legal restrictions on firms buying and selling their own shares further complicated matters by creating technical difficulties in the organization of stock option plans. Moreover, German works councils strongly resist efforts by management to institute performance related pay, especially on an individual basis. Although most small German technology firms established during the early 1990s and during the recent boom have not created work councils (*Wirtschaftswoche* 2000), if they do begin to form, similar restraints on performance pay and similar schemes might emerge.

In sum, core German market institutions are primarily geared toward the creation of firm-level competencies needed to create sustained, incremental innovation patterns in industries with lower scientific intensity. The result during the 1980s and early 1990s was poor performance in most sectors with technological profiles that are best advantaged through the creation of entrepreneurial business models (see Casper, Lehrer, and Soskice 1999). Germany lacks institutions to nurture *systematically* the development of entrepreneurial competencies.

Technology Drivers

Institutional explanations ignore the importance of technology drivers in fostering growth. They neglect the role of entrepreneurs—especially when facing potentially vast new markets—in engineering successful organizational structures in the face of inhospitable business climates. Germany's oldest new economy firms, although now large, emerged as entrepreneurial start-ups in the 1980s and early 1990s to exploit technology innovations by their founders. These include Europe's most successful biotechnology firm, Qiagen, as well the software giant SAP. Both firms were founded in an era where few if any of the "appropriate" institutions for entrepreneurial technology businesses existed.

Although explanations focused on the activities of individual entrepreneurs are difficult to sustain, it is possible to examine the role of technology drivers. How do patterns of technological leadership—for example, in telecommunications technologies—influence patterns of technological specialization within the Internet economy? Can large firms playing dominant roles in the provision of particular technologies provide spillovers within regional economies that can override normal institutional constraints?

Technological hubs created by dominant firms can dramatically change "normal" institutional incentives within economies. The Swedish example is indicative. Although Sweden has a national institutional infrastructure similar to Germany, Ericsson's current leadership in third generation wireless technologies has helped create a technology hub in the Stockholm area that has a technological intensity far more similar to Silicon Valley than normal patterns of industrial organization in Sweden. In Ericsson's case, hub effects created by the firm's lead in developing important next generation wireless standards such as WAP and Bluetooth, and a switch during the late 1990s from property to open development standards, have allowed local start-up ventures easily to develop technologies compatible with Ericsson's technologies. Technology spillovers have been complemented by a major change in employment policy at Ericsson. Resignations of several key systems engineers during the late 1990s compelled the firm to switch from a relatively closed to open employment policy. This has dramatically lowered the career risk of talented engineers working in Internet technology firms in the Stockholm area—if start-up ventures fail, engineers retain the possibility of returning to a "normal" large firm career at Ericsson. Within normally conservative labor markets, this employment insurance is a key catalyst for creating extremely active labor markets necessary to sustain competency destroying technology strategies (see chapter 4, this volume, and Casper and Glimstedt 2000).

In contrast to the Swedish case, the technological intensity of the German Internet economy has suffered from a lack of important "upstream" firms in either the network or connectivity layers of Internet-based telecommunications. Although German firms are minor players in some areas, they have not become dominant forces in the creation of system architectures and related standards in core emerging network or connectivity markets. This point is best made through an overview of the activities of large German firms within the context of telecommunication network infrastructure markets.

The Network Layer During the 1970s and 1980s, Siemens was Germany's quasi-monopoly provider of telecommunication switches and a strong international player in centralized switching systems for voice traffic. As mentioned above, Siemens emerged as an important player in the development of ISDN switching systems during the early 1980s. As ISDN was the dominant early digital telephone switching technology (i.e., one that could accommodate data and voice traffic), this investment could have given Siemens a strong position in the manufacture of digital networking equipment. However, over the past several years, Siemens has emerged as only a weak player in a number of high-capacity digital networking technologies, and only recently, through purchasing several U.S.-based companies, has emerged as a competitor in Internet-based switching technologies.

The development of fixed network technology parallels wireless equipment as the other truly massive network equipment market within the Internet economy (Cisco's dominance of the router segment of this market has transformed it into the firm with the world's highest market capitalization). During the 1990s, ever increasing network traffic created widespread latency concerns over pure Internet protocol (IP) based networks. This created demand by large corporations and governmental customers for telecommunication equipment providers to develop a range of high-capacity "overlay" networks that could provide higher network capacity and reliability (see Dodd 1999). To compete successfully in these markets, established telecommunication equipment manufacturers including Lucent, Nortel, and Alcatel generally compete with Cisco and other providers of cheap IP-based routing equipment to provide more expensive but also more intelligent networking capacity to corporate and other large clients. This has led to the development of frame relay, ATM, and other networking technologies that attempt to provide rapidly increasing levels of bandwidth capability and reliability.

During the mid to late 1990s, a high-end switching technology called ATM (asynchronous transfer mode) was widely heralded as the most important broadband networking technology. ATM switches repackage variable-length IP data packets into fixed-length packets that are then sequentially channelled over fixed network channels at very high bandwidth. The low latency provided by sequential transmission of packets allows the reliable channelling of high-quality video and other data-rich multimedia content. Combined with the development of a large market for leased network capacity (spearheaded by WorldCom, Global-Crossing, and others), it allowed large corporate clients to create geographically dispersed intranets with very high functionality that could simultaneously connect to often overcrowded public networks. North American firms have become key providers of ATM technologies—above all Ascend, but also Fore Networks, Bay Networks, and Newbridge Networks. Large telecommunication switch providers quickly formed alliances with and eventually acquired each of these firms.

During the mid 1990s, Siemens decided to develop switches with ATM technologies as one of its core moves on the Internet. To do so it developed an alliance with Newbridge Networks, a Canadian firm that for a time was a leading provider of high-end ATM switching equipment for very large corporate networks and governments. The alliance floundered. Although corporate culture conflicts played a strong role (see Meissner and Naschold 1999), on-going corporate restructuring within Newbridge has been a central problem (Saunders 1998). Weaknesses within its manufacturing division and an inability to compete in fast-growing markets for lower-end ATM equipment severely depressed Newbridge's share price (Greene 2000), leading to a management reorganization as well as widespread speculation during 1997 and 1998 that Siemens would acquire the firm. However, during late 1999, following Lucent's acquisition of Ascend, Alcatel, the last major telecoms giant without a strong presence in ATM markets, successfully negotiated to acquire Newbridge. Although Alcatel has allowed Newbridge to continue work with Siemens in marketing some high-end products, the acquisition can only hurt Siemens' long-term prospects in developing overlay technologies, particularly for corporate markets.

Siemens has also failed to emerge as an important player in the wireless equipment industry. Siemens was late to develop wireless technol-

ogies using GSM technologies—in part through adopting an early strategy to convince the German government to adopt rival standards that
Siemens would have a better chance of controlling. The weakness
of Siemens in the wireless area is currently so large that wireless
telecommunications consultancies such as the Yankee Group do not currently include Siemens in their semi-annual ranking tables of firm performance in this area (Yankee Group 1999). Although currently a strong
player in the chipset market for handsets, the firm has failed to capture
expanding markets for third generation wireless switching systems dominated by Ericsson. Siemens recently shifted its core wireless R&D center
to a wireless technology hub in Aalborg, Denmark. No other German
firm currently has a strong position in wireless infrastructure technologies; Bosch attempted to enter the handset market during the mid 1990s
but failed.

Siemens has recently developed competencies in increasingly IP-driven
network equipment markets. Over the last few years, large infrastructure
investments in network capacity have combined with the maturation of
optical networking technologies to increase the reliability of so-called
"dumb" networking technologies based solely on IP switching (see Gilder
2000). Siemens has become increasingly committed to adopting Internet-
based standards as the core of its switching technologies. To do this, it
has spent $950 million to acquire three small US-based Internet equip-
ment start-ups: Argon Networks, Castle Networks, and Redstone Communications, the activities of which will become integrated into a newly
expanded US research and development center in Burlington, Massachusetts (Economist 1999).

These investments signal an increased internationalization of Siemens.
Following a similar strategy of Hoechst in the area of biotechnology
(Sharp 1999), Siemens has increasingly decided to locate research competencies for important newly emerging technologies in the United
States. The success of this new strategy is undetermined—critics note
much higher investments in IP technologies by Siemens' core network
switching rivals; Cisco Systems alone acquired two dozen network
switching start-ups during the late 1990s, while Lucent is spending $20
billion on its acquisition of Ascend (*Business Week* 1999). However, the
transfer of leading edge R&D activities in data-driven network equip-

ment to the United States will surely minimize what were already weak technology spillovers around Siemens' core R&D sites in Munich.

The Connectivity Layer As discussed above, the German deregulation process has given Deutsche Telekom large if not dominating stakes in most core broadband connectivity technologies. Most technologies associated with the connectivity layer, such as the upstream provision of broadband connectivity standards (Qualcomm), chipsets for cable modems (Broadcom), or "last mile" transmission technologies (TeraBeam) have developed outside Germany. Few if any German firms are currently playing major roles in the deployment of these technologies, though both Deutsche Telecom and its Internet spin-off T-Online have large R&D budgets that could conceivably spin off new innovations. Deutshe Telekom has focused primarily on creating a dominant position within German network infrastructure provision, which it has leveraged into a number of ISP and content services now developed at T-Online. Although the success of these ventures is important for the long-term development of the German network infrastructure, they are primarily sunk-cost related businesses relying on technologies developed at the network layer; they lack significant standard-creating externalities leading to the types of technological entrepreneurism characterizing Silicon Valley, Stockholm, or other hot beds of innovation within the Internet economy.

Overall, neither of Germany's former telecom-based monopolists has developed technological trajectories that could lead to local agglomerations of technology start-ups in core Internet infrastructure technologies. Recent research by Sternberg and Tamasy (1999) on the impact of Siemens on the development of Munich's industrial structure concludes that Siemens is primarily oriented toward outsourcing complex semiconductor components and related electrical parts. This is driven in part by the decentralization of Siemens into several major electronics groups, all of which depend on a variety of relatively complex components. Sternberg and Tamasy view this as a positive development, in that Siemens does not "make or break" firms in the Munich area. Elements of hierarchy often found in more vertical supplier networks, such as those found in the automobile industry, are removed. Creating a large demand for intermediate electronic components has increased the technological intensity of the Munich area. Similarly, through creating a huge market for engineers, developers, and applied research scientists, Siemens has surely contributed to the size and leading reputations of Munich's two large universities.

The lack of technology drivers reinforces constraints created by "normal" institutional frameworks in Germany. Of particular importance, the absence of technology hubbing within local regions influences the development of active labor markets for engineers and developers within important technological fields. "Competency destroying" R&D is hard to sustain without very active labor markets for experienced scientists and engineers. Idiosyncratic evidence from interviews with Munich Internet start-ups suggests that Siemens has failed to develop either technological spillovers or human resource policies that could precipitate more technologically intense clusters of software firms in Munich. Although technological weaknesses dampened Siemens' capacity to play this role in the Munich area, Siemens has a reputation for long-term employment— generally hiring engineers early in their career, and developing their careers internally—thus muting the creation of active labor markets for high-profile scientists and engineers.

Although Munich became the main technology hub in Germany, very little of this activity is in software or equipment-related networking technologies. No software or Internet firms listed on the German stock exchange for growth stocks are currently involved in the development of new network telecommunications technologies, and less systematic evidence from field research suggests that few if any private start-ups in these areas exist in Munich. Largely due to its technological weaknesses in data telecommunications technologies, Siemens has not been able to assume a role in Germany similar to other large telecommunication equipment players, and in particular Ericsson in the Stockholm area.

Implications—German Venture Capital Markets during the 1990s

During the 1980s to mid 1990s, a combination of institutional and technological drivers created disincentives for entrepreneurial technological firms to develop. To provide an indication of the low level of entrepre-

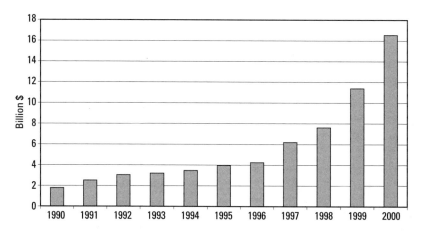

Figure 7.2
Total German VC fund size

neurial technology activity in Germany during the early 1990s, as well as highlight significant developments that have taken place during the last few years, figures 7.2 through 7.5 survey the German venture capital scene over the last decade.

During the early 1990s, a relatively low level of venture capital was available in Germany, growing incrementally from less than $2 billion in 1990 to $4 billion in 1996. Of these funds, only a small amount of venture capital was invested in new economy industries—biotechnology, information technology, or communications. Although not shown in figures 7.2 and 7.3, German Venture Capital Association data show that the vast majority of venture capital during the early 1990s was invested in engineering related industries—most typically machine tool companies seeking funds for expansion, acquisitions, or management buyouts (German Venture Capital Association 1999). Furthermore, only a paltry amount of available venture capital in Germany was invested in higher-risk start-up investments. Most money was invested in expansion activities or (the missing percentages not shown in figure 7.4) in management buy-outs and replacement capital. Business expansion and buy-out activity is far less risky than start-up financing. Business models are generally proven at expansion stages and less technical knowledge is needed by venture capitalists.

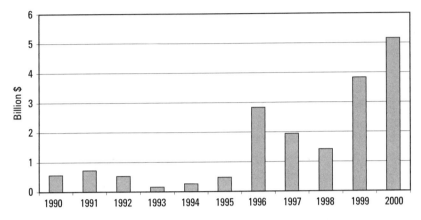

Figure 7.3
Annual growth in German VC funding

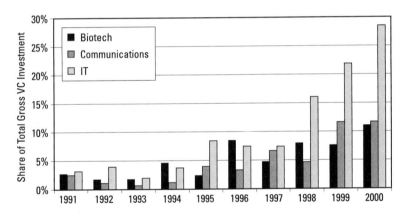

Figure 7.4
Distribution of German VC investment—Selected sectors

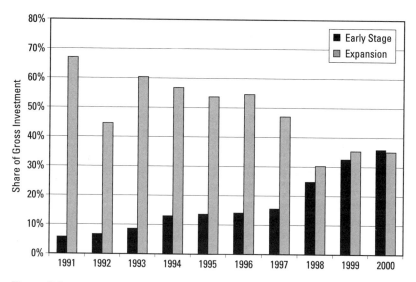

Figure 7.5
Share of German VC investment by stage

The conservative structure of the German venture capital industry is broadly consistent with the view that the country has lacked key institutions—particularly follow-on capital markets—needed to sustain the widespread growth of high-risk technology firms. Starting in roughly 1996, however, incremental expansion in German venture capital was replaced by much more rapid growth. Total funding rose from about $5 billion in 1996 to over $16 billion available in 2000. Much of this money was targeted at new economy industries. In 2000, roughly 40 percent of German venture capital was invested in communications and information technology, the two industries strongly associated with the Internet. Finally, as seen in figure 7.5, much of this investment has shifted from expansion to more risky early phase financing—well over one-third of all German venture capital was targeted at early stage financing in 2000, compared to about 6 percent in 1991.

To interpret these changes, the remainder of this chapter examines the emerging German Internet software sector in more detail. It focuses on patterns of subsector specialization within the broad Internet sector. From analyzing these patterns, we can examine the role of the interaction of institutional incentives and corporate demonstration effects in shaping key areas of competitive advantage.

The Emerging German Internet Economy

Important success stories do exist within the German Internet sector. Interestingly, large firms have played an important role. Important large-firm corporate role models have emerged from the software rather than the telecom industry, leading to an important specialization in many areas of the Internet impacting enterprise software processes. After briefly describing a series of governmental technology policies and private sector reforms designed to stimulate German entrepreneurship, we examine patterns of specialization and related corporate strategies by German Internet software developers.

The Creation of Financial Institutions to Support "New Economy" Firms

Combinations of governmental technology policies and private sector financial reforms have, since the mid 1990s, created the minimal institutional environment to systematically sustain entrepreneurial technology firms in Germany. In 1996, the German federal government, wary of criticisms of the lack of venture capital, decided to systematically provide "public venture capital" in the form of "sleeping" or silent equity partnerships from federal sources. Figure 7.6 surveys these investments. German state or *Laender* governments have organized similar programs, often providing additional funding for local firms supported by federal venture capital subsidies (see Adelberger 2000). The federal agency created to oversee this program, the Technology Holding Association (*Technologie-Beteiligungs-Gesellschaft*, known commonly as the *Tbg*), has provided on average $165 million to new start-up firms per year between 1998 and 2000, spread over roughly four hundred firms per year. Government investments are relatively small, typically about $500,000 per firm, and provided only on a matching basis when the firm has obtained private venture capital. To reduce opportunism, the Technology Holding Association relies on due diligence performed by the firm's primary venture capital sponsor to make assessments.

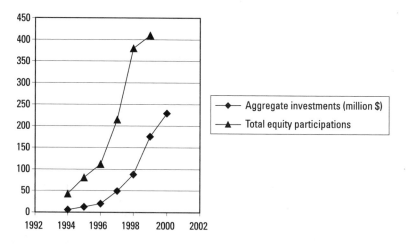

Figure 7.6
Growth of German federal "public venture capital"
Source: Tbg 2001.

A primary goal of German technology policy is to channel venture capital investments into new economy sectors. As of late 1999, about 45 percent of total investments were provided to software, information technology, and Internet businesses, with an additional 27 percent flowing into the biotech sector (*Tbg* 2001). The program is advantageous to the firms involved. In addition to dramatically reducing the cost of start-up capital, "public venture capital" investments are structured so that the recipient firm can buy back the government owned stake at any point during the first seven years of the investment. This allows firms to exploit insider knowledge of firm performance to buy back equity before public announcements that important milestones have been met.

Firms acquiring public venture capital are often also involved in a dense array of complementary programs to spur entrepreneurship, often organized by local governments within German states. These include business plan competitions promising seed-capital to winners, programs to encourage the transfer of university technology into start-ups, as well as cluster policies developed by local economic development offices to promote partnering and provide very basic consultancy advice concerning the formation of new ventures (see Adelberger 2000).

Technology policy has provided an important catalyst, but alone cannot explain the recent upsurge in German high-technology entrepreneurism. At only about $200 million in 1999, federal funds form less than 5 percent of the total sum of venture capital currently available in Germany. Private sector investments in new financial markets, coupled with supportive financial regulatory reforms, have proven much more important in creating institutions for sustainable venture capital finance in Germany. The cornerstone of these initiatives was the 1997 creation of a new technology oriented stock exchange, the *Neuer Markt*, with substantially less burdensome listing requirements than those that exist for the main stock market. As of December 2000, about 270 firms had taken initial public offerings on the *Neuer Markt*, 30 of which were initially backed by federal public venture capital programs (*Tbg* 2001). The vast majority of these firms are in technology-related businesses. In addition to numerous semiconductor and computer hardware firms and over a dozen biotechnology firms, 64 software firms with substantial Internet activities had listings on the *Neuer Markt* at year's end 2000.

The *Neuer Markt* has become Europe's leading technology stock market, spearheading the growth of investment banking activities in Germany. By providing a viable exit option to investors in technology start-ups, the *Neuer Markt* has created a financial environment more conducive to high-risk venture capital investments. The huge increase in available venture capital funding in Germany directly mirrors the introduction and success of the *Neuer Markt*. About half of all *Neuer Markt* firms in IT-related sectors currently have equity stakes held by venture capitalists—a strong indication that equity leveraged financing models are increasingly viable in Germany.

Reforms have also helped German technology start-ups introduce higher performance incentives to employees. There have been changes in financial market regulations, and the introduction in March 1998 of a change in corporate law allows firms to more easily buy and sell their own shares—a prerequisite for stock option plans. Combined with the introduction of viable initial public offering possibilities through the *Neuer Markt*, this new law has precipitated a widespread dispersal of options and related share dispersal schemes in German technology firms. Though systematic evidence on stock option plans is unavailable, each of the dozen Internet software developers interviewed for this project has implemented them. This signifies an important shift in employee motivation incentives used by German technology firms, allowing many of these firms to introduce the extreme dedication to work commonly found in Silicon Valley–type start-ups.

An environment more hospitable to technology start-ups in Germany has been created through recent technology subsidies and financial reforms. However, important continuities remain. Lack of reforms to the highly regulative German industrial relations or labor market systems, and related long-term oriented career structures continue as the norm at virtually all firms within old economy sectors. These continuities are crucial, as they have strongly influenced patterns of corporate organization and competitive advantage that are developing within the German Internet sector.

Subsector Specialization by German Internet Software Firms
A good methodology to examine the development of the German Internet software industry is to look at the performance of German firms in various market segments, such as enterprise software or packaged software. Table 7.1 contains patterns of submarket specialization of all software firms based in Germany currently listed on the *Neuer Markt* that include Internet activities in their core business.

Although only a small number of packaged software vendors exist in Germany, firms in the enterprise software category comprise over half of all German software firms listed on the *Neuer Markt*. Enterprise software

Table 7.1
Patterns of Sub-market Specialization of German Neuer Markt Software Firms

Category	Number	Percentage
Enterprise software	31	51
Network application software	16	27
Packaged software	3	5
Internet software	10	17

Source: Compiled by author through Web page searches of all software firms with listings on the Frankfurter Neuer Markt (60 total). Several listed firms were excluded due to foreign ownership or because the Internet had not significantly influenced their business activities (this includes, for example, two firms that develop specialized software for precision manufacturing activities).

firms develop customizable software platforms shifting standard business processes into information technology systems. Firms in this category include enterprise resource planning (ERP), customer relationship management (CRM), groupware, systems integration, and a variety of firms creating sector-specific enterprise tools. As we will see in more detail below, most firms in this category are relatively mature. The Internet has strongly influenced their areas of activity, but primarily in an evolutionary rather than transformative trajectory.

The second category, network application software, includes two main firm types: vendors of security software and document management specialists. Firms in this category are very similar to enterprise software vendors, in that they also often create customizable software applications sold primarily to business clients. The Internet has created a large market for corporate firewalls and related software to protect intranets, and there is a high demand for a variety of secure transaction and authentication software to strengthen the reliability of electronic commerce. Document management includes a variety of firms creating software to help increase the efficiency and reliability of electronic document exchange. Although the German firms in this category have not been innovators in creating important electronic types (e.g., PDF) or document transmission and compression protocols, several of these firms have developed application software to help businesses effectively manage electronic document systems, particularly in the storage area. Firms in this category can be quite technologically intensive and tend to have better defined technological competencies than other enterprise software firms.

The number of "pure" Internet firms listed on the *Neuer Markt* is rising rapidly. Of the 10 Internet software firms listed in table 7.1, seven specialize in e-commerce software applications, whereas three firms develop middleware software, software technologies developed primarily to help vendors of application software easily interact with the network layer of the Internet. Several of the most successful German Internet software firms, in terms of market capitalization and international market presence, are in the e-commerce software segment. These firms are covered in detail below.

Firms in the middleware segment compete in markets to develop new interface technologies used to link telecommunication networking protocols to application software. This is one of the most technically intensive areas of Internet software, in which start-ups usually work in the shadow of larger firms active in the creation of new network layer standards. Technological volatility and high failure rates create managerial dilemmas that are best resolved in regions with highly flexible labor markets and rich venture capital markets resembling ideal-typical Silicon Valley patterns of entrepreneurial organization (see Casper and Glimstedt 2001).

The small number of middleware firms (three of 60) strongly supports the argument that neither technology drivers nor institutional conditions in Germany support technologically intensive activities within the Internet economy. Two of these firms are in the wireless area. The first, Wapme, is a recent start-up specializing in the development of connectivity platforms for application vendors developing WAP-enabled software. The second firm, Condat, was originally a mainframe systems integrator for Bosch and several other large firms. From Bosch, Condat obtained a contract to develop stack protocol software for mobile headsets for its wireless venture during the early 1990s. Although Bosch failed, Condat secured the intellectual property for this endeavor, and has used *Neuer Markt* IPO funds to expand through offering services to other mobile handset providers, as well as leverage its systems integration business into the provision of wireless business solutions more broadly. This is a rare if somewhat exceptional example of a technological spillover from a large to small firm in Germany. The third firm, Infomatec, is an older enterprise software firm that has used IPO funding from the *Neuer Markt* to transform into a specialist in the production of broadband video streaming technology.

To help examine the performance and activities of these firms in more detail, table 7.2 provides a statistical overview of firms in each category, grouped by subsector, as of early 2000. Structural characteristics include age from founding, employment, and sales. Licensing measures as a percentage of sales is a broad indicator of business activity—firms involved in customizable software activities tend to have a high percentage of sales from licensing. Research and development as a percentage of sales and costs are both measures of R&D intensity. This is one of the most important ways to estimate the technological intensity of particular firms. Finally, EBIT, or "earnings before interest and taxation," is a measure of profitability. EBIT figures tend to be more reliable for technology enter-

Table 7.2
Structural Characteristics of German Internet Software Firms by Subsector, 1999

		Age	Employ-ment	Sales (million $)	License Rev as % of sales	R&D as % of sales	R&D as % of all costs	EBIT
Enterprise resource planning	N	4	4	4	4	4	4	4
	Average	18	476.0	43.4	42.8	3.0	2.6	−9.3
	Median	20.5	320.5	26.8	39.6	2.9	2.4	−6.3
Customer relationship management	N	5	5	5	2	3	3	5
	Average	17.6	367.6	31.5	38.0	15.1	16.8	2.3
	Median	21.0	306.0	29.7	38.0	8.3	8.9	6.6
Enterprise tools	N	8	8	8	5	8	8	8
	Average	19.8	154.6	14.7	42.3	13.3	11.4	−14.3
	Median	20.5	150.0	14.5	33.5	10.7	11.6	5.2
Systems integration	N	7	7	7	6	6	6	7
	Average	15.9	313.0	24.8	40.7	22.6	15.5	−53.9
	Median	17.0	249.0	10.0	42.3	14.7	11.2	−29.7
Groupware	N	6	6	6	3	6	6	6
	Average	12.7	161.3	16.1	34.2	7.7	6.5	−14.3
	Median	11.5	163.5	15.9	37.9	7.7	6.5	−11.2
All enterprise software	N	30	30	30	20	27	27	30
	Average	16.8	271.3	24.0	40.3	12.8	10.5	−20.1
	Median	17.0	186.5	16.0	35.7	8.4	9.1	−6.3
Document management	N	9	9	9	6	9	9	9
	Average	16.2	433.3	46.2	28.3	14.7	13.7	−5.3
	Median	15.0	357.0	40.8	29.5	14.7	13.6	−7.3
IT/Network security	N	7	7	7	6	7	7	7
	Average	14.0	135.3	12.0	36.1	17.5	14.1	−24.0
	Median	9.0	113.0	40.8	25.0	18.0	19.7	−1.7

	N							
Packaged software								
N	3	3	3	1	3	3	3	
Average	20.7	478.7	48.5	29.6	22.1	23.3	-0.4	
Median	21.0	300.0	29.5	29.6	24.2	26.8	9.7	
E-commerce software								
N	7	7	7	5	6	6	7	
Average	7.4	217.1	16.7	53.4	45.3	18.1	-115.1	
Median	6.6	120.0	4.5	53.6	39.7	20.2	-68.6	
Middleware								
N	3	3	3	3	3	3	3	
Average	13.3	211.3	20.0	47.3	18.4	201.0	-13.4	
Median	13.0	170.0	13.3	46.9	13.5	12.7	-6.6	
Total								
N	59	59	59	41	55	55	59	
Average	15.3	280.9	26.1	39.8	18.1	13.6	-28.2	
Median	15.0	170.0	16.0	37.9	13.5	11.3	-6.9	

Sources: Information compiled from company annual reports and IPO prospectuses as part of a collaboration with Sigurt Vitols of the Wissenschaftszentrum Berlin. I'd like to thank Lutz Engelhard and Jana Meier for considerable research assistance in compiling these figures. One publicly listed firm, Telesens, has been omitted from the enterprise tools section to minimize an outlier effect. This firm is a recent spin-off of Deutsche Telekom, which has injected very substantial amounts of capital into the firm in an effort to capture market share in the telecommunications billing software market.

prises than simple earnings, as it excludes what can be substantial interest earnings from IPO proceeds.

Although information for all firms is provided, the following focuses on firms in the enterprise software and e-commerce software segments. Doing so helps us compare the fortunes of two dramatically different generations of German start-up firms. Most German enterprise software firms were established in the 1980s, in many cases following the lead of worldwide ERP leader SAP. These firms were founded well before the current entrepreneurial technology boom in Germany, and developed business models and related growth strategies accordingly. Initial Public Offering opportunities created by the rise of the *Neuer Markt* have created opportunities for these firms to become retooled for the Internet economy. The e-commerce software firms are much younger firms, founded explicitly to exploit market opportunities created by the Internet as well as venture capital-financed rapid growth opportunities. Although these firms have used the increased viability of venture capital-based growth models to expand rapidly, we'll see important continuities compared to enterprise software in both the business models and underlying patterns of human resource deployment. This continuity has significant implications for the broader shape of the emerging Internet economy in Germany.

Enterprise Software

Enterprise software firms comprise over half of German software firms on the *Neuer Markt*. Although substantial demand by German corporations for enterprise software services presumably has driven many of these firms into existence, the stunning success of SAP in dominating the international market for enterprise resource planning software during the 1980s has been the most crucial factor. Although few if any technological spillovers have been created by SAP's dominance of this market, the firm has produced an important demonstration effect within the German technology sector. Initially backed by IBM, SAP was one of Germany's first firms to loudly proclaim itself "entrepreneurial" in organization. In addition to an early IPO and the widespread use of stock options and performance-based incentives, the firm has actively distanced itself from the German industrial relations system, in particular through refusing to organize an employee works council.

SAP's innovative business model established it as the only non-American firm to be counted in the top 10 world software giants in terms of market capitalization; it was the fourth largest in 2000. SAP's core business is the periodic updating of a spreadsheet-based software system called R/3 that allows corporations manage a huge array of corporate controlling functions within an integrated system. Corporations installing R/3 require often massive and costly implementations, as corporate process information is translated and customized into R/3 software modules. Although implementation work for very large (and thus profitable) customers is provided by SAP itself, the vast majority of R/3 implementations are performed by software consultancies accredited by SAP to install the system. Several of the older ERP-based enterprise software firms listed on the *Neuer Markt* started as dedicated R/3 implementation firms, often with sector-specific expertise.

A key factor of this business model is that the software used to run most enterprise software systems is not particularly technologically intensive. This can be seen in table 7.2 by the relatively low R&D intensity of most enterprise software firms—the median R&D as a percent of total costs was only 8.4 percent for enterprise software firms as a whole in 1999, with variance across subsectors. Although the emergence of Internet-based corporate networking has created a technological shock to most enterprise software firms, most of this software is fairly simple in orientation: firms develop libraries of software modules that are then customized and licensed to firms as part of implementation contracts.

Appropriability issues thus dominate the strategic calculations of most enterprise software firms. How can firms generate rents from rather low-cost and generic technological investments? Teece (1986) suggests that firms specializing in generic technologies must develop "co-specialized" assets, tying the generic assets with other corporate competencies that are more difficult for competitors to easily mimic. SAP has managed appropriability risks through the creation of a huge user-base of firms that, once they have undergone expensive R/3 customizations, face high switching costs in changing to alternative systems. SAP can also generate long-term revenues through adding new functionality to its software, which is then re-sold to customers through periodic upgrade cycles.

Complementing this installed base has been the creation of a huge network of smaller firms involved in the distribution and installation of

SAP software. The existence of a well-developed distribution aids the marketing of SAP products and expedites the availability of SAP-based ERP software. Building this network is difficult, as the primary software provider must convince these satellite firms to develop specialized installation skills that might not be easily transferable to systems sold by competitors.

This business model is important, as it demonstrates that large-scale success within the international software market is possible without the development of market leading technologies. This helps explain why so many firms are in the German enterprise software segment: the competencies needed to succeed, although complex, do not depend on the creation of privileged access to newly emerging technology. Returning again to table 7.2, one indicator of the widespread diffusion of this business model is the very high percentage of sales through licensing by most enterprise software firms (about 40 percent on average).

The human resource organization of enterprise software firms typically includes a cadre of software developers that create and maintain software libraries. Developers work intensively with a larger group of technicians, consultants, and marketing personnel involved in implementation and customization work. This human resource structure is broadly consistent with restraints on "competency destruction" that have long characterized German business institutions. Technology within these firms is relatively cumulative, evolving as new functions are designed to include in periodic upgrades. As a result, the ability to hire and fire to rapidly change the technological orientation of most enterprise software firms is rare. Rather, more "competency preserving" personnel practices are important. Teams of technicians, consultants, and sales people must work in conjunction with software engineers to quickly customize software libraries for use by clients, while ensuring that innovative routines developed through particular projects feed back into the firm's repertoire of enterprise software solutions.

How has the Internet influenced software firms? The vast majority of firms were founded before either the Internet era or the current availability of entrepreneurial venture financing in Germany. All firms included in this survey have adopted Internet technologies into their core businesses, often using funds from initial public offerings to finance these investments. However, the timing and scale of this technological transformation have varied. For many firms, particularly in the area of enterprise software tools, the inclusion of Internet-based software has been gradual, first offered as an area of enhanced software functionality. One of the firms visited, ATOSS Software, for example, produces employee time management software to help managers organize production schedules more effectively. For this firm, Internet technologies have not changed the core business or software systems. Rather, they have created an opportunity to integrate plant-specific installations into global systems managed through corporate intranets, as well an opportunity to extend the range of options extended to customers through the creation of software to allow traveling employees to use the system through developing wireless applications. In cases such as this the Internet can be viewed as primarily competency enhancing, rather than destroying.

For some enterprise software firms, Internet technologies have created a more profound shock. Systems integration is a good case in point. This area has been among the most strongly impacted by the Internet, as centralized mainframe and minicomputer networks are being replaced by client server networks used to manage corporate intranets. Interview research at several of these firms suggest that this switch in network architecture generates human resource challenges created by the switch from linear languages (C, Cobol, etc.) used to support mainframe and minicomputer networks to object-oriented languages (C++, Java, etc.) used to develop software architectures for Internet-based applications. Transformation costs are illustrated by the existence of moderately high R&D intensities (22 percent as a percent of sales) for systems integrators, whereas the very poor profitability figures (an average loss of 53 percent of sales, with a mean of 30 percent) illustrate the competitive challenges currently facing these firms. An additional difficulty for older firms such as these is the availability of highly skilled programmers with object-oriented language skills; few of these firms can lure such programmers over "pure" Internet start-ups. Facing labor market hurdles, in addition to hire-and-fire constraints, at least two of the systems integration firms visited as part of this study have adopted the costly solution of retraining in-house programmers in object-oriented languages.

E-commerce Software Firms

E-commerce software firms are the most successful group of German entrepreneurial start-ups designed from infancy to exploit Internet economy markets. The e-commerce market is one of the largest application-based infrastructure areas within the Internet sector. According to estimates by Forrester Research, the e-commerce software market was worth $1.7 billion in 1999, but is projected to increase to as much as $13.2 billion by 2003. E-commerce software firms develop customizable software modules designed to help client firms organize e-commerce. The business model here involves the creation and updating of a kernel of e-commerce applications—inventory tracking, accounting, order completion, as well as the creation of visible web-interfaces used by customers—which are typically installed and customized by third-party software consultancies trained and accredited by the e-commerce software producer.

E-commerce software is one of the only core Internet infrastructure areas in which German firms have established substantial market shares in non-German language markets. Although American firms dominate several segments, particularly in the provision of software for business-to-business transactions (e.g., CommerceOne) in the business-to-consumer area, as well as finance dominated "vertical" markets, several German firms are strong. These include most importantly Intershop, a global market leader in the provision of B2C e-commerce software to medium to large firms, as well as firms such as Internolix and Openshop, both of which have developed similar business models for related markets. Another firm with a strong international presence is Brokat, a Stuttgart-based firm that integrates secure transaction software into e-commerce platforms sold to financial institutions.

Over the late 1990s, Intershop emerged as Germany's most successful Internet start-up. It has developed a successful series of integrated e-commerce packages combining back-end inventory and accounting support with front-end web interfaces. In addition to offering integrated packages, the firm has been a leader in exploiting XML scripting technology to allow customers a wide degree of leverage in customizing the basic software. The firm's curious history is also notable. The firm was founded in 1992 in Jena, one of the technology centers of the former East Germany, by several people with expertise in organizing inventory tracking and accounting systems gleaned from prior experience developing software to manage East European trade flows. Although the firm's research and development center remains in Jena, it has shifted its corporate headquarters to joint offices in Hamburg and San Francisco.

The business model underlying e-commerce software is virtually identical to the one SAP pioneered for the ERP market. The core software platforms rely on middleware software and standards developed elsewhere. Important examples include the SET electronic payment protocols, encryption tools, and related Web site security software, as well as commonly used database software from Oracle and other vendors. Despite being strongly dependent on the existence of middleware to integrate the firm's application software into Internet applications, the e-commerce software platforms themselves are proprietary systems completely owned and maintained by the developer. Patenting over core e-commerce processes appears weak; a quick Web search reveals dozens of e-commerce software firms, most of which offer relatively similar technologies.

Although e-commerce software firms may compete to introduce software with enhanced functionality, especially in the "ease of use" area, the software itself is relatively generic. Interestingly, despite the clustering of German firms within e-business software areas, little if any geographical proximity unites these firms, which are scattered across Munich, Stuttgart, Hamburg, and Frankfurt. At least two of these firms (Intershop and Internolix) also seem to have little problem locating their software development offices far away from their corporate headquarters. This lack of regional clustering suggests a low degree of technological interdependence among software standards developed by e-commerce firms.

As in the enterprise software area, appropriability concerns dominate. Firms must tie relatively generic technological assets with more specialized competencies in marketing, sales, and distribution. As with SAP's R/3 platform, creating large user bases facing high switching-costs that can then be captured into long-term upgrade cycles is a central strategy. Creating strong third-channel distribution channels is an additional goal. Intershop boasts of having nearly four thousand consultants trained in the installation of its two core e-commerce platforms. Customer-sharing through corporate alliances with producers of complementary software products is an additional tactic. Intershop has developed an alliance with CommerceOne, one of the leading B2B e-commerce software providers. Internolix, a German e-commerce firm specializing in software for small business, has had its fortunes enhanced through a deal with Microsoft to become the exclusive supplier of e-commerce software for firms using

Microsoft NT-based web servers. Although Microsoft hopes to expand the relatively weak presence of NT servers in small business, the inclusion of Internolix as a partner in various Microsoft developers conferences and related marketing activities has been a huge benefit for the firm. According to interviews with managers at Internolix, it has also invigorated the firm's activities in creating a distribution network of independent contracts specializing in the installation of its software.

Overall, it would be fair to categorize e-commerce software primarily as a marketing and distribution dominated application area, sharing broadly similar business models with enterprise software specialists. This is evident in the R&D intensity and licensing figures for German e-commerce firms from table 7.2. Research and development as a percent of costs is only 18 percent on average and 20 percent for the median firm—only marginally higher than R&D intensities for the much older enterprise software firms. The figures from licensing are also indicative: a relatively small amount of sales come from complete software packages. Rather, about 54 percent of sales are in the form of licensing software to clients; interview evidence from visits to several of these firms suggests that consulting and implementation are related fees.

These firms are much younger on average than the enterprise software firms, in all cases founded with the exploitation of Internet markets as a core goal. Most have received substantial private venture capital placements, facilitating much faster growth before initial public offerings. Rather than relying on "organic" growth based on earnings, they have had the opportunity to invest lavishly to create large organizational structures in an attempt to quickly grab substantial market shares. This reliance on equity leveraged growth models is a good example of how the growth of technology-driven capital markets has allowed more aggressive start-up strategies to flourish in Germany. The very high EBIT statistics for the seven e-commerce software firms confirm their ability to spend lavishly in order to quickly scale up. Intershop, the oldest of these firms (founded in 1992), came close to the break-even point in 1999; the rest took huge losses in attempts to build market share (-115 percent losses on average, with about 69 percent as the median figure). The relatively low R&D intensities suggest that much of this investment was used for the creation of sales and marketing organizations.

Field research at several of these firms suggests that new economy forms of entrepreneurial start-up organization are far more prevalent than at older German software firms. Each of these firms has stock option plans with very wide dispersal across employees, as well as relatively flat managerial hierarchies to help enable a more decentralized, employee-empowered work environment. One enterprise software firm visited for this study, for example, had seven layers of management to govern under five hundred employees; the newer Internet-driven startups generally had fewer (three to four). This has facilitated faster growth and a clearer new economy focus in terms of personnel organization, particularly with regards to relatively intense work environments.

However, Germany's e-commerce software specialists also resemble most German firms in developing human resource policies that are broadly competency enhancing in nature. Human resource competencies are similar to those in enterprise software. Firms usually organize a group of programmers with advanced degrees who update the software platform, along with a much larger group of lower trained technicians involved in implementation and service issues. Proprietary programming environments tend to keep competency destruction low—new programmers may be added to accommodate inevitable "feature creep," but existing staff should have high job security due to the need to periodically update the code. The trade-off is that, compared to more technologically volatile sectors, extremely challenging technical challenges will be few. Although this might keep the best programmers away from these firms, in terms of skill-requirements, "good" should suffice.

In sum, e-commerce software firms are primarily marketing and distribution driven entities. Interestingly, both Intershop and Internolix have located their software development labs in different parts of the country than their corporate headquarters. They can succeed in Germany precisely because the core business model does not depend on the creation of world-beating technology. Rather, competitive success is driven by the bundling of rather generic technologies into proprietary systems promoted through marketing and sales organizations designed to create large user-bases facing high switching costs.

Conclusion

As suggested in this book's introductory chapter, the Internet economy in many ways is as much a cultural as a technological upheaval. In Germany, the widespread diffusion of entrepreneurial business models embodies this transformation. For example, in a recent survey of European dot.com firms (PriceWaterhouseCoopers 2001), 91 percent of German respondents agreed that working in these firms was "fun"—quite a statement given the usually stolid German business culture. In this same survey, however, only 45 percent of respondents claimed they were working in a dot.com company because they "like to take risks" (compared to 73 percent in the United Kingdom and 71 percent in France). When managers of these firms were surveyed concerning their growth prospects for the forthcoming year, German firms targeted growth at a "mere" 93 percent, compared to 173 percent in France and a rather staggering 1,745 percent in the United Kingdom.

This survey evidence resonates with the more systematic evidence presented for the Internet software companies: Internet companies do represent the banner of change in Germany, but of a particular kind. The trailblazing success of SAP in the ERP market and more recently Intershop in e-commerce software have provided corporate sirens that could guide the construction of business models sustainable within the present German institutional landscape. Their success likely indicates an extension of the German business system to include new organizational structures, rather than a transformation into something new. Particularly in the key area of human resource development, German Internet software firms generate competency enhancing employment and knowledge development patterns similar to most old economy firms in Germany.

German software firms have gravitated primarily to segments with relatively low technological intensity. Important constraints currently exist on the feasible technological intensity of German firms. Due to the generally unchanging structure of German labor markets and the lack of important technological drivers by large firms (i.e., as in Sweden), new German start-up firms cannot expect to be competency destroying at the firm level. German technology start-ups cannot easily hire and fire personnel, in large part because labor markets for highly experienced technical staff and managers are limited due to the long-term employment equilibrium throughout the economy. This creates important limitations on the strategic orientation of German Internet firms, in that they cannot engage in projects in which necessary human resource competencies could shift quickly. Rather, German firms must anticipate that most engineers hired into the firm will have a relatively long employment tenure within the firm.

However, embedded within this constraint may be opportunities for German Internet firms to develop patterns of knowledge investment among employees that are difficult to sustain by firms depending on hire-and-fire to achieve flexibility. Turning to the dominant U.S. case, a contradiction exists within the incentive structures most high-technology enterprises offer to employees. Top management expect skilled employees to commit to the very intense working conditions needed to win innovation races with competitors, but also reserve the right to hire and fire at will. This incentive conflict is reduced through offering very high-powered short-term performance incentives to employees (stock options, bonuses, and the like). Although effective, hire-and-fire practices create strong incentives for employees to invest in skills that can easily be transferred to other firms. Within the U.S. context, the development of firm-specific skills is risky, in that they cannot be easily transferred to other firms when the current firm fails or the employee is laid off or fired.

In sum, within liberal-market institutional environments, it is difficult for high-technology firms to engage in technology profiles that generate substantial amounts of firm-specific skills or knowledge that cannot be codified in the relatively short term. German national institutional frameworks, on the other hand, strongly encourage competency preserving human resource development through restraints on hire and fire that facilitate long-term employment. This presents a second explanation of why so many German firms have selected areas of the Internet dominated by more generic, customizable software. In addition to the lower financial and competency destruction risks, it is likely that the higher degree of technological cumulativeness in these markets creates a combination of tacit, firm-specific knowledge risks. As a result, German entrepreneurial technology firms should enjoy a comparative institutional advantage in the creation of competencies needed to support innovation in areas where long-term knowledge investments are important.

At present, technology drivers appear to be the dominant basis for competition in the Internet economy. This strongly advantages firms in economies that can develop institutions to mimic the Silicon Valley model in its entirety. Although the Ericsson example in Stockholm shows that technological externalities can spur technological spin-offs, this analysis in general does not bode well for the ability of Germany and other "organized economies" to compete in technologically turbulent areas of the Internet economy. However, as technology drivers stabilize, Internet businesses may increasingly thrive in "hybridized" environments combining new economy financing and growth with old economy human resource stability. Although the successes of Germany's e-commerce software firms are relatively small, this formula could eventually provide a model for longer-term success in the Internet economy.

8

The Internet Economy of Korea

Sea-Jin Chang

Introduction

Korea showed signs of a strong Internet economy by the end of 2001. According to the Ministry of Information and Communication, 16.4 million Koreans, or 36 percent of the population, were Internet users. This penetration ratio was tenth among OECD countries.[1] In addition, more than 60 percent of the population was equipped with mobile phones, nearly all of which could log on to the Internet. More than 60 percent of stock trading was done online, which was the highest ratio among all nations. Korea also boasted one of the highest penetrations of broadband services. It was during this time that unprecedented numbers of Internet start-ups were formed.

This chapter pursues two broadly defined research questions. First, it explores how Korea developed a strong Internet economy. In Korea, economic development relied mainly on low-cost manufacturing, which was dominated by large conglomerates called *chaebols*. Corporate venturing was limited and venture capital firms were almost nonexistent. The strong Internet economy in Korea was possible not only because of the sound infrastructure but also due to the collapse of the old economy during the Asian Crisis. This chapter examines how the 1997 Asian crisis shattered the old economy model and helped install the new economy model. Second, this chapter examines how chaebols moved quickly into the Internet realm as Korea recovered from this crisis. Therefore, two different breeds—pure Internet start-ups and chaebols—populated

Korea's Internet economy. This chapter will examine how these two very distinct camps influence Korea's Internet industry.

The Antecedents of the Internet Economy

Every Korean knows what price the country paid for being a late-comer to industrialization. Throughout the Chosun Dynasty, Korea was known as a hermit kingdom, secluded from the rest of the world. Korea maintained a trade relationship only with China. In the late nineteenth century, however, imperialistic western countries and Japan, which rapidly industrialized after the arrival of Commodore Perry in 1840, claimed Korea as its own. After a series of wars with China and Russia, Japan emerged as the winner and annexed Korea in 1910. Koreans suffered greatly during the Japanese occupation. After liberation in 1945, Korea later fell victim to the Cold War. It has remained a divided country ever since.

After such hardships, Koreans might have unconsciously decided not to fall behind again when the next industrial revolution occurred. Pundits predicted that this revolution would be based on information processing technology (Naisbitt 1990). Some authors, such as Hagel and Armstrong (1997), suggested that the Internet might represent the next revolution, and envisioned a new economy based on Internet technology that was completely different from the old economy, which had diminishing returns to scale. Evans and Wurster (1999) warned that new economy firms would quickly obliterate the competitive advantages held by old economy companies. In these developments, Koreans might have perceived the opportunity to catch up with more industrialized countries and possibly even take the lead in this new economy. Certainly, Korea has been a leader in embracing the Internet economy.

Telecommunication Deregulations and Industrial Policies

The emergence of a strong Internet economy in Korea would not have been possible without sound telecommunication infrastructure. Needless to say, the Korean government provided a solid physical infrastructure for this economy. The Ministry of Post and Telecommunication, which used to regulate postal and telephone services, decided to take the lead in the information revolution and renamed itself the Ministry of Information and Communication in 1994. Until the 1970s, it had focused on providing telephone services to every household. In the 1980s, it deregulated the telephone industry and brought in competition. It set up DACOM in 1982 to provide long distance telephone services and data communication services. DACOM has been in competition with Korea Telecom over long distance and international telephone services ever since. DACOM has also been a major ISP via Chollian, equivalent to AOL, with 4.3 millions subscribers as of September 2001, and also a provider of data communication services for businesses. Deregulations in the early 1980s brought competition and contributed to provide a strong voice and data communication infrastructure in Korea.

Furthermore, the government's industrial policies played a pivotal role in building a strong telecommunication industry. The government set up a research institute, ETRI (Electronics and Telecommunication Research Institute), in 1976. With the government funding, ETRI developed full digital telecommunication exchanges and licensed them to four major telecommunications equipment manufacturers, Samsung Electronics, LG Telecom (now LG Electronics), Daewoo Telecom, and Dongyang Telecom. They then developed their own models and competed in the world marketplace. Electronics and Telecommunication Research Institute continued to be a source of technology development by developing fundamental technology in optical transmissions systems, ATM switching systems, and mobile telecommunication equipment, which were transferred to private companies for commercialization. Overall, the government's industrial policy in the telecommunication industry proved to be successful in providing a strong telecommunication infrastructure in Korea.

The 1990s observed the further deregulation of communication services, particularly in the area of mobile phone services and of broadband Internet services. In 1991, the Korea Mobile Telecom (now SK Telecom) was privatized. In 1996, the ministry gave mobile phone licenses to four other carriers. While allocating licenses to those new entrants, the government imposed on them a national standard, CDMA (code divisional multiple access), technology developed by the U.S. company Qualcomm, over the European GSM standard. Although CDMA was an unproven technology at that time, it was evident that it could potentially handle a larger call volume than GSM. The government's push for a CDMA standard helped Korean firms avoid problems that came from multiple standards as in the United States and helped them be leaders in commercializing CDMA technology. As a consequence, Samsung Electronics and LG Electronics became worldwide leaders in supplying CDMA equipment, as well as handsets. SK Telecom actively sought foreign markets to exploit its know-how in mobile phone services based on the CDMA standard.

Given the huge installation costs and scale economies, five mobile phone operators competed fiercely with each other to attract customers with generous subsidies for phone equipment and aggressive marketing campaigns. Owing to this competition, 28.2 million subscribers, more than 60 percent of the population, used mobile phone services as of September 2001.[2] In 2001, the government selected three licensees for the third generation wireless services that enable broadband Internet access through mobile phones. The wide penetration of mobile phones in Korea created a strong infrastructure for mobile Internet services.

The government also contributed to diffuse broadband Internet services. The ministry selected the Hanaro Telecom as the second local call carrier in 1997. Hanaro Telecom focused on broadband service in order to penetrate the local loop service market that Korea Telecom had monopolized previously. Hanaro Telecom offered local loop service at a nominal fee if a customer signed up for broadband service. Korea Telecom reacted to this competitive threat by accelerating the deployment of broadband services. In addition, several companies such as Dreamline initiated broadband Internet services through cable networks. Korea Power, a power utility company, announced broadband Internet access service through its electric power network. Because two-thirds of the South Korean population lives in large apartment complexes, installation of broadband services was not as expensive as it was in other countries such as the United States. According to the ministry, the number of broadband Internet subscriptions exceeded 7 million as of September 2001.[3] Among them, 4 million subscribers used DSL, and the rest used cable modems and local area networks.

The Role of Universities

Experiences in other countries suggest that universities were the sources for innovations and new ideas that became a basis of pushing for the

Internet economy. The Korean universities, however, did not play any important role. It was rather the government that played a pivotal role in pushing for deregulation and funding R&D. Unlike their counterparts in other countries, Korean universities adhered solely to teaching. There were only very rare cases of university professors starting companies. Although some universities encouraged start-ups on the university premises by their faculty members subsequent to the Internet boom, few did so prior to that event. Universities focused on teaching fundamental theories and left private companies to perform R&D. Most college graduates joined large, established firms upon graduation. Prior to the Internet boom, there was virtually no venture capital financing. The Silicon Valley model (Kenney 2000) simply did not exist prior to 1997.

Furthermore, a Korean education system that emphasized rote memorization often stifled the creativity of students. As a consequence, Korean firms excelled in process innovation but not in product innovation. Although many Korean firms distinguished themselves in manufacturing computers, electronic equipment, and telecommunication systems, they lagged behind in areas such as software design and content that required employee creativity.

The Collapse of the Old Economy and the Emergence of the New Economy

Chaebols: Korean Business Groups

The flourishing of the Internet economy in Korea amazed many Koreans because the country had long been dominated by a few large business groups, known as chaebols. In 1996, the top 30 chaebols accounted for 40 percent of Korea's output in the mining and manufacturing sectors. They enjoyed a dominant position in the Korean market. According to a report by the Korea Development Institute, in 1994, the 30 largest chaebols participated in 2,465 of 3,168 mining and manufacturing markets and ranked first in market share in 566 of those markets, second in 312, and third in 221.[4] This report also points out that chaebols' power increased significantly from 1982 to 1994. Chaebols were criticized for driving out small- and medium-sized companies in almost all markets they entered.

Chaebols are creatures of underdeveloped markets and industrial policies pursued by the Korean government (Amsden 1989; Kim 1997;

Chang, in press). After liberalization, the Korean government sold off reverted property to a small number of firms. Such preferential treatment provided a foundation for the chaebols to grow. The government's economic development plans after 1961 provided huge subsidies for expansion into strategic industries such as heavy equipment and chemicals, and export-oriented industries. The government also effectively nationalized all banks by denying them the right to examine the validity of investment projects. Instead, the banks were compelled to raise and allocate funds according to plans established by the government. Most large-scale investments were allocated to only a few companies. The Korean government also adopted the Japanese export-oriented economic development policy. Chaebols set up general trading companies, modeled after the Japanese *sogo shosha.*

Not only did the Korean government follow the Japanese industrial policies, but Korean business also adopted several Japanese management systems. The chaebol business model was based on mass production of commodity products. Chaebol firms borrowed heavily from both local and foreign banks and invested in production capacities. Emulating Japan's system, Korean enterprises preferred debt financing to equity financing. Internally, chaebol firms followed the Japanese firms' seniority system, lifetime employment, and bureaucratic organizational structures (Steers, Shin, and Ungson 1989). Under the chaebol system, young recruits went through a long socialization process and were not given any responsibilities. They were expected to follow orders from superiors. Creativity or initiative were not expected nor encouraged.

The Asian Crisis and the Collapse of Chaebols

The emergence of the Internet economy in Korea, however, coincided with the Asian Crisis that led to the collapse of the chaebol system. The crisis, which started with the plunge of the Thai baht in July 1997, spread quickly to other Asian countries.[5] Unstable foreign exchange rates caused a foreign currency exodus from the region, which resulted in a sweeping instability throughout Southeast Asia. Foreign investors began reexamining the fundamentals of the Korean economy. They then started withdrawing their funds from Korea en masse, liquidating their investments at a loss and converting them to dollars. Foreign financial institutions also sharply reduced advances to Korean companies and began calling in their loans to Korean financial institutions. These actions in turn created even larger contractions in the stock and foreign exchange markets and induced the bankruptcies of larger Korean firms. The Bank of Korea vainly intervened in the market to protect the won's value, thereby reducing its foreign currency reserves to $5 billion at one point.[6] During the crisis, foreign exchange rates soared from 864 won per dollar in January 1997 to 1,695 won per dollar by December 1997. Concurrently, the Korean stock exchange index tumbled from 669 to 390, and the number of Korean companies going bankrupt increased from a thousand per month to thirty-five hundred per month. Thirteen of the top 30 chaebols either went bankrupt or were under bank-sponsored workout programs.

The International Monetary Fund demanded that the Korean government adopt draconian measures in return for the bailout. It wanted to restore confidence in the Korean economy and to fundamentally restructure Korea's financial and corporate sectors. It induced the Korean government to restructure the chaebols. During this process, many financially weak companies went bankrupt and many had to lay off employees. The crisis and the subsequent restructuring shattered several conventional beliefs that had been important building blocks for the Korean economy.

First, most Koreans believed that the bigger the firms were, the less likely they were to fail. In the past, the government had traditionally rescued large firms from bankruptcy. Under this assumption, banks advanced loans only to large firms. Smaller firms could not secure loans from banks or raise money from the stock market. The job security and the prestige of working for large chaebols attracted talented employees to large companies. Small firms found it hard to recruit employees. The crisis, however, overturned this belief. It demonstrated that chaebols were no more secure than smaller firms.

Second, the crisis and subsequent restructuring broke the promise of lifetime employment. Large Korean firms had followed the Japanese model, guaranteeing job security. Top college graduates favored such corporations. In return, these companies demanded absolute loyalty and dedication from their employees. Promotion was based strictly on seniority. Starting a new venture was neither well regarded nor popular. After these firms laid off employees, however, their remaining workers no longer believed they had job security and became more willing to assume the risk of beginning a new venture or working for one in order to reap better pay and quicker promotions. This opening up of the labor market was an important development for the Internet economy in Korea. In contrast, Japan, which maintained the seniority system and lifetime employment despite the decade-long recession, did not show active entrepreneurial activities to the extent Korea did.

More fundamentally, the crisis raised questions about the validity of the economic model that Korea had followed. Until the crisis, Korea emulated Japan's economic policies, management practices, and business strategies as it attempted to replicate Japan's economic success. The crisis shook the belief in the fundamentals of this system. Japan itself had been in a deep recession since the early 1990s. During the same period, U.S. companies fared well, particularly in the high-technology sector. As an alternative to the Japanese economic model, Koreans began to admire the US model, which was typified by Silicon Valley's many start-ups and abundant venture capital (see chapter 3, by Kenney).

The Emergence of Internet Start-ups and Venture Capital Industry

As the Korean economy recovered from the crisis, there were sudden changes in business environments.[7] From the perspective of employees, capital markets, and even the government, the center of gravity shifted from the old economy, dominated by chaebols, to the new economy, led by Internet start-ups. This shift was most evident in the capital market, where the fortunes of firms listed on the KOSDAQ, a market modeled after the NASDAQ and devised for technology and small start-up firms, rapidly outpaced the fortunes of the conventional brick and mortar firms, which were generally listed on the Korea Stock Exchange (KSE). Figure 8.1 shows that the KOSDAQ index skyrocketed from 60 in September 1998 to 266 in February 2000. Initial public offerings (IPO) have been concentrated on the KOSDAQ. The number of listed companies on the KOSDAQ increased from 329 in 1999 to 612 in 2001, while the number of firm listed on the KSE dropped from 776 in 1999 to 704 in 2000. Table 8.1 shows the top 10 industry areas that had IPOs during January 1999–February 2001. As the table shows, audio, video, and telecommunication equipment areas and information processing were the two main

The Internet Economy of Korea

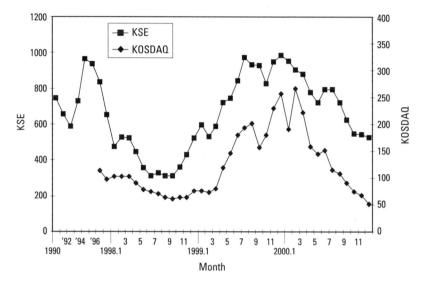

Figure 8.1
The market indices of KSE and KOSDAQ

areas for recent IPOs. As a consequence, more capital flew into the KOSDAQ than into the KSE. Figure 8.2 shows how the trading volume of the KOSDAQ, which was miniscule prior to 1999, skyrocketed and exceeded that of the KSE. Figures 8.3a and 8.3b show that the number of start-up foundings has increased sharply since 1997. The valuation of start-ups, particularly Internet companies, was extraordinarily high. Table 8.2 compares the market valuation of major Internet companies in Korea and the United States.

Figures 8.3a and 8.3b also classify Internet start-ups according to their business areas. In Korea, the proportions of Internet start-ups in portals and e-commerce products and services had been much higher than those in United States, where a large portion of Internet start-ups had been concentrated in infrastructure technology and Internet-related software and technology. This may reflect a relative backwardness of Korean firms in technology and software as of 2001. There existed no equivalents to technology pioneers such as Cisco, Sun, Broadvision, and Oracle. Most software firms in Korea imported software packages from overseas and adapted them to the Korean environment. Without accumulated

Table 8.1
Comparison of Major Internet Companies between the United States and Korea

	United States				
Business Type	Company	Year Founded	Sales in 1999 ($ millions)	Sales Growth Rate (percent)	Market Capital- ization ($ millions)
Portal	Yahoo!	1994	588	140	77,000
Commerce	Amazon	1994	1,639	169	16,000
Intermediary	eBay	1995	224	160	16,000
Contents	New York Times	1896	3,130	6.2	69,000
ISP	AOL	1985	4,777	55	125,000
	Korea				
Business Type	Company	Year Founded	Sales in 1999 ($ millions)	Sales Growth Rate (percent)	Market Capital- ization ($ millions)
Portal	Daum	1995	0.069	352.6	96
Commerce	Interpark	1997	0.089	593.6	8
Intermediary	Auction	1996	0.003	n.a	62
Contents	Digital Chosun	1995	0.324	15	18
ISP	KT Hitel	1991	0.550	22.6	75

Note: Market capitalization as of June 2000.

technology in infrastructure and Internet technology and software, Korean Internet start-ups tended to be heavily populated in application areas such as portals and e-commerce, where there were fewer barriers to entry. Figures 8.3a and 8.3b, however, show that the number of start-ups in infrastructure and Internet-related technology and software has been increasing since 1999.

Another notable change in the capital market was the sharp growth of the venture capital industry. The number of venture capital companies grew from 51 in 1996 to 87 in 1999. The annual venture capital investment grew from 350 billion won ($437 million) in 1993 to 1.4 trillion won ($1.2 billion) in 1999, as shown in figure 8.4. The new fund raised in 1999 was up 158 percent to 1.7 trillion won ($1.4 billion) from the previous year (Asian Venture Capital Journal 2001). Successful IPOs, which

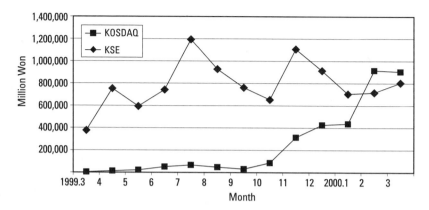

Figure 8.2
Trading volumes in KSE and KOSDAQ

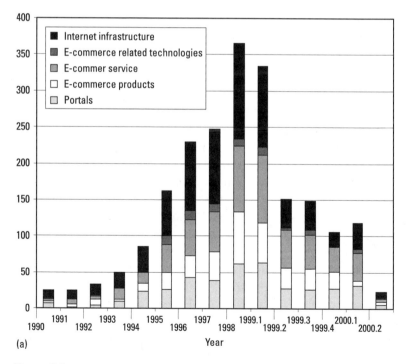

(a)

Figure 8.3a
Business areas of Internet start-ups in Korea

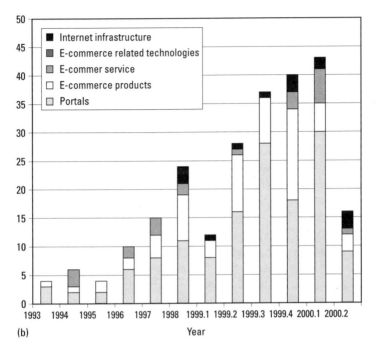

Figure 8.3b
Business areas of Internet start-ups in the United States

numbered 160 firms on the KOSDAQ in 1999, attracted a large sum of money to venture capital funds. The majority of the capital raised by Korean funds came from local sources, which took up 75 percent of total funds raised. It is, however, notable that the other 25 percent of funds came from foreign sources. Several US and Japanese venture capital firms such as Bowman Capital, Goldman & Sachs, and Softbank set up branches and started to invest in Korean startups. Among the 10,993 start-up firms that were officially recognized by the government, fifteen hundred firms were funded by venture capital firms.

A corresponding shift occurred in the Korean labor market. The prospect of getting rich quickly induced an exodus of entrepreneurs, as well as many engineers and managers, who left established firms to set up their own ventures. Venture capital firms and wealthy individuals were eager to fund ex-chaebol employees and even college graduates who had

Table 8.2
Top 10 Industries That Experienced Most IPOs in KOSDAQ during January 1999 and January 2001

Industry	No. of firms in the industry as of January 1999	No. of firms in the industry as of January 2001	IPO count
Audio, video, telecommunications equipments	35	93	58
Information processing	7	53	46
Financial services	35	76	41
Equipment manufacturing	22	51	29
Chemicals	14	34	20
Medical and precision manufacturing	4	17	13
Other electronic equipments	12	22	10
Wholesales	13	23	10
Broadcasting	0	8	8
Communications	5	12	7
Other industries	182	223	41
Total number of companies listed in KOSDAQ	329	612	283

Source: KOSDAQ.

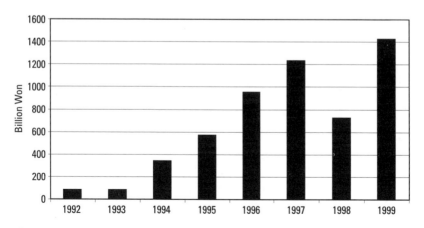

Figure 8.4
Annual venture capital investment

business plans. According to statistics by the Korea Small & Medium Business Administration, in 2001, 31 percent of presidents of start-ups were from large corporations, 38 percent from other small- and medium-sized firms, 10 percent former researchers at the research institutes, 6 percent former professors, and 15 percent others. It is worth noting that not only employees of large corporations and research institutes quit their jobs to start their own ventures but university professors did as well. Moreover, several universities set up their own venture incubating units for their students and faculty to develop marketable ideas prior to venture capital funding.

The Government Policies toward Start-ups
The government also shifted its attention from the old economy to the new economy. The Korean government's attempts to induce economic development from 1961 on were indispensable to the creation and growth of the chaebols. Through various forms of assistance, the government induced chaebols to invest in designated strategic sectors and export-oriented industries (Amsden 1989; Kim 1997). After the crisis, however, faced with the daunting task of easing unemployment, it sought relief by supporting the start-ups with various modes of funding and subsidies.

The government came up with the following conditions for firms to qualify as start-ups: 1) more than 10 percent of the firm's equity issue is assumed by venture capitalists, 2) the firm spends more than 5 percent of its revenues on R&D, 3) the firm possesses at least one patent, and 4) various government agencies such as the Small Business Administration approves of the firm's qualification. For officially recognized start-ups, the government provided funding of 50 billion won ($41 million) in 1999 and 315 billion won ($262 million) in 2000. It also gave officially recognized ventures special treatment in securing bank loans, lowered these firms' minimum incorporation capital requirement from 50 million won to 20 million won, and provided start-ups with various income tax breaks, favorable treatment in building regulations, and lower requirements for being listed on the KOSDAQ. In addition, it eased the regulations on the bond issuance of the venture capital firms and provided various tax credits to such firms in order to stimulate their investment in startups. As of November 2001, the government officially recognized 10,993 start-ups, which included Internet firms and among which 3,705 firms (33 percent) were in the computer and information processing industry. It is worthwhile to emphasize that the government played an important role in the growth of the Internet economy in Korea by providing direct funding and by helping start-ups secure loans from banks, just as it did to chaebols in the 1960s and 1970s.

Yet these government policies provided wrong incentives to start-ups. Many firms were formed to tap the funding and various subsidies from the government. Whereas venture capital firms in the United States provided seed money for start-ups and subsequent funding upon their progress, the government had no capacity to evaluate the business plans and the progress of start-ups. It ended up providing support to all that satisfied formal requirements. Consequently, many firms without any economic merit were funded and granted subsidies, which resulted in many of these firms eventually ending up in failure. It should be emphasized that the government initiated these policies mainly to address unemployment problems. By engaging in industrial policies to support start-ups, the government might have temporarily eased unemployment problems but it encouraged moral hazard of would-be entrepreneurs, thus resulting in a waste of resources.

The Internet Industry in Korea

B2C Sector
DACOM, a leading ISP provider, opened the first Internet shopping mall, named Interpark, in 1996. Since then, the number of Internet shopping malls has been increasing at an astounding speed. A survey by Korea Information Society Development Institute in 2000 revealed that there were a total of 7,951 e-commerce firms in Korea, among which 3,101 were in the business-to-business (B2B) sector, 4,694 in the business-to-consumer (B2C) sector that included Internet shopping malls, 383 in the consumer-to-consumer (C2C) sector, and 114 in other areas.[8]

According to the survey by the Korean Chamber of Commerce (2000), the number of Internet shopping malls increased from 375 in 1998 to 1,700 by June 2000.[9] These malls achieved sales of 50 billion won ($41 million) in 1998 and 246 billion won ($205 million) in 1999. Another survey from the National Statistical Office (2000), a government agency, indicated a total of 1,846 Internet shopping malls in 2000 and estimated the size of B2C sector to be $564 million in that year. The same statistics, however, point out that the proportion of the sales of Internet shopping malls relative to the entire retail industry is only 1.3 percent, thereby suggesting that e-commerce was still in its infancy in Korea as of 2000.

The Korea National Statistical Office showed that 1,583 of the 1,846 Internet shopping malls (85.8 percent) were geared to particular products or services, and the other 263 sold a variety of products. Five hundred and seventy-nine Internet shopping malls were Internet-only firms, whereas the other 1,267 have both online and offline operations. All the chaebols created their own online shopping malls and concentrated on retailing. For instance, Samsung Corporation, a general trading company of the Samsung Group, extended its retail operations to include the online Samsung Mall. Similarly, LG, Hyundai, SK, and Lotte followed similar courses of expansion. The average Internet shopping mall run by chaebols had sales that were far greater than those of independent online shopping malls. Virtually all online shopping malls, large and small, however, were reported to have lost money in 2000.[10]

Table 8.3 shows the distribution of sales of Internet shopping malls into product categories. The table shows that computers and accessories represent 32.2 percent of total sales. Computer software represents an additional 3.5 percent. The next largest segment is consumer electronics, with 18.2 percent, followed by books, representing 5.5 percent. According to the Japanese Ministry of Trade and Industry and Anderson Consulting, in the United States, automobile sales, travel services, and PCs represent 35.5 percent, 21.9 percent, and 10 percent of online sales, respectively. In Japan, personal computers (30.5 percent) and travel services (18.8 percent) take up the largest portion.[11] This comparison shows that the B2C market in Korea was focused on the sales of tangible products that were standardized and required less effort to sell in cyberspace. The Internet market for services such as travel and complex products such as automobiles had not yet been developed in Korea. Online stock trading was, however, growing quickly in Korea, probably due to the stock market rally during 1999–2000, as shown in figures 8.1 and 8.2.

Table 8.2 compares major Internet companies in the United States and Korea as of 2000. Daum is a major portal, equivalent to Yahoo!, with 21 million subscribers. Interpark was the first Internet shopping mall in Korea. Auction provided an online service similar to that of e-Bay.[12] The

Table 8.3
Sales of Internet Shopping Malls by Product Categories ($ million)

Product categories	Sales in October 2000	Percentage
Computer and accessories	51.5	32.2
Software	5.6	3.5
Consumer electronics	29.1	18.5
Books	8.8	5.5
CD/video	3.7	2.3
Travel services	8.5	5.3
Toys and baby products	3.8	2.4
Food	3.9	2.5
Flowers	0.9	0.5
Sports and leisure products	3.1	1.9
Home products/automobiles	10.6	6.7
Clothing/fashion products	5.5	3.5
Cosmetics	4.9	3.1
Stationary	3.0	1.9
Other	16.7	10.5
Total	159.6	100.0

Source: Korea National Statistics Office 2000.

Digital Chosun converted its offline newspaper to an online version. KT Hitel is the second largest ISP in Korea after DACOM. There are two interesting points of comparison in table 8.2. These Korean firms were founded right after their U.S. counterparts began operating. For instance, Daum was founded in 1995; it was modeled after Yahoo! and followed Yahoo!'s strategy rather closely. This example suggests the Internet business model is relatively easy to copy or emulate, and that the barriers to entry are relatively low, and that the Silicon Valley Internet firms are the main sources for ideas. Second, the valuation of Internet-based companies in Korea is extremely high, much higher than that of comparable U.S. firms. For instance, Daum, with only $69,000 in revenues in 1999, was valued at $96 million, or a market valuation to sales ratio of 1,391. On the other hand, the same ratio for Yahoo! was 130. Similarly, Auction had only $3,800 revenue, but was valued at $62 million, a whopping 16,315 value to sales ratio, whereas eBay had a more modest ratio of 71.

These comparisons were done on June 22, 2000, thus reflecting some adjustments on both the NASDAQ and KOSDAQ after the April 2000 crash. Internet stocks were clearly overvalued in Korea.

B2B Sector

Even as late as 2000, B2B e-commerce was still in its infancy in Korea. The National Statistical Office estimated the size of the B2B market in Korea to be $40.2 billion. The NSO, however, defined B2B very broadly, encompassing all transactions using computers and networks. The electronic marketplaces, which can be a narrower definition of B2B, amounted to $398 million, roughly less than 1 percent of what NSO estimated to be the overall B2B sector in Korea. According to the same statistics, there were 191 electronic marketplaces in Korea at the end of 2000, but only 86 of these had any business transactions.[13] There are 35 e-marketplaces in the trading industry, 18 in the chemical, 17 in MRO (maintenance, replacement), 15 in industrial machinery, 15 in electronics, 14 in textiles, 12 in computer manufacturing, 11 in steel, and others.

A critical reason why the B2B sector in Korea did not explode as it did in the United States lies in the closeness of supply networks. Most big chaebol companies were highly vertically integrated. Core manufacturing firms were integrated upstream with many parts-supplying affiliates and integrated downstream with general trading companies and domestic distributors. It is critical to have an open network to get the most benefit out of B2B. The closeness of supply networks in chaebols did not allow firms to buy from suppliers associated with other business groups, although they planned to have an open network in the future. The chaebol network was much more stringent than the keiretsu (see chapter 9, by Sako). Another reason for backwardness in B2B was that most businesses had been handled by paperwork. Even EDI was relatively new to most Korean firms. Chaebol firms, however, were busy converting their existing intragroup EDI systems to Internet-based systems or building new ones based on Internet B2B technology.

For instance, in the electronics industry, incumbent electronics producers such as Samsung, LG, and Daewoo were converting their EDI networks of suppliers to the e-marketplace (Ministry of Commerce, Industry, and Energy 2000a). (See chapter 11, by Helper and MacDuffie, for a discussion of this transformation in the auto industry.) Samsung

Electronics converted the Smartnet, its in-house supply networks, to the Glonet and linked it to its ERP (enterprise resource planning) system. It had plans to conduct all its procurement and orders on the web. It was also trying to link its system to the various shopping malls operated by Samsung affiliates. In the automobile industry, assemblers such as Hyundai Motor and Daewoo Motor were converting their closed EDI networks so that they could adhere to more international standards, which were web-based, open, and included overseas suppliers. In the steel industry, POSCO, a dominant steel producer, at one point operated its own VAN (value-added network). It attempted to extend its network to outside suppliers and buyers to create its own e-marketplace. In the trading industry, conventional general trading companies were transforming their businesses into web-based exchanges by opening web homepages and showrooms from which they solicited inquiries and executed business transactions.

An interesting feature of the B2B segment in Korea was that the general trading companies were rapidly taking the lead as they did with Internet shopping malls. The general trading companies, all of which were associated with chaebols, had been engaged in importing raw materials and intermediate goods to their affiliates and exporting their final products to overseas markets. Because the Internet technology and the emergence of e-commerce were rapidly making their main trading businesses obsolete, their actions in the online world were necessary for them to remain viable. Although the general trading companies had traditionally competed fiercely with each other, they were seeking to collaborate in some industries to convert their trading businesses into large electronic marketplaces. For instance, in the chemical business, the general trading companies of Hyundai, LG Group, and SK Group combined their chemical trading businesses into Chemround, an electronic marketplace. Samsung, Kumho, Kohap, and several other companies launched Chemcross, a competing e-exchange. In steel trading, however, SK, Hyundai, Samsung, and LG all launched their own separate exchanges.

The Emergence of E-chaebols

Until 1999, chaebols seemed to be stunned by the sudden shift in the center of gravity to the new economy. They were heavily indebted and were undergoing serious restructuring to lower debts through asset sales. Their best and brightest employees were leaving them en masse to join start-ups. Investors were shunning their stocks for start-ups listed on the KOSDAQ. As a result, chaebols had neither cash nor talented employees to compete seriously in the Internet economy, and thus seemed unable to respond to this turn of the events.

They managed, however, to slowly move into Internet businesses. Their general trading companies spearheaded such efforts. As mentioned above, the general trading companies had export/import trading businesses and participated in a variety of domestic businesses, most importantly in the retailing sector. For instance, when Samsung Corporation launched Samsung Mall in March 1999, it had 61,000 visitors to its site and 3.3 billion won ($2.8 million) in sales within a month. The sales of Samsung Mall increased from 72 billion won ($55 million) in 1999 to 180 billion won ($138 million) in 2000. Such growth can be attributable to the loyalty of customers, who trusted Samsung's brand name and found its shopping mall as a place that would be safer than unknown start-ups. As the revenue of all Internet shopping malls, compiled by National Statistical Office, was 2.2 trillion won ($1.8 billion) in 2000, Samsung Mall commanded an 8 percent market share in Korean Internet shopping malls. Other leading Internet shopping malls in 2000 were chaebol affiliates such as Hansol CS Club ($115 million), a subsidiary of Hansol Group. The sales of non-chaebol affiliated Internet shopping malls were much smaller in scale, such as Daum ($21 million) and Interpark ($18 million).

Samsung's Traport.com is a travel-specialized Web site, modeled after the Expedia or Travelocity. Cresens is an online bookstore. Samsung Corporation also runs a premier auction site called Samsungauction, an entertainment site called Doobob.com, and several other specialty shopping malls. In addition, Samsung Corporation operates a venture capital arm, GoldenGate, to invest in promising start-ups that capitalize on the booming Internet IPO market (see figure 8.5).

Samsung Corporation also translated its offline business expertise to B2B e-commerce. Among its various e-marketplaces is Fishround.com, an online trading system of fishing products, with suppliers in Asia and customers in Western countries. Fishround.com is converting Samsung's incumbent offline fish products trading business to the e-marketplace.

B2B	Industry Vortals -Domestic (ichemnet, Carecamp) -Global (Textopia, Chemcross, Global Steel Exchange) e-OSN Samsung Corp.'s online trading catalog
B2C	Samsung Mall
Corporate Venture Capital	Golden Gate
Others	CV Net Visacash HTH

Figure 8.5
Samsung Corporation's Internet businesses

Textopia.com is the online version of the textile trading business unit of Samsung. CareCamp.com is the importing and retailing business unit of medical products, which has been one of Samsung Corporation's most profitable business units. Chemcross.com engages in the wholesale trading of petrochemical products. It was established as a consortium with Samsung's petrochemical trading unit and other partners. Ichemnet.com is the domestic retailing business of specialty chemical products. Global Steel exchange is a joint venture with Samsung and Cargill, a global trader of agricultural product and steel products, as well as Duferco and TradeARBED, both of which are independent global steel traders. B2Bsamsung Mall is the B2B exchange of MRO suppliers, similar to Ariba or CommerceOne in the United States. Samsung Corporation also has a site called FindKorea to help small- and medium-sized companies market their products around the world. For products offered by its other trading divisions, Samsung Corporation is operating an online trading catalog called Merchant Intelligence System, which has detailed information on over a thousand products.

SK Group also focused on the mobile Internet services via SK Telecom, which holds a more than 50 percent market share in mobile phone service. SK Telecom has plans to augment the mobile service with offline businesses in the SK Group. SK Global and SK Corporation, which operate convenience stores and gas stations throughout the country, plan to provide offline customer interfaces for customers of SK Telecom. For instance, customers who order merchandise from SK's Internet shopping malls can pick it up from nearby gas stations and convenience stores, paying for it at the time of pickup. LG Telecom, which held a 15 percent market share in mobile phone services, also plans to provide similar services.

As table 8.4 suggests, other chaebols are engaging in similar activities. Possibly because they lacked the engineers and prowess in Internet technology, chaebols actively sought alliances with global Internet companies that wished to enter the Korean market. These global Internet firms lacked the knowledge of local customers and needed the strong brand names possessed by chaebols. For instance, Amazon.com entered into an alliance with Samsung Corporation, selling its books through Samsung's Internet shopping mall. Samsung sells Korean books on its own site, but when a customer searches non-Korean title, he on she is connected to Amazon's database. Samsung Mall then aggregates all the orders to Amazon through its website, thereby saving on mailing costs. E*trade entered a joint venture with LG Investment and Securities, and began a discount trading business. Therefore, in Korea, two groups of Internet firms were in fierce competition with each other—start-up companies and chaebols' Internet business affiliates, which were often allied with global Internet firms.

These forays by chaebols into Internet businesses represented the creation of "e-chaebols." Samsung Corporation's e-chaebol is a prime example. Chaebols that invested heavily in Internet businesses had some common traits. First, chaebols with general trading companies had been particularly active in transforming their trading businesses into Internet platforms, as addressed above. Second, chaebols with young heirs to the chairmanship were most active in Internet business. For example, in 2000, Samsung Group reorganized various Internet initiatives of individual affiliates into e-Samsung, a separate company headed by Jae-Yong Lee, a son of the current group chairman Kuen-Hee Lee. E-Samsung presented itself as a holding company for all Internet businesses run by various Samsung affiliates including Samsung Corporation. Similarly, Taewon Choi, the eldest son of the late chairman Jong-Hyun Choi, who is being groomed as the next chairman of the SK Group, managed the group's Internet business initiatives.

Table 8.4
E-marketplace of General Trading Companies

Industry	Site	Participants	Business
Chemistry	www.chemround.com	Hyundai Corporation/LG International Corporation/SK Global	Distribution and marketing of chemical product
	www.chemcross.com	Samsung Corporation/Kumho Chemical/Kohap/LG Caltex/Hanwha/SK/Ssangyong. Etc (Domestics 14, Foreigns 20)	Initiate the "chemcross" with 20 domestic firms and 20 foreign firms
	www.polyolefin.com	Daerim Corporation	Distribution and marketing of chemical product
Steel/nonmetal	www.isteelasia.com	SK Global/Sambo Computer/Thrunet/iSteel Asia (Hong Kong)	Initiating joint venture with iSteel Asia
	www.steelnmetal.com	Hyundai Corporation/Walnet Holdings (Hong Kong)	JV with Walnet Holdings
	www.tradesteel.com	Samsung Corporation	Samsung Corporation lead this new venture
	www.steelround.com	LG International Corporation	LG International lead this new venture
Medical	www.carecamp.com	Samsung Corporation, Samsung Medical Center, Gil Hospital	EDI system, credit and estimation information, etc.
	www.emedicals.com	SK Global/Bit Computer/Chunneung Medical SW/Brain Consulting/Medidas/SQL	Order, distribution, sign, etc., through the Internet
Finance	www.visacash.co.kr	Samsung Corporation/Visa International	Financial portal

Source: Electronic Commerce Research and Development Association of Korea, ⟨http://www.b2b.or.kr⟩.

The Future of Korean Internet Economy

Internet stocks were highly valued until early 2000. The NASDAQ reached its historical peak of 5,132 in March 2000 but plunged to 3,300 by April. As of November 2001, the NASDAQ composite index was around 1,800. The KOSDAQ has plummeted from a high of 280 in February 2000 to 60 in November 2001. Due to this collapse, Internet start-ups in Korea and the United States faced an unexpected capital crunch in the latter half of 2000. The IPO window closed for most Internet companies, forcing start-ups to survive on their own revenue, sell out, or go bankrupt. For many Internet start-ups, which were in their expansion stage, revenues were not high enough to sustain operations. Thus, many of these firms face bankruptcy. In Korea, some of these firms might be acquired either by chaebols or foreign Internet giants.

For instance, Serome Technologies, which pioneered free Internet phone service, sold 10 percent of its equity to Samsung Electronics in 2000. Although there is no official statistic on the bankruptcies of Internet start-ups, several went under and were acquired by chaebols at heavily discounted prices.[14] Chaebols had good opportunities to acquire technology and personnel from troubled start-ups at a bargain. Many second-tier Internet start-ups simply went bankrupt because they were unlikely to find buyers. In parallel, foreign Internet giants were buying up indigenous start-ups for bargain prices. In December 2000, eBay acquired Auction, a leading auction firm, for $130 million. EBay must have found it cheaper to enter the Korean market by purchasing Auction rather than building a brand and operating from scratch. Similarly, Internet start-ups in other Asian countries were acquired by big conglomerates from the old world or by foreign giants. For instance, Tom.com acquired several Internet start-ups in Hong Kong after the stock market crash.[15]

It is critical to understand whether the blooming of Internet startups was just one of the events facilitated by the Asian Crisis. After the crisis is over, will Korea once again be dominated by chaebols? Will the Internet economy in Korea be shaped by the start-ups or by the e-chaebols? If e-chaebols dominate this sector, the Internet business in Korea will likely be just another addition of business units to the conglomerates.

By the end of 2001, it seemed likely that electronic commerce areas including B2C and B2B would be dominated by chaebols. Although start-ups were early entrants, they failed to build up entry barriers to chaebols. Because most Korean start-ups lacked deep technology and they mainly entered into application areas such as portals or Internet shopping malls, it was not difficult for chaebols to penetrate those markets despite their late entry. Chaebols could therefore take large market shares in the B2C sector with their own brands. Brand awareness and consumer trust turned out to be critical success factors. Consumers found it more comfortable to shop at chaebol-operated Internet retailers such as Samsung Mall or at online extensions of brick and mortar retailers, most of which were chaebol affiliated, than at obscure Internet startups.

The B2B sector developed in an extension to firms' existing supply networks. Thus, each chaebol formed its own network while creating possibilities to share some commodities with other chaebols. In particular, chaebols are expected to excel in the area of mobile Internet. Samsung and LG Group had accumulated competences in CDMA-based telecommunication exchanges, data transmission equipments, and handsets, and they have been actively penetrating export markets. SK and LG Groups owned mobile phone operators. They actively sought after partnerships in other countries to leverage their expertise in operating large-scale CDMA networks.

It is not, however, true that chaebols will dominate the entire Internet space. The Internet has made some fundamental changes in the Korean business practices. First, the Internet boom has contributed to the growth of the venture capital industry. Before the Asian Crisis and the subsequent Internet boom, the venture capital industry was all but nonexistent in Korea. During 1999, however, a total 1.7 trillion won ($1.4 billion) was raised. The establishment of the venture capital industry represented a diffusion of the Silicon Valley model to Korea. Korea's venture capital industry will continue to finance entrepreneurs despite the collapse of Internet start-ups. Second, it created an army of entrepreneurs who pursue their ideas rather than being employees of chaebol companies. Some entrepreneurs became very successful, becoming role models for young would-be-entrepreneurs. The opening up of a labor market in Korea provided a basis for strong entrepreneurial activities. Third, there are some fundamental changes in the corporate culture.[16] Young entrepreneurs in the start-ups are putting more emphasis on profits and making business more transparent. Start-ups have a more open and collegial environment, encouraging creativity and initiative. Perhaps the financial crisis and the subsequent Internet boom has opened a small window of opportunity to Korean people, showing the way for radical changes that would have been unthinkable a few years ago. Many Koreans are undergoing a fundamental change in mindset. After experiencing entrepreneurship, instant access to information, access to venture capital, and new tools such as the Internet, Korea will not be the same as before.

Start-ups might be able to find their niches in some areas such as infrastructure technology, Internet software, and content. As figures 8.3a and 8.3b show, start-ups in those areas have been increasing rapidly since 1999. These are the areas where creativity and entrepreneurship play a critical role, and therefore the areas where chaebols cannot do well. It is questionable whether chaebols, which are products of an industrial economy with a rigid employment system and bureaucratic control, will be able to transform themselves easily into knowledge-based, high-tech firms. Chaebols operate under autocratic, capricious controls. Subordinates find it impossible to go against wrong decisions by their superiors. Chaebols rarely use stock options or pay for performance. Many start-ups that initially operated portals and e-commerce sites, are restructuring their business domain. Many focus on developing contents for mobile Internet services, as Korean mobile service providers are busy developing 2.5G services modeled after the Japan's I-mode success. Young entrepreneurs are starting up new ventures with the backing of venture capitalists. Start-ups might have found a small beachhead in Internet industry that now is spreading to other industries traditionally occupied by chaebols.

Notes

1. The Ministry of Information and Communication, November 2000.

2. The Ministry of Information and Communication, November 2000, available from ⟨www.mic.go.kr⟩.

3. The Ministry of Information and Communication website.

4. Korea Development Institute, internal memorandum.

5. See Corsetti, Pesenti, and Roubini 1998 for a survey on this topic.

6. At the end of 1996, the foreign currency reserve of Korea was $32 billion. At the end of 2000, it increased to $96 billion, according to the *Financial Statistics Yearbook*, Bank of Korea.

7. The source of the relief was unexpected. The Asian economic malaise started to infect Russia and South America. It then afflicted advanced countries, including the United States. For example, one of the biggest hedge funds in America, Long-Term Capital, was saved from insolvency by the U.S. government in 1998. Eventually, the Federal Reserve Bank of the United States lowered the interest rate to keep the crisis under control. See Frankel and Roubini 2000 for an in-depth discussion of this topic.

8. Available on its website, ⟨http://www.kisdi.re.kr⟩.

9. Ministry of Commerce, Industry and Energy 2000a, p. 125.

10. *IT Business* newsletter, December 10, 2000.

11. KISDI, "Trends in B2C e-commerce," report on e-commerce, September 1, 2000.

12. Auction was acquired by eBay in December 2000.

13. Ministry of Commerce, Industry, and Energy 2000b, "B2B e-marketplace Will Be in Operation in Later 2000," press release, August 18, 2000.

14. The *Chosun Ilbo*, December 29, 2000.

15. *Business Week*, "In Asia, the Dot-Coms Are Clicking on 'Exit,' " September 18, 2000.

16. *The Economist*, "South Korea: Entrepreneurial Fresh Air," January 13, 2001; *Business Week*, "Korea's Digital Quest," September 24, 2000.

9

Between Bit Valley and Silicon Valley: Hybrid Forms of Business Governance in the Japanese Internet Economy

Mari Sako

Japan has experienced the beginning of a take off in its Internet economy since the mid 1990s, despite a prolonged macroeconomic recession. Business enterprises enthusiastically endorsed the Internet, as the usage rate went up from 12 percent in 1995 to 95.8 percent in 2000 (MPHPT 2001, 5). At the end of 2000, 34 percent of Japan's population, or 47 million users, were connected to the Internet, up from 3.3 percent in 1996 and 19.1 percent in 1999. This adoption rate is not high compared to the United States or Scandinavian countries with over 40 percent penetration rates. But NTT DoCoMo's highly successful i-mode—mobile Internet services—is expected to further accelerate the pace of wireless access to the Internet. Japan is the first country in the world to introduce third generation (3G) mobile services, in October 2001. The year 2001 was also the first year of broadband service, which is expected to diffuse rapidly.

What explains such growth in Internet-related business activities in Japan? And what is the impact of the Internet on the Japanese business system? These are the questions that this chapter addresses.

The stylized facts about the classical Japanese business model pose a challenge to answering the above questions. In general, the Japanese model is characterized by long-term commitments in the labor market (i.e., lifetime employment), financial markets (i.e., the main bank system and cross-shareholding within corporate groups), and inter-firm relations (i.e., relational contracting in product markets). These different spheres of the business system complement each other to facilitate flexible production based on teamwork and long-term investment financed by "patient capital." Given these characteristics, Japanese firms are internationally competitive in assembly-based manufacturing sectors, in which product and process innovation tends to be of the incremental sort, as similar strengths (e.g., close cross-functional coordination) are used to reduce development lead times and enhance design for manufacturability. Even in more basic R&D, engineers and scientists are given incentives and develop norms similar to other employees as company-wide organizational patterns diffuse to R&D labs. As long as the best and the brightest continue to be hired by large Japanese corporations that retain them for their lifetime, the engine of innovative activities remains within large corporations.

This characterization of the Japanese model is a useful benchmark to investigate whether or not the Internet phenomenon will drive a fundamental shift. At one extreme, one might predict that Japan will continue to be a laggard in the Internet economy because of the relative absence of venture capital and features of the Japanese model that accounted for many of the sources of Japanese competitive advantage (e.g., Aoki and Dore 1994; Dore 2000). But the world has moved on fast, and Japan is left behind with an inhospitable institutional climate for entrepreneurship, radical innovation, and high risk-taking associated with the U.S.-style new economy. By emphasizing the embeddedness of firms in national institutions, this analytical perspective focuses on the resilient nature of national business systems, with path dependency, complementarity of different elements of the system, and high switching costs (Kogut 1993).

An alternative view, at the other end of the spectrum, predicts that the Internet, together with the globalization of financial markets, is a powerful trigger to dislodge the Japanese economy from its traditional institutional rut. According to this perspective, the Internet, regardless of geographic location, facilitates efficiency improvements in the form of reduced transaction costs, increased transparency in transactional content, and better customer satisfaction. The market forces will ensure that the Japanese business system will be transformed in one best way toward more flexible market exchanges, leading to the breakdown of *keiretsu* trading and of long-term commitments in finance and labor. This perspective is predicated on technological determinism and a belief in convergence toward a single form of global capitalism.

Between the two extreme views of universal convergence and complete institutional resistance to change is a series of more nuanced middle positions that may be categorized as the adaptive hybridization perspective. Over time, despite institutional complementarities and distinct national trajectories, hybrids—combining elements from more than one model—have occurred not least in firms' attempts to transfer practices across national borders (Boyer et al. 1998; Zeitlin and Herrigel 2000). A notion that the process of imitation necessarily involves innovation is not new (Westney 1987). But what is more novel is the recent greater attention given to the extent to which actors, be they firms or regulators, can work toward triggering a dynamic change in the national business system in which they operate. Firms are strategic actors that do not passively embed in national institutions, but negotiate between the existing institutions and new opportunities by devising a new corporate strategy. In this sense, firms treat national institutions as a tool kit to influence the governance costs they face. Therefore, apart from a national or an industry level analysis, corporate actions must be analyzed at the micro level in order to explain dynamic changes (Hall and Soskice 2001).

So far, however, this sort of analysis, linking micro-level actions to national institutions, is easier said than done. This is in part due to disciplinary segmentation in academic study. Political scientists and industrial relations scholars may see more embedded resistance to change than others simply because their studies of corporatist and other forms of governance tend to stop at either national or sectoral levels. By contrast, business historians with detailed knowledge of the trajectory of a particular multinational corporation may observe more instances of innovative adaptation at the firm level, but tend to stop short of exploring the impact of corporate action on national institutions.

Moreover, the concept of hybridization is underdeveloped. Hybrid forms of governance are everywhere, but the trick is in being able to distinguish between viable and unstable hybrids. At the corporate level, an incompatibility between corporate strategy and national institutions may be resolved by a search for a functional equivalent on either side of the equation. For example, it might be possible for a firm to combine venture capital finance with long-term employment relations for a while, but this combination is not likely to perform as well as a package of venture capital finance and flexible labor. The resolution of this sub-optimal combination might be a new form of governance, but whether it works or not appears to be a matter of ex-post discovery through trial and error rather than strategic choice by the firm.

Here lies the problem with attributing too much intentionality in the process of arriving at hybrid solutions. If it is believed that the use of the Internet can realize its full benefits only if accompanied by more fluid product, financial, and labor markets, a firm might not go for a hybrid but instead attempt to create a local pocket of new practices (see the discussion of Sweden by Glimstedt and Zander, chapter 4 in this book). That is to say, a firm or a set of firms might simultaneously exploit equity finance and flexible entrepreneurial labor in a sea of bank finance and life-long employment in Japan. The ability of firms to mobilize resources in this way would appear to be high either if they are confined to a certain sector or geographical location, or if a firm is large enough and well connected to international financial and labor markets.

This chapter is structured as follows. The first section outlines when and how the Internet economy began to take off in Japan. Government policy and the role of NTT (and its reluctant yet successful "start-up" NTT DoCoMo) are recounted here. The second section focuses more closely on Internet start-ups, in order to investigate the extent of hybridization of Japanese and Silicon Valley models of business. The third section turns to a case study, namely the analysis of Softbank Group, arguably the most significant corporate player that is using the Internet to transform Japanese business.

The Japanese Takeoff: When, How, and Why?

The origin of the Internet in Japan may be traced back to 1984, when JUNET (Japan University/Unix NETwork) was launched to facilitate electronic links for research collaboration among three Tokyo-based universities, the University of Tokyo, Keio University, and Tokyo Institute of Technology. Beginning in 1988, private sector enterprises participated in a government-led WIDE project (Widely Integrated Distributed Environment) to improve network technologies, but their use for commercial purposes was prohibited. It was only in 1993 that the Japanese government lifted this restriction, following the U.S. decision in

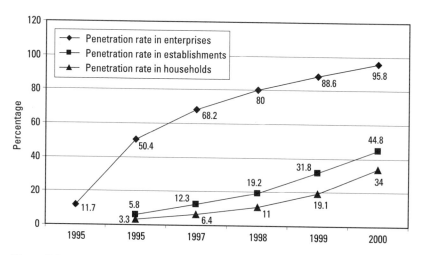

Figure 9.1
Trends in Internet penetration in Japan
Source: MPT 2000.

1990 to open Internet subscription to private users beyond government agencies and research organizations. Thus, the public and research roots of the Internet are similar in Japan and the United States.

Since then, the use of the Internet by households and businesses has grown considerably in the latter half of the 1990s (see figure 9.1). At the end of 2000, there were some 47 million Internet users aged 15–79 in Japan; one in three Japanese households is connected to the Internet. The rate of diffusion among large businesses, however, has been much more rapid than that among households, as was the case in the United States. By 2000, nearly all (95.8 percent) business enterprises in Japan used the Internet.

The purpose of this section is to account for when and how the Internet took off in the Japanese economy. The discussion begins with an examination of the patterns of consumer demand, followed by an investigation of the "Internet industry" and the regulatory changes facing the telecommunication infrastructure providers. There will be a critical evaluation of the timing of indigenous activities and of entry of foreign telecom and Internet companies in stimulating the demand for, and supply of, Internet-related activities.

Consumer Demand: Mobile Triggers a Takeoff

In Japan, the relatively late timing in the spread of the Internet among individual consumers is commonly attributed to the low diffusion of personal computers (PCs) at home. Personal computers in Japan suffered from relatively high prices, keyboard phobia (associated with a general lack of familiarity with typing skills and the cumbersome way in which the QWERTY keyboard is used to generate Japanese scripts), the advent of word processors that were sufficient for most user's needs, and the Japanese manufacturers' persistent adherence to proprietary standards. As figure 9.2 shows, only 16.3 percent of households owned a PC in 1995, and the ownership rate, at 37.7 percent in 1999, is not much higher than that of facsimile machines, a popular piece of equipment that enables users to retain the aesthetic pleasure of handwriting. In this climate, a diverse range of alternative online networked terminals emerged in the late 1990s. In particular, game consoles such as SEGA's Dreamcast, the Nintendo Entertainment System, and Sony's PlayStation, originally used cartridges and CD-ROMs that plugged into the console, but are increasingly linked to online terminals such as cable TVs and to broadband Internet Web pages, to fuel a $15 billion video game market.

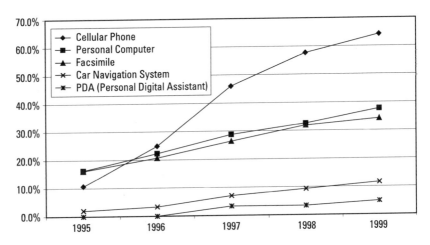

Figure 9.2
Ownership of household information-communications equipment in Japan
Source: MPHPT 2000.

But by far the most significant platform for triggering Internet connection in Japan is the mobile phone. By 2000, some 23.64 million out of the 47.08 million Internet users gained access via cell phones; moreover, Internet users who could not handle a keyboard accounted for more than 75 percent of cell phone Internet usage (MPHPT 2001, 5, 10). As shown in figure 9.2, more people owned cellular phones than PCs as early as 1996. The number of mobile telephones has increased rapidly to 60.88 million by August 2000, overtaking the number of fixed line telephone subscribers in March 2000 (JIPDEC 2000, 138). April 1994 marked the switch from rental to the introduction of a COAM (customer owned and maintained) system for mobile phones, and therefore is considered the start year for the general usage of mobile telephones in Japan. After that, it took a mere six years for mobile phone service to catch up in its usage level with a 110-year record of the fixed line telephone service (Yoshimura 2000, 19). What accounts for this rapid diffusion of mobile telephones in Japan?

Mobile telephones at an affordable price in Japan started with the introduction of PHS (Personal Handy phone System) in 1995. From the latter half of 1997, non-voice services began to be offered by mobile communications carriers, first with short messaging service, then electronic mail exchanges using the Internet. Once this habit of reading short messages on a compact screen on the mobile phone was inculcated, NTT DoCoMo launched its i-mode in February 1999. I-mode refers to Internet services using mobile telephones. DoCoMo's conception of i-mode as a marketing tool, just like a game console, was a complete break from the mode of operation of its parent, NTT, as an infrastructure provider. The popularity of this "browser phone" is manifested in the explosion in its use, shooting past 1 million users in the first six months after its launch, reaching 5 million users in March 2000 and 16 million in December 2000. In the year 2000, 59 percent of mobile phones sold in Japan were for i-mode. When i-mode was launched, it was considered a stop gap before the PC-based Internet would really take off. It seems that this was not a correct assumption, as i-mode is more likely to accelerate the use of mobile phones for Internet access than to diffuse the use of PCs (Yoshimura 2000, 71). Moreover, an early setback in choosing PDC as a standard incompatible with the U.S. or European 2G mobile standard seems to explain NTT's wish to push for 3G mobile services quickly.

The i-mode was intended to be a lifestyle gadget; nowhere was there a notion that it be used as a work or business tool. On fashionable street corners in Tokyo, young *yamanba* women, sun-tanned, with bleached blonde hair, primary color clothes, and high platform shoes, must have their thumb busily tapping a translucent i-mode phone. They mainly use the phone to download their favorite Hello Kitty screen saver, or a favorite tune that would play on receipt of a message, or to send a simple social message to friends. This is just the tip of the iceberg of all Japanese Internet users, who tend to surf the Internet more to obtain information about hobby or travel than business data (JIPDEC 2000, 505). The Internet culture is led by the youth all over the world, but Japanese Internet consumers in particular are distinctively young—in their teens —and female (Yoshimura 2000) (76 percent of Internet users are in their teens, 20s, or 30s [MPT 2000, 13].) A "mobile culture" is fashionable, out there on the streets, and affecting language as well as lifestyle.

Despite the enormous success of i-mode as a socio-cultural phenomenon in Japan, there is doubt about its universal applicability to other parts of the world and to business. Most of the i-mode contents, geared specifically to the Japanese taste for trivia and games, may not sell at all well outside of Japan. Moreover, the launch of FOMA, NTT DoCoMo's 3G phone, in October 2001, is limited in its technical capability by its use of NTT's existing telephone networks. Last but not least, it is important to note that NTT DoCoMo has built a profitable business by going against the trend of open access and standard access protocol. This means that i-mode users can browse only those websites that conform to DoCoMo's proprietary i-mode access protocols. Japanese users are therefore in a cumbersome position of having two systems in parallel, the convenient yet proprietary i-mode and open standards giving access to a broader range of Web sites.

But what is clear is that i-mode has made an irreversible impact on the Japanese mode of Internet access for the forseeable future. Specifically, the main platform is likely to remain the phone with its ten keys rather than the PDA, such as the Palm Pilot, which continues to rely on the QWERTY keyboard.

Internet Industry

This subsection follows the definition by the Ministry of Posts and Telecommunications (MPT) (MPHPT from January 2001) to capture all businesses that are involved in commercial transactions using computer networks based on TCP/IP. Two broad areas of business are identified: 1) Internet-mediated commerce (involving both B2B and B2C), and 2) Internet-related businesses involving markets for Internet connection, and the production of hardware and software used for Internet connection. According to the MPHPT's estimate, the total value of the Internet industry in 2000 was 47,803.1 billion yen ($425.3 billion), more than double the value in the previous year (MPHPT 2001, 16). This sum consists of 623.3 billion yen ($5.5 billion) for B2C commerce, 38.1 trillion yen ($339.0 billion) for B2B commerce, and 9,079.8 billion yen ($80.8 billion) for Internet-related businesses (an exchange rate of $1 = 112.4 yen was used). Between 1998 and 1999, B2C commerce grew two-fold, while B2B commerce grew six-fold. Between 1999 and 2000, B2C grew 78 percent, but B2B experienced a 2.5-fold growth. As in other countries, the size of B2B, accounting for 80 percent of the Internet industry, is much bigger than that of B2C.

One indication of the rise of B2C commerce is the number of retail shops (including "virtual shops") that operate on Internet sites. According to one estimate, only 216 such shops existed in 1995, but the number grew to 2,264 in 1996, and grew a further ten-fold to 27,279 by May 2000 (⟨http://www.ccci.or.jp⟩). This acceleration of online shopping has some universal drivers, not least the example of the success of U.S. companies entering the Japanese market in Internet auctions (e.g., eBay Japan in October 1999, Onsale Japan in July 1998), car sales (e.g., Autobytel Japan in June 1999, CarPoint Japan in November 1999) and Internet banking (e.g., E*Trade Japan in June 1998). Nevertheless, a small number of local successes also exist. In particular, Rakuten Ichiba, founded in 1997 by an ex-Industrial Bank of Japan employee with a Harvard MBA as a cybermall where individuals and businesses can buy and sell, boasts second or third place in popularity in Japan's ranking of all Internet sites.

Retail distribution is one of the most inefficient sectors in Japan, with only 50 percent of U.S. productivity (McKinsey Global Institute 2000). A major reason for this is the predominance of mom and pop shops as compared to large-scale stores, and Japanese consumers' preference for higher levels of convenience and service. Would e-commerce replace unproductive mom and pop shops? It seems that the retailing revolution is taking a distinctively Japanese turn, based on pre-existing patterns of trade and consumption. In particular, mom and pop shops are being transformed into convenience stores, such as 7-Eleven and Lawson, with a national network of fifty thousand outlets in total (Arthur Andersen 2000, 58). Multimedia terminals placed in these seven-day-a-week, 24-hour-a-day convenience stores are used to settle payments more securely for orders placed online; the stores are also pick-up points for goods ordered online. With refrigerated delivery services, online shopping of perishable local speciality food and drink is also on the rise. Thus, convenience stores at every street corner are likely to stay part of the e-commerce infrastructure in Japan, rather than being replaced by large-scale stores in suburban shopping malls.

For manufacturing companies, B2C is being adopted in Japan, as elsewhere, in order to access more information about consumer behavior and preferences that might have typically been held solely by retailers or dealers. But as their interest shifts toward B2B, attention is likely to descend on the power of the Internet to potentially bring about major changes in the way intermediate goods are traded in Japan. First, e-marketplaces where multiple seller and buyer companies engage in trading, typically by auction or reverse auction, may develop. But like consumers, Japanese manufacturing companies place a high priority on security within a closed network rather than the advantages of open market exchanges (MPT 1999, 20). Moreover, relational contracting as the predominant mode of trading in intermediate goods has deterred Japanese firms from actively participating in auctions. It is therefore not surprising that as of 2000, only 83 billion yen out of the total of 83.1 trillion yen generated in B2B e-commerce is accounted for by e-marketplaces (MPHPT 2001, 16).

Second, although it is difficult for public e-marketplaces to take root in Japan, the prevailing trading norm may blend more easily with e-marketplaces that place greater emphasis on collaboration among members. One notable example is E2open Japan Corporation for trading in electronic components, launched as a fully owned subsidiary of E2open U.S. in May 2001, with Hitachi, Matsushita, and Toshiba as Japanese founding members. Through collaboration among member companies, E2open intends to bring about standardization in a country where each major electronics company tends to have its own proprie-tary middleware, applications, and component design. Standardization will lower entry barriers and enable trading across so-called *keiretsu* groupings.

Thus, the Internet potentially has the effect of making intermediate goods trading in Japan more fluid, but the weakening of long-term committed trading relationships would be a consequence of standardization and not the intended outcome of the use of the Internet. The speed with which this may happen depends on the ability of private e-marketplace corporations to promote standard-setting just as industry associations have been attempting to do for some time. Moreover, it is quite possible, as Helper and MacDuffie (chapter 11 in this book) argue, that the prevailing emphasis on long-term committed relationships would bias Japanese manufacturers toward using the Internet more for intensifying the sharing of confidential information for product development than for mere price comparisons. If so, it is not at all evident that the diffusion of the Internet would fundamentally undermine relational contracting in Japan.

Regulatory Changes and Restructuring in Telecommunications
In 1985, Japan became the third country in the world to liberalize its telecommunications sector, after the United States and United Kingdom. Before 1985, the telecommunications industry in Japan was highly regulated, consisting of Nippon Telegraph and Telephone Public Corporation, which had a monopoly over domestic operations, and Kokusai Denshin Denwa Co. Ltd. (KDD), which had a monopoly for international operations. In April 1985, all legally approved monopolies in telecommunications were abolished in Japan, and the Nippon Telegraph and Telephone Public Corporation was gradually privatized as NTT (KDD's legal status has been a private company from the beginning) (Nakamura 1997). The main objectives of liberalization and privatization were to introduce competition into the market with a view to reducing customer charges and to improve the business performance of NTT and KDD.

With the regulatory reform, the Ministry of Posts and Telecommunications (MPT) introduced a distinction between Type I carriers that offer telecommunications services over their own networks, and Type II carriers that provide services over networks and facilities leased from Type I carriers. As table 9.1 shows, there has been a rapid increase in new entrants for both types in the years since the regulatory change in 1985. By September 2000, there were 301 Type I carriers and 8,273 Type II carriers. Of the latter, 3,320 (February 1999 figure) were Internet Service Providers (ISPs), according to the MPT's ISP Survey; 27 percent of ISPs had Internet service provision as their main business, whereas the rest had something other than ISP as their core business (MPT 1999, 24).

Competition began initially in separate segments of the market, namely domestic local, domestic long distance, domestic mobile, and international. The MPT, through its administrative guidance, encouraged new common carriers (NCCs) to enter one of the market segments in the belief that segmentation would safeguard NCCs against undue competition from NTT or KDD. But the segmentation of markets eventually became infeasible with subsequent alliances and mergers. Main investors in the new carriers are regional electric power companies, trading companies, car manufacturers (esp. Toyota), and foreign telecommunication companies. In domestic long-distance services, NTT initially faced competition with the entry of DDI in 1988, and subsequently Japan Telecom (established by the Japanese National Railways) and Teleway Japan (established by Toyota and the Japanese Highway Public Corporation). Similarly, in international Type I business, KDD was challenged by the entry of ITJ and IDC. In December 1998, KDD merged with Teleway Japan. Then DDI announced its merger with KDD and IDO, to form KDDI in October 1999. Also, 1999 saw the UK's Cable & Wireless triumph over NTT in its acquisition of IDC. Thus in 2001, the major players were NTT, KDDI, Japan Telecom, and C&W IDC.

In the mobile phone market, NTT DoCoMo competed with J-Phone, DDI Cellular, IDO (owned by Toyota Motor, Tokyo Electric Power Co., and Chubu Electric Power Co.), and Tu-Ka (majority owned by Nissan). Of these, DDI and IDO were merged as KDDI, as mentioned above, and Tu-Ka was absorbed by J-Phone in 1999. By August 2000, of the 55 million cellular subscribers, 32.1 million were with NTT DoCoMo, 13.9 million with KDDI, and 8.9 million with J-Phone. J-Phone, originally created by Japan Telecom, is now 26 percent owned by Vodafone and 20 percent by BT, two rival companies that are likely to treat Japan as a battleground and a source of learning in competition for 3G mobile

Table 9.1
Number of Telecommunications Carriers in Japan

Beginning of each FY	1986	1987	1988	1989	1990	1991	1992	1993	1994	1995	1996	1997	1998	1999	2000	9/1/01
Type I Carriers[1]	7	12	37	45	63	68	70	80	86	111	126	138	153	178	246	301
NTT	1	1	1	1	1	1	1	1	—	—	1	1	1	1	3[3]	3
NTT DoCoMo, Inc. and group companies	—	—	—	—	1	—	1	1	9	9	9	9	9	9	9	9
KDD	1	1	1	1	1	1	1	1	1	1	1	1	1	1	1	1
New Type I Carriers	5	10	35	43	61	66	68	77	75	100	115	127	142	167	236	288
Long-distance/international carriers	3	3	5	5	5	5	5	5	5	5	5	5	6	12	21	27
Regional Carriers	—	3	4	4	7	7	7	8	10	11	16	28	47	77	159	217
Satellite carriers	2	2	2	2	2	2	3	3	2	2	4	4	5	6	5	5
Mobile communications	—	2	23	31	46	52	53	61	58	82	90	90	84	72	51	39
Others	—	—	1	1	1	—	—	—	—	—	—	—	—	—	—	—
Type II Carriers[2]	209	356	530	693	841	943	1036	1179	1589	2107	3134	4588	5871	6602	7651	8273
Special Type II carriers	9	10	18	25	28	31	36	36	39	44	50	78	95	88	101	105
General Type II carriers	200	346	512	668	813	912	1000	1143	1550	2063	3084	4510	5776	6514	7550	8168
Total	221	378	602	781	965	1077	1174	1336	1750	2318	3375	4853	6166	6947	8133	8862

Notes: (1) Type I carriers offer services by establishing their own telecommunications circuit facilities; (2) Type II carriers offer services by leasing telecommunications circuit facilities; (3) NTT was reorganized into two regional Type I carriers (NTT East Corp. and NTT West Corp.) under one holding company (NTT) on July 1, 1999
Source: MPT 2000.

markets. (It was only in 1998 that the foreign ownership restriction was eliminated for Type I carriers.)

Reflecting the Ministry of Posts and Telecommunication (MPT)'s focus on market segmentation, NTT divestiture became a policy focus. First, in 1987, MPT ordered NTT to separate its data communications arm into a subsidiary as NTT Data Corporation. In 1992, it also requested the separation of the mobile communications portion, and NTT DoCoMo was established as a separate company. But it was not until July 1999 that a new structure was finally imposed on the core part of NTT with the passing of the revised NTT Corporation Law in June 1997. NTT has been reorganized into a company (NTT Communications Corp.) that deals with the trunk network and two regional companies that deal with local telephone services (NTT East Corp. and NTT West Corp.). The three companies come under control of a pure holding company, a corporate form made legal again in Japan very much with the NTT case in mind.

Despite these structural changes, NTT East and NTT West each continue to be a *de facto* monopoly with 90 percent market share in local networks. This is due to the fact that unlike in the United States, cable TV is much less widely used in Japan. Moreover, electric utility companies in Japan are also organized in large regional blocs, thus giving them no edge over NTT in becoming providers of comprehensive local networks. Consequently, NTT, with its pre-privatized bureaucratic stance, could easily delay negotiations in the installation of new subscriber lines for new carriers. NTT is also in a powerful position to influence the direction and speed of adoption of broadband access to the Internet through its capacity to set access charges for different services.

The year 2001 in Japan marked a concerted government campaign to enable broadband access to the Internet, with the desirable characteristics of constant connections and fast speed. For instance, in March 2001, NTT East and NTT West began their 10 mbps Fibre to the Home (FTTH) service, and Usen Broadnetworks inaugurated its 100 mbps high-speed transmission services in the Tokyo metropolitan area. Japan had long suffered from one of the highest telecommunications tariffs among the major OEDC countries. Particularly damaging for the Internet users was NTT's adoption for the dial-up service of its long-standing policy to charge according to the length of time users were on the telephone. NTT finally gave in to political pressure to charge flat rates for Internet users in 2001; flat rates had been applied from the start for ISDN, ADSL, and FTTH services. The charges, estimated by MPHPT (2001, 10) range from 6,000 yen per month for 1.5 mbps service to 6,950 yen per month for the 10 mbps FTTH service in mid-2001, not so different from charges for similar services in the United States, United Kingdom, and France. In the broadband age, the alternatives in Japan are between ADSL and FTTH, both relying on NTT's local networks. Thus, the relative balance in the usage of these alternatives will depend on NTT's pricing policy.

Given NTT's continued *de facto* monopoly in major chunks of the Internet infrastructure, NTT has not had to change its corporate behavior much. It is therefore all the more remarkable that NTT DoCoMo was transformed into a highly successful spin-off as a result of the combination of chance and determination. Like a start-up, DoCoMo was able to make decisions speedily, and was determined to become independent of its parent company by investing in its own wireless network rather than leasing from NTT. The chance element was in the evolution of mobile standards. In particular, i-mode was predicated on making the best use of a packet exchange network that NTT DoCoMo already had to provide to Dopa, a rather unsuccessful PC-based wireless communication service. DoCoMo rejected WAP (wireless applications protocol) in favor of its proprietary standard, but no one foresaw the failure of WAP and the subsequent development of making WAP 2.0 compatible with i-mode in May 2001 (Ikeda 2001, 159).

Is ICT Contributing to Growth in Japan?

The new economy is said to exist when ICT brings about growth without inflation (U.S. Department of Commerce 1998). What contribution does growth in ICT make to the overall growth of the economy in Japan? The real gross domestic output of the info-communications industry in 1998 was 112.9 trillion yen, accounting for 12.5 percent of real GDP, up from 7.7 percent in 1985 and 9.3 percent in 1990 (MPT 2000, 38). Not surprisingly, the fastest growing segment of this sector was software, achieving an annual real output growth of 15.9 percent between 1980 and 1997 (MPT 199, 89). Much of the software growth is accounted for by the popularity of game consoles. Game software, in contrast to PC-based packed software, can thrive on closed standards and bundling (Anchor-doguy 2000). Employment in the sector also rose at an annual rate of 2.1 percent during 1980–1998, as compared to 1.6 percent for all industries, so that by 1998, some 3.8 million people, or 6.7 percent of all industrial workforce, were employed in this sector. Labor productivity (as measured by real gross domestic output divided by total employed) in the info-communications industry amounted to 29.48 million yen in 1998, nearly 2.5 times the level in 1980, or an annual increase of 5.1 percent during 1980–1998. Lastly, about 10.4 trillion yen was invested in info-communications equipment by all industries in 1998, accounting for 2.2 percent of GDP, 1.7 times the level in 1990. Thus, despite the prolonged recession in the 1990s, the impact of ICT industries on economic growth, employment, and business investment has been positive.

Capital investment in the telecommunications and broadcasting industries took off after 1994, whereas investment in all other industries continued to be sluggish. By 1996, investment in telecom and broadcasting, amounting to 4,900 billion yen, was nearly double the level in 1989, whereas the investment in all industries remained at a level no higher than that in 1989. However, since 1996, the telecom and broadcasting sector have also suffered a decline in its capital expenditure, down to 4,000 billion yen by 1999 (see figure 9.3). Thus, according to this indicator, it looks as though the ICT-led economic recovery is not assured.

What is different from the United States is not so much the timing of the take off, in the mid 1990s, as the slower pace at which ICT investment is increasing (see fig. 9.4 and 9.5). Moreover, the figures indicate that the impetus was already running out of steam in Japan by the late 1990s. Although the relation of ICT industries to the health of the overall economy is likely to continue to be debated, one possible interpretation of the Japanese phenomenon is that ICT investment in itself is necessary but not sufficient to bring about economic growth (in the sense of Ragin 1987, as discussed by Kogut's introduction to this book). The Internet may be used as a trigger to redefine corporate goals and conceive new ways of creating and maintaining competitive advantage. Unless these concomitant changes occur, "the Internet in itself will not rescue the Japanese company" (Porter, Takeuchi, and Sakakibara 2000, 180) nor the economy.

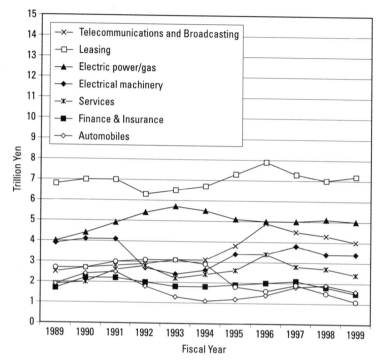

Figure 9.3
Capital investment by the telecommunications and broadcasting industries, compared with major industries, in Japan
Source: MPT 1999.

Summary

To summarize the state of the Internet economy in Japan, it is evident from the discussion above that telecommunications investment started to accelerate in 1995, preceding the consumer demand boom in 1999 with the launch of the i-mode. The Internet economy was relatively slow to take off due to (1) lack of diffusion of PCs in Japanese households, (2) relatively high access charges for dial-up users of the Internet, and (3) a decline in private investment in information technology after the bursting of the 1980s bubble. The first factor was rendered irrelevant by cheap wireless access to the Internet. Here, NTT DoCoMo, an ex-public corporation start-up, played a significant role in making mobile phones the main platform for wireless access in Japan. The second factor is being

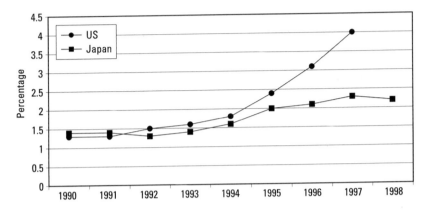

Figure 9.4
Investment in info-communications equipment as percent of GDP
Source: MPT 1999.

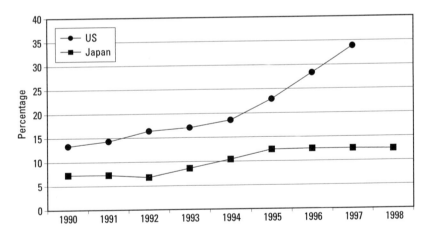

Figure 9.5
Investment in info-communications equipment as percent of total private sector capital
investment
Source: MPT 1999.

addressed by NTT's adoption of flat rates for both narrow and broadband services. Although the pace of capital investment by the telecom sector dipped by the late 1990s, the increasing availability of broadband access is likely to lead to a further increase in Internet users.

Is the Silicon Valley Model Relevant in Japan?

Journalistic accounts of the Internet economy in Japan in the late 1990s used to zoom right into Bit Valley—a literal rendition of Shibuya (Bitter Valley)—in Tokyo. Networking among entrepreneurs and venture capitalists, either through all night parties or through more sober meetings organized by the Bit Valley Association (established in spring 1999), and of incubators founded by individuals with strong links to Silicon Valley, gave a reassuring picture of the buzz of the new economy. According to a recent survey conducted by the Fujitsu Research Institute (FRI 2000), approximately thirteen hundred new media companies are located within Tokyo's 23 wards. Of those, one in four companies are clustered in the Minato and Shibuya wards, the geographical area identified as Bit Valley. Companies in the survey are generally small (39 percent employed 30 workers or fewer) and relatively new (49 percent were founded after 1994). But how does this Bit Valley phenomenon compare with the Silicon Valley model?

The Silicon Valley model is here understood to be an interactive entity with institutions and social norms that encourage the creation of technology-based start-ups (Kenney 2000 and chapter 3 in this book). These start-ups constitute loosely integrated inter-firm networks in a specific locality. The provision of risk capital in the form of venture capital and high growth stock markets, and the availability of mobile labor out of universities and existing firms are two important features of Silicon Valley. Although the urban Bit Valley may be more closely aligned to New York's Silicon Alley, involving less deep technology, the model for high-tech start-ups in Japan is the Silicon Valley. Benchmarking against Silicon Valley is useful insofar as we can gauge the extent to which the governance of Japanese start-ups approaches, or diverges from, the U.S. model.

In the last 50 years, large Japanese industrial firms have been funded primarily by committed creditors through the main bank system and committed shareholders often in a cross-shareholding arrangement (Aoki and Patrick 1994). Although stock market capitalization, at 63 percent of GDP in 1995, is not as low as in Germany (27 percent), around a quarter has been accounted for by such "patient" industrial capital. For small enterprises, finance has traditionally come from family and friends, and from commercial banks and government financial institutions that advanced collateral loans. The relative absence of equity capital to finance small entrepreneurial companies led the Japanese government to devise various measures to encourage the growth of venture capital and initial public offerings. As early as 1983, JASDAQ was created as an OTC (over the counter) market for small- and medium-sized venture companies. By 1999, with a total of 868 listings, JASDAQ's market capitalization grew to be twice the size of the Second Section of Tokyo Stock Exchange. Investors in this market tend to be individuals rather than institutional; in fact, over 70 percent of traded volume is accounted for by individuals (⟨http://www.jasdaq.co.jp⟩).

More recently, in December 1999, the Tokyo Stock Exchange launched its Market for High Growth and Emerging Stocks (MOTHERS) to provide easier funding for emerging companies with high growth potential. This was in anticipation of the opening in June 2000 of NASDAQ Japan at the Osaka Stock Exchange, a joint venture between Softbank Corp. and the National Association of Securities Dealers (NASD). At the time, it was thought that there would be horizontal competition among the three marketplaces, each with slightly different listing criteria. In particular, as compared to JASDAQ and MOTHERS, NASDAQ Japan is noted for its stricter disclosure and delisting requirements. In calendar year 2000, the number of IPOs in JASDAQ, NASDAQ Japan, and MOTHERS was 97, 33, and 27, respectively. For 2001, the numbers changed to 73, 43, and 7. The increasing popularity of NASDAQ Japan relative to the other two markets was notable, yet by fall 2002, it closed.

The "financial reform" policy focuses on the supply of funds as a precondition for entrepreneurship. It is assumed that an active stock market is vital for inducing a bustling venture capital industry, which in turn is essential for financing start-ups. Given this line of logic, there exist two alternative hypotheses about the future of corporate governance for start-ups in Japan. One possibility is that the "open, fair, and global" marketplaces in Japan will be sufficient to bring about a major transformation in corporate finance, and that they will effectively remove the only barrier to the development of high-tech, high-growth industries in Japan. In this view, the shortage of early stage venture capital will be solved by offering an easy exit option for harvesting investments through IPOs. An alternative possibility derives from noting that the financial market reform in itself is not sufficient to bring about fundamental changes to corporate governance. Japanese start-ups would, in this view, still be constrained by existing institutions and practices, including the types of venture capital and career incentives of managers and technologists. The ensuing investigation of the characteristics of the IPO companies listed on the three markets gives some evidence in favor of the second hypothesis.

Characteristics of IPOs in the New Stock Markets

The Silicon Valley model of company governance may be operationalized along the following dimensions: (1) development of new technologies by young companies in high-growth, high-risk markets; (2) the significant role of private venture capital as a major shareholder, often represented on the company board; and (3) pronounced regional agglomeration that affects access to labor and information. These dimensions will be discussed for the population of IPO companies at the end of June 2001, namely 55 firms in NASDAQ Japan, 31 in TSE MOTHERS Market, and 131 in JASDAQ. (JASDAQ as a whole is a much bigger market, but we counted only those IPOs that took place during the period December 1999 and June 2001 to provide a fair comparison with the other two marketplaces). In many respects, MOTHERS and NASDAQ Japan are both very young markets, too young to make any definitive statements about their likely achievements in the future. The results drawn below are therefore tentative, but are consistent with Vitols's (2000) findings for Germany.

As shown in table 9.2, the total market capitalization of the three markets is 278.1 billion yen in 2000. The average size of the firm is quite large, ranging from 113 employees in the TSE MOTHERS market to 373 in the JASDAQ market. Notably, not many IPOs are start-ups as such; the average time elapsed between the establishment of the firm and the IPO date was eight years in the MOTHERS market, 14 years in NASDAQ Japan, and 28 years in JASDAQ.

Table 9.2
Characteristics of IPO Companies in Three Markets in Japan

	NASDAQ Japan	TSE MOTHERS	JASDAQ
Market opened	June 2000	December 1999	1983
# of IPOs (as of June 30, 2001)	55	33	92*
# of IPOs (Dec. 1999–May 2000)	0	10	NA**
# of IPOs (June 2000–June 30, 2001)	55	23	92
Total capitalization 2000*** (billion yen)	63.5	144.3	70.3
Employees (average per firm)	341	113	373
Average years elapsed from founding to IPO	13.7	7.4	28
Location clustering (# with HQ in Tokyo)	37	25	40
(% located in Tokyo)	(67)	(76)	(43)

Notes:
* From June 1, 2000 to June 30, 2001 only.
** There were 39 IPOs during December 1999 and May 2000, but the data analysis for this table excludes them.
*** Fiscal year ending 2000 (1999–2000).

The sectoral distribution of IPO companies in figure 9.6 indicates a different pattern in each market. In both the MOTHERS and NASDAQ Japan markets, the Internet and IT sectors predominate, although NASDAQ Japan has attracted IPOs in other sectors as well (but not in biotechnology). By contrast, the predominance of the retail sector and a relative absence of IPOs in the Internet sector are notable in JASDAQ. Thus, although the total number is quite small, there appears to be a degree of self selection in different markets. There is also evidence of regional agglomeration among the IPO firms. Two-thirds of IPO companies in NASDAQ Japan and MOTHERS are headquartered in Tokyo (see table 9.2). JASDAQ companies, by contrast, are more geographically dispersed, which may be a function of the sectoral distribution of firms.

Lastly, the IPO companies may be classified according to their founder's background. Of the 29 companies in NASDAQ Japan for which we have some information, 20 were founded by owner-managers who have had work experience in large established companies. Twelve of those had an engineering or other technical background, seven had ex-

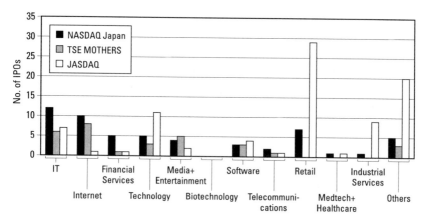

Figure 9.6
Sectoral distribution of IPOs in three markets in Japan

perience in financial services, and one in a trading company. Only two componies were classified as family businesses, and none was a start-up in a university environment.

Characteristics of Venture Capital Activities in Japan

Another sign of why the Japanese Internet economy would not replicate the Silicon Valley model, despite the greater availability of stock markets intended for start-ups, lies in the different mix of venture capital funds available in Japan. Private venture capital has grown in three phases in Japan, starting in the early 1970s when eight VCs, including Nippon Enterprise Development (now NED) and JAFCO, were established to finance rapidly expanding small firms. After the two oil crises, a second phase of growth in the 1980s saw banks, securities, trading companies, regional banks, and insurance companies set up their VC subsidiaries. In the third phase, since the mid 1990s, venture capital funding has grown in size in response to the legalization of stock options for all firms in 1995, the establishment of TSE MOTHERS and NASDAQ Japan, and the growth of Internet-related firms. Nevertheless, the VC industry is still quite small, with an annual investment of 230 billion yen ($2 billion) (during FY 2000) and a total investment balance of 815.5 billion yen ($7.3 billion) (as of June 2000), according to the Venture Enterprise Centre survey (VEC 2001).

It is peculiar in a nation of associational networks that there is no single industry association that would be the equivalent of the US Venture Capital Association. The Venture Enterprise Centre, set up in 1975 as an organization approved by MITI to guarantee unsecured loans for small- and medium-sized enterprises has a directory that listed 149 VC firms in 2001. The Bit Valley Association website has a more comprehensive list of 208 venture capital firms. Broadly speaking, there are four types of venture capital and private equity investment firms in Japan. First, there are the "old-style VCs," such as Jafco, which take small positions in an investee and then invite other Japanese VC firms to take similar positions, "convoy style." The old-style VCs are typically subsidiaries of banks and other financial institutions. They do not provide much in the way of incubation services; instead, they provide "legitimacy" to attract follow-up investors. Second, there are corporate VCs such as Softbank and Hikari Tsushin, which have their own business operations but invest directly in other companies, seeking to create value through the stock appreciation of their investments. These companies have tended to focus on high-tech investments, often related to their own enterprise specialty. Third, there are large, mostly foreign, private equity investment firms such as Prudential Asset Management Asia (PAMA) and Warburg Pincus. These firms do not provide management assistance, but they do provide some supervision and financial advice, more than do old-style Japanese VC. Some of the larger of these firms, once interested in leveraged buyout and merger opportunities, are turning their attention to start-ups. Fourth, there are "Western-style" Japanese and foreign venture capital firms, large and small, that provide management oversight.

As compared to VC funds in other major countries such as the United States, United Kingdom, and Germany, Japanese VC funds may be characterized by the following. First, except for a few giants (the top four—Softbank Investment Corp., JAFCO, NIF Ventures Co. and Worldview Technology Venture Capital—account for 50 percent of total amount invested in FY 1999), Japanese VC companies are relatively small. Second, Japanese VC firms are typically joint stock companies, although they establish VC funds with a limited liability, as is common in the United States after the introduction of a new law in 1998. Third, VC funds in Japan rely significantly on bank, securities, and insurance finance; as compared to the United States, wealthy individuals (1.8 percent of total funds in 2000) and institutional investors (pension funds accounted for 10 percent in 2000) play a less significant role. Fourth, few VC firms are independent, with over half of them being affiliated to a bank-centered corporate group. Fifth, 70 percent of VC firms in Japan engage in the lending business, so that the VC firms' income from interest on loans exceed their income from capital gains on the sale of public stocks and dividends put together. Sixth, Japanese VC firms tend to invest in a variety of sectors at any one time, and only since the late 1990s have there been VCs that specialize in software and Internet-related businesses (a recent METI survey [2001] found that 126 out of the 206 VC funds identified by the survey were of the multiple-sector sort).

These structural characteristics of Japanese VC firms render their investment activities much more conservative than otherwise. In particular, Japanese VC funds are predominantly directed at companies in later stages of development, with very little support for seed and start-up companies. The relative absence of management oversight on start-ups by VC firms is due to a combination of structural and regulatory factors. Until August 1995, the antitrust law prohibited venture capital investors from taking board seats at the companies in which they had invested. Even with the lifting of this barrier, venture capitalists with the relevant managerial and technological expertise are in short supply. Typically, venture capital fund managers are on temporary transfer (*shukko*) from their parent firms for a period of seven to eight years; these parent financial institutions tend to be the major source of ideas for new VC investment opportunities; once an investment is made, each VC manager looks after ten or more companies, resulting in little time to guide each company toward an initial public offering (SMEA 1998, 308, 313). As individuals, VC managers are "salarymen" who are unlikely to take any risk in their investment decisions that would jeopardize their chances of promotion back at the parent company. It is not surprising that Japan has few incubators that provide close mentoring and start-up seed capital.

It is evident by now that venture capital as one of the key institutions of the Silicon Valley model functions differently in a bank-centered system in Japan. According to a conventional line of reasoning, an active stock market would be a sufficient condition for encouraging the development of early stage venture capital, supply of which in turn would facilitate the proliferation of business start-ups. Such a process would be most pronounced in new sectors such as the Internet. In Japan, recently opened stock markets have attracted some start-ups as well as older companies dispersed in various sectors. Reflecting this, Japanese VC firms have had an interest in creating new companies across the full spectrum of the economy—not just the Internet and information technology, but also retailing, financial services, and health care. Investment in the United States in communications, software, and data processing accounts for more than 50 percent of total venture capital investment, but the proportion of investment in these areas in Japan is less than 10 percent (MPT 2000, 40).

In fact, the term *benchaa bizinesu* (venture enterprise) is defined too broadly to include many of the traditional small businesses such as retailing, sake brewing, and shiitake mushroom growing. This blurring in public policy parlance of the dot.com phenomenon and traditional small businesses more generally reflects the relative absence of free-wheeling venture capital funds and the close links most VC firms have to Japan's old mainstream economy: trading companies and banks, manufacturers and consumer companies. In Japan, potential business partners are far less willing to give a chance to a new company or an unknown entrepreneur. So in a country of relational contracting, the support of an established Japanese firm will lower risk, speed up the launch time, and increase the success rate. Establishing a new operation in partnership with a Japanese bank, for example, will provide access to the personnel, knowledge, resources, and business networks that cross dozens of industries and hundreds of companies throughout Japan. Softbank, as discussed in the following section, has exploited this resource from the old economy to its maximum advantage. This strategy has its advantage in winning credibility and reputation quickly, but it also begets the unenviable pressure to conform to existing patterns of corporate behavior.

Softbank: Transformation of the Old Economy?

The nature of the Internet economy in Japan is incomprehensible without identifying the strategy and structure of Softbank Group. With businesses in e-commerce, e-finance, media and marketing, broadcasting, and Internet technology, Softbank Group has an all pervasive presence in the Internet economy in Japan and increasingly in the United States, Asia, and Europe. What are its sources of competitive advantage? In analyzing Softbank's business model—to use a hackneyed term—this section treats Softbank as a means of gauging the extent to which firm-level actions are overturning the existing business system in Japan. In other words, Softbank in action is an ideal case to investigate the process of hybridization, as it takes on the task of fundamentally transforming Japanese business for the digital age while working within the confines of existing financial and labor market institutions.

Softbank Corp. was founded in 1981 as a distributor of pre-packaged software. The founder, Masayoshi Son, grew up a second-generation Korean Japanese in a country that has traditionally had little tolerance for immigrants, least of all Koreans. Son began taking initiative early in life and at the age of sixteen moved from Japan to California. He went to the University of California, Berkeley, and graduated with a BA in economics. While at the university, Son earned his first million by importing second-hand arcade games from Japan for the US market. His entrepreneurial drive led him further to commission a patent for a multilingual pocket translator that he sold to Sharp Corporation.

Back in Japan, Son's business diversification took on an unprecedented momentum from the late 1980s into the 1990s, the "lost decade" of post-bubble recession in Japan. In 1988, the company began multinational activities by establishing Softbank America, which coordinated Softbank's business in North America. From then on, Softbank expanded into international markets through a series of joint ventures, partnerships, and acquisitions. With the benefit of hindsight, the most important move that swung the subsequent fortune of Softbank was its decision to provide early stage financing of Yahoo!, emerging as a primary shareholder with a 37 percent equity stake in 1996. Thereafter, an earlier acquisition of Ziff Davis, the U.S. publishing business, financed Softbank's replication of the Yahoo! business model to Japan, South Korea, Germany, France, and the United Kingdom in partnership with Yahoo! Inc. of the United States. Other subsequent examples include CarPoint K.K. (a joint venture with Microsoft), E*Trade Japan, Morningstar Japan, GeoCities Japan, broadcast.com Japan, and ONSALE JAPAN, all of which are joint ventures with the founding companies in the United States (see table 9.3 for dates of entry of these companies into the Japanese market). Moreover, by March 2001, Softbank had invested nearly 700 million yen

Table 9.3
Entry of U.S. Internet Companies into Japan

Company	Established (Chronological Order)	Shareholders
Yahoo! Japan	January 31, 1996 (JASDAQ November 1997)	Softbank (51%), Yahoo! Inc. (32%)
E*Trade Japan	June 5, 1998	Softbank Finance (46%), E*Trade Group Inc. (32%)
Onsale Japan	July 1, 1998	Softbank E-Commerce, Indigo, Egghead.com (ex Onsale US Inc.)
AutoByTel Japan	June 1999	autobytel.com Inc., Intech, Itoh Chu, Trans Cosmos, Recruit, GE Capital
eBay Japan	October 19, 1999	eBay Inc., NEC
Car Point Japan	November 1, 1999	Softbank, Microsoft
Nasdaq Japan	June 2000	Softbank (42.5%), NASD

($6 billion) as venture capital in 531 start-ups, of which around a hundred are located in Japan; in total, 32 out of the 531 have had an IPO. An overwhelming proportion of Softbank's VC investments are concentrated in U.S. firms; however, its sole domestic VC firm, Softbank Investment, is the biggest in the Japanese VC industry. Thus much of the engine of growth for Softbank is relational financing (Aoki 2001) as venture capital in the United States.

What strategy underlines this rapid expansion by Softbank? It appears that while assisting Yahoo! in its globalization process, Softbank adopted Yahoo!'s business model. It consists of (1) financing operations out of advertisements to provide free service to users; (2) a good classification system for the search engine; and (3) a strong brand image. With this model, the opportunities for sales growth initially appear endless, because the overhead can be kept low and constant. Geographical coverage can be spread by giving autonomy to local companies to choose their own contents but using the same standardized classification system.

Softbank has labeled its own strategy "time machine management," a strategy to "foster the global incubation of superior business models found through its venture capital operations in the United States." (Softbank corp. 2000, 4). Thus, Softbank's entrepreneurial drive, and its source of profit, has focused around the importation and adaptation of U.S. business models into Japan and elsewhere. But there are at least two respects in which Softbank's own business model differs from that of U.S. venture capitalists. First, profit is generated by the stock appreciation of acquired and joint venture businesses that in turn finance further acquisitions and joint ventures. But instead of looking for exit options in the form of IPOs, Softbank has engaged in an expansionary "empire building" by retaining many companies in the group's portfolio. Second, Softbank is not renowned for close incubation, although incubation programs (another joint venture, this time with IFC) have been in place since the late 1990s. This, in part, arises from Softbank's origins in distribution and services rather than hardware or technology. Softbank certainly prides itself on promoting the idea that profit opportunities exist without new technology. But the focus on information services also led to some recent ventures whose sole purpose was to generate cash flow for further acquisitions; both Kingston Technology Company and Ziff-Davis Inc., acquired then disposed of by April 2000, may fall into this category.

The empire building has necessitated putting in place an elaborate organizational structure (see figure 9.7). In 1996, within Japan, there was only Softbank Inc, the software distribution business, and Yahoo! Japan. By 2000, there were more than a hundred operating companies within the Softbank Group. As shown in table 9.3, Softbank adopted in October 1999 a three-tier organizational structure within a holding company structure, after the 1998 revision to the Anti-Monopoly Law re-legalized pure holding companies in Japan. At the apex is a slim pure holding company employing only 60 workers. It focuses on establishing a strategy for the group as a whole, developing new business areas, and utilizing the tiered structure to manage and align the direction of each group company. The middle tier consists of seven key consolidated divisions, namely e-Finance, e-Commerce, Media & Marketing, Technology Services, Internet Infrastructure, Broadmedia, and Internet Culture within Japan; global operations are separate from this divisional structure. At first, the middle tier was intended to be no more than a divisionalization of operations, each division establishing strategy for its respective business domains, assisting operating companies within the division, and facilitating intra-divisional coordination to exploit synergies. Nevertheless, by May 2000, Softbank decided to develop five of the seven divisions into "operational holding companies" publicly quoted in their own right: Softbank Finance, Softbank e-Commerce, Softbank Media & Marketing,

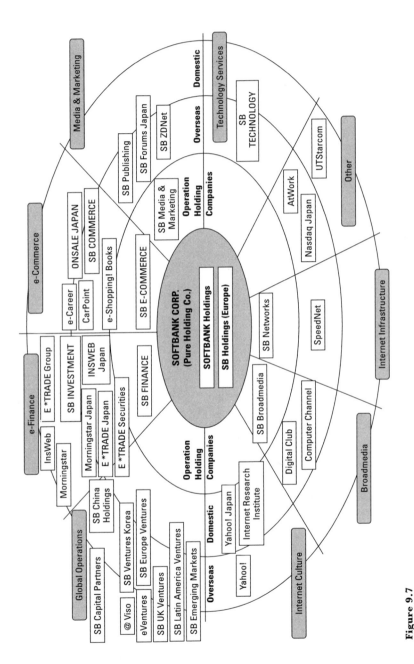

Figure 9.7
Softbank group organizational chart
Source: Softbank Corp. 2000.

Softbank Networks, and Softbank Broadmedia. This structure of a pure holding company overseeing a group of operational holding companies is a unique pattern of corporate control. By making operational holding companies responsible for partly raising their own finance, the pure holding company intends to benefit from even more rapid business expansion (Nikkei 2000). Lastly, many of the operating companies, particularly in the e-finance and e-commerce areas, are joint ventures with domestic or foreign partners. As intended, 37 out of the total of 334 operating companies are now publicly quoted on one of the stock markets.

Softbank Group is often described as a cyber keiretsu (Whittington 2001, 106) or an Internet zaibatsu (Asahi Shimbun Weekly 2000). The adoption of a holding company structure makes the label of zaibatsu (a pre-1945 corporate structure, common before holding companies were made illegal) most apt. Softbank Group is keen to promote an image for the Softbank Group of agile strategy and open corporate networks that is diametrically opposed to that of the traditional keiretsu: "Because companies in the Softbank Group are not affiliated with any existing Japanese *keiretsu* (corporate group), they can share a vision of creating open cross-industry alliances with any enterprise" (Softbank Annual Report 2000, 11). Certainly, Softbank Group does not have cross-shareholding among the group's operating companies, criticized for being a closed and non-transparent ownership structure that makes takeovers by outsiders difficult. But ironically, it is precisely the web of joint ventures and partnerships in the creation of operating companies that make Softbank Group's own finances appear "convoluted and opaque" (Tett and Harney 2000). The bases for making this point may be understood with reference to financial markets and labor markets in turn.

So far, Softbank has taken two major initiatives that would potentially transform the workings of the financial markets in Japan. The first is the aforementioned creation of NASDAQ Japan, made possible by Softbank stepping in as a joint venture partner when NASDAQ approached, and faced relative hostility by Japan's established authorities. With the NASDAQ brand name and the favorable listing requirement for high-tech/high-growth firms, this market is expected to expand, and Softbank is in a position to benefit as the owner of the market, as a venture capital fund that finances start-ups with IPO plans, and as shareholder of operating companies that list on the market. Already, Morningstar Japan, E*Trade Japan, Softbank Investment, and Softbank Frontier have listed on NASDAQ Japan.

Softbank's second move to transform Japanese financial markets is through the purchase of the failed Nippon Credit Bank (NCB) from the Japanese government as part of a consortium. This marks an important step in the Japanese government's efforts to clean up its troubled banking sector, but it is also the first time that a non-financial group has been allowed to buy a Japanese bank. Because none of the consortium members (including Orix and Tokio Marine and Fire) have experience in managing loan portfolios, Softbank appointed a former bank of Japan official as president to deal with the immediate task of minimizing losses from existing loans estimated to total 6,000 billion yen ($56 billion). Softbank bought NCB to access a limited stock of banking licenses and to exploit new business opportunities by creating a new type of bank in Japan. This involves developing two new lines of business. The first is in retail banking, linked to the Internet, and combining Softbank's own expertise in online finance businesses such as E*Trade with other consortium members' interest in online sales of insurance products. The second is more controversial, involving lending cash to starved small- and medium-sized companies. This is badly needed given the traditional unwillingness of commercial banks to lend to these companies. Nevertheless, this plan begets the question why a commercial bank should take the risk of using depositors' money to lend to Internet firms when venture capital funds should be available to finance them. Nippon Credit Bank has already established a VC fund for biotech start-ups. Softbank is treading the grounds carefully, lest it might be accused of advancing favorable loan terms to companies that it invests in as a venture capitalist. It is possible that NCB would develop into a "main bank" for the growing Softbank Group.

The long tail of joint venture firms within the Softbank Group necessitates building an open architecture for the management of employees. In mid 2000, Softbank Group probably employed around two thousand workers. But it was only in August 2000 that the pure holding company instituted a system for the middle-tier operational holding companies to report their workforce size. Such reporting is, however, not straightforward. At the operating company level, there are a variety of forms of employment, including the use of agency labor. Moreover, in joint venture companies, the employment status of joint venture managers, as to which of the JV partner is the employer, may be left undefined. Typically, it is the middle-tier operational holding companies that provide some managerial labor for new ventures. Essential expertise in financing and substantive business operations for Softbank Group ultimately comes from mid-career hiring from existing established businesses. In particular, the middle-tier holding companies hire mid-career employees for their management team, employ them for no more than three months, and send them out to manage newly established operating companies. In the case of Softbank e-Finance, its CEO, Mr. Kitao, who was originally headhunted from Nomura Securities, attracted his ex-colleagues from Nomura to establish Softbank's financial expertise. Softbank originally came across Nomura Securities as a funder of SkyPerfect Communications, a Softbank operating company. Although headhunting for individuals is not unknown, an important source of talent for Softbank Group more commonly comes in connection with business deals involving partner companies from the old economy of Japan.

Softbank's internal accounting is opaque because its unlisted companies' financial performance is not made public. According to one estimate, the collapse of technology stocks in 2000 vaporized $180 billion worth of Softbank's market capitalization, leaving it with a $21 billion valuation (Bremner and Kunii 2001). To conclude, Softbank is not a company with deep technology. It found its niche in VC investments starting with Yahoo!, then in proactively assisting U.S. Internet firms enter the Japanese market. Whatever the state of health of Softbank Group as a whole, Softbank has made some marks on Japanese institutions, most notable of all being in facilitating the creation of the short-lived NASDAQ Japan.

Conclusion

This chapter discussed three interrelated topics. First, economy-wide government statistics indicate that the Internet economy began to take off in Japan in the mid to late 1990s. It is not so much the timing of the take off as the mode—wireless access using mobile telephones—that is notable here. The liberalization of the Japanese telecommunications industry since 1985 has led to new entry from both domestic and foreign service providers, but nothing is more significant than NTT DoCoMo's transformation from being part of a bureaucratic public corporation to the start-up that pioneered the i-mode as a social-cultural phenomenon.

Second, characteristics of the IPO companies on JASDAQ, TSE's MOTHERS market, and NASDAQ Japan were compared against the Silicon Valley model. It was found that Japanese IPO companies were generally older, more spread out in sectoral coverage, and benefited from venture capital funds that were closely linked to existing financial institutions. Initial Public Offering companies are just the tip of the iceberg of all venture business activities in Japan. Nevertheless, a survey of venture capital activities indicates that institutional isomorphic pressures are much stronger than the mechanisms for economic isomorphism—that is, the diffusion of the U.S. model by example of its superior performance. The establishment of stock markets for start-ups is a necessary, but not a sufficient, condition for venture capital to develop. To make it a sufficient condition, we also need the supply of entrepreneurs demanding VC funds and labor market changes to transform the incentives of VC fund managers. As long as the majority of new business start-ups are with the blessing of previous employers, and as long as the movement of labor between companies is mediated by the large company personnel system of temporary transfers (shukko), the scope for maneuvering to create pockets of new institutional logic is limited.

Third, Softbank Group was taken up as a case study to gauge the extent to which firm-level actions can lead to hybridization of institutions. Softbank Group has had a direct hand in transforming national institutions in financial markets by creating NASDAQ Japan and buying the failed Nippon Credit Bank. Within the corporation, Softbank Group certainly has some characteristics of the new economy, with close links to the U.S. venture capital industry and flexible labor, but also those of the old economy, having an elaborate holding company structure with a large number of operating companies. It is precisely the tight links between the new and the old economies that Softbank Group has exploited to its advantage, to secure access to personnel and resources at the heart of Softbank's core competence.

The Internet permitted the creation of a new corporate group but did not lead to new corporate forms nor broader institutional restructuring.

Even among IPO companies listed on NASDAQ Japan, labor markets remain well linked to established firms and relatively closed at the borders (with no sign of an increase in immigrant population in start-ups, for example). Borders are more open for stock markets, telecommunications infrastructure, and Internet start-ups. But for the moment, economic isomorphism due to the glittering attraction of the U.S. model appears to be weaker than institutional isomorphism for existing Japanese patterns.

Acknowledgments

The author acknowledges helpful research assistance by William Kelly, Shahin Mansuri, and Emma Rosvall.

II

Cross-Cutting Themes

10

Is There Global Convergence in Regulation and Electronic Markets?

Bruce Kogut

Do these differences point to the persisting influence of national specificities? Or do they reflect the confounding of national institutional differences with sectoral differences? Perhaps, for example, India looks very
different because its comparative advantage lies in software development,
not because it develops software different from other countries. To explore more narrowly the sectoral effects, chapter 11, by Susan Helper
and John Paul MacDuffie looks at the development of business to business (B2B) in the automobile industry in Japan and in the United States,
and then expands this analysis to other sectors. They find rather star-
tlingly that national differences, despite two decades of convergence in
supplier practices, still have an important influence on the design of
auction systems and supplier chain management.

Because of the importance of the state and global regulatory policies,
two chapters turn to in-depth studies on the relationship of regulation to
the development of the Internet. Hervé Dumez and Alain Jeunemaître
take on the task of explaining the complicated dynamic between national
regulation and the European Commission in setting out a competition
policy for the Internet in chapter 12. They describe a history that suggests that the Internet was an opportunity to further existing policies
in Europe. National governments were reactive; the European Union
saw the Internet as a passage around the national telecommunication
monopolies that have been slow to dissolve. In other words, the EU interest in the Internet primarily was built around their larger competition
concerns in the domain of telecommunication deregulation.

Dennis Yao's chapter provides a forward looking analysis of critical regulatory issues. He focuses in chapter 13 on the United States and its free market philosophy regarding consumer protection and privacy. In the absence of a global regulatory agency, the U.S. model of self-regulation poses a coherent though controversial view of how Internet policies might evolve internationally. His analysis pits a self-regulatory regime of the United States that is often in conflict with European regulation. Yao proposes three types of outcome by which the conflict in regulatory systems might be managed. The most interesting of these solutions is the case where one system relies upon another to enforce a regulatory policy that is not politically feasible.

In the final chapter, I summarize the results of the studies as pointing to the continuing role of national specificities, but also to a growing convergence in institutions and economic experiences. The Internet served to encourage pockets of experimentation that promoted the "recoupling" of national institutions. In some countries, such as Sweden and India, these experiments were substantial enough to lead to tangible institutional changes by which new sets of actors emerged. For others, the Silicon Valley model did not diffuse per se, so much as it occasioned the strategic repositioning of actors in different national environments. There is, however, a larger issue that transcends the usual discussion of national systems in a global economy, for the Internet poses a globalizing force that is, in many ways, distinct from national institutions and trajectories. Indeed, the shift toward digital technologies in many industrial sectors poses profound opportunities for a global economy. In particular, I ask what are the implications of technologies that rest increasingly upon intelligent agents and business disintermediation for national systems. The development of communities, such as open source software and Napster, are examples where business is disintermediated in the production of economic and cultural exchange. I propose that this disintermediation lessens the importance of differences in national institutions relative to the convergent expectations of individuals.

11

Suppliers and Intermediaries

Susan Helper and John Paul MacDuffie

The realm of e-business known as "business-to-business," memorably captured in the acronym B2B, has already passed through its first cycle of hype to disparagement, following closely on the heels of its near-relative, B2C ("business-to-consumer"). This is useful, for it means that the spirited but ultimately limited debate about whether new economy firms powered by new business models would overpower and displace old economy firms is largely closed. Instead, we can focus attention on a broader inquiry into the ways that the capabilities of the Internet can alter the modes of exchange among firms.

As the dust settles from the dot.com bust, B2B emerges as an enduring feature of the Internet economy in most of the countries featured in this volume. The Internet offers new tools that can be readily combined with the assets and capabilities of incumbent firms to transform the business processes of procurement and supply, or at least to make them much faster and more efficient. Whether these effects are evolutionary or revolutionary—and whether they lead to convergence or preserve divergence across industries and nations—is the central focus of investigation in this chapter. In this sense, our analysis of B2B provides an opportunity to understand how historical and institutional differences among countries affect the development of the Internet economy.

Initial predictions about B2B, as for the Internet overall, were deterministic in nature. Many argued that B2B would sweep away national differences in purchasing patterns; one representative quote states that "a supply chain revolution is underway.... The Internet will reduce search and price discovery costs to a minimum. . . . The cost of changing suppliers will be zero" (Cohen and Agrawal 2000). In contrast, our view, encouraged by recent history, is that B2B will be evolutionary, not revolutionary. Business-to-Business reduces costs of transferring most types of information and, therefore, reduces the costs of most modes of exchange. Because switching to a new mode of exchange is expensive, most firms will develop B2B consistent with their existing mode. In this way, B2B will preserve divergence in modes of exchange.

We use the term "mode of exchange" to convey a set of standard procedures, common practices, communication patterns, and norms governing routine behavior in the value chain relationship between a supplier and its customer. We intend a meaning broader than a purely monetary definition of exchange, because we include the exchange of information and "know-how," the development of trust, and the influence of norms of reciprocity. A mode of exchange has a "legacy" that influences its future development; this legacy includes managerial mindsets—cognitive ways of characterizing means and ends, problems and solutions—as well as long-standing relationships embedded in incentive systems, procedures for transactions, regulation, and law.

Business-to-Business potentially affects the mode of exchange in two ways. First, it can alter how core tasks are accomplished. Second, it can change the infrastructure that underpins transactions. The legacy of a mode of exchange will generally tolerate changes of the first kind and be more resistant to changes of the latter kind. Thus we must also investigate what forces or factors, independent of B2B, may affect the infrastructural aspects of modes of exchange. Where the legacy of a particular mode is disrupted, it may create greater opportunities for B2B to have a more transformative impact.

In this chapter, we focus on incumbent firms in well-established industries whose historical patterns of exchange, generally grounded in national infrastructure and institutional norms, can provide the baseline for evaluating B2B's impact. The analytical exercise first takes the form of examining how different models of B2B affect core procurement tasks at firms that have a dominant mode of exchange. The second step is asking how various external factors will influence the infrastructural aspects of a given firm's mode of exchange and hence the potential impact of B2B. We will focus particularly on three factors: the consolidation and re-

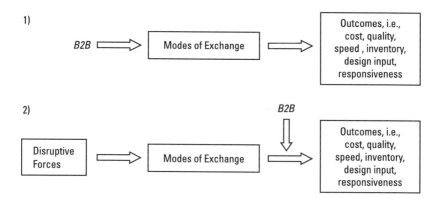

Figure 11.1
Two steps in analyzing B2B's impact on modes of exchange

structuring of incumbent firms; the deverticalization, global extension, and reconfiguration of supply chains; and changes in product markets and product architecture. Figure 11.1 displays the logic of this two-step analysis.

We will use the world automotive industry as our primary case for this analysis. Not only are the historical modes of exchange well documented in the industry, at both national and company levels of analysis, but the recent move by a majority of the world's largest automakers to establish an industry-wide B2B exchange (Covisint, which stands for Cooperation, Vision, and Integration) provides us with a specific B2B model to consider. By examining Covisint against the background of historically based modes of exchange in the auto industry, we can gain an excellent window into the potential impact of B2B on global industries and national economies. The dynamic task is to speculate (for B2B is in its infancy) on how national infrastructure, industry structure and competitive dynamics, and firm strategies for this particular industry will both shape and be shaped by the diffusion of B2B.[1]

We will address these questions: Will technical change in the form of the Internet transform relationships that automakers such as Toyota have for decades nurtured with their suppliers, replacing close ties with cutthroat auction markets? Will the strategies of multinational companies take precedence over national differences in infrastructure? Or will

distinctive patterns of supplier relations remain, with companies and nations developing e-business tools in ways that reinforce old paradigms?
In short, will the Internet overwhelm historical choices, facilitating the
convergence of national and firm approaches to procurement, or will
it reinforce existing differences? Although we mostly anticipate the reinforcement of existing differences, as noted above, we are alert to particular external changes that, by fundamentally disrupting current modes of
exchange, would facilitate a more transformative impact for B2B.

This chapter is structured in the following way. In the first section, we
define "mode of exchange" more precisely and describe the potential
impacts of B2B on the technological and institutional characteristics of
different modes. In the second section, we differentiate the historic modes
of exchange in the auto industry along a continuum from "exit" (in which
automakers resolve problems with a supplier by finding a new supplier) to
"voice" (in which automakers work with an existing supplier to resolve
problems) and use them to characterize the U.S. and Japan cases at a
national level. We also draw attention to the interaction between national infrastructure and company strategies. As companies expand their
operations globally, the exit and voice models confront each other more
directly and, to some extent, blend together.

In the third section, we bring the pieces of the argument together to
make predictions about the impact of B2B in the automotive industry
over the next 10–15 years. We start by identifying the specific contributions to performance improvement that B2B can offer the auto industry, given past legacies of exit and voice modes of exchange. Then we
explore the history and structure of Covisint, and assess its prospects
given our foregoing analysis of the industry. Finally, we describe how the
three potentially disruptive factors described above will interact with the
new capabilities provided by the Internet.

The fourth section extends the implications of our in-depth examination of the auto industry to other industries attempting to organize
industry-wide B2B exchanges. We pay particular attention to the dynamics
between exchanges set up on the industry consortia model and private
exchanges set up between individual firms and their closest suppliers. We
also probe the issue of where benefits are likely to accrue more or less
evenly to all exchange participants versus where use of the exchange can
generate a differentiated source of advantage.

The Impact of B2B on Modes of Exchange

We organize our notion of "mode of exchange" around four technological and institutional characteristics: (1) organization of the procurement process; (2) degree of standardization of transactions, interfaces, and products; (3) incentives for supplier investment; and (4) mechanisms and norms affecting the flow of knowledge in the supply chain.

Organization of the procurement process refers to the nitty-gritty details of how customers make their purchasing needs known, the form in which bids and proposals are received, the procedures for selecting among competing suppliers, the contracting arrangements governing a successful bid and the establishment of pricing, the formal (legal) rules affecting how disputes and problems are handled, the manner in which contracts are ended or extended, and so forth. These elements may take different forms at different firms and in different countries, depending on legal and regulatory statutes, the founding conditions under which the supply chain emerged, and the norms generated through years of repetitive procurement tasks.

In our view, the most significant short-term gain of B2B comes from exploiting the Internet's open architecture to automate the purchasing process across the different firms involved. An integrated e-procurement system allows manual, paper-based, labor-intensive processes such as purchase orders and invoices to be generated electronically. With data put into the system only once, data entry costs plummet, but even more significantly, data error problems, which can be tremendously difficult to find and eliminate, are minimized. Open-architecture information technology (IT), easily accessible by all parties in a supply chain, should also allow a reduction in inventory held as a buffer against uncertainties created by inaccurate or out-of-date information and, in turn, to reductions in scrap. For procurement of rarely needed goods and services, suppliers and customers can draw on shared expert systems that facilitate processes such as need identification, vendor selection, receiving, and accounts payable.

Standardization of transactions, interfaces, and products refers to the extent to which transactions can be completely defined; the extent to which interfaces can be completely specified to facilitate greater supplier independence in meeting customer requirements, hence reducing interdependence, asset specificity, and transaction costs; and the extent to which products are commoditized to allow price competition that drives down costs.

Standardization of information is a prerequisite for B2B to work, because information must be encoded in ways that mean the same thing to multiple parties for the benefit of its open architecture to be realized. The use of XML (eXtensible Markup Language) in a B2B exchange provides data tags that can be read by the operating systems or applications of all exchange participants with minimal translation effort. This makes it possible to put all participants in a supply chain—large or small and located anywhere in the world—on the same information system with access to real-time data without expensive investment. All transactions involving that information can benefit from this standardization of format and process.

This standardization facilitates greater reliance on market mechanisms in procurement, most notably auctions of various forms. Auctions present huge opportunities for customers by reducing prices on well-specified parts that can potentially be made by several suppliers. Although the gain for customers may often come at the expense of supplier margins, the ready availability of auctions as a procurement mechanism can benefit suppliers, too; they may find it easier to bid into new markets where they have had no prior access, and they can also use auctions in their own procurement. Auctions can also facilitate greater efficiencies across the supply chain, for example, as a means to sell excess production capacity. Indeed, these savings create incentives for still greater standardization of products and interfaces as well.

Incentives for supplier investment can take two forms. If customers require specific assets, they may provide financial incentives to subsidize those investments by suppliers, yet if customer requirements can be met via non-specific assets (e.g., general-purpose machine tools), suppliers have the incentive to make investments that meet the needs of multiple customers, thus reducing total outlays.[2] In the former case, if customers purchase physical assets for suppliers, the incentives for suppliers to invest in complementary capabilities may be low, because customer control means that the physical assets could be removed.

B2B potentially affects supplier incentives to invest in two ways. The open architecture characteristic of the web allows suppliers to exchange design and schedule information with their customers without making large, often customer-specific, investments in proprietary systems for EDI (electronic data interchange) and CAD (computer-aided design). Thus, the Internet offers the possibility of *de-specifying* assets while providing the same (or greater) functionality at a lower investment cost. Under this scenario, overall investment levels by suppliers might fall. Supplier investment could also fall for a less favorable reason: greater information transparency means that customers face lower costs of switching suppliers, making suppliers reluctant to invest for fear of being left with excess capacity.

Mechanisms and norms affecting the flow of knowledge in the supply chain refers to the non-contractual understandings of whether or not knowledge is shared freely between customers and suppliers (or across functions, i.e., design and manufacturing, within a firm) or protected fiercely as a potential source of advantage in a largely zero-sum relationship. This includes both information that is critical to negotiations conducted and decisions made during the procurement process (see above) and knowledge related to complex tasks where shared responsibility and task interdependence is high, such as product design. Mechanisms are characterized by the frequency of information-sharing and the variety of channels through which information flows, whereas norms apply to such areas as trust, gain- and risk-sharing, and how closely the parties adhere to contractual terms.

Although auctions are a prominent feature of B2B, they clearly cannot be used for procurement of all products. Many complex products and services are rarely sourced entirely on the basis of price, nor are bids sought very often, as relationship-specific knowledge must be extensive for suppliers to fulfill customer requirements. In these cases, the value of B2B is as a source of timely and accurate information that aids coordination and collaboration. For example, the posting of production schedules on the web, updated in real time, would significantly reduce communication costs and delays from a change in the schedule. The asynchronous nature of web communication can facilitate interaction with a global supply base. Imagine a customer sending a real-time video of a quality problem whose cause was unknown to the set of suppliers whose parts might be involved. With all the parties able to access the same information, problem-solving speed and efficacy should be enhanced.[3]

Designs can also be posted on the web, eliminating the expense of proprietary design software. As with a quality problem, having common access to the same design information could facilitate discussions about design problems with all the relevant parties. However, technical barriers are not the largest obstacles to posting design data. Suppliers do not want their competitors to see their designs without some assurance that they would not lose business to a firm that could cheaply imitate it. Protection of proprietary information will certainly be required. But no technological security mechanism can fully substitute for the presence of trust between supplier and customer. Collaborative mechanisms will need reinforcement from other aspects of the customer-supplier relationship; B2B alone can't provide trust.

Summary

This analysis suggests that electronic procurement and collaborative planning through B2B will result in significant savings over current systems. Some are one-time savings, whereas others will affect every transaction. Because B2B facilitates both market mechanisms (e.g., auctions), and collaborative activities (e.g., joint product development), it can potentially reinforce whatever modes of exchange are already dominant in a particular industry, country, or firm—a point we develop further below.

Legacies of Past Modes of Exchange: Comparing the U.S. and Japanese Auto Industry

Two different modes of exchange emerged historically in the auto industry.[4] Following Hirschman (1970), these can be characterized as "exit" and "voice." In the exit model, automakers solve problems with suppliers (regarding price, quality, etc.) by replacing them with another supplier. In the voice model, an automaker works with the original supplier to resolve problems. The advantage of the voice model is a rich flow of information that can eliminate unnecessary or expensive process steps, whereas the advantage of exit for the automaker is that it is not locked in to any supplier. Since the 1930s, the U.S. auto industry has generally been characterized by exit relationships, whereas the Japanese industry has historically been characterized more by voice. Some convergence has been evident in recent years, towards voice in the United States and exit in Japan.[5]

Business-to-Business can readily reinforce and amplify either the exit or the voice approach because, by cutting communication costs of all kinds, it facilitates both auctions and collaboration. Firms typically move away from their historically dominant mode of exchange only in the face of evidence that they suffer a cost disadvantage large enough to offset the cost of switching to another mode. We turn now to examine the legacy of these dominant modes of exchange for U.S. and Japanese firms.

Exit Mode and U.S. Automakers

Given their history, U.S. automakers, can use B2B to exit more efficiently and more thoroughly than in the past. We can see the legacy of incentives and capabilities created by exit in each of our four characteristics.

Organization of the Procurement Process   Maintaining a credible threat of exit is crucial for this mode. Thus, as GM vertically integrated complicated parts of its value chain (such as product design and the management of subassemblies) from the 1920s on, this partly served to minimize barriers to entry into supplier industries. A legacy of this strategy is that there are many suppliers capable of making simple parts, and GM retains in-house capability to design and integrate these parts. These conditions greatly facilitate auctions, because auctions work best if buyers can make "apples-to-apples" comparisons of bids submitted by a large number of potential suppliers.

Standardization of Transactions, Interfaces, and Products
Historically, GM set the norm for the industry by devoting considerable effort to formalizing transactions with suppliers.[6] Designs were well documented, contracts had standard provisions, and purchasing agents had clear rules for supplier selection—they were to go with the low price, as long as finance and engineering thought that the firms were qualified to produce the parts (i.e., would not go bankrupt or be unable to deliver parts). Non-codifiable factors, such as responsiveness to engineering changes or quality problems, played a very small role. In the 1910s, these firms established the Society of Automotive Engineers (SAE) to promote standardization. Early projects focused on standardizing large parts such

as carburetors. But as Ford and GM grew, their engineers increasingly staffed the SAE's committees, and pursued a different agenda. Ford and GM had the volume to make carburetors and other important components in-house, and wanted to be able to compete on the basis of a superior design of these parts. So they narrowed the SAE's standardization efforts to parts such as nuts and bolts, and grades of steel (Thompson 1954).

Barriers to entry in the auto assembly business went up dramatically, as the firms that became the "Big Three" purchased independent suppliers of carburetors, bodies, and engines. In contrast, barriers to entry into the lower tiers of the supply chain dropped, but these were low-margin businesses that, under an exit system, lived from year to year with the anxiety of losing a contract. Only suppliers that diversified into other industries (such as Timken and TRW) remained independent and profitable. Thus standardization efforts first expanded and then contracted. These competitive dynamics had a significant impact on automobile design, moving it from "modular" to "integral." We expand on this point below.

Incentives for Supplier Investment Under exit, incentives were low, as suppliers knew they could easily be replaced. Incentives for investments that were specific to one automaker were particularly low. Fierce competition among suppliers led to the creation of two distinct types of firms. The first group was small suppliers who kept prices low due to minimal overhead and a willingness to accept small margins. The second group (mostly firms that had developed during the early voice period) tried to make profits by developing slightly improved products that could justify a higher profit margin. Often these firms obtained their new ideas from outside the auto industry; for example, TRW, Bendix, and Rockwell all participated significantly in aerospace.

The legacy of this low investment is positive for auctions in several ways. First, as mentioned above, low barriers to entry means more suppliers. Second, suppliers have been slow to adopt early versions of computer-aided manufacturing (CAM), computer-aided design (CAD), and electronic data interchange (EDI) that are to some extent made obsolete by e-business. A potential negative effect is that experience with these technologies is useful in adopting their Web-based successors.

However, it is not clear how much an automaker using an auction-based e-business strategy will be able to use these technologies anyway, as they require the supplier to trust the automaker with proprietary information.

Mechanisms for Knowledge Flow throughout the Industry
Mechanisms for knowledge flow were not well developed during the exit period, and were hampered by a lack of trust. For example, when an OEM accepted a supplier's design, the design had to be copied onto the OEM's paper to protect the OEM's property rights. In the days of hand copying, this requirement frequently introduced errors—and certainly added costs.

Predicted levels of demand were often disputed. OEMs wanted suppliers to tool their plants so that they would have the capacity to meet even the most optimistic forecasts. Large suppliers such as TRW and Eaton employed their own economic forecasters so they would not be left with idle capacity.

Desire to maintain a credible threat of exit from any one supplier also hampered communication within the OEMs. Great efforts were made to prevent suppliers from going around purchasing agents to try to influence engineers to design a part in a favorable way (Corey 1977). This compartmentalization made it difficult to share information about different aspects of supplier performance. For example, there was no standard procedure for making sure that the assembly plant could make the purchasing department aware of a supplier's quality and delivery performance, or that engineering could systematically provide information to purchasing about responsiveness to engineering changes.

Voice Mode and Japanese Automakers
We predict that Japanese automakers will find that voice relationships with suppliers can be maintained more effectively than in the past, and they will be reluctant to interfere with these relationships by developing B2B capabilities that point toward exit. Thus, like Sako (chapter 9 in this volume) we see Japanese institutions shaping the way the Internet is adopted, and disagree with the polar views that these institutions will block Internet use altogether, or that the Internet will cause these institutions to look more like their Western counterparts.

Like the U.S. industry, the Japanese auto industry started with collaborative relations with suppliers. But whereas the U.S. industry evolved toward a combination of vertical integration and arm's-length relations with outside suppliers, voice has proven relatively stable in Japan.

Organization of the Procurement Process The procurement process was organized to facilitate collaboration between OEMs and suppliers. As discussed below, automakers (particularly Toyota, Nissan, and Honda) spent a great deal of time learning about (and improving) the details of suppliers' operations—a strategy that was feasible only with a small number of suppliers. Contracts were almost always for the life of the car model (typically four years), and were renewed if performance was satisfactory. If performance was not satisfactory, automakers sent teams of engineers to improve the operation, and would reduce the firm's market share (rather than cut them off completely) as a sign of displeasure (Nishiguchi 1994). Japanese automakers typically did not rely on market competition among suppliers to set prices; instead, prices were set using target costs, which were derived from a combination of marketing decisions about what consumers would pay, historical costs, and engineering determinations of what individual process steps would cost (Asanuma 1985).

Levels of Standardization of Transactions, Interfaces, and Products There has been little standardization of these elements, making it difficult to set up an auction market. As in the United States, products were not very standardized, though for different reasons. Particularly at Toyota, engineers saw their competence as integrating supplier-provided parts so as to produce excellent fit and finish, and relatively little noise, vibration, and harshness (NVH). However, component design is not as idiosyncratic as in the United States. First, Toyota in particular has focused on re-using parts across models to save design time and improve quality (Cusumano and Nobeoka 1997). These efforts at parts carryover mean that interfaces between different generations of the same model must have some commonality. Second, the low levels of vertical integration have made it possible for smaller automakers to survive by sharing suppliers of parts with a high minimum efficiency scale. (Japan has nine domestic automakers sharing a total production smaller than that of the

U.S. Big Three). Particularly for smaller automakers such as Subaru and Isuzu, parts have more in common across automakers than they do in the United States or Europe (Takeishi, personal communication).

The criteria for awarding business to a supplier were not at all standardized. A supplier's bid was important, but automakers (particularly Honda) also considered such intangibles as the supplier's "attitude" (whether they were interested in learning Honda's methods of continuous improvement and in working hard to meet Honda's targets). Honda did not try to cost every aspect of a transaction, thus reducing the value of B2B's ability to categorize costs thoroughly. For example, if a problem arose during launch, Honda expected suppliers to pitch in to solve it, and worry about how much it cost later. Similarly, Honda would provide technical assistance (valued at $1 million by one supplier) without charge, and would sometimes award "good" (high-margin) jobs to a supplier in compensation for a job that had turned out to be unexpectedly low-margin (MacDuffie and Helper 1997). All of these discussions and trade-offs across transactions would be very difficult to encode in an automated "business rule."

Yet some Japanese automakers (especially Honda and Toyota) have invested a great deal in standardizing data on quality and delivery performance. These data facilitate identification of problems, evaluation of experiments to improve performance, and discussion of results. Thus, Japanese automakers have invested in standardization to improve collaboration with long-term partners who are willing to share a great deal of data about their operations, but they have not invested in the standards that would facilitate easy comparison of, and switching between, alternative suppliers (MacDuffie and Helper 1997).

Incentives for Supplier Investment In the early days of the Japanese auto industry, Japanese auto suppliers used cheap, general-purpose equipment and sold only a small portion of their output to the auto industry. Suppliers gradually developed knowledge and equipment specialized to the auto industry, receiving financial and technical assistance from their customers. Because suppliers knew they would not suddenly lose all of an automakers' business, they were willing to invest in both general and automaker-specific machinery. For example, adoption of computer-numerically controlled machine tools (CNC) was much higher in Japan than in the United States. On the other hand, with few exceptions (Nippondenso, Yazaki), suppliers let automakers take the lead in developing new applications and new products; they did not actively sell new engineering approaches to automakers in the way that large U.S. suppliers did.

Mechanisms for Knowledge Flow throughout the Industry
Suppliers' trust in their customers grew over time, given the low frequency of switching and high technical assistance from customers. This made suppliers more willing to share detailed information about their costs and processes, without worrying that this information would be used to deprive them of what was considered a fair return on their investments.

Initially, suppliers served as buffers, simply providing capacity when the OEM could not meet demand. But in the 1950s, Nissan and Toyota, aided by local governments and unions, began to provide extensive technical assistance to suppliers, gradually spreading knowledge about the philosophies of just-in-time and continuous improvement throughout the supply chain. Many suppliers became involved in "black-box" product development, in which the OEM specified only performance requirements and exterior dimensions, while the supplier did the rest of the design work, yielding a product tuned to the supplier's production process, thus increasing productivity and quality. As long as these requirements were met, the OEM often did not keep a close watch on the exact specifications of what a supplier was making. And, with an experienced supplier, OEMs often did not bother clearly to spell out their requirements, because the supplier had an intuitive knowledge of how to interpret vague OEM drawings (Cole 1986; Nishiguchi 1994; Odaka, Keinosuke, and Fumihiko 1988; Sako 1996, 1999). This lack of clarity became a problem when designs were transferred to local suppliers as automakers globalized their production (Helper 1998; Couch 1999); it would be an even bigger problem in trying to put specifications on the Internet and conduct an auction. To run an auction, they would have to invest in documenting more fully (and more centrally) the details of design, and building suppliers' capabilities for responsiveness to formal engineering changes.

The automakers did conduct design competitions. In some cases, assemblers would take an aspect of a supplier's design that they liked, and provide it to a supplier whose overall design and price they liked better. However, the OEM would compensate the losing supplier in some way, by providing either some volume of the part under license from the winning supplier, or extra business on another part (MacDuffie and Helper 1997).

Japanese automakers are much less compartmentalized than U.S. firms, with a great deal of emphasis on cross-functional teams and job rotation. Supplier selection and evaluation is done with input from production planning and quality control as well as purchasing. At Honda, suppliers receive a monthly report listing numerical performance measures, plus comments from each group on ways to improve. As discussed above, decisions on how to respond to these numbers are not based on preset rules, but rather are discussed in frequent meetings.

U.S. and Japanese Cases Compared

Compared to Japan, the U.S. auto industry has had relatively adversarial and arm's-length relationships with outside suppliers for most of its history. This strategy has had several negative consequences for the U.S. industry: less willingness by most suppliers to invest in product design capabilities and capital equipment, less information flow between suppliers and customers, higher inventories, and lower quality. It has also had some neutral or positive consequences, such as a compartmentalized organization, integral designs, and a small group of suppliers whose competitive advantage increasingly depends on their ability to come up with new products. Conversely, the Japanese industry is characterized by a large number of suppliers skilled in black-box design and just-in-time production. On the negative side, few Japanese suppliers are experienced in selling their ideas to customers, and the automakers are not skilled in selecting new suppliers.

Now that the auto industry is global, U.S. and Japanese modes of exchange no longer exist in isolation from each other. Under pressure from Japanese competition, the U.S. industry has moved toward voice in the last 15 years. Collaborative problem-solving within and across firms, spurred by the efforts of Japanese transplants to develop local supply chain capabilities, is increasingly common (MacDuffie 1997; MacDuffie and Helper 1997; Dyer 2000). Suppliers have taken on more of a role in design, and contracts now usually last four or five years, rather than one, as was typical before the 1990s. However, the parties continue to talk about their relationship in adversarial terms, and describe competition as fierce. These moves toward voice have been strongest at Chrysler (until the 2001 DaimlerChrysler financial crisis), and weakest at GM.

As they globalize, Japanese automakers have moved somewhat toward exit, scaling back the role of traditional suppliers in favor of U.S. or European firms discovered during their expansion overseas. In addition, Japanese suppliers have become somewhat more independent, for example breaking (outside Japan) an informal ban on supplying to both Nissan and Toyota (Ahmadjian and Lincoln 2001). However, ties between customers and suppliers remain in general much closer than in the United States.[7]

With the increasing consolidation of the world's automakers (as we discuss in more detail below), fewer cases of "pure" exit or voice approachs can be found. Although suppliers tend to remain more strongly identified with national boundaries, their exposure to the demands of multiple customers operating production facilities in multiple countries also increases their responsiveness to different modes of exchange. Furthermore, to the extent that different kinds of components require different procurement processes, both U.S. and Japanese automakers may gain more choices from B2B that would allow them to mix modes of exchange under a hybrid strategy.[8]

This greater latitude, combined with the blurring of dominant modes of exchange, may reduce but will not eliminate national differences. Indeed, which B2B capabilities are developed first and the priority given to their use will be affected by the institutional norms associated with historically dominant modes of exchange in different countries. In this way, B2B's reinforcing and amplifying effect could contribute to strategic differentiation based on national differences. In other words, an American, German, or Japanese firm—finding themselves able to pursue their preferred mode of exchange more easily and at lower cost—may well choose to adhere to those historical patterns rather than sampling from the broader choice set that B2B offers them.

It is important to note, however, that not all configurations of practices are feasible. One cannot expect suppliers to make large investments, or to provide proprietary information, without some security that they will receive a return for their efforts. To some extent, B2B helps with this. By lowering the costs of information flow, B2B makes more collaboration possible with fewer long-term safeguards, because Internet-based technologies for computer-aided design and for exchanging scheduling information are much less customer-specific than their predecessors. And, if B2B makes it easier to find new customers or suppliers, then the risks of dedicated capacity becomes less severe. However, if the barrier to exchanging information is trust, then even if the cost of transmission is zero, firms will not do so. Participating in B2B will not, in itself, generate trust; indeed, as we will see, it can threaten trust.

Predictions for Automotive B2B: Evolutionary or Transformative?

In this section, we will focus on three issues: (1) our evaluation of how automotive B2B can contribute to performance improvements along various dimensions; (2) our view of the strengths and weaknesses of Covisint's industry consortium structure; and (3) our assessment of possible disruptive developments in supplier relations that could affect our primary hypothesis about B2B as an evolutionary extension of already dominant modes of exchange.

Sources of Performance Improvement

A large subset of the improvements from B2B—particularly those related to automation of the procurement process and to standardization of transactions, interfaces, and products—accrue to firms regardless of their dominant mode of exchange. These savings are likely to be one-time, transitional gains rather than providing a source of continuous improvement. Even so, they will powerfully fuel the diffusion of B2B in the next five years. Gains due to increased supplier investment and improved information flow may be harder to obtain at first, but should provide opportunities for continuing improvement in cost, quality, and delivery performance—especially for firms operating in collaborative mode.

We discuss five potential sources of performance improvement from B2B: (1) automating procurement processes; (2) interoperability; (3) auctions; (4) collaborative planning; and (5) collaborative design. We also estimate total savings from all these sources. We draw here on interviews with managers at both automotive and IT firms and on data from early auto industry experiments in order to predict B2B's future trajectory.

Automating Procurement Processes   In the traditional purchasing process, a purchasing manager issues a request for quotes, acknowledges receipt of quotes, chooses a supplier, gets approval from a supervisor, and notifies the winning supplier. Meanwhile, a marketing manager at a supplier is preparing a quote, getting approval from a supervisor, and, if the supplier wins the order, acknowledging receipt of a purchase order. Each of these steps generates paper that must be filed, and time is lost in sending the message (either by fax or phone), and finding a supervisor to sign off on decisions. Dan Jankowski, head of corporate communications for Covisint, explained the expense involved in just the request for quote stage. "The automaker FedExes a binder, which can be 3 inches thick, to each of a dozen suppliers. If they change a specification, then they have to redo the whole thing, each time introducing the possibility of errors in collation, and losing lots of time" (Jankowski 2001).

E-business offers the potential to dramatically reduce both the lead time and the cost involved in purchasing. Notifications can be sent instantly via e-mail, and the approval process can be automated with software that incorporates "business rules." These rules can be simple (Manager X is authorized to spend up to $10,000) or complicated (a set of criteria for actually choosing among the bids); the rules can incorporate any procedure that can be codified into software. The rules can also ban purchases from non-authorized suppliers, leading to further savings if the authorized suppliers are cheaper (which they may be if the firm has negotiated quantity discounts).

Estimates of the impact of reduced paperwork suggest that costs may fall from $75–150 to $10–30 per purchase order (Marti 2000). A similar estimate, from Kevin Prouty of AMR, predicts that an online exchange can bring purchase order costs down from their current level of $125–145 to $30–35 (Kisiel 2000b).

Interoperability In order to achieve these savings, the buyers' and suppliers' computers need to be able to communicate with each other. With electronic data interchange (EDI), the pre-Internet application of information technology to this problem, each party signs up with a vendor who provides software and a communications link; either all must use the same vendor or the vendors must use compatible software.

Starting in the 1960s, EDI systems were developed to help firms substitute information for inventory. These systems speeded up the transmission of information dramatically, and by eliminating the need for re-keying data, also cut errors by orders of magnitude. However, the technology was enormously expensive; in the mid 1990s, a small supplier might spend $45,000 per year in EDI-related expenses. These expenses included software for communications, special training for EDI operators, and payments to a value-added network (VAN) provider to transmit the documents and to translate them for computers of many different kinds. In addition, there were large up-front costs, including custom programming to connect the EDI system to the company's billing and inventory management systems (Marti 2000).

Because of the expense, only 30–40 percent of automotive suppliers use EDI, according to Peter Weiss, former co-CEO of Covisint (Konicki 2001a, 5). As a result, even by the late 1990s, large suppliers typically received scheduling information directly from automakers via EDI, and then transmitted the schedules to second- and third-tier suppliers via fax and phone, because these lower-tier firms in the supply chain did not have the capital to invest in EDI.

At TRW, we learned that this process of migrating the information all the way down the chain could take 5–10 days, a delay adding significantly to inventory (author interviews 2000 at TRW; Jansen, CommerceOne; Ford). On Monday morning, TRW would receive a weekly schedule from its automotive customers via EDI and would feed this information into its Materials Resource Planning (MRP) system, which would figure out what TRW needed from suppliers to meet the automakers' requirements for seat belts, and send the information (often by fax rather than computer) to these suppliers. These second-tier suppliers would wait for their other customers to send them production requirements before coming up with a schedule. Based on this information, a supplier (say a seat belt buckle provider) would send its requirements to its suppliers in the third tier, and so on.

How could it take so long? First, the updating process at each firm can take a day. When TRW receives its customers' requirements, it must translate the entire document it receives from Ford in order to understand what has changed. Second, it is often not possible for a firm to skip a link in the chain. For example, suppose Ford plans to increase its production of the Focus by one unit compared to last week. This information by itself isn't useful to the seat belt buckle provider, because it doesn't know how many seat belt buckles TRW has in inventory, how many seat belt buckles TRW will need next week, whether the seat belt buckle might be the same for a Nissan seat belt, what Nissan's production levels are, and so on.

Two developments, both based on open standards, promise easier communication among many users. The Internet offers a significantly cheaper way of communicating with other firms compared to VANs. First, Internet access fees are 50–80 percent lower than those charged by VAN providers, and almost all firms now have access to the Internet. It is cheaper largely because the transmission lines are shared across many people; the Internet is more like a highway, and a VAN is more like a private road. Also, use of a web browser provides universal access to multiple servers, a huge improvement over each user having to customize each EDI link.

Second, the Internet's open standards mean that document translation is less complicated. For example, a standard Web browser such as Internet Explorer can translate documents written in HTML, meaning that (in contrast to EDI) little special training to operate the system is needed. (Marti 2000; Glushko 1999). The development of XML (Extensible Mark-up Language) allows computers to communicate with each other in a more advanced way than does HTML (Hyper-Text Markup Language). While HTML contains tags that describe typography—for example, $\langle i \rangle$ 5.95 $\langle /i \rangle$ would tell the receiving computer to italicize *5.95*. In contrast, in XML, tags refer to characteristics of the item. For example, $\langle price \rangle$ 5.95 $\langle price \rangle$ and $\langle product\ description \rangle$ radio $\langle product\ description \rangle$ says that "5.95" is a price and "radio" is a product description. With a program called a parser, it is easy to sort radios by price— very useful if one wants to compare bids. The fact that each element of data has a tag greatly eases translation. By contrast, in a traditional database (e.g., an Excel spreadsheet), items are described only by their location (e.g., column B row 5) and are only subsequently tied to a variable name. Thus, the entire database must be brought into the host computer and translated before any of it can be understood—dramatically slowing the pace of communication.

Although the future vision of XML anticipates full interoperability, the current reality is more complex. There are issues of transition from EDI to XML. "We used to be XML purists," said Bob Glushko, CommerceOne's VP of document engineering (August 2000). "But now we see that firms are not going to abandon their investments in EDI." At CommerceOne and elsewhere, lots of code is being written to translate EDI messages into XML, and to allow communications from firms with EDI to firms that do not have EDI.

XML itself is far from encoding a standard set of business processes. To take just one example, at the present time, XML data tags are not standard. For one buyer or e-marketplace, ⟨price⟩ may refer to a retail price stored in some database, whereas another may use the same tag to refer to the wholesale price. Even if the message content encoded by XML is standardized, there is no guarantee that it will satisfy the processing expectations of a trading partner. For example, Business A may expect an acknowledgement when it sends a purchase order to Business B, but Business B's practice is to send an invoice and a shipping notice (Global Trading Web Association 2001). This lack of standardization means that suppliers to different exchanges and customers must have translators between their form of XML and the one used by each of their potential customers (or be prepared to retype information manually upon each request for a quote). The expense of these steps may limit the number of new bidders, a barrier to realizing the "zero switching cost" ideal.

The reality of needing to make XML operable in a world with substantial prior investment in EDI has given rise to different visions of how extensive interoperability must be for e-markets to work. We describe two distinct strategies below, associated with Oracle and CommerceOne, the primary software providers to Covisint.

Auctions The ability to exchange price data quickly greatly facilitates auctions. In theory, an OEM should be able to search for suppliers all over the world and easily compare bids submitted in XML format. Early experiments revealed the tremendous potential for auctions to reduce prices. In one dramatic example (Colvin 2000), an automaker was buying plastic parts through FreeMarkets.com (GM's original B2B partner, before the announcement of Covisint). It had paid $745,000 for the last pre-auction batch of parts. After 33 minutes of bidding by 25 suppliers, the price came down to $518,000. That auction was one of five run that day for that automaker. Parts that would have cost $6.8 million under the old procurement system sold for $4.6 million after the auctions. Small wonder that many interpret B2B as primarily a means, through auctions, for OEMs to squeeze supplier margins even more successfully than in the past (Taylor 2000).

Yet the applicability of auctions is more limited than it first appears. The key issue is the desirability of standardization (necessary for automated comparisons across bidders) from the point of view of various actors. Automation works less well when a firm wishes to incorporate tacit knowledge or discussion into a decision. For example, one automaker tried using an auction to source printed circuit boards in 2000. But they had to withdraw the auction, because they decided that the low bidder would not meet their needs. According to the CEO of Solectron, who eventually won the business, "We asked them, 'Do you want to fly first class or coach?' Sure, it's cheaper in coach, but you know we treat you first-class. We always deliver on time, and never charge you for engineering changes. A printed circuit board is way too complicated for an auction—the specs are always changing," (Ko Nakamura, CEO of Solectron, Sloan Foundation Annual Meeting, April 2001).

This incident suggests three problems with auctions. First, a customer may have criteria other than price (such as delivery or responsiveness). One way to handle this is to limit bidding only to approved bidders. All auctions on Covisint have done this; few have had more than eight bidders. Another remedy is to weight the different criteria. In principle, this problem is not too difficult to solve if the trade-offs among the criteria can be quantified. For example, CommerceOne's Auction Services 4.0 allows for comparison of bids across multiple criteria. However, so far it has been used only for trade-offs on terms of payment, and even so has had to be shut down several times because the software cannot handle the complexity (authors' interviews at CommerceOne).

Second, bidders can feel manipulated, even when the pool of bidders is pre-qualified and when criteria (and trade-offs among them) are clearly identified and quantified. One reason is that when auctions take place in real time (eBay style), the only attribute that other bidders can see is the price being bid. So a bidder does not know if a low bid is being submitted by a high-quality competitor, or by a ringer incapable of meeting all the performance expectations of the customer. We heard numerous examples in which the supplier awarded a bid through auction was later eliminated on performance grounds (authors' interviews; Akira Takeishi, personal communication).

Third, the customer may find it costly to quantify trade-offs across criteria in advance. Indeed, the customer may find that discussion of potential trade-offs both internally and externally generates valuable data for choosing a supplier. Using auctions can both preclude this discussion and may alienate potential partners on other projects. Early evidence suggests that supplier participants in auctions perceive their relationship with customers with less trust and more dissatisfaction, and state a desire to differentiate their products and/or services so they cannot be procured through auction (Jap 2000). Given the risk for voice-mode firms of alienating their close supplier relationships, they will be less inclined to use auctions, except perhaps for non-vital procurement, such as office and cleaning supplies.

Collaborative Planning   The Internet offers the promise of "visibility throughout the supply chain," through which participants could continuously update each other about their production plans. Much of this could be done in an automated way. Because translating and updating can be done so quickly, real time operations are possible. For example, Ford would send its schedule to TRW's computer, which would check that TRW's plants had the capacity to meet Ford's requirements. If so, the computer would create a production schedule, without need for human intervention. If not, the computer would generate an exception notice.

Information could flow the other way as well. Suppose the second-tier supplier decides to shut down for deer-hunting season. It could send a notice to TRW saying that it will not produce anything the first week of November, but could ship extra in each of the last two weeks of October.

TRW could approve this new schedule, and then confirm to Ford that the schedule will be met.

The above represents a technical challenge—large, but one that can be handled. Some pieces of the new vision are already in place. SupplySolution offers a web-based product that enables a supplier to see its customers' level of inventory for the supplier's component in real time, leading to 20–40 percent declines in inventory within a few months of adoption (⟨www.supplysolution.com⟩; interviews with users).

However, before capacity planning can become truly collaborative, several strategic issues must be resolved. First, "capacity" is not entirely technically determined. How much does a supplier say it has available to allocate to TRW versus to its other customers? If it says it has a lot of capacity, TRW may think the supplier is desperate for work and ask for a price cut. If it says it has only scant capacity, TRW may take that as a signal to find another source. A supplier might be tempted to allocate the same capacity to two customers, and simply hope that they won't ask for it at the same time. Furthermore, a supplier's capacity may depend on the price; the suppliers may be willing to schedule production on relatively inefficient machines or run a second shift and pay operators overtime if the price were high enough.

Thus B2B doesn't allow a second-tier supplier to skip links in the chain—it just offers information flow in seconds instead of days. To know how it should react to a change in production at Ford would require TRW to let the entire supply chain see Nissan's production schedule as well. This may be technically feasible before long, but a great deal of trust would be necessary across the industry for this to occur.

If a key legacy of exit is lack of investment by suppliers in information systems, the move to B2B might provide an opportunity to leapfrog over the EDI stage; suppliers' lack of prior investment in EDI would mean less has to be thrown away. But the business process reengineering done to facilitate the transition to EDI is crucial for the success of collaborative planning over the Web. This reengineering was done because linking EDI systems with internal order management and production scheduling processes required extensive custom programming. The rationalization and customization of these linkages may be necessary even for suppliers that skip the EDI stage.

In any case, much of the investment in EDI is not wasted. According to Bob Jansen (formerly of CommerceOne, now at VIA systems), "Collaborative planning has a tremendous number of challenges—it is only as good as the information being transmitted. If the information isn't right, then with the Internet, I'm just communicating bad information faster. EDI is treated as software, but it is really a tool for reengineering business processes.... Firms that haven't gone through this process can mess up the whole chain" (personal interview, August 2001). Jansen provided the following example:

I had a customer once that was always making manual interventions to his MRP system, because, he said, "its numbers are wrong." It turns out that there were a lot of data entry errors in the Bill of Materials, for example saying it took 50 gallons of oil to make one part rather than to make one batch of parts. Also, this firm didn't report scrap until the end of the week. So all week long, you'd be thinking you had a lot more parts than you did, or that the MRP system was wrong, because you couldn't find the parts. So if we set up a system where every day this firm is sending information to Ford about its inventory levels, but it is only updating scrap once a week, we're just transmitting bad information faster. The delay is not in the software application, as in getting accurate information from the shop floor into the computer. This is the key to supplier participation in the [capacity] planning aspects of Covisint.

Supply chain management software also offers the opportunity to shift costs, as well as to reduce them. "If you set up a build-to-order system, you cut the reaction time of your suppliers. If you link them in when the customer orders, then the suppliers, on their nickel, can see when your inventory of their part reaches a critical level, so you don't need release analysts to go over stock levels" (Paul Hebeler, Automotive Director, Oracle Corporation 2001).

Whether the EDI or XML path is chosen, IT infrastructure and capability must be built into the automotive supply base for collaborative planning to advance. A survey of 434 Ohio auto suppliers in early 2001 found that only 82 percent used computers in their business, 34 percent had access to the Internet, and 20 percent had a Web site. (For those firms with over a hundred employees, the figures were 95 percent, 52 percent, and 42 percent.) It is interesting to note that these figures are below those for U.S. households, 45 percent of whom claimed to have Internet access in March 2001 (Furchgott 2001). Of those firms that had

Internet access, 71 percent used a modem—far from a high bandwidth connection (Sabety 2001).

In summary, we agree with observers who claim that the potential benefits of collaborative planning over the Internet are huge. But this aspect of B2B will require two things: first, long enough time horizons that even small suppliers can develop capabilities for accurate reporting of inventory and link their business systems to the Internet; and second, enough trust within the supply chain that parties will reveal their capacities accurately. Both are attributes of the voice mode of exchange, suggesting that the benefits of collaborative planning will disproportionately accrue to firms operating in voice mode.

Collaborative Design E-business also offers the opportunity for designers (either in the same firm or different firms) to work in parallel. As with EDI and inventory planning, a pre-Internet technology based on proprietary software already exists—computer-aided design (CAD). In the United States alone, GM, Ford, and Chrysler each chose a different CAD standard, requiring suppliers that wished to have a design relationship with all of the automakers to maintain three different CAD systems, at a cost of about $100,000 per year per seat in software and (more importantly) time for engineers to acquire and maintain familiarity with the software.

The savings from collaborative design tools are difficult to estimate, although most observers agree they will be substantial. The primary gain will come from avoiding the delays and errors associated with today's exchange of design information, which happens imperfectly because of the different proprietary CAD systems, and by eliminating many of the face-to-face meetings between supplier and customer engineers that are now the mainstay of product development.

Intertwined technical and organizational barriers prevent collaborative design from becoming common practice. First, having a collaborative design space on an Internet server is not the same as having a common product design program. Although the different designers working on a project will have a common area to store documents, and can change the documents located in the central file, these changes will not affect the files in the designers' own CAD system. These will still have to be entered manually (Jankowski 2001; Oracle interview), reducing productivity and leading to the possibility of errors.

Second, suppliers are very worried about data security (Reuters 2001). "If there is concern, it's one of data ownership, what happens to that data," says John Van Alstyne, president of e-business technology for supplier Freudenberg-NOK. "We don't want people mining our data" (Milligan 2001).

Some of these problems can be addressed technically. Some collaborative software makes it possible to add and delete features of a design according to the identity of an individual user. For example, a designer at an automaker could see how several parts mesh together, whereas each of the suppliers might be able to see only their own part (Jankowski 2001). But other security issues have more to do with trust in the customer. Suppliers were very angry in 1993 when GM purchasing czar Jose Ignacio Lopez in several cases turned over supplier designs to their competitors, hoping to generate lower bids—well before e-business was underway. Collaborative design tools cannot, through technical means, prevent this from happening again.

Total Savings Current estimates of the savings from automotive B2B span a considerable range. Goldman-Sachs estimates total savings of over $2,000 per vehicle, with more than half of these savings occurring post-factory, in distributing cars to consumers. Procurement-related supply chain savings are estimated at $807 per vehicle, or more than 7 percent of the cost of purchased parts and 4.4 percent of the total cost of a $20,000 car (Lapidus 2000). We believe a more accurate figure might be around $500 per vehicle—still a large number. Almost one-quarter of the potential supply chain savings come from improved timeliness and accuracy of information that allows the reduction of inventory held in the supply chain—benefits experienced under both exit and voice modes.[9]

Although all parties potentially benefit from these savings, the advantage that information transparency gives to the large automakers and first-tier suppliers in managing the complexity of their operations and pressing for cost reductions from lower-tier suppliers (in either exit or voice mode) suggests that the majority of the benefits will accrue to them. Assuming the persistence of present-day competitive intensity, a sizable portion of the gains may well be passed on to consumers.

Covisint—History, Structure, and Prospects

As described above, B2B offers a huge potential for performance improvements of various kinds, the achievement of which is stymied less by technical issues than by conflicting strategies, both across exit and voice modes of exchange and between OEMs and their suppliers. Can Covisint, the automakers' online exchange, overcome its own technical and organizational challenges while also helping align these strategies? In the section below, we briefly sketch the history and structure of Covisint and assess its prospects from the perspective of modes of exchange.

History and Structure In November 1999, Ford and General Motors simultaneously announced separate plans to put virtually all of their global purchasing activity into huge web-mediated exchanges called AutoXchange and TradeXchange, respectively. Suppliers howled, because they feared that, as with CAD, they would have to maintain multiple expensive interfaces. As a result of this fear, and of the automakers' realization they could save money by pooling investment in infrastructure, Ford and GM abandoned their separate exchanges and began secret meetings to form an industry-wide consortium. In February 2000, Ford, GM, and DaimlerChrysler announced the unified exchange called Covisint and invited the rest of the world's automakers to join as well; Renault and Nissan joined in April, with Toyota and Peugeot following suit several months later. As of April 2001, this left only VW, BMW, and Honda as holdouts among the major OEMs.

The potential of this new exchange was heralded as enormous: it would handle $240 billion in purchasing for ninety thousand companies worldwide (some estimates range as high as $750 billion, depending on assumptions about how much lower-tier suppliers will use the exchange for their own purchasing), generate transaction fees of $3 billion per year (if suppliers were mandated to use the exchange, and were charged standard e-marketplace fees of 0.5 to 1.5 percent of transaction value), and cut $3,000 from the price of an average car. There was excited talk of a Covisint IPO, whose stock price would soar due to its revenue-generating potential. The exchange quickly secured $240 million in corporate funding, hired two hundred consultants and loaned employees, and signed an equity deal with CommerceOne that valued Covisint at $59 billion (Baer and Davis 2001).

Suppliers remained skeptical. In February 2000, soon after Covisint was announced, and at the height of the dot.com boom, a group of suppliers asked for an equity stake, but were rebuffed. A group of eight large suppliers subsequently announced they might form their own online exchange concept. Covisint began attempts to woo this group of suppliers back, offering them profit-sharing in June and inviting 18 suppliers onto a Customer Council in July that began meeting monthly to get input from the supplier perspective (Kisiel 2000b). Thus mollified, the eight suppliers disbanded their initiative, and one by one, agreed to join Covisint (Milligan 2001). About forty suppliers now belong to the exchange.

In a concession to suppliers, Covisint has backed away from its initial idea that sellers would cover most of the costs of using the exchange by paying the transaction fees. Talk of an IPO disappeared even before the Internet bubble burst, because its revenue model only served to confirm the worst fears of suppliers that these revenues would be drawn directly out of their margins. Instead, fees will be paid by buyers, not on transactions per se but whenever they use a supplier's online catalog, or originate an auction.

Covisint also faced antitrust scrutiny. In September 2000, the U.S. Federal Trade Commission and German Bundeskartellamt agreed that the venture had, at least for the time being, met their antitrust concerns—but they will continue to monitor the exchange to make sure there is no sharing of price information among the exchange's owners.[10]

In December 2000, Covisint began operating, and in January 2001, it announced its board of directors. The board has 12 members, including two each from the founding automakers and one from Renault. Five seats were left open—one for the CEO (who was not named until May 2001), with the remaining seats to go to suppliers. The additional seats were created so that founding automakers would not have a majority on the board (Jankowski 2001).

The early attention to Covisint emphasized its exit features heavily —particularly auctions, which offer the most visible source of savings. This is partly because the IT firms involved in Covisint, Oracle and CommerceOne, have both developed software for auctions in the past, but don't have much experience with supply chain management software. Increasingly, however, statements from Covisint executives have shifted gears to emphasize the tools that support collaborative knowledge exchange among suppliers and their customers. This has been necessary to attract suppliers to participate in the mammoth task of establishing the IT infrastructure and XML overlay for Covisint. But it also points out the tension between the exit and voice views of what Covisint can—and should—be.

Assessing Covisint's Propects With many of the independent B2B exchanges founded in the late 1990s now closed for lack of revenues, certain strengths of Covisint's consortium structure are clear: given commitments from its equity partners, the exchange will have both guaranteed transactions and financial liquidity. Indeed, Covisint's progress to date is striking, given that only 10 percent of the thousand B2B exchanges launched in the past 18 months are processing any transactions whatsoever (International Data Corporation study, cited in *The Economist* 2001).

During the first six months of 2001, Covisint managed transactions worth more than $33 billion (13 percent of the $240 billion that Ford, GM, and DaimlerChrysler buy annually). Fully 2.5 million items were bought (primarily strategic materials) using the exchange's two hundred catalogs, in 420 auctions conducted by the exchange's one thousand registered users. The auctions were not just for standard parts; Daimler-Chrysler used the exchange to buy $3 billion in "highly engineered parts" during four days in May. (Sources did not explain how the auctions worked.) Moreover, two hundred subscriptions had been sold for Covisint's collaborative design software, the Virtual Project Workspace (Jankowski 2001).

The main equity partners report that they are already seeing results from their investment. For example, DaimlerChrysler purchased over $100 million in components through Covisint between December 2000 and March 2001, saving on average 17 percent, even though, the company complained, they were limited to the small number of suppliers who have joined the exchange (Milligan 2001). In July, Ford announced that it had saved $70 million by using the exchange (in reduced paperwork and lower supplier prices), much more than the cost of its investment in Covisint (Konicki 2001a, 2001b; Grande 2001).

It is the automakers' clout and purchasing volume that keeps Covisint powerful, but that also keeps it divided. The consortium approach must confront the tremendous differences in organizational culture and modes of exchange among the equity holders. Even among the founding partners—GM, Ford, and DaimlerChrysler—there are big differences in their approaches to procurement and supplier relations, given Chrysler's shift toward voice and GM and Ford's shift toward exit in the 1990s. Unless Covisint can support either mode of exchange equally well, it may come to be dominated by certain automakers and shunned by others; the latter may pursue alternate exchanges, most likely private networks of their own design and including only their suppliers.

Toyota offers one case in point. Although it was reported in May 2000 that Toyota would join (Kisiel 2000a), rumors later in the year asserted that this decision would be reversed. For now, Toyota is still officially a member but does not hold an equity stake (*Manufacturing Engineering* 2001). But our interviews with consultants to Covisint suggest that although Toyota has closely followed what was going on at Covisint, it is not likely to join in any substantial way. During the early months of Covisint, Toyota proceeded to set up its own exchanges, for both OEM and after-market parts. Although the OEM parts exchange will involve bidding, "this is not an open bidding system," said Gene Tabor, Toyota general manager for purchasing. "We are not changing the way Toyota selects suppliers. We will still decide upfront who will be a Toyota supplier, and we wouldn't go to them for a sourcing quote until we have had discussions with them, and they've understood our strategies and philosophies." Sources of savings mentioned in the article were fewer mistakes in paperwork and data re-entry, and did not include lower prices from suppliers due to auctions (Chappell 2000).

Certain automakers have stayed aloof from Covisint from the start. VW and BMW have announced they would each set up their own exchanges (Kisiel 2000e). BMW worries that "Covisint is too controlled by our friends in America. We don't want our secrets in the hands of competitors," said William Becker, senior vice president of purchasing. And Bertil Thoren, head of purchasing at Volvo (now owned by Ford) said, "There is a risk [with Covisint] that relationships with suppliers could be affected. We don't want to destroy these relationships. We don't think we will ever take online quotes for parts" (Catterall and Chew 2000).[11]

Indeed, even Covisint's founding partners are pursuing other options. In August 2000, the U.S. arm of DaimlerChrysler announced that it was developing its own system called FastCar to use the Internet to link design, engineering, finance, procurement, and manufacturing, with other divisions and with suppliers. "Covisint will never host our geometry [product design specifications]. Covisint will never host our business. Covisint will be our communications portal for suppliers," said Karenann Terrell, described by *Automotive News* as "DaimlerChrysler's B2B guru." DaimlerChrysler wants to develop this software itself because it sees it as a competitive advantage, she added (Kisiel 2000d, 2001b). GM is also developing its own exchange (GM SupplyPower) for most functions; GM views Covisint only "as a trading site for auctions and e-procurement," says GM chief information officer Ralph Szygenda (quoted in Joachim and Moozakis 2001; see also Wecker 2001).

Suppliers remain skeptical, even though Covisint has toned down its rhetoric about the power of auctions, preferring to discuss its supply chain management and design services instead. At a Covisint briefing in May 2001 that one of us attended, during a break a representative of a major supplier first looked around nervously to make sure Covisint representatives were not within earshot, and then said, "You do a dance [with Covisint]. On the one hand, you don't want to alienate your largest customers. On the other, you don't want to get locked into something that might not work, or might not meet your needs." In a confidential survey of 434 Ohio auto suppliers conducted in early 2001, only 24 percent of first-tier auto suppliers said they planned to join; 0 percent of third-tiers did (calculated from Sabety 2001). Dana, a $13 billion supplier with eighty-two thousand employees and a notable holdout from Covisint, has been running its own exchange, in partnership with FreeMarkets and Ariba (Baer and Davis 2001).

It may well be the code writers at Oracle and CommerceOne that have the most influence over how much Covisint affects the mode of exchange of these different companies (Lessig 1999b). (Indeed, the actions of these players have important implications for how Internet capabilities evolve and for regulatory requirements; see Yao, chapter 13, and the book's concluding chapter.) If the code writers emphasize exit-type capabilities first, it will make Covisint all that much more useful to firms already inclined toward exit, and less so for those inclined toward voice.

So far, the different strategies pursued by the two major software providers have been a major source of tension within Covisint. In 1999, GM had chosen CommerceOne and Ford had chosen Oracle to power their independent sites. When the automakers decided to join forces, they simply ordered their software partners to work together. It was decided that there would be a UNIX platform, with basic infrastructure from Oracle, transactional capabilities provided by CommerceOne, and other firms providing software for supply chain management (Jankowski 2001).

These two IT firms have very different business models. CommerceOne envisions a process of "reintermediation" based on open standards and creation of common business libraries using XML. Firms would communicate with each other through an e-marketplace that provides translators converting various legacy databases into a standard form of XML, in addition to procurement services related to currency conversion, tax law advice, shipping, and financing (interview, CommerceOne April 2001). This infrastructure is intended to support an Internet business model in which "relationships are experimental and evolving, and have shorter lifetimes.... The goal is 'describe once, {sell, buy} anywhere,' which won't be met through point-to-point coupling approaches" (Glushko 2000).

CommerceOne franchised its MarketSite technology to a variety of e-marketplaces, some organized regionally (such as those organized by British Telecom and NTT), and some organized by industry (such as the Apparel Buying Network). Any type of procurement system could operate over a MarketSite network, including those offered by CommerceOne competitors Oracle or Ariba. CommerceOne is actively working with international standard-setting bodies to create a Global Trading Web, in which XML tags would be standardized enough so that if, for example, USX prepared a catalog for one e-marketplace (such as eSteel), it could be linked to another e-marketplace (such as Covisint) and USX's back office operations without re-keying. CommerceOne would make money by charging a fee (ranging from $.25 to $2) to suppliers for each transaction (Marti 2000; interview, CommerceOne, April 2001).

In contrast, Oracle's view is that most communication will take place directly between companies. The translation problem won't be so hard, because in their view, Oracle software will become the standard at most companies (just as Microsoft is the de facto standard for word-processing and spreadsheet applications). Larry Ellison, CEO of Oracle, has said publicly that he believes that CommerceOne will soon be out of business.

In response, CommerceOne believes that Oracle's strategy dooms users to inferior applications, because they won't be able to pick "best of breed" products that aren't Oracle-compatible (CommerceOne, Oracle interviews). So much for partnership!

So far, it seems that Oracle's business model is winning. Oracle and CommerceOne each own 2 percent of Covisint. (Ford and GM, in turn, each own 14 percent of CommerceOne [Kisiel 2001a]). However, Oracle will be paid a one-time fee for its software and will also get an (undisclosed) share of Covisint's gross revenue, whereas CommerceOne elected to get paid on a per-transaction basis. Because there have been relatively few transactions and few members, CommerceOne has not made as much money as expected.

CommerceOne is also suffering from other strategic decisions by Covisint. One of the key benefits of CommerceOne's global XML approach for users is the ability to connect across many e-marketplaces. But in an effort to keep transaction volume on its own exchange high, Covisint has opted not to make interconnection available (Jankowski 2001). Furthermore, the key software that CommerceOne is providing Covisint is for auction-based procurement, which is slated to become a less important piece of the site as collaborative tools are added. To strengthen its involvement in key Covisint functionality, CommerceOne is working at present on a supply chain management application for direct materials in partnership with SAP. (For more on the German firm SAP, and the high degree of complementarity between its products and traditional competencies in production scheduling, see Casper, chapter 7 in this volume.)

By inviting these "code writers" in, the automakers have placed a wild card in their future. Their choice may not affect just the structure of Covisint, but of other e-marketplaces as well, due to the huge size of Covisint. If the Oracle model wins, the B2B experience could end up being similar to consumers' experience with Microsoft: the software is relatively standardized and well integrated, but lock-in is high, and much of the profit from efficiency gains will go to the software firm, rather than to automotive suppliers, OEMs, or consumers. If CommerceOne's more open source vision wins, B2B exchanges and users may well need to spend more time sitting on standardization committees and integrating their own set of software applications, but will spend significantly less money.

Another issue is proprietary versus public exchanges. Both Commerce-One and Oracle are benefiting from the pursuit of private online solutions by firms unwilling to put all their eggs in the Covisint basket. Both firms sell applications that customers can use behind their own firewall, and help customers move applications back and forth between a proprietary exchange and a secure network host belonging to Covisint. In fall 2001, Covisint began to accept this option as well, signing contracts with Delphi to host the supplier's private exchange, and agreeing to become a portal for Ford's Supplier Network purchasing site, offering a single sign-on to the site and to Covisint, even though the site uses technologies that aren't on Covisint's list of preferred platforms. As *Internetweek* pointed out, these moves raise a question: "Are Covisint's two priorities—creating a self-sustaining business and setting technology standards for the auto industry—in direct conflict?" (Joachim and Moozakis 2001).

The promise of B2B was that firms would agree on HTML-like standards that would allow them to avoid the expense of a software Tower of Babel, in which a firm has to invest in many different programs to be able to communicate with all of its business partners. Yet recent developments show that this feature is not a given part of the Internet. Even Covisint's chief technical officer, Kevin Vasconi, is worried: "Left to our own devices, we'll do to XML what we did to EDI, and that would be a travesty," he said (Joachim and Moozakis 2001).

Thus, one possibility is that battles over standards and open sourcing will have as great an effect on the structure of B2B as they will in the public sphere. As Lessig (1999b) points out, the more open source code is, the more difficult it is for government to dictate how software must be written (e.g., whether it must include features to enable government monitoring of users), because many people could modify the code to defeat the government's purposes. In the case of B2B, the more open the code, the more profits are likely to accrue to traditional players in the industry (rather than software developers), and the less integrated the offerings are likely to be (meaning compatibility problems are more likely to arise, and that individual manufacturers may be able to reap competitive advantage from how well they use a common service like Covisint). (For more on the power of code writers, see the introduction to this volume.)

Another scenario is that the ultimate outcome is not path-dependent. In this view, held strongly by CommerceOne, firms initially start out with private exchanges and gradually move more functions over to the public e-marketplace as they realize that it is reliable and secure—and much cheaper (CommerceOne interviews, March 2001). Note that in this case, however, firms still incur the huge upfront cost of setting up a network.

Are there national differences reflected in the strategies of these code writers? Almost all of the major B2B firms are U.S.-owned. However, we do not think that this necessarily means that the software reflects American business culture more than others. Above, we have discussed two key strategic differences in code writing: whether the purpose of the software is collaboration or auctions, and whether its architecture is open or proprietary. As we have seen, US firms are active in all four areas: CommerceOne promotes open architecture and auctions, whereas Oracle's software is proprietary. And SupplySolution's open-architecture collaboration tool is part of both Covisint (a public exchange) and JCI's proprietary exchange.

With respect to architecture, European programmers in other types of software use both proprietary architectures (SAP) and open (Linux). The key determinant of strategy appears to be not nationality, but timing: first-movers appear to aim for proprietary standards, whereas open architecture is a feature that later entrants can use to woo customers. Some German companies are developing private exchanges utilizing both in-house software development and the capabilities of U.S. software firms; VW is working with MatrixOne and EDS, and Bosch with Ariba and CommerceOne (Joachim and Moozakis 2001). Such a strategy is slower than immediately buying and utilizing an existing open architecture product but may allow for customization while avoiding the mistakes of early adopters.

However, if U.S. exit-influenced preferences for auctions are likely to be embedded in software from U.S. software providers, this could influence the options available to global firms that would prefer to pursue voice mode. Those companies (e.g., Toyota) may simply develop their own private exchanges with software developed specifically to support voice mode. However, if many suppliers are signed up by Covisint and operating more in exit mode, they may not be so ready to work with firms in voice mode. Or Toyota may miss out on the opportunities of auctions by not having ready access to the prevailing auction software, and not making complementary investments in the necessary business processes.

An alternate path could emerge from supplier attempts to achieve competitive advantage within a network of firms following the voice mode. Johnson Controls Inc. (JCI) has set up its own exchange, called NexCommerce, containing a mix of software packages, integrated by JCI, to support "Collaborative Commerce" or "C-commerce." Suppliers who are "Peer Partners^{TM}" of JCI will get access to a pre-engineered software and procedural toolset for product design, schedule fulfillment, and so on, optimized for use with JCI. "Early adopters of C-commerce in automotive will achieve first-mover advantages, much like their counterparts Cisco, Celestica, and others have already achieved in high-tech by using their supply and netbatsu partners to achieve profitable scalability and growth," writes John Waraniak, director, E-Business Speed, Johnson Controls Inc. (Waraniak 2001).

According to Tom Hachiya, a partner with Computer Sciences Corporation's Consulting Group:

The challenge to JCI is, just as the industry is finally understanding the role of the systems integrator, they are moving to a network integration business model. JCI is setting up a virtual keiretsu, evolving their supply base from a sandlot baseball metaphor (where teams are assembled using available players on a happenstance basis) to a business model more closely resembling the organized "big leagues." JCI's goal is first to establish and then to optimize commercial, technical, and procedural connections with the best n-tier suppliers. The first mover advantage for JCI is that competitors like Magna, Delphi or Visteon will be handicapped by having to a) do business following JCI's processes, b) find alternate (lesser) suppliers or c) bear the cost of installing their own infrastructure.

JCI has an incentive to make their mix of technical and procedural components somewhat unique, i.e., a blend of "off the shelf" technologies and proprietary intellectual capital, not entirely compatible with whatever Covisint eventually gets around to offering. Wherever Covisint is successful in establishing the de-facto standard, the benefit or value will inure to Covisint's OEM sponsors. JCI is betting on obtaining a return on their infrastructure development investments by superior access to their preferred suppliers' capabilities due to the reluctance and difficulties in replicating comparable (expensive) connections with Delphi, Covisint, etc. As JCI begins to compete more on the capabilities of their proprietary network than their internal competencies, it also commits them to more collaboration with *their* suppliers. There is a significant disincentive to working with supplier partners not on the network due to the friction of incompatible processes and technologies.

Ultimately, then, the race is between the commoditization acceleration effects of open standards versus the derivative value of collaborative supplier networks. The success of these proprietary networks in delivering customer value will largely be a function of their ability to outmaneuver Covisint and the open standard model. (Personal interview, December 2001)

In summary, auctions are still the most advanced application at Covisint, although collaborative planning and design tools are under development. Customers seem to be using auctions as a winnowing device, rather than binding themselves to select the low bidder, even from among the suppliers they themselves have declared qualified. Often what happens is that customers hold an auction among eight suppliers, and then negotiate among the top two or three firms. This suggests that even U.S. firms do not want to take advantage of the Internet's capabilities to pursue a pure exit model, and will be interested in Covisint's collaborative planning and design tools—or in developing their own such tools in a private exchange. One possible outcome is that B2B tools take on the disadvantages of the lack of standardization of their predecessors (EDI, CAD), and that the promise of cheap communication will not be realized. Whether firms use private exchanges or Covisint, software with open or closed architecture, we expect that automakers and suppliers will find ways to encode their historically dominant mode of exchange because of the high organizational costs of switching.

Disruptive Pressures to Modes of Exchange

So far, we have primarily considered how B2B directly affects modes of exchange; the first step in our analysis, as portrayed in figure 11.1. Now we turn to the second step in our analysis, considering how external factors affecting modes of exchange might alter our main prediction that B2B will reinforce historical dominant practices, relationships, and mindsets. These disruptive pressures could alter organizational switching costs and could also change the cost/benefit ratio for implementing various B2B capabilities. Here we continue our focus on the automotive industry case; in the next section, we consider these issues more broadly.

Global Restructuring and Strategic Alliances   As firms from different countries and exchange traditions are linked through mergers and alliances of various kinds, the dynamics of restructuring and of global strategy-making will affect their future trajectory in unpredictable ways. In the auto industry, DaimlerChrysler and Renault-Nissan provide two contemporary examples. In both cases, financial crises led to mergers in which the dominant partner insisted on a shift from voice to exit.

Chrysler's very early history was more consistent with voice than either GM or Ford, yet it spent more than fifty years operating under the dominant exit approach of the U.S. industry. When near-bankruptcy in 1979 forced Chrysler to work collaboratively with its suppliers and unions simply to survive, historical patterns were broken. Chrysler sought to make its collaborative "extended enterprise" the basis for competitive advantage in the mid 1990s, under the leadership of Thomas Stallkamp (Dyer 2000). Yet in the management crisis of late 2000 that brought Daimler into direct control of Chrysler (following the exit of Stallkamp and many other Chrysler executives), the first-announced decisions were directed at cutting procurement costs by edict—all suppliers were instructed to reduce their prices to Chrysler by 10 percent if they wanted any future business. Consulting studies were produced that suggested suppliers had taken advantage of the collaborative regime to gain or maintain unreasonably high prices, and suddenly exit arguments and mechanisms had high legitimacy again. This is noteworthy because Daimler-Benz has hardly been a strong advocate of a strict exit approach in its German operations, nor would it be likely to propose similar measures to its German supply base in a similar situation.

Renault-Nissan is an even more intriguing case. Nissan's financial crisis, sustained over many years of decline and failed management initiatives, managed to discredit the entire Japanese approach to management, enabling Carlos Ghosn to enter from Renault and demand the breakup of Nissan's keiretsu purchasing arrangements. How will this sudden move toward exit be perceived in a country that still highly values voice (and whose two most successful automakers, Toyota and Honda, are very visible practitioners of this mode of exchange)? Will access to B2B capabilities make it easier or more difficult for Renault-Nissan to make this transition in Japan? If we are right that Covisint will initially lean toward procurement mechanisms such as auctions—and given Renault-Nissan's early and enthusiastic support for taking an equity stake —then we predict its participation will in fact speed movement toward exit.

Transfer of Responsibility from OEMs to Suppliers   Our second factor pulls toward the voice mode of exchange. As OEMs transfer more responsibility for design, manufacturing, and logistics to first-tier suppliers, the exit mode with suppliers will be less viable.

This deverticalization is a relatively recent trend. Over the past 15 years, many suppliers have invested heavily in design capabilities in order to take over design tasks from OEMs. Suppliers have hoped to persuade automakers of the benefits of sourcing full modules (such as complete interiors) from one firm. The central argument has been one of "core competence"—design and production would be integrated on a large scale, by firms that specialized in all the relevant technologies. Wall Street looked favorably upon this strategy, and a great wave of consolidation occurred among auto suppliers in the 1990s. In some cases, small suppliers were bought by large suppliers aiming to provide "full service" design, production, and logistics services. In other cases, they remained independent, but increasingly supplied to a large, "first-tier" supplier rather than directly to the automaker.

This emergence of "mega-suppliers" at the first tier calls into question the hypothesis that Covisint's primary effect will be to squeeze supplier margins. These suppliers will design and coordinate the production of complete modules and subsystems (more on this below) that are too complex and idiosyncratic, given current product architecture, to be put out for auction. Furthermore, the number of suppliers capable of providing these bundles of products and services are too few in number to support much price competition. These suppliers are big enough that they could benefit greatly from using Covisint's capabilities to organize their own purchases from second- and third-tier suppliers. So although there is still considerable suspicion about Covisint among these new mega-suppliers, they may turn out to be more natural allies of the automakers than is now apparent.

National differences in modes of exchange will affect these power dynamics (Fine 1998), which will in turn affect the adoption and diffusion of B2B. If B2B involved only traditional industry players, it might simply recreate the current industry structure, particularly the dominance of the OEMs. However, the development of B2B capabilities will require that IT and logistics firms—with their very different product development rates, product architectures, and approaches to standardization—become intertwined with the OEMs and their suppliers. As noted above, given that these outside firms will be helping to establish the protocols and write the code for the auto industry's B2B tools, their predilection for particular modes of exchange will be highly influential (Lessig 1999b).

Changes in Product Architecture The "dominant design" for automobiles has been quite stable for most of the past century, but now automakers and suppliers alike are investigating the potential gains and liabilities of moving toward a more modular product architecture. To the extent that this trend continues, the procurement requirements for modules are sufficiently different from that for simple components that it will disrupt current modes of exchange; this disruption will be accentuated if industry standards are identified for even a subset of those modules. The modular approach faces a number of obstacles, but the fact that modularity could facilitate the move toward a "build-to-order" system may increase the incentives to shift product architecture in this direction (Helper and MacDuffie 2001).

Discussions of modularity are often confounded by confusion about terminology. Following Ulrich (1995), we distinguish between a system, defined as the totality of components, interfaces, and software providing a key vehicle function, and a module, defined as a physically proximate "chunk" of components, typically from multiple systems, which can be assembled into the vehicle as one unit. The product architecture is the scheme by which functional elements are arranged into physical chunks and by which the chunks interact. It can range from modular to integral, and also from open to closed, in terms of whether standards are industrywide or proprietary.

In contrast to the current personal computer industry, which is highly modular and open, the current dominant product architecture for automobiles is substantially integral rather than modular, and closed rather than open. That is, most components are not standardized across products or companies and have no common interface; hence, they are highly interdependent with other components and idiosyncratic to a particular model. The specifications for components are typically treated as proprietary and model-specific, shared only between an OEM and a supplier, rather than being widely known and accessible to a wide range of suppliers. Components from different companies or even different models within the same company cannot be easily combined, so customization requires idiosyncratic modifications (Sako and Warburton 1999).

This product architecture is partly the result of the history of the industry, as described above. But some integrality seems inherent to the functioning of a modern car. For example, in designing a safety system, seat belts and airbags need to be in the interior, where the passengers are. But sensors need to be near the outside of the car, where the obstacles are. In contrast, it is relatively easy for computer makers to unite system functions and geography, for example, to put all functions related to typing in the single physical unit of the keyboard.

We believe that the extent to which the product architecture of an automobile moves toward modularity will be yet another influence on whether B2B will be primarily directed toward exit or voice modes of exchange. Modules can vary on two dimensions: (1) they can be produced either by vertically integrated or independent suppliers, and (2) they can be designed to fit only one OEM (or only one car model), or to be standardized across models and OEMs. If modular designs are outsourced to suppliers but remain nonstandard and OEM-specific, extensive interaction during design between OEMs and suppliers will be required. Similarly, if vehicle design remains integral, yet the production of OEM-designed components is outsourced extensively to suppliers, extensive interaction will be needed. In both cases, voice mode would be indicated, and would favor B2B capabilities that support collaborative product design.

In contrast, an exit strategy works well if: (1) there are many suppliers who can make a particular part (so the threat to leave is credible), and (2) there is little payoff to interaction between automaker and supplier, so frequent switching does not harm quality. If modular designs are kept vertically integrated (because control of modules is seen by OEMs as a "core competence"), the outsourced components would be relatively simple parts procured more readily via the exit model. An intermediate case might occur if module designs are standardized across the products of different automakers. On the one hand, this would reduce the need for communication between OEM and supplier as in the exit mode; on the other hand, these parts would be more complicated to make than individual components, with fewer suppliers capable of making them, reducing the automakers' ability to switch, as in voice mode.

Automakers may well vary in their choices about outsourcing and parts standardization. If a given module design is standardized, made interchangeable across products of two customers, then the supplier of that module to both customers would be hedged against sales declines at either one.[12] However, agreeing on a module standard across the industry limits any single automaker's freedom to design new capabilities into their vehicles. For example, a firm such as Toyota, which favors more integral designs and a voice approach to suppliers, would most likely move toward modules by doing the design work internally, maintaining model-specific idiosyncrasies to insure the integrity of the overall design, and working closely with its long-term suppliers on accomplishing production performance targets. On the other hand, GM—which favors a more modular product architecture, the outsourcing of modules, and an exit approach to suppliers—would prefer standardized modules available from multiple suppliers, so it could use its volume purchasing power and threat of exit to drive down module prices.

Summary

If one thing is clear from this complex summary of a complex industry, it is that the impact of B2B on modes of exchange is not by any means technically determined. For maximum effect, the nature of a firm's B2B investment should be complementary to its other investments, the investments of its competitors, and the nature of its competitive environment. In this sense, the effects of B2B will depend on the extent to which complementary changes occur in product design strategy (modular versus not, standardization versus not) and procurement strategy (voice versus exit), not to mention retail strategy (build-to-order, factory direct, dealer direct), which concerns B2C modes of exchange and is not our focus here.

These e-effects could be path-dependent: the order in which these changes occur could affect the ultimate outcome. For example, if the short-term effects of the Internet are to promote exit relations with suppliers, the scenario of moving toward complex modules sourced to powerful first-tier suppliers would become less likely than if voice-inspired information exchange with suppliers were to dominate. The reason is that the less tightly linked suppliers would probably not develop the skills to produce complex modules.

B2B's Next Phase: Implications for Modes of Exchange

B2B will have a staying power that will outlast the dot.bust that has afflicted B2C but, as the auto industry case makes clear, it will take forms very different from those first heralded by e-business proponents. Independent public exchanges, never a factor in autos, are failing at a rapid rate. The most visible failure, Ventro (previously Chemdex), a public B2B exchange for the life sciences and medical equipment industries, held its IPO in July 1999 and saw its share price rise from $15 to a high of $240. Its revenues in 1999 were $30.8 million. Yet at the end of March 2001, Ventro reported its second straight quarter of zero revenues; its marketplaces are shut down, three-quarters of its staff laid off, and its stock trading below $1.

With sellers and buyers under no obligation to transact through Ventro's public catalogs and procurement software, the exchange was unable to maintain the liquidity necessary to support its increasingly expensive infrastructure. Both suppliers and customers were able to reach better deals on commodity products through more specialized exchanges,[13] and able to build specific exchanges for longer-term relationships with more sophisticated supply chain management services. These problems are not unique to Ventro; observers now predict that fewer than 20 percent of the thousand B2B public exchanges founded in the last two years will survive in any form.

Ventro's experience highlights the advantages of the consortia approach at the industry level. These include a guaranteed source of transactions, financial liquidity, and a higher probability of achieving standards that facilitate interoperability. Other prominent B2B consortia include:

• Worldwide Retail Exchange, founded in March 2000 by more than fifty large multinational retailers, including Best Buy, Kmart, J.C. Penney, Safeway, and Target in the United States, Delhaize in Belgium, Auchan and Casino in France, Jusco in Japan, Royal Ahold in the Netherlands, and Kingfisher, Marks and Spencer, and Tesco in the United Kingdom. A competing exchange, Global Net Exchange, was founded at about the same time by Sears Roebuck (United States) and Carrefour (France); Kroger in the United States, Metro AG in Germany, and Sainsbury's in the United Kingdom have all joined subsequently. Wal-Mart is the exception, choosing to run its own B2B exchange with its vendors.

• Transora, a consumer products marketplace created in June 2000 by over fifty companies, including Kraft, Proctor and Gamble, and General Mills in the United States; and Cadbury Schweppes, Nestlé, and Unilever in Europe.

• Metalspectrum, a raw materials marketplace, is backed by over twenty of the leading firms in the metals industry, including aluminum giants Alcoa, Kaiser, and Reynolds. Its suppliers offer over 180 different metal products, from copper to aluminum and stainless to carbon steel.

• Pantellos, a consortium of 21 energy and utility companies, including Entergy Corp. and PG&E Corp.

These consortia share with Covisint the massive task of building the necessary infrastructure, deciding on the degree of interoperability they want, winning cooperation from both buyers and sellers, and deciding on the appropriate revenue model. So far, auctions are the most developed features of these exchanges and, as we would predict, the exchanges handling the most commodity-like products, such as Metalspectrum, have advanced the fastest. Although firms such as Target have increased their purchasing through Worldwide Retail Exchange, half of the volume so far has been for general and administrative items, such as plastic clothes hangers and office supplies. This category represents about 25 percent of Target's total procurement, or $8.2 billion. Much of the "cost of sale" purchases—those items for resale that make up the other 75 percent— are still not easily amenable to procurement on the exchange, because of the overwhelming variety Target sells (Totty 2001).

New revenue models are emerging from these consortia exchanges. One service offered by Transora is the Collaborative Planning, Forecasting, and Replenishment (CPFR) system designed by Syncra. Users of this service pay no fees whatsoever for transactions. What they pay for is the service of having accurate information generated instantaneously for buyer and seller alike, and their associated supply chains, through a web-based interface. This model is collaborative by design. Trading partners must reach an up-front agreement about confidentiality and dispute resolution, develop key metrics to track progress, and establish any financial incentives and penalties. Plans for promotions, inventory policy changes, store opening/closings, and product changes must be shared, as well as demand forecasts and replenishment plans. Then when real time data on transactions are fed to all trading partners, they understand enough of the context to make sense of the data to adjust inventories, highlight over/understock conditions, and initiate replenishment (Johnson 2001).

Collaborative Planning, Forecasting, and Replenishment makes explicit a central truth about the consortia exchanges—that they will provide efficiencies through automation and standardization of the procurement process, while greater value-added activities, allowing more differentiated competitive advantage among their members, will arise from collaborative planning and design.

The consortia exchanges very much want to be the nexus of these latter activities. They are working hard to develop collaborative software tools and to persuade their trading partners that they will handle confidentiality and intellectual property issues appropriately. Yet some believe that collaborative planning and design will be better obtained through private exchanges between a focal firm and its supply chain and design partners. In a phrase from a recent Boston Consulting Group report on B2B, the goal will be "to exploit public exchanges to create private sources of advantage" (Elkington, Rasch, and Mosquet 2001). A firm could invite a supplier first encountered through an open auction on the industry exchange to join their private network for projects involving more complex procurement criteria and coordination requirements, more proprietary knowledge content, and a longer-term relationship.

There will be no shortage of software vendors rushing to support private network activities of this kind. L. M. Ericsson, which recently outsourced the building of mobile phone handsets to an electronics contract manufacturing firm, still runs five factories making cellular-network base stations. It recently installed supply chain software from Chicago-based PipeChain Inc. to aid collaborative planning. As Michael Totty (2001) reports:

With the software, an Ericsson vendor can tell just by looking at a Web browser how rapidly Ericsson factories are using suppliers of a certain material, how many hours of inventory the factory has on hand, and how much the factory projects to use over the next several days and weeks based on actual orders and forecasts. The supplier can then adjust its production and shipping schedules accordingly, permitting it to make and deliver the component only as it's needed. What's more, the plants that supply the vendor can also use the software to adjust their production and shipping schedule.

This approach essentially adds new functionality and easier, lower-cost accessibility to the EDI model; database structure and variable definition are likely to be proprietary, at least initially. Ericsson (and PipeChain) might eventually benefit from the standard-setting activities of Rosetta-Net, the effort by a consortia of electronics companies to achieve XML-based global interoperability. This would increase the range of vendors available to Ericsson and the market for PipeChain's products. But until that time, Ericsson can achieve supply chain efficiencies on its own.

The future of industry consortia exchanges will involve complex governance issues. The basis for industry-wide collaboration is somewhat fragile, and developing industry-wide interoperability will require huge investments of time and money. They may well be undercut by the restlessness of individual firms to make progress through private exchanges developed with independent software firms. However, such specialized software firms may find they lack the capabilities to provide integrative tools for the full range of supply chain activities. The efforts of a firm such as Oracle to establish its approach as the database standard for B2B might help the industry consortia move more quickly, or simply make it easier for firms to opt out of the consortium exchange while still gaining access to a de facto standard.

What we don't know is whether the knowledge of industry context, procurement norms, and design processes that seems essential to apply B2B to collaborative planning and design is more likely to be established within an industry consortium or within private networks of trading partners. If multiple private networks thrive, it is possible that suppliers to multiple customers will face the same duplicate investment requirements that slowed the diffusion of EDI—even if the Internet makes the investment threshold easier to attain. As firms explore various exchange options, incentives for investment in getting the industry-wide exchanges up and running will be affected.

Ultimately, firms will probably hedge their bets, and not belong to only one exchange. There will be competition among types of exchange, along many different dimensions, that will greatly affect firms belonging to multiple exchanges. In short, B2B's next phase will have inter-firm dynamics, involving both competition and cooperation, that will be far more complex and intriguing than the horse race between incumbents and startups that was the initial preoccupation of participants in this arena.

Conclusion

We have advanced in this chapter a central hypothesis about B2B—that it will have an evolutionary effect by accentuating and reinforcing existing modes of exchange. We see the largest impact of B2B as a significant reduction in the information costs of performing certain core procurement, planning, and coordination tasks between customers and suppliers. These gains will accrue, by and large, to all industry participants willing (and able) to make the initial investment to migrate these tasks to the Internet. This investment is already less for the Internet than for past electronic networks, such as traditional EDI, because of inexpensive hardware and open software protocols. However, considered across entire industries, these investment costs are still substantial, and much of the potential savings could be lost if firms choose proprietary rather than independent public exchanges. The degree of progress toward standardization of B2B protocols (including data labels in XML) will also have a tremendous impact on conversion costs and the ultimate level and distribution of benefits from B2B.

Regardless of whether the cost improvements for core tasks occur quickly versus slowly, or are large versus very large, these are primarily one-time gains associated with conversion to these new technological capabilities. The more substantial and lasting economic impacts of B2B will result from changes in the underlying transactional infrastructure of procurement. Here the legacy of past modes of exchange, both at individual companies and at the level of the nation-state, is powerful. Switching costs from a firm's dominant mode of exchange (or a nation's) to some other mode are extremely high. Given that B2B lowers information costs for any mode of exchange, the financial incentives to make the infrastructural shift are low.

This is true, in our view, as long as the environmental conditions supporting a given mode of exchange are stable. Once disruptive pressures affect a dominant mode of exchange, a firm may suddenly find the tools and capabilities associated with B2B provide options for change that were previously unpalatable. At the country level, even more so, disruptive forces that challenge or invalidate the dominance of historical patterns of exchange will be needed before B2B is likely to have a transformative rather than an evolutionary impact.

It is a fluid time, when firms are experimenting with many kinds of B2B exchange and trying to figure out which mix will best support their procurement needs and strategic goals. Amid this experimentation, and in the absence of a strongly shared vision of what kind of exchange will best meet the interests of key stakeholders, investment incentives are very likely to be inadequate to allow pursuit of the most ambitious levels of standardization. Thus although private networks may be appealing because they overcome the governance problems of consortia, they may well lead to the problems of non-standard software that the open architecture of the Internet was supposed to prevent.

In summary, B2B demonstrates the powerful complementarities that exist between traditional capabilities and so-called "new economy" capabilities. These complementarities favor a strong continued role for incumbent firms and preservation of the historical legacies of different modes of exchange. Although the savings from B2B may increase the tenacity of these legacies in the short term, B2B does offer firms a wider range of feasible choices for procurement, collaborative planning, and co-design activities. The key to an effective supply chain is being able to respond flexibly to changes in conditions that are difficult to specify in advance, rather than the ability to automate routine tasks or run online auctions. B2B can be an important source of that flexibility.

Acknowledgments

Thanks to Bob Jansen, Bob Glushko, Bruce Kogut, Mike Smitka, and Tom Hachiya for many helpful discussions. Remaining errors are our responsibility.

Notes

1. For analysis of the development of different historical trajectories in the auto industry, see Freyssenet et al. 2000.

2. Note that if a supplier cannot quickly replace a lost customer order, assets that could in principle be general purpose (such as a machine tool, or a broadly trained engineering staff), become in effect "dedicated capacity" (Williamson 1985; Helper 1995). A supplier will be less likely to invest in such capacity without contractual safeguards.

3. Note, however, that the video would not substitute completely for being at the actual site, because problem-solvers would not be able to pick up clues based on the senses of touch or smell, on chance conversations with people not participating in the video conference, or on intuition from the general factory environment.

4. This section draws on Helper, MacDuffie, and Sabel 2000; Hochfelder and Helper 1996; and Helper 1991.

5. Europe is an intermediate case, but has typically been closer to the US mode of exchange. For more on this point see Helper 1991; Sako 1992; Ahmadjian and Lincoln 2001.

6. For insight on the advantages and disadvantages of standardization for different economic agents, see Farrell and Saloner 1992; and Shapiro and Varian 1999.

7. For example, when a fire stopped production at Aisin Seiki, a firm that provided a brake component for 90 percent of Toyota cars, suppliers spent millions of dollars in inventing ways to make the component using general-purpose equipment (sometimes spending vastly more than the $2 price of the part), without negotiating any form of compensation in advance.

8. For example, Toyota may find it easier to experiment with auctions, because Covisint makes it easy to set up such transactions and find suppliers willing to participate. Conversely, the availability of cheap, general-purpose design tools may cause GM to experiment more with black-box design (of a type that does not involve information that suppliers consider to be their intellectual property).

9. For more detail, see the long version of Helper and MacDuffie 2001, posted at ⟨http://weatherhead.cwru.edu/helper⟩; and Fine and Raff 2001.

10. But this doesn't mean the Big Three do not face legal hurdles. In January, the aftermarket e-marketplace operated by Ford, GM, and DCX was sued by Choice Parts LLC for allegedly withholding access to industry parts data (Karpinski 2001).

11. Brian Kelley, former head of e-business for Ford, said it was a "myth" that "B2B is only about procurement and buying goods cheaper. It will start with procurement as the path of least resistance, but quickly move on to supply chain management and and product development, and, ultimately to complete integration of this ecosystem called the auto industry" (Kisiel 2000c). This view represents the convergent perspective of e-business champions rather well but neglects, in our view, the legacies of modes of exchange and pressures for competitive differentiation.

12. If a module supplier was owned by an automaker, other automakers might be reluctant to buy large amounts of parts from it, for fear of dependence and revealing proprietary information, so common interfaces would have less impact in the modules-with-vertical-integration scenario.

13. One reason why specialized exchanges can be more efficient is that their managers have the industry knowledge to screen information, in contrast to more general exchanges that send their members many RFQ's or supplier catalogs that are of no interest, because the only screening device they use is SIC code.

12

Regulation in Europe

Hervé Dumez and Alain Jeunemaître

Introduction

The Internet has taken over the mindset of the European business and political community as a cause for the unprecedented economic growth that the United States experienced in the 1990s and that Europe failed to achieve. Therefore, in the recent years, the European equation might be summed up into one motto: "Jump on the Internet and NTIC bandwagon or undergo economic decline."

But as the Internet crosses the boundaries of sectors, the e-economy is not only about the Internet. It is also an opportunity for Europe to create a liberalized economy for entrepreneurship, to support the small- and medium-sized enterprises in their attempts to access venture capital, and to ease the administrative burden for their creation and development. There is a wide recognition in the European Commission and in individual nation states that policies must be changed and adapted to encourage fundamental changes. However, here lie the hard facts. In their efforts, European policymakers have seemed to be left with one available option: push the different public policies levers more or less at random and hope for results without knowing in advance which one will prove successful.

Even if the gap with the United States shrinks, it would be unreasonable to assume that particular targeted policies have so far produced a significant impact. First, the inception of Internet technology goes back to the mid 1980s. All available indicators from a decade later suggest that

Europe failed to promote the Internet. The European Internet penetration level (number of users) is less than 30 percent, compared to more than 50 percent in the United States (Commission 2000). According to the OECD, the United States has, on average, 2.8 times the number of Internet hosts per thousand inhabitants than the European Union has.

Secondly, EU members' governments and the European Commission took action to change this state of affairs only recently. For example, it was only in 1997 that the Lionel Jospin government launched a "Programme d'Action Gouvernemental pour la Société de l'Information" (PAGSI), which proposed to develop an information society for France. In 1998, the Blair government issued a White Paper on "Our Competitive Future: Building the Knowledge Driven Economy," which set out a U.K. strategy for closing the productivity gap between the United Kingdom and other leading countries. The European Commission launched the eEurope initiative in December 1999 and followed it with the Lisbon European Council on March 23–24, which endorsed the objective of narrowing the gap between Europe and the United States so that Europe could become the most competitive and dynamic trading block. It was only after that summit that the Feira European Council (June 19–20, 2000) agreed on an action plan—"eEurope 2002: An Information Society for All." As a comparison, the Clinton administration released its report on the information technology highway by 1993.

This chapter addresses two questions: did regulation contribute to the development of the Internet in Europe, and were these regulatory influences operative at the national or European level? After all, the speed and quality of the growth of the Internet economy appears, by the force of the chapters included in this book, to differ by European country. We address these questions by analyzing the core challenges that faced European and national regulatory authorities. For purposes of analysis, it suffices to look primarily at two cases, the United Kingdom and France.

The first challenge for Europe has been to devise a public policy suitable for the Internet and the e-economy. This policy is reviewed and discussed in the first section, which stresses recent developments that have occurred in the United Kingdom and France and gives an account of the work in progress in Europe. The second e-economy challenge concerns Internet access and the use of traditional regulatory tools to deal with it. This is reviewed in section two. Finally, the third section sets out the current European thinking about the e-economy and makes clear the shift from regulation to facilitation.

The Internet as a Public Policy Issue

The e-economy is not sector based. The Internet crosses the boundaries of sectors. In this regard, there is not a concept of the old economy to oppose to the new economy. There is little public policy that focuses on the Internet economy as such. A recent U.K. survey of European policies toward the Internet illustrates this point.

The U.K. government think tank on "Better Regulation" has surveyed the various regulations relevant to Internet and the e-economy. Its findings are summarized below.

Existing regulations an e-business needs to think about:

Consumer protection legislation—e.g., Trade Descriptions Act, Consumer Protection Act, including new Distance Selling regulations

Contract law

Advertising codes of practice

Data Protection Act

Company law

Tax and VAT requirements

Regulation of Investigatory Powers Act—e.g., Lawful business practice regulations

Electronic Communications Act

Employment law

Sector specific regulation—e.g., the Financial Services and Marketing Act

Foreign laws—the implications of cross-border trading, advertising laws

Planning laws

Health and safety laws (e.g., display screen equipment regulations).

(Better Regulation Task Force 2000)

Regulations in the pipeline that e-businesses need to think about:

EC E-Commerce Directive

Internal Market Directives

Dual Use Regulation

Proposed amendments to regulations under the Brussels Convention

Waste Electrical Equipment Directive.

(Better Regulation Task Force 2000)

Other issues that affect e-commerce include:

Funding

Government as exemplar—government's adoption of electronic methods of working

Skills shortage

Trust

Single currency

IR 35—tax treatment of IT consultants

Competition/monopoly issues introduced by collaborative e-markets

National insurance on share options

Internet access and usage charges

Internet surveillance and interception policy.

(Better Regulation Task Force 2000)

The lists invite comments.

In the first place, there are many regulations that are relevant to e-commerce. Moreover, e-commerce is itself only part of the e-economy. The task of listing all regulations that could apply in the Internet economy would be arduous. It would entail including all regulations attached to property and copyrights, including the circulation of information, pictures, sounds, and texts going through the Internet (Benghozi and Paris 1999). At one extreme, it is questionable whether any regulation can be applied and enforced in the Internet economy if this economy is defined in isolation. In short, the e-economy is a transverse phenomenon anchored in all parts of society and economic activities.

Subsequently, the Better Regulation Task Force rightly points out that regulations that could be enforced toward e-commerce have not been specifically devised for it. There are regulations that have attempted to adapt to the new environment with some specific alterations. Mainly, however, there has been tinkering to adjust to the legal challenges raised by e-commerce. Few specific legal mechanisms have been implemented to deal with the radical changes brought about by the new technology. In other words, assessing the significance of the European Commission and Member States' public policies toward the Internet economy involves evaluations of the flexibility of already existing legal tools to deal with the Internet.

In this regard, two particularly significant outcomes of the debate on Internet regulation are worth highlighting. The first relates to competition policy, the second to setting up specific Internet regulatory agencies.

The former issue has been raised in the United States and Europe. Would the existing legal competitive policy framework be robust enough and relevant to the Internet economy? Both the United States and Europe have concluded that the Internet is not so revolutionary that it would entail changing competitive appraisals. Particularly telling was the recent report of the U.K. Office of Fair Trading, which produced an in-depth analysis of existing procedures and concepts of competition policy and their relevance to the Internet. It found that there was no need to rethink legislation and introduce amendments (Office of Fair Trading 2000).

There has also been consensus in Europe on the latter issue. No Internet regulator has been set up. Considering that the Internet economy goes across borders and involves different parts of the law, the United Kingdom, France, and the European Commission had developed a similar "co-regulation" approach (Tronc 1999). Competition authorities already "cohabit" alongside regulators in sectors particularly relevant to the Internet; especially broadcasting and telecom. Self-regulatory bodies also emerged to discipline business and the dissemination of information on the Internet (Foster, Rutkowski, and Goodman 1997; Brousseau 2000). Thus, co-regulation means defining a regulatory mode that accommodates the Internet by combining a mix of statutes and self-regulation on a national as well as an international basis. The U.K. government merely went a step further in creating a specific body in charge of coordinating and analyzing the Internet, the "e-Envoy." This body is not, however, regulatory:

The purpose of the office of the e-Envoy is to lead the U.K. in its drive to be the best place in the world for e-commerce. It will work with partners in the public, private and voluntary sectors, and internationally to develop:

1. Modern Markets—developing a legal, regulatory and fiscal environment in the U.K. and globally that facilitates e-commerce.

2. Confident People—helping individuals and businesses take full advantage of the opportunities opened up by information and communication technologies and ensuring that those opportunities are available to all.

3. Government is a global exemplar in its use of information and communication technologies.

4. Analysis and Benchmarking—ensuring that government and business decisions are informed by reliable, accurate e-commerce monitoring and analysis. (Better Regulation Task Force 2000)

By the same token, subsequent to a report commissioned by its prime minister, France supported the view that it was necessary to coordinate and create an ad hoc structure between existing regulatory bodies. Self-regulatory bodies and stakeholders would meet in this ad hoc structure. They would make their opinions clear and confront elaborate regulatory approaches on practical issues raised by the Internet economy. Here again, there is no question of whether to create an Internet regulator. Instead, the focus is on establishing a forum of ideas, the "Forum des droits de l'Internet," which can be compared under French law to a non-profit organization with no governmental mandate or duties (Paul 2000).

Therefore, the regulatory tools that have been used by Member States and the European Commission to promote the development of the Internet economy have generally been vague. Internet regulations have usually relied on already existing regulation devised for the old economy, although laws have been modified slightly from time to time to adapt to the new Internet environment.

Thus, the logic has been because the Internet economy has no fixed limits, European public policies toward the Internet should have no clear boundaries. Facing unclear regulatory issues, European governments have been reactive and cautious about the Internet. They have, under pressure, used particular regulatory tools, but have not set up a clear and coherent perspective or a framework specifically dedicated to the Internet. As part of this reactive stance, two public policies have been particularly relevant. One focuses on regulation, particularly Internet access and pricing; the other one emphasizes facilitation, which entails removing hurdles and creating a propitious environment for Internet expansion.

Regulating Internet Access and Pricing

Regulating Internet access and pricing raises multiple issues that range from technical issues to the exercise of market power (Crémer 2001). Until recently, regulatory decisions have focused on telecom and the Internet, competition policy, and Internet service provision.

Internet and Telecom

A key issue regarding the Internet is access to users. In Europe, this issue has translated into concerns about pricing of Internet access.

Until the 1980s, telephony services were provided by a national monopoly in all Member States. In 1984, the U.K. government of Mrs. Thatcher privatized British Telecom without separating infrastructure from service provision. British Telecom has retained the ownership of what is called the "local loop," which denotes telephony access to households. The U.K. government also set up an independent regulator, the director general of telecom, backed by an office, OFTEL (Dumez and Jeunemaître 1999).

From the end of the 1980s onward, liberalization of the European telecom markets occurred with a similar pattern of monopoly privatization (Cave 1997). National monopolies were privatized, and national independent regulatory bodies were created. Europe did not create a European telecom regulator. From then on, national telecom regulators had to deal with the crucial issue of pricing access to the infrastructure for new telecom entrants.

Because the national privatized telecom monopolies have market power in all Member States, they charge high access prices. Not surprisingly, household penetration rates for the Internet are low. In the meantime, mobile telephony markets are highly competitive and mobile phones have a high penetration rate. For Member States, the mobile phone penetration rate ranges from 39 percent to 70 percent (Commission 2000). Moreover, Internet growth (portals and services) has been controlled by the incumbent national monopolies. The largest European

Internet Service Providers (ISPs) are subsidiaries of the old Telecom monopolies (Wanadoo—France Telecom; T-online—Deutsche Telekom; Terra—Telphonica; Tin-in—Telecom Italia; etc.). In most cases, the market share of the ISP owned by the historically dominant monopoly is in excess of 50 percent, and all subsidiaries have a significant foothold in all Internet market segments: dial-up retail, corporate web-hosting, website design, backbone operations, wholesale packages for ISPs. Competitors are far behind. The first non-historical competitor, AOL, has only 3.8 million Internet subscribers across Europe. T-online Deutsche Telekom has 5.3 million subscribers for Germany alone.

In drawing lessons from the US experience and the 1996 US Telecom Act, and in seeking to promote the Internet by means of increased competition, the European Commission has focused on opening competitive access to the telecom infrastructure by requesting the unbundling of the local loop (Bomsel and Le Blanc 2000; de La Rochefordière 2000). On April 26, 2000, it issued a recommendation addressed to Member States to unbundle the local loop so that competitive entry in the use and management of infrastructure can occur (de la Rochefordière 2000). In the future, European households are expected to benefit from unbundling by paying lower access charges to the Internet. Compared to the description of Sweden in this volume, these efforts clearly lag the early pioneers of deregulating the national monopolies.

The commission has made three alternative recommendations by which the local loop can be opened to competition:

1. The historical incumbent telecom monopoly withdraws from managing the business relationship with households. The household rents the telephone line from a new entrant, which rents or leases the line to the incumbent monopoly. This approach is workable only if the new entrant can offer the whole spectrum of telecom services: local and international telephony, and high-speed and high-density Internet connections.

2. The historical incumbent monopoly shares the local loop with competitors but retains the low-density lines and local calls. New entrants are allowed to provide high-speed and high-density Internet connections, but have to invest in new commuting devices and therefore make profitable infrastructure improvements. In other words, new entrants concentrate on high value-added segments, although incumbent monopolies have

leeway in offering joint services for voice telephony and their own high-speed Internet connections. This alternative makes it possible for the historical incumbents to protect their positions by exercising market power. The U.S. experience suggests, however, that such deregulation can result in swift new entry.

3. The third option, which cannot properly be called unbundling, consists of incumbents investing in high-speed connections and renting them to interested new entrants.

Whatever the alternative, achieving local loop competition is not straightforward. Germany mandated unbundling in 1998. Two years later, Deutsche Telekom remained dominant with a 99 percent market share in local telephony and Internet access. This experiment happened when ADSL (Asymmetric Digital Subscriber Line) was not made available in Germany. Therefore, high-speed lines dedicated to the Internet did not exist and could not attract potential new entry. Additionally, the German telecom regulator made new entry unprofitable by setting retail prices that were lower than the price that new entrants had to pay to access the local loop. Deutsche Telekom's competitors lodged complaints with the European Commission against the regulator decision, contending that it was a case of anti-competitive practice.

The German case also illustrates the tricky situation in which the European Commission is enmeshed. The European Commission's efforts to liberalize and foster competition in the Member States' telecom markets may face adverse decisions from national regulators, which face pressure from the dominant historical incumbent. It is therefore most likely that the development of a truly competitive European telecom market will come primarily from market forces and deregulation.

U.S. firms have so far proposed the most promising market arrangements, but this market arrangement contradicts the dominant one in Europe. In Europe, local calls and Internet connections are billed per minute. Accordingly, European consumers cannot get an unlimited access Internet connection, which is a major impediment to the development of the Internet. In September 1999, MCI Worldcom asked BT to offer an unmetered access scheme, known as FRIACO (Flat Rate Internet Access Call Origination). Under this arrangement, MCI Worldcom would handle the Internet service to the customer (marketing, billing, etc.). In December 1999, BT rejected this proposal and announced that by mid 2000 it would propose an unmetered Internet offer to U.K. customers, called Surftime. British Telecom anticipated that the Internet market growth would be driven by such offers and that 50 percent of the Internet users in the United Kingdom would have subscribed by the end of 2000 to unmetered offers. MCI Worldcom complained before the U.K. telecom regulator, David A Edmonds. The regulator decided in support of MCI Worldcom (May 26, 2000 decision, OFTEL): "BT (The Licensee) shall offer to enter into an agreement with MCI Worldcom." A particular number, 0 808 99, has been assigned to the FRIACO offers. The number indicates that the billing is no longer handled by the local telecom provider BT. MCI Worldcom has entered the Netherlands market under a similar agreement.

Thus, the European telecom market is evolving under business pressure from U.S. companies, which seek to undermine the dominant position of national European incumbents in their home markets. However, it is unclear to whom these deregulatory spoils will in fact accrue.

Internet and Competition Policy   Has competition policy played a crucial role in regulating the Internet in Europe? At first glance, it seems as if there have only been a few competitive cases involving the Internet. Yet it would be underestimating the influence of competition policy with regard to promoting the Internet.

The European Commission   Only one major Internet-related decision has been made under the leadership of the European Commission, the MCI Wordcom case described above. In coordination with the U.S. antitrust authorities, the European Commission cleared the merger but required the merged firm to divest its Internet business. But the case was a straightforward merger control case that had no general implications.

From the broader perspective outlined above, the European Commission has had to face the development of the Internet that has been shaped by various speeds and contents of national regulations. To impose coherence, the commission has used the competition policy framework to bind national regulations to common objectives and procedures. It has been handicapped in two respects. In application of the subsidiarity principle of a federal system, the commission could not step in directly with regard to national issues. Moreover, the boundaries of the e-economy being hazy, there was an intrinsic difficulty in defining the different relevant Internet markets that would be subject to competitive assessments.

Therefore, bereft of the means of direct intervention, the European Commission had to invent a particular line of action. It did so, on the one hand, by reactivating old procedures on sector-base and competition inquiry. It has only twice used the procedure since the 1960s—in margarine and beer markets. On the other hand, it has developed policies in a more usual move by implementing directives and guidelines to bind national regulators to a common European regulatory framework.

Competition Inquiry The European Commission competition inquiry was filed on July 27, 1999. The commission wanted the inquiry to establish whether the current commercial practices and pricing in the telecommunications sector infringed the EU competition rules, in particular the prohibition of restrictive practices and abuses of dominant position (articles 81, 82, and/or 86 of the EC Treaty). The inquiry has dealt with the provision and practice of leased lines, mobile roaming services, and the provision of access to and use of the residential local loop. All of these areas are vital for the creation of e-Europe, as they involve the pricing of important elements that enable Europe's citizens to access the Internet and all the services accessible on it.

Investigations were launched on the grounds of "article 11 of Regulation 17." Under article 11, the commission sent a questionnaire to the parties. Responses by these parties were mandatory and binding. In the leased lines inquiry, a hundred questionnaires were sent to national competition authorities, Member States' telecom regulators, incumbent firms, and new leasing lines entrants (in the supply and/or the purchase of lines). The commission findings about leased lines provide insights about the Internet-related competitive issues and the European Commission's reasoning.

The commission stresses how quickly new business practices are emerging and the extent to which they could impact Internet growth. Demand for leased lines is dramatically increasing, with the biggest driver being the Internet. Secondly, it pays special attention to Internet fragmentation and competitively assesses relevant market niches. Third, it intends to use pricing studies and benchmarking as markers of competition.

Harmonizing and Developing a Common Regulatory Framework

To address the regulatory divergence between NRAs, the European Commission put forward a directive proposal organising a common regulatory framework for electronic communications networks and services (Commission of the European Communities 2000b). In a supplement, it drew guidelines on market analysis and the calculation of significant market power when applying the directive (Commission of the European Communities 2001). One aim of the directive was to recall the commission goals: promote competition and freedom of access to networks, develop the internal market, promote the interests of European citizens. But above all, the directive and guidelines have been drafted so as to ensure diligence, consistency, and commitment toward Internet competitive issues. In particular, the NRAs have the duty to act swiftly once the commission refers a case to them, with a six-month deadline after notification. Moreover, the objective is to standardize competitive assessments. The guidelines detail the methodology to apply when defining the relevant market and assessing market power. The methodology itself is derived from and in line with competition policy analysis of dominance.

In its guidelines, the commission recalls the main relevant markets it has considered in its different decisions. There are defined in a voluntary narrow sense to make assessment on dominance effective. The list also illustrates the complexity of market definition:

International voice-telephony services

Advanced telecommunications services to corporate users

Standardized low-level packet-switched data-communications services

Resale of international transmission capacity

Audioconferencing

Satellite services

Enhanced global telecommunications services

Directory-assistance services

Internet-access services to end users

Seamless pan-European mobile telecommunications services to internationally mobile customers.
(European Commission COM2001 175, 16)

As can be seen, the European Commission (that is, in the case of competition policy, the Competition Directorate) has had to cope with the room for maneuver of NRAs and to detail a clear approach applicable to the Internet. Currently, the initiatives have not had time to bear fruit and it is still a gamble to think that national regulators will easily agree to give up part of their freedom and prerogatives to the benefit of a centralized European direction. The European Commission itself can provide guidance but it has not had the resources to substitute those of the NRAs.

By way of conclusion, if the European competition policy has played little role in promoting the Internet, it remains a credible threat to prevent deviating national regulations. These effects are hard to estimate, so consequently, we review select national cases below.

Member States: The French Case

As far as Members States' competition policy, there are only a few competition cases that address the perennial problem of defining the difficulty of assessing the relevant market. France is given as way of illustration by stressing an insightful complaint lodged before the French Conseil de la Concurrence.

The case involves a company named "Concurrence," which filed a complaint with the Conseil de la Concurrence on two grounds. First, it contended that the Association Française pour le Nommage Internet en Coopération, AFNIC, a self-regulatory body that managed the French domain name (.fr) by delegation of the Internet Assigned Numbers Authority, IANA, had abused its dominant position. Concurrence was refused the Internet address "concurrence.com," as the AFNIC had considered that "concurrence" (the word translates into English as "competition") was a generic term and, as such, not possible to use as a business address. AFNIC had proposed that the company change concurrence.com to concurrence-sa.com, "sa" standing for Société Anonyme (the French acronym for company limited or corporation).

Secondly, Concurrence argued that search engine companies, among them Altavista.fr, Nomade.fr, Voila.fr, and Yahoo.fr, were behaving as a cartel. It provided evidence that these search engines organized to exclude Concurrence from proper indexing. It also claimed that search engines are a prerequisite for being known on the web and are neither objective nor exhaustive, giving preference to companies sponsoring them through advertising.

Concurrence's complaint was ill conceived. Although Concurrence complained about these search engines, it also acknowledged that similar queries for "Concurrence" on the different search engines resulted in different answers.

Although the case was dismissed, it did raise key competitive issues.

The first issue is the definition of relevant Internet markets and the nature of the relationship between the European Commission and national competition authorities. In making its decision, the Conseil de la Concurrence considered the online market for a product as but one segment of the broader relevant market. It therefore had to include the product and competing products and its distribution channels in defining a market. The case law thus suggests that a dominant position in the online distribution of a product or service is not itself a competitive issue, particularly if other distribution channels are available for supply.

The second concerns the dominance of the self-regulatory organizations in allocating domain names and the potential for anti-competitive practices in such allocation. This issue is all the more topical since the creation of Internet Corporation for Assigned Names and Numbers, ICANN, which superseded IANA on October 1, 2000.

Regulating access and applying competition policies have been only one part of the European and Member States' public policies toward the Internet. The second part has involved facilitation.

Facilitating Regulation

Facilitation is reviewed for two significant Member States, the United Kingdom and France, and the European Commission.

The United Kingdom

The U.K. experience is a vivid example of a European Member State's strategy to promote Internet growth. Officially, the U.K. government is in support of a market "laissez faire" approach that a priori excludes specific support and targets for particular industries and relies on light regulation. With regard to the Internet, the U.K. government has nevertheless put forth a structured political scheme that focuses on five core dimensions that are consistent with the European Commission's approach: confident consumers, successful businesses, government as exemplar, world class supply sectors, and modern markets. As we have already reviewed analyses of regulation, we will concentrate in this section on issues more related to Internet facilitation: the need for an exemplar government, fostering consumer confidence in the Internet, and fostering the relationship between SMEs and the Internet.

Government as Exemplar The European Commission has made clear its intention to use the administrative procedures of Member States as a lever to get European citizens accustomed to the Internet. The commission has proposed an e-government initiative: "The challenge for administrations is to adapt quickly to the new methods of working" (Council and Commission 2000, 22). The U.K. government has been a leading European country in this respect. In March 2000, Tony Blair, prime minister of the United Kingdom, set three Internet targets: make 100 percent of government services available online by 2005; make access to Internet purchasing possible for 90 percent of low-value goods and services (by volume) by March 2001; and offer access to 100 percent of civil central government procurements, which are to be tendered via Internet by 2002.

Building Consumer Confidence With a 30 percent Internet penetration level, the United Kingdom ranks among the most advanced European countries. As in most other Member States, however, the Internet is used above all for e-mail. Less than 3 percent of U.K. Internet users buy online products (versus 29 percent of the 53.5 million U.S. Internet users). Of these, 28 percent place orders only for recognized brand names and 22 percent buy online only from already known High Street retailers.

To create an enlarged Internet business environment, the U.K. government introduced Distance Selling regulations, which took effect on October 31, 2000. The U.K. consumer benefits now from a seven-day cooling off period after buying on the Internet (i.e., he or she has seven days to cancel the order), and the credit card companies have agreed to take on the risk of fraudulent selling. Therefore, the United Kingdom now has a selling environment comparable to that of the United States'.

The U.K. government is also seeking to improve consumer information about buying online but also agrees that only light regulation is needed.

The Government is committed to a light touch regulatory approach to e-commerce. We agree that any further consumer protection regulation would not be helpful and that it could stifle the growth of UK e-commerce as well as proving to be unforeseeable. Only businesses themselves can win consumer products and services in a secure environment—and by respecting their customers' privacy. (Better Regulation Task Force 2000, 21).

Even if such documents are already available, however, (e.g., "Shopping on the Internet—Better Safe Than Sorry," issued in October 2000 by the Trading Standards Institute, and a research survey carried out by the National Consumers Council, "E-commerce and Consumer Protection," August 2000), U.K. consumers are not aware of their rights.

To improve consumer confidence in the Internet, the government also promotes hallmark schemes:

Self regulatory (industry led) and co-regulatory (Government in partnership with industry) trust or hallmark schemes are developing to support consumer confidence in on-line shopping. A hallmark scheme operates by allowing businesses which meet its consumer protection standards to display their seal or emblem on their website. Although consumers may already trust established brands, this kind of hallmark scheme may help to enhance consumer confidence in smaller, less well known e-businesses. (Better Regulation Task Force 2000, 22)

Building Trust for Small- and Medium-Sized Enterprises In 2000, about 70 to 85 percent of e-commerce was B2B in the United Kingdom. Large companies and the biggest retailers are the primary drivers of this market. One characteristic of B2B is that the Internet does not alter the business relationship between suppliers and buyers. In the B2B market segment, online and offline deals are complementary and are based on accumulated trust. Moreover, the largest businesses have organized to negotiate agreements across countries by creating a robust Internet business framework, the Global Business Dialogue on electronic commerce (GBDe), launched under the initiative of Martin Bangemann, the European commissar, who asked for an international e-forum where world business leaders would gather and discuss appropriate ways to reinforce international cooperation in the online e-economy. The first roundtable discussion was hosted in Paris on June 29, 1998. Subsequently, the prominent chairpersons of world companies active in Internet business made the GBDe official in New York on January 14, 1999. The purpose of the GBDe is to limit business to minimum Internet regulation and above all to avoid disparate regulations, which entails harmonizing regulations where necessary. The GBDe counts 72 CEO and board members from companies all over the world. "The GBDe's mission is to work in co-operation with businesses, governments, nongovernmental organizations, private foundations, consumer organizations, and multilateral institutions to broaden the involvement of key stakeholders in creating an environment to ensure that e-commerce can reach its full economic and social potential" (⟨www.gbde.org⟩).

In contrast to large businesses, SMEs have entered the Internet economy cautiously. Small- and medium-sized enterprises sell offline to chosen outlets and locations. In the online market, however, consumers are scattered across countries. They can access their website and place orders. If an order goes awry, an e-consumer can sue an SME from its home country, making the latter liable to overseas legislation. An SME might thus have to enter litigation in countries where it has no foothold. Actually, SMEs have little knowledge about restrictions on their sales. For example, they are legally entitled to offer their products and services in a reduced number of countries.

To the promote Internet and ease the access to the web for SMEs, the U.K. government has created a ministerial position, the minister for small business and e-commerce, which has been entrusted to Patricia Hewitt. The first initiatives of the minister have been to improve information about e-commerce regulation. The plan aims at gathering available information that is dispersed among various bodies onto one website of the Department of Trade and Industry and to make it especially dedicated to SMEs.

France

Since the launch of PAGSI, the Ministry of Economy, Finance and Industry (MINEFI) has undertaken several initiatives. A political milestone was the Francis Lorentz report (Lorentz 1998). In September 1997, Lorentz was commissioned to report on e-commerce. The minister of finance at the time, Dominique Strauss-Kahn, referred to it as the "Lorentz process" (Strauss-Kahn 1998). This process relied first on extensive consultation between the different departments of the ministry and the private sector, and second, on directly receiving feedback from Internet users by creating a website and an Internet forum. Based on these consultations, several actions were suggested in March 1998. Most centered on the safety of transactions, support for entrepreneurship and SMEs by reducing red tape, making venture capital available, giving support to exports by offering free access to information on foreign markets from embassies, and creating one-stop shopping for financial assistance to exporters.

In many respects, the French experience is similar to the United Kingdom's, with identical stress placed on consumer protection and confidence and the use of e-government policy to promote the Internet (SESSI 2000). Still, perhaps as can be expected, a more radical management is observed. For example, on November 27, 2000, a supervisory body for e-commerce was created and directly attached to the SMEs and consumer affairs minister—Ministre des PME, au commerce, à l'Artisanat, et à la Consommation. Specially trained civil servants, a sort of police surveillance group, are responsible for keeping close watch over e-commerce and for handling e-mail complaints from consumers and SMEs. This surveillance is, however, conducted by only 10 public servants and is limited, as these individuals can monitor only so much.

Two other points are worth noting. First, the Internet is considered a public service that merits free access in schools and in public areas and the creation of Internet kiosks to provide access for people that do not have a personal computer. The underlying principle is that all French citizens should have access to an e-mail address. France has nevertheless found it hard to convince its European counterparts that it is necessary to make the Internet a universal service. Incidentally, early studies on the use of Internet show that access to the Internet does not guarantee use and that use of Internet kiosks is disappointing. This universal service policy will probably reinforce the dominant position of the historical operator, France Telecom.

Second, the French government is attempting to provide political guidance regarding the Internet. It is measuring and monitoring Internet growth and the changes it introduces in the economy through a "Tableau de Bord de l'Innovation"—the economic dashboard of innovation. It has selected eighteen key indicators on the development of technological innovation and grouped them into four key areas: new capital, new entrepreneurs, new technologies, and new uses of technology (SESSI 2001). The tableau de bord has been in existence for two years. It enables France to benchmark international Internet expansion.

Finally, short-term, medium-term, and long-term strategies toward the Internet have not received much attention. PAGSI hoped to promote and disseminate a framework for developing NTICs throughout the administration. It hoped to use an adviser from each minister's office to coordinate and formulate development projects. The end result of the PAGSI process has materialized through the Thierry Carcenac report on e-administration (2001). It proposes a four-step approach: (1) to create as many websites as necessary to enable a direct dialogue between the government and citizens; (2) to use websites as a substitute for usual administrative procedures (electronic sending of administrative forms); (3) to fully integrate administrative information systems to websites in order to enable the complete management of administrative procedures on the web without any external assistance; (4) to create one-stop shopping for all administrative procedures. Steps 3 and 4 would be regrouped in the future under a specific program, the Programme Unifié Gouvernemental pour la Naissance d'une Administration Citoyenne (PUGNACE, which means pugnacious and says much about the determination of the French government!). Hence, although not markedly different from the Blair proposals, the French program for promoting the Internet emphasized the Internet as a public good. Under the French perspective, the Internet is too important to be left to market forces. Therefore it is up to the State to give impetus and direction in order to ensure that French citizens will benefit equally from the new technology.

European Initiatives
The European Commission has put forward an action plan for the Internet (Commission 2000). This plan is consistent with Member States' objectives and supports their pre-existing arrangements. It has initiated an e-confidence forum to follow up on this plan (⟨http://econfidence. jrc.it/⟩). Many of its other initiatives have been more specific to its own concerns.

For instance, it has attempted to resolve consumer problems with cross-border transactions. E-commerce usually involves business transactions of low value. Legal fees to file a complaint and sue are disproportionate with the financial value of the transaction. Therefore, attempts have been made at the international level to develop alternative dispute resolution, ADR, which proposes quick and cheap settlement of disputes. At the European level, a European extra-judicial network (EEJ-Net) has been established. It entails setting up clearinghouses in each Member State to facilitate consumer access to the country ADR where the product was purchased.

In this area, there is strong cooperation between Europe and the United States to define common principles and rules. On December 18, 2000, the Washington summit issued a joint declaration on ADR (Statement of the U.S. and the European Union on Building Consumer Confidence in e-Commerce and the Role of Alternative Dispute Resolution).

There are also concerns that personal information will be misused. This issue is more complex to deal with in Europe than it is in the United States, as European legislation is more stringent. (See the discussion in the chapter 13.) An agreement has been reached, however, that allows for transfer of personal data from Europe to the United States only if the U.S. company has signed an agreement to protect data. The European Commission is also about to launch a "smart card" program, and it emphasized that it will be more active in cooperating against cybercrime.

To help researchers and students, the European Union will finance high-speed networks to connect to the worldwide grid. Europe will also massively invest in the development of faster Internet backbones. Furthermore, it will financially support the creation of software interfaces and innovative forms of services such as learning through the Internet.

In terms of services, health systems have been high on the European political agenda. The national health service of Member States is rigid and costly. Europe hopes to use new information technology to develop electronic health services, which will be closely monitored and supervised. Different Internet tools will improve patient and doctor information. The e-health industry already accounts for 6 percent of the IT market.

Content circulating on the Web is another concern in Europe, particularly as it involves copyrights and property rights. There is little cooperation, however, among Member States and between cultural and teaching institutions on what the appropriate position toward copyright should be. Also, relatively little online information and content are available.

Finally, transportation is a main focus. Europe is experiencing congestion in all transport infrastructures, as well as problems with safety and a lack of new services. Massive investments are required, particularly with regard to a Single Sky for Europe, Galileo, Rail, and urban transport services. Member States have to ensure that the barriers to a single European transport market have been removed. The Internet can help such efforts. For example, in rail transport, the Internet can be used as a booking mechanism for freight, thus giving information about the availability of trains, their position, congested areas, and so on, in real time.

European initiatives have therefore been manifold but rather than stemming from an explicit ex ante plan, it has been a matter primarily of searching for support and intervention wherever possible. It has been as if the European initiatives would consist in reacting—finding ways of settling disputes, of dealing with property rights—and in inventing all possible important uses for the Internet—education, health, transport. In these efforts, the commission has been preaching for a one-go move toward the Internet but without clear understanding about the best way and resources to achieve that goal.

Impact of European Policies on the Internet Economy

Member States governments and the European Commission are not convinced that public policies affect the Internet economy. Bauer, Berne, and Maitland (2000) have sought to explain why the Internet economy is so much more robust in the United States than it is in Europe. They have identified three main causes:

Structural Factors: Income (GDP per capita); education and computer literacy; market size; local/accessible content; existing competing systems; and cultural factors.

Access Conditions: Regulatory framework; access business model; and telecom infrastructure and tariffs.

Corporate Strategies: Telecommunication companies; ISPs; and business firms.

Figures about the European Internet economy are frequently misleading, as average data do not account for large discrepancies among Member States. By the end of 1999, Greece reported four Internet hosts per thousand inhabitants, whereas Finland had 91. Two European countries, Denmark and Sweden, have a penetration rate that is comparable to the U.S. figure of 50 percent, whereas Greece's rate is less than 10 percent, and the larger Member States' rates are about 25 percent (Commission 2000).

According to Bauer, Berne, and Maitland (2000) these differences are due largely to structural factors, with Internet penetration and GDP per capita being significantly correlated. Another relevant factor is the potential Internet market size of each European Member State, which in turn relates to cultural factors. The Internet expanded in the United States from an English language base. The United Kingdom, Ireland, and Northern European Anglo-Saxon countries were de facto integrated to the English Internet community. Southern European countries were in this regard at a disadvantage because they have smaller, more fragmented markets in which there is less opportunity for economies of scale and network effects in the production of Internet content and software dissemination. France itself has been distinctive. It had the Minitel prior to the Internet and had to shift from an old technology to a new one that has involved additional costs and certainly handicapped Internet growth (see Benghozi and Licoppe, chapter 5).

European public policies toward the Internet are therefore one among several drivers of the European Internet economy. In the Bauer, Berne, and Maitland analysis, a second set of factors includes access conditions, and a third involves corporate strategies. This categorization of factors is probably a bit blunt. In many cases, there are interactions between public policies, access regulation, and corporate strategies. As Bauer, Berne, and Maitland point out, the most important European ISPs are subsidiaries of historical incumbent telecom companies. The new Internet economy is more an outgrowth of the old economy than it is a stand alone phenomenon. Member States where Internet penetration has been the most successful are also those where liberalization of fixed telephony has been the most advanced; Sweden is at the forefront of both liberalization and Internet penetration (Cohen and Henry 1997; Henry 1997; Anderson 2001).

Conclusion

In contrast to the United States, which has focused on creating markets (see chapter 13), the European Union has focused on somewhat hands-on policies that have been an opportunity to foster a more unified Europe. Hands-on policies could be thought of as paradoxical as Internet growth is primarily about spontaneous decentralized initiatives. However, the interventionist stance has been vindicated by the existing gap with the United States, the failure to develop high-speed telecommunications networks, and the significant variation in Internet penetration among Member States, particularly between the north and south of Europe.

The hands-on policies refer to regulations, directives, and government plans, which have been put forward at the European and Member States levels. The European Commission and the Member States have used all the political levers. They have intervened in all areas where there was scope for Internet growth. In particular, the EU Commission has created a transverse directorate, the DG Infso, dedicated to Internet. The DG Infso has targeted all economic sectors (education, health, etc.). The strange thing is that rather than obvious success, it has led to a catalog of measures that has not been supported by a clear-cut rationale for embracing the Internet cause. For instance, the European B2B growth is comparable to the United States. It has been spurred by companies and decentralized initiatives. The European policies have had little to do with this success. Business-to-Consumer is lagging and Internet use is in Europe above all dedicated to e-mail. There is no clear indication of European policy success in this regard. So how far have European policies and differences in national policies mattered?

We have considered that the hands-on policies consisted of two political streams, regulation and facilitation. To sum up, it appears that the disappointing European Internet performance has primarily been due to a European regulatory failure in the telecommunications sector.

With regard to regulatory policies, a first target was to properly address the deficit in high-speed telecommunications network. The

European Commission has striven to impose a common framework on access, but it came late and has so far failed to materialize a clear outcome. Telecom markets are driven by national monopolies that have footholds in the various Member States and reciprocal interests in maintaining their respective home market share dominance. End-user prices vary significantly across European countries and remain particularly high with poor quality connection regarding speed and reliability. High prices and poor quality are the major impediments to Internet growth.

Particularly striking for the years to come is the case of the next Universal Mobile Telecommunications System mobile telephony generation. It was assumed that the so-called third generation mobile technology would allow Europe to leapfrog the United States on the Internet. But the UMTS licences have been allocated nationally under different procedures. In many countries, such as Germany, the United Kingdom, the Netherlands, and France, these licenses were auctioned at high prices, contributing to the pessimism that the operators have the financial incentives to make the complementary investments to initiate service. These national policies missed an effective central European regulatory framework to avoid divergence and create coherence. Therefore, it is expected that future high prices to end users and increased divergence in telecom prices in Europe will work contrary to Internet growth.

The second point about regulatory policies applies to the content and behavior of the parties taking part in Internet growth. Regulators find it difficult to deal with the cross-sectoral nature of the e-economy. This difficulty is noticeable in the attempt the European Commission and National Competition agencies made to define relevant markets related to Internet competitive issues. To be effective, competition policy requires narrow delineation of the different markets. In other words, competition policy illustrates the difficulty of isolating and assessing the cross-cutting effects of the Internet on the economy. But even on these grounds, only recently did the European Commission move toward organizing regulatory convergence by means of directive and guidelines.

Finally, as for facilitating policies, it has been said that they were second to access, which is the engine of Internet growth. At equal access conditions, they create confidence and determine the "tipping point" (Gladwell 2000) where the final consumer starts making intense use of the technology. A good number of initiatives have been launched to reach that tipping point. Governments of the Member States and the European Commission have developed similar approaches targeting e-government, support to SMEs, easing access to venture capital, and so on. Facilitating policies cannot be assessed in isolation, since they require other complements in order to be effective (see chapter 2). Besides, there is frequently a lack of available metrics as assessments entail quality measurements. For example, the French government has recently launched an administrative fiscal plan on the Internet. Each year the French have to fill out a fiscal form for inland revenue purposes. The administration aim was to make the form available and to allow French citizens access to the form directly on the Internet. But it fell short of achieving that goal. Eventually the only form that was made available on the Internet was one that could be downloaded and printed at the household premises. The French carry on having to fill their forms manually and sending them by back by post! In short, the Internet came less as a revolution than as an set of incoherent advances that varied widely by sector and, contrary to the claim of a unified Europe, by national arena.

13

Non-market Strategies and Regulation in the United States

Dennis A. Yao

The development of the Internet, Internet technologies, and electronic commerce has exhibited path dependence in which governmental regulation—or lack of it—has played a major role. Sometimes the role has been direct, as in the development of the Minitel in France, the creation of a European mobile telecommunications standard, or the impact of regulatory discretion in Sweden in fostering Ericsson's growth and technological strength. Other times the impact has been indirect: India's pool of software engineers is an outgrowth of an education policy that stressed higher education in engineering, German industry's relative focus on more predictable technologies was arguably influenced by German labor policy, and, of course, the initial development of Internet technologies was funded by the United States Defense Department.

This chapter provides a base for understanding how regulation works in the United States and what can be expected with respect to future regulation of electronic commerce. The effects of previous regulatory policy, especially on telecommunications, have been covered in earlier chapters. Although the discussion is U.S.-centric, the analysis suggests why the United States is often at logger-heads with other regulatory bodies, such as with the European Union in reference to privacy policy. Two perspectives are emphasized in my analysis: regulation is part of a system that includes self-regulatory actions, and the design and implementation of this system is open to political influence.

The regulation of the Internet and electronic commerce—where the new economy hits the old regulation—covers a panoply of topics, public and private interests, and players. Rather than offering a broad survey, this chapter focuses on regulatory interventions involving protection of consumers against online marketing misrepresentations (e.g., deceptive advertising) and misuse of consumer information (e.g., invasion of privacy). These interventions involve a broad spectrum of problems and solutions relating to consumer protection in cyberspace, offer simple, but instructive, examples of the interplay among market forces, technology, and regulation, and highlight the differences between the conventional and e-commerce worlds.

There are three main sections to this chapter. The first section provides a brief overview of U.S. regulation and its institutions, focusing primarily on consumer protection and the Federal Trade Commission (FTC). The second section has a normative flavor. It assumes that the political will and control is available to legislate and implement a desired form of regulation. What is at issue is the appropriate form of regulation. The third section considers the political economy of regulation and its implications for the outcome of government attempts to regulate electronic commerce. The section will also consider international conflicts over e-commerce regulations.

A Brief Overview of Federal Regulation in the United States

Regulation of markets in the United States takes place at all levels of government; the jurisdiction of the various regulatory agencies is often overlapping. In this section I focus on the federal level, noting, however, that state regulators frequently have similar regulatory powers and that regulatory laws also frequently allow for a private right of action whereby injured private parties (e.g., firms or buyers) can initiate lawsuits within the judicial system.

At the federal level, regulation is conducted by both executive branch agencies (e.g., Environmental Protection Agency, Antitrust Division of the Department of Justice, Food and Drug Administration) whose leaders serve at the pleasure of the president, and by independent regulatory agencies (e.g., Federal Communications Commission, Federal Trade Commission, Securities and Exchange Commission) whose leaders are nominated by the president with the consent of the Senate, but once in office, are (theoretically) independent of the executive, legislative, and judicial branches of the U.S. government. Congress determines the budgets of these agencies and exercises oversight.

Agency regulatory powers are derived from laws passed by Congress. Although some laws are quite detailed, it is also common for the laws to leave considerable discretion to the agencies in terms of the implementation. For example, Section 5 of the Federal Trade Commission Act gives the commission the power to prevent "unfair methods of competition" (e.g., antitrust and competition issues) and "unfair or deceptive acts and practices in or affecting commerce" (e.g., deceptive marketing). Such broad statutory language is not uncommon in common law countries where law is often made through judicial decisions.

Typically, U.S. regulatory agencies will issue rules (with the force of law) that flesh out the authorizing law. The rule-making procedure is subject to an administrative process that ensures transparency and allows for limited public participation. Resulting rules are often challenged in the courts as exceeding authority granted by the underlying law or as conflicting with other rules and laws. Independent regulatory commissions are unusual in typically having a judicial function through which cases are brought before an administrative law judge within the agency itself, with appeal possible to the full commission and then, perhaps, to a federal appeals court.

The U.S. FTC is a key regulator in the marketing practices area. The agency has two major missions: a competition (antitrust or antimonopoly) mission and a consumer protection (marketing practices, advertising, etc.) mission. Protecting or enhancing consumer welfare is the underlying goal of the agency and the basic philosophical starting point is a belief that a properly functioning market will produce the best outcome for consumers. Federal Trade Commission Commissioner Andrew Strenio (1990, 147) states:

I am market oriented. In my view, markets should be allowed to work their magic to the maximum amount possible. The government usually should intervene only to the minimum extent necessary to correct market failures. Even then, the government should intervene only when such intervention is not likely to be counterproductive. . . . From that perspective, I am convinced that the analytical methods employed at the Commission are roughly correct.

The FTC's regulatory approach in the consumer protection area has evolved toward an information and consumer choice perspective—where possible, mandatory information disclosure is preferred over minimum quality standards. The FTC expects that this information will lead consumers to make good choices and that these choices will induce manufacturers to produce consumer-desired products at appropriate prices and qualities. Economics-based assessments are typically most influential for selecting enforcement targets and for developing remedies, though an explicit cost-benefit criterion is a key element to finding a law violation under the FTC's "unfairness" power. This market-oriented philosophy is also consistent with the American approach to competition policy that emphasizes one-time structural interventions (e.g., preventing an acquisition that might reduce competition) into the market.

Of the regulatory agencies in the United States, the FTC and the Antitrust Division of the Department of Justice are arguably the most market oriented. They frequently submit market competition-based advocacy comments on draft rules of other regulatory agencies and are usually on the market side of policy disputes with sister agencies such as the Department of Transportation and the Food and Drug Administration. Nonetheless, the policies of American regulators and politicians (holding subject matter constant) are typically more trusting of the market and less trusting of governmental intervention than their non-American counterparts (Swire and Litan 1998).

This may be due in part to the historical development of the business-government relationship in the United States. McCraw (1984) argues that the American adversarial business-government relationship—and hence a distrust of government and perhaps a greater faith in the market —developed because U.S. business, unlike their counterparts in Europe, became powerful when the U.S. federal government was relatively weak. Business, therefore, was not only forced to cooperate with government; it attempted to resist government interference in the market. Lack of good working relationships led to distrust of regulators and regulatory solutions (Vogel 1981). As a result, government is not typically viewed as a partner by business.

In addition, American concern with transparency and legal process makes the regulatory system slower and more unwieldy. Further, it is often argued that the U.S. government is less able to attract personnel as talented as the bureaucracies in countries such as France and Japan where government service is thought to be more highly respected. Given the relative competitiveness of most American markets, then, it is not surprising that the United States is more inclined to favor market solutions while resisting calls for government-led industrial policies.

Market Ecology of E-commerce

Markets function within a legal, governmental, and social infrastructure that is often taken for granted. Critical elements of this commercial infrastructure include property rights (e.g., the right to private property, exclusion of others from using patented intellectual property, etc.) and contract enforcement. This infrastructure consists of local, national, and regional legal institutions (e.g., U.S. Federal Trade Commission), norms governing the proper conduct of business in various countries, industries, or membership groups (e.g., industry "codes"), and institutions such as industry self-regulatory groups (e.g., TRUSTe Program).

With respect to the legal infrastructure of conventional commerce, most countries have formal consumer protection laws that make fraudulent and deceptive acts and practices illegal. The laws are typically enforced by a governmental agency, though it is common to allow for private enforcement as well.[1] Various industries also have self-regulatory codes for marketing conduct (e.g., television network broadcasters) or self-regulatory institutions (e.g., National Advertising Division).

Consumers in most countries are protected to varying degrees in their e-commerce transactions by consumer protection laws that exist for conventional transactions. Deceptive marketing representations in e-commerce have much in common with those in conventional markets. However, differences between conventional and e-commerce markets affect how well consumers are protected in cyberspace. These differences include the availability and organization of relevant product (or service) information, applicability and efficacy of various political jurisdiction rules and laws, and boundaries or constraints that partition or limit transactions in cyberspace. Further, underlying technology and production factors as well as regulatory factors create a different context for e-commerce and have the potential to lead to substantially different market outcomes for a given regulatory and legal infrastructure. Electronic commerce markets may therefore function differently than conventional markets.

In this section, I begin with a quick examination of marketing practice-oriented market imperfections in conventional markets. A market imperfections approach (see, for example, Baron 2000) focuses on the reasons that an unregulated market will not perform efficiently and ways in which government intervention might mitigate the identified inefficiencies. Next I explore how the electronic commerce marketplace differs with respect to these market imperfections, look at the incentives and prospects for industry self-regulation and formal governmental regulation, and consider how the pieces work as a system. Finally, I examine privacy issues and then comment on regulation's general impact on electronic commerce.

Marketing Representations and Information Market Imperfections

In recent years there has been an increasing reliance on market mechanisms and market-based thinking at the business-government interface of the U.S. economy. This tendency is most evident in new laws deregulating industries such as electric power and telecommunications. It also appears in the exercise of regulatory discretion by federal and state agencies with respect to less market-oriented laws. United States policy with respect to the use of market thinking is inconsistent, however, and in many policy areas (e.g., social regulation such as environmental protection, drug and product safety regulation) economic cost-benefit and market imperfection analyses often take a secondary role.

My starting point is to presume that markets have general efficiency properties. I then analyze where this efficiency presumption is likely to fail, examine market imperfections associated with marketing and privacy in conventional markets, and see how those failures are exacerbated or mitigated in cyberspace. This market-based approach is helpful in identifying problems that might justify intervention and provides a useful baseline against which to compare intervention strategies.

Although this idealized analysis of the unregulated e-commerce market does not directly comport with the regulatory analysis used by U.S. governmental officials in practice, such analyses are important intellectual bases on which the commonly held faith of American and FTC policymakers in a lightly regulated market have been developed. This market orientation is evident in a comment by FTC commissioner Christine Varney (1996):

> I approach this issue with three working assumptions. First, government should step in to regulate only when there has been an identifiable market failure or where an important public policy goal cannot be achieved without government intervention. Second, the pace of change in the information industry is unprecedented. Government regulation, on the other hand, moves very slowly, and the predictive skills of government agencies are notoriously limited.... Third, I believe that the electronic medium itself offers new opportunities for consumer education and empowerment, which, in turn increases the likelihood that self-regulatory regimes can be effective.

Other supporting elements are a belief that less-regulated markets are more innovative, a general distrust in government efficiency and government restraint, and fears that rent-seeking will dictate the legislative outcome.

The market-based approach begins with consideration of an unfettered market. A market imperfection based on transaction costs of obtaining information exists when buyers lack important information that would have altered their purchase choices and buyers choose not to obtain this information because of location, acquisition, and/or processing costs. Marketing, in theory, can mitigate this problem. For example, a buyer does not know if frequent consumption of a ready-to-eat cereal product will have health benefits, yet such information may be decisive in the choice of that cereal. The seller benefits from supplying this information to consumers.

But sellers have the incentive to provide biased information or worse —reintroducing information problems as buyers now must determine whether the information is truthful. Public policy may mandate a standard for truthful representations. A good standard will balance the benefits of deterring representations that provide deceptive information or make unsubstantiated claims with the costs of deterring the marketing of valuable purchase-relevant information (see, for example, Ippolito 1984).

To what extent will the market self-correct, absent regulation? The first defense against misrepresentation is an educated consumer. The easier it is for consumers to determine the truth of a representation, the more likely that market responses by consumers will prevent firms from making deceptive representations. Unfortunately, many representations about products are difficult for a consumer to verify (e.g., the cancer reducing effects of eating whole grain cereals) and it is with those products that the potential for market self-correction via direct consumer response is the smallest. Consumers will also adapt their purchase behavior if they know that they cannot rely on vendor representations. They may rely on vendor reputation (e.g., Sony) or perhaps retailer reputation (e.g., Tiffany). Consumers will chat more with their friends about products.

Second, vendors can provide guarantees or warranties on performance. But here, too, there are often issues of verifiability, buyer moral hazard, and costs of dispute resolution. The actions of competitors or other parties can also partially police deceptive marketing representations. Competitors may directly or indirectly correct misrepresentations; retailers may screen the products they sell or provide various guarantees or information that exceeds that provided by the manufacturer alone (e.g., Sears).

Information can also be supplied by third-party information intermediaries who may review (e.g., *Consumer Reports, Wine Spectator, Nutrition Action Newsletter*, user reviews), or rate (e.g., an environmental seal, Good Housekeeping seal, social investing) some aspect of the quality of a given product or service. Third-party reviews may, however, be underprovided in the market because users may benefit from the review without paying the reviewer for it and consumers may lack confidence in the accuracy of the reviewer. This situation is most likely for services (products) that are quite complex and very individual specific.

Thus, there are numerous incentives for self-interested market participants to partially or fully discipline deceptive marketing representations. Yet deceptive representations are still made in the marketplace, suggesting a role for self-regulation and/or governmental regulation.

Representations in Cyberspace: A More Efficient Market?

What makes electronic commerce different with respect to product misrepresentations? First, the apparent and sometimes actual virtualness of vendors creates consumer concerns about the virtuousness of the retailers on the Internet. Second, there is more than an order of magnitude difference in the availability of information on suppliers—and on buyers—in the online world. Information collection and flow, though, is a two-way street: ready information about suppliers eases information problems for buyers and information about individual buyers improves marketing, but collection and availability of buyer information can be exploited by suppliers and can invade a buyer's privacy.[2]

Unlike local retailers that signal their expectations about longevity by location-specific investments in physical structures, an untested virtual cybermerchant—one that subcontracts almost all of the activities of the business—may appear similar to a long-established vertically integrated merchant. The lack of physical signals about a vendor is, of course, not a new situation: telemarketing and mail order industries have similar characteristics.

In the conventional marketplace, information bearing on purchase decisions suffers from being too costly to find, acquire, and digest relative to its value and may not be timely. In cyberspace it is technologically and economically feasible to collect considerable review information in a timely fashion. The ready availability of such information alters the context of the consumer's reception to a vendor's online representation. Retail sites can reassure the wary by offering links to third-party evaluation sites with relevant information on consumer experiences. The market has also responded to consumer concerns about reliability with third-party seal programs (e.g., BBBOnLine's reliability seal, TRUSTe seal). As reliability seals and links to evaluation organizations become accepted, even required ways of doing business, consumers may shun merchants who lack such reassurance.

Electronic commerce without regulation, therefore, operates in an environment sufficiently different from real space that the same outcomes with respect to deceptive or fraudulent marketing representations may not obtain. The web offers a means through which careful consumers can make more informed purchase decisions and can penalize vendors who misrepresent themselves or their products. In some ways, the cyberspace market will likely do a better job at policing deception than the conventional market. Whether enough consumers will take advantage of this information to reduce substantially the level of misrepresentations is an open question.

Self-regulation: Marketing Representations

Where individual firm or consumer actions to cure market ills fall short, incentives may exist for industry or cross-industry self-regulatory action.

Industry self-regulation has sometimes proven valuable in policing deception. In the United States, the Council of Better Business Bureaus runs a well-regarded voluntary cross-industry advertising self-regulation program via its National Advertising Division (NAD), Children's Advertising Review Unit (CARU), and the National Advertising Review Board (NARB). Organized in 1971, the NAD investigates about 150 deceptive advertising cases annually in response to its own monitoring efforts and complaints from consumers and businesses (Council of Better Business Bureaus 2000). The investigations are rapid, rely on voluntary cooperation of the affected party, and detailed decisions are made public but are not binding. The NAD standards follow that of the current national advertising law with additional consideration of good industry practice.

The NAD self-regulation program may be the poster child of the self-regulatory world, but many believe its effectiveness requires the regulatory backbone of law and enforcement agencies (i.e., the FTC).[3] Voluntary compliance is in large part due to the formal regulatory threat—NAD refers cases to the FTC—and to the legitimacy that is given to the standard employed in the self-regulatory process by the existing law. Thus, the success story is arguably one of co-regulation rather than one of self-regulation.

Forces favoring self-regulation of marketing representations in cyberspace include the substantial interest among many firms in creating some level of transnational uniformity and a desire to preempt problematic formal regulation. Self-regulation also has advantages because, at least in principle, it is not confined to national boundaries, implementation involves fewer political and legal obstacles, it can be more flexible, and development involves informed players.[4] This is presumably one reason the European Union, whose members often disagree on consumer issues, has begun to push a co-regulation model. Against self-regulation is the likely heterogeneity of interests and views of firms in cyberspace, the relative lack of a tradition of self-regulation in many countries, and, in many geographical locations, the lack of strong law enforcement institutions.

Because self-regulation is voluntary, it is more likely to be successful when there is a strong majority supporting a particular standard; this majority is more likely in the shadow of an existing law.[5] Absent a consensus-forcing law, a mix of firms possessing different resources and strategies will have difficulty finding agreement. The potential for disagreement among sellers in cyberspace is arguably greater than in real space. Start-up firms often rely more heavily on marketing representations, especially when competing against firms whose real space reputation is transferable to cyberspace. These start-ups are less likely to have experience with marketing representation standards, probably rely less on lawyers, and can therefore be expected to see the world differently than the established firms. Finally, with political and cultural geography removed as market isolating factors, we can expect substantial variation across firms with respect to their consumer protection-related attitudes and actions. The problem is exacerbated with legally gray area choices that have differential impacts across industry participants. Those who are disadvantaged are unlikely to participate unless the market forces them to do so. Alternatively, if penalties for violating the self-regulatory code are small, such firms may join, but not comply.

Self-regulation has emerged (1) when the growth of that industry was perceived as being undermined by consumer mistrust, and (2) under the threat of regulation or because existing regulations have deficiencies. For example, the Direct Marketing Association (DMA) has gotten almost all of its more than two thousand members to agree to its Privacy Promise program, which includes opt-out notice and choice (Swindel 2000). This behavior is perhaps unsurprising even when viewed through the lens of collective action theory. The negotiation and set-up of the system does not require substantial participation. The real problem may emerge in the compliance and enforcement stage where, for example, firms may be reluctant to contribute funds for enforcement and may care little for how their possible lack of compliance will impact the overall self-regulatory program. Along these lines, one early problem faced by NAD in its conventional advertising self-regulatory program was the tendency of some challenged advertisers to drag out proceedings until the challenged ad became moot (McGrew 1991).[6]

Given the need for self-regulation and some positive experiences with it, self-regulatory efforts against deceptive marketing have a chance for some limited success on a worldwide basis, especially given a background of formal consumer protection laws. A basic problem is that there are significant differences worldwide in existing legal standards (and penalties) and e-vendors have lower costs of moving than do conventional vendors. But even if a substantial fraction of vendors worldwide do not participate, a self-regulatory system will provide benefits within a combination self-regulation and formal regulation system. Both U.S. and EU government agencies have worked informally with self-regulatory groups in a "co-regulation" mode.[7]

The importance of near-complete coverage is arguably reduced in cyberspace because technological rules make it possible for a firm to set up a "gated community" that limits vendor membership to merchants that subscribe to a self-regulatory scheme involving marketing representations, reliability, and privacy standards (Lessig 1999b). Such a community might be attractive to consumers and conceivably these gated communities might gain substantial market share. Of course, such communities only protect those that choose to be protected and would not be seen as a complete solution in political jurisdictions with paternalistic leanings. Nonetheless, this is an intriguing possibility.

Governmental Regulation of Marketing Representations

Marketing law for conventional commerce applies in cyberspace. In this regard, the United States, like Europe, did not view the Internet as substantially different than traditional markets. (See the discussion in Dumez and Jeunemaître, chapter 12 in this volume.) In the online world, misrepresentations can be made in the same manner as in the offline world. The context is different, but dealing with such differences has long been a part of the advertising landscape. Consider the differences among print advertising, television advertising, and telemarketing. The U.S. FTC, for example, employs the same principles to online advertising as to other advertising, though it provides additional guidelines for non-deceptive qualifying disclosures in online ads.

The basic question with marketing representations is whether consumers are misled by the claims. Claims that are taken by a consumer depend on a host of factors, including the context, the consumers experience and gullibility, and so on. A literally truthful advertisement, for example, may be read by some small but significant proportion of the population to make an "implied claim" that is untrue. Or a claim might lack "adequate" substantiation. Thus, what constitutes a deceptive representation involves judgment calls on who will be deceived (which varies by person and by culture), what proportion of the population should be protected, and the standard of evidence necessary to substantiate a claim (see, for example, Yao and Vecchi 1992). This legal analysis does not appear to directly reflect economic trade-offs or market imperfections analyses. Those considerations are, however, apparent in the regulatory discretion the FTC employs in selecting cases for prosecution and in negotiating settlements.

Countries vary in how far they are willing to go to protect the more gullible consumers from being misled. In the United States, consumers acting "reasonably" are protected; in Australia, consumers of "less then average intelligence" but not those who are "unusually stupid" are protected; and some countries such as Italy have taken an almost caveat emptor approach (Petty 1994). There are also disagreements in suitable remedies for violations of the law. This heterogeneous starting point makes international harmonization of laws difficult. Harmonization of cyberspace laws internationally also complicates domestic harmonization between real space and cyberspace laws (Goldsmith 1998).

Regulatory, Technological, and Political-social Systems
Having explored the pieces of the regulatory system, it is now useful to think about how these pieces relate. Market self-correction, self-regulation, and regulation are endogenous to one another. The absence of self-regulation may not indicate an inherent impossibility but may merely reflect a lack of need. These systems, too, are part of larger systems that develop and apply relevant technologies and that control the use of such technologies.

Markets respond to a lack of formal regulation by, for example, developing alternative consumer assurance institutions such as third-party reviewers or firm reputations. Firms respond to private litigation threats. Consumers adjust their purchasing behavior, becoming more skeptical absent effective formal regulation or more credulous given faith in an existing regulatory regime. The effectiveness of self-regulation may depend on the existence of formal regulation, whereas effective market mechanisms or self-regulation will sometimes preempt strong formal regulation.

The endogeneity of consumer beliefs about the truth of representations to the perceived regulatory regime poses particular problems in the cyberspace environment. In cyberspace, vendors located in a country different than the buyer may be subject to more lax substantiation requirements. Some consumers may incorrectly believe that the real space rules also hold for all vendors in cyberspace. Because implied claims also depend on the cultural context, it may be difficult for a vendor to avoid deceiving some portion of its potential customer base even when it is fully compliant with the laws of a relatively strict country.

Effectiveness of regulation depends not only on law but the implementation and enforcement of that law. The same law implemented by a more interventionist agency would have different consequences than one implemented by a conservative agency. Similarly, a law that gives legal rights to consumers might be expected to give headaches to firms in proportion to the underlying litigiousness of the relevant society.

To understand consumer protection in cyberspace it is also critical to consider the interrelationships between technology and regulatory systems. Internet technology poses critical challenges quite different than that of the offline world. Many commentators (e.g., Johnson and Post 1997) have stressed that electronic commerce lacks borders. Some argue that attempts by countries to strictly regulate such commerce are likely to be unsuccessful because retailers can always move to jurisdictions that allow more lax practices.[8] What is clear is that the current lack of borders combined with the enormous growth in worldwide electronic commerce has greatly increased the friction between nation-based consumer protection systems using different principles and enforcement mechanisms.

Technology offers, however, potential remedies to some of the problems. Lessig (1999b) suggests some ways in which technology might provide ways to recreate borders in cyberspace.[9] Cyberspace "digital identification cards" could be encoded with information that allows vendor sites and ISPs to screen access on a country of origin or age basis. Vendors would incorporate software in their sites to take advantage of these digital IDs. Assuming that such identification would be politically acceptable and that vendors could be persuaded to adopt screening technology, this combination of technologies might go far to reassert the borders that were run over in cyberspace. Technology is also being developed that will allow a consumer's computer to check a site's privacy policy and then release information in accordance to the consumer's preferences (e.g., the Platform for Privacy Preferences project).

The deeper point here is that regulation and the workings of the marketplace are endogenous to the technology and to technological change. The architecture of cyberspace changes the impact of law and its effectiveness and architecture is also a choice that can be influenced by regulation (Lessig 1999a). Technology also alters the market conditions of competition, indirectly shaping market structure, providing levers and remedies to regulatory agents, and changing consumer and producer behavior. Yahoo!, for example, which reluctantly found a technological solution that allowed it to meet French regulatory concerns over unacceptable content, is now developing this technology as a market opportunity.

Technology can also be used to circumvent regulation or at least to change the nature of marketing. Legal principles developed by reference to old-style "broadcast" marketing may miss nuances introduced by e-commerce's emphasis on customized marketing. One wonders if traditional standards defining misrepresentation are fully applicable to e-vendors that employ software programs designed in part to exploit a particular consumer's perceptual weaknesses (as well as their interests) on the basis of some historical pattern of purchases and clicks.

But the existence of technology does not imply that it will be used in expected ways. Technology that has the potential to solve various market problems might be used instead to push an existing socio-political agenda or solidify an economic status quo. Hughes (1987, 340), in commenting on the history of electric power, argues that "Another explanation for the flawed predictions of the past—and probably of the present—is the failure to realize how powerfully existing persons with deeply held traditional values and established institutions can shape new technology to their ends and trends. Instead, therefore, of new technology acting as a force for radical change it reinforces the status quo." An older, but quite striking example is provided by the two-century-plus period in which Japan gave up firearms and reverted to traditional means of warfare. Firearms had the annoying property that unskilled peasants could use them to kill members of the warrior class (Perrin 1979). The parable as applied to cyberspace: although digital identification allows for efficient sorting of various categories of people, it may encounter resistance from those who hold privacy to be a greater priority or might be used to facilitate a purpose such as taxation or immigration violations.

The Unregulated Market and Privacy

The flip side of information availability in cyberspace is the comparative ease with which information about specific consumers can be collected, used, and distributed with little or no knowledge of the affected consumer. This concern is but one aspect of the larger privacy problem affecting citizens in the digital age, but it is an important one. The privacy issue with respect to information disclosed in commercial transactions is not new. Firms that collect credit information, for example, are restricted by law as to the purposes for which this information can be used and there are rules that dictate consumer rights with respect to disputes about the accuracy of this information. Retailers and marketers have long created and sold customer lists to one another. Some fraudulent telemarketers have even been known to sell lists of gullible consumers to other telemarketers!

What is new—and disconcerting—is the extent and ease with which individualized records about consumer characteristics and purchase behaviors are collected, analyzed, used, and even transferred to other parties without the knowledge of the consumer. An FTC survey indicates that over 90 percent of Web sites are capturing this type of information (Bernstein 2000), and numerous surveys have demonstrated strong and pervasive consumer concern about privacy in cyberspace.

Putting aside for the moment the question of what actions are appropriate if privacy is seen as a right that trumps commercial concerns, I start by focusing on what can be expected of an unfettered market. A privacy-preferring consumer would prefer to buy from a privacy-sensitive company than from a company that freely shares consumer information, all other things being equal. Thus, a competitive market with perfectly informed consumers has the potential to generate a menu of product plus privacy (and price) choices that will succeed in protecting privacy in the consumer interest. In practice, we do observe variation over privacy policies that are offered by vendors.

There are many reasons to think, however, that the real market does not closely approximate this ideal portrayal of market competition. First, strong competition (with its buyer-favoring characteristics) is an important assumption underlying this outcome (see Kang 1998). Second, and perhaps more importantly, the informed consumer assumption is likely to be substantially violated. Although online merchants often state their privacy policies, consumers have reason to be skeptical (at least absent legal enforcement) because they have no easy way to determine whether these merchants follow their stated policies and in some cases may be confused as to what the stated policy really means.

Self-regulation, the Threat of Regulation, and Indirect Regulation—Privacy in Cyberspace

As of the writing of this chapter, the approach of the United States toward privacy protection in cyberspace has been to rely on a patchwork of sector-based regulation (e.g., credit, finance and insurance, government dissemination of personal information, medical data) with respect to privacy problems relating to adults, and more aggressive regulation with respect to children. General privacy protection is provided via market-induced company action and development of industry self-regulation programs. Vendor claims concerning their privacy policies ("notice") become regulated under existing laws regarding marketing representations.

Unlike in the European Union, the approach of the United States has been to view privacy not as a consumer right that trumps other considerations, but as only one, albeit critical, element in a choice about how to handle consumer information in the marketplace (Cate 1999).[10] Once one admits to a trade-off across numerous values, there is no obvious preferred policy.

In the cyberspace context, effective self-regulation to protect consumer privacy seems more problematic than protection of marketing deception. One major difference between privacy self-regulation and marketing deception self-regulation is the newness and rapid evolution of the problems posed by privacy in the digital world and the consequent lack of existing formal protection and of consensus on what formal protection is needed. Without at least partial consensus, molding an agreeable policy and enforcement regime that can gain widespread adoption is difficult. What has been the record of self-regulation of privacy? Overall, with respect to adult privacy issues, an FTC commissioned survey found limited evidence of effective self-regulation in 1998 ("while almost all Web sites [92%] were collecting great amounts of personal information from consumers, few [14%] disclosed anything at all about their information practices"). A year later, the survey (U.S. FTC 2000) found evidence of self-regulation in 66 percent of the Web sites.

This progress was made through a wide variety of individual and industry self-regulation programs and initiatives. A number of privacy seal programs have been launched (e.g., TRUSTe and BBBOnline), some industry associations and alliances (e.g., Direct Marketing Association, Online Privacy Alliance, Network Advertising Initiative) have devised privacy guidelines for their membership, and some companies (e.g., Intel, Microsoft, Disney) have made commitments to privacy programs that include avoiding advertising on sites that have inadequate privacy policies.

Criticisms of these self-regulatory programs are that the programs are voluntary and skewed to business interests. Most programs make heavy use of "opt-out" rather than the more protective "opt-in" provisions for determining if consumer information can be used for profiling purposes. Enforcement is seen as a major question mark, especially given the fact that funding for these programs is typically provided by the firms that are monitored (Shaffer 2000). Industry spokespersons, however, argue that industry will be forced to respond to consumer privacy demands (see, e.g., Peterson 2000). Even with these weaknesses, many of these self-regulatory programs (e.g., NAI, and the EU-compliant privacy seal programs) exceed the standard that many industry leaders would prefer (Stone 2000) and claims about privacy are legally actionable if they are deceptive.

Conservatively, the law plus the self-regulatory programs provide only indicators of the upper bound of privacy protection. Much of the effort has been on trying to ensure that input measures of privacy control are in place, but a real question—especially given the changing nature of technology in this area—is the actual effect of these policies.

Regulation and Electronic Commerce
Before moving to a discussion of the political economy of e-commerce regulation, it is useful to briefly consider the general relationship between regulation and e-commerce.

As discussed in other chapters in this book, the development of the Internet and electronic commerce and its uneven progress in various parts of the world has its roots in a wide range of government policies, differing business cultures, preexisting business infrastructures, and underlying demand. Arguably, the American business environment with its immense potential customer base, vibrant financial markets and technological base, competitive manufacturing and retailing sectors, and a pro-business regulatory environment, has been and will continue to be more ideally situated for the development of electronic commerce than its European or Asian counterparts.

In chapter 3 in this book, Kenney notes a variety of U.S. public policies that have created a relatively more favorable environment for the development of electronic commerce. In the telecommunications area, for example, Kenney argues that "early and gradual deregulation" was instrumental in creating an impetus for innovation that pushed costs down and usage up. He goes on to note the historical evolution of telecommunications regulation in the United States, in conjunction with a universal service goal, created an untimed local call tariff structure that, in turn, significantly reduced the price of online access for consumers. Lower access prices in an enormous consumer market implies greater demand and with various supply-side factors also favoring both technological and business innovation, it is no surprise that the United States pioneered electronic commerce. Although some of these policies are serendipitous from the viewpoint of e-commerce development, others merely reflect a general U.S. preference for less government intervention, which benefits, on average, development of emerging technologies and industries.

The initial advantage provided to firms in the United States will persist for U.S.-based electronic commerce firms that operate in markets characterized by features favoring first movers. There will also be some advantage in terms of capability (but note the European advantages in wireless technology) and knowledge that comes from the U.S. strength in various areas such as software tool development and e-marketing. At least until the electronic commerce sector matures, I believe that the American business environment—including the relatively more flexible regulatory environment—will continue to provide advantage by allowing firms operating in U.S. markets more freedom to be innovative.[11]

Major innovation can be stifled by regulations (e.g., quality standards) based on a mature status quo technology. Abernathy (1980), for example, argues that quality-constraining regulation reduced innovation in the automobile industry because it made it tougher for a new unrefined technology to compete with a relatively well-developed conventional technology. Regulations increase the entry cost for new technologies that provide exceptional performance on one dimension while falling below regulation-mandated quality on another. Such technologies may need a more permissive regulatory environment that allows early adopter sales necessary to sustain further development.

A similar problem may occur with new business models. As pioneering electronic commerce and ISP firms experiment with various ways of making profits in what would otherwise appear a highly competitive area, the development of long-term sustainable business models may be promoted by allowing these firms (and their financial backers) latitude for experimentation. As a general matter, then, the more (business) flexible American-style regulation may prove advantageous in cultivating attractive business models in economic spheres such as electronic commerce that involve new markets and new technologies.

The Political Economy of Electronic Commerce Regulation

The previous section pursued the role of regulation in electronic commerce without considering political constraints. Political constraints are important because the political process and the implementation and enforcement of political direction commonly fall short of producing the socially best outcome. In this section I explore three factors that mold regulatory outcomes and consider what these factors mean for the future regulation of this part of the economy. First, the business and technical environments are rapidly changing. Second, e-commerce regulation of marketing representations cuts across industries, and, finally, e-commerce regulation cuts across political jurisdictions. This last factor will receive the most emphasis.

The Rapidly Emerging Marketplace: New Business Models and Technologies

According to the market-based approach discussed above, the role of government in the market should be to mitigate market imperfections without introducing more costly government failures. One problem with early intervention in an emerging marketplace is that the market has not reached equilibrium. What business models will succeed, how the e-commerce markets work, where they fail and why are not fully understood. Immediate intervention will be based on a transition model of e-business and on projections of the future.

Action (or inaction) by governmental entities changes both the long-term marketplace equilibrium and the political economy environment for further regulation. Inaction opens the door to opportunities for preemptive self-regulation by business, which alters the political and economic status quo. Such action can delay legislators who are anxious to pass bills on privacy to satisfy constituents.[12] Regulatory action, on the other hand, may force the adoption of ultimately inferior technologies or technical standards and create interest groups for their maintenance.

Technology provides both the tools for misuse and the tools to ensure adequate protections or remedies. A major problem for policymakers in technologically dynamic settings is that interventions tend to focus on current problems and current solutions, but the product of such interventions may be rapidly outdated. Attempts to deal with future problems involve leaps of faith and offer fewer political (reelection) benefits.[13] Swire and Litan (1998) point out the example of a pioneering regulation on digital signatures passed by the State of Utah in 1995 in hopes that it would become a standard facilitating general use, but which by 1998 was already beginning to be out of step with technology and business developments. In rapidly changing technological environments, businesses usually prefer performance-based laws over specification-based laws (which will probably have at their heart some assumptions about technology), but such laws often make enforcement more difficult.

Cross-subject Jurisdiction: Convergence

Because regulation of electronic commerce cuts across industries, many of which are currently regulated on an industry basis, it is likely that general electronic commerce regulation will be influenced by industry-oriented regulation. There are two ways in which this might occur. First, regulatory substance and approaches may be extended or adapted from existing industry-based regulations (e.g., financial services regulation), even where somewhat inappropriate.[14] At a minimum, existing industry-based regulation establishes the status quo threat point for legislative negotiations. Second, existing regulators with different regulatory perspectives may fight over the electronic commerce regulatory space. The starting points for this convergence of cross-subject jurisdiction will differ by country and therefore one should expect—even for the same overall social preferences—differences to emerge through the implementation of developing e-commerce rules.

Multiple Jurisdictions and Harmonization

Given the physical borderless aspect of cyberspace, each country's or region's laws have potentially awkward consequences for electronic commerce businesses in other countries. Consider a world in which no borders can be maintained in cyberspace and in which the current country-based standards on advertising representations are applicable for the electronic marketplace. Comparative advertising that is permissible in the United States is considerably more restricted in Europe. A direct conflict that had been mediated through geography now has the potential to be directly confrontational. Europe has a legitimate concern that geographically limited laws will be ineffective in protecting its citizens in cyberspace and might like to expand the "reach" of its marketing laws. But it may be (socially) cost-ineffective for e-businesses to be forced to accommodate widely differing standards given difficulties in determining, at an acceptable legal standard, the country of origin of the customer. In any event, the ability of a country to enforce its laws extraterritorially often requires an in-territory credible threat or cooperation of other countries. An important example of international conflict along these lines is the EU privacy directive, which will be discussed below.

There are at least three steps associated with smoothing interjurisdictional conflict among laws. First, countries (or other political entities) can identify what is common, publicize this, and begin to harmonize some of the procedural and compliance elements in these common laws.[15] This action provides a least common denominator for businesses. Second, countries can agree about how to disagree. Given laws in conflict, which laws take precedence in what situation? What level of cooperation will there be across jurisdictions? Such actions will oftentimes be implemented through informal understandings among various government enforcement agencies. Third, there is actual harmonization of laws that will require changes to various countries' laws.

Facing conflict among laws is not uncommon for multinational businesses. In the antitrust arena, for example, an acquisition that involves companies with effects on consumers in multiple countries is theoretically subject to being blocked by each of those countries. Because antitrust standards are somewhat different across the world, theory suggests that the business entities must meet the most stringent standard to gain ultimate regulatory approval. In practice, however, antitrust enforcement agencies commonly operate under a principle of "comity" in which countries with limited interest defer to the entity with the greatest interest and those with no effective enforcement possibility do not intervene. In many instances, understandings about technical and political cooperation have been developed. This is how antitrust enforcers have agreed to disagree. Actual efforts at harmonization, however, have not been so successful, but at least have been on the agenda during bilateral and multilateral trade talks (see, for example, Yao and Krauss 1994).

Returning to consumer protection and privacy laws, it is clear from the above discussion that there is a substantial amount of conflict—arguably more than with respect to antitrust laws—among national legal regimes. Although various international consumer protection issues existed prior to electronic commerce, the rise of e-commerce has moved the international consumer protection issues and the conflict among laws to center stage. An important step toward making the international consumer protection system work more efficiently would be some agreement on how to disagree. One way to do this would be to agree to some system that determines which law applies (exclusively) under what circumstance. This would follow common business contracting practice in which firms dealing with partners in another country routinely agree on which law will be in force and often make use of third-party alternative dispute resolution methods. Many online businesses have favored a related approach with respect to online consumer transactions in which the applicable law would be "prescribed-by-seller." Others, typically governments and consumer interest groups, would prefer a system based on "country of destination" or possibly "country of origin."[16] At this point only limited progress has been made on the agreement to disagree, and this seems mostly under duress (EU–U.S. privacy safe harbor). Many officials are not particularly sanguine about prospects of consumer protection harmonization (see, for example, Pitofsky 2000). Obstacles include that consumer protection is politicized, settings in which the comity principle could apply are not many, cooperation among relevant agencies is weak, and the basic philosophies of consumer protection differ.

The EU–U.S. negotiations concerning EU implementation of the 1995 Privacy Directive is illuminating. To protect the interests of its citizens, the EU directive prohibits transfer of European data to firms in countries that have inadequate privacy protection. As the United States has no general privacy regulation, many sectors of its economy appear to fall under the inadequate protection category and hence many U.S. firms will be forced to change their information handling and protection practices (and maybe the location of their data storehouses) in order to comply with the directive.

At first blush, the impact of the Directive is far-reaching, though exactly how far-reaching depends on subsequent legal interpretations and enforcement. As part of an argument for regulatory flexibility, Swire and Litan (1998) describe a number of potential negative consequences of the directive. These include altering and interfering with information management systems and global outsourcing strategies of firms, as well as impacting industry structure, for example, by changing the size of entry barriers, and firm strategy—smaller firms are less likely targets for enforcement and so may choose less strict compliance. Whether or not the problems will turn out to be as dire as in the worst-case scenarios posed by Swire and Litan, there seems little doubt that the directive poses transition issues and will reduce flexibility and add to the overhead costs of global companies.

Firms could, of course, adopt a strategy of global compliance to the European standard. But this seems unlikely as well as inefficient for most firms. Further, there is the basic question of why a stricter standard should be "imposed" on the rest of the world. Along these lines, Cate (1999) and others see the EU–U.S. conflict over privacy as a collision of a system that treats privacy as a right with a system that treats privacy as being in tension with other concerns such as free information flow and expression.[17] Both parties have strong interests in reaching an agreement so as to avoid a trade war.

After three years of negotiation, a "safe harbor" agreement was reached that allows individual U.S. firms to meet the EU privacy protection standards through adoption of a suitable self-regulatory system (e.g., the cBBBOnline privacy seal). General compliance by non-European firms is not required, so firms are free not to participate in appropriate self-regulation efforts. Penalties for those publicly adopting the safe harbor but not complying include loss of the transfer of European data, penalties associated with deceptive representations under the FTC act, private litigation, and in some cases deletion of data.[18] In terms of the steps to resolving interjurisdictional conflicts, I interpret this agreement as agreeing how to disagree.

After so much negotiation and compromise, it is no doubt annoying to the EU and U.S. governments that fewer than a hundred firms have taken advantage of this safe harbor through August 2001 (Loomis 2001). It is still early, however, and enforcement of the directive vis-à-vis the United States was not expected until mid 2001 at the earliest. United States business seems to be worried that adopting the EU safe harbor will not only make information handling more cumbersome, but will make the companies more vulnerable to private and government lawsuits in the United States and may weaken their lobbying position with respect to a general privacy law that is under consideration (Shaffer 2000). The companies are also waiting for a test case that will show how far the European Union will go in prosecuting a partially compliant firm and the extent and system by which the directive will be enforced (Loomis 2001). Some may be delaying to see the outcome of U.S. congressional action so they can develop a strategy suitable to both U.S. and EU requirements.

At the same time as firms seem reluctant to sign on to the safe harbor, there is a movement toward embracing self-regulation. Much of this self-regulation may have been induced by the European Union and by the looming threat of U.S federal and patchwork state privacy regulation. Shaffer (2000, 74) argues that "the timing of these multiple efforts [in self-regulation] in conjunction with the EU Directive's coming into force in October 1998 is no coincidence. These self-regulatory schemes are the EU Directive's bastard offshoots—the unplanned offspring of the EU directive's encounter with U.S. business." I think, however, that it is difficult to untangle the EU effect from market and political effects stemming from an upsurge in public concern over privacy. Shaffer believes the EU directive may provide some political cover for U.S. legislators and administrators that desire additional privacy protection, but want to avoid antagonizing industry. Further, firms that have a substantial fraction of their business in Europe anyway will now be less resistant to U.S. privacy regulations. At least in these respects, we might expect the borderlessness of cyberspace to exhibit a "ratcheting up effect" rather than a fall to the least common denominator. Large vendors and advertisers who adopt strong privacy policies may also ratchet standards upwards.

Conclusion: Some Thoughts on Regulation in a Dynamic World

There are no easy answers for politicians who wish to regulate a dynamic marketplace. How much and when are questions for which current experience may be unreliable. But current experience (or current fear) is the fuel to political action. And political action, once taken, is not easily reversed. Technological and market dynamism and governmental inertia would not seem to be ideal complements for the electronic commerce world.

Complete reliance on a dynamic marketplace has substantial defects as well. Unregulated markets may have imperfections, and the markets of cyberspace are not different in this regard. Although new technologies offer opportunities for the market self-corrections that benefit consumers, new technologies also offer opportunities by which existing regulations and the consumer interest can be circumvented.

If regulatory action is flexible or correctible, the efficiency costs of enacting a poor system to protect consumers (or to pass any law entitled "a law to protect consumers in cyberspace") might be an acceptable risk. But legislators do not usually write laws with that much flexibility, groups that benefit from the regulation will fight to maintain it, and companies will build their longer-term technical and business strategies using the regulation as a baseline. A legislature is unlikely to revisit quickly an issue that it has recently "disposed" of and for which numerous policymakers have taken credit. And, to the extent that flexibility is written into the law, it would be naïve to suppose that the interest group battles would not just shift from the legislature to the implementation agency and the courts.

If quick adjustments to an existing regulatory scheme cannot be expected, then it would make sense to go somewhat slower in imposing regulations and to rely on more flexible mechanisms. This approach amounts to taking the short-term risk of inadequate consumer protection in order to protect the longer-term interest of consumers: give the market more time to sort itself out; have the political patience to let the market self-corrections develop and to let self-regulation experiment and provide some solutions. This has been the prevailing U.S. perspective. The prevailing European approach is more aggressive with respect to early regulatory intervention. Thus, although many European countries are keen to "catch up" to the Americans in technology, they are also running ahead of the Americans in direct regulation of the impacts of that technology. The degree to which a country or region can make proper midcourse corrections is important to the question of when to intervene.

Fortunately, on the marketing representation problem, basic consumer protection laws are already in place, though interjurisdictional conflict looms. Currently, in the United States the most salient consumer protection problem in cyberspace is privacy. The market is taking many self-interest-based strides that will provide consumers a modicum of privacy protection, but I do not think it will be enough. Timely, inclusive, and effective self-regulation needs formal regulation as its backbone or the threat of regulation as its stimulus. The European Union Privacy Directive is one such stimulus, as are the Federal Trade Commission and the threat of state and federal privacy laws. To get the best out of the market with respect to consumer protection, some prodding from the government sector is needed and, ultimately, as the market becomes more predictable, additional formal regulation may be needed for the infrastructure for electronic commerce.

Acknowledgments

The author would like to thank Rebecca Crane, Bruce Kogut, Felix Oberholzer-Gee, Frederique Sachwald, and participants in the Global Internet Economy project for helpful comments.

Notes

1. In the United States, for example, the Lanham Trade-Mark Act allows injured parties to sue rivals for false advertising. Because of differences in incentives for bringing and resolving the disputes, a private right of action overlaps with but is not a good substitute for governmental enforcement.

2. For now I will adopt a US perspective on buyer information that trades off commercial value of information and privacy.

3. The FTC notes that the NAD is a "model self-regulatory program that complements the Commission's authority to regulate unfair and deceptive advertising" (U.S. FTC 2000, 55)

4. Many commentators (e.g., Johnson and Post 1996; Aguilar 1999) argue that a self-regulation system is appropriate for cyberspace because it can transcend territorial boundaries. Government officials in the United States have viewed self-regulation very favorably (e.g., Valentine 2000).

5. Sometimes government delegates actual enforcement power to industry self-regulation groups (e.g., National Association of Securities Dealers).

6. There is some history of self-regulation emerging in industries that were threatened by formal regulation (liquor, financial derivatives), in industries that are under formal regulation but wanted the flexibility of a quicker, more informal mechanism (advertising), and in industries that felt the need for a yet unprovided standard (network television broadcasting, professional organizations, ISO standards organization).

7. Commissioner Byrne (EU Health and Consumer Protection DG) noted that the commission is taking efforts to create a core code for various Internet trustmarks as a prelude to code accreditation that is being developed in some Member States. The commission is also working on various alternative dispute resolution systems to help support cross-border disputes that may arise through Internet and other transactions (Byrne 2000).

8. But see Burk (1997), who argues that firms will choose location based on the "bundle" of laws offered by a particular jurisdiction, not necessarily on a single lax law.

9. See also "Stop Signs on the Web," *Economist*, January 13, 2001, 21–25 for a discussion of other technologies that can partially filter web users by country and other characteristics.

10. The FTC (2000) has recently recommended that legislation be passed that requires websites to provide notice (of their information practices), choice (with respect to how information can be used), reasonable access (to information collected), and security (of information collected). Note that these recommendations are market-oriented in that they allow consumers to choose based on provided information but do not dictate a specific policy.

11. Where ability to navigate the myriad of regulatory rules becomes important, as might be the case in some markets in some countries and regions (e.g., EU), European firms may have an advantage.

12. Bell (1991, 3), in discussing the NAD self-regulation program, believes that "had the industry not acted when it did we would have seen an avalanche of regulation of advertising from the Congress and FTC."

13. This problem may be further exacerbated by the legal system in place. It is sometimes said that civil law countries write laws that specify what can be done, whereas common law countries write what cannot be done. Reidenberg (1998) argues that the EU system of directives may be too rigid to deal with a rapidly changing technological environment. Cate (1999, 231) notes that the Privacy Directive was developed before the Internet and had in mind centralized approaches to privacy protection, but with the Internet real enforcement of this would be very difficult.

14. Jeunemaître and Dumez (chapter 12 in this book) note that this is also occurring in Europe.

15. Many business and cross-governmental groups have put together basic codes or recommendations to serve as a template for worldwide cooperation. See, for example, OECD 1999b. Actions that support the infrastructure of self-regulation such as encouragement and development of ADR systems are something over which most countries seem to agree.

16. See Pitofsky 2000 for a nice summary of cyberspace jurisdictional issues from the viewpoint of the US FTC. The EU Brussels I regulation passed in late 2000 gives consumers the ability to sue in the country of destination.

17. See, e.g., U.S. Department of Commerce 2000a, "Safe Harbor Privacy Principles," July 14, 2000; and Letter from John Moog (Director-General, EU Internal Market DG) to Robert LaRussa (U.S. under secretary for international trade, US Department of Commerce) July 27, 2000. Gellman 1997 provides a valuable look at conflict across various regulatory systems.

18. U.S. Department of Commerce 2000b, "Damages for Breaches of Privacy, Legal Authorizations and Mergers and Takeovers in U.S. Law," July 14, 2000; and letter from Robert Pitfosky (chairman U.S. FTC) to John Moog (EU director general DG XV), July 14, 2000, which details FTC enforcement powers and jurisdiction.

14

Conclusion

Bruce Kogut

What an odd dénouement to this study: the global Internet economy has not yet arrived! But this conclusion is not entirely our intention. The first phase of the commercialization of the Internet has had two effects on national economies: it has accelerated processes of institutional change by providing a chance to sample the Silicon Valley model, and it has defined more clearly roles in the global supply chain of information technologies. There is, though, a more powerful lesson from this first phase than these effects. The Internet has sparked the emergence of global communities that permit the harnessing of a distributed intelligence with potentially far-reaching implications. The cultural, sociological logic of these communities has proven difficult for business to penetrate or to embrace; we see these conflicts most clearly in the cases of open source software and music exchange communities. These effects, national and global, deserve our attention in summarizing the studies in the book.

They also raise a larger point: today's national economies belong, in varying degrees, to a global system. I address these issues of national and global in two distinct parts. The first stresses the cultural dimension of the Internet explosion and then turns to analyzing systematically the extent that a global Internet economy and, in particular, a Silicon Valley model diffused across these countries. The second part is a more prospective reflection on the surprising emergent properties of the Internet as illustrated by P2P communities and the global implications they hold for private and public conflicts over intellectual property and social

norms. The Internet economy evidenced a clear paradox: it was a remarkable social success, with rapid global penetration, but largely a
business failure. The explanation for this gap is the myopia of business
against the development of policies to harness the social dynamics of
affiliation, identity, and status.

Retrospective Analysis

Cultural Happening and a Financial Bubble

We spent the next half-hour going over the timeline. Boo would launch in May
1999. Our IPO would come six to nine months later, once revenues hit $5 million
on an annualized basis.

"We'll also need to draw up a contract," Paulmichl said. "What's the proper
name of your company. Is it boo.com Ltd.?"

"We haven't actually set up a company yet," Patrick said. "All we have is the
name."

Paulmichl's eyebrows shot up. Here they were about to raise $100 million for a
company that didn't even exist. "That's one of the things you'll have to sort out
soon," he said.

(Discussion between Patrick Hedelin, a founder, boo.com and Thomas Paulmichl,
investment banker, J.P. Morgan. [Malmsten, Portanger and Drazin 2001, 50–
51])

The Internet technology was a massive storm that rained for a handful of
years on the national topographies, carving deep caverns in one country,
broad wetlands in another, flash floods with no residues but for whitened
sculls of bankrupt companies in a third. The waters found their way
along the paths of least resistance, wireless technologies, gaming sector,
infrastructure, and software. Or perhaps the metaphor for the Internet
bubble is a river itself, that tossed a drunken boat, as in Rimbaud's *Le
Bateau Ivre*, from one shore to the next, driven by a will of its own. To
paraphrase the advertising of one software company, a drunken boat
powered by the Internet.

The aftermath of the party is still not over, but the patterns are fairly
predictable. Established and surviving firms do not withdraw from the
Internet, they reassemble its remains. For 2001, the estimates are that
1,289 U.S. Internet companies were acquired for $39.7 billion; most of
these investments by value were in infrastructure and software; destination sites such as portals and e-commerce were relatively shunned.[1] The

valuations of many companies remain high by historical standards, but the multiples of the Internet boom are no longer to be seen.

The traditional multiples were completely absent during the boom itself. Few companies serving the new market ecologies made earnings, so the classic P/E ratios could not be calculated. Amazon.com, with negative profits (a.k.a. losses), had higher valuations than the incumbent book retailer Barnes Noble that had profits, not to mention stores. SAP, the German logistics software company, was worth more than Siemens, which not only had stores, but also the hundred-plus-year money machine, the light bulb business. In chapter 3, Kenney provides the chilling figure for March 2000 of a $1.5 trillion valuation of the 370 public U.S. Internet start-ups that had $40 billion in sales. This provides a ratio of about 37 of price to sales; we should keep in mind this is not price to earnings.

The cultural history of this period has yet to be written, though the chapters of this book are, we hope, a good place to begin. The list of business terms that sought to justify—one would think with guile, if not for the evidence of universal gullibility—Internet investments on the basis of future growth rates that would imply market shares more than the world population is instructive: in the absence of rates of return or P/E ratios, we had price to revenues, or price to eyeballs. Or failing any evidence, we had valuation by "benchmarking," used by famous American investment bankers that visited the offices of recent graduates in Stockholm and placed a million dollar valuation on them because a similar company was floated on the stock market for this valuation last week. Timing was everything.

If the cyber rhetoric of consulting and investment banking firms did not suffice, there were the cultural machines of the popular press and, alas, the business school. Online electronic magazines and new atomic rags such as *Wired* produced a refined cultural and business blend that seemed to move with the tempo of the time.[2] The observation that a few recent graduates were already fabulously wealthy was not lost on MBA students, some of whom left midway in their studies to join new companies. Stories blossomed of summer jobs for which MBA students asked for options to be exercised at the end of August. Faculty took leaves of absence, joined the boards of new firms, and invested like everyone else.

There is a hysteretic hangover from the financial hysteria. The great valuations placed on companies created substantial cash reservoirs for

Table 14.1
Rough Estimates of B2B and B2C in Seven Countries for Year 2000

Country	B2B	B2C	Internet Users per capita*	Hosts per capita*	Domain Names per capita**
France	6.098 billion $5.49 billion[1]	0.670 billion $0.6 billion	14	2	5
Germany	$60 billion[2]	$3.87 billion[3]	29	2	14
Japan	$339 billion	$5.5 billion	37	4	3
India	$90 million	$12 million	0	0	0
Korea	$40.2 billion[4]	$564 million[4]	40	1	8
Sweden	$2.12 billion	$530 million	46	7	15
United States	$251 billion	$43 billion	35	29	25

Notes: (1) NFO Infratest 2001 (estimate does not include EDI transactions, estimated at $120 billion); (2) Mid-point of 1999 estimate given in chapter; (3) July 2000 to June 2001; (4) 1999.
* From ITU 2001b.
** From Zooknic Internet Intelligence, ⟨http://www.zooknic.com⟩.
Source: See country chapters unless noted otherwise.

many companies. A few used this cash to buy into something more stable, as when AOL used its valuation to swap shares with Time Warner, buying into cable, media content, and communications. But in case one credits its visionaries with too much vision, they also valuated their joint venture with Bertelsmann at the height of craze, leading to a buy-out of the German company at about three times comparable value in January 2002. Others were less lucky. Such cyber hothouses as CMGI watched their investments fall to a fraction of their former value. The high flyers, Softbank of Japan and Intershop of Germany (with a name of some nostalgic value) also saw a rapid shift in their valuations.

Table 14.1 offers the summary from the country chapters with this caution of reader beware. The data on B2B and B2C reflect different measurements; the reader is encouraged to review the chapters for details. The ITU provides data on Internet penetration and hosts (which include computers to web servers); these data also differ from other available estimates, though there is agreement among the ordinal rankings. Because hosts (e.g., .org or .edu) do not always identify accurately the country of the owner, domain names (.de or .fr) are also given for the per capita density.

Despite the flaws in measurement, the table is useful in providing ordinal rankings and also in showing the gap between overall Internet penetration and commercialization for some countries. The number of domain names and hosts provides an independent measure by which to triangulate the transaction figures. Japan and Korea particularly appear to have a high Internet penetration but rather low consumer commercialization. Germany shows the reverse trend, with one of the lower rates of penetration in our sample (but not globally) and yet one of the highest rates of commercialization. Sweden, a country one-tenth the size of Germany and one-fourth of Korea, shows a remarkable Internet penetration as well as consumer commercialization. Though currently experiencing high growth rates, the Internet economy in France is small, as is the degree of Internet penetration.

At the end of the day, the Internet wave crashed primarily on the shores of B2B. The Gartner Group estimates world B2B at about $145 billion in 1999, with $91 billion in the United States; they estimate transactions of $430 billion for 2000 (Gartner 2001). In some countries, these transactions have not been very important. Chang notes that though B2B is estimated at $40 billion, electronic marketplaces are rather small, accounting for less than $400 million. Benghozi and Licoppe also supply a low number that captures only the transactions on electronic exchanges; we have also included an estimate for B2B from an additional source to increase the comparability of the French case. Sako estimates Japanese B2B as larger than the United States. Yet Helper and MacDuffie and she both claim that traditional personal relationships persist in the Japanese supply networks. The logical reconciliation of this claim with the empirical assessment is to infer that the electronic transactions are the back office work to the handshakes that still characterize Japan.

The variances in estimates raise two important insights. The first is simply the difficulty of sorting out the estimates across countries. Gartner, for example, reports the size of Japanese B2B as $11.2 billion for 1999, 3 percent of the figure given by Sako in her chapter.[3] Internet figures give rough comparisons and should be taken in that spirit. The variance in figures reflects an important sociological observation: B2B is yet to be given a standard definition.[4]

The second insight is the importance of prior technologies and user experience that guide subsequent technological trajectories, for B2B was built on the back of existing electronic data systems such as EDI. Thus, the Internet diffused along the greased rails of an earlier technology. B2C had largely to build afresh, with the exceptions of the Minitel in France, by phone transactions, and automatic teller machines and equivalents. This no doubt explains why B2B is estimated to be a large share of the world Internet commerce, despite the variations in the estimates as to its actual market importance. The large share of B2B also suggests that diffusion is faster along supply chains than through markets, reflecting the role of global supplier relationships in the current world economy.

The consumer space reflects the differences in national cultures. In Korea, it was car sales and shopping malls, especially for electronic goods; in the United States, online shopping malls, gambling, and auctions proliferated. For India, the Internet drove software demand; the problem of logistics and reliable access to a communication network as well as, one suspects, the large availability of domestic labor services, made the Internet less interesting for the famed, but unmeasured, middle class. In Europe, online shopping is well established, with 31 percent and 26 percent of the Swedish and German populations, respectively, estimated to have bought from an e-retail site; France lags at 18 percent. Germany represents the largest online market outside the United States, estimated at $13.2 billion by Gartner for 2001 (Gartner 2001, 2002). Books, CDs, travel, electronics and software, and sports and entertainment tickets dominate sales. The lead of Germany is also suggested by its ranking in domains per capita, as summarized in table 14.1. In Sweden, online financial trading boomed. Web-enabled devices have yet to be important platforms for e-commerce sales. It is in Japan that the wireless access reached the heights of a cultural phenomenon, with Nokia testing its latest products and designs in this market. Japan is one of the few countries where female (and teenage) use of the Internet outpaces male, at least in the domain of wireless use. Japanese retail e-commerce is estimated as rather small. The success of web-enabled communication and the paucity of e-commerce underscores the relevance of the Internet's history and the dominance of communication by e-mail and related content. The Internet is packet switching with a thousand blossoms, their density and variety depending upon national soils and environments. But the constant across countries is social communication and the value of convenience for enjoying social events: travel, entertainment, gambling.

A primary effect of the Internet has been to render "back-office" operations, such as customer service, more efficiently. These activities are not captured by the definitions of B2B and B2C but may in fact constitute the bulk of the explanation for the increase in productivity observed in the 1990s. Companies such as General Electric and Cisco claim to have realized billions of dollars in savings by replacing less efficient information systems (such as EDI) with internet-based solutions. These savings do not show up in some definitions of market transactions, and yet they constitute some of the more important economic effects of the Internet. Certainly, an index of these changes has been the rapid growth in call centers—operators located in different parts of the country or world handle customer requests. These operations are aided through the rapid retrieval of personal information and imaging from central servers. The operators can also identify the caller's location and provide friendly chat regarding local weather and events. In this way, the Internet is able to enrich online conversations and *simulate* contextual cues by which communication is tacitly facilitated among strangers.

Financing Social Experimentation
Beyond all this hype and cultural experimentation is the question if these stock market booms left behind them the pieces and bits of a new recoupling of institutions and the generating of new organizational forms. I noted in chapter 2 that one way in which national institutions evolve is through changes in cultural expectations. Beneath the faddish trends in business lies the possibility that new visions of careers, markets, and the nature and role of firms have been created that can alter the institutional landscape. In most of the countries we studied, it is hard to see much evidence for radical change. One is left with the hypothesis that if not for the financial bubble, these experiments would not have been possible. The interesting question is whether these experimental seeds grew to institutional change that is irreversible.

Deregulation, Pockets of Competition, and Technological Paths
For experiments to take place, the national landscapes had to first make room for them. Above all, the first observation that can be made on diffusion is that, besides income, deregulation matters most to the speed and extent of penetration. All of the non-U.S. countries in this study entered

the 1990s with monopoly telecommunications champions, though Sweden had left a door open through which wireless competitors passed. By the time of this writing at the start of 2002, all the countries except for India had deregulated their telecommunications sector; some had privatized their national companies. In addition, many countries had national champions for the provision of telecommunication equipment, or had strong tariffs and non-tariff barriers to foreign imports and direct investment.

The effect of national preferences is not only perceptible in diffusion rates, but also in terms of technological choices. Benghozi and Licoppe, for example, explain how the installed base of the Minitel slowed the diffusion of Internet usage in France. Similarly, the initial decision of Japan to develop national standards for wireless transmission lead to rather slow growth of this technology until two policy changes were made: world standards were chosen for later generations and the sector was deregulated, with DoCoMo spun off from the national telecommunication provider that itself was privatized.

A revealing history of how national champions reduce the internal variety required in a period of technological uncertainty is Siemens' choice to pursue the X.25 protocol standard suited to the large German investments in ISDN. The Integrated Service Digital Network is a circuit-switch digital service. According to ITU (2001) statistics, Germany had the most ISDN subscribers in the world, after Japan! In 1997, they both had each more than 4 million subscribers, whereas the United States had only 2 million. Thus, both countries had existing infrastructure permitting high-speed digital transmission. The German government and Siemens supported a software protocol called X.25 that was well suited to the ISDN installed base. (See the introduction for a discussion of X.25.) However, compared to the TCP/IP alternative, the X.25 was over-engineered and designed for a different regulatory logic. German telecommunication authorities consequently faced the difficult decision to accommodate the global (i.e., U.S.) standard that reduced their lead in X.25 enabled communication.

It is interesting that Sweden and India, two countries at the economic periphery, both developed leading positions in specific sectors. Glimstedt and Zander describe the Swedish success based on two factors. The first is the loophole in the regulatory regime that allowed wireless operators to connect to the installed fixed network. This loophole permitted a pocket of competition to survive and eventually expand as the Internet technologies competed with the point to point operators. In turn, this local market gave a boost to regional equipment manufacturers to produce for the wireless sector.[5] Second, Ericsson understood early on that Sweden could set neither global standards, nor viable national standards, without vigorous participation in foreign regulatory bodies. With one foot in Stockholm and another in its foreign development sites, Ericsson profited from the textbook description of that theoretical multinational corporation that benefits globally from its dispersed and yet coordinated national investments. But as important, the combination of its adoption of international standards and integrated research activities served to coordinate the development efforts of smaller Swedish firms that innovated around Ericsson's core technologies. In effect, Sweden enjoyed both the benefits of agglomeration of firms clustering in the Stockholm area and globalization as mediated by Ericsson, which aligned the path of Swedish technological developments to an emerging world market for the Internet.

India, of course, does not boast a large penetration of the Internet, measured either by users or domain sites. Domestic communication has been also under the monopoly of the state operator. However, satellite communication escaped this monopoly, as did the emergent software sector. Because Indian policy had been oriented to large capital-intensive businesses, the software industry flew under the radar to become a sizeable contributor to export earnings, with annual growth rates of nearly 50 percent in the 1990s. As with Sweden, software vendors aligned themselves entirely on international standards and were fast adopters of ISO and other standards, providing products that complied with foreign customer needs. As Zaheer and Rajan note, multinational corporations aided the process by establishing development subsidiaries in Bangalore and other locations. With turnover rates of 25 percent being reported, human capital flowed to new start-ups.

The Swedish and Indian cases illustrate the importance of two factors. First was the presence of dormant technological variety preserved in pockets of competition that escaped the regulatory environment and dominant position of encumbents. Second, these resident technologies were developed for a world market, allowing for rapid expansion outside national markets that were too small. However, this combination of technological capability and market opportunity does not explain entirely the success of these two countries. A third factor of finance was also critical. For small companies to emerge from these pockets, financing for small- and medium-sized enterprises is required. One form of this financing is venture capital.

Venture Capital, Exit, and Start-ups Let's turn then to our stylized Silicon Valley model and its emphasis on venture capital financing. Zook (2002) provides an unusually detailed snapshot of the relationship between venture capital and the Internet in the United States. Five U.S. urban centers (Los Angeles, New York, San Francisco Bay, Seattle, and Washington, D.C.) account for 38 percent of the top 1,000 Web sites; the Internet business is highly agglomerated in regions. He notes that between 1995 and 2000, venture capital investments in the United States grew by 1,300 percent, with almost 90 percent of this investment in Internet-related companies. The correlation of venture capital location and the region of their target investment is 80 percent. These results lend support to Kenney's argument that venture capital was the critical institution to the rapid development of the Internet in the United States.

By the year 2000, the venture capital form of financing was prevalent in all seven countries, though with wide variations. Because the chapters in this book used different sources, and hence different definitions for venture capital, it is useful to review independent studies comparing the countries. Gompers and Lerner (2001) provide estimates for many countries for early stage capital. They offer the caveat that international figures often include management buyouts, investments by consolidators, turnarounds, and late-stage financing prior to the IPO. Column 2 in table 14.2 provides their figures for early stage per capita calculations. We collected data for 1998, the most recent year available for most countries. We caution the reader that venture capital is not defined the same way, with our data reported in column 3 representing early and late stages. For European countries and Singapore, the figures are for "available" capital, not committed funds. In column 4, we report the venture capital figures cited by the authors of this book.

Given these cautions regarding the 1998 figures, we can make only a few inferences. The first is that even though the figures for 1998 are generally based on more expansive definitions than those used for 1995, the vast difference in the columns surely reflects the expansion of venture capital over this period of time. The importance of venture capital in Israel relative to other countries stands out, and this is unlikely to be an artifact of the data. Interestingly, countries begin to report large increases in venture capital, reflecting the diffusion of the idea that venture capital is not only a necessary component to innovation but also a symbol of a country's innovation policy. For example, the figure for available venture capital for Singapore is over $1,300 per person, indicating a government policy far in excess of actual entrepreneurial opportunities.

The figures from the book chapters are more comparable and intuitively correct. The United States stands out far above the pack. It is surprising, given Casper's rather dire assessment of German innovativeness in Internet software, that venture capital is remarkably more important in Germany than in other countries, including Sweden. France is strikingly far behind, confirming Benghozi and Licoppe's overall evaluation. Gompers and Lerner (2001) estimate that German early venture capital investments were double those of France (€1 billion to €519 million). Korea and Japan do not rely to any considerable extent on venture capital, though both experienced positive trends.

The Indian figures look quite low, but there are two important qualifications. The first is that India is obviously poorer than the other countries, with a much larger population. The second is that we might look instead at the share of venture capital in overall investment. Zaheer and Rajan estimate, for example, that 15 percent of new investment in the B2B and B2C sectors is raised by venture capitalists. This is indeed a high figure that needs to be taken with caution given the many broad definitions of venture capital, but it nevertheless signals the importance of these funds to the Internet sector in India.

These data show an expanded role of venture capital in most countries of our study, a growth that can be seen also in the figures we collected for a larger sample of countries. Many of the chapters note that foreign, primarily American, venture capital firms played an important role. Gompers and Lerner (2001) observe that studies of the top investment firms show that about 18 percent of their investment by the end of the 1990s targeted non-American companies. Chang finds that about 25 percent of venture capital money is foreign, and Glimstedt and Zander

Table 14.2
Global Expansion of Venture Capital Markets and Entrepreneurial Development

Country	Gompers-Lerner esitmates per capita for 1995	Total venture capital per capita for 1998	Chapter estimates (in $ billions)	NASDAQ-like stock markets	Start-ups in Internet sectors
Australia	$2.99	$16.75*		Enterprise Market	
Austria	$.05	$17.08		Austria Growth Market 1997	
Belgium	$.79	$45.97		Second Marché, 1985; expanded 1990s	
Canada	$6.20	$36.68		1999 restructuring to encourage VC	
Denmark	$.77	$9.62		No	
Finland	$.19	$70.83		No	
France	$.61	$73.27**	4 (1999 new investments, early stage)	1996 Nouveau Marché	250 new internet firms 1999, 30 IPOs total in 99
Germany	$1.42	$26.36**	16 (1999)	Neuer Markt 1997	65 in internet related, total 270 IPOs in Neuer Markt, 1998–2000
India	NA	$0.09*	2.5 newly committed (2000)	None	146 start-ups received venture capital financing in 2000
Ireland	$.28	$49.30		ITEQ, 2000	
Israel	$97.88	$98.94*		No	
Italy	$1.05	$0.02		Nuovo Mercato, 1999	

Japan	$.09	$7.17*	7.3 (2000)	MOTHERS, 1999; JASDAQ, 1993	217 total IPOs 1999–2001, IPOs in NASDAQ Japan, 8 in MOTHERS and 1 in JASDAQ, making a total IPO of 19.
Korea	NA	$26.24*	1.2 (1999)	KOSDAQ, 1991	1500 firms venture capital financed
Netherlands	$6.45	$75.61		NMAX, 1997	
New Zealand	$.28	$6.33*		No	
Norway	$1.60	$113.49		Small firm exchange	
Portugal	$.91	$5.22		OTC market created 1991	
Singapore	NA	$1,340.30**			
Spain	$.61	$19.74***		Nuevo Mercado 2000	
Sweden	$1.02	$126.41	21 (Jan. 2001)	Small firm exchange part of OME	35 IPOs in Internet and telecom in 2000
Switzerland	$.14	$34.88		Swiss New Market 2000	
United Kingdom	$.61	$170.72**		AIM, part of LSE	
United States	$13.88	$72.03*	$103 (2000)	NASDAQ, 1971	1044 and 1546 Internet start-ups and 134 and 56 IPOs in 1999 and 2000, respectively

Sources: EVCA 2000; Asian Venture Capital Journal 2000; World Bank 2000; Jeng and Wells 2000, as amended by Gompers and Lerner 2001; Ventresca 2002; otherwise from chapters in this book.

point out that 20 percent of the venture capital firms in Sweden are foreign. Many of the largest venture capital firms in all of these countries are multinational investment firms, such as APAX.

An argument is that venture capital without equity markets by which to exit are not effective (Black and Gilson 1998). The countries in our study had existing equity markets, and several of them adopted NASDAQ-like exchange in the 1990s. NASDAQ itself was founded in 1971 with the listing of Intel, and it has been active in forming alliances to build similar exchanges abroad, such as the JASDAQ in Japan. By 2002, only India did not have a NASDAQ equivalent exchange, if we allow for the expansion of the Swedish exchange to incorporate small firm trading. The German case is especially interesting, as the Neuer Markt has become the dominant small firm exchange in Europe; one-sixth of the listed firms are non-German (Vitols 2000).

How then are these events related to the importance of start-ups? As the final column of table 14.2 shows, start-up and IPO activity was reasonably strong in the United States, Sweden, Germany, and India. Start-ups played a rather minor role in Korea, where many of the new major entrants were joint ventures between chaebols and foreign entrants. The high figure for Korean start-ups financed by venture capital reflects again the hazards of cross-country studies; few of these investments, notes Chang, are early stage capital investments in Internet-related companies. France is clearly a case where start-ups were relatively unimportant, as they were also in Japan.

Table 14.2 suggests as well that venture capital is related to one particular path of technological development, namely by start-up formation. Venture capital and start-ups are both present in three of our non-U.S. countries, and they are largely absent in the other three: France, Korea, and Japan. We will refer to the first grouping as relatively succeeding in developing nascent venture capital markets, and the latter three as traditional in their capital market financing. Do these differences in entrepreneurial patterns matter to the development of the Internet and broader institutional change?

Broader Institutional Change   Let's turn then to the summary of the individual country analyses, paying attention to the institutional factors that influenced the development of the Internet economy. Japan and

Korea did not, according to our studies, undergo clear institutional changes that influenced organizational forms and their relative impor- tance and *cultural* attractiveness. Sweden and India show more evidence of a change. France is intermediate and arguably so is Germany. These are the qualitative conclusions of our authors, with the exception of Casper. In large part, these conclusions reflect the larger tendencies in each of these societies. They are open to challenge, as they are based, after all, on only a few years of observations.

The striking aspect of these accounts is active government policy in many of these economies. There is an institutional logic that marks all countries, including the role of the state. In addition to a common trend toward deregulation and, in some cases, privatization, the countries differ in the extent that government supported by active intervention the cre- ation of a new high-tech Internet sector.

Germany is a case where government policy is proactive. The waters of the Internet, according to Casper, found the fastest path through the channels of software development. Casper clearly discounts the German efforts to encourage radical innovation, stressing the failure of Siemens to support a regime whereby engineers can leave, succeed or fail, and then return. Not all will agree with this analysis and others might, as I do, look more toward the cultural expectations of Germany society and education for bell weathers of change. There are signs of evolutionary change: the world dominance of a SAP—started by former German IBM employees —the new stock exchange, being the leading European country in num- ber of Internet domains, changes in the tax codes, and Germany's rank as having one of the highest per capita densities of domain sites in the world. And then there is also MP3, the revolutionary compression tech- nology developed by a German research institute (see the discussion below). Still, the growth of venture capital notwithstanding, the emer- gence of new organizational forms or start-ups appears modest against the larger backdrop. German capitalism consists of a set of corporate ties at the owner and bank level, along with dense supplier chains among the Mittelstand industrial firms, with close ties to applied research institutes and government investment policies. But the global cultural model has entered the system, ironically because the state has subsidized start-ups and is responsible for 5 percent of venture capital investment. This probably understates the state's role, because this funding is early stage;

using Casper's data, it would then represent 15 percent of early stage financing. How ironic, for Germany is the country that gave the world the alliance of the banker Bleichroeder and Chancellor Bismarck. It is this alliance that informs the Gerschenkron thesis on bank finance to accelerate late capitalist development. Today, the German states recapitulate this history through incentives for venture capital markets! If there will be a change, it will come through further state-enacted reforms in the corporate governance laws and tax policies that have supported large firm capitalism.

Korea has surely started down this road, though the change is evolutionary. It remains in many ways a young capitalism, unable to permit young and old firms to go bankrupt, and yet increasingly wary of the economic and social costs of maintaining the status quo. The state support for underwriting the costs of wiring residences resulted in one of the most connected populations, with access to high bandwidth connections. Consequently, three Korean ISPs are listed among the world top 10 leaders. However, online sales make up only a bit over 1 percent of retail. Overall, Chang concludes, it is the chaebols that dominate, partly on the basis of their alliances with American firms, partly because capital and labor markets have yet to offer sustainable alternatives to entrepreneurs. The Internet economy in Korea reflects, in short, the hand of the state and large firm, even if the promise had been momentarily for a different path.

Though Mari Sako did not discuss the political economy of Japan, the political stalemate echoes in the background. The interesting cases occur outside the traditional keiretsu, such as Softbank. The perennial innovation leader Sony rides upon a strategy of unbundled and emergent game design to complement its game console standard. And yet there is also DoCoMo, an offshoot of the national monopoly, that develops a technology, i-mode, that provides Japan with its most promising product in the Internet domain. It is of interest, notes Sako, that the reasons to be sceptical of B2B exchanges in Japan provide support for the eventual development of venture capital. For if personal relationships deter B2B exchange development (see also Helper and MacDuffie), such relationships are often the basis of venture capital transactions. Japan is a case of slow development, with promising avenues of technological expansion and, less obviously, of institutional change.

France is an intermediate case, insofar as the authors describe a learning dynamic that had preceded the Internet itself and that had laid the foundation for the development of technologies well oriented to the Internet, such as linguistic translators. The government is an actor via the role played by its state-owned enterprises. Benghozi and Licoppe argue that France Telecom played an important role in providing the organizational context by which learning in the Minitel arena could be used to support a French position in Internet markets. The more obvious evidence is that France started late in the Internet space, though it eventually caught up in terms of the standard statistics of penetration; however, it still has one of the lowest uses of online commerce of any large European country. The tear on the system was reflected in the many debates inside the higher educational system, as the graduates of the Ecole Polytechnique often chose to pay back the state their tuition fees (that is, their hiring investment bank and consulting firm) rather than enter into public service following graduation. Indeed, the exodus of French talent for London and the Silicon Valley was a source of concern for the French government, as well as a source of some benefit as these expatriates returned to participate in the new economy (Weil 2000). Some of these reforms are still underway, but the labor market pressure is no longer the source of the momentum. It could well be that broad institutional evolution is underway, but likely by a French logic of state subsidies for industrial parks (broadening from Toulouse, Grenoble, Nice to Marseille, and other regions). In this sense, the evolution follows the institutional pattern that struck Frank Dobbin (1994) in his comparative study of the development of railroads as the persistent principle of French industrial policy.

The countries that suggest the greatest institutional and technological evolution to our authors are India and Sweden, and they deserve our attention. In both of these countries, the historical institutional consensus had already been challenged. India is perhaps the most spectacular of our studies, for in the midst of one of the poorest regions of the world emerged a vibrant software sector, increasingly centered in Bangalore. To visit Bangalore is to see a strange blend of impressions of a traditional India with industrial parks, served by satellite dishes and back-up energy suppliers, including batteries located in the back of rows of Internet-capable computers. The strategy of software development led to the creation of silos, or Offshore Development Centers, that operated under the internal rules and specifications of the contracting multinational or foreign contractor. There would be the Cisco ODC, the GE Capital ODC, and Lucent ODC, subdivided within the same physical premises, the assigned engineers guarding the intellectual property right agreement but also mingling over lunch, in bars, in each others' homes. Did this internal variety mix and brew like an ancient alchemy to evolve rapidly the technical capabilities and innovation of a few firms? Surely something was created, as the founder of Wipro joined for a while the ranks of Bill Gates of Microsoft and Larry Ellison of Oracle as the richest industrialist in the world. Infosys boasted a thousand millionaires made rich by their American IPO. A combination of permitting the duty-free import of computers at the federal level and the decisions of Bangalore to leverage its technological strength of its Indian Institute of Science and invest in a digital network with a satellite port to the world created a dynamic by which Indian entrepreneurs and engineers found an institutional island within the regulated industry of a developing country. But as important, stress Zaheer and Rajan, has been the flow of Indian engineers to and from the United States. The overall percentage of these "returnees" may not be particularly high relative to the work force, but their impact is important not only in terms of their social contacts and acquired skills, but also in terms of the cultural images transported of successful Indian entrepreneurs, working in the Silicon Valley model.[6] We observe in these patterns the emergence of a global labor market for talent, as well as convergence in cultural expectations.

Though some categorize Sweden as a coordinated economy (Hall and Soskice 2001), Glimstedt and Zander describe a broad cultural change that can be traced in the technological trajectories that moved from bundled to unbundled systems. They argue that a hidden diversity within the Swedish regulatory and technological regime—"a pocket of competition" —became a source to experiment with the new Internet and wireless technologies. As in the case of the French analysis, the Swedish study points to specific technologies that were favored by the deregulation of telecommunications and, by chance, critical to the subsequent evolution of the Internet. Indeed, it could well be that the dominance of a home multinational player, LM Ericsson, plus the often exercised option of

Swedish talent to emigrate, forced the Swedish system to generate and sustain new organizational forms. It is hard to make the case on the basis of venture capital figures alone, though the larger cultural argument appears to pertain to Sweden. The image of the start-up firm, with entrepreneurs who look quite different than the traditional managers of Swedish industry, and that promised and sometimes gained a fortune by a public offer on the Internet clearly appealed to young Swedish engineers and managers, and to a few enterprising angel investors.

And there is the United States itself. Silicon Valley ran the economic cycle that, in hindsight, was inevitable. As the real estate costs of a closet appeared to be out of the financial reach of guards, custodians, janitors, and housekeepers who serviced the local economy, equilibrium raised its head. Was this excess? Did the massive write-offs of assets signal the folly of too much investment? Did the hardship of bankruptcy offset the welfare gains of new technologies? These are not the pertinent questions for many. For them, Silicon Valley is a "pocket of competition and competing technologies" in a world system. A country that cannot educate its population is yet a magnet for human capital; in return, it offers the world innovation and diffusion. It is hard to infer any larger institutional message for change for a region that is unique in its innovatory performance, and successful because it is a globally open system.

The more important question to pose is if the world needs a second Silicon Valley. Our country studies largely observe the answer: "not for us." For the global Internet economy did seed local Silicon Valley institutions in these national settings: unplanned and designed experiments with start-ups, venture capital, equity-based governance, fluid labor markets. That the seeds of these institutions, though still persisting, have yet to alter the dominant ecospheres of these national economies does not mean that innovation remains a provenance of the United States. Rather, it may mean that innovation proceeds by *functional equivalence*; there is more than one route to innovation. Foreign models, more as cultural norms, diffuse and release an evolutionary change that uncouples and recouples practices, firms, and institutions. Europe may have missed the early commercialization of the revolutionary technologies in the Internet, but it has been a contributor of major innovations regarding MP3 software, the World Wide Web, Linux, and wireless systems and products. No matter how one evaluates this record, it is myopic to extrapolate linearly from the past, a danger perhaps all the more dangerous to countries such as India or China whose institutions are still nascent. It would be reassuring to anchor these qualitative assessments in observations of statistical trends. Outside of the emergence of start-ups and venture capital, perhaps the more interesting figure would be the expectations of skilled workers entering labor markets and, more broadly, changes in educational curriculum and the university orientation toward research. We are too early to make such assessments, but we do note the changes in French legislation to permit their CNRS (Centre National de Recherche Scientifique) laboratories to file for patents on their discoveries. Whereas neither Korea nor Japan have undergone similar transformations (in part because research has been primarily an activity of private enterprise), India and Sweden have both harnessed their educational facilities to feed labor to the new sectors and enterprises. Germany surely has a remarkable body of applied research institutes (e.g., Frauenhoefer). It has also a tradition of highly defined work categories and scientific disciplines—reinforced by an apprenticeship system—that may interfere with the fluid definitions required by an evolving economy. These are areas deserving further study.

Global Regulation

National systems exist within a world economy that is itself institutionally evolving, both in its public regulatory spheres as well as the growing importance of private standards. The chapters by Yao and Dumez and Jeunemaitre document these tensions. Yao describes the clash between the United States and Europe in the cultural understandings of "privacy." Artistic property in France remains the property of the artist; in the United States, companies are valued in the billions for their rights to film, music, and literature.[7] Regulatory bodies do not fight wars, nor in a time where American technological dominance is either less pervasive, or less desired, can the United States dictate global standards; markets may "impose" standards and very often these are American standards such as TCP/IP, Ethernet, and the ubiquitous Microsoft standards. In some cases, national regulatory agencies converge or decide to neglect benignly each other. The intrusiveness of the Internet does not always permit these resolutions. Occasionally, self-regulating industry boards have emerged along with government participation, such as in the example of ICANN given in the introduction.

There remain, though, areas of cultural and legal disagreement that will not be settled by self-regulation. The study by Dumez and Jeunemaître is of broad interest in revealing the dilemma of the regulatory agencies of the European Union in, first, understanding the Internet, and second, deciding on the implications for its jurisdiction. The decision was to focus primarily on the traditional policy of deregulation of the telecommunication monopolies, a goal almost reached in Europe by 2002. These operators were ambivalent toward the Internet, especially in encouraging IP voice transmission that would substitute for the toll-fees earned on circuit calls. It is not surprising that the main ISP champions in Europe, outside of AOL, are affiliated with national telecom companies, except for a few important cases, such as Terra in Spain.

The alternative to these regulatory dilemmas is to allow the code to regulate. This solution by "private ordering" echoes the incisive analysis of Lessig that the code is what counts in this world of the Internet. If you are concerned about violence on the Internet, join an ISP that filters out violent content. If countries cannot create standards, then companies will. Indeed, the analysis by Helper and MacDuffie is impressive in suggesting how the Internet subtly alters the power of self-regulation. Of all sectors of the Internet, B2B has emerged as the dominant commercial sector. Their study of Covisint, in part, is the traditional analysis of whether supplier auctions run by an alliance among dominant assemblers is monopolistic. Yet beneath this antitrust concern is the issue of code and "value migration." For it is the sellers of proprietary software, CommerceOne, Ariba, and Oracle, that set the standards by which suppliers and assemblers will coordinate. Who gains the profits from these innovations? Potentially, those who gain are the buyers of lower priced parts, possibly suppliers who can more efficiently plan their production, and surely the software vendors.

If one places their study of B2B exchanges in the auto industry against the backdrop of Sako's analysis of Japan, the power of national models appears as both impressive and yet increasingly fragile. For although Sako and Helper and MacDuffie agree that Japanese relational contracting is not well suited to B2B auction exchanges, their forecasts are less certain. Nissan is partly owned by Renault, which has aggressively sought to reduce supplier costs in Europe. The supply chains of Toyota, Honda, and other companies are international. It may be that at the sectoral level, the momentum for institutional changes in Japan will be observed over time. But more broadly, the implication is that national models cannot be studied now, if ever, in isolation from the global system of multinational corporations and transnational supply chains.

The chapter by Yao confirms the importance of placing nations within the context of a global system. His chapter presents an economic study of the ideological and cultural conflict between the United States and Europe in a few areas, such as privacy, while also documenting the considerable convergence in views regarding deregulation and competition policy. The Internet rides upon global standards such as TCP/IP, HTML, domain addressing, and even ISO—the industrial standards that permit Indian software firms to demonstrate the quality of their practices. These standards are not set by a government authority, they are set by non-governmental organizations. Thus, the Internet brings us two differing models of regulation: the private ordering by companies such as Oracle, and the industry standard-setting bodies. These models are not always in agreement. With the recession of coordinated government action in the international sphere, the disagreement among these models promises to pose deep challenges to the evolution of the Internet, as analyzed below.

Prospective Analysis

Have We Understood the Internet?

There is an odd sense of déjà vu in the cultural observations of this first period. Boltanski and Chiapello (1999) put forth the argument that because capitalism cannot culturally justify itself, it must borrow its justification from other domains. For the capitalism of the 1990s, this justification came belatedly from the cultural imagery of the 1960s and the themes of self-actualization, community, and self-employability. Indeed, some of the cultural icons of the 1960s found themselves suddenly recycled. Thus, Peter Max of glow paint poster fame discovered his old work being auctioned off on eBay for more money than in a retail store. He hurried to put his mothballed inventory on the electronic market. This cultural hybridization is echoed in Sweden. For a country that is the third largest exporter of music (usually rock) in the world, the cultural fusion of the Internet decade was an odd echo back to the 1960s culture of their parents and 1980s financial obsession of their older siblings. Fashion harked back to bellbottoms, Austin Powers glared at us from the DVD player, and Bill Clinton reflected a Kennedyesque magnetism, on some.

These observations are not without consequence in understanding the paradox of the investment disappointment and yet the high usage rates of the Internet. The Internet has the property, even if illusory, of both engaging peripheral communities and exuding a sense of no boundaries. It rose, as we saw, out of scientific and research networks that were increasingly global in their expanse. The early success was e-mail, or USENET, or MUDs, that is, those uses that fostered social exchange. Membership in the Well experience of northern San Francisco has an association with stereotypes of the California lifestyle, but for others, is a valued entry on the consulting resume and list of credentials.

For the wider public, the Internet is a convenient research source that substitutes for the public or school library, or for the trip to the auto lot or electronics shop to ascertain prices. It is this convenience value, as Litan and Rivlin (2001) note, that is often undervalued in Internet productivity statistics. For many, the Internet is a social community built around a hobby or communication with people sharing similar traits and predilections. For those without long experience with paid television or cable, it is a *free* home entertainment and communication center. In every country, users come to the Internet with a different history, yet while often sharing the belief that the Internet is a public resource. The cultural baggage of consumers recalls the early history of markets, such as life insurance for which companies had to overcome the cultural resistance to thinking about death as a probability (Zelitzer 1983). Users came to the Internet with varying notions that reflect their life experiences and cultural apprehensions.

Business has had a difficult time inserting itself into the cultural roots and dynamics of the Internet. One of the more interesting business books on the Internet is *Blown to Bits* by two consultants, Evans and Wurster (1999), who note that the Internet is about different types of information. Information can be analyzed by two dimensions of reach and richness; the latter dimension captures what is commonly called "tacit," "sticky," or "contextual" knowledge. Consumers must be able to access the information, and the information must be able to be communicated easily by text, pictures, and context. These simple dimensions capture well why consumers tend to use the Internet for trading stocks but not for making financial decisions. Airline booking is easily done online if you know where you want to go, but not if the trip is complex, filled with connections or possible route changes. In these cases, human intervention by voice helps. The technological forecast is that the integration of voice and Internet imaging will resolve some of these problems. Perhaps this is true, but I suspect that technologists neglect other consumer preferences such as offline purchases; technology is unlikely, for example, to satisfy shoppers who enjoy the post-holiday crush of bodies.

However, these helpful business insights understate the underlying sociology of the role of identity, association, and community. Much like fashion, users of the Internet are sensitive to changing status, with some e-mail addresses becoming low real estate while others suddenly become hip. Yet, Internet businesses have not done well in establishing neighborhoods based on the social and economic divisions in society. There is a digital divide in access and use, but we have yet to see many successful strategies in which certain addresses have the ability to exploit the more traditional divides and to earn high rents of exploiting social distinction, such as those earned by platinum credit cards. No doubt, there will be a time when some business will figure out how to append a brand label after the @, and yet it is striking that few if any examples of this kind come to mind.

The developers of many of the sites are blind to the fact that people's self-perception differs from their revealed consumption behaviors. Economics has discarded the former by developing theories of choice on observable action, but most people resist being classified by their consumption decisions alone; the pejorative term *the new rich*, or *nouvelle bourgeoisie*, is given to those who appear to want to rise in status by virtue of their consumption. The progression of life is marked by social differentiation: where to live, where to educate children, what to wear, how to vote, and, as the French sociologist Pierre Bourdieu never failed to emphasize, by language. This differentiation does not descend from above, nor does it coincide with grocery purchases; unfortunately, the contents of the supermarket bag are not an adequate passport into high-status communities. People's public consumption decisions are not sufficient to understand their private identities and self-perceptions. An online bookseller's attempt to tell readers that "other readers who bought this book" also liked these other books provides a useful service, but to many readers, they care about who these other readers are and how they stand socially in relation to them. It is perhaps the arbitrariness of social-status distinctions that render efforts to exploit private information by Internet participation deeply repugnant to users who take comfort in anonymity and perhaps role playing. This arbitrage of public association and private preference (the other side of the Internet not discussed in this book) is a delectable pleasure for many not easily ceded to intrusive cookies.

This issue of the public and private character of the Internet is far from settled internationally, as Yao's chapter explains. Consider two of the most successful projects launched on the Internet, both of which pose challenges to prevailing law on property rights. These projects are essentially peer-to-peer (not surprisingly abbreviated as P2P) communities in which users volunteer their labor or property. Napster and open source, especially software, are of interest because they express the emergent characteristic of the Internet and the potential for the Internet to connect otherwise anonymous individuals along the lines of their cultural preferences and professional identities.

The origins of Napster lie first in Erlangen, Germany, where the Fraunhofer Institut Integrierte Schaltungen and Dieter Seitzer, professor at the University of Erlangen, developed a compression technology in the late 1980s. MP3—or MPEG-1 Layer III—is an audio subset of the MPEG industry standard registered with the ISO (Industry Standard Organization). Frauenhofer in Erlang received a German patent in 1989 and a U.S. one in 1995; it also spun off a company to profit from the technology. With the introduction of MP3 decoding software by a Zagreb computer scientist in 1997, the MP3 standard diffused widely among a user population.

The potential of these European technologies took off in the hotbeds of universities. College students armed with computers and CD burners could "rip" music from their proprietary collection and share CDs with each other. (These activities were fairly oblivious to the 1998 Digital Millennium Copyright Act, ratifying the United States' signing of the intellectual property treaties in 1996 that dealt mainly with software piracy and publishing copyrighted material on websites.) This dynamic has a classic tipping point potential to it: intense local activity with far fewer connections between the communities.

This largely local sharing of music suddenly was turbo-charged in May 1999. Shawn Fanning, a 19-year-old freshman at Northeastern University, founded the Napster online music service. The service, known as peer-to-peer (P2P) file sharing, allows users to easily trade music encoded in the MP3 format. Music listings are maintained on central servers under the control of Napster. By February 2001, Napster had recorded over 26 million unique users, with 13.6 million in the United States.[8] By comparison, Napster captured more users in less than two years than AOL had paying customers at that time.

This success occurred against the backdrop of a significant number of court cases regarding intellectual property. The decision of the 9th U.S. Circuit Court of Appeals in 1999 ruled positively that Diamond Multmedia's portable MP3 player did not violate the Audio Home Recording Act, because it used copies made from computer drives, not digital musical recordings. But this positive ruling was not replicated for Napster, which beginning in December 1999 was sued by several recording companies, including Bertelsmann. In July 2000, U.S. Judge Marilyn Patel issued an injunction against Napster, prohibiting it from listing copyrighted songs; Napster appealed and stayed the injunction. In October 2000, the U.S. Circuit Court ruled against Napster's appeal. In the same month, Bertelsmann formed a partnership with Napster to develop a service for fee. In February 2001, the 9th U.S. Circuit Court of Appeals ruled that Napster knew its users were violating copyright laws through its music file-sharing service. The court cited a memo drafted by Napster's co-founder Sean Parker as evidence. The court found that Napster was involved in "contributory and vicarious infringement," and had full knowledge that it was allowing its users to infringe upon copyright laws. Infringement requires less evidentiary proof, requiring that the liable party knew or should have known if end-users infringed on copyrights.

However, the demise of Napster did not immediately decrease P2P sharing of music. Alternative file-sharing systems avoid Napster's use of central servers. For example, the alternative system Gnutella renders the user both a server and a client—a server when he or she sends out information and a client when he or she retrieves information from another user's computer. More files were downloaded in August 2001 than ever before. At the same time, surveys report that less than a quarter of the people who download music are interested in paying for it. Given that nearly a third of these users are younger than 17 years old, these habits indicate a fairly potent and sustained cultural phenomenon.[9]

The open source movement reflects as well this opposition between intellectual property and communities. Open source began in the 1960s with the Freeware movement in reaction to AT&T's successive decision to release UNIX as a proprietary software. This move threatened the hacker community that relied upon open standards and access to the source code. However, countering this factor was the gradual loss of IBM's domination in the development of software, especially for the personal computer. With the ubiquity of computers and the fragmentation of integrated software, programmers could "hack" at new software, sharing knowledge of bugs and improvements. E-mail and the Internet provided a vital technology to support this community.

It as in this environment that Linus Torvalds, a Finnish computer scientist in Helsinki, released the following e-mail:

Hello everybody out there using minix—
I'm doing a (free) operating system (just a hobby, won't be big and professional like gnu) for 386(486) AT clones. This has been brewing since April, and is starting to get ready. I'd like any feedback on things people like/dislike in minix, as my OS resembles it somewhat (same physical layout of the file-system (due to practical reasons) among other things). (DiBona, Ockman, and Stone 1999)

The e-mail takes for granted a number of remarkable expectations: computers are connected, ubiquitous, and users anonymous but willing to volunteer and capable of communicating in a distributed environment. In other words, it presumes an engaged community and a common language and expertise. In 1991, Torvalds released the kernel of his system, which became Linux. By 1993, there were twenty thousand users and over a hundred programmers contributing changes. By 1998, there were 7.5 million, and 15 million by 2000. The kernel has now grown to 2.9 million lines of code.[10]

Linux is then a software with European origins that was developed in an open community, protected by a General Purpose License. The GPL places the ownership of the software in the public domain and also requires that companies incorporating this software cannot render it private. Linux can be bundled with proprietary software applications and interfaces. The contributors to Linux are of two types: programmers who work directly with Torvalds and users who identify bugs and suggest fixes. Many of these contributors are located in Europe (Dempsey et al. 1999), though Linux has been most aggressively developed commercially in the United States by such companies as Redhat and VA Linux.

Linux is by no means unique. Apache is a "patchy" web server software that has a larger share of the market than competing products, including that offered by Microsoft. Though these open source software projects are often protected by differing licenses, they share the trait that they rely upon distributed users for debugging and upon a core set of programmers for fundamental upgrading. Because of their value as an alternative to Microsoft's products, large companies such as IBM and Sun have made considerable investments in supporting these open source communities.

Open source is a P2P phenomenon, where users can freely download the software and share ideas among themselves. Its rapid diffusion was bootstrapped in a hacker community first, and then spread to an increasingly wider population of users. For many, the puzzling question has been why should programmers and users donate their time. Part of the answer is that IBM and Redhat pay them to do so, now. But for much of the first decade, contributions were voluntary and reflected the norms of a professional community of practice that enjoyed hacking and vying for prestige. Again, we see the norms of community operating as a substitute for the pecuniary rewards of the market.

We flag the caution that distributed networks confront important limits. Knowledge is not always amenable to codification and often resides in spontaneous and situated exchange among practitioners. Problem solving is dynamic, requiring resort to writing boards and objects one can touch, taste, and smell. Yet we are still early in the social life of the Internet. Language for online exchange is still in development, as any user of a wireless web device can attest. And the obstacles may be more anchored in emotion than conscious cognition. Metiu (2001) looked, for example, at the activities of distant and co-located software teams and found that the sense of foreignness and the lack of shared ownership were the primary defects of globally distributed teams. The Internet does not eradicate the meaning of proximity and foreign.

The Napster and Linux cases represent the emergent potential of the Internet. The Internet economy rose and fell in its first phase, but the emergence of communities of users, as well as overall penetration rates, indicate that the Internet has been a considerable cultural and social force. But more importantly, these communities are international, though for different logics. Napster is the expression of a global culture, built around the diffusion of popular music, of MTV programming, that has strong youth demographics. Linux and open source are, in many ways, the more fascinating, for as a production model, they represent the potential of the Internet to benefit from distributed innovation. Though the vast numbers of contributors were located in wealthy countries, programmers and users located in India, China, South America, and elsewhere made contributions. Linux provides the leading experiment for the implications of global distributed innovation that can be released when property rights are placed in the public domain.

These implications are not minor. The primary lesson of this first phase of the global Internet economy is that business remains national and stalled in its attempts to harness the potential of social networks. But the Internet itself provides striking examples of the power of emergent global communities. These cases suggest that, cognitively, users do not see the Internet the way that business, and sometimes the law, do. If but for these differences, we would see more examples of companies employing a blend of proprietary and public domain strategies.

Should public policy support these communities? There is, in fact, the threat that Microsoft has publicly acknowledged regarding the power of open source software to displace private property. Government support, such as massive purchases of Linux by the military, may be effective in tipping the Internet economics away from one standard toward another. Open source may constitute interference in the market and it also can, by detracting from universal acceptance of a standard, decrease social welfare. After all, the advantage of a standard is that software engineers know the architecture and the interfaces, thus lowering the costs of innovation. The observation that Microsoft offers free instant messaging, e-mail, and browser software dilutes this particular argument. Moreover, such solutions as government support for competing standards might be more attractive than antitrust sanctions that offer, among alternatives, the messy solution of dismembering a highly innovative firm by a cost/ benefit analysis that no one can credibly calculate.

The more far-reaching concern is the long-term effect on the U.S. near-monopoly on certain critical technologies in the distributed network: the microprocessor, the operating systems, the security applications, and so on. The benefits hearken back to the theory of strategic trade policy, by which the monopoly losses are borne partly by foreign consumers whereas the benefits accrue to American shareholders and workers. This is a complicated (and dubious) calculus under the best of circumstances.

Globalization denigrates such arguments for two reasons. First, shareholders and workers are increasingly international and firms located in the United States are often foreign multinational subsidiaries. One cannot assume the benefits flow uniquely to the United States. Second, it may be in the interests of developed countries to encourage the participation of poor regions in world innovation. This is an old sawhorse, going back at least as far as the machinery debates of the 1830s in Britain. Yet surely, as the global population compounds, policies that promote growth in the poorer regions of the world have an urgency that calls for lenient experimentation along these lines.

Globalization and Digital Property Rights

The rapid emergence of global communities raises the cautionary flag that a globally connected world may be capable of broad social and cultural changes that are unanticipated. It was unanticipated, for example, that terrorists would coordinate their activities by embedding encrypted messages in images (such as jpeg files) transmitted by the Internet. The Internet empowers coordination among distributed groups, and has influenced ironically the organization of political protests against globalization, as well as the emergence of cultural and innovative communities that we discussed earlier.

Yet it also enhances the power of surveillance and control. The digitalization of content and media, coupled with the increasing power of computing, permits police enforcement, national security agencies, and militaries to data mine massive amounts of information. The increasing development of digital signatures allows firms to send out bots to visit web servers and personal computers, to check for unlicensed use of proprietary materials, such as music, literature, or economic analysis. These powers, argues Lessig (1999b), endanger the doctrines of "fair use" and enable a far more restrictive control of intellectual property than has been previously possible.

Whether this outcome is good or bad depends partly upon the murky debates over the welfare properties of strong intellectual property right regimes. Suffice it to say that the case for strong patent regimes is far less established academically than in the law and economic textbooks.[11] Indeed, the missing element in the American, and Silicon Valley, model is the wide agreement that knowledge moves surprisingly rapidly among competing firms, often by the poaching of intellectual talent.[12]

The digitalization of knowledge is often the outcome of investments to codify intellectual materials in order to charge for it. The great danger of private ordering through establishing proprietary ownership over knowledge is exactly that the public commons moves to a fee basis. There is a benefit to these trends, as private industry has resources to digitalize content that many governments do not have. But the issues at hand are complex and explosive.

Of course, privatization increases this trend, as does the policy to make government services fee-based. We noted in the introduction to this book that the United States privatized the agency responsible for domain name registration, which is now in the private sphere, though under self-regulation. The privatization and commercialization of public resources, such as airwaves, occasionally creates critical conflicts between government policy objectives. For example, the United States bought monopoly rights to all satellite images by a private company of Afghanistan during the 2001 conflict. The alternative was to issue an injunction against private companies to sell, or offer, such images during a national crisis, risking a challenge in court. This transaction would be harder to enforce if the technology, satellites, and service providers were not American. To the Europeans, the U.S. monopoly is not only undesirable from the point of view of security, but also of their commercial interests. However, beyond this debate is the wider issue of whether satellite positioning and imaging, developed by government subsidies, should be commercialized. Digitalization coupled with the distribution of the Internet changes the economics of this sleepy business. If the conduct of war is a public good that justifies "eminent domain" policies for intellectual property, then do other public good activities, such as research, require similar safeguards?

For example, should researchers be required to pay for images that previously were in the public domain?

The digital warfare between property regimes and notions of public domain and community is still in its infancy. No sooner does Hollywood finance a new encryption tool to prevent abuse of copying DVD recordings than a hacker releases a digital key to decode the recordings. Intrusive bots visiting computers, unwanted cookies, are defeated by software—increasingly commercially sold—to set up firewalls and to seek and destroy foreign files. Self-regulators may argue that this warfare reaffirms the belief that markets are the solution. Governments concerned about security, consumers concerned about privacy, and banks paranoid over electronic financial transactions will most likely not agree.

Whether new technologies will enhance property right enforcement or destroy it is a fascinating question that emphasizes our primary conclusion of the overriding role played by community culture in the first phase of the Internet. The frustrations of business to make profits from the Internet has led to an increasing concern to strengthen digital property rights to content, one of the few areas where profits can be clearly earned in the future. These efforts obviously threaten P2P communities such as those found in the sharing of music. And yet, it is these communities that represent the most radical implications of a connected and distributed world economy in this first phase of the Internet. It is this potential of exploiting distributed human intelligence and nascent identity that has always existed that makes the open source movement so interesting. It is vital to understanding this potential that the evolution of new institutional solutions, such as the general purpose licenses (GPL), has been the critical factor permitting the emergence of a distributed software community. And it is the lack of new institutions, and the reliance on traditional intellectual property protection, that threatens the P2P music communities. This may be a necessary step in permitting business to earn profits, but because it represents a restriction of the potential use of the Internet, it should be viewed skeptically and with an eye toward other institutional solutions such as those found in open source licensing.

Webs of Bots in Small Worlds

The full implications of digital technologies and ubiquitous interconnection are intimated in these early experiments. Though many electronic sites do not welcome shopbots, most sites do, though they cunningly confuse these bots and the consumer. But shopbots also pose an interesting thought experiment. What should happen if shopbots were fully intelligent, that is, they completely represented the preferences of the owning consumer by Bayesian learning from previous experience. What if they were also empowered to identify the tricks of electronic marketing, such as baiting strategies that lure consumers to a site by a low-price, low-quality product and then lures them to buy the high-price product? What would be the counter strategy? It seems as if the vision of the future is indeed that of Bill Joy or Ray Kurzweil—one negative, the other positive but still the same: technology will increasingly drive out human participation and sooner than we forecast.[13]

In my introduction to this volume, I argued that the Internet was built by webs of people. It is this idea that is challenged by these technological musings. We could imagine a cyberspace populated by bots that owe their fidelity to computers. Already computers are fully authorized to carry out arbitrage trading with one another on the basis of trading programs. In this world, the connections traced by these intelligent agents create networks and patterns in the absence of human actors. Indeed, these patterns generate *structurally equivalent* clusters among bots who share similar preferences. In this space, the networks of things and people that have so fascinated some schools of social network studies (Latour 1987; Callon 1986) evolve to the next step: humans are absent from the analysis; technical agents and artifacts have taken over.

I like a contrary image, the robot tailor in Woody Allen's movie *Sleeper*, who speaks with a New York Jewish accent. Or that of the Sony dog that comes in multiple breeds, except for pit bull terriers. The lesson of the Internet has been that it was built within distributed communities, it diffused along the "superhighways of social connections," and it has most impressively innovated through its emergent properties to activate preexisting communities of hackers, of participants in popular culture, of scientists. The global technology of shopbots confronts the same social forces described by the adherents of the social construction of technology. Much as the bicycle evolved to meet the social standards of its era, all the evidence of the development of the Internet points to the dominant role of human culture and society.[14]

As it evolves, its connections reveal the elective affinities among social preferences and relationships. The global Internet is, in many regards, quite small. Consisting of millions of sites, its diameter (i.e., the minimum number of sites on which you need to click to trace the path between two sites the "furthest away" in the Internet) is about 16, or a bit more if we include those sites to which no one links. This is a surprisingly small number, suggesting a high degree of order in the overall structure. It is not hard to think of why this order should be found. The Internet connections show statistical properties similar to human communities: small worlds by which hyperlinks and packet traffic generate intense clusters of activity, with a few bridges between them. The tendency of people to find others who are similar, or to find common interests (called "homophily" by social network theorists), generates a power law distribution. A few sites are vastly more popular than others.[15] The power law distribution is of interest, because it reaffirms the early prediction of a tendency toward "winner takes all" markets.

These statistical properties of what are called "small worlds" are exploited by search engines, which initiate their search by going to the most popular sites. A small world consists of clusters of people who interact intensely with each other; friends are friends of friends. Yet because a few people span these clusters, the distance between any two randomly chosen people is not likely to be large. These observations are the structure behind the famed Milgram (1967) experiments that found on average six degrees of separation between people given an unaddressed envelope and the named recipient; that is, it took six steps to get the letter to a stranger. These experiments carry an important implication: a technological network grows by adding sites that are weaved by the social relationships among users.

Small worlds work because of this power law distribution, whereby certain people and certain websites are highly connected. Of importance to note is that small worlds, both in terms of hyperlinks and e-mail addresses, reflect how social and cognitive affinities weave the physical web. (Of course, packet switching means that the actual routing of mail may provide little information on these social connections.) Oddly, these patterns create a technological infrastructure that is both robust yet fragile. The small world structure is of concern to public authorities who worry about the vulnerability of the Internet to viral attacks, some of which may strategically target popular sites. The spread of computer viruses over the Internet is yet perversely interesting, because they flow along the social networks of communication. They are also the stuff of the enlightenment for Internet strategies, as these relationships reveal emergent communities of people.[16] What the evidence shows is a few cases where remarkable user communities have emerged—such as the Linux and Napster communities—but even they bootstrap from existing networks of people who knew each other, or knew their colleagues.

By and large, the small worlds of Internet communication and business are prescribed within national boundaries because social networks and their institutions are geographically local and national. The studies by Zook (2000) show that domain names are located largely in a few countries and, moreover, within a few cities. As noted above, these patterns appear to correspond to the presence of venture capital angels in the same community (Zook 2002). Although it is notoriously difficult to pin e-mail traffic to a location because of the distributed nature of packet switching, the evidence on domain names points to location as an enduring feature of commerce and social exchange.

We began by noting that national systems are not mere reflections of institutions, they are the acoustic chambers in which the echoes of human action resound depending upon the national contours of the walls and ceilings and the material composites of the structure. These social networks that modulate the effects of institutions are also the channels of human agency in the undulations of the Internet. Just as the Silicon Valley is made of the diversity of human agency scurrying along social corridors, the superhighways of the Internet speed the light of human discourse in clustered and local neighborhoods, occasionally illuminating the world's landscapes as a parade of flashlights at night. For the vast proportion of all traffic, these lighted messages are among acquaintances, family, and friends. And yet, perhaps for that curious mind born in a locale too impoverished to promise an education and future, the light along the fiber could be the energy for a life filled with a greater opportunity than ever before imaginable.

Notes

1. Reported by Yahoo!, January 9, 2002, ⟨http://biz.yahoo.com/rf/020109/n09197574_2. html⟩.

2. For a first-rate analysis of these cultural roots, see Flichy 2001.

3. See ⟨http://www.e-economie.com/articles/0200/210200-gartnerbtob.htm⟩.

4. An excellent discussion of the lack of agreement is given in "B2B-Umsätze: Wo laufen sie denn?" 2001, Electronic Commerce InfoNet, ⟨http://www.ecin.de/marktbarometer/b2b-umsatz/⟩. One reputable information consultancy reports Europe B2B e-commerce at €81 billion and world at $22 billion, on the same page of their report!

5. This explanation ignores, however, that the Swedish military had long stressed wireless communication among isolated units as part of their strategy to use distributed tactics to defeat a numerically stronger Soviet army.

6. See Saxenian 1999 for a recent study of emigrants in the Silicon Valley and those that return home.

7. For a discussion, see Benghozi and Paris 1999.

8. See ⟨http://www.jmm.com/xp/jmm/press/2001/pr_040501.xml⟩, Jupiter Media Metrix.

9. See ⟨http://www.webnoize.com/item.rs⟩, Webnoize Research, for file data; ⟨http://www.jmm.com/xp/jmm/2001/pr_101001a.xml⟩, Jupita media metrix, for demographic information.

10. This history and the key documents are recorded in the collection of articles in DiBona, Ockman, and Stone 1999. These data and the following analysis are drawn from Kogut and Metiu 2001; see also Lerner and Tirole 2000. For an interesting study on the motivations of users, see Lakahani and von Hippel 2000.

11. For a review, see Mazzoleini and Nelson 1998, and for a discussion of the privatization of open science, see David 1998.

12. Gilson 1999 offers a legal analysis of how weak intellectual property regimes are a prerequisite to the success of the Silicon Valley; Almeida and Kogut (1999) show statistically the importance of mobility to innovation.

13. Bill Joy, chief scientist for Sun Microsystems and of considerable fame for his UNIX contributions, launched a debate over the potential of self-replicating technologies in *Wired* magazine, April 2000, "Why the Future Doesn't Need Us," ⟨http://www.wired.com/wired/archive/8.04/joy.html⟩. Ray Kurzweil's response is presented at length in his 1999 book *The Age of Spiritual Machines: When Computers Exceed Human Intelligence*.

14. See the classic study by Pinch and Bijker (1987).

15. This and the next paragraph draw on reviews by Reka and Barabasi (2001) and Huberman (2001). This particular definition of small worlds as consisting of short path lengths and clustered neighborhoods is proposed by Watts and Strogatz (1998).

16. See, for example, the studies by Rocha (2001), and Flake, Lawrence, and Giles (2000).

References

Abbate, Janet. 1999. *Inventing the Internet.* Cambridge, Mass.: MIT Press.

Abernathy, William J. 1980. "Innovation and the Regulatory Paradox: Toward a Theory of Thin Markets." In Douglas H. Ginsburg and William Abernathy (eds.), *Government, Technology, and the Future of the Automobile,* New York: McGraw-Hill.

ActivMedia. 2000. *Real Numbers Behind Business-to-Business Online 2000,* report, available from ⟨http://www.activmediaresearch.com/business-to-business_2000.html⟩.

Adelberger, Karen E. 2000. "Semi-sovereign Leadership? The State's Role in German Biotechnology and Venture Capital Growth." *German Politics* 9:103–122.

AFNIC (French Network Information Center). 2001. ⟨www.nic.fr/statistiques/afnic/fr-host.html⟩.

Aguilar, John R. 1999. "Over the Rainbow European and American Consumer Protection Policy and Remedy Conflicts on the Internet and a Possible Solution." *International Journal of Communications Law and Policy* 4:1–57.

Ahmadjian, Christina L., and James R. Lincoln. 2001. "Keiretsu, Governance, and Learning: Case Studies in Change From the Japanese and Automobile Industry." *Organization Science* 12(6):683–701.

Alfred, Berg. 1999. "Untangling the Web: Internet Story Underpins Value Case," report. Stockholm: Alfred Berg.

Allen, Franklin, and Douglas Gale. 1999. "Diversity of Opinion and Financing of New Technologies." *Journal of Financial Intermediation* 8:68–89.

Almeida, Paul, and Bruce Kogut. 1999. "Localization of Knowledge and the Mobility of Engineers in Regional Networks." *Management Science* 45:905–917.

Amazon.com. 1997. "SEC S-1 Filing," March 24.

References

Amsden, Alice. 1989. *Asia's Next Giant: South Korea and Late Industrialization.* New York: Oxford University Press.

Anchordoguy, Marie. 2000. "Japan's Software Industry: A Failure of Institutions?" *Research Policy* 29:391–408.

Anderson, Curt. 2001. "Sweden—A Case of Lighter or Tighter Telecom Regulation?" In Claude Henry, Alain Jeunemaître, and Michel Matheu (eds.), *Regulating Network Utilities: The European Case.* Oxford: Oxford University Press.

Angel, David P. 1989. "The Labor Market for Engineers in the U.S. Semiconductor Industry." *Economic Geography* 65:99–112.

Aoki, Masahiko. 1990. "Toward an Economic Model of the Japanese Firm." *Journal of Economic Literature* 28:1–27.

Aoki, Masahiko. 2001. *Towards a Comparative Institutional Analysis.* Cambridge, Mass.: MIT Press.

Aoki, Masahiko, and Ronald P. Dore (eds.). 1994. *The Japanese Firm: The Sources of Competitive Strength.* Oxford: Oxford University Press.

Aoki, Masahiko, and Patrick, Hugh (eds.). 1994. *The Japanese Main Bank System.* Oxford: Clarendon Press.

Apte, Uday, and Richard Mason. 1995. "Global Disaggregation of Information-intensive Services." *Management Science* 41:1250–1262.

Arora, Ashish, V. S. Arunachalam, Jai Asundi, and Ronald Fernandes. 2001. "The Indian Software Services Industry." *Research Policy* 30:1267–1287.

Arora, Ashish, V. S. Arunachalam, Jai Asundi, and Ronald Fernandes. 2000. "The Globalization of Software." Final report submitted to the Sloan Foundation, available at ⟨www2.heinz.cmu.edu/project/india/index.html⟩.

Arora, Ashish, and Jai Asundi. 1999. "Quality Certification and the Economics of Contract Software Development: A Study of the Indian Software Services Companies." NBER Working Paper no. W7260. Cambridge, Mass.: National Bureau of Economic Research.

Arthur Andersen. 2000. "E-business" (in Japanese). Tokyo: Toyo Keizai Shinposha.

Artus, Patrick. 2001. "Téléphone mobile: la coûteuse erreur de l'Europe." *Sociétal* 31:21–24.

Asahi Shimbun Weekly. 2000. Series on Softbank, ⟨www.asahi.com/shimbun⟩.

Asanuma, Banri. 1985. "The Organization of Parts Purchases in the Japanese Automotive Industry." *Japanese Economic Studies* 13:32–53.

Asian Venture Capital Journal. 2000. *The 2000 Guide to Venture Capital in Asia.* Hong Kong: AVCJ.

Asian Venture Capital Journal. 2001. *The 2001 Guide to Venture Capital in Asia.* Hong Kong: AVCJ.

References

Baer, Martha, and Jeffrey Davis. 2001. "Some Assembly Required: Can Covisint Show Other Industries How B2B Really Works?" *Business 2.0* 20:76–85.

Bahrami, Homa, and Stuart Evans. 2000. "Flexible Re-Cycling and High-Technology Entrepreneurship." In Martin Kenney (ed.), *Understanding Silicon Valley: The Anatomy of an Innovative Region.* Stanford, Calif.: Stanford University Press.

Baker, Wayne. 1984. "The Social Structure of a National Securities Market." *American Journal of Sociology* 89:775–811.

Balakrishnan, Ajit. 2000. Personal interview, August.

Balasubramanian, Sridhar, Vish Krishnan, and Mohanbir Sawhney. 1999. "The Implications of Digitization for Markets and Marketing." Chicago, Ill.: Northwestern University Kellogg GSB Working paper.

Baring Private Equity Report. 2000. New Delhi: Baring Private Equity Partners (India) Ltd.

Baron, David P. 2000. *Business and Its Environment,* 3d ed. New York: Prentice-Hall.

Baron, James, Diane Burton, and Michael Hannan. 1996. "The Road Taken: The Origins and Evolution of Employment Systems in High-Tech Firms." *Industrial and Corporate Change* 5:239–275.

Bartlett, Christopher, and Sumantra Ghoshal. 1989. *Managing Across Borders: The Transnational Solution.* Boston: Harvard Business School Press.

Bauer, Johannes, Michel Berne, and Carleen Maitland. 2000. "Internet Access in the European Union and the United States," presented at Regulating the Internet: EU and US Perspectives, Seattle, University of Washington, April 27–29.

BBBOnline. ⟨www.bbbonline.org⟩.

Beaudouin, Valérie. 1999. "Wanadoo ADSL chez les résidentiels," *Usages.* 3:1–5.

Beaudouin, Valérie, and Julia Velkovska. 1999. "Constitution d'un Espace de Communication sur Internet." *Réseau* 97:121–177.

Bell, Howard H. 1991. "History of the NAD/NARB Self-Regulatory Program." In *Proceedings NAD Workshop III: Advances in Claim Substantiation.* New York, April 29–30, pp. 1–4.

Bendix, Richard. 1956. *Work and Authority in Industry: Ideologies of Management in the Course of Industrialization.* New York: Wiley.

Benghozi, Pierre-Jean. 1990. "Managing Innovation: From ad hoc to Routine in French Telecom." *Organization Studies* 11:531–554.

Benghozi, Pierre-Jean. 2001. "Relations interentreprises et nouveaux modèles d'affaires." *Revue économique* 52:165–190.

Benghozi, Pierre-Jean, Patrice Flichy, and Alain d'Iribarne (eds.). 2000. "Le développement des NTIC dans les entreprises françaises." *Réseaux* 104:31–58.

References

Benghozi, Pierre-Jean, Petros Kavassalis, and Richard Jay Solomon. 1996. "The Internet: A Paradigmatic Rupture in Cumulative Telecom Evolution." *Industrial and Corporate Change* 5:1097–1126.

Benghozi Pierre-Jean, and Thomas Paris. 1999. "Authors' Rights and Distribution Channels: An Attempt to Model Remuneration Structures." *International Journal of Arts Management* 1:44–58.

Berger, Suzanne, and Ronald Dore (eds.). 1996. *National Diversity and Global Capitalism.* Ithaca, N.Y.: Cornell University Press.

Berners-Lee, Tim, with Mark Fischetti. 1999. *Weaving the Web: The Original Design and Ultimate Destiny of the World Wide Web by Its Inventor.* San Francisco: HarperSanFrancisco.

Bernstein, Jodie. 2000. "Online Profiling: Benefits and Concerns." Prepared Statement of the Federal Trade Commission before the U.S. Senate Committee on Commerce, Science, and Transportation, June 13.

Better Regulation Task Force. 2000. *Regulating Cyberspace: Better Regulation for E-commerce.* London: The Cabinet Office Publications.

BITCOM. 2001. "Statistical Overview." BITCOM (German IT Industry Trade Association) web site, ⟨http://www.bitcom.de⟩.

Black, Bernard, and Ronald J. Gilson. 1998. "Venture Capital and the Structure of Capital Markets: Banks Versus Stock Markets." *Journal of Financial Economics* 47:243–277.

Boltanski, Luc. 1982. *Les cadres: la formation d'un groupe social.* Paris: Editions de Minuit.

Boltanski, Luc, and Eve Chiapello. 1999. *Le nouvel esprit du capitalisme.* Paris: Gallimard.

Bomsel, Olivier, and Gilles Le Blanc. 2000. "Dynamiques industrielles et réglementaires des télécoms: une comparaison Etats-Unis/France." In *Le nouveau défi américain. Les Notes de l'IFRI no. 29.* Paris: La Documentation Française.

Boorman, Scott, and Paul R. Levitt. 1980. *The Genetics of Altruism.* New York: Academic Press.

Bowker, Geoffrey C., and Susan Leigh Star. 1999. *Sorting Things Out: Classification and Its Consequences.* Cambridge, MA: MIT Press.

Boyer, Robert. 1996. "The Convergence Hypothesis Revisited: Globalization but Still the Century of Nations?" In Suzanne Berger and Ronald Dore (eds.), *National Diversity and Global Capitalism.* Ithaca, N.Y.: Cornell University Press.

Boyer, Robert. 1998. "Hybridization and Models of Production." In Robert Boyer, Elsi Charron, Ulrich Juergens, and Steven Tolliday (eds.), *Between Imitation and Innovation: The Transfer and Hybridization of Productive Models in the International Automobile Industry.* Oxford: Oxford University Press.

Boyer, Robert, Elsie Charron, Ulrich Jurgens, and Steven Tolliday (eds.). 1998. *Between Imitation and Innovation: The Transfer and Hybridization of Productive Models in the International Automobile Industry.* New York: Oxford University Press.

References

Boyer, Robert, and André Orléan. 1991. "Les Transformations des conventions salariales entre théorie et histoire." *Revue Economique* 42:233–272.

Boyland, Oliver, and Giuseppe Nicoletti. 2000. *Regulation, Market Structure and Performance in Telecommunications.* Paris: OECD.

Brannen, Mary Yoko, Jeff Liker, and Mark Fruin. 1999. "Recontextualization and Factory-to-Factory Knowledge Transfer from Japan to the US: The Case of NSK." In Jeffrey K. Liker, W. Mark Fruin, and Paul S. Adler (eds.), *Remade in America: Transplanting and Transforming Japanese Production Systems.* New York: Oxford University Press.

Bremner, Brian, and Irene Kunii. 2001. "The Last True Believer." *Business Week* online, ⟨http://www.businessweek.com⟩, January 22.

Breton, Thiérry. 1994. *Les Téléservices en France: quels marchés pour les autoroutes de l'information.* Paris: La Documentation Française.

Brousseau, Éric. 2000. "What Institutions to Organize Electronic Commerce? Private Institutions and the Organization of Markets." *Economics of Innovation and New Technology* 9:245–273.

Brousseau, Eric, and Alain Rallet. 1999. "Technologies de l'information et de la communication, organisation et performances économiques." Commissariat Général du Plan 1999, ⟨http://atom2.univ-paris1.fr/FR/membres/eric/tic.htm⟩.

Brown, John Seely, and Paul Duguid. 2000. *The Social Life of Information.* Boston: Harvard Business School Press.

BSE (Bombay Stock Exchange). 2001. The Stock Exchange Mumbai, ⟨http://www.bseindia.com⟩.

Buigues Pierre A., and Urrutia Bernardo. 2000. "Les enjeux pour la concurrence des marchés liés à Internet et au commerce électronique." *La Gazette du Palais* 23/24:6–17.

Burk, Dan L. 1997. "The Market for Digital Piracy." In Brian Kahin and Charles Nesson (eds.), *Borders in Cyberspace: Information Policy and the Global Information Infrastructure.* Cambridge, Mass.: MIT Press.

BusinessWeek. 1999. "Lucent's Ascent." *Business Week* (February 8): 111–114.

BusinessWeek, 2000a, "Where the Dot-Coms Are Clicking on 'Exit.'" *Business Week* (Industrial/Technology ed.) (September 18):16.

Business Week, 2000b, "Korea's Digital Quest." *Business Week* (September 24):68–72.

Byrne, David. 2000. "Cyberspace and Consumer Confidence." Speech before the Annual Conference of the Kangaroo Group of MEPs, September 18, Brussels, Belgium.

Callon, Michel. 1986. "The Sociology of an Actor-Network: The Case of the Electric Vehicle." In Michel Callon, John Law, and Arie Rip (eds.), *Mapping the Dynamics of Science and Technology.* London: Macmillan.

References

Carcenac, Thierry. 2001. "Pour une administration électronique citoyenne." Report to the Ministère de la Fonction Publique, April 19, Paris.

Casper, Steven, and Henrik Glimstedt. 2001. "Economic Organization, Innovation Systems, and the Internet." *Oxford Review of Economic Policy* 17:265–281.

Casper, Steve, and Hannah Kettler. 2000. "National Institutional Frameworks and the Hybridization of Entrepreneurial Business Models within the German and U.K. Biotechnology Sectors." Mimeo, Judge Institute, Cambridge University.

Casper, Steven, Mark Lehrer, and David Soskice. 1999. "Can High-technology Industries Prosper in Germany? Institutional Frameworks and the Evolution of the German Software and Biotechnology Industries." *Industry and Innovation* 6:6–23.

Castells, Manuel. 2000. *The Rise of the Network Society*, 2d ed. Oxford: Blackwell.

Castells, Manuel. 2001. *The Internet Galaxy: Reflections on the Internet, Business, and Society*. Oxford: Oxford University Press.

Castilla, Emilio, Hokyu Hwang, Ellen Granovetter, and Mark Granovetter. 2000. "Social Networks in Silicon Valley." In Chong-Moon Lee, William Miller, Marguerite Gong Hancock, and Henry Rowen (eds.), *The Silicon Valley Edge: A Habitat for Innovation and Entrepreneurship*. Stanford, Calif.: Stanford University Press.

Cate, Fred H. 1999. "The Changing Face of Privacy Protection in the European Union and the United States." *Indiana Law Review* 33:174–232.

Cats, Baril William, and Towsik Jelassi. 1994. "The French Videotext System Minitel: A Successful Implementation of National Information Technology Infrastructure." *MIS Quaterly* 18:1–20.

Catterall, Mark, and Edmund Chew. 2000. "Europeans Seeking Alternative." *Automotive News*, accessed June 26, ⟨http://www.autonews.com⟩.

Cave, Martin. 1997. "Telecommunications Regulation: National, European and International Perspectives." In Michael E. Beesley (ed.), *Regulating the Utilities: Broadening the Debate*. London: Institute of Economic Affairs, London Business School.

Cawson, Alvin, Kevin Morgan, Douglas Webber, Peter Holmes, and Anne Stevens. 1990. *Hostile Brothers: Competition and Closure in the European Electronics Industry*. Oxford: Clarendon Press.

Chandler, Alfred. 1990. *Scale and Scope: The Dynamics of Industrial Capitalism*. Cambridge, Mass.: Belknap Press of Harvard University.

Chang, Sea-Jin. In press. *Financial Crisis and Transformation of Korean Business Groups: The Rise and Fall of Chaebols*. Cambridge: Cambridge University Press.

Chappell, Lindsay. 2000. "Toyota Develops Its Own Online Purchasing System." *Automotive News*, accessed October 30, ⟨http://www.autonews.com⟩.

Charles, Carol. 1999. *GIIC Report on E-commerce in Developing Countries: Enabling E-commerce in India*. Washington, D.C.: Center for Strategic and International Studies.

References

Charon, Jean-Marie. 1987. "Teletel, de l'interaction homme-machine à l'interactivité médiatisée." In Marie Marchand (ed.), *Les paradis informationnels: du minitel aux services de communication du futur.* Paris: Masson.

Chosun Ilbo. 2000. "There is Also a Hope for Dot-Coms." (December 29):43.

Christensen, Clayton M. 1997. *The Innovator's Dilemma: When New Technologies Cause Great Firms to Fail.* Management of Innovation and Change Series. Boston: Harvard Business School Press.

Cisco Systems, Inc. 2000, "E-commerce—Best Practices @ Cisco." Accessed June 16, ⟨http://www.cisco.com/warp/public/779/ibs/solutions/ecommerce/practices/⟩.

Cohen, Don, and Laurence Prusak. 2001. *In Good Company: How Social Capital Makes Organizations Work.* Boston: Harvard Business School Press.

Cohen, Élie. 1992. *Le Colbertisme "high-tech": économie des télécom et des grands projets.* Paris: Hachette.

Cohen, Élie, and Claude Henry. 1997. *Service public, secteur public.* Rapport au Premier Ministre, Conseil d'Analyse Economique. Paris: La Documentation Française.

Cohen, Morris, and Vipul Agrawal. 2000. "All Change in the Second Supply Chain Revolution." *Financial Times,* October 2, Mastering Management supplement.

Cohen, Stephen S., J. Bradford DeLong, and John Zysman. 2000. "An E-conomy?" *Milken Institute Review* 2:16–22.

Cole, Robert. 1986. "The Macro-politics of Organizational Change: Comparative Analysis of the Spread of Small-group Activities." *Administrative Science Quarterly* 30:560–585.

Colvin, Geoffrey. 2000. "Seller Beware." *Fortune* 1:74.

Commission of the European Communities. 2000a. *Organisation and Management of the Internet—International and European Policy Issues 1998—2000.* Report from the European Commission to the European Council and the European Parliament, COM(2000) 202–C5-0263/2000, July 4, Brussels.

Commission of the European Communities. 2000b. *Sixth Report on the Implementation of the Telecommunications Regulatory Package.* Report, December 7, Brussels.

Commission of the European Communities. 2001. *Commission Working Document on Proposed New Regulatory Networks and Services. Draft Guidelines on Market Analysis and the Calculation of Significant Market Power,* COM (2001) 175, March 28, Brussels.

ComputerWorld, ⟨www.computerworld.com/home/emmerce.NSF/All/pop⟩, accessed February 2001.

Conseil de la Concurrence. 2000. Décisions n 2000-D-32 du Conseil de la Concurrence en date du 9 juin 2000 relative à une saisine au fond et une demande de mesures conservatoires présentées par la société Concurrence. Paris: Conseil de la Concurrence.

Corey, E. Raymond. 1977. "General Motors (A): Organization of the Procurement Function." Harvard Business School, case 9-576-251.

Corsetti, Giancarlo, Paolo Pesenti, and Nouriel Roubini. 1998. "What Caused the Asian Currency and Financial Crisis?" Manuscript, New York University.

Couch, Christopher. 1999. "Promoting Competency Development Through the Design and Management of a Multinational Supply Chain." Ph.D. diss., Sloan School, Massachusetts Institute of Technology.

Council of Better Business Bureaus. 2000. *Fairness in the Marketplace.* Arlington, Va.: CBBB.

Council of the European Union/Commission of the European Communities. 2000. *E-Europe: An Information Society for All.* Action plan, June 19–20, Brussels.

Crémer, Jacques. 2001. "Regulating the Internet?" In Claude Henry, Alain Jeunemaître, and Michel Matheu (eds.), *Regulating Network Utilities: The European Experience.* Oxford: Oxford University Press.

Curry, James, Oscar Contreras, and Martin Kenney. 2001. "The Internet and E-commerce Development in Mexico." May 19 project report to UCMexus-Conacyt, ⟨http://hcd.ucdavis.edu/faculty/kenney/InternetEcommerce.pdf⟩.

Curry, James, and Martin Kenney. 1999. "Beating the Clock: Corporate Responses to Rapid Change in the PC Industry." *California Management Review* 42:8–36.

Cusumano, Michael, and Kentaro Nobeaka. 1997. *Thinking Beyond Lean: How Multi-project Management Is Transforming Toyota and Other Companies.* New York: Free Press/Simon & Schuster.

Cusumano, Paul, and David Yoffie. 1998. *Competing on Internet Time.* New York: Free Press.

David, Paul A. 1985. "Clio and Economics of QWERTY." *American Economic Review* 75:332–337.

David, Paul. 1998. "Common Agency Contracting and the Emergence of 'Open Science' Institutions." *AEA Papers and Proceedings* 88:15–21.

David, Paul. 2001. "The Evolving Accidental Information Super-highway." *Oxford Review of Economic Policy* 17:159–188.

Davies, Andrew. 1994. *Telecommunications and Politics: The Decentralized Alternative.* London: Pinter.

de la Rochefordière, Christophe. 2000. "Le dégroupage de la boucle locale: un pas de plus dans la libéralisation des télécommunications. Exemple de complémentarité entre la régulation sectorielle et les règles de concurrence du Traité." *Competition Policy Newsletter* 2:34–40.

de Sola Pool, Ithiel. 1977. *The Social Impact of the Telephone.* Cambridge, Mass.: MIT Press.

Dempsey, Bert J., Debra Weiss, Paul Jones, and Jane Greenberg. 1999. "A Quantitative Profile of a Community of Open Source Linux Developers." Report, UNC Open Source Research Team, School of Information and Library Science, University of North Carolina at Chapel Hill.

Deutsche Bundesbank. 1998. *Monthly Report*, April.

References

DiBona, Chris, Sam Ockman, and Mark Stone. 1999. *Open Sources: Voices from the Open Source Revolution*. Sebastopol, Calif.: O'Reilly.

DiMaggio, Paul, and Eszter Hargittai. 2001. "From the 'Digital Divide' to 'Digital Inequality': Studying Internet Use as Penetration Increases." Working paper #15, Department of Sociology, Princeton University.

DiMaggio, Paul J., and Walter W. Powell. 1991. "Introduction." In Walter W. Powell and Paul J. DiMaggio (eds.), *The New Institutionalism in Organizational Analysis*, Chicago: University of Chicago Press.

Djelic, Marie-Laure. 1998. *Exporting the American Model: The Postwar Transformation of European Business*. Oxford: Oxford University Press.

Dobbin, Frank. 1994. *Forging Industrial Policy: The United States, Britain, and France in the Railway Age*. New York: Cambridge University Press.

Dodd, Annabelle. 1999. *The Essential Guide to Telecommunications*. New York: Prentice Hall.

Dordick, Herbert. 1990. "The Origins of Universal Service." *Telecommunications Policy* 14: 223–231.

Dore, Ronald. 2000. *Stock Market Capitalism: Welfare Capitalism Japan and Germany Versus the Anglo-Saxons*. Oxford: Oxford University Press.

Dosi, Giovanni. 1984. *Technical Change and Economic Transformation*. London: Macmillan.

Dosi, Giovanni, and Bruce Kogut. 1993. "National Specificities and the Context of Change: The Coevolution of Organization and Technology." In Bruce Kogut (ed.), *Country Competitiveness*. New York: Oxford University Press.

Dumez, Herve, and Alain Jeunemaître. 1994. "Privatization in France: 1983–1993." In Vincent Wright (ed.), *Privatization in Western Europe: Pressures, Problems and Paradoxes*. London: Pinter.

Dumez, Hervé, and Alain Jeunemaître. 1999. "La régulation des marchés. Réflexions à partir de l'expérience du premier régulateur britannique, Sir Bryan Carsberg." *Gérer et Comprendre* 56:31–35.

Dyer, Jeffrey. 2000. *Collaborative Advantage*. Boston: Harvard Business School Press.

eBay, Inc. 2001. ⟨http://www.ebay.com⟩.

ECIN. 2001. "B2B-Umsätze: Wo laufen sie denn?" Found at ⟨http://www.ecin.de/marktbarometer/b2b-umsatz/⟩.

Economist. 1999. "Communications: And Then Came the Europeans," *The Economist* (March 13):73–74.

Economist. 2001a. "South Korea: Entrepreneurial Fresh Air." *The Economist* (January 11):60.

Economist. 2001b. "Stop Signs on the Web." *The Economist* (January 11):21–23.

Economist. 2001c. "Time To Rebuild: B2B Exchanges." *The Economist* 19:55–56.

Edwards, Jeremy, and Klaus Fischer. 1994. *Banks, Finance and Investment in Germany*. Cambridge: Cambridge University Press.

Edwards, Paul N. 1998. "Y2K: Millennial Reflections on Computers as Infrastructure." *History & Technology* 15:7–29.

E-economie.com. 2000. ⟨www.e-economie.com/articles/0200/210200-gartnerbtob.htm⟩, accessed February 21.

Electronic Commerce InfoNet. 2001. "B2B-Umsätze: Wo laufen sie denn?" ⟨www.ecin.de/marktbarometer/b2b-umsatz⟩.

Electronic Commerce Research and Development Association of Korea, ⟨www.b2b.or.kr⟩.

Elkington, Henry, Stefan Rasch, and Xavier Mosquet. 2001. "Incumbents Take the Initiative: Harnessing the Power of Business to Business." Report, Boston Consulting Group.

Engstrand, Åsa-Karin. 2002. "The Road Once Taken: Business, Politics and Promotion in Post-War Karlskrona and Uddevalla," Ph.D. diss., Department of History, Göteborg University, Göteborg, Sweden.

eStats, ⟨www.estats.com⟩.

European Private Equity and Venture Capital Association (EVCA). 2000. *EVCA Yearbook 2000*. Brussels: EVCA.

Evans, Philip, and Thomas Wurster. 1999. *Blown to Bits: How the New Economics of Information Transforms Strategy*. Boston: Harvard Business School Press.

Farmer, Melanie, and Sandeep Junnarkar. 2000. "Amazon-Toysrus.com Deal Signals Strategy Shift." Accessed at ⟨http://www.news.CNET.com⟩, August 10.

Farrell, Joseph, and Garth Saloner. 1992. "Converters, Compatibility, and the Control of Interfaces." *Journal of Industrial Economics* 401:9–35.

Federal Express, Inc. 2001. ⟨http://www.fedex.com⟩.

Feldman, Stuart. 1999. "E-commerce Applications in Sectoral Perspective." Presentation to The Digital Economy in International Perspective: Common Construction or Regional Rivalry conference, May 27, Washington, D.C.

Ferguson, Charles. 1999. *High Stakes, No Prisoners*. New York: Times Business.

Feuvrier, Paul, and Raymond Heitzmann. 2000. "L'inernet dans l'industrie française: une révolution en marche." *Le 4-Pages* no. 136 août 2000. Paris: Sessi.

Finansinspektionen. 2000. *Internet Och Finansiella Tjänster*. Report. Stockholm: Finansinspektionen.

Fine, Charles. 1998. *Clockspeed: Winning Industry Control in the Age of Temporary Advantage*. New York: Perseus Books.

Fine, Charles, and Daniel Raff. 2001. "Internet-Driven Innovation and Economic Performance in the American Automobile Industry." In Robert Litan and Alice Rivlin (eds.), *The Economic Payoff from the Internet Revolution.* Washington D.C.: Brookings Institution.

Flake, Gary, Steve Lawrence, and C. Lee Giles. 2000. "Efficient Identification of Web Communities," Proceedings of the Sixth International Conference on Knowledge Discovery and Data Mining, Boston, pp. 150–160.

Flamm, Kenneth. 1988. *Creating the Computer.* Washington, D.C.: Brookings Institution.

Flichy, Patrice. 1999. "Internet ou la communauté scientifique idéale." *Réseaux* 97:77–120.

Flichy, Patrice. 2001. *L'imaginaire d'Internet.* Paris: La Découverte.

Fligstein, Neil. 1990. "Markets as Politics: A Political-Cultural Approach to Market Institutions." *American Sociological Review* 61:656–673.

Fligstein, Neil. 2001. *The Architecture of Markets: An Economic Sociology of Twenty-First Century Capitalist Societies.* Princeton, N.J.: Princeton University Press.

Florida, Richard, and Martin Kenney. 1991. "Transplanted Organizations—The Transfer of Japanese Industrial Organization to the United States." *American Sociological Review* 56:381–398.

Forrester Group. 1999. *Europe: The Sleeping Giant Awakens.* Cambridge, Mass.: Forrester Group.

Forster, Richard. 1986. *Innovation: The Attacker's Dilemma.* New York: Summit Books.

Foster, Will A., Anthony M. Rutkowski, and Seymour E. Goodman. 1997. "Who Governs the Internet?" *Communications of the ACM* 40:15–20.

Frankel, Jeffrey, and Nouriel Roubini. 2000. "The Role of Industrial Country Policies in Emerging Market Crises." Manuscript, presented at the NBER Conference on Economic and Financial Crises in Emerging Market Economies, October 20–21, Woodstock, Vt.

Fransman, Martin. 2002. "Evolution of the Telecoms Industry in the Age of Internet." In Gary Madden (ed.), *The International Handbook on Telecommunications Economics,* vol. 3. Cheltenham: Edward Elgar Publishing.

Freyssenet, Michel, Andrew Mair, Koichi Shimizu, and Guiseppe Volpato (eds.) 2000. *One Best Way? Trajectories and Industrial Models of the World's Automotive Producers.* Oxford: Oxford University Press.

FRI (Fujitsu Research Institute). 2000. "The Cluster of New Media Companies in Tokyo." ⟨http://www.bitvalley.org⟩.

Fridlund, Mats. 1998a. "Shaping the Tools of Competitive Power: Government Technology Procurement in the Making of the HVDC Technology." *Tema-T Arbetsnotat 192.* Linköping: Tema University.

Fridlund, Mats. 1998b. "Switching Relations: The Government Development Procurement of a Swedish Computerized Electronic Telephone Switching Technology." *Tema-T Arbetsnotat 191.* Linköping: Tema University.

Funk, Jeffrey L. 2002. *Global Competition Between and Within Standards*. London: Palgrave Press.

Furchgott, Roy. 2001. "The Clicks and Bricks Way to Buy That Car." *BusinessWeek* May 7, 128–130.

Garfinkel, Harold. 1967. *Studies in Ethnomethodology*. Englewood Cliffs, N.J.: Prentice-Hall.

Garner, Rochelle. 2000. "Online Beauty Gets Ugly." *Upside* January, 63–74.

Gartner. 2001. Growth Pauses, But Expansion Is on the Horizon. Report.

Gartner. 2002. Strategic Planning Forecast, German Online Retail 2000–2005, New Platforms for New Revenue. Report.

Gellman, Robert. 1997. "Conflict and Overlap in Privacy Regulation: National, International, and Private." In Brian Kahin and Charles Nesson (eds.), *Borders in Cyberspace: Information Policy and the Global Information Infrastructure*. Cambridge, Mass.: MIT Press.

German Venture Capital Association. 1999. "Venture Capital in Europe 1998." Special Report, July 9.

Gensollen, Michel. 2000. "Internet: marché électronique ou réseaux commerciaux?" Presented at Economie de l'Internet workshop, June 22–23, ESNT Bretagne, Brest, France.

GfK Gruppe. 2001a. "E-Commerce-Markt in Deutschland wächst im ersten Halbjahr 2001." Found at ⟨http://www.gfk.com⟩.

GfK Gruppe. 2001b. "GfK-Web*Scope: Rekordumsatz im Online-Weihnachtsgeschäft 2000." Found at ⟨http://www.gfk.com⟩.

Gibson, William, 1984, *Neuromancer*, New York: Ace Books.

GIIC (Global Information Infrastructure Commission). 1999. *A Survey of E-commerce in India*. Indian Market Research Bureau, ⟨http://www.giic.org/events/ec990615survey.html⟩.

Gilder, George. 2000. *Telecosm: How Infinite Bandwidth Will Revolutionize Our World*. New York: Free Press.

Gillies, James, and Robert Cailliau. 2000. *How the Web Was Born: The Story of the World Wide Web*. Oxford: Oxford University Press.

Gilson, Ron. 1999. "The Legal Infrastructure of High Technology Industrial Districts: Silicon Valley, Route 128, and Covenants Not to Compete." *New York University Law Review* 74:575–629.

Gittelman, Michelle. 2000. *Scientists and Networks: A Comparative Study of Cooperation in the French and American Biotechnology Industry*. Ph.D. thesis, Wharton School, University of Pennsylvania.

Gladwell, Malcolm. 2000. *The Tipping Point: How Little Things Can Make a Big Difference*. New York: Little, Brown.

Glete, Jan. 1983. *Asea Under Hundra År 1883–1983: En Studie I Ett Storföretags Organisatoriska, Tekniska Och Ekonomiska Utveckling*. Västerås: Asea.

References

Glete, Jan. 1994. *Nätverk I Näringslivet: Ägande Och Industriell Omvandling I Det Mogna Industrisamhället 1920–1990*. Stockholm: SNS.

Glimstedt, Henrik. 2000. "Creative Cross-Fertilization and Uneven Americanization of Swedish Industry: Sources of Innovation in Post-war Motor Vehicles and Electrical Manufacturing." In Jonathan Zeitlin and Gary Herrigel (eds.), *Americanization and Its Limits: Reworking US Technology and Management in Post-war Europe and Japan*. Oxford: Oxford University Press.

Glimstedt, Henrik. 2001. "Competitive Dynamics of Technological Standardization: The Case of Third Generation Cellular Communications." *Industry and Innovation*. 8:49–78.

Global Trading Web Association. 2001. "White Paper on XML Standards." Santa Fe, NM: Global Trading Web Association.

Glushko, Robert J. 1999. "How XML Enables Internet Trading Communities and Marketplaces." Working paper, CommerceOne, Cupertino, Calif.

Glushko, Robert J. 2000. "XML, Document Engineering, and New Business Services: Overview & Introduction." *CommerceOne*, ⟨www.commerceone.com⟩.

Goldsmith, Jack. 1998. "Regulation of the Internet: Three Persistent Fallacies." *Chicago-Kent Law Review* 73:1119–1131.

Gompers, Paul A., and Josh Lerner. 2001. *The Money of Invention: How Venture Capital Creater New Wealth*. Boston: Harvard Business School Press.

Grande, Carlos. 2001. "Ford Recoups Investment in Covisint Web Exchange." *Financial Times*, accessed July 2, ⟨http://www.ft.com⟩.

Granovetter, Mark. 1973. "The Strength of Weak Ties." *American Journal of Sociology* 78:1360–1380.

Granstrand, Ove, and Sven Alänge. 1995. "The Evolution of Corporate Entrepreneurship in Swedish Industry—Was Schumpeter Wrong?" *Evolutionary Economics* 5:133–156.

Grant, Linda. 1997. "Why FedEx Is Flying High." *Fortune*, November 10, 155–160.

Greenan, Nathalie, and Jacques Mairesse. 2000. "Computers and Productivity in France: Some Evidence." *Economics of Innovation and New Technology* 9:275–315.

Greene, Tim. 2000. "Newbridge Sells Out After Years of Missed Chances." *Network Word* February 28, 16.

Gustafsson, Per, 2000. "The E-Venture Capital Explosion, Sweden 2000." *BrainHeart Magazine*, ⟨http://www.brainheartmagazine.com⟩.

Hachiya, Thomas. 2001. Personal interview, December.

Hafner, Katie, and Matthew Lyon. 1996. *Where Wizards Stay Up Late: The Origins of the Internet*. New York: Simon & Schuster.

Hagel, John, and Arthur Armstrong. 1997. *Net Gain: Expanding Markets Through Virtual Communities*. Boston: Harvard Business School Press.

Hagel, John III, and Mark Singer. 1999. *Net Worth: Shaping Markets When Customers Make the Rules*. Boston: Harvard Business School Press.

Hagström, Peter. 1991. *The Wired Multi-national Corporations: The Role of Information Systems for Structural Change in Complex Organizations*. Philadelphia: Coronet Books.

Hagström, Peter. 1997. *International Data Communications*. Cambridge, Mass.: Harvard Business School.

Hall, Peter, and David Soskice. 2001. "Introduction." In Peter Hall and David Soskice (eds.), *Varieties of Capitalism*. Oxford: Oxford University Press.

Hall, Peter, and David Soskice (eds.). 2001. *Varieties of Capitalism: The Institutional Foundations of Comparative Advantage*. Oxford: Oxford University Press.

Hamao, Yasushi, Frank Packer, and Jay R. Ritter. 1999. "Institutional Affiliation and the Role of Venture Capital: Evidence from Initial Public Offerings in Japan." Mimeo, University of Southern California.

Hamilton, Gary, and Nicole W. Biggart. 1988. "Market Culture and Authority: A Comparative Analysis of Management and Organization in the Far East." *American Journal of Sociology* 94:52–94.

Hebeler, Paul. 2001. "Elements of a B2B Model: Successfully Transforming Your Company to an E-business." Presented to Covisint: A B2B Primer for Original Equipment Automotive Suppliers, May 10, Cleveland, Ohio.

Heeks, Richard. 1996. *India's Software Industry: State Policy, Liberalization and Industrial Development*. New Delhi: Sage.

Helgesson, Claes-Fredrik. 1999. *Making a Natural Monopoly: The Configuration of a Techno-economic Order in Swedish Telecommunications*. Stockholm: Economic Research Institute, Stockholm School Of Economics.

Helper, Susan. 1991. "Strategy and Irreversibility in Supplier Relations: The Case of the US Automobile Industry." *Business History Review* 65:781–824.

Helper, Susan. 1995. "Supplier Relations and Investment in Automation: Results of Survey Research in the US Auto Industry." National Bureau of Economic Research Working Paper 5278.

Helper, Susan. 1998. "Japanese 'Transplant' Supplier Relations: Can They Be Transferred? Should They Be?" In Massimo Colombo (ed.), *The Firm and Its Boundaries*. Oxford: Oxford University Press.

Helper, Susan, and John Paul MacDuffie. 2001. "E-volving the Auto Industry: E-business Effects on Consumer and Supplier Relationships." In Michael Cohen and John Zysman (eds.), *Tracking a Transformation: E-commerce and the Terms of Competition in Industries*. Berkeley: Berkeley Roundtable on the International Economy.

References

Helper, Susan, John Paul MacDuffie, and Charles Sabel. 2000. "Pragmatic Collaborations: Advancing Knowledge While Controlling Opportunism." *Industrial and Corporate Change* 10:443–483.

Henrekson, Magnus, and Ulf Jakobsson. 2000. "Where Schumpeter Was Nearly Right: The Swedish Model and Capitalism, Socialism and Democracy." Stockholm: SSE/EFI Working Paper Series in Economics and Finance no. 370.

Henrekson, Magnus, and Nathan Rosenberg. 2000a. "Designing Efficient Institutions for Science-based Entrepreneurship: Lessons from the US and Sweden." Stockholm: SSE/EFI Working Paper Series in Economics and Finance no. 410.

Henrekson, Magnus, and Nathan Rosenberg. 2000b. "Incentives for Academic Entrepreneurship and Economic Performance: Sweden and the United States." Stockholm: Studieförbundet Samhälle Och Näringsliv, Occasional Paper no. 84.

Henry, Claude. 1997. *Concurrence et services publics dans l'Union européenne.* Paris: P.U.F.

Hirschman, Albert. 1970. *Exit, Voice, and Loyalty.* Cambridge, MA: Harvard University Press.

Hochfelder, David, and Susan Helper. 1996. "Joint Product Development in the Early American Auto Industry." *Business and Economic History* 29:35–51.

Hollingsworth, J. Rogers, and Robert Boyer. 1997. *Contemporary Capitalism: The Embeddedness of Institutions.* Cambridge: Cambridge University Press.

Howe, Walt. 2000. "A Brief History of the Internet." Accessed April 18, ⟨http://www0.delphi.com/navnet/faq/history.html⟩.

Huberman, Bernardo A. 2001. *The Laws of the Web: Patterns in the Ecology of Information.* Cambridge, Mass.: MIT Press.

Hughes, Thomas P. 1987. "Visions of Electrification and Social Change." In Fabienne Cardot (ed.), *L'Électricité et ses consommateurs.* Paris: AHEF.

Hughes, Thomas P. 1993. *Networks of Power. Electrification in Western Society, 1880–1930,* 3d ed. Baltimore: Johns Hopkins University Press.

Hunt, Courtney Shelton, and Howard Aldrich. 1998. "The Second Ecology: The Creation and Evolution of Organizational Communities as Exemplified by the Commercialization of the World Wide Web." In Barry Staw and Lynn Cummings (eds.), *Research in Organizational Behavior,* vol. 20. Greenwich, CT: JAI Press.

Hyde, Alan, 1998. "Employment Law After the Death of Employment." *University of Pennsylvania Journal of Labor Law* 1:105–120.

IDC 2001. "eCommerce Applications Market Forecast and Analysis, 2000–2005." Confidential report, accessed June, ⟨www.idc.fr⟩.

Ikeda, Nobuo. 2001. *Burodo bando senryaku shohai no wakareme* (The Turning Point in Broadband Strategy). Tokyo: Nihon Keizai Shinbunsha.

Indian Venture Capital Association. 1998. *IVCA Venture Activity*. Ahmedabad, India: IVCA.

International Data Corporation. 2001. World Times Information Society Index. Washington, D.C.: IDC.

International Telecommunications Union (ITU). 2000. *Yearbook of Statistics*. Geneva, Switzerland: ITU.

International Telecommunications Union (ITU). 2001a. *Yearbook of Statistics*. Geneva: ITU.

International Telecommunications Union. 2001b. *World Telecommunication Indicators Database*, 5th ed., available from ⟨http://www.itu.int⟩.

Internet Access Provider French Association. 2001. ⟨www.afa-france.com/html/chiffres/index.htm⟩.

Internet Capital Group. 2001. ⟨http://www.icg.com⟩.

Internet Software Consortium, ⟨www.isc.gov⟩.

Ippolito, Pauline M. 1984. "Consumer Protection Economics: A Selective Survey." In Pauline M. Ippolito and David T. Scheffman (eds.), *Empirical Approaches to Consumer Protection Economics*. Washington, D.C.: FTC Bureau of Economics.

Isaksson, Anders. 1999. *Effekter Av Venture Capital I Sverige—Vad Betyder Venture Capital För De Små Bolagens Tillväxt?* Stockholm: NUTEK Förlag.

IT Business. 2000. ⟨www.itbiz.co.kr⟩, accessed December 10.

Jagrén, Lars. 1993. "De Dominerande Storföretagen." In Thomas Andersson, Pontus Braunerhjelm, Bo Carlsson, Gunnar Eliasson, Stefan Fölster, Lars Jagrén, Eugenia Kazamaki, and Kent Rune Sjöholm (eds.), *Den Långa Vägen: Den Ekonomiska Politikens Begränsningar Och Möjligheter Att Föra Sverige ur 1990-talets Kris*. Stockholm: The Research Institute of Industrial Economics.

Jain, Rekha. 2001. "A Review of the Indian Telecom Sector." In Sebastian Morris (ed.), *India Infrastructure Report 2001: Issues in Regulation and Market Structure*. Delhi: Oxford University Press.

Jankowski, Dan. 2001. "Covisint Overview: Product Development, Procurement, & Supply Chain Management." Presented to Covisint: A B2B Primer for Original Equipment Automotive Suppliers, May 10, Cleveland, Ohio.

Jansen, Robert. 2001. Personal interview, August.

Jap, Sandy. 2000. "Going, Going, Gone." *Harvard Business Review* 78:30.

Jeng, Leslie, and Philippe Wells. 2000. "The Determinants of Venture Capital Funding: Evidence Across Countries." *Journal of Corporate Finance* 6(1):241–89.

Jenkinson, Tim J. 1990. "Initial Public Offerings in the United Kingdom, the United States, and Japan." *Journal of the Japanese and International Economies* 4:428–499.

References

Jimeniz, Ed, and Shane Greenstein. 1998. "The Emerging Internet Retailing Market as a Nested Diffusion Process." Manuscript, Department of Management and Strategy, Northwestern University.

JIPDEC. 2000. *Johoka Hakusho 2000*. White paper. Tokyo: Computer Age.

Joachim, David, and Chuck Moozakis. 2001. "Can Covisint Find Its Way?" *Internet Week*, ⟨http://www.internetweek.com⟩, September 17.

Johnson, David R., and David G. Post. 1996. "Law and Borders: The Rise of Law in Cyberspace." *Stanford Law Review* 48:1367–1402.

Johnson, David R., and David G. Post. 1997. "The Rise of Law on the Global Network." In Brian Kahin and Charles Nesson (eds.), *Borders in Cyberspace: Information Policy and the Global Information Infrastructure*. Cambridge, Mass.: MIT Press.

Johnson, Eric J., Wendy Moe, Peter S. Fader, Steven Bellman, and Jerry Lohse. 2002. "On the Depth and Dynamics of Online Search Behavior." Working Paper, Wharton School, University of Pennsylvania, Philadelphia, Pa.

Johnson, Matt. 2001. "Transforming B2B Exchanges into Collaborative Trading Communities." White paper, ⟨http://www.transora.com⟩.

Jorde, Thomas M., and David J. Teece. 1992. *Antitrust, Innovation, and Competitiveness*. New York: Oxford University Press.

Joy, Bill. 2000. "Why the Future Doesn't Need Us." *Wired* (April), ⟨www.wired.com/wired/archive/8.04/joy.html⟩.

Jupiter Media Metrix. 2001a. "Jupiter Media Metrix Reports Multi-country Napster Usage Statistics for February 2001." Press release, April, ⟨www.jmm.com/xp/jmm/press/2001/pr_040501.xml⟩.

Jupiter Media Metrix. 2001b. "Users of File-Swapping Alternatives Increase Nearly 500 Percent in the U.S., Surpassing Napster, Reports Jupiter Media Metrix." Press release, October, ⟨www.jmm.com/xp/jmm/press/2001/pr_101001a.xml⟩.

Kang, Jerry. 1998. "Information Privacy in Cyberspace Transactions." *Stanford Law Review* 50:1193–1294.

Kaplan, David A. 1999. *The Silicon Boys: And Their Valley of Dreams*. New York: William Morrow.

Karaömerlioglu, Dilek, and Staffan Jacobsson. 2000. "The Swedish Venture Capital Industry." *Venture Capital* 2:66–88.

Karlsson, Magnus. 1998. "The Liberalisation of Telecommunications in Sweden: Technology and Regime Change from the 1960s to 1993." *Linköping Studies in Arts and Science 172*. Linköping: Tema T, Linköping University.

Karpinski, Richard. 2001. "Net Market Slaps Big 3 with Lawsuit." *B to B Chicago*, January 21.

References

Katz, Harry P. (ed.). 1997. *Telecommunications: Restructuring Work and Employment Relations Worldwide.* Ithaca, N.Y.: ILR Press.

Kenney, Martin. 1986. *Biotechnology: The University-Industrial Complex.* New Haven, CT: Yale University Press.

Kenney, Martin. 2000. *Understanding Silicon Valley: The Anatomy of an Entrepreneurial Region.* Stanford, Calif.: Stanford University Press.

Kenney, Martin, and James Curry. 1999. "E-commerce: Implications for Firm Strategy and Industry Configuration." *Industry and Innovation* 6:131–151.

Kenney, Martin, and James Curry. 2000. "Beyond Transaction Costs: E-commerce and the Power of the Internet Dataspace." In Thomas R. Leinbach and Stanley D. Brunn (eds.), *Worlds of E-commerce: Economic, Geographical and Social Dimensions.* New York: John Wiley.

Kenney, Martin, and James Curry. 2001. "The Internet and the Personal Computer Value Chain." In BRIE-IGCC E-conomy Project (eds.), *Tracking a Transformation: E-commerce and the Terms of Competition in Industries.* Washington, D.C.: Brookings Institution.

Kenney, Martin, and Richard Florida. 2000. "Venture Capital in Silicon Valley: Fueling New Firm Formation." In Martin Kenney (ed.), *Understanding Silicon Valley: Anatomy of an Entrepreneurial Region.* Stanford, Calif.: Stanford University Press.

Kenney, Martin, and Urs von Burg. 1999. "Technology and Path Dependence: The Divergence Between Silicon Valley and Route 128." *Industrial and Corporate Change* 8:67–103.

Kim, Eun-Mee. 1997. *Big Business, Strong State: Collusion and Conflict in South Korean Developments, 1960–1990.* New York: State University of New York Press.

King, Mervyn A., and Fullerton, Don T. (eds.). 1984. *The Taxation of Income from Capital: A Comparative Study of the United States, the United Kingdom, Sweden and West Germany.* Chicago: University of Chicago Press.

Kinsey, Jean. 2001. "The Internet and the Grocery Store." In BRIE-IGCC E-conomy Project (eds.), *Tracking a Transformation: E-commerce and the Terms of Competition in Industries.* Washington, D.C.: Brookings Institution.

Kipping, Matthias. 1999. "American Management Consulting Companies in Western Europe 1920 to 1990: Products, Reputation, and Relationships." *Business History Review* 73:190–220.

Kisiel, Ralph. 2000a. "What's Behind Plan by Tier 1's?" *Automotive News,* ⟨http://www.autonews.com⟩, May 29.

Kisiel, Ralph. 2000b. "Covisint Profit Sharing Offered to 40 Suppliers." *Automotive News,* ⟨http://www.autonews.com⟩, June 26.

Kisiel, Ralph. 2000c. "Ford Executive Dispels Myths Surrounding E-business." *Automotive News,* ⟨http://www.autonews.com⟩, July 10.

Kisiel, Ralph. 2000d. "DaimlerChrysler Uses Net to Rewire Itself." *Automotive News,* ⟨http://www.autonews.com⟩, August 21.

Kisiel, Ralph. 2000e. "VW Going Its Own Way on E-auctions." *Automotive News*, ⟨http://www.autonews.com⟩, December 11.

Kisiel, Ralph. 2001a. "2 Roads to Covisint." *Automotive News*, ⟨http://www.autonews.com⟩, January 1.

Kisiel, Ralph. 2001b. "Study: Web Collaboration Could Yield Big Savings." *Automotive News*, ⟨http://www.autonews.com⟩, May 7.

Klepper, Steven, and Elizabeth Graddy. 1990. "The Evolution of New Industries and the Determinants of Market Structure." *The Rand Journal of Economics*, 21:27–44.

Kogut, Bruce. 1991. "The Permeability of Borders and the Speed of Learning Among Countries." In J. H. Dunning, B. Kogut, and M. Blomstrom (eds.), *Globalization of Firms and the Competitiveness of Nations*. Lund, Sweden: Institute of Economic Research, Lund University.

Kogut, Bruce. 1992. "National Organizing Principles of Work and the Erstwhile Dominance of the American Multinational Corporation." *Industrial and Corporate Change* 1:285–325.

Kogut, Bruce (ed.), 1993. *Country Competitiveness: Technology and the Organizing of Work*. Oxford: Oxford University Press.

Kogut, Bruce. 1997. "Identity, Procedural Knowledge, and Institutions: Functional and Historical Explanations for Institutional Change." In Frieder Naschold, David Soskice, Bob Hancké, and Ulrich Jürgens (eds.), *Ökonomische Leistungsfähigkeit und Institutionelle Innovation. Das deutsche Produktions—und Politikregime im Internationalen Wettbewerb*. WZB-Jahrbuch, Berlin: Sigma.

Kogut, Bruce. 2000. "The Transatlantic Exchange of Ideas and Practices: National Institutions and Diffusion." In Frederique Sachwald (ed.), *A New American Challenge and the Organization of Transatlantic Learning*. Paris: Institut Francais des Relations Internationales.

Kogut, Bruce, and Paul Almeida. 1999. "Localization of Knowledge and the Mobility of Engineers in Regional Networks." *Management Science* 45:905–917.

Kogut, Bruce, and Anca Metiu. 2001. "Open Source Software Development and Distributed Innovation." *Oxford Review of Economic Policy* 17:248–264.

Kogut, Bruce, and Udo Zander. 1992. "Knowledge of the Firm, Combinative Capabilities, and the Replication of Technology." *Organization Science* 3:383–397.

Kollock, Peter. 1999. "The Economies of Online Cooperation: Gifts and Public Goods in Cyberspace." In Marc Smith and Peter Kollock (eds.), *Communities in Cyberspace*. London: Routledge.

Konert, Bertram. 1999. "Western Europe and North America." In *The World Communication and Information Report 1999–2000*. Paris: UNESCO.

Konicki, Steve. 2001a. "Covisint's Big Deal," ⟨http://www.infoweek.com⟩, May 21.

Konicki, Steve. 2001b. "Covisint Books 'Impressive' Procurement Volume," ⟨http://www.infoweek.com⟩, July 18.

References

Korea Information Society Development Institute, ⟨www.kisdi.re.kr⟩.

Korea National Statistical Office. 2000. "Survey on Electronic Commerce." Press release, December. Seoul: Korea National Statistics Office.

KOSDAQ, ⟨www.kosdaq.or.kr⟩.

Kurzweil, Ray. 1999. *The Age of Spiritual Machines: When Computers Exceed Human Intelligence*. New York: Penguin.

Lakhani, Karim, and Eric von Hippel. 2000. "How Open Source Software Works: 'Free' User-to-User Assistance." Working Paper no. 4117, MIT Sloan School of Management, Cambridge, Mass.

Landell, Elin. 1998. *Entreprenörsfonder: Riskkapital I Växande Företag*. Stockholm: NUTEK.

Landström, Hans. 1993. "Informal Risk: Capital in Sweden and Some International Comparisons." *Journal Of Business Venturing* 8:525–540.

Langlois, Richard. 1992. "Creating External Capabilities: Innovation and Vertical Distintegration in the Microcomputer Industry." *Business and Economic History* 66:93–150.

Langlois, Richard, and David C. Mowery. 1996. "The Federal Government Role in the Development of the U.S. Software Industry." In David C. Mowery (ed.), *The International Computer Software Industry: A Comparative Study of Industry Evolution and Structure*. New York: Oxford University Press.

Lapidus, Gary. 2000. "Gentlemen, Start Your Search Engines." Goldman Sachs Investment Research, January.

Lappin, Todd. 1996. "The Airline of the Internet." *Wired* December, 234–241.

La Recherche. 2000. *Spécial Internet*, no. 328.

Latcovich, Simon, and Howard Smith. 2001. "Pricing, Sunk Costs, and Market Structure Online: Evidence from Book Retailing." *Oxford Review of Economic Policy* 17:217–234.

Lateef, Asma. 1997. "Linking up with the Global Economy: A Case Study of the Bangalore Software Industry." Geneva: ILO, ⟨http://www.ilo.org/public/english/bureau/inst/papers/1997/dp96/⟩.

Latour, Bruno. 1987. *Science in Action*. Cambridge, Mass.: Harvard University Press.

Lee, Chong-Moon, William Miller, Marguerite Gong Hancock, and Henry Rowen. 2000. *The Silicon Valley Edge: A Habitat for Innovation and Entrepreneurship*. Stanford, Calif.: Stanford University Press.

Leijonhufvud, Jonas. 2001. "IT-Jättar Fortsätter Att Växa I Sverige." *Svenska Dagbladet* (May 23):31.

Leiner, Barry M., Vinton G. Cerf, David D. Clark, Robert E. Kahn, Leonard Kleinrock, Daniel C. Lynch, Jon Postel, Larry G. Roberts, and Stephen Wolff. 2000. "A Brief History of the Internet," ⟨http://www.isoc.org/internet-history/brief.html#Initial_Concepts⟩.

References

Lerner, John, and Jean Tirole. 2000. "The Simple Economics of Open Source." NBER Working Paper 7600.

Lessig, Lawrence. 1999a. "Commentary: The Law of the Horse: What Cyberlaw Might Teach." *Harvard Law Review* 113:501–549.

Lessig, Lawrence. 1999b. *Code and Other Laws of Cyberspace*. New York: Basic Books.

Levy, Steven. 1994. *Hackers: Heroes of the Computer Revolution*, 2d ed. New York: Delta.

Licoppe, Christian. 2002. "La conception et le développement des sites Internet pour les entreprises: une épreuve continue et dialogique d'objets intermédiaires dans un processus où ne se distinguent plus technologie et marché, itérativité et interactivité, conception usages." In Philippe Geslin and Pascal Salembier (eds.), *La co-construction des connaissances autour de l'objet technique*. Paris: La Découverte.

Lindbeck, Assar. 1997. *The Swedish Experiment*. Stockholm: Studieförbundet Samhälle Och Näringsliv.

Lindholm Dahlstrand, Åsa. 1997. "Growth and Inventiveness in Technology-based Spin-off Firms." *Research Policy* 26:331–344.

Lindström, Karin. 2001. "KTH Noc Svenska Internets Vagga." *Computer Sweden* 2001-04-02.

Lipartito, Kenneth. 1997. "'Cut-throat' Competition, Corporate Strategy, and the Growth of Network Industries." *Research on Technological Innovation, Management and Policy* 6:3–53.

Lipartito, Keneth. 2000. "Failure to Communicate: British Telecommunication and the American Model." In Jonathan Zeitlin and Gary Herrigel (eds.), *Americanization and Its Limits*. Oxford: Oxford University Press.

Litan, Robert, and Alice Rivlin. 2001. *The Economic Payoff from the Internet Revolution*. Washington D.C.: Brookings.

Locke, Richard. 1995. *Remaking the Italian Economy*. Ithaca, N.Y.: Cornell University Press.

Loomis, Tamara. 2001. "Data Privacy; A Few Companies Have Complied with EU Law." *New York Law Journal*, ⟨http://www.law.com⟩, August 30.

Lorentz, Francis. 1998. "Rapport sur le commerce électronique." Report to MINEFI (Ministère de l'Economie, des Finances et de l'industrie), March 15, Paris.

Lorentz, Francis. 1999. "La nouvelle donne du commerce électronique." Report, Mission Commerce Electronique, présidée par F. Lorentz, Ministère de l'économie des finances et de l'industrie, Les Ed. de Bercy, ⟨http://www.finances.gouv.fr/mission_commerce_ electronique⟩.

MacDuffie, John Paul. 1997. "The Road to 'Root Cause': Shop-floor Problem-solving at Three Auto Assembly Plants." *Management Science* 43:479–502.

MacDuffie, John Paul, and Susan Helper. 1997. "Creating Lean Suppliers: Diffusing Lean Production Through the Supply Chain." *California Management Review* 39:118–151.

References

Malmsten, Ernst, Erik Portanger, and Charles Drazin. 2001. *Boo Hoo: A dot.com Story from Concept to Catastrophe.* London: Random House.

Manufacturing Engineering. 2001. "Covisint Moves Ahead." *Manufacturing Engineering* March, 22–23.

Manzar, Osama, Madanmohan Rao, and Tufail Ahmad (eds.). 2001. *The Internet Economy of India.* New Delhi: INOMY Media.

MarketManager. Version 2000-1. Stockholm: MM Pactner. ⟨www.mmp.se⟩.

Markoff, John. 1993. "A Free and Simple Computer Link." *The New York Times,* December 8, D1.

Marti, Eric. 2000. "SAP and the Online Procurement Market." Case #EC-5:Version (C), Center for Electronic Business and Commerce, Stanford Graduate School of Business, Stanford University.

Mazzoleni, Roberto, and Richard Nelson. 1998. "Economic Theories About the Benefits and Costs of Patents." *Journal of Economic Issues* 32:1031–1052.

McCraw, Tom. 1984. "Business and Government: The Origins of the Adversary Relationship." *California Management Review* 26:33–52.

McGrew, Thomas J. 1991. "Twentieth Anniversary of the NAD/NARB Industry Self-regulatory Program: Remarks." In *Proceedings NAD Workshop III: Advances in Claim Substantiation,* New York, April 29–30, pp. 9–14.

McKelvey, Maureen, François Texier, and Håkan Alm. 1998. "The Dynamics of High Tech Industry: Swedish Firms Developing Mobile Telecommunication Systems." Linköping: University Of Linköping, Department of Technology and Social Change, Systems of Innovation Research Program (SIRP).

McKenna, Chris. 1999. "Economics of Knowledge: A Theory of Management Consulting." Mimeo, ESSEC.

McKinsey Global Institute. 2000. *Why the Japanese Economy Is Not Growing: Micro Barriers to Productivity Growth.* Washington D.C.: McKinsey & Co.

Media Metrix, ⟨www.mediametrix.com⟩.

Médiangles. 1999. "Les Français et Internet." Paris: Conseil Supérieur de l'Audiovisuel, ⟨http://www.csa.fr/html/etude.htm⟩.

Mehta, Dewang (ed.). 1999. *Nasscom's Handbook: IT-enabled Services.* Delhi: NASSCOM.

Mehta, Dewang (ed.). 2001a. *Indian IT Software and Services Directory—2001.* Delhi: NASSCOM.

Mehta, Dewang (ed.). 2001b. *The IT Software and Services Industry in India—Strategic Review 2001.* Delhi: NASSCOM.

References

Meissner, Heinz-Rudolf, and Frieder Naschold. 1999. "Internationalisierung durch strategische Allianzbildung zwischen Siemens und Newbridge: Aus dem monopolitschen Heimatmarkt auf den kompetiven nordamerikanischen 'Lead-Market' in einem neuen Technologiefeld." In Frieder Naschold, Christoph Doerrenbaecher, Heinz-Rudolf Meissner, and Leo Renneke (eds.), *Kooperieren ueber Grenzen: Evolutionsprozesse globaler Produktentwicklungsverbuende in der InfoCom-Industrie.* Heidelberg: Physika Verlag.

METI. 2001. "Nihon no Benchaa Kyapitaru ni kansuru Hokokusho" (Benchmarking Report on Venture Capital in Japan). Tokyo: METI Agency for Small and Medium Enterprises.

Metiu, Anca. 2001. "Faraway, So Close: Code Ownership Over Innovative Work in the Global Software Industry." Ph.D. diss., Wharton School, University of Pennsylvania, Philadelphia, Pa.

Meurling, John and Richard Jeans. 1995. *A Switch in Time: AXE—Creating a Foundation for the Information Age.* London: Communications Week International.

Meurling, John, and Richard Jens. 1994. *The Mobile Phone Book: The Invention of the Mobile Phone Industry.* London: Communications Week International.

Meyer, John W., John Boli, George M. Thomas, and Francisco O. Ramirez. 1997. "World Society and the Nation-State." *American Journal of Sociology* 103:144–181.

Milgram, Stanley. 1967. "The Small World Problem." *Psychology Today* 2:60–67.

Miller, Gary. 1992. *Managerial Dilemmas.* Cambridge: Cambridge University Press.

Milligan, Brian. 2001. "What is Covisint." *Purchasing* March 8. ⟨www.manufacturing.net/pur/⟩

Ministère de l'Economie et des Finances. 2000. *L'industrie française des technologies de l'information et de la communication en chiffres (edition 2000).* Paris: SESSI.

Ministère d'Economie, des Finances, et de l'Industrie, ⟨www.minefi.gouv.fr/minefi/chiffres/comelac/tbce/indi/indi.htm⟩.

Ministry of Commerce, Industry and Energy. 2000a. *A White Paper on Electronic Commerce.* Seoul: Ministry of Commerce, Industry and Energy.

Ministry of Commerce, Industry, and Energy. 2000b. "B2B e-Marketplace Will Be in Operation in Later 2000." Press release, August 18.

Ministry of Information and Communication. 2000. "Report on Communication Services Subscribers." Press release. Seoul: Ministry of Information and Communication.

Mishra, Asim Kumar. 1996. *Venture Capital Financing in India.* New Delhi: Shipra Publications.

Mölleryd, Bengt G. 1999. *Entrepreneurship in Technological Systems: The Development of Mobile Telephony in Sweden.* Stockholm: EFI, Stockholm School Of Economics.

Moore, Richard K. 1996. "Telecom Regimes," ⟨http://www.cni.org/Hforums/roundtable/1996-02/0056.html⟩.

Moran, Nuala. 2000. "Don't Forget the Little Guy," *Financial Times* (November 15), available from ⟨specials.ft.com/eprocurement/FT39UWWXKFC.html⟩.

Mowery, David C., and Timothy Simcoe. 2001. "Is the Internet a U.S. Invention? An Economic and Technological History of Computer Networking." Mimeo, Haas School of Business, University of California, Berkeley.

MPHPT. 2000. *Communication Usage Trend Survey.* Tokyo: Ministry of Public Management Home Affairs, Post and Telecommunications.

MPHPT. 2001. *Information and Communications in Japan: 2001.* White paper. Tokyo: Ministry of Public Management, Home Affairs, Posts and Telecommunications.

MPT. 1999. *Tsushin Hakusho.* White paper. Tokyo: Ministry of Post and Telecommunications.

MPT. 2000. *Communications in Japan 2000,* ⟨http://www.mpt.go.jp/eng/⟩.

Myers, Stewart C., and Nicolas Majluf. 1984. "Corporate Financing and Investment Decisions When Firms Have Information that Investors Do Not Have." *Journal of Financial Economics* 13:187–221.

Naisbitt, John. 1982. *Megatrends: Ten New Directions Transforming Our Lives.* New York: Warner Books.

Närings-Och Teknikutvecklingsverket. 1993. *Datornät Och Telekommunikationer: Infrastruktur För Informationssamhället.* Stockholm: NUTEK.

Näringsdepartementet. 2000. "IT Som Tillväxtmotor: Rapport Från Näringsdepartementet Om Informationsteknikens Betydelse För Tillväxt Och Sysselsättning I Sverige." Stockholm: Näringsdepartementet.

NASSCOM. 2001. National Association of Software and Service Companies Web site, ⟨http://www.nasscom.org⟩.

NASSCOM-McKinsey Study. 2000. *Indian I.T. Strategies.* Delhi: NASSCOM.

National Consumers Council. 2000. "E-commerce and Consumer Protection," ⟨cgi.www.ncc.org.uk⟩.

Negroponte, Nicholas. 1995. *Being Digital.* New York: Knopf.

Nelson, Richard R. (ed.). 1993. *National Innovation Systems: A Comparative Analysis.* New York: Oxford University Press.

NetValue, ⟨www.netvalue.com⟩.

Newbizz. 2001. "Au secours, le Minitel revient!" edited by Pierre Agède, ⟨www.01net.com/rdn?oid=135094&rub=1569&page=0-135094⟩, January 25.

NFO Infratest. 2001. *Monitoring Information Economics: Third Core Report,* available from ⟨http://193.202.26.202/bmwi/index.htm⟩.

References

NFO-MBL Research and Consultancy Group. 2000. *The Indian Internet User Survey 1999*. Hyderabad, India: MBL.

Nie, Norman, and Lutz Erbring. 2000. *Internet and Society. A Preliminary Report*. Stanford, Calif.: Stanford Institute for the Quantitative Study of Society.

Nielsen Netratings. 2001. "International Top Ten Properties." November 2001, ⟨http://www.nielsen-netratings.com/hot_off_the_net.jsp⟩.

Nikkei. 2000. *Shido: Netto Bizinesu* (Internet Business has Begun). Tokyo: Nihon Keizai Shinbunsha.

Nishiguchi, Toshihiro. 1994. *Strategic Industrial Sourcing: The Japanese Advantage*. New York: Oxford University Press.

Nishiguchi, Toshihiro. 1998. "Case Study: The Toyota Group and the Aisin Fire." *Sloan Management Review* 40:49–53.

North, Douglass, and Robert Thomas. 1973. *The Rise of the Western World: A New Economic History*. Cambridge: Cambridge University Press.

Nua Internet Surveys, ⟨www.nua.ie⟩.

NVCA (National Venture Capital Association). 2000a. "Venture Capital Funds Raise a Record $46.55 Billion in 1999." Press release, March 27.

NVCA. 2000b. *2000 National Venture Capital Association Yearbook*. Washington, DC: NVCA.

NVCA. 2001. *2001 National Venture Capital Association Yearbook*. Washington, DC: NVCA.

Odaka, Konosuke, Keinosuke Ono, and Fumihiko, Adachi. 1988. *The Automobile Industry in Japan: A Study of Ancillary Firm Development*. Oxford: Oxford University Press.

OECD (Organisation for Economic Co-operation and Development). 1996. *Information Infrastructure Policies in OECD Countries*. Paris: OECD.

OECD. 1998. *France's Experience with the Minitel: Lessons for Electronic Commerce Over the Internet*. Report. Paris: OECD.

OECD. 1999a. *Building Infrastructure Capacity for Electronic Commerce: Leased Line Developments and Pricing*. Paris: OECD Working Party on Telecommunications and Information Service Policies.

OECD. 1999b. *Recommendation of the OECD Council Concerning Guidelines for Consumer Protection in the Context of Electronic Commerce*. Paris: OECD.

OECD. 2000. *A New Economy? The Changing Role of Innovation and Information Technology in Growth*. Paris: OECD.

OECD. 2001. *Understanding the Digital Divide*. Paris: OECD.

Office of Fair Trading [OFT]. 2000. *E-commerce and Its Implications for Competition Policy*. London: HMSO.

Office of Telecom [OFTEL]. 2000. "Determination of a Dispute Between BT and MCI Worldcom Concerning the Provision of a Flat Rate Internet Access Call Origination Product (FRIACO)," ⟨http://www.oftel.gov.uk/publications/internet/fria0500.htm⟩.

Pastore, Michael. 2000. "European Shoppers Moving Online." *Cyberatlas*, ⟨http://www.cyberatlas.com⟩.

Paul, Christian. 2000. *Du droit et des libertés sur l'Internet. La corégulation, contribution française pour une régulation mondiale*. Paris: Rapport au Premier Ministre.

Perkins, Anthony. 2000. "Investors: Brace Yourselves for the Next Bubble Bath." *Red Herring* (November 13):21–22.

Perlmutter, Howard V. 1969. "The Tortuous Evolution of the Multinational Corporation." *Columbia Journal of World Business* (January/February):9–18.

Perrin, Noel. 1979. *Giving Up the Gun: Japan's Reversion to the Sword, 1543–1879*. Boston: David Godine.

Peterson, Molly M. 2000. "E-commerce: Growing Concern in Cyberspace." *National Journal* September 2, 2718–2719.

Petty, Ross D. 1994. "Advertising Law and Social Issues: The Global Perspective." *Suffolk Transnational Law Review* 17:309.

Piore, Michael, and Charles Sabel. 1984. *The Second Industrial Divide: Possibilities for Prosperity*. New York: Basic Books.

Pinch, Trevor J., and Wiebe Bijker. 1987. "The Social Construction of Facts and Artifacts." In Wiebe Bijker, Thomas P. Hughes, and Trevor J. Pinch (eds.), *The Social Construction of Technological Systems: New Directions in the Sociology and History of Technology*. Cambridge, Mass.: MIT Press.

Pitofsky, Robert. 2000. "Balancing the New Powers and Interests of Consumers and Business in Cyberspace Commerce." Speech at American Bar Association 2000 Annual Meeting, July 17, London.

Pontusson, Jonas. 1992. "The Limits of Social Democracy: Investment Politics in Sweden." *Cornell Studies in Political Economy*. Ithaca, N.Y.: Cornell University Press.

Pontusson, Jonas, and Peter Swensson, 1996, "Labour Markets, Production Strategies and Wage Bargaining Institutions: The Swedish Employer Offensive in Comparative Perspective." *Comparative Political Studies* 29:223–250.

Porter, Michael. 1990. *The Competitive Advantage of Nations*. Boston: Harvard Business School Press.

Porter, Michael E., Hirotaka Takeuchi, and Mariko Sakakibara. 2000. *Can Japan Compete?* London: Macmillan Press.

Post- och Telestyrelsen. 2000. *IT-infrastrukturen i Sverige*, Stockholm: PTS.

References

Press, Larry, William Foster, and Seymour E. Goodman. 2000. "The Internet in India and China." Manuscript, Tucson: University of Arizona.

PriceWaterhouseCoopers. 2001. "Internet 150 Report," October.

Putnam, Robert. 1993. *Making Democracy Work: Civic Traditions in Modern Italy.* Princeton, N.J.: Princeton University Press.

Ragin, Charles. 1987. *The Comparative Method.* Berkeley: University of California Press.

Rallet, Alain. 2001. "Du commerce électronique à l'électronisation du commerce." In Pierre-Jean Benghozi, Christian Licoppe, and Alain Rallet (eds.), *Réseaux Special Issue: Internet et le commerce électronique* Paris: Hermès Science Publications.

Ramamurti, Ravi, and Devesh Kapur. 2001. "India's Emerging Competitive Advantage in Services." *The Academy of Management Executive* 15:20–32.

Rapport AFTEL. 1994. *La télématique française en marche vers les autoroutes de l'information.* Paris: les Éditions du Téléphone.

Regnér, Patrick. 1999. *Strategy Creation and Change in Complexity: Adaptive and Creative Learning Dynamics in the Firm.* Ph.d. diss., Institute Of International Business, Stockholm School Of Economics, Stockholm.

Reidenberg, Joel R. 1997. "Governing Networks and Rule-making in Cyberspace." In Brian Kahin and Charles Nesson (eds.), *Borders in Cyberspace: Information Policy and the Global Information Infrastructure.* Cambridge, Mass.: MIT Press.

Reka, Albert, and Albert-Laszlo Barabasi. 2001. "Statistical Mechanics of Complex Networks." Manuscript, University of Minnesota/University of Notre Dame.

Reuters. 2001. "Automakers Must Explain Covisint Better—Study." Press release, January 13.

Rheingold, Howard. 1993. *The Virtual Community: Homesteading on the Electronic Frontier.* Reading, Mass.: Addison-Wesley.

Roberts, Larry. 2001. "Opportunities in Internet Access Infrastructure, and E-commerce— What's Alive, What's History." 2001 AVF/U.S. The Asia-Silicon Valley Venture Capital Forum, Palo Alto, California, May 21–23.

Rocha, Luis M. 2001. "Adaptive Webs for Heterarchies with Diverse Communities of Users." Paper prepared for the workshop, From Intelligent Networks to the Global Brain: Evolutionary Social Organization Through Knowledge Technology, Brussels, July 3–5.

Rogers, Juan. 1998. "Internetworking and the Politics of Science: NSFNET in Internet History." *The Information Society* 14:213–228.

Rowen, Henry. 2000. "Serendipity or Strategy: How Technology and Markets Came to Favor Silicon Valley." In Chong-Moon Lee, William Miller, Marguerite Gong Hancock, and Henry Rowen (eds.), *The Silicon Valley Edge: A Habitat for Innovation and Entrepreneurship.* Stanford, Calif.: Stanford University Press.

Sabety, Pari. 2001. "B2B Practices in the Automotive Sector." Presented to NEOSA Monthly Meeting, May 2, ⟨http://www.neosa.org⟩.

Sagari, Silvia B., and Gabriela Guidotti. 1992. "Venture Capital: Lessons from the Developed World for the Developing Markets." IFC Discussion Paper no. 13, Washington, D.C.: The World Bank.

Sagatel. 2001. Confidential report, ⟨www.sagatel.com/fr/fr_etudes&prod.asp?action= teleseeq⟩.

Sako, Mari. 1992. *Prices, Quality, and Trust: Inter-firm Relations in Britain and Japan.* New York: Cambridge University Press.

Sako, Mari. 1996. "Supplier Associations in the Car Industry: Collective Action for Technology Diffusion." *Cambridge Journal of Economics* 20:651–671.

Sako, Mari. 1999. "From Individual Skills to Organisational Capability in Japan." *Oxford Review of Economic Policy* 15:114–126.

Sako, Mari, and Max Warburton. 1999. "MIT International Motor Vehicle Programme Modularization Project: Preliminary Report of European Research Team." IMVP Annual Forum, October 6–7, Boston.

Sams Publishing. 1994. *The Internet Unleashed.* Indianapolis: Sams Publishing.

Saunders, John. 1998. "Newbridge Stock Tumbles After Ominous Prediction." *Computing Canada* February 23, 34.

Sawhney, Mohanbir, and Steven Kaplan. 1999. "Let's Get Vertical." *Business 2.0*, September, ⟨http://www.business2.com⟩.

Saxenian, Annalee. 1994. *Regional Advantage.* Cambridge, Mass.: Harvard University Press.

Saxenian, AnnaLee. 1999. *Silicon Valley's New Immigrant Entrepreneurs.* San Francisco: Public Policy Institute of California.

Schelling, Thomas C. 1960. *Strategy of Conflict.* Cambridge: Harvard University Press.

Schmidt, Susanne K., and Raymond Werle. 1998. *Coordinating Technology: Studies in the International Standardization of Telecommunications.* Cambrdige, Mass.: MIT Press.

Seabright, Paul, and Jennifer Halliday. 2001. "Networks Good, Cartels Bad: But How Could Anyone Tell the Difference?" In *Fighting Cartels—Why and How?* Stockholm: Konkurrensverket.

Servan-Schreiber, Jean-Jacques. 1967. *Le défi américain.* Paris: Denoël.

Service des Etudes et des Statistiques Industrielles (SESSI). 2000. *Le 4 Pages des Statistiques industrielles* no. 128.

SESSI. 1997. "Technologies de l'information, Insee-Sessi-SJTI." *Chiffres clés Analyse.* Paris: Ministère de l'économie, des Finances et de l'industrie.

SESSI. 1999. "Technologies et société de l'information, Insee-Sessi-SJTI." *Chiffres Clés Analyse* no. 207, Paris: Ministère de l'économie, des Finances et de l'industrie.

SESSI. 2000. *L'industrie française des technologies de l'information et de la communication en chiffres.* Paris: Ministère de l'économie, des finances et de l'industrie.

SESSI. 2001. *Tableau de bord de l'innovation,* no. 5. Paris: SESSI.

Shaffer, Gregory. 2000. "Globalization and Social Protection: The Impact of EU and International Rules in the Ratcheting Up of U.S. Privacy Standards." *Yale Journal of International Law* 25:1–89.

Shapiro, Carl, and Hal R. Varian. 1999. *Information Rules: A Strategic Guide to the Network Economy.* Boston: Harvard Business School Press.

Sharp, Margaret. 1999. "The Science of Nations: European Multinationals and American Biotechnology." *International Journal of Biotechnology* 1:132–162.

SMEA. 1998. *Chusho Kigyo Hakusho* (White Paper on Small and Medium Enterprises). Tokyo: Small and Medium Enterprise Agency.

Smith, Michael, Joseph Bailey, and Erik Brynjolfsson. 2000. "Understanding Digital Markets: Review and Assessment." In Erik Brynjolfsson and Brian Kahin (eds.), *Understanding the Digital Economy.* Cambridge, MA: MIT Press.

Söderlund, Peter. 2001. "En Internetpionjär Talar Ut." *Computer Sweden,* ⟨computersweden.idg.se⟩, January 21.

Södersten, Jan. 1984. "Sweden." In Mervyn A. King and Don Fullerton (eds.), *The Taxation of Income from Capital: A Comparative Study of the United States, the United Kingdom, Sweden and West Germany.* Chicago: University of Chicago Press.

Söderström, Hans Tson (ed.). 2001. *Kluster.Se.* Stockholm: SNS Förlag.

Softbank Corp. 2000. *Annual Report 2000,* available from ⟨www.softbank.co.jp⟩.

Sorenson, Olav, and Toby Stuart. 2001. "Syndication Networks and the Spatial Distribution of Venture Capital Investment." *American Journal of Sociology* 106:1546–1588.

Soskice, David. 1990. "Wage Determination: The Changing Role of Institutions in Advanced Industrialized Countries." *Oxford Review of Economic Policy* 6:36–61.

Soskice, David. 1997. "German Technology Policy, Innovation, and National Institutional Frameworks." *Industry and Innovation* 4:75–96.

Standage, Tom. 1999. *The Victorian Internet: The Remarkable Story of the Telegraph and the Nineteenth Century's Online Pioneers.* New York: Berkley Books.

Stark, David. 1996. "Recombinant Property in East European Capitalism." *American Journal of Sociology* 101:993–1027.

Statens Institut För Kommunikationsanalys. 2001. *Fakta Om Informations—Och Kommunikationsteknik I Sverige 2001.* Stockholm: Sika.

References

Steers, Richard, Yookeun Shin, and Gerardo Ungson. 1989. *The Chaebol: Korea's New Industrial Might.* New York: Harper & Row.

Sternberg, Rolf, and Christine Tamasy. 1999. "Munich as Germany's no. 1 High Technology Region: Empirical Evidence, Theoretical Explanations and the Role of Small Firm/Large Firm Relationships." *Regional Studies* 33:367–337.

Stinchcombe, Arthur. 1965. "Social Structure and Organizations." In James G. March (ed.), *Handbook of Organizations.* Chicago: Rand McNally.

Stone, Peter H. 2000. "Allaying the Fear of Big Brother, Inc." *National Journal* June 17, 1924–1925.

Strauss-Kahn, Dominique. 1998. "Dix mesures pour le développement du commerce électronique MINEFI." Report to MINEFI (Ministère de l'Economie, des Finances et de l'industrie), May 6, Paris.

Streeck, Wolfgang. 1984. *Industrial Relations in West Germany: A Case Study of the Car Industry.* New York: St. Martin's.

Streeck, Wolfgang. 1992. "On the Institutional Preconditions of Diversified Quality Production." In Wolfgang Streeck (ed.), *Social Institutions and Economic Performance.* London: Sage.

Strenio, Andrew J., Jr. 1990. "The FTC in 1989: Rising from the Ashes?" In Patrick E. Murphy and William L. Wilkie (eds.), *Marketing and Advertising Regulation: The Federal Trade Commission in the 1990s.* Notre Dame: University of Notre Dame Press.

Stuart, Leslie. 2000. "The Biggest 'Angel' of Them All: The Military and the Making of the Silicon Valley." In Martin Kenney (ed.), *Understanding Silicon Valley: The Anatomy of an Entrepreneurial Region.* Stanford, Calif.: Stanford University Press.

Suchman, Mark. 2000. "Dealmakers and Counselors: Law Firms as Intermediaries in the Development of Silicon Valley." In Martin Kenney (ed.), *Understanding Silicon Valley: Anatomy of an Entrepreneurial Region.* Stanford, Calif.: Stanford University Press.

Svensk Handel. 2001. "Internetindikatorn." 3:E Kvartalet, ⟨http://www.svenskhandel.se/Filer/internetkv301.pdf⟩.

Svensson, Viktor. 2000. "Telelogic Lovar Stark Tillväxt." *Finanstidningen*, ⟨www.finanstidningen.se⟩, October 24.

Sveriges Tekniska Attachéer. 1999. "IT-Mognaden I Världen—En Jämförande Analys Mellan Europa, USA Och Sydostasien." Stockholm: Sveriges Tekniska Attachéer.

Swedish Venture Capital Association. 2000. ⟨www.vencap.se⟩.

Swidler, Ann. 2001. *Talk of Love: How Culture Matters.* Chicago: University of Chicago.

Swindel, Orson. 2000. "Dissenting Statement of Commissioner Orson Swindel." In U.S. Federal Trade Commission, *Privacy Online: Fair Information Practices in the Electronic Marketplace.* Washington, D.C.: FTC.

References

Swire, Peter P., and Robert E. Litan. 1998. *None of Your Business: World Data Flows, Electronic Commerce, and the European Privacy Directive.* Washington, DC: Brookings Institution.

Tapscott, Don. 1998. *Growing Up Digital: The Rise of the Net Generation.* New York: McGraw Hill.

Tate, Jay. 2001. "National Varieties of Standardization." In Peter. A. Hall and David Soskice (eds.), *Varieties of Capitalism: The Institutional Foundations of Comparative Advantage.* Oxford: Oxford University Press.

Taylor, Alex III. 2000. "Detroit Goes Digital." *Fortune* April 17:173–176.

Tbg. 2001. "Sectoral Distribution of Public Venture Capital," ⟨http://www.tbgbonn.de/info/index.html⟩.

Teece, David. 1986. "Profiting from Technological Innovation: Implications for Integration, Collaboration, Licensing, and Public Policy." *Research Policy* 15:285–305.

TELDOK. 2000. *Teldoks Årsbok 2000.* Stockholm: TELDOK.

Telegeography, Inc. 2000. *Hubs and Spokes: A Telegeography Internet Reader.* Washington, D.C.: Telegeography, Inc.

Tett, Gillian, and Alexandra Harney. 2000. "Japan Awaits Buyer's Vision for Bank," *Financial Times* (June 7):36.

Thelen, Kathleen. 2000. "Why German Employers Cannot Bring Themselves to Abandon the German Model." In Torben Iversen, Jonus Pontusson and David Soskice (eds.), *Unions, Employers and Banks.* New York: Cambridge University Press.

Théry, Gérard. 1994. *Les autoroutes de l'information.* Paris: La Documentation française.

Thompson, George V. 1954. "Intercompany Technical Standardization in the Early American Automobile Industry." *Journal of Economic History* 14:1–20.

Tilly, Charles. 1984. *Big Structures, Large Processes, Huge Comparisons.* New York: Russell Sage.

Tolliday, Steven, Robert Boyer, Elsie Charron, and Ulrich Jürgens. 1998. "Introduction: Between Imitation and Innovation: The Transfer and Hybridization of Productive Models in the International Automobile Industry." In Robert Boyer, Elsie Charron, Ulrich Jürgens and Steven Tolliday (eds.), *Between Imitation and Innovation.* Oxford: Oxford University Press.

Toth, Bob. 1996. "Putting the US Standardization System in Perspective." *Standard View* 4:169–178.

Totty, Michael. 2001. "The Next Phase: Contrary to Rumor, B-to-B E-commerce is Showing Surprising Signs of Life." *Wall Street Journal* (May 21):R8.

Trading Standards Institute. 2000. "Shopping on the Internet—Better Safe Than Sorry," ⟨www.tradingstandards.gov.uk/fife/shopping.htm⟩.

Tronc, Jean-Noël. 1999. "Le rôle conjoint de la puissance publique et des acteurs de l'Internet: la corégulation." In Premières rencontres parlementaires sur la société de l'information et l'Internet: *Internet, la révolution numérique crée-t-elle une révolution juridique?* Paris, Assemblée nationale, Octobre 5.

Turkle, Sherry. 1995. *Life on the Screen: Identity in the Age of the Internet.* New York: Simon & Schuster.

Tylecote, Andrew, and E. Conesa. 1999. "Corporate Governance, Innovation Systems, and Industrial Policy." *Industry and Innovation* 6:25–50.

Ulrich, Karl. 1995. "The Role of Product Architecture in the Manufacturing Firm." *Research Policy* 24:419–440.

UMTS Intellectual Property Association. 2001. "Industry Group Plans a 5% Maximum Royalty for 3G Systems 2001." Accessed 9/20/2001, ⟨http://www.3gpatents.com/Press/99109d.htm⟩.

Upin, Eric. 1999. "The B-to-Bs Are Coming." Presentation to November 2 Venture Capitalist Luncheon, Menlo Park, Calif.

U.S. Department of Commerce. 1998. "The Emerging Digital Economy." Report, ⟨http://www.ecommerce.gov/emerging.htm⟩.

U.S. Department of Commerce, 2000a. "Safe Harbor Privacy Principles," July 14, ⟨www.export.gov/safeharbor/SHPRINCIPLESFINAL.htm⟩.

U.S. Department of Commerce. 2000b. "Damages for Breaches of Privacy, Legal Authorizations and Mergers and Takeovers in U.S. Law," July 14, ⟨www.export.gov/safeharbor/PRIVACYDAMAGESFINAL.htm⟩.

U.S. Federal Trade Commission. 2000. *Privacy Online: Fair Information Practices in the Electronic Marketplace, A Report to Congress.* Washington, D.C.: GPO.

Uzzi, Brian. 1996. "The Sources and Consequences of Embeddedness for the Economic Performance of Organizations: The Network Effect." *American Sociological Review* 61:674–698.

Valentine, Debra. 2000. "Privacy on the Internet: The Evolving Legal Landscape." Prepared remarks at Santa Clara University, February 11–12.

Varney, Christine A. 1996. "Consumer Privacy in the Information Age: A View from the United States." Prepared remarks before the Privacy and American Business National Conference, October 9, Washington, D.C.

VEC. 2001. *Japanese Venture Capital Investment Survey.* Tokyo: Venture Enterprise Centre.

Ventresca, Marc. 2002. "Why So Many Organizational Forms? The Global Proliferation of Exchange-Traded Growth Markets, 1993-2002." Working paper, Kellogg School of Management, Northwestern University, Chicago, Ill.

Verma, J. C. 1997. *Venture Capital Financing in India.* London: Sage.

VerticalNet. 2001. ⟨http://www.verticalnet.com⟩.

References

Vietor, Richard H. K. 1994. *Contrived Competition: Regulation and Deregulation in America.* Cambridge, Mass.: Belknap Press of Harvard University Press.

Vitols, Sigurt. 2000. "Frankfurt's Neuer Markt and the IPO Explosion: Is Germany on the Road to Silicon Valley Yet?" Mimeo, Wissenschaftszentrum Berlin für Sozialforschung, Berlin.

Vogel, David. 1981. "The 'New' Social Regulation in Historical and Comparative Perspective." In Thomas K. McCraw (ed.), *Regulation in Perspective: Historical Essays.* Boston: Harvard Business School Press.

Vogel, Steven. 1996. *Freer Markets, More Rules.* Ithaca, N.Y.: Cornell University Press.

von Burg, Urs. 2001a. *The Birth of the Local Networking Industry.* Stanford, Calif.: Stanford University Press.

von Burg, Urs. 2001b. *The Triumph of Ethernet: Technological Communities and the Battle for the LAN Standard.* Stanford, Calif.: Stanford University Press.

von Hippel, Eric. 1988. *The Sources of Innovation.* New York: Oxford University Press.

von Hippel, Eric. 2001. "Perspective: User Toolkits for Innovation." Journal of Product Innovation Management 18:247–257.

Wall Street Journal. 2000. "No Fun and Games." *Wall Street Journal* (October 23):R21.

Wallerstien, Michael. 2000. "Post-war Wage Setting in the Nordic Countries." In Torben Iversen, Jonus Pontusson, and David Soskice (eds.), *Unions, Employers and Banks.* New York: Cambridge University Press.

Waraniak, John. 2001. "Lean Thinking: Creating a No Fear Value Chain Based on Collaboration." Accessed January 10, ⟨http://www.sae.org/topics/leanapr01.htm⟩.

Watts, Duncan J., and Steven H. Strogatz. 1998. "Collective Dynamics of 'Small-World' Networks." *Nature* 393:440–442.

Waxer, Cindy. 2000. "Wal-Mart Takes Another Crack at the Net." *Business 2.0* January:82–85.

Webmergers. 2001. "Mid-year Report: Internet Shutdowns Appear to Reach Plateau." ⟨http://www.webmergers.com/editorial/article.php?id=37⟩.

Webnoize Research, ⟨www.webnoize.com/item.rs⟩.

Wecker, Daniel. 2001. "Role of the E-Marketplace." Presented to Covisint: A B2B Primer for Original Equipment Automotive Suppliers, May 10, Cleveland, Ohio.

Weil, Thierry. 2000. *Why and How European Companies Reach Out to Silicon Valley.* Notes de l'Ifri no. 25. Paris: La Documentation Française.

Wellman, Barry. 1999. *Networks in the Global Village: Life in Contemporary Communities.* Boulder, Colo.: Westview Press.

Wellman, Barry, and Milena Gulia. 1999. "Virtual Communities as Communities: Net Surfers Don't Ride Alone." In Marc Smith and Peter Kollock (eds.), *Communities in Cyberspace*. London: Routledge.

Westney, D. Eleanor. 1987. *Imitation and Innovation: The Transfer of Western Organizational Patterns to Meiji Japan*. Cambridge, Mass.: Harvard University Press.

White, Alissa, and Roberto Coronado. 2000. *Networks.Com—A Study of Interlocking Directories in the Swedish Internet Industry*. Master's thesis, Stockholm School Of Economics, Stockholm.

Whitley, Richard (ed.). 1992. *European Business Systems: Firms and Markets in Their National Contexts*. London: Sage.

Whitley, Richard. 1999. *Divergent Capitalisms: The Social Structuring and Change of Business Systems*. Oxford: Oxford University Press.

Whittington, Richard. 2001. *What Is Strategy?* 2d ed. London: Thomson Learning.

Williamson, Oliver. 1985. *The Economic Institutions of Capitalism*. New York: Free Press.

Wirtschaftswoche. 2000, "Aktien statt Mitbestimmung," March 9, ⟨www.wirtschaftswoche. de⟩.

Wittke, Volker, and Heidemarie Hanekop. 1999. "National Divergence in Developing Broadband Internet Access: The Specifics of the German Case." Paper presented at the Telecommunications Policy Research Conference, Alexandria, Va, September 25–27.

Woolgar, Steve. 2000. "The Virtual Society." Presented to British/French Doctoral Seminar, Fédération de Recherches sur les Organisations et leur Gestion/Said Business School, Oxford, November 21.

World Bank. 2001. *World Development Indicators*, Washington, D.C.: World Bank Group.

Wright, Mike, Andy Lockett, and Sarika Pruthi. 2001. "Internationalization of Western Venture Capitalists into Emerging Markets: Risk Assessment and Information in India." Nottingham, U.K.: University of Nottingham Business School Working Paper.

Wright, Vincent (ed.). 1994. *Privatization in Western Europe: Pressures, Problems and Paradoxes*. London: Pinter.

Yahoo!. 2002. ⟨biz.yahoo.com/rf/020109/n09197574_2.html⟩, accessed January 9.

Yankee Group. 1999. "Telecommunications Ranking Charts." New York: Yankee Group.

Yao, Dennis A., and Christa van Anh Vecchi. 1992. "Information and Decisionmaking at the Federal Trade Commission." *Journal of Public Policy and Marketing* 11:1–11.

Yao, Dennis A., and Joseph G. Krauss. 1994. "Prospects for Harmonization of United States and European Union Antitrust Laws Concerning International Strategic Alliances." In Chia-Jui Cheng and Lawrence S. Liu (eds.), *Proceedings of the Symposium on International Harmonization of Competition Laws*. Taipei: ROC Fair Trade Commission.

References

Yolin, Jean-Michel. 1999. "Internet et Entreprise: mirage ou opportunité pour les PME? Pour un plan d'action. Contribution à l'analyse de l'économie de l'Internet." Report, Paris: Ministère de l'Economie, des Finances et de l'Industrie, Secrétariat d'Etat à l'Industrie, ⟨http://www.ensmp.fr/industrie/jmycs/⟩.

Yoshimura, Katsumi. 2000. *I-mode Business Model Impact* (in Japanese). Tokyo: H&I.

Zaheer, Srilata. 2000. "Time Zone Economies and Managerial Work in a Global World." In P. Christopher Earley and Harbir Singh (eds.). *Innovations in International Management.* Thousand Oaks, Calif.: Sage.

Zaheer, Srilata, and Shalini Manrakhan. 2001. "Concentration and Dispersion in Global Industries: Remote Electronic Access and the Location of Economic Activities." *Journal of International Business Studies* 32:667–686.

Zander, Udo, and Bruce Kogut. 1995. "Knowledge and the Speed of the Transfer and Imitation of Organizational Capabilities: An Empirical Test." *Organization Science* 6:76–92.

Zeitlin, Jonathan, and Gary Herrigel (eds.). 2000. *Americanization and Its Limits: Reworking U.S. Technology and Management in Post-war Europe and Japan.* New York: Oxford University Press.

Zelizer, Viviana. 1983. *Morals & Markets: The Development of Life Insurance in the United States.* New York: Columbia University Press.

Zook, Matthew A. 2000. "Internet Metrics: Using Hosts and Domain Counts to Map the Internet Globally." *Telecommunications Policy* 24:613–620.

Zook, Matthew A. 2002. "Grounded Capital: Venture Financing and the Geography of the Internet Industry 1994–2000." *Journal of Economic Geography*, vol 2(2):151–177.

Zooknic Internet Intelligence, ⟨http://www.zooknic.com⟩.

Zuboff, Shoshana. 1988. *In the Age of the Smart Machine: The Future of Work and Power.* New York: Basic Books.

Index

Abbate, Janet, 15–16, 81
Access time, 10
Address, IP, 14
Advanced Research Projects Agency (ARPA), 15–16
Advertising, 412–419
Afghanistan, 467
Akamai, 81, 103
Alando.de, 94
Alcatel, 162, 237
Altavista, 86
Alternative dispute resolution (ADR), 400
Amazon.com, 30, 96–99, 284, 439
American Bell Company, 113
Andhra Pradesh (AP), 207
Andreesen, Marc, 4, 22, 83, 88
Antitrust law, 72, 76
  Covisint, 359
  technical collaboration, 142
AOL, 28, 85, 388, 440
Apache, 464
APAX, 34
Appropriability, 253, 257
Ariba, 103
ARPANET, 16–20, 82
Ascend, 238
Asian Crisis, 268–270, 286
Asset recycling, 231
AT&T, 56, 82, 113
  deregulation, 74–77
  UNIX, 463
ATM (asynchronous transfer mode), 237
ATOSS Software, 255
Auctions, 278, 279, 286
  automobile industry, 351–353

consortia exchanges, 375
Covisint, 359, 364–368
  and design, 344–345
  procurement, 336–337, 339
  supplier investment, 340
Australia, 94, 419
Automobile industry, 333–334, 338–373
  auctions, 351–353
  B2B savings, 357
  collaborative planning and design, 345–347, 353–357, 368
  Covisint, 333, 358–368
  exit/voice mode, 334, 338–346, 354, 356, 361–362, 366–373
  Internet usage, 355–356
  Japan, 338–339, 341–347, 457–458
  product architecture, 371–373
  regulation, 425–426
  software, 363–368, 370–371
  standardization, 339–340, 342–343, 349–351, 364–368
  United States, 338–341, 345–347
Automobile safety systems, 133
AXE, 114

Back-office operations, 443
Bandwidth, 204–205, 237
Bangemann, Martin, 21, 396
Banking system, 32, 34–35
  vs. equity system, 52
  Japanese, 60, 322
  Sweden, 127–128
Bankruptcy law, 58
Baran, Paul, 16
Barnes & Noble, 439

Bechtel, 198
Becker, William, 361
Benghozi, Pierre-Jean, 55, 65, 153–190,
441, 444, 447, 453, 472
Berger, Suzanne, 45
Berners-Lee, Timothy, 20–22, 83
Bertelsmann, 462
Bezos, Jeff, 4, 96
Billaut, Jean Michel, 172
Bina, Eric, 83
Biotechnology industry, 70
Bit Valley, 309
BITNET, 82
Blown to Bits, 459
BMW, 361
Bolt, Beranek, and Newman, 18
Bonnier, 147
Boo.com, 31–32
Bosch, 238, 249
Boston, 51–52, 79
Bourdieu, Pierre, 460
Boyer, Robert, 45, 49
Branding, 220
Britain. *See* United Kingdom
British Telecom, 387, 389–390
Broadband, 11–12
Germany, 227–228
Japan, 304–305, 309
Korea, 266
Brokat, 256
Browser, 14, 21–22, 35, 88, 350
Browser phone, 297
Business-to-Business (B2B) e-commerce, 24-
26, 32, 70, 440–442. *See also* Automobile
industry
Europe vs. U.S., 167, 403
France, 155
Germany, 226–227
India, 194–195
Japan, 299–301
Korea, 280–281
modes of exchange, 332–338, 373–379
national differences, 331–332, 346
Sweden, 128
and trust, 347, 354, 356–357
United Kingdom, 396–397
United States, 100–102, 441
and venture capital, 100–102
Business-to-Consumer (B2C) e-commerce,
24, 26–31, 440
Europe vs. U.S., 167, 403
France, 155, 184–187, 442
Germany, 227, 256, 442
India, 194–196

Japan, 299–300
Korea, 277–280, 442
Sweden, 128, 442
United States, 95–100, 442

Cable & Wireless IDC, 302
Cable modem, 11–12, 228
California, 79
Canada, 94
Capitalism, 458
Carnegie Mellon University (CMU), 205
Carterphone ruling, 76
Casper, Steven, 65, 104, 150, 223–262,
364, 447, 451–452
Castells, Manuel, 7, 40, 179–181, 188
Castilla, Emilio, 39, 51
Causality, 46–47, 50, 52
C-commerce, 367
CDMA (code divisional multiple access),
265–266, 287
Cellular phones. *See* Mobile phone services
Cerf, Vinton, 18
CERN, 18, 20
Chaebols, 263, 267–269, 276, 281–288
Chandler, Alfred, 45
Chang, Sea-Jin, 65–66, 96, 263–290, 441,
447, 450, 452
Chemcross, 281
Chemdex, 101, 374
Chemround, 281
Choi, Jong-Hyun, 284
Choi, Taewon, 284
Chollian, 265
Chrysler, 360–362, 369
Circuit switching, 121–122
Cisco Systems, 19, 86–87, 198, 236, 238
Clark, Jim, 22, 88
Collaborative planning, 338, 345–347,
353–357, 368
Collaborative Planning, Forecasting, and
Replenishment (CPFR), 375–376
Comity principle, 429–430
CommerceOne, 103, 257, 352, 359, 362–
366
Commercialization, 23–33, 437, 459–460.
See also E-commerce
and communities, 26–30
comparison shopping, 31
foreign markets, 31–32
and Internet penetration, 441
network externality, 27–28
in U.S., 69–70, 83–86, 91
Communities, Internet, 26–30, 465, 471
virtual communities, 28–30, 149

Commuted access, 171
Compaq, 86–87
Competency development, 229–234
competency destruction, 254–255, 260–261
high-risk finance, 230, 233
human resource development, 230–231, 233–234
motivational incentives, 231–232, 234
Competition, 74–77
pockets of, 444–445, 454
policy, 385, 388–394, 404, 409
Computer-aided design (CAD), 340, 356
Computer-aided manufacturing (CAM), 340
Computer-numerically controlled machine tools (CNC), 343–344
Condat, 249
Consortia
exchanges, 374–378
standards, 138, 142–143, 149
Consulting companies, 34
Consumer protection, 411, 419–421
EU Privacy Directive, 429–433
FTC, 409–410
privacy, 422–424
Consumer-to-consumer (C2C) e-commerce, 24, 94–95
Convenience stores, 300
Cookies, 14
Cooperation, 53–54
Copyleft, 20
Copyrights, 400–401
Co-regulation, 385, 416, 418
Cosmetic stores, 98
Country suffix, 14, 36
Covisint, 333, 358–359
mega-suppliers, 370
and proprietary exchanges, 365–366
Credit card usage, 71, 105
Credit information, 422
Credit transaction, 30
CSNET, 82
Cultural prototyping, 57–59
Customer service, 443
Cyberspace, 4
Cybersquatting, 37
Cyclades network, 16–18, 155

DACOM, 265, 277
DaimlerChrysler, 360–362, 369
Data communications, 76
Sweden, 117–118, 121
telecom deregulation, 227–228

Database, 186–187
DATEX network, 122
Daum, 278–279
David, Paul, 15, 136
Davies, Donald, 16, 17
DEC, 72, 86
Dell, 86–87
Demographics, user, 23–24
Denmark, 402
Department of Electronics (DOE), 202
Deregulation, telecom. *See also* Regulation
European Union, 160, 329
Germany, 227–228
India, 204–205
and institutional change, 56–57
and Internet penetration, 443–444
Korea, 264–266
Sweden, 109–110, 113–115, 118–120, 148
U.S., 73–77, 104–105, 425
Deutsche Bundespost, 228
Deutsche Telecom, 227–228, 239, 389
Development pairs, 134
Diffusion, 1, 33–34, 47–50
and cultural change, 60
multinational corporations, 48
opposition to, 49
Digital certification, 37
Digital Chosun, 279
Digital convergence, 176
Digital ID, 420
Digital Millennium Copyright Act, 461
Digital signal processing (DSP), 220
Digital signature, 427, 466–467
Digital subscriber line (DSL), 11
DiMaggio, Paul, 67
Dimensional space, 59
Direct Marketing Association (DMA), 417
Disbundled network, 113–114, 124, 148
Disintermediation, 330
Distance Selling, 395–396
Distributed model, 19–20, 72
Diversified quality production, 232
Document management, 248, 348
Documentation conversion, 25
Domain Name, 14, 35–37, 73, 393–394, 471
Dore, Ronald, 45, 292
Dosi, Giovanni, 45, 47, 72, 107
Dumez, Hervé, 329, 381–406, 418, 434, 456, 457

E2open, 300
eBay, 30, 89, 94, 100, 279, 286

EBIT (earnings before interest and
taxation), 249–252
Ebone, 123
E-chaebols, 281–284
E-commerce. *See also* Business-to-Business
(B2B) e-commerce; Business-to-
Consumer (B2C) e-commerce;
Commercialization
C2C, 24, 94–95
Europe vs. U.S., 167, 403
France, 155, 181, 184–187
Germany, 226–227, 255–261, 441
India, 191–192, 194–196, 442
Japan, 299–301, 441–442
Korea, 271–272, 277–281, 286–287,
441–442
market ecology, 411–412
product misrepresentations, 414–415
regulation, 385, 415–421, 424–432
software development, 218, 248, 255–261
Sweden, 128, 441–442
United States, 69–70, 83–86, 91, 94–102,
424–426, 441–442
Economic sociology, 54
EDI (electronic data interchange), 87, 105
automobile industry, 340, 349, 351
Korea, 280–281
Edmonds, David A., 390
e-Envoy, 385–386
E-Hand, 141
EIN, 16
Electronic documentation, 25
Ellemtel, 114
Ellison, Larry, 363, 454
E-mail, 19, 82, 196, 403
Employment policy, 235, 240
England. *See* United Kingdom
English-language market, 91–92, 93–95
Enterprise software, 247–248, 252–255
Entrepreneurship
competency development, 229–232
France, 164–165
Germany, 232–234, 240–241, 244–246
India, 213–214
Korea, 274–276, 287
E.piphany, 103
Epoch, 139
Equity financing, 52, 230, 246
Ericsson, 64, 114, 130, 443
employment policy, 235
and Microsoft, 134
mobile telephony, 117
and PipeChain Inc., 376–377
standardization, 133, 139, 141

Ericsson, Björn, 123
eToys, 100
ETRI (Electronics and
Telecommunications Research Institute),
265
Europe, 16–17
B2B, 167, 403
government policy, 401–403
Internet penetration, 382, 387
mobile phones, 404
telecom sector, 75, 104, 329, 387–390,
401–404
and U.S., 167, 382, 401–402, 430–433
European Commission, 386, 403–405
competitive policy, 388–394
e-Europe initiative, 382
facilitation, 399–401
European Union (EU)
co-regulation model, 416
deregulation, 160, 329
domain names, 36
Privacy Directive, 430–433
Evans, Phillip, 459
Excite, 81, 89
Exit mode, 334, 338–341, 346
Covisint, 361–362, 366, 368
industry strategies, 369
supplier responsibility, 354, 372–373
Eyeball count, 29

Fabmart, 196
Facilitation, 403–405
European Commission, 399–401
France, 399
United Kingdom, 394–397
Fanning, Shawn, 462
Federal Express, 87
Federal Trade Commission (FTC), 409–
410, 418–419, 433
Fiber optics, 120–121, 205
File sharing, peer-to-peer, 462–463
Filo, David, 4
Financing. *See* Venture capital
Finland, 402
First Tuesday, 34–35
Fishround.com, 282
FOMA, 298
Ford, 358, 360–361
France, 153–189. *See also* Minitel
biotechnology in, 58
Breton report, 179
components, 164
Concurrence case, 393–394
e-commerce, 155, 184–187, 442

entrepreneurship, 164–165
France Telecom, 168–173, 182–184
government policy, 382, 397–399, 405,
  453
ICT sector, 157–159
information technology, 163
Internet penetration and usage, 155–157,
  169–170
kiosks, 398
Lorentz report, 177, 397–398
national Web sites, 167
R&D, 182–184
regulation, 386
start-ups, 450
telecom sector, 159–162
Thierry Carcenac report, 399
university network, 155
venture capital, 166–167, 447
Yahoo!, 92–93, 421
Yolin report, 177
Free services, 28
FreeMarkets.com, 352
FRIACO (Flat Rate Internet Access Call
  Origination), 389–390

Games, 140, 296, 305–306
Gandhi, Indira, 201
Gated community, 30, 418
Gates, Bill, 22, 86, 454
General Electric, 197–198, 214
General Motors, 339–340, 358, 361–362,
  373
General Purpose License (GPL), 463–
  464
Geocities, 94
Germany, 5, 65, 223–262
  competency destruction, 254–255, 260–
    261
  connectivity technology, 239–240
  Deutsche Telecom, 227–228, 239, 389
  eBay, 94
  e-commerce, 226–227, 255–261, 441–
    442
  entrepreneurship, 232–234, 240–241,
    244–246
  government policy, 244–246, 451–452
  institutional characteristics, 232–234
  Internet usage, 156, 170, 225–226
  IT employment, 225
  network technology, 236–239
  Neuer Markt, 246, 250
  software industry, 247–261
  telecom deregulation, 227–228, 389
  venture capital, 233, 240–245, 258, 447

wireless technology, 249
Yahoo!, 93
Ghosn, Carlos, 369
Gibson, William, 4
Glimstedt, Henrik, 35, 39, 55, 64, 109–
  151, 227, 235, 249, 294, 444, 447,
  454
Global Business Dialogue on electronic
  commerce (GBDe), 396–397
Global Net Exchange, 374
Global Technology Ventures (GTV), 209–
  211
Globalization. *See also* Diffusion
  economy, 6–7
  modes of exchange, 368–369
  regulation, 456–458
Glushko, Bob, 351
Gnutella, 462
Google, 81
Gopher, 82
Government policy. *See also* Deregulation,
  telecom; Regulation
  France, 332, 397–399, 405, 453
  Germany, 244–246, 451–452
  India, 200–207
  Korea, 265, 268, 276–277, 452
  United Kingdom, 382, 394–397
  United States, 410–411
Graphics, 84
Gray Cell, 215–216
Greece, 402
Grif, 21–22
GSM standard, 133, 265
Gulia, Milena, 26

Hachiya, Tom, 367
Hagel, John, 27
Hagstrom, Tony, 119–120
Hall, Peter, 46, 66, 232, 293, 454
Hanaro Telecom, 266
Health services, electronic, 400
Helper, Susan, 70, 100–102, 106, 280, 301,
  329, 331–380, 441, 452, 457
HEPNET, 82
Hewitt, Patricia, 397
Hierarchical management, 51–52
Hindustan Lever, 195
Hi-Tech-City, 202
Holding company, 319–321
Homophilous network, 28–29
Hotmail, 28
HTML, 13–14, 20, 180–181, 350
HTTP, 13–14, 20
Hughes, Thomas, 17

Human resource developments, 230–234, 261
e-commerce software, 259
enterprise software, 254
Hush-a-Phone decision, 76
Hybridization, 49, 111
Japan, 293–294, 317, 324
Sweden, 148–150, 458–459
Hypertext Markup Language (HTML), 13–14, 20, 180–181, 350
Hypertext Transfer Protocol (HTTP), 13–14, 20

IBM, 72
Icon MediaLab, 147
ICQ, 29
Immigration, U.S., 6, 51, 71, 211–212
i-mode, 291, 297–298, 305, 324
India, 5, 65, 191–222
  e-commerce, 191–192, 194–196, 442
  e-mail, 196
  entrepreneurship, 213–214
  government, 200–207
  Internet penetration, 191
  local services, 194–196
  Offshore Development Centers, 453–454
  remote services, 196–199, 214
  software industry, 196–199, 212–221, 445
  technical education, 201, 211–212
  technological imprinting, 216–220
  telecom sector, 202–206
  venture capital, 192, 195, 208–211, 447
Infomatec, 249
Infomediary, 27
Information and communication technologies (ICT), 153–154
  France, 157–159
  Japan, 305–306
Infosys, 218, 220
Initial public offerings (IPOs), 166–167
  Germany, 234, 246
  Japan, 310–313, 324
  Korea, 270
  U.S., 91, 232
Inktomi, 81, 103
INRIA, 21
Instant messaging, 28
Institutional change
  causality, 46–47, 50, 52
  configurations, 46–47
  cultural prototyping, 57–59
  deregulation, 56–57
  diffusion, 47

evolutionary, 59–60
  and national systems, 44–46
  pockets of competition, 56, 109, 112, 115–119, 148, 150, 169, 443–446, 454–455
  recoupling, 8
  Silicon Valley model, 50–53
  technology, 55
Integral product architecture, 371–373
Intel, 87
Intellectual property rights, 461–462, 466–468
Interlocking directorates, 146–147
International Telecommunications Union (ITU), 114
Internet
  communities, 26–30, 465, 471
  as cultural event, 3–4
  diffusion, 1, 33–34, 47–50, 60
  history, 2–4, 15–23, 81–84
  levels of, 92
  modular system, 8–9, 18
  perceptions of, 459
  pricing, 10, 24, 31, 205–206, 387–390, 404, 425
  protocols, 12–15
  user demographics, 23–24
  user self-perceptions, 460–461
Internet Architecture Board (IAB), 13
Internet Assigned Numbers Authority (IANA), 36, 393
Internet Capital Group (ICG), 101
Internet Corporation for Assigned Names and Numbers (ICANN), 36, 394
Internet Protocol (IP), 14, 122–123
Internet Service Provider (ISP), 10, 12
  Europe, 388
  India, 204–205
  U.S., 73
Internolix, 256–259
Interoperability, 12–13, 124. See also Standardization
  automobile industry, 349–351
  Minitel, 187
  open standards, 136–143
Interpark, 277, 278
Intershop, 256–259, 440
Investment banking, 34–35
IP address, 14
IP protocol, 14, 122–123
Ireland, 217
ISDN technology, 228–229, 236, 444
Israel, 77, 209, 217, 447
Ittiam, 220–221

JANET, 17
Jankowski, Dan, 348
Jansen, Bob, 355
Japan, 5, 66, 291–325
  automobile industry, 338–339, 341–347,
    457–458
  banking system, 60, 322
  business model, 291–292
  complementary institutions, 45
  e-commerce, 299–301, 441–442
  and foreign institutions, 49
  ICT sector, 305–306
  Internet usage, 291, 295
  Japan Telecom, 302
  and Korea, 268, 270, 278
  mobile phone services, 297–298, 307,
    442, 444
  PC ownership, 296, 307
  production model, 48
  start-ups, 450
  stock markets, 310–313, 321–322
  telecom sector, 301–307
  and U.S., 314–316
  venture capital, 310–316, 318–319, 322,
    324, 452
  Yahoo!, 93, 317–319
JASDAQ, 310–312
Jeunemaître, Alain, 329, 381–406, 418,
  434, 456, 457
Johnson Controls Inc. (JCI), 366–368
Jonströmmer, Ulf, 144
J-Phone, 302
JUNET (Japan University/Unis
  NETwork), 294

Kahn, Robert, 18
Kana Communications, 103
KDD, 302
Keio University, 21
Keiretsu, 321
Kenney, Martin, 15, 39, 63–64, 69–108,
  146, 147, 229, 267, 270, 309, 425, 439,
  446
Kogut, Bruce, 1–40, 43–67, 111, 216, 229,
  292, 306, 329–330, 379, 433, 437–472
Korea, 5, 65–66, 96, 263–288
  chaebols, 263, 267–269, 276, 281–288
  e-commerce, 271–272, 277–281, 286–
    287, 441–442
  entrepreneurship, 274–276, 287
  government policy, 265, 268, 276–277,
    452
  history, 264
  Internet usage, 263

and Japan, 268, 270, 278
  mobile phones, 265–266, 283
  software industry, 271–272
  start-ups, 450
  stock market, 270–271
  telecom deregulation, 264–266
  universities, 266–267
  and U.S., 278–279
  venture capital, 272–274, 287, 447
KOSDAQ, 270–271, 286
KT Hitel, 279

Labor markets, 235, 240, 260
Langlois, Richard, 18, 40
Law firms, 78
Layered functional model, 124
Lee, Jae-Yong, 284
Lee, Kuen-Hee, 284
Legacy systems, 216, 218–220
Levi Straus, 96
LG Electronics, 266
Licklider, Joseph C. R., 17
Licoppe, Christian, 55, 65, 153–190, 441,
  444, 447, 453
Linux, 463–465
Local area network (LAN), 72
Local loop, 387–389
Lopez, Jose Ignacio, 357
Lucent, 105, 238
Lycos, 81, 85, 89

MacDuffie, John Paul, 70, 100–102, 106,
  280, 301, 329, 331–380, 441, 452, 457
Makitalo, Östen, 116
Marketing representations, 412–419
  market imperfections approach, 412–
    413
  regulation, 415–419
  self-correction, 413–414
Markoff, John, 84
Mauritius, 208
MCI, 76, 389–390
Messaging service, 28
Metalspectrum, 375
Metcalfe, Robert, 18
Metcalfe's Law, 28, 107
MFENET, 82
Microsoft, 28, 72, 83, 85–86
  and Ericsson, 134
  and Internolix, 257–258
  and open source software, 465
  PocketPC, 139
Middleware, 8, 132, 248–249, 257
MindTree, 195, 214–215

Minitel, 17, 55, 174–187, 402, 444
and e-commerce, 155, 181, 184–187
electronic directory, 183–184
kiosk billing system, 172, 175–176, 180
national learning, 65, 154
Mobile Games Interoperability Forum, 140
Mobile phone services, 11, 63, 104
Europe, 387, 404
France, 159–160
Germany, 249
i-mode, 291, 297–298, 305, 324
Japan, 297–298, 307, 442, 444
Korea, 265–266, 283
Siemens, 237–238
Sweden, 55, 115–117, 132–134, 444–445
Mockapetris, Paul, 18
Modems, 118
Modes of exchange, 332–338. *See also*
Automobile industry
consortia, 374–378
globalization, 368–369
knowledge flow, 337–338, 341, 344–345
procurement, 335–339, 342, 348
standardization, 335–336, 339–340
supplier investment, 336–337, 340–344
Modular product architecture, 371–373
Modular system, 8–9, 18, 124
Monopolies, 56, 113, 115, 467
Europe, 387–390, 404
France, 169–173
India, 204
Japan, 304
Mosaic browser, 22, 83, 88
MOTHERS (Market for High Growth and
Emerging Stocks), 310–313
Motivational incentives, 231–232, 234,
261
Motorola, 162
Mowery, David, 18, 24
MP3, 451, 461
MUD (multi-user dungeon), 19
Multi Protocol Layer Switching (MPLS),
138
Multinational corporation, 33, 48, 214
Munich, 239–240
Music file sharing, 462

Naidu, Chandrababu, 221
Name registry, 35–37
Napster, 94, 461–462, 465
NASDAQ, 79, 98, 232, 286, 450
NASDAQ Japan, 310–313, 321–322
National Advertising Division (NAD), 416–
417

National Center for Supercomputing
Applications (NCSA), 22
National Physical Laboratory (NPL), 16–18
National Science Foundation (NSF), 18, 20,
82
National System of Innovation (NSI), 70
National systems, 5–8, 329–330, 471
B2B, 331–332, 346
diffusion, 47
economic and social networks, 53
evolutionary change, 59–60
institutional change, 44–46
NEC, 94
Negroponte, Nicholas, 1
Nehru, Jawaharlal, 211
Nelson, Richard, 45, 50
Netscape, 2, 22, 81, 88
Network Solutions, Inc., 36–37
Networks, social, 53–54
e-mail, 19, 23, 28, 72, 82, 103, 205, 348,
403, 442, 459, 463, 465, 470–471
Gulia, Milena, 26
homophilous, 28, 470
Peer-to-Peer (P2P), 437, 461–462, 464,
468
recoupling, 5, 8, 59, 330, 443
small worlds, 468, 470–472
USENET, 19, 82, 459
webs of people, 15, 22, 34, 469
Wellman, Barry, 26
Networks, technical, economic
disbundled, 113–114, 124
externalities, 27–28, 136
layers, 113–114
packet switching, 16, 56, 121–122
software, 248
trunk, 113
Neuer Markt, 246, 250
New York, 79
Newbridge Networks, 162, 237
Nippon Credit Bank (NCB), 322
Nissan, 344, 369
NMT 450 system, 117
Nobel Prize winners, 48
NORDUNET, 123
Noyce, Robert, 51
NSFNET, 18, 20, 82
NTT (Nippon Telegraph and Telephone),
301–305, 309
NTT DoCoMo, 297–298, 302–305, 307,
324

Object-oriented languages, 255
Offshore Development Center (ODC), 454

Oligopolists, 101–102
Open source software, 20, 366, 463–466
Open standards, 16–17, 136–143
  automobile industry, 364–368
  document translation, 350
Open System Integration (OSI), 121–122
Openshop, 256
Oracle, 86, 103, 198, 362–366
  and Covisint, 359
  Sweden, 133–134
Outlocating, 198–199

Packet switching, 16, 56, 121–122
Pantellos, 375
Parker, Sean, 462
Parser, 350
Patents, 142–143
P/E ratios, 439
Peer-to-peer (P2P) communities, 461–462,
  468
Performance incentives, 231–232, 234, 261
Personal computers, 72
Pet stores, 98
PHS (Personal Handy phone System), 297
PipeChain Inc., 376
Plastics Network, 101
PocketPC, 139
Portals, 93–95
POSCO, 281
Postel, Jon, 19
Pouzin, Louis, 16
Powell, Walter W., 67
Power law distribution, 31, 470
Pricing, Internet, 10, 24, 31
  Europe, 387–390, 404
  India, 205–206
  United States, 425
Privacy, 420, 422–424, 429–433, 456
Private ordering, 457
Privatization, 141–143, 467. See also
  Deregulation, telecom
Procurement process, 335. See also Auctions
  automation, 348
  B2B savings, 357, 378
  exit/voice mode, 334, 338–346, 354, 356,
    361–362, 366–373
  software, 363–368
Project-based management, 51–52
Property rights, 461–462, 466–468
Protocols, 12–19, 108, 121–123, 149, 182,
  378
Prototyping, cultural, 57–59
Prouty, Kevin, 348

PSINET, 82, 88
Public venture capital, 244–245
Pure holding company, 319–321
Push technology, 89

Qiagen, 234–235
Qualcomm, 265

R/3 system, 253
Radio technology, 117
Ragin, Charles, 46
Rajan, Radhika, 65, 191–222, 445, 447,
  454
Rakuten Ichiba, 299
RamsinCoMedia, 147
Regulation, 329–330, 381–405. See also
  Deregulation, telecom
  automobile industry, 425–426
  competition, 385, 388–394, 404, 409, 445
  conflict among laws, 427–429
  consumer protection, 409–411, 419–421
  co-regulation, 385, 416, 418
  and facilitation, 394–401
  France, 386
  global, 456–458
  government, 418–419, 426–427
  and Internet technology, 420–421, 432
  Japan, 301–305
  privacy, 420, 422–424, 429–432, 456
  property rights, 461–462, 466–468
  self-regulation, 415–419, 423–424, 431
  telecom sector, 12, 387–390, 403–404
  United Kingdom, 383–385
  United States, 35–37, 73–77, 104–105,
    330, 407–411
Reliability seals, 415
Renater, 155
Renault-Nissan, 369
Rennes center, 182–183
Research and development (R&D)
  France, 182–184
  German software, 253, 258
  Japan, 292
  Sweden, 129–130, 134–136
Research, university, 71
Retail commerce. See Business-to-Consumer
  (B2C) e-commerce
Rheingold, Howard, 26
Roberts, Lawrence, 17–18, 76
RosettaNet, 377
Route 128 model, 51–52, 79
Royal Institute of Technology (KTH),
  122–123

Sako, Mari, 66, 104, 206, 280, 291–325,
   341, 344, 372, 380, 441, 452, 457
Samsung Corporation, 266, 278, 280–284
SAP, 103–104, 234–235, 252–254, 439
Satellite technology, 11, 206
Satyam, 195, 218
Seal programs, 415
Search engine companies, 393–394
Security, 248, 400. *See also* Privacy
Selective adaptation, 111–112
Self-regulation, 415–419, 423–424, 431
Servers, 14–15, 35, 63, 81–83
Shopbots, 469
Shopping, online, 95, 442
   Japan, 299–300
   Korea, 277–278, 282
Siemens, 228, 236–240, 439, 444
Silicon Automation Systems, 214
Silicon Valley model, 5–8, 44, 215, 223
   and Bit Valley, 309–311, 324
   and innovation, 455–456
   institutional change, 50–53
   project-based management, 51–52
   venture capital, 64, 79–81, 88
Simcoe, Timothy, 24
Singapore, 447
Singer, Mark, 27
SK Group, 283–284
Small and medium-sized enterprises
   (SMEs), 159, 162, 164, 396–397
Small worlds, 470
Society of Automotive Engineers (SAE),
   339
Softbank Group, 66, 316–323, 440
Software development, 65, 79, 102–104
   automobile industry, 363–368, 370–371
   e-commerce, 218, 248, 255–261
   games, 305–306
   Germany, 247–261
   India, 196–199, 212–221, 445
   Korea, 271–272
   middleware, 8, 132, 248–249, 257
   private exchanges, 376–377
   revenue per employee, 217–218
   standardization, 140–141
Software Technology Parks (STP) scheme,
   202
Solectron, 352
Solow, Robert, 25
Son, Masayoshi, 317
Sony, 452
Soskice, David, 45–46, 66, 150, 232–234,
   293, 454
Speed, transmission, 11

Spyglass, 83
Stallkamp, Thomas, 369
Standardization
   automobile industry, 339–340, 342–343,
      349–351, 364–368
   consortia, 138, 142–143, 149
   ex-ante, 138
   GSM, 133
   Japan, 300–301
   open standards, 16–17, 136–143, 350,
      364–368
   private exchanges, 379
   privatization, 141–143
   procurement process, 335–336
   product architecture, 371–373
   software, 140–141
Stenbeck, Jan, 116–117, 119–120, 123
Sticky knowledge, 29
Stock markets, 3, 32, 34–35
   France, 166–167
   Germany, 240
   India, 208–209
   IPOs, 91, 166–167, 232, 234, 246
   Japan, 310–313, 321–322
   Korea, 270–271
   NASDAQ, 79, 98, 232, 286, 450
   Neuer Markt, 246, 450
   Sweden, 146
   United States, 63, 89–91, 98–99
Stock option plans, 246
Strauss-Kahn, Dominique, 398
Strenio, Andrew, 409
Stuart, Leslie, 6
Sun Microsystems, 72, 86
Supplier investment, 336–337
   exit mode, 340–341, 354, 372
   voice mode, 370, 372
SupplySolution, 354, 366
Svenska Radio Aktiebolaget (SRA), 115,
   117
Sweden, 64, 109–150, 454–455
   data communications, 117–118
   e-commerce, 128, 441–442
   economy, 110–111
   hybridization, 49, 111, 148–150, 458–459
   Internet penetration and usage, 125–128,
      156, 402–403
   IT industry, 125, 129–132
   mobile telephony, 55, 115–117, 132–134,
      444–445
   R&D, 129–130, 134–136
   selective adaptation, 111–112
   standardization, 136–143, 149
   stock market, 146

Swedish Telecom, 114–119
TCP/IP, 121–123
technology hubs, 235
telecom deregulation, 109–110, 113–115,
  118–120, 148
venture capital, 143–147, 447, 450
Swissair, 198
Symbian, 139–140
Systems integration, 255
Szygenda, Ralph, 362

Tabor, Gene, 361
Tata Consultancy Services (TCS), 196,
  213, 217, 220
TCP/IP, 13–14, 82, 122–123
Technology Holding Association (Tbg), 244
Technology hubs, 235
Telecommunication services, 10–12, 43. See
  also Deregulation, telecom; Mobile phone
  services
  equipment, 236–238
  Europe, 75, 104, 329, 387–390, 401–404
  France, 159–162
  Germany, 227–228, 389
  India, 202–206
  Japan, 301–307
  Korea, 264–266
  Sweden, 109–110, 113–115, 118–120,
    148
  unbundling, 388–389
  U.S., 71, 73–77, 104–105, 425
Teledensity, 204
Telematics. See Minitel
Telia, 123
Terrell, Karenann, 362
Third generation (3G) mobile services, 291
Thoren, Bertil, 361
3G Patent Platform, 142
Tokyo Stock Exchange, 310–313
Tomlinson, Ray, 19
T-Online, 239, 388
Torvalds, Linus, 463
Toy stores, 98
Toyota, 344, 361, 373
Toys "R" Us, 99
Trademarks, 37
Transmission Control Protocol (TCP), 13
Transmission speed, 11
Transora, 375
Transpac, 17
Transportation, 401
Trunk network, 113
TRW, 349–350
Turkle, Sherry, 39

Unified Modeling Language (UML), 141
Unimobile, 215–216
United Kingdom
  British Telecom, 387, 389–390
  ebay, 94
  e-commerce, 227, 396–397
  government policy, 382, 394–397
  Internet usage, 156
  NPL, 16–18
  regulation, 383–385
  Yahoo!, 93
United States, 5, 43–44, 69–107. See also
  Silicon Valley model
  antitrust law, 72, 76, 359
  ARPA, 15–16
  automobile industry, 338–341, 345–347
  bankruptcy law, 58
  biotechnology in, 58
  business-government relationship, 410–411
  company acquisitions, 438
  e-commerce, 69–70, 83–86, 91, 94–102,
    424–426, 441–442
  education, 50–51
  established firms, 86–88, 101–103
  and Europe, 167, 382, 401–402, 430–433
  and Germany, 225–226
  human capital, 48
  immigration policy, 6, 51, 71, 211–212
  inequity in, 50
  Internet pricing, 10, 425
  and Japan, 314–316
  and Korea, 278–279
  marketing representations, 415–419
  portals, 93–95
  privacy protection, 423–424
  regulation, 35–37, 73–77, 104–105, 330,
    407–411
  software tools, 102–104
  start-up firms, 88–93
  stock markets, 63, 89–91, 98–99
  telecom deregulation, 73–77, 104–105,
    425
  university system, 71, 81
  venture capital, 52, 77–81, 90–91, 105–
    106, 232, 446–447
  Web servers in, 63, 83
Universal Mobile Telecom Services
  (UMTS), 136
Universal Resource Identifier, 20
Universal Resource Locator (URL), 20–21
University system
  France, 155
  Sweden, 135
  United States, 71, 81

UNIX, 83, 463
USENET, 19, 82, 459
Users, Internet, 23–24
UUNET, 82, 88

Valuation, company, 439–440
Varney, Christine, 413
Vasconi, Kevin, 365
Ventro, 374
Venture capital, 34–35, 230
  B2B, 100–102
  biotechnology industry, 70
  competency development, 230, 233
  France, 166–167, 447
  Germany, 233, 240–245, 258, 447
  India, 192, 195, 208–211, 447
  Israel, 447
  Japan, 310–316, 318–319, 322, 324, 452
  Korea, 272–274, 287, 442
  public, 244–245
  push technology, 89
  Silicon Valley, 64, 79–81, 88
  software, 103
  Sweden, 143–147, 447, 450
  in U.S., 52, 77–81, 90–91, 105–106, 232,
    446–447
VeriSign, 37
Vernon, Ray, 198
VerticalNet, 101
Video games, 296
Videsh Sanchar Nigam Limited (VSNL),
  204–206
Virtual community, 28–29
Voice mode, 334, 338–346, 356
  Covisint, 361–362, 366–367
  supplier responsibility, 370, 372–373
Volvo, 361
VW, 361

Wal-Mart, 96, 99
Wanadoo, 168
WAP (wireless applications protocol), 123,
  305
Wapme, 249
Waraniak, John, 367
Web consultants, 131
Web design, 185
Web servers, 14–15, 35, 63, 83
Weiss, Peter, 349
Wellman, Barry, 26
Western Electric, 113
Westney, Eleanor, 48
Whitley, Richard, 45

WIDE (Widely Integrated Distributed
  Environment) project, 294
Wipro, 195, 218
Wireless technology, 11–12. See also Mobile
  phone services
WirelessCar, 133
Works councils, 233–234
World Wide Web, 20–21, 72–73, 83, 131.
  See also Internet
World Wide Web consortium (W3C), 21
Worldwide Retail Exchange, 374
Wurster, Thomas, 459

X.25 protocol, 16–17, 121–123, 444
XML (eXtensible Markup Language), 336,
  350–351

Yahoo!, 81, 85, 89, 279
  foreign markets, 93
  France, 92, 421
  and Softbank, 317–319
Yang, Chih-Yuan "Jerry", 4
Yao, Dennis, 32, 74, 92, 330, 362, 407–
  435, 456, 458, 461

Zaheer, Srilata, 65, 191–222, 445, 447,
  454
Zaibatsu, 321
Zander, Udo, 35, 39, 55, 64, 66, 109–151,
  294, 444, 447, 454
Zook, Matthew, 52, 74, 446, 471